FABULISTS FRENCH   VERSE FABLE
S OF NINE CENTURIES

SHAPIRO, NORMAN R

The Fabulists French

Woodcuts by David Schorr

THE FABULISTS FRENCH
Verse Fables of Nine Centuries

Translated, with Prologue and Notes, by Norman R. Shapiro

University of Illinois Press   *Urbana and Chicago*

Publication of this work has been aided by a grant from the Thomas and Catharine McMahon Fund, of Wesleyan University, established through the generosity of the late Joseph McMahon.

© 1992 by Norman R. Shapiro

Manufactured in the United States of America

C 5 4 3 2 1

This book is printed on acid-free paper.

The several fables of the following authors, from the works indicated, are reproduced with permission:

Jean Anouilh, *Fables,* © La Table Ronde, 1962 (by arrangement with Michael Imison Playwrights, Ltd.)
Gabriel Audisio, *Fables,* © Editions Pierre Belfond, 1966
Yves-Emmanuel Dogbé, *Fables africaines,* © Editions Akpagnon, 1978
Eugène Guillevic, *Fabliettes,* © Editions Gallimard, 1981
Jacques Prévert, *Histoires et d'autres histoires,* © Editions Gallimard, 1963

The fables of Jean-Luc Déjean and Jean-Charles Talmant (pseud. Gomar) are published with the kind permission of the authors, whose generosity I am happy to acknowledge.

Library of Congress Cataloging-in-Publication Data

The Fabulists French : verse fables of nine centuries /
translated, with prologue and notes, by Norman R. Shapiro ;
illustrations by David Schorr.
     p. cm.
English and French.
Includes bibliographical references.
Includes index.
ISBN 0–252–01756–0 (alk. paper)
    1. Fables, French—Translations into English. 2. Fables,
English—Translations from French. 3. French poetry—
Translations into English. 4. English poetry—Translations
from French. 5. Fables, French. 6. French poetry. I. Shapiro,
Norman R.
PQ1170.E6F3 1991
841'.0308—dc20
                                  90–46363
                                     CIP

Contents

Prologue

THE VERSE FABLE is a persistent little genre. Inherited from Antiquity, with its cast of animal heroes, villains, and victims, it has known periods of robust good health and seemingly imminent demise, never quite willing to gasp its last, however. Persistent, but all too unrealistic, I'm afraid, and much too ambitious. It has purported to exist in order to do its bit in correcting Humankind's flaws, and has been at it for ages, changing its aspect here and there with the changing times. A casual glance at the state of the race will reveal its success. Obviously the fable is no guarantor of moral correction. Nor would I, realistically, expect it to be one. After all, I must have read a few thousand of these apologues myself over the years, all offering incontrovertible proof of their individual theses and holding out the tacit promise of mini-salvation in this or that area of behavior; and, frankly, I'm quite as imperfect now as I was when I began. Not that I fail to recognize the moral truths the fable preaches; only that, like all of us I imagine, I always recognize those truths as valid for somebody else.

Still, through its ups and downs of greater and lesser vogue, the fable, even in France alone, has flourished for many centuries, spreading its recipes for moral rectitude to appreciative and admiring audiences.[1] But audiences unregenerated nonetheless. How come? I suppose because, for the most part, the very quality intended to coat the moral pill—the artistry of the individual fabulist, his (and rarely her) skill in dramatizing the scenario, in crafting the self-contained little opus with an eye toward colorful description and an ear toward colorful sound—has tended to get in the way and call more attention to the coating than to the pill itself. The "how" has won out over the "why": the medium has subverted the message. Naked Truth—especially the moral truth of the fable—may be, in the words of the chevalier de Boufflers, "la seule vierge, en ce vaste univers, / Qu'on aime à voir un peu vêtue"; but her dress, necessary to attract us to her in the first place, can distract us from her just as easily.[2] Personally, I find no fault at all with that. For my own tastes, didactic literature is, by its very nature, more often than not a bore. And the most agreeable literary didacts are not those who use their art as a pretext for their preachments, but those, vice versa, whose ethical truisms serve as an excuse to fashion a work of art.

Persistent, the fable is also a modest genre. Perhaps therein lies its charm and its tenacious longevity. It is undemanding. It does not ask to be deconstructed, psychoanalyzed, or otherwise dismembered to death in order to be "appreciated." Not, of course, that it cannot be. The ingenuity of critics and theoreticians is boundless; and even the straightforward and unassuming little fable has,

of course, been subjected to its scrutinizing light.[3] Whether to wither under it or to flower is a matter for the individual reader to decide, and for personal predilection. As for the fable itself, it simply says—and, at its best, says simply—what it has to say; usually tells us why, or at least hints broadly; then finishes almost as quickly as it began and goes away. That is not to imply that all fables are brief, lapidary of form (in the best Babrian tradition), and crystal clear of message. Some—not usually the most aesthetically attractive—have erred on the side of long-winded complexity, entangling their supposed moral raison d'être in excessive and convoluted verbiage, often dragging in a panoply of Olympian gods, goddesses, and assorted Abstractions to drive their point home, or making not-so-veiled allusions to contemporaneous personalities and political events.

Few of such intellectually interesting but aesthetically ponderous fables will be found in these pages. Still, the reader should be aware that they do, indeed, exist; that not every French verse fable over the last nine centuries is under two pages long; that some fabulists, even the best, seem to forget at times that their genre had its beginnings as, essentially, a brief oral medium intended to make a quick point with an unsophisticated (but not artistically obtuse) listener, in whom protracted excess might provoke only a counterproductive yawn. Fables, perhaps more than any other verse form, are still best read aloud.[4] I think that La Fontaine, the often imitated but inimitable, must have realized that fundamentally oral nature of the fable when he opted, in writing his, for the so-called *vers libres,* the closest that the seventeenth-century French poet could come to the naturalness of prose speech while still writing in recognizably measured and rhyming verse. Especially in his earliest books, where the fables are disarmingly simple; before he too would let himself be carried away, on occasion, into the headier realms of philosophical and moral speculation.

La Fontaine... The name has become virtually synonymous with the verse fable in the Western world, French and otherwise, second only to the prototypic and probably mythic Aesop himself. He is the reference point of every fabulist who comes after; the standard by which all his followers are measured, and by which, indeed, they usually measure themselves. Even when they try not to. For even those who pretend to ignore him utterly—not an easy task—call attention, ironically, to his presence by his very absence. Most, however, will acknowledge his preeminence by attempting to copy that typical easygoing La Fontaine gait: his leisurely digressions and casual asides, his intimacy with the reader.[5] And those who do not will pay him frequent homage in their prefaces, *avertissements,* and the like. But however obviously they flatter him by imitation, or however sincere their praise and deep their salaams at the shrine of his incomparability, they must all, it seems to me, be of two minds in the matter, realize it or not. In a literary love-hate relationship, as it were. With filial affection for their spiritual progenitor, on the one hand, and resentment at the same time—in Bloomian terms—toward the all-powerful and threatening castrating Fabulist-Father, on the other. "Also-rans" by definition, and condemned to remain such, they are caught (if I may make a pun) between their cerebral urge to run toward him in love and their visceral urge to run from him in hate. The fabulist Florian, I think, gives us a telling glimpse of that ambivalence. "La Fontaine parut," he admiringly exclaims (through the fictional lips of a wise old man), "et La Fontaine fit oublier toutes les fables passées, et, je tremble de vous le dire, vraisemblablement aussi toutes les fables futures."[6]

To call La Fontaine's legion of followers also-rans is not to deprecate them or to suggest that they have not, in their own right, added to the literature a substantial body of fables well worth the reading (or, if possible, the hearing): aesthetically witty, stylistically elegant and often even virtuosic, on occasion profound... Or, at the very least, historically and socially significant, or otherwise satisfying on intellectual grounds. Readers will encounter many in this collection. (They will find fewer by La Fontaine's predecessors, however; which is not to say that the genre didn't flourish before him, but rather that, for me, his literary descendants are more varied and exciting a lot than most of his medieval and Renaissance ancestors, for all their rich antiquarian interest.)[7]

That abundance reflects the objective facts. The heyday of the French verse fable began in the eighteenth century, when every poet and his proverbial brother seemed eventually to try his hand. Even theoreticians graced the fable—never a major or "noble" genre, but respected all the same—with its share of analysis.[8] More recent generations, too sophisticated for traditional moralizing, have seen the La Fontaine form wryly bent to parodic self-imitation, or set aside entirely in favor of more modern trappings. But, although less robust today than in its glory years, the fable still continues, unpretentious and indomitable, along its "petit bonhomme de chemin," less to enlighten but no less to delight. It doesn't seem ready just yet for obituaries.

Excuse and apology, it seems, are the inevitable lot of every anthologist. I am no exception. Fortunately, though, I am probably less open than many to the usual queries: "Why So-and-So?... Why not Such-and-Such?... Why this one?... Why not that?..." The field of the French verse fable, after all, is not an especially well trodden one, and there are few to do the asking. Still, some may well question my inclusions and exclusions.[9]

No one, I'm sure, will object to La Fontaine, or, for that matter, to Marie de France, Florian, Anouilh, Guillevic—all prominent enough names in French letters, ancient to modern; or even to Baïf, Furetière, Perrault, Benserade, Boursault, or Houdar de La Motte—by no means unknown quantities. But some may ask, if I honor Madame de Villedieu, who published a scant eight—long—fables, why I ignore La Fontaine's no-less-prolix and more productive contemporary La Barre, who wrote a heftier thirty. Others will wonder, if I present the Provençal poets Tandon and Diouloufet, for example, why I leave out the better-known Roumanille and Morel, or many of the score of latter-day patois troubadours for whom the fable had a special attraction but whose names—D'Astros, Martin, Reymonenq, Castela, Foucaud, et al.—have long since faded gently into oblivion. Or why, if I favor the obscure Thierry-Faletans, I omit the prolific Lachambeaudie, much admired in his day. Few and far between, I daresay, are those who will complain of my slight to such as Barbe, Hérissant, Grenus, Agniel, La Louptière, Fumars... (Or even Jussieu, who performed the admirable tour de force of translating his own fables into Italian.) The list could fill several pages. But an occasional specialist may well wonder, with good reason, why I neglect the likes of Le Bailly, Imbert, the duc de Nivernais, the baron de Stassart, or the prominent fabulist-cum-theorist Richer, among others; while curiosity-seekers might even lament the exclusion of such intriguing works as the late eighteenth-century apologues of Edme Billardon-Sauvigny, wrought from the French and American revolutions, or of Nobel laureate physician Charles Richet's pacifistically inspired fables of the early twentieth.

Besides proffering in reply the timeworn but still valid excuse of limited space, I could retreat behind some unassailable aesthetic criteria, constructed for the occasion. But frankly they would be factitious. The plain (Naked) Truth of the matter—and where is "she" more appropriate than in discussing the fable?—is that the works of many fabulists, failing heroic measures, are virtually *introuvables.* And for those that are, more or less, reasonably accessible—thanks to the miracle of xerography, the blessing of interlibrary loans, and the agency of kind and cooperative friends—I admit unabashedly that I have chosen the ones that strike my personal fancy for any number of reasons. Among them, a certain historico-literary interest (such as the dramatic fables in the Aesop-plays of Boursault and his emulators); a taste for the esoteric (like Roger's adaptations from the Wolof, and the several examples of patois and Creole fables, or Saint Gilles's fables in *rondeau* form and Deschamps's in *ballades,* or even Benserade's and Vaudin's wonderfully absurd little quatrains); a charming simplicity, or even a blatant pomposity of subject; a neat turn of phrase here, wit and whimsy there; elegance, tone, style... Some je ne sais quoi. Whatever... Personal preference may be the anthologist's vice; but it is one, I think, that doesn't need much defending. Nor does, I hope, the translator's vice of liberal rendition. My aim, I need hardly repeat, is to bring across the sense, style, and spirit of the originals, in all their variety, not to provide servilely faithful equivalents. To do the latter would be to undo the former. And so, like any translator worth his or her salt, I ask that my renderings be taken occasionally with appropriate grains of same.

If excuses are a formality, acknowledgments are a pleasure. At the risk of compiling a list longer than my Contents, let me take that pleasure in acknowledging here the many who have, in measure large or small, offered their help in this enterprise of the last five years. Foremost among them is Evelyn Singer Simha. Unfailing in her insight and judgment, she has unstintingly spread her encouragement from cover to cover, and I thank her heartily for it. My gratitude, also, to the many knowledgeable library and book professionals who have smoothed over the numerous bumps along the way: to the gracious and accommodating staff of Harvard's Widener and Houghton libraries; to Steven Lebergott, of Wesleyan's Olin Library, for his frequent and utterly indispensable assistance, and to Connie Fraser for hers, as well as to Joan Jurale, Lisa Degnan, and Carol Terzini; to Stephen Ferguson and Nancy Pressman, of the Princeton University Library; to Anthony Bogucki, of the Library of Congress; and to David Leyenson and Dan Cianfarini, and their associates of Schoenhof's Books,

Cambridge. This work, quite literally, could not have been completed without them all.

Thanks, too, to my Wesleyan colleagues, departmental and extradepartmental, who indulgently listened— and particularly to Susan Frazer, Sheila Gaudon, Joyce Lowrie, and Howard Needler, who helped track down recalcitrant volumes and references—and to Andrée Kekeh, Glenn Young, Alex Dupuy, Gloria Quintana, Noreen Baris, Mary Lou Nelles, and Lisa Fleury. Likewise to helpful colleagues and friends at other institutions: Caldwell Titcomb, Seymour O. Simches, Lillian Bulwa, John DuVal, Paul Ruffin, Annegret Bollée, Gérard L. St. Martin, David Kozubei, Dudley Knight, Franklin Smith, Jon Weiss, and Graham Falconer; to Robert Gorman, for his advice in guiding me safely around legal thickets; to Peter O'Malley, always generous with his aesthetic acumen and worldly wisdom; and to Sylvia and Allan Kliman for continuous encouragement. To Lisa Meyers, J. French Wall III, and Sarah Dawidoff, my appreciation for early editorial chores, as well as to Christopher Caldwell for expert assistance with the Bibliography; Marc David Carnegie for help in proofreading the final manuscript; and, copiously, to my long-suffering editor, Elizabeth Dulany, and her capable staff—Jessica Moseley, Becky Standard, and my copyeditor, Pat Hollahan—as well as to Christie Schuetz and her staff, for putting up with me well beyond the call of duty.

Very special thanks to my late father; and, as ever, to the memory of my mother, for her own poetic gifts.

NOTE: I have seen fit not to presume to "correct" any of the original texts, or, especially, to update those of more remote periods. With a few minor exceptions, such as regular use of quotation marks, I have reproduced them as they appear in the editions used, going so far as to retain their orthographical, punctuational, and even typographical idiosyncracies. While this may disconcert some readers unfamiliar with premodern French, to whom I offer my apologies, it should, I imagine, please the scrupulous purist.

1. Adult audiences, by the way. Despite popular misconception, relatively few serious fabulists over the years have written primarily for children; and most of those few have set store by the artistic approbation of their mature contemporaries. Many observers have voiced the opinion, in fact, that the traditional fable is quite inappropriate for the juvenile mentality. As an example of one of the more concisely expressed, one can cite the following passage by the early nineteenth-century abbé Pierre-Philibert Guichellet, himself a prolific (if little-known) fabulist: "Non seulement la Fable n'a point été inventée pour l'instruction des enfans; mais les leçons qu'elle présente sont en général au-dessus de leur portée. Les acteurs que l'on introduit dans la Fable sont d'une espèce si éloignée de la leur; leurs mœurs, leurs appétits si différens des leurs, qu'ils ne peuvent s'imaginer que les discours et les actions des bêtes, des oiseaux et des êtres inanimés, que l'on fait parler et agir dans la Fable, doivent les concerner" (*Fables nouvelles, suivies de pièces fugitives en vers*, p. viii). As for the prototypic La Fontaine himself, it is quite well established that, while his earliest fables were, indeed, generally intended for the edification of the young, he soon came to realize that the seriousness of his philosophy and the sophistication of his art were really well beyond their immaturity.

2. On Boufflers, see pp. 129–30. The lines are from his "Vers à Madame D***, en lui envoyant un exemplaire d'une nouvelle édition des *Fables* de La Fontaine," in his *Œuvres*, I:20.

3. While most such theoretical studies seem, predictably, to be Germanic, several recent French examples suggest themselves. Inter alia: Jean Batany, "Détermination et typologie: l'article et les animaux de la fable (de

Marie de France à La Fontaine)"; and Genette Ashby-Beach, "Les *Fables* de Marie de France: essai de grammaire narrative." Though the latter limits her structuralist analysis, replete with "Propp-erly" pseudoscientific formulas and diagrams in the best narratological tradition, to only four of Marie's fables, she promises us, reassuringly, a vaster array forthcoming: "Parce qu'il existe probablement d'autres modèles narratifs de la fable que nous n'avons pas encore étudiés, il nous reste, par conséquent, une vaste recherche à faire" (p. 26).

4. The same, I daresay, was true of all verse in its beginnings, back when there was no clear-cut distinction between "verse" and "poetry." But somewhere along the way an aesthetic and intellectual split occurred. As a student of mine simplistically put it: "Poetry is verse that's hard to understand." Today most "poetry" is written primarily to be read, not heard. Poets write to be printed on pages and pored over. Only seldom and secondarily, to be listened to. (And yet we continue to indulge in the ceremonial "poetry reading"; usually an exercise in personality-worship more than in aesthetic comprehension, since we never do to the oral poem what we always do to the written; namely: stop, reread, reflect, half-decipher, ponder, reread again, and again...)

5. Fernand Vandérem once astutely and picturesquely divided the French verse fable into two basic types. The first, in the La Fontaine manner, like a schoolboy playing hooky, "ne se hâte point, s'avance nonchalamment en tunique légère et lâche, butinant à toutes les pentes de la pensée ou du rêve." The second, more typical of a Florian or an Arnault, different though those two are from each other, is more proper in its dress and demeanor: "Soigneusement corsetée et poudrée, étroitement serrée dans ses atours dont pas un fil ne dépasse, elle court d'un seul élan à son but, la moralité, et ne perd ni un instant ni un mot en route." (See *Le Miroir des lettres*, IV:161.)

6. See his "De la fable," the prefatory essay to his own celebrated fable collection, third paragraph from the end.

7. Furthermore, some of the works I might have wanted to see represented are almost impossible to lay hands on. Among them, such

sixteenth-century collections as Pierre Heyns's *Esbatiment moral des animaux* (see p. 24) and Etienne Perret's *Vingt-cinq fables des animaux.* For erudite studies on the French verse fable prior to La Fontaine, see, inter alia, the following: A.-C.-M. Robert, "Essai sur les fabulistes qui ont précédé La Fontaine," preface to his pioneering *Fables inédites del XIIe, XIIIe et XIVe siècles, et Fables de La Fontaine,* I:xiii–ccxl; Prosper Soullié, *La Fontaine et ses devanciers;* and the recent comprehensive, well-documented study of Gianni Mombello, *Le Raccolte francesi di favole esopiane dal 1480 alla fine des secolo XVI.* The reader especially interested in translations from the medieval corpus may wish to consult my *Fables from Old French: Aesop's Beasts and Bumpkins,* which includes, in addition to a number of Marie de France's fables, examples from the *Isopet I,* the *Isopet II de Paris,* and the *Isopet de Chartres.*

8. "Il est peu de poètes du XVIIIe siècle qui n'aient écrit des fables," Emile Faguet tells us. "Il était, du reste, aussi nécessaire à un écrivain, pour se faire classer parmi les hommes de talent, d'avoir écrit des fables que d'avoir écrit des tragédies. De sorte que, si l'on voulait faire sa carrière dans les lettres, on commençait par faire une tragédie; puis, si l'on échouait, on composait alors des poésies légères, et parmi celles-ci, des fables." (See his *Histoire de la poésie française de la Renaissance au Romantisme,* VIII:270.) In her brief but insightful article on the eighteenth-century fabulists, their fables, and their foibles, Roseann Runte places their number at over two hundred. (See "The Paradox of the Fable in Eighteenth-Century France.") Regarding that period's theoreticians of the fable, in France and elsewhere, see Thomas Noel's well-documented and informative study, *Theories of the Fable in the Eighteenth Century.* The author dismisses the later fable rather too cavalierly, however, when he writes that "the fable in the nineteenth century no longer ranked among the practiced literary genres" (p. 157). The copious (and very far from exhaustive) examples in this collection will speak for themselves.

9. It will be obvious from my title that I have chosen to omit examples of the less-practiced prose fable; works that, like their counterparts in verse, also span the centuries: from the late medieval prose recensions of the Isopets (see p. 7) and the likes of Julien Macho's popular fifteenth-century translations of Aesop, through the rather turgid moralizings of Fénelon's seventeenth-century fables written for the edification of the young duc de Bourgogne, and even down to such more recent but lesser-known collections as the *Fables comiques* of prolific animal illustrator Benjamin Rabier.

The Fabulists French

The Fabulists French

Marie de France   Fables (late twelfth century)

ALTHOUGH she enjoys the distinction of being the first identifiable woman writer in French, and certainly one of the first (if not the very first) extant fabulist of either sex in any of the western vernaculars, and although her work has generated a vast bibliography of scholarly studies,[1] the poet called "Marie de France," like many medieval writers, remains an enigmatic figure. We know her to be the author (or translator-adapter) of three works, composed probably in this order: her best-known Breton-inspired *lais*—brief sentimental romances recounted with many a subtle insight and artistic nuance, despite the limitations imposed by the traditional octosyllables; her Aesopic fables, briefer still—straightforward adaptations of the classical (and classical-type) corpus; and her lengthy *Espurgatoire Seint Patriz* ("The Purgatory of Saint Patrick"), a religious tale of adventure and spiritual revelation.[2]

The few solid details that we have about Marie's person are those that she herself provides in her writings or that can be deduced from them. With none of the self-effacing anonymity common to many medieval predecessors, contemporaries, and successors, she readily identifies herself in her works, specifying, in the epilogue to her fables, not only her name but also her place of origin: "MARIE ai nun, si sui de France" (l. 4). This geographical indication, probably referring narrowly to the region of Ile-de-France, implies that she was, at least at the time of writing, an expatriate of sorts. Further evidence in the same epilogue—her reference to one Count William, "the noblest of any realm," for whom she translated her fables from English (i.e., Anglo-Saxon) into Romance[3]—suggests that she was, indeed, a member of the Norman aristocracy that ruled England after the battle of Hastings in 1066. It is also of interest, and typical of the often naive medieval acceptance of hearsay, that she attributes her English model to King Alfred the Great (871–901), "Li reis Alvrez" (l. 16), who had allegedly translated it from the Latin. The attribution is rejected, however, by present-day scholars. (See *Marie de France: Fables,* ed. Ewert and Johnson, p. xi.)[4] Modern scholars, likewise, tend to believe, from complex deductions, that Marie spent her artistic life, all or in part, at the French-speaking court of the Plantagenet kings of England, Henry II (1154–89) and Richard I, "the Lion-Hearted" (1189–99). (See Richard Baum, *Recherches sur les œuvres attribuées à Marie de France,* and Emanuel J. Mickel, Jr., *Marie de France.*) But despite much learned speculation and erudition, the only details that can be advanced with assurance are that "Marie wrote in the last third of the twelfth century, that she composed the *Lais* at some time before 1189, that this work was followed by the *Fables*, and that the *Espurgatoire* was composed after 1189" (*Marie de France: Fables,* ed. Ewert and Johnson, p. x). (Some commentators, in fact, extend her probable productive years through the first decade of the thirteenth century.)[5]

The reader, however, will appreciate that, notwithstanding all the biographical uncertainty surrounding Marie, her works—and, of especial interest here, her fables—remain and speak for themselves in a language that transcends conditions temporal and geographic. One of her recent translators puts the matter neatly into perspective: "Fortunately, particular details of time, place and author are in a sense irrelevant to fables. Fables maintain their identity always, whether borrowed by a Marie de France, a Rudyard Kipling, or a Walt Disney."[6]

Marie's fables translated in these pages are numbers 1, 10, 31, 38, 59, and 81 of the Warnke edition.

1. See Glyn S. Burgess, *Marie de France: An Analytical Bibliography.*
2. For authoritative editions of Marie's works, see the following: *Die Lais der Marie de France,* ed. Karl Warnke; *Marie de France: Lais,* ed. Alfred Ewert; *Les Lais de Marie de France,* ed. Jeanne Lods; *Les Lais de Marie de France,* ed. Jean Rychner; *Die Fabeln der Marie de France,* ed. Karl Warnke; *Marie de France: Fables,* ed. Alfred Ewert and Ronald C. Johnson; *Marie de France: Fables,* ed. and trans. Harriet Spiegel; *L'Espurgatoire Seint Patriz,* ed. Thomas Atkinson Jenkins; and *Das Buch vom Espurgatoire S. Patriz des Marie de France und seine Quelle,* ed. Karl Warnke. For recent observations on the text of the *Fables*, see also Karen K. Jambeck, "The *Fables* of Marie de France: Base Text and Critical Text."
3. "Pur amur le cunte Willame, / Le plus vaillant de nul realme, / M'entremis de ceste livre feire / E de l'engleis en romanz treire." For one of the more recent of the several hypotheses concerning this inspiring—if enigmatic—count, see Madeleine Soudée, "Le Dédicataire des *Ysopets* de Marie de France," in which the author identifies him with Guillaume le Maréchal, or William Marshal, of the Plantagenet court.
4. It is thought that the ultimate source of many of Marie's fables—at least the first forty—through several lost reworkings, was the Latin prose Aesopica collection known as the *Romulus Nilantii.* (See Urban T. Holmes, Jr., *A History of Old French Literature from the Ori-*gins to 1300, pp. 207–10; *Marie de France: Fables,* ed. Ewert and Johnson, pp. xi–xii; and *Marie de France: Fables,* ed. Spiegel, pp. 6–11.)
5. For rather early speculation on Marie's identity see A.-C.-M. Robert's seminal study of the predecessors of La Fontaine, *Fables inédites des XIIe, XIIIe et XIVe siècles, et Fables de La Fontaine,* I:clii–clix.
6. The quotation is from the introduction to a collection of thirty fables translated into free verse by Jeanette Beer and sumptuously illustrated by Jason Carter: *Medieval Fables: Marie de France,* p. 9. For other translations, in rhyming octosyllabic couplets, see the literally accurate but rather bland renderings of the entire collection by Harriet Spiegel (*Marie de France: Fables*), and eleven examples in my *Fables from Old French: Aesop's Beasts and Bumpkins.* Seven unrhymed translations are also found in Joan M. Ferrante, "The French Courtly Poet Marie de France." For a complete prose version see *The Fables of Marie de France,* ed. and trans. Mary Lou Martin. As for the literary value and aesthetic implications of Marie's work, opinions vary widely. On the one hand, historian of the fable Jacques Janssens tells us to expect to find in it "ni poésie véritable ni richesse dans les développements." (See his *La Fable et les fabulistes,* p. 35.) On the other, it is obviously considered sophisticated enough to have yielded up—or to have had imposed upon it—the detailed structuralist analysis referred to above (see p. xv, n. 3).

De Gallo et Gemma

Del coc recunte ki munta
sur un femier e si grata;
sulunc nature purchaçot
sa viande, si cum il sot.
Une chiere gemme trova;
clere la vit, si l'esguarda.
"Jeo quidai," fet il, "purchacier
ma viande sur cest femier.
Or t'ai ici, gemme, trovee;
ja par mei n'en iers remuee!
S'uns riches huem ci vus trovast,
bien sai que d'or vus honurast,
si acreüst vostre clarté
par l'or, ki mult a grant bealté.
Quant ma volenté n'ai de tei,
ja nule honur n'avras par mei."

Altresi est de meinte gent,
se tut ne vait a lur talent,
cume del coc e de la gemme.
Veü l'avuns d'ume e de femme:
bien ne honur nïent ne prisent;
le pis pernent, le mielz despisent.

The Cock and the Gem

About a cock the tale is sung,
Perching upon a pile of dung,
And searching for his daily ration
With peck and scratch, as was his fashion.
At length he found an object, shining—
A rare and precious gem! And, whining:
"I meant to make my meal," he said,
Here on the dungheap. But, instead,
I find a jewel!" With moan and groan,
Disgruntled, he addressed the stone:
"If some rich human being had found you,
Doubtless indeed he would surround you
Straightway with priceless gold, and thus
Make you shine yet more luminous.
Well, fiddlesticks and fiddle-de-dee!
You'll get no such respect from me!"

As with our cock who chanced to find
A gem, so too with humankind,
When plans and wishes turn askew.
Many's the man and woman who
By excellence are unimpressed:
They prize the worst and scorn the best.

De Vulpe et Aquila

D'un gupil cunte la maniere,
ki ert eissuz de sa tesniere;
od ses enfanz devant jua.
Uns aigles vint, l'un en porta.
Li gupiz vet aprés criant
que il li rende sun enfant;
mes il nel volt mie esculter,
si l'en cuvint a returner.
Un tisun prist de feu ardant
e seche busche vet cuillant:
entur le chesne le meteit,
u li aigles sun ni aveit.
Li aigles vit le feu espris;
al gupil prie e dit: "Amis,
estein le feu! Pren tun chael!
Ja serunt ars tuit mi oisel."

Par cest essample entendum nus
que si est del riche orguillus:
ja del povre n'avra merci
pur sa pleinte ne pur sun cri;
mes se cil s'en peüst vengier,
dunc le verreit l'um suzpleier.

The Fox and the Eagle

This fable tells the tale about
A fox who, with his brood, was out
One day, disporting by his lair,
When, all of a sudden, then and there,
An eagle soared, swooped down, swept up
A tender, unsuspecting pup,
And bore him off. The fox, distraught,
Pleads for his cub, so cruelly caught.
The eagle pays him little mind.
"Very well, then, be paid in kind,
My feathered friend!" So saying, the fox
Runs off... Returns with twigs, sticks, stalks...
Spreads them about the eagle's tree...
Sets fire... "Oh no! My family..."
Bewails the bird—aghast, distressed.
"Take back your babe! Just spare my nest!"

The haughty and rich will ever wreak
Relentless power upon the weak.
But keep in mind this caveat:
Give blow for blow and tit for tat,
Uneven though your controversy.
Hit where it hurts: they'll beg for mercy.

De Pavone et Junone

Uns poüns fu forment iriez
vers sei meïsme e curuciez
de ceo que tel voiz nen aveit
cum a lui, ceo dist, avendreit.
A la deuesse le mustra,
e la dame li demanda
s'il n'ot asez en la bealté
dunt el l'aveit si aürné;
de pennes l'aveit fet plus bel
que ne veeit nul altre oisel.
Li poüns dist qu'il se cremeit,
de tuz oisels plus vils esteit
pur ceo que ne sot bien chanter.
Ele respunt: "Lai mei ester!
Bien te deit ta bealtez suffire."
"Nenil," fet il, "bien le puis dire:
quant li russignolez petiz
a meillur voiz, jeo sui huniz."

Juno and the Peacock[1]

A certain peacock, discontented,
Hated his voice, and much resented
Having one less mellifluous
Than he, indeed, found fit. And, thus,
He took the matter up with Juno.
"Come now," she chided him, "you do know,
Surely, how exquisite you are—
Finer of feather, fairer far
Than all my wingèd retinue.
Is that not quite enough for you?"
The peacock sighed: "If only I
Could sing aright and not awry!
What pain to hear the nightingale!
I try... But no... To no avail...
Poor me! Poor me!..." "Yes yes, I heard you,"
Juno replied. "You silly bird, you!
Leave me alone! Enough!" she cried.
"You're beautiful! Be satisfied!"

1. I have taken the liberty of reversing the elements of Marie's—or, more likely, her scribe's—Latin title, "De pavone et Junone," perhaps through a subconscious association with Sean O'Casey's play *Juno and the Paycock* (with which, I hasten to add, the fable has nothing in common but the fortuitous title). Marie is indebted to Phaedrus (III, 18): "Pavo ad Junonem venit, indigne ferens / Cantus luscinii quod sibi non tribuerit"; but O'Casey is indebted to nobody.

De Pulice et Camelo

Une pulce, ceo dit, munta
sur un chameil, sil chevalcha
des i qu'en une altre cuntree.
Dunc s'est la pulce purpensee,
si a mercië le chameil,
ki si suëf dedenz sun peil
l'aveit ensemble od lui portee;
"ja mes par sei n'i fust alee:
pur sun travail le servireit
mult volentiers, s'ele poeit."
Li chameiz li a respundu,
qu'unkes de li chargiez ne fu
ne ne sot qu'ele fust sur lui
ne qu'el li fesist nul ennui.

Issi vet de la povre gent:
s'as riches unt aprismement,
forment les quident curucier,
damage faire e ennuier.

The Flea and the Camel

They tell about a flea, a-flit,
Who sprightly on a camel lit
And rode his host abroad. The flea
Thought it was only fit that he,
Alighting at his destination,
Voice his sincere appreciation:
"Never, I vow, could I have gone
So long a distance all alone.
Now tell me, how can I repay you?
Pray, name your favor, friend! What say you?"
"What?" sneered the camel in reply.
"You thank me, but I can't guess why!
I had no notion you were there—
And, had I known, I wouldn't care!"

The poor have little strength with which
To press their weight upon the rich.
Try though they may, they merely flatter
Themselves—like fleas—to think they matter.

De Lupo et Corvo

D'un lou cunte ki vit jadis
u uns corbels esteit asis
desur le dos d'une berbiz.
Li lous parla od nobles diz:
"Jeo vei," fet il, "mult grant merveille:

The Wolf and the Crow

A wolf, they tell us, gazed in awe
And disbelief, to see a daw
Perching upon a sheep. "Ah me!"
Complained the wolf, bombastically.
"A sight to shock the eyes! A crow—

le corp sur le dos d'une oweille.
Siet la u siet, dit ceo que dit,
fet ceo que fet senz cuntredit:
mal ne crient il de nule rien.
Se j'i seïsse, jeo sai bien
que tute genz me huëreient:
de tutes parz m'escriëreient
que jeo la voldreie mangier;
ne m'i larreient aprismier."

Issi est il del tricheür:
en esfrei est e en poür
—sa cunsciënce le reprent—
que tuit cunuissent sun talent.
Forment li peise del leial,
que hum ne tient ses fez a mal.

Calmly, politely, poised just so—
Atop a sheep! And look!... Without
The slightest qualm, the merest doubt...
Doing what suits his fancy, freely...
Ah! If *I* chose to sit there, really
I can just hear the hue and cry!
Let me approach him... dare draw nigh...
Folks will expect I must mistreat him.
Worse, they suspect I'm going to eat him!"

Thus does the felon live in fear
Lest all his purposes appear
Base and unworthy, even though
He may behave quite *comme il faut*.
The traitor is his own worst victim:
Conscience will prick him; grief, afflict him.

De Presbytero et Lupo

Uns prestre volt jadis aprendre
un lou a letres faire entendre.
"A," dist li prestre, "a" dist li lous,
ki mult ert fel e engignous.
"B," dist li prestre, "di od mei!"
"B," dist li lous, "la letre vei."
"C," dist li prestre, "di avant!"
"C," dist li lous, "a i dunc tant?"
Respunt li prestre: "Or di par tei!"
Li lous li dist: "Jeo ne sai quei."
"Di que te semble, si espel!"
Respunt li lous: "Aignel, aignel!"
Li prestre dist que verté tuche:
tel en pensé, tel en la buche.

De plusurs le veit hum sovent:
cel dunt il pensent durement
est par lur buche cuneü,
anceis que d'altre seit seü;
la buche mustre le penser,
tut deïe ele d'el parler.

The Priest and the Wolf

A priest there was, in days gone by,
Who took upon himself to try
To teach a certain wolf to spell.
"A," says the priest; the beast, as well.
"Good!" Now say 'B,'" exhorts the teacher.
"B... B..." repeats the crafty creature.
Likewise, in turn, with letter C.
"Oh," groans the wolf, "my goodness me...
Is there much more?" The priest: "Now, now...
All by yourself..." The beast: "But how?
I'm just a wolf; that's all I am..."
"Spell something... Try..." The wolf cries: "Lamb!"
"Ah," sighs the priest, "how true to kind!
Your mouth, I fear, betrays your mind."

So too it is, indeed, among
The race of man, whose wagging tongue,
In time, is certain to reveal
What mind demands that it conceal.
Persistent thought, or passion strong,
May seal man's lips—but not for long.

Anonymous   Isopet de Lyon (thirteenth century)

MARIE DE FRANCE, if the first, was far from being the only purveyor of Aesopica to the French Middle Ages. The corpus ascribed to the half-legendary Phrygian slave whose name would become synonymous with the genre he supposedly created had been handed down to the West through a chain of intermediary translations stemming, themselves, from two basic compilations: the third-century prose collection of the Greek Babrius and, especially, that of the Latin poet Phaedrus in the first century A.D. It is, in fact, from Phaedrus that most of the medieval French collections—called Isopets, for obvious reasons—derive; not directly, but rather through a pair of Latin adaptations known, for historical reasons peculiar to medieval bibliography, as the *Romulus Neveletii* (ca. 1175), in verse, and the *Romulus Nilantii,* in prose, of uncertain date. The latter, as previously noted (see p. 3, n. 4), was the ultimate source for at least a number of Marie's fables. The former, written in elegiacs now generally attributed to one Walter the Englishman (Galterus Anglicus, or Walter l'Anglais)—bishop of Palermo and chaplain to Henry II Plantagenet—is the direct ancestor of the *Isopet de Lyon.*[1]

This collection, as well as several others of various provenance, was published for the Société des Anciens Textes Français—along with the sixty-eight Latin fables of Walter's *Romulus*—by Julia Bastin in her two-volume *Recueil général des Isopets.*[2] In her introduction she indicates that a detailed linguistic analysis of the Franche-Comté dialect of this Isopet suggests that it dates from the thirteenth century (see II:xix–xxv). The absence of internal evidence makes further precision speculative at best.

The *Isopet de Lyon,* named after the city where it was discovered, contains sixty fables in traditional octosyllabic couplets and of widely varying lengths, ranging from twenty lines (excluding a fragment) to two hundred and fifty-eight. They are introduced by a brief prologue in which the anonymous translator-poet espouses the time-honored principle that the more a work pleases, the better it will instruct: "Raisons qu'est de solez paree / Est plus voluntiers escoutee" ("Reason adorned with entertainment is more willingly listened to"); going on to compare his apologues to a garden in which, attracted by the beauty of the flowers, one will more readily feed on the nourishing fruit.

The three fables translated here are numbers 25, 26, and 52 of the Bastin edition.

---

1. Regarding the attribution to Walter, see Julia Bastin, *Recueil général des Isopets,* II:ii–iii.

2. For another, earlier, critical edition of this collection, see *Lyoner Yzopet. Altfranzösische Übersetzung des XIII. Jahrhunderts,* ed. Wendelin Foerster. For a detailed study, see also Bruno Herlet, "Studien über die sogenannte Lyoner Ysopet, Ysopet I und Ysopet II."

Dou Lou et de la True

Une True danz soi portoit
Porceax. Li Lous la confortoit
Et li disoit: "Dame! acouchiez,
Et je, doucemant, ce saichiez,
De mon pouoir vos aiderai
Et vos porcelaz bien norrai."
Cele dit: "Gloz ploins de malice!
N'ai que faire de ton office.
Vai loin de ci et tien ta voie,
Si que suremant enfantoie.
Se tu faire me vuez servise,
Va t'en, bien conois ta fointise!"
A la True avoir fit Nature
De garder ses porceas grant cure.
Li Lous s'an part et tient sa vie,
La True anfante sa lignie.

Garde lou tens et la persone
En conoistre parole bone;
Quar traïtour lo tens esgaitent
Ou lour mançonges miez effaitent.

The Wolf and the Sow

A wolf went calling on his neighbor—
A pregnant sow, about to labor—
Saying how happy he would be
To help with her delivery.
"Go have your piglets, friend," he said.
"I'll see that they're well housed and fed."
"Oh yes, I'm sure!" replies the sow.
"What do you take me for? Come now,
I know your help, and I don't need it!
False is your talk, and I'll not heed it,
Vile hypocrite! You can't deceive me.
I'll not give birth until you leave me."
Nature endowed the sow with sense
Against the wolf's blandiloquence;
And he, seeing he can't outwit her,
Leaves her in peace to have her litter.[1]

Beware those treacherous rogues malicious,
Who watch for circumstance propitious
When best to gull and cozen you.
Learn how to tell false words from true:

Bien mostre sa fole meniere,
Qui tost croit parole legiere.

Only the arrant fool, unthinking,
Blindly accepts his own hoodwinking.

1. In these pages the reader will find two other treatments of this classic Aesopic confrontation, each stylistically very different from the present medieval version, as well as from one another. (See pp. 13–14 and 47.)

De la Terre Qui Anfante la Rate

La Terre s'enfla grossemant
Et dona grant gemissemant,
Con famme qui doit anfanter.
La gent s'en prist a gaimanter:
Faire doit, ce samble, mervoille
La Terre, qu'ensinc s'avantroille.
Bien cuide ce soit demostrance
Ou novele senefiance.
Chescuns tremble, fuit et fremit,
Quant voit la Terre qui gemit.
En ris torne ceste dotance;
Quar, quant la Terre ovre sa pance,
Ele enfante une grosse Rate:
Chescuns rit de ceste barate.

Qui en mout perler se travaillent,
Ce sont cilz qui, en fait, moins vaillent.
Por une cause mout petite
Est tost fole gent desconfite.
Tost fait sa litiere et s'estable
Paour en cuer qu'est trop muable.

The Earth That Gives Birth to the Mouse

The earth, one day—or so they tell—
Began to grumble, tremble, swell
Like pregnant woman giving birth.
Round and about there was no dearth
Of tearful, fearful conversation.
The village folk, in consternation,
Pictured the earth, in her travail,
About to spawn some woeful bale,
Some new and awesome prodigy.
A-quake, aghast, they turn to flee.
But lo! earth's belly opens wide,
And suddenly their fears subside:
A mouse appears!... A mouse!... Soon after,
Fright turns to glee; and gloom, to laughter.

Foolish are they who chitter-chatter
Over those woes that little matter;
Prattling with fright—distressed, distraught—
For what might well amount to nought.
Faint hearts give fear a place to dwell,
All for the merest bagatelle.

De la Vivre et de la Lime

Morant de fain vient une Vivre
Chies un fevre querant son vivre;
La Lime comancë a rore.
La Lime perlai a cele hore:
"Vivre, tu n'as sent ne memoire,
Por savoir mon pooir ne ma gloire.
Ta denz ne me grieve riens, fole,
La moie ront la tue mole.
Dou fert fait la farine dure
Ma denz, tant est forz sa morsure.
Les choses aspres e lè plainne
Deront ma force soverainne.
Lo fert dur et lo fort acier
Puis je per ma force percier.
Tu me morz de dant desarmee,
Bien pert que tu n'es pas sannee.
Tu te quasses, s'an es grant ire,
De ta folie me fais rire."

La Vivre mostre en sa folie
Folz est qui plus fort contralie.
A son paroil contretenir

The Viper and the File

A viper, fairly dead from hunger,
Happens upon a costermonger.
Spying a file, he starts to chew it.
"Fool that you are! You'll live to rue it!"
(So chides the tool.) "Can you be so
Devoid of wit as not to know
How strong I am, you stupid snake?
You can't hurt me, but I can make
Short work of you, I guarantee!
I bite so sharp that, one two three,
Everything yields before my power,
Crumbling to dust like pastry flour!
Nothing, however smooth or rough—
Hard iron, stout steel—is tough enough
To take my measure. Yet *you* would!
What utter, sheer foolhardihood!
Gnash, nibble, gnaw... I'll twit and chaff:
The more you chew, the more I'll laugh!"

The viper, in his folly, shows
How daft the man who would oppose
Those of a mightier bent than his.

Se puet li forz, et convenir.
Mais li fort ne puet lo plus fort
Soffrir, quant il fait son effort.
Li foibles se doit mout doter ·
Qu'a fort ne l'estuisse joter.

Madness it ever was—and is—
When weak attack the strong. They never
Last very long in their endeavor.
If proof you need, behold the viper:
He played too bold... and paid the piper!

1. For a strikingly terse rendition of this often-treated subject, see p. 48.

Eustache Deschamps (ca. 1346–ca. 1406)

ALTHOUGH one of the most important links between the French poets of the early Middle Ages and the great François Villon, towering giant of their waning years, Eustache Deschamps, famous during his lifetime, was virtually forgotten for four centuries after his death. It took devoted nineteenth-century scholars to dust off his prodigious *œuvre* and rediscover it for posterity.

A disciple (and, according to some, a nephew) of poet-musician Guillaume de Machaut, Deschamps, besides authoring several rather ponderous didactic works, was an indefatigable practitioner and developer of the *formes fixes* that his mentor had introduced into French prosody in the mid-fourteenth century: brief stanzaic set pieces, composed according to formal conventions of rhyme and repetition, in contrast to the lengthier and generally amorphous verses of an earlier age.[1] Deschamps tailored his *rondeaux* and *chants royaux,* his *lais* and *virelais*—and especially his literally thousand-plus *ballades*—to the many demands of his varied inspiration and vigorous style. In them he expressed not only the inherited lyric themes of love, death, and the like, but also, and more characteristically, a whole gamut of emotions from patriotic fervor to bitter personal resentment. The result was a vast body of verse—subjective but often objectively informative as well—in which the poet, as both victim and observer, passes in review the events of the day, voicing his satirical recriminations against an unkind Fate, in general, or his (and Society's) enemies, in particular. It is, in fact, primarily through a study of the historical allusions and personal references in his works that his biography can be sketched.[2]

Deschamps, known also by his sobriquet Morel—"dark-skinned"—was a native of Champagne, born around 1346 to a well-to-do bourgeois family in the town of Vertus. After studying law for a time in Orléans, he abandoned his studies to accept an appointment as king's messenger, and went on to serve at the court of Charles V in a variety of governmental functions from 1367 until that monarch's death in 1380. Continuing his service under Charles VI, he traveled extensively on official missions, possibly as far afield as Egypt and Syria. Deschamps married in 1373, fathered two or three children—sources differ—and was widowered three years later. If one can take his cynical and often earthy (not to say obscene) *Mirouër de mariage* as a reflection of personal experience and not merely a conventional antifeminist salvo in the ongoing medieval debate known as the Querelle de la Femme, his brief marriage could not have been an especially happy time.[3] Nor were his latter years, marked by his progressive fall from royal grace at the hands of the mad king's manipulating courtiers. Disillusioned, disgruntled, and already en route to oblivion, Deschamps died in the early years of the fifteenth century, probably in 1406 or 1407.

Tucked away here and there in his *Œuvres complètes,* among the more than eighty thousand lines of verse that constitute his "espèce d'encyclopédie morale du siècle où il a vécu" (see Deschamps, *Poésies morales et historiques,* ed. Crapelet, p. xiii), are a dozen or so fables set in the form of *ballades*—some with, some without the codalike envoi that Deschamps is credited with having introduced—clearly inspired by the tradition of the Isopets. Most had been included in the collection of Crapelet, who noted, with some pride, in his introduction that he was the first biographer to realize that Deschamps was, indeed, a fabulist: "On a bien souvent, sans doute, ouvert l'énorme manuscrit des poésies d'Eustache Deschamps sans soupçonner que des fables y fussent cachées sous les titres de ballades ou de rondeaux" (p. xxiv). According to him, all of Deschamps's apologues, like so much of his work, were inspired by specific personal grievances. Only a few of them, however, can be readily identified. If, as Crapelet observes, they clearly pose no threat to La Fontaine's hegemony in the genre (pp. xxiv-xxv), they are nevertheless picturesque examples in their own right of the versatility of the fable, no less at home in the Procrustean formalism of Deschamps's *ballades* than in the octosyllabic couplets of his predecessors and, eventually, the "free verse" of La Fontaine himself and his many emulators.[4]

The three fables translated in our collection are the *ballades* numbered 36, 58, and 1253 in the *Œuvres complètes.*

1. Deschamps enunciated the formalities of his poetics—under the rubric "Musique," in a discussion of the medieval trivium and quadrivium—in his prose *Art de dictier*. This brief, rambling treatise, dated 1392 at the end of the text, is the first of a long line of French *arts poétiques*.

2. For one of the earliest see the pioneering collection edited by Georges-Adrien Crapelet, *Poésies morales et historiques d'Eustache Deschamps*, pp. i–lvi. It was this publisher-scholar who was largely responsible for exhuming the poet's work for the modern world, showing him in sharp contrast with most of his poetic contemporaries, who, in the words of bibliophile Emmanuel-Louis-Nicolas Viollet Le Duc, "se sont bornés à célébrer leurs belles ou à rimer des aventures allégoriques" (*Catalogue des livres composant la bibliothèque poétique de M. Viollet Le Duc*, p. 65). Crapelet's work was followed by Prosper Tarbé's two-volume collection, *Œuvres inédites d'Eustache Deschamps*, containing a brief biography, a few hundred poems, notes, and glossary. Amédée Sarradin based his biography, *Etudes sur Eustache Deschamps*, on the poems in Crapelet and Tarbé, only a fraction of Deschamps's *œuvre*, however. Publication of the entire available corpus was undertaken for the Société des Anciens Textes Français by Auguste de Queux de Saint-Hilaire and completed after his death by Gaston Raynaud (*Œuvres complètes d'Eustache Deschamps*). It contains some fifteen hundred poems in all, various collateral materials, but no biography as such. For the latter, see Ernest Hoepffner, *Eustache Deschamps, Leben und Werke*.

3. The *Mirouër*, begun around 1381, was left unfinished after some thirteen thousand lines. A number of *ballades* in which Deschamps deplores his married state would indicate that it was, in fact, no mere fashionable fiction. (It is ironic that the poet Christine de Pisan, author of the *Epistre au dieu d'amours* [1399] and other pro-Woman works, could be one of Deschamps's most devoted admirers and disciples. Surely it was not for the ideas in the *Mirouër*.)

4. Important recent studies of Deschamps are found in Daniel Poirion, *Le Poète et le prince: évolution du lyrisme courtois de Guillaume de Machaut à Charles d'Orléans*; Henrik Heger, *Die Melancholie bei den französischen Lyrikern des Spätmittelalters*, chap. 3; and Christine M. Scollen-Jimack, "Marot and Deschamps: The Rhetoric of Misfortune."

Le Paysan et le Serpent[1]

J'ay leu et veu une moralité
Ou chascuns puet assez avoir advis,
C'uns paisans qui, par necessité
Cavoit terre, trouva un serpent bis
Ainsis que mort, et adonques l'a pris
Et l'apporta, en son celier l'estent;
La fut de lui peus, chaufez, nourris;
Mais on rent mal en lieu de bien souvent.

Car li serpens plains de desloyauté,
Roussiaulx et fel, quant il se voit garis,
Au paisant a son venin getté.
Par lui li fut mal pour bien remeris,
Par bien faire est li povres homs peris
Qui par pitié ot nourri le serpent;
Moult de gens sont, pour bien faire, honnis,
Mais on rent mal en lieu de bien souvent.

C'est grant doleur quant l'en fait amisté
A tel qui puis en devient ennemis;
Ingratitude est ce vice appellé,
Dont pluseurs gens sont au monde entrepris,
Retribuens le mal a leur amis
Qui leur ont fait le bien communement.
Ainsis fait on, s'en perdront paradis;
Mais on rent mal en lieu de bien souvent.

1. Although some of Deschamps's *ballades* and other pieces bear titles seemingly of his own invention, the title of the present fable (and of the one following) were apparently added by the modern editor.

The Peasant and the Snake

I found a fable once—and read it, too—
That might, in fact, to good effect be read
By everyone; about a peasant, who,
Turning the soil, turns up a snake instead:
A serpent dark of hue and well-nigh dead.[2]
He takes him to his pantry, where we find
The dying beast well cared for, coddled, fed...
Kindness is seldom recompensed in kind.

The snake—a viper, vicious through and through—
Nursed back to health and risen from his bed,
Suddenly strikes, as snakes are wont to do,
And kills the peasant, who, as I have said,
Has done such good—and been so much misled!
Many there are who, selflessly inclined
To worthy deeds, reap woe unmerited:
Kindness is seldom recompensed in kind.

Others there are, I fear—and not a few—
Who ill repay such noble-spirited
And generous-hearted souls, fair friends and true;
Others who, in this world—foul and ill-bred—
Reward our charity with not one shred
Of human gratitude. Vile sinners blind!
For them is Heaven forever forfeited.
Kindness is seldom recompensed in kind.

2. If we can believe him, Deschamps would have read his fable in one of the Isopets, several of which include it. For one version, with translation, see my *Fables from Old French: Aesop's Beasts and Bumpkins*, pp. 62–63.

Le Chat et les Souris[1]

Je treuve qu'entre les souris
Ot un merveilleux parlement
Contre les chas leurs ennemis,

The Cat and the Mice

The mice—they tell us, verily!—
Once had a wondrous rendezvous:
Plotting to foil their enemy,

A veoir maniere comment
Elles vesquissent seurement
Sanz demourer en tel debat;
L'une dist lors en arguant:
Qui pendra la sonnette au chat?

Cilz consaulz fut conclus et prins;
Lors se partent communement.
Une souris du plat pais
Les encontre et va demandant
Qu'om a fait: lors vont respondant
Que leur ennemi seront mat:
Sonnette aront ou coul pendant.
Qui pendra la sonnette au chat?

"C'est le plus fort," dist un rat gris.
Elle demande saigement
Par qui sera cilz fais fournis.
Lors s'en va chascune excusant;
Il n'y ot point d'executant,
S'en va leur besongne de plat;
Bien fut dit, mais, au demourant,
Qui pandra la sonnette au chat?

L'ENVOY

Prince, on conseille bien souvent,
Mais on puet dire, com le rat,
Du conseil qui sa fin ne prant:
Qui pendra la sonnette au chat?

They sought some path they might pursue
Against the cats, who, thitherto,
Had terrorized their habitat.
Said one: "I know just what to do:
Who's going to go and bell the cat?"

Excellent plan, they all agree!
And when their colloquy is through,
A neighbor mouse comes by, and she
Inquires of them: "Well, friends, what's new?"
Reply the mice without ado:
"The cats have had their day! That's that!
We're going to bell them!..." "Really? Who?...
Who's going to go and bell the cat?"

"Aye, there's the rub!" sighs cynically
An old grey rat. "I wish I knew!"
Again the mouse asks: "Who will be
Our catbell-hanger?... You?... You?... You?..."
But one by one, bidding adieu,
Our mice withdraw... Their plan falls flat.
And yet, the question still rings true:
"Who's going to go and bell the cat?"

ENVOY

Prince, when advice unstintingly
Flows from loquacious diplomat,
Best is the old rat's repartee:
"Who's going to go and bell the cat?"

1. For an admittedly incomplete list of over four dozen Oriental
and Occidental antecedents and adaptations of this popular fable,
probably introduced from Arabic sources into the West in the early
thirteenth century, see Paul Franklin Baum, "The Fable of Belling the

Cat," in *Proverbia in Fabula: Essays on the Relationship of the Proverb
and the Fable*, ed. Pack Carnes, pp. 37–46. (Baum's paper first appeared in *Modern Language Notes* 34 [1919]: 462–70.)

D'un Paisant et de Son Chien[1]

Un paisant avoit un chien
De grant exploit, jeune et puissant,
Fort et hardi, si l'ama bien,
Car toute beste fut prenant,
Et si gardoit diligemment
Son hostel de jour et de nuit;
Manger lui fist de maint deduit,
Et des loups son tropiau garda.
Or devint vieulx; lors le destruit:
Quant fruit fault, desserte s'en va.

Son vivre en son aage ancien
Lui restraint et le va foulant
Pour en chaiel qui ne vault rien,
Dont le viel chien est moult dolent
Et dit: "J'ay perdu mon jouvent,
Qui cuidoie cueillir le fruit
De mon jeune temps; or suy vuit
D'avoir guerdon. Advisez la;

A Peasant and His Hound

A peasant had a hound: young, bold,
Victor against his every prey.
Fearless protector of the fold,
Staunch sentinel—by night, by day—
He kept the fearsome wolf at bay,
Guarding the household, snug abed.
Loved by his master, he was fed
None but the finest fare... But he
Grows old. He might as well be dead:
When gone the fruit, farewell the tree.

Where now those meats and sweets untold?
Where now the love, the work, the play?
A callow pup has been enrolled
To take his place; some worthless stray!
Laments the hound, in disarray:
"My youth, with all its pleasures? Fled!
Now, only hollow days ahead...
Look at my plight and chastened be!

Notez bien ce proverbe tuit:
'Quant fruit fault, desserte s'en va.' "

Bien voy ceste figure et tien;
Reduire la puis proprement
A mon service, et pour ce vien
A conclure semblablement:
Quant j'ay servi treslonguement,
Lors vient ingratitude et bruit;
D'estat me despointe et me nuit.
Las! ma viellesce que fera?
Bien puis dire com vray instruit:
"Quant fruit fault, desserte s'en va."

L'ENVOY

Prince, faictes faire autrement
A ceuls qui servent loyaument,
Vostre regne mieulx en vauldra;
Ne faictes com le paisant
Fist a son chien mauvaisement.
Quant fruit fault, desserte s'en va.

How true the saying, often said:
'When gone the fruit, farewell the tree!' "

I see this fiction, and behold
The hound's dejection with dismay:
Undone, unwanted, unconsoled...
That peasant and his hound portray
My plight as well. Ah, welladay!
Cast out, scorn heaped upon my head...
Where now the loyal life I led?
Ah, age! What sport you make of me!
And so I sigh, dispirited:
"When gone the fruit, farewell the tree."

ENVOY

Prince, let not faithful liege, I pray,
Be cast so carelessly away,
Like hound, though fine his pedigree.
Pay loyalty its due; thus may
Your reign be praised, and none may say:
"When gone the fruit, farewell the tree."

1. The title of the original appears to be one of those appended by the poet himself.

Gilles Corrozet   Les Fables du Très-Ancien Esope Mises en Rithme Françoise (1542)

UNLIKE his predecessor Eustache Deschamps (see pp. 9–10), who merely inserted an occasional fable here and there, almost inconspicuously, into the vast body of his verse, Gilles Corrozet devoted a whole volume—one of his many—to a collection of Aesopic translations. If we can believe Auguste de Queux de Saint-Hilaire, the editor of a nineteenth-century republication of that volume, *Les Fables du très-ancien Esope mises en rithme françoise,* he was, in fact, the first published poet to do so, clearly taking advantage of the contemporary popularity of the Phrygian fabulist.[1] At the same time, Corrozet was giving natural expression to his own moralistic leanings, as evidenced by a number of his other works in verse and prose. He could, furthermore, indulge his proclivities with relative ease, materially speaking, being himself a member of the burgeoning sixteenth-century book trade: a bookseller, certainly, and possibly also a printer.[2] Be that as it may, without imputing to him only crass pecuniary motives, we are justified, I think, in suspecting that at least some of the author's inspiration was due to the astute bookseller's appraisal of public taste; a taste to which he catered as well with the profusion of illustrations that adorned his writings. Many of his texts, in-

deed, would seem almost to be pretexts for the elegant woodcuts that illustrated them, most of which belonged to the stock of celebrated Parisian printer Denis Janot, on whose presses much of our author's work was executed. Corrozet is said to have amassed a considerable fortune from the sale of his books, thereby apparently becoming one of the earliest authors to support himself by his publications.[3]

Corrozet was born in Paris on January 4, 1510.[4] With little formal education, but with proper Renaissance spirit, he is said to have taught himself Latin, Italian, and Spanish, as well as history and geography, all eminently useful in his later profession. It is thought that he began his career as a guide for foreign visitors, a supposition encouraged by the publication, in 1532, of his first important work, the *Fleur des antiquitez de Paris,* both a history of the capital—in prose, with verse interspersed—and a kind of Baedeker *avant la lettre* to its points of interest. The volume's many editions, during his life and after, attest to its success. (See the modern edition by François Boucher.) It was, in fact, to sell copies of that book that he supposedly first set up shop, in 1535. Biographical accounts tell us little more about his personal life, except that he lost his wife in 1562, and remarried shortly before his own death on July 4, 1568. Corrozet left several children—among them two sons who continued his prosperous trade for a time—and several dozen published (and often republished) works: translations, moralistic verse, historical prose, occasional and religious pieces, and a variety of *blasons, sentences, apophtegmes,* and the like, whose titles fill several pages of bibliography.[5]

Owing to numerous editions, presenting a maze of differing details—variations in title, printer, ancillary matter—as well as to works of questionable attribution, that bibliography is a thicket of knots and tangles through which I would not attempt here to lead the reader. Ancient, less ancient, and modern bibliographers, aiming at completeness, face inevitable frustration. Some settle for listing only Corrozet's most important works.[6] As for his *Fables du très-ancien Esope,* Queux de Saint-Hilaire cites only three editions, those of 1542, 1544, and 1583. His text reproduces the hundred fables of the first,

with variants from the second, plus twenty-three additional fables and a prose *Vie d'Esope* from the third.[7]

As might be expected, much of the interest in Corrozet's text derives from a comparison with analogues in La Fontaine.[8] But while it is generally agreed that the latter knew the work of some of his sixteenth-century predecessors—the "modernes" he refers to in the third paragraph of the preface to his first collection (Books I–VI), in 1668—there is no real certainty as to which ones he knew, nor to what extent (if at all) any may have inspired him.[9] Such imponderables aside, Corrozet's fables deserve a reading on their own merit, perhaps less for their sober but not wholly colorless moralizing than for the unusually rich variety of rhythmic patterns that he introduces into his narrations.

Both that sobriety and diversity are reflected in the five translated here: numbers 20, 47, 54, 83, and 91 of the Queux de Saint-Hilaire edition.

---

1. "Ce petit livre . . . est, à notre connaissance, la première version poétique qui ait été, sinon faite, du moins publiée, du recueil des fables d'Esope, qui avait joui d'une si grande popularité pendant tout le moyen âge; de nombreuses traductions en prose, publiées au XVe et au commencement du XVIe siècle, en sont la preuve ainsi que les traductions en vers du XIIIe et du XIVe siècle, que l'on a publiées depuis quelques années . . ." (Corrozet, *Les Fables du très-ancien Esope,* p. i).

2. Sources differ. Many early observers indicate that Corrozet was an "imprimeur" as well as a "libraire." (See among others, the abbé Claude-Pierre Goujet, *Bibliothèque françoise, ou Histoire de la littérature françoise,* XIII:99; and Jean-Pierre Niceron, *Mémoires pour servir à l'histoire des hommes illustres dans la république des lettres, avec un catalogue raisonné de leurs ouvrages,* XXIV:150. They possibly took their cue from François Grudé de La Croix du Maine, who, in his *Premier volume de la bibliothèque du Sieur de La Croix du Maine,* writing on Corrozet, refers to "plusieurs liures que luy-mesme a imprimez" [p. 128].) Others, especially more recent scholars, specifically deny that he was himself a printer. (See, for example, Charles Oulmont's preface to his edition of Corrozet's 1540 collection of *emblèmes* [see pp. 20–21], entitled *Hécatomgraphie,* p. viii, n. 1.)

3. See the revised *Biographie universelle, ancienne et moderne,* IX:264. This biographical dictionary is a revision of the eighty-five volume work of the same name, commonly referred to as the "Biographie Michaud."

4. Here too there is disagreement, some sources citing the date as July 4.

5. For a brief and readable sketch of his life and work, more informative than those in the many biographical dictionaries, see Charles Oulmont's above-mentioned preface to the *Hécatomgraphie;* and for a recent study devoted to his fables and *emblèmes,* see Barbara Tiemann, *Fabel und Emblem. Gilles Corrozet und die französische Renaissance-Fabel.*

6. His earliest bibliographer, Grudé de La Croix du Maine (see above), cites some thirty-nine titles, admitting that his list is probably incomplete: "Il peult auoir escrit plusieurs autres liures, soit de son inuention ou autrement, desquels ie n'ay pas cognoissance." (See

Antoine Rigoley de Juvigny's augmented revision of La Croix du Maine's original 1584 edition, *Les Bibliothèques françoises de La Croix du Maine et de Du Verdier,* I:286–89.) Niceron lists about the same number. The nineteenth-century bibliophile Jacques-Charles Brunet cites only some fifteen—not including the fables, curiously—but does so in minute detail. As for modern bibliographical help, in addition to the relatively useful entries in *Dictionnaire des lettres françaises: le seizième siècle,* pp. 203–4, and Alexandre Cioranescu, *Bibliographie de la littérature française du seizième siècle,* pp. 219–20, see the study by S.-M. Bouchereaux, "Recherches bibliographiques sur Gilles Corrozet."

7. Other sources indicate two more sixteenth-century editions (1548 and 1549) as well as another from the early nineteenth century. (See the above-mentioned citations in Niceron, Cioranescu, and the *Dictionnaire des lettres françaises: le seizième siècle.*) There is also a selection of fifteen fables accompanying Ferdinand Gohin's edition of Corrozet's verse-tale of love and honor, *Le Compte du Rossignol,* first published in 1546 by Jean de Tournes. To complicate matters further, a recent researcher claims that the collection had a total of twelve editions between 1542 and 1587, and refers to the edition of 1548 as a second, separate, collection. (See Adriana Stramignoni, "Les Fables de Gilles Corrozet," p. 586; also the chapter on Corrozet in Gianni Mombello, *Le Raccolte francesi di favole esopiane dal 1480 alla fine del secolo XVI,* pp. 108–21.)

8. It is also worth noting in this regard that a number of the moralistic *emblèmes* of the *Hécatomgraphie* (see above) are fables of sorts. Several of them have parallels in La Fontaine (e.g., "Contre les astrologues," pp. 142–43), which, along with many other models, may possibly have caught his fancy.

9. Although A.-C.-M. Robert, in his *Fables inédites des XIIe, XIIIe et XIVe siècles, et Fables de La Fontaine,* calls attention to occasional parallels between Corrozet and La Fontaine, he does not discuss the former's work at length. He does, however, go into considerable detail regarding his contemporary Guillaume Haudent, for whom a strong case can, in fact, be made. (See pp. 17–18.)

De la Truye et du Loup

La promesse bien souvent
Est plus legiere que vent,
Tel ayder aultruy promet
Qui pour luy nuyre s'y met.

The Sow and the Wolf[1]

False friends make promises galore,
But only wind and little more;
Or else they promise help, then do
Their best to work their worst on you.[2]

Une Truye cochonnoit,
　　Sy venoit
Ung Loup qui en sa finesse
　　Feit promesse
A la Truye de l'ayder,
　　Et garder
Les Cochons à leur saillir
　　Sans faillir.
Lors luy respondit la Truye,
　　Esbaye,
Qu'el n'avoit de luy affaire
　　Necessaire,
Qu'il la voulloit decevoir
　　Pour avoir
Ses Cochonnetz tant petis
　　Et gentilz.
Et luy pleust sans plus parler
　　S'en aller,
Car trop mieulx en son absence
　　Qu'en presence
Ses petits cochonneroit,
　　Et seroit
En plus grande liberté,
　　Seureté:
Lors s'en va le Loup honteux
　　Marmiteux.
En faulx amy, quoy qu'il die,
　　Ne te fie.

A pregnant sow goes into labor.
　　Comes friend neighbor,
The wily wolf, who, all the while
　　Full of guile,
Tells her that he might well be helping
　　With the whelping:
That he will gladly hold her young,
　　Newly sprung,
Each one by one. "How now! How now!"
　　Gasps the sow,
Aghast. "That really won't be very
　　Necessary!"
Ah no! For she knows well and good
　　How he would,
In turn, quickly turn tail and quit her
　　With her litter.
And so she asks the vile deceiver
　　Please to leave her.
Yes, surely she would do much better
　　If he let her
Labor alone, in peace, without
　　Wolves about,
Safe and secure in solitude
　　With her brood.
Ashamed, the wolf, in disarray,
　　Skulks away.
Indeed, don't trust false friends, no matter
　　What they chatter!

1. I have omitted from my translations the one-line prose summary with which the author introduces each of his fables. In the originals, both that single line and the opening quatrain, accompanied by an appropriate woodcut and placed before the title, occupy the left-hand page of text.

2. In the second couplet of the introductory quatrain, as well as in lines 25–26 of the fable proper, I translate the variants from Corrozet's revised edition of 1544 rather than the original 1542 version.

De la Chate Muée en Femme

　　A grand peine sçauroit-on faire
　　D'ung Chahuan ung Esprevier,
　　Et qui se pense contrefaire
　　Ne peult à son blasme obvier.

The Cat Turned Woman

　　By no endeavor, I'm afraid, you
　　Ever turn owl to hawk; and hence,
　　I pray you stay as Nature made you,
　　Free of the taint of false pretense.

Ung jouvenceau, trop fol et mal apris,
Fut de l'amour d'une Chate surpris
Qu'il nourrissoit, voire sy ardemment
Qu'il supplia affectueusement
Venus affin qu'elle muast icelle
Chate amoureuse en tresbelle pucelle.
Venus, voulant plaire au vouloir infame
Du jouvenceau, lors transmua en femme
La beste mue, et la feit acomplie
Au faict d'aymer, et de beaulté remplie.
Le jeune amant adonc se resjouyst,
Et de la dame à son aise jouyst;
Mais il advint que, pour sçavoir si elle
Estoit de mœurs femme bien naturelle,
Venus laissa passer une Souris
Par devant elle. O qu'il y eut de ris!
Icelle femme, aussy tost qu'elle veid
Ceste Souris, elle la poursuyvit
En oubliant sa beaulté corporelle,
Et ensuyvant sa vertu naturelle.
Doncques Venus, de cela despitée,
Sa forme humaine alors luy a ostée.
Ainsi aulcuns, qui font mutation
De leur estat, sont en complexion
Sy depravez que de tout bien s'estrangent,
Et leur malice en bonté point ne changent.

A youth there was, of wit bedulled and dim,
Who kept a cat that doted so on him—
Because, forsooth, he fed her well—that he
Prayed to the goddess Venus, earnestly,
To turn the fawning feline then and there
Into a living, loving lady fair.
Venus, to serve his lecherous intent,
Transformed the beast into a beauty, bent
On making love, and doing so quite well—
As well as any human damosel!—
Such that our boor, a-twitter and a-stir,
Eagerly did his lustful will with her.
Now then, it happened that, to ease her mind
And test the new-made mortal's humankind,
Venus let loose a mouse before the creature,
Who, still the cat in all but form and feature—
Doing what any cat was wont to do,
Without so much as "what?" or "why?" or "who?"—
Threw beauty to the winds, went chasing after,
Amid haws and guffaws and gales of laughter.
Venus, irate, observing, jaws agape,
Forthwith returned her to her former shape.
Those who would play at Nature's counterfeit
Debase themselves and profit not a whit.
No good can come of ill; nay, not a jot:
So be yourself and not someone you're not.

Du Lion et du Regnard

Tout ce qui n'est hanté
Est trouvé bien estrange;
Mais, s'il est frequenté,
L'oppinion se change.

Le Regnard au chemin trouva
Le Lyon, beste fort terrible,
Qui luy sembla sy treshorrible
Que de grand peur fuyt et s'en va.

Il le trouva secondement
Une aultrefois, dont il eut crainte,
Mais non pas de sy forte attainte
Qu'il avoit eu premierement.

La tierce foys le rencontra.
Donc, pour l'avoir veu si souvent,
Il meist hardiesse en avant,
Et sans peur à luy se monstra.

Avecques luy se meist en voye.
Lors il le trouva si privé
Que d'estre vers luy arrivé
Il eut grande liesse et joye.

S'aprivoiser est difficile;
Mais, quand on a prins cognoissance,
L'amytié prend pleine croissance,
Et le hanter en est facile.

The Lion and the Fox

Things unfamiliar will
Always confound us, for
What's new seems strange until
We see it more and more.

A fox out strolling happened on
A lion, who appeared to him
So cruel of face, so fierce and grim,
That in a trice the fox was gone.

A second time his luck was such
That he encountered him again,
And found him fearsome... Yes... But then,
To tell the truth, not quite as much.

He saw the beast a third time yet;
But, having seen him twice before,
This time, intrepid, he forswore
His fear... Drew near... And so they met.

Lion and fox soon came to be
As friend to friend, brother to brother;
And when the one would join the other,
Joyous would be their company.

When intercourse seems fraught with danger,
The first step is the hardest one;
But friendship blossoms once begun
And makes a comrade of the stranger.

L'acoustumance en plusieurs lieux
Avec les grandz nous aprivoise,
Lesquelz n'ausions, de peur de noise,
Regarder entre les deux yeulx.

Little by little, by the by,
Even those born of high degree
Seem less and less aloof, though we
At first scarce looked them in the eye.

De l'Enfant et de Fortune

Ordinairement par nous mesmes
Nous tumbons en perilz extremes,
Nostre faulte et coulpe excusons
Et la fortune en accusons.

Prés d'ung puys estoit
Et s'y esbatoit
Ung beau jeune filz;
Sommeil le surprint,
Et dormir s'en vint
Au bord de ce puys.

Fortune, qui va
Au lieu, arriva
Et celluy resveille,
Disant: "Mon amy,
Ne sois endormy
Et plus ne sommeille.

"Sy tumbé tu fusses,
Excusé ne m'eusses,
Et chascun eust dict
Que trop importune
Luy estoit Fortune,
Qui mort le rendit.

"Moy donc accusée,
Ta faulte excusée
Tousjours eust esté;
Mais l'homme imparfaict
Luy seul mal se faict
Par sa lascheté."

Dame Fortune and the Child

In dangers dire, too often we
View our own actions blamelessly.
Fortune it is who stands berated
For ills our frailties have created.

A youth, beside a well,
Close—too close, truth to tell—
    Was hard at play,
When, rather by surprise,
Sleep came and closed his eyes
    As down he lay.

Dame Fortune passed, espying
The edge where he was lying,
    And warned: "Nay, nay! You
Mustn't lie sleeping there!
Beware, fair lad! Beware!
    Wake up, I pray you!

"For if you slip, and fall,
And drown, then one and all
    Will rail at me.
Fortune will be reviled
For cutting down a child
    Mercilessly.

"Ah, yes, they'll curse my name,
But not find you to blame
    For thoughtlessness!
Yet none but Man's own flaws
And failings are the cause
    Of his distress."

De la Femme et de la Geline

L'homme est maintesfois trop expert
En exerçant son avarice,
Dangereux est tel exercice,
Car tel cuide gaigner qui perd.

Quelque femme une Poulle avoit
Qui luy portoit grand advantaige,
Chascun jour pondre luy devoit
Ung œuf d'or comme elle pouoit,
C'estoit son naturel usaige:
Dont fut augmenté le mesnaige,
Et riche grandement devint
Pour ce beau thresor qui luy vint.

The Woman and the Hen

Often is man, to his chagrin,
Too skillful in the ways of greed.
A skill most dangerous indeed:
He loses, who had thought to win.

A certain woman once there was
Who had herself a wondrous hen,
One unconstrained by nature's laws—
Prodigious fowl in fact—because
Each morning, time and time again,
It laid a golden egg. Now then,
In time the woman's daily treasure
Brought her great wealth and worldly pleasure.[1]

Ceste femme avaricieuse,
Pensant la Poulle estre au dedans
Toute dorée et precieuse,
La tua comme furieuse,
Sans adviser les accidentz;
Mais à l'œil de tous regardantz
Fust trouvée dans sa poictrine
Tout ainsi qu'une aultre geline.

En pensant doncques s'enrichir
Elle perdit par convoitise.
Avarice nous faict fleschir,
Et nous augmente le desir
Qui nous faict perdre chose acquise.
Desir de gaing faict entreprise,
Qui est cause de perte à mainctz
De ce qu'ilz tenoient en leurs mains.

But being of a greedy bent,
Thinking the bird must surely be
Crammed full of gold magnificent,
She wrung its neck, impenitent,
And slit its throat for all to see.
What met their eyes? Well, actually,
No more nor less that one sees when
One opens any other hen.

More and more wealth she wanted. Thus
Our woman lost, alas, the source
Of all her gold miraculous.
Greed makes such blessèd fools of us!
Many there are who, in due course,
Gain much; want more; lose all, perforce.
Not satisfied with what they've got,
They covet more, and lose the lot.

1. Many Aesopic antecedents present the hen's owner as a man. La Fontaine (V, 13) and many other fabulists will do likewise. As for the type of fowl in question, some identify it as a goose, more famil- iar to our ears. (See, for example, Ben Edwin Perry, *Aesopica*, p. 355.) Others, like Babrius, 123, refer merely to an *ornis* 'bird', though the Greek word often does refer specifically to the hen.

Guillaume Haudent   Trois Cent Soixante et Six Apologues d'Esope Traduicts en Rithme Françoise (1547)

Guillaume Haudent was virtually unknown, even in his native city of Rouen, when Robert exhumed him from oblivion in his volume devoted to the fabulists before La Fontaine.[1] And this despite the fact that, of all the latter's precursors, Haudent's claim to direct, discernible "influence" appears to be the most well established. (See A.-C.-M. Robert, *Fables inédites des XIIe, XIIIe et XIVe siècles*, pp. clxxxviii–cxciii; and Charles Lormier's introduction to his reedition of *Trois cent soixante et six apologues d'Esope traduicts en rithme françoise*, pp. xxii–xxvi.) Robert, however, gives him rather short shrift artistically, calling attention to "l'excessive platitude des vers" and "l'absence totale de génie poétique." It is not surprising that, piqued by such a negative appreciation, several *rouennais* compatriots would spring to Haudent's posthumous defense; not surprising either that they would tend to compensate appropriately by exaggerating his merits. The result, besides the above-mentioned edition, was an enthusiastic reappraisal of his contribution to the fable literature.[2]

Haudent, for all his subsequent eclipse, appears to have been reasonably well known during his lifetime, though admittedly not a literary giant. (See Millet-Saint-Pierre, "Guillaume Haudent," pp. 195–201, 211–12.) Born in Rouen in the early years of the sixteenth century, he was apparently a minor cleric, who indulged his poetic aspirations in his youth by participating in the yearly poetic competitions—"Palinods"—held in the Normandy towns of Rouen, Caen, and Dieppe in honor of the Virgin.[3] We know too that he was employed from 1537 to 1545 as preceptor to the choirboys of his city's cathedral. Resigning from that post, possibly with the intention of devoting himself to literature, he was, however, appointed "maître de grammaire" to novices of the Carmelite order. (See *Trois cent soixante et six apologues d'Esope*, ed. Lormier, pp. viii–ix.) Nevertheless, despite his continuing religious and pedagogical obligations, he spent the next dozen years translating a variety of moralistic works, including his Aesopic apologues.[4] He died in his native city, probably in or around 1557.

Haudent's modern editor, Lormier, goes to some length to show that he was familiar with the fables of his contemporary Corrozet, even suggesting that it was the latter's success that moved him to adapt the genre to his own didactic purposes (see pp. xiv–xviii). Not unexpectedly, Lormier concludes that a comparison of the two fabulists does not disadvantage his poet. On artistic grounds that subjective judgment seems overly partisan and not a little exaggerated. What can be said objectively, however, is that Haudent not only wrote many more fables than Corrozet but that he did so with far less inventive flair, at least insofar as formal elements of prosody are concerned. Even a superficial observation reveals that he seldom varies the rather doggedly determined pace of his collection. It is clear that his purpose is an eminently didactic one, and that art and style, if at all a consideration, are strictly secondary. Still, in all fairness, it has to be admitted that this pious moralizer does have his moments: as the reader will appreciate, an occasional bit of Rabelaisian ribaldry lightens his otherwise pedestrian—though historically significant—contribution to the fable literature.

Haudent's apologues are divided into two books, containing, for no apparent reason, 206 and 160, respectively. My five translations are numbered as follows: I, 95; I, 114; II, 45; II, 79; and II, 122.

1. "Vers la première moitié du seizième siècle, la ville de Rouen se trouvait posséder... un poète fabuliste et traducteur, nommé Guillaume Haudent, dont elle n'a gardé le moindre souvenir. Dans sa bibliothèque publique il n'y a rien de cet auteur, et on ne le voit cité dans aucune des excellentes biographies et bibliographies normandes que nous possédons." (See J.-B. Millet-Saint-Pierre, "Guillaume Haudent, poète normand du XVIe siècle," p. 193.)

2. See the Marquis de Gaillon's brief article, "Un Fabuliste du XVIe siècle"; and, especially, the very detailed article, cited above, chronicling the literary detective work of Millet-Saint-Pierre (pp. 193–214). The latter seems particularly carried away by regional pride, however, when he suggests that Haudent's alleged "badinerie naïve" may have encouraged La Fontaine's characteristic easygoing bonhomie (p. 207).

3. See the abbé A. Tougard's edition of Joseph-André Guiot's work on the subject, *Les Trois siècles palinodiques, ou Histoire générale des Palinods de Rouen, Dieppe, etc.*

4. For as complete a bibliography as is available, see Verdun L. Saulnier's entry on Haudent in the *Dictionnaire des lettres françaises: le seizième siècle*, pp. 372–73; and Alexandre Cioranescu, *Bibliographie de la littérature française du seizième siècle*, p. 363. (Both should be supplemented by information contained in Millet-Saint-Pierre and Lormier, as well as in Gianni Mombello, *Le Raccolte francesi di favole esopiane dal 1480 alla fine del secolo XVI*, pp. 122–27.)

D'un Asne Vestu de la Peau d'un Lyon

Vn asne vestu de la peau
D'un lyon, faisoit crainte auoir
A mainte aultre beste & trouppeau
Tant il sembloit cruel a veoir,
Mais il fault entendre & scauoir
Qu'un regnard luy dist, "tes effroys
Me feroient paour, sans concepuoir
Que n'es qu'un asne a ouyr ta voix."

LE MORAL

Par la fable il est manifeste
Que souuent vn asne & indocte
Porte l'habit d'un homme docte
Mais son parler le manifeste.

The Ass Dressed in the Lion's Skin

The beasts grew fearful, far and wide,
When ass dressed up in lion's skin.
None but the fox, indeed, defied
His fierce appearance leonine.
Said he: "I could be taken in,
Like all the rest, by your charade;
And, I admit, I would have been...
If only, friend, you hadn't brayed."

MORAL

So too when, from the vulgar masses,
Crass and uncultured, nonetheless,
Some human ass wears scholar's dress:
His tongue, alas, is still an ass's.

D'une Grenoille, d'une Souris & d'une Escoufle

Vne grenoille eust quelque foys
Contre vne souris grosse guerre,
Tant qu'ilz vindrent par deux ou trois
Assaultz, s'entre empoigner sur terre.
Or pendant qu'estoient en telle erre
Lescoufle vint qui les rauist
Et dedans son ventre les serre
Si qu'oncques puis on ne les veist.

LE MORAL

Ceste fable nous determine
Que quand gentz d'une mesme ville
Menent entre eulx guerre ciuille
Aisément on les extermine.

The Frog, the Mouse, and the Kite

A frog and mouse were once engaged
In battle long and arduous.
Twice, thrice already they had waged
Their hand-to-hand attacks. As thus
The pair warred on, a ravenous,
Rapacious kite swooped down and bore
Them off in his esophagus:
None saw the warriors evermore.

MORAL

This lesson, then, may be inferred:
When two compatriots choose to be
Each one the other's enemy,
Both may be crushed by yet a third.

De Iuppiter Faisant vn Bansquet aux Bestes

Iadis fut faict vn bansquet treshonneste
Par iuppiter le souuerain des dieux
Auquel conuint, en effect toute beste
En luy donnant presentz delicieux
Lesquelz il print d'un vouloir gracieux
Sans nul d'iceulx refuser, fors la rose
Que luy offrit le serpent vicieux
La desdaignant, ainsi qu'infecte chose.

LE MORAL

  Ceste fable icy nous aprend
  Qu'a fuire soyons diligentz
  Les presentz de meschantes gentz
  Veu le dommage qu'on en prend.

Jupiter and the Banquet of the Beasts

Olympus' sovereign, Jupiter by name,
Once gave a splendid feast. From everywhere
Beast after beast, without exception, came,
Offering him their presents, fine and fair.
Each one he took, gracious and debonair,
Refusing none of them—except, that is,
The wicked serpent's rose, quick to forswear
As vile and loathsome any gift of his!

MORAL

  This fable teaches us to be
  Deaf to the generosity
  Of evil men who make too free
  With gifts that hide their villainy.

D'un Asne, d'un Singe & d'une Taulpe

Ainsi que l'asne d'auanture
Se plaingnoit qu'il n'estoit cornu
Le singe aussi contre nature
Murmuroit d'auoir le cul nu,
Le filz de la taulpe est venu
Qui leur a dict "soyez contentz
Voyantz m'estre pire aduenu
Qui est d'estre aueugle en tout temps."

LE MORAL

La fable nous apprend a estre
Bien contendz de nostre fortune
Par considerer l'infortune
Et d'aulcuns le malheureux estre.

The Ass, the Ape, and the Mole

Because he had no horns, an ass
Found fault with Nature, moaned and whined.
An ape bewailed no less, alas,
That she gave him a bald behind.
Then said the mole: "I think you'll find
She treats you better, far, than me.
You see, my friends, she made me blind:
Be satisfied that you can see."

MORAL

This fable shows that one should not
Deplore one's fate, however ill.
Many's the lot more grievous still:
Be happy with the one you've got.

D'un Homme Refusant vn Clistere

Ainsi que plusieurs medecins
Estoient venuz reuisiter
Vn patient, qu'a toutes fins

The Man Who Refused an Enema

A group of doctors stood about
As patient on his sickbed lay,
Trying their best to figure out

S'efforçoient a bien visiter,
Penser aussi solliciter,
Pourtant qu'il estoit homme riche
Selon qu'ilz l'ouoient reciter
Et que d'argent n'estoit point chiche.
Or par aprez que tous ensemble
Eurent bien consulté, l'un d'eulx
A dict, "il conuient se me semble
Luy bailler vn clystere ou deux."
Mais ce propos fut si facheux
A ouyr au patient, qu'allors
Il commanda chasser iceulx
Et sans argent les mettre hors,
En leur disant "vous monstrez bien
Chascun de vous estre vne beste
Et a guarir n'entendre rien
Entendu que c'est a la teste
D'ou vient le mal qui me moleste
Qu'applicquer debuez medecine
Non a mon cul ou n'est moleste
Ny de maladie aulcun signe."

LE MORAL

Par cest apologue il appert
Que conseil salubre & utile
Semble a homme qui n'est expert
Souuent estrange & inutile.

What remedies might save the day,
Eager to cure their protégé,
Man of great wealth—so it was said—
And one who would be quick to pay
Could they but raise him from his bed.
And so, in proper consultation,
Said one: "I know what we should do
To rectify his situation:
Give him an enema or two."[1]
The patient, when he heard him, flew
Into a rage and sent them packing—
And, what was worse, without a sou.
"I fear, my friends, you're sadly lacking!
What stupid fools you are, for sure!
It's clear your science is a fake!
You should be giving me a cure
To help my head: that's where I ache!
I'd take your medicine to make
Me lose this aching head of mine—
My head, messieurs, for goodness' sake!—
But not my ass! My ass feels fine!"

MORAL

Often when man—callow, naive—
Is offered counsel salutary,
His ignorance makes him believe
It's foolish and unnecessary.

1. I hasten to point out that the pun implicit in the verb "rectify" is not gratuitous on my part. Though I hesitate to attribute to Haudent more linguistic finesse than he probably deserves, the verb

bailler of the original, "to give," is homonymous with *bâiller* 'to gape', not entirely inappropriate, given the anatomical context.

Guillaume Guéroult   Premier Livre des Emblèmes (1550)

A CONTEMPORARY of Corrozet and Haudent (see pp. 12–13 and 17–18), Guillaume Guéroult was not nearly as prolific a fabulist as either one.[1] Still, he is of no lesser interest among the sixteenth-century predecessors of La Fontaine in that several of his fables too are thought by some to have served as specific models.[2] Even without that distinction, however, he deserves a place, albeit a modest one, among the early French practitioners of the genre. His fables, if not outstanding, are pleasantly didactic, not overly heavy-handed or without flashes of humor, and present a balance of narrative and dialogue in a variety of rhyme schemes and meters.

Guéroult was born in Rouen around 1507, though the exact date is not certain, and died, probably in Lyon, around 1564, possibly in the epidemic that ravaged the city at that time.[3] Details of his life between these two vague termini were, for a long time, almost equally vague:

either incorrectly known or not known at all. As late as the middle of the nineteenth century, Théodore Lebreton, while able to list a number of Guéroult's principal works in his *Biographie rouennaise*, could state that his life was "inconnue des biographes" (II:184). Some fifty years ago, however, a French professor at The Phillips Exeter Academy uncovered a number of facts and clarified others, calling attention, for one thing, to the confusion that had existed between this author and an older contemporary of the same name, professor at the Université de Caen.[4] DeVaux de Lancey's facsimile of *Le Premier livre des emblèmes,* published under the auspices of the Société Rouennaise de Bibliophiles, offers probably the most detailed and reliably documented biographical account available, though it too remains necessarily incomplete.[5]

Lancey's study chronicles Guéroult's career as classical scholar, translator, poet, and—not the least important—member of the thriving printing profession, which he practiced in Paris for a time, and especially in the cities of Geneva and Lyon.[6] As a Protestant, he had taken temporary refuge in Calvin's city-state in 1544. His subsequent anti-Calvinist persuasion and "libertine" behavior, however, incurred the displeasure of the city fathers and, soon after, of Calvin himself. For his part in the clandestine printing of Michael Servetus's anti-Trinitarian *Christianismi Restitutio,* Guéroult became embroiled in the celebrated persecution of the ill-fated theologian and doctor, who was condemned for heresy and burned at the stake in 1553. Guéroult himself emerged unscathed, but in 1556 further difficulties with the authorities obliged him to leave Geneva for good. He eventually returned to Lyon, where several years earlier he had produced many of his writings, notably his *emblèmes.* It was in that city that he published the rest of his works, including a variety of Protestant-inspired verse.[7]

With the exception of one entitled "Aenigme"—a poetic *devinette* or riddle—the twenty-nine poems in *Le Premier livre des emblèmes* (which, incidentally, does not appear to have been followed by a second) are examples of a genre that flourished during the sixteenth century in the wake of the immense success of the brief didactic aphorisms, in Latin, by the Renaissance legal scholar Andrea Alciati (1492–1550), of Milan. His *emblemata,* widely republished and translated after their first appearance in 1522, took their name from the Greco-Latin word for the woodcuts that accompanied his verses; but the term soon came to designate the poems themselves.[8] Six of Guéroult's examples present animal characters. The rest are peopled by human beings; but they are no less fables for that, unless we adopt a definition so narrow that much of La Fontaine—and, indeed, even of Aesop—would be excluded. Their moral intent, if ever in doubt, is made obvious from the outset in Guéroult's dedicatory verse to one comte de Gruyère, in which he proclaims that their aim is to "enseigner la vertu / Dont vostre cœur heroique est vestu . . ."

The pair translated here, numbers 2 and 28, are examples of the animal and the human, respectively.

1. One nineteenth-century observer voiced his regrets at this disparity in no uncertain terms, at least insofar as Haudent was concerned: "Si en lisant Guillaume Guéroult, on regrette quelquefois qu'il n'ait pas composé plus de fables, on éprouve un sentiment tout contraire, quand on parcourt les trois cent soixante-six apologues versifiés par Guillaume Haudent, en 1547" (Prosper Soullié, *La Fontaine et ses devanciers,* p. 227).

2. See, for example, the entry on the author in *La Grande Encyclopédie* (XIX:527); and, more specifically, the list of the six fables with corresponding La Fontaine subjects in DeVaux de Lancey's preface to his reedition of Guéroult's 1550 collection. Like Corrozet, Guéroult is not, however, one of the sixteenth-century predecessors discussed by Robert. (See p. 3, n. 5.)

3. A recent source specifies the date as October 7, 1569, though without giving any authority. (See T. de Morembert's entry on Guéroult in the *Dictionnaire de biographie française,* XVI: 1526.)

4. It is no doubt for this reason that some sources (including the *Dictionnaire de biographie française*) list Caen as our Guéroult's birthplace.

5. Of special interest to scholars is the appendix: an apprecia-
tion of Guéroult by the seventeenth-century poet Guillaume Colletet, part of his unpublished manuscript, *Vie des poètes français,* most of which was destroyed by the fire, set by the Communards, that burned the Bibliothèque du Louvre in May of 1871.

6. He may also have studied medicine, although the sources that suggest this are more likely confusing him with his namesake. (Guéroult, *Le Premier livre des emblèmes,* ed. Lancey, p. xi.)

7. For a bibliography of Guéroult the reader should consult both *Dictionnaire des lettres françaises: le seizième siècle,* p. 367, and Alexandre Cioranescu, *Bibliographie de la littérature française du seizième siècle,* p. 356, which complement one another (although the latter's final entry represents a confusion with the other Guillaume Guéroult). Several individual poems appearing in other authors' works are also cited in Guéroult, *Le Premier livre des emblèmes,* ed. Lancey, p. xli.

8. See Guéroult, *Le Premier livre des emblèmes,* ed. Lancey, pp. xlii–xlv; Henry Green, ed., *Andreae Alciati Emblematum fontes quatuor; namely, an account of the original collection made at Milan, 1522, and photo-lith fac-similes of the editions, Augsburg 1531, Paris 1534 and Venice 1546*; and Georges Duplessis, *Les 'Emblèmes' d'Alciat.*

Du Coq & du Cheual[1]

Si tu te veux associer
D'un plus que toy autorisé,
En fin tu seras mesprisé:
Ne t'en vueilles doncq soucier.

Le Coq de famine pressé,
Dans vne estable s'en alla,
Pensant estre bien adressé:
Mais vn Cheual il trouua la.
Lequel humblement il salue
Luy disant. "Cheual de value
Icy suis venu à recours:
Pour receuoir de toy secours.

The Cock and the Horse

You who crave the society
Of those who boast a higher station,
Desist lest, in the end, you be
Undone by your humiliation.

A cock, by hunger sore distressed,
Went to a stable where, perforce,
He thought he might be sated best;
But there, forsooth, he found a horse.
In manner most obsequious
He gives the beast his greeting, thus:
"I stand before you, noble steed,
To seek your succour in my need.

"Souffre moy l'auoyne manger
Qui est esparse dessous toy,
Tu n'en auras mal, ny dangier.
Et si m'osteras hors d'esmoy,
Mais premier (pour plus grand fiance)
Nous deux ferons vne alliance,
Par laquelle m'accorderas:
Que sur moy tu ne marcheras.

"Et ie promets de mon costé
Que le semblable ie feray,
Ie te garderay loyaulté:
Dessus toy point ne marcheray.
Et promets encor d'auantage,
Que (si ie ne meurs auant aage)
Le bien que m'auras dispensé:
Te sera bien recompensé."

Le Cheual fier & glorieux
Respond lors. "O coq insensé
Marche dessus moy si tu veux,
Point ne crains en estre offencé.
Car par trop mince est ta puissance
Pour me faire tort ou greuance,
Mais en mon pouuoir il est bien:
De te nuire ou faire du bien."

Cette brusque & rude harengue
Auec ce vigoureux reffus,
Rendist le poure Coq sans langue:
Et en son cœur triste & confus.
Parquoy c'est chose fort louable
De s'accointer de son semblable,
Mais bien folz on repute ceux:
Qui s'accointent de plus grands qu'eux.

"Suffer me but to eat, I pray,
The oats that round your feet lie spread.
Nought can it harm you, sire. Nay, nay!
You'll not be hurt, and I'll be fed...
But first, I think it meet, in fact,
That you and I conclude a pact
Whereby you promise, solemnly,
To take care not to step on me;

"Whilst I for my part likewise swear
To be your loyal friend and true,
Ever to try, with no less care,
Never, indeed, to step on you.
I promise, sire—unless I die
Before my proper time—that I
Shall show you my appreciation
For your most kind consideration."

Answered the horse, vaingloriously:
"Step on me all you like! There's little
The likes of you can do to me,
You stupid cock! Nor jot nor tittle!
Whilst I for my part—if I would—
Could choose to do you harm or good.
So, I repeat, do what you will:
Nought you can do can do me ill."

Thus did the horse, in accents gruff,
Rebuke the cock, poor foolish one,
Who stood before his rude rebuff,
Speechless, chagrined, done in, undone.
Witless are they, of low degree,
Who choose their betters' company.
Rather should man his equals seek:
The strong, the strong; the weak, the weak.

---

1. About one-half of Guéroult's apologues do not have a title, as such, although all are introduced by a one-line prose summary followed by a moralizing quatrain, as in the next poem. In the other half, however, as here—more in the fable tradition—he inserts a specific title after the moral, in the manner of his contemporary Corrozet and his follower Guide (see pp. 12–13 and 25–26). In this edition, while I preserve the vagaries of sixteenth-century orthography and punctuation, I opt for typographical consistency rather than historical precision. (I also take the liberty, in both this poem and the next, of justifying Guéroult's rather capricious margins and of inserting spaces between obvious stanzas.)

En Putain N'Ha Point de Foy

Putain qui s'abandonne,
Ne garde non plus foy
A vn autre personne:
Comme elle fait à soy.

Vn iour Lays ce vieux cabas rusé'
Contre quelqu'vn forma grosse complainte,
Qui contenoit que de l'homme accusé,
Ou de son fait: el' se sentoit enceinte.
Le bon hillot veit que ce n'estoit fainte,
Et qu'il falloit repousser ceste offence:
Si allegua pour raison & deffence,
Qu'a vn chascun elle s'abandonnoit,

The Faithless Whore

The wanton jade, abject—
Shameless and faithless whore—
Has little self-respect;
For others, little more.

One day a dried-up prune, Laÿs by name,
Crafty old jade, decided to bring suit
Against a village lad. The strumpet's claim:
That she was pregnant; and that he, the brute,
Had done the deed. He, eager to refute
Her charge, saw that she was, in truth, with child.
Still, in defense, bemused but not beguiled,
He told the court that she, time and again—

En concluant que par maliuolence,
Et à grand tort: tel blasme luy donnoit.

Ceste deesse alors se prend à braire,
Voire & maintient, qu'elle est femme de bien,
Le compaignon replique le contraire,
Et si maintient qu'il le prouuera bien.
Le iuge alors fasché (Dieu sait combien)
Commande à l'homme amener ses tesmoings,
Qui vindrent tost: quinze ou vingt pour le moins.
L'enqueste faicte en forme iuridique,
Il se trouua que pour beaucoup de points:
La femme estoit vne putain publique.

Le iuge adoncq prest à donner sentence
Fit vn fardeau d'espines amener,
Et la putain (pardeuant lassistence)
Fit par dessus (les piedz nuds) cheminer.
Nauree feust. Et pour mieux l'estonner
Luy demanda. "Or monstre nous icy
L'aguillon seul qui ta picquee ainsi:"
"Ie n'en ay pas" (respond el') "la puissance."
"Ha ha" (dist il) "ie ne puis pas aussi:
Iuger, qui c'est qui t'ha emply la pance."

No shrinking lass, no maiden undefiled—
Had done as much or more with many men;

That it was wrong to lay on him the blame.
Whereat our goddess pure shrieks out that she
Has led an honest life, and free from shame.
The lad objects, and says that presently
He will show proof of her debauchery.
"Be quick!" orders the judge in angry tone.
(God knows how they can be!) "Let proof be shown!"
Wherewith a troupe of men come forth—a score—
Each swearing to have dallied with the crone,
Clearly a common slut, and little more.

The judge thereat asks that some thorns be spread
Before the whore. Then, as all eyes look on,
He summons her to bare her feet and tread
Unshod, forthwith—up, down, back, forth—thereon.
Much to her woe, she does so; whereupon,
Seeing her pain, the judge commands straightway:
"Show us the thorn that pricked your foot, I pray."
Says she: "The one? But one?... I cannot tell."
"Ha ha!" he laughs. "Nor likewise can I say
Which swain it was that made your belly swell!"

1. The entry for the word *cabas* 'prune' in Edmond Huguet's authoritative seven-volume *Dictionnaire de la langue française du seizième siécle,* II:36, cites precisely this line. It apparently errs, however, in that it quotes the accompanying epithet as *usé* 'worn out' rather than *rusé* 'crafty', both being equally applicable. This is undoubtedly a misreading rather than a variant, since the reference in Huguet's preface (I:lxx) is, indeed, to the 1550 edition of Guéroult, the only edition prior to that of DeVaux de Lancey in 1937. In any event, my translation attempts to reconcile both possibilities.

Jean-Antoine de Baïf   *from* Les Mimes, Enseignements et Proverbes (1576–97)

CLASSICAL scholar Jean-Antoine de Baïf, though one of the more prolific of the Pléiade poets, is usually remembered only for his ill-fated spelling reform and, especially, for the rhythmic innovations he attempted to introduce into French poetry, based on the measured verse of Greek and Latin prosody.[1] All the more reason that he is not generally recognized for his fables. While he is not properly speaking a fabulist, in the sense that one would apply the term to the other sixteenth-century adepts of the genre—authors of individual, self-conscious collections—the fable does crop up inconspicuously in his work, much as it does, here and there, in the vast *œuvre* of his medieval predecessor Eustache Deschamps (see pp. 9–10).

Some twenty such apologues are sprinkled among the almost 1250 heterogeneous octosyllabic sestets—moral and religious maxims, anecdotes, and other diverse didactic forms—that make up Baïf's last (and, according to some, his most significant) opus, *Les Mimes, enseigne-ments et proverbes.* "Dans cette suite de petits discours, l'élégie alterne avec la satire, avec l'épître, avec l'ode; une morale, digne d'une âme chrétienne, tantôt s'y développe librement et souvent avec éloquence, tantôt s'y dérobe habilement sous l'allégorie et sous la fable." (See *Poésies choisies de J.-A. de Baïf,* ed. Louis Becq de Fouquières, p. xxxi.) If it is, surely, rather a partisan exaggeration to claim for these dry little fables, varying in length from a single sestet to as many as eight, "une grâce légère et une bonhomie digne de La Fontaine," one can agree that they are, indeed, characterized by "concision" and "sobriété," and even, on occasion, by "le pittoresque de l'expression."

The future colleague of Ronsard and Du Bellay was born on February 19, 1532, in Venice, where his father, the eminent humanist and diplomat Lazare de Baïf, was ambassador from the court of François I. Baïf's early teachers were among the most celebrated of the day: Charles Etienne, Ange Vergèce, Jacques Toussaint; and especially Jean Dorat (or Daurat), whose Collège de

Coqueret was the intellectual and artistic nursery of the Pléiade. It was no doubt his colleague the young Ronsard who developed and refined his taste for poetry; a taste to which he would devote the rest of his life, in a broad variety of forms. At his death in October of 1589, in the siege of Paris during the Wars of Religion, he had to his credit not only the founding, with musician Thibault de Courville, of an academy of poetry and music (later to become the Académie du Palais) but also a reputation as one of the foremost French poets of his day. He owed his renown to several collections of rather conventional Petrarchian love poetry, octosyllabic adaptations of three classical plays (the most successful of which was *Le Brave,* his gallicized version of Plautus's *Miles Gloriosus,* performed for the king, Charles IX, in 1567), a translation of the Psalms, and numerous other miscellaneous compositions.[2] That reputation did not long survive him. But Baïf deserves to be remembered, if not for any notable subtlety, finesse, or depth of poetic sentiment, at least for the humanistic fervor of his typically Renaissance production; and, especially, for his often audacious originality. "Pour être juste envers Baïf, il faut considérer que ses innovations témoignent d'un esprit actif, curieux, entreprenant, ou, pour reprendre son propre terme, véritablement 'inventif'." (See *Dictionnaire des lettres françaises: le seizième siècle,* p. 73.)

Les Mimes, enseignements et proverbes, the collection that includes Baïf's twenty-odd fables—not twelve, as indicated by Chamard (*Dictionnaire des lettres françaises: le seizième siècle,* p. 76)—went through a number of editions. The first consisted of a single book, according to Chamard, and was published in 1576, in Paris, by Lucas Breyer.[3] A second volume, expanded to two books, appeared five years later (Paris: Mamert Patisson, 1581); and a third, consisting finally of four, was published posthumously (Paris: Mamert Patisson, 1597). Four seventeenth-century editions, which seem to have escaped the notice of both Cioranescu and Chamard, are cited by Blanchemain (Baïf, *Les Mimes,* I:x): 1608, 1612, and 1619 (Toulouse: Jean Jagourt), and 1619 (Tournon: Guillaume Linocier). As for more modern editions, besides that of Blanchemain, *Les Mimes* is included in volume 5 of Marty-Laveaux's reedition of *Euvres en rime.*

The four fables presented here in translation are taken from Blanchemain's reproduction of the four books of the 1597 edition, where they are, respectively, sestets 73, 170, and 177 of Book I, and sestet 112 of Book III.

---

1. "Baïf ne possédait ni le puissant coup d'aile de Ronsard, ni la force élégante de Joachim du Bellay, mais c'était un *oseur*. Ses essais ne furent pas toujours heureux; mais il a plus tenté à lui seul que les autres poètes de la Pléiade." (See Prosper Blanchemain's introduction to his edition of Baïf's *Les Mimes, enseignements et proverbes,* I:vii.) Regarding the author's so-called *vers mezurés* and spelling innovations, see Mathieu Augé-Chiquet, *La Vie, les idées et l'œuvre de Jean-Antoine de Baïf,* pp. 338–74.

2. Only one collected edition of Baïf's work was published during his lifetime: *Euvres en rime,* 4 vols. (1573). A modern five-volume edition was published under the same title by Charles Marty-Laveaux, with biographical introduction and notes. For bibliographical references see Alexandre Cioranescu, *Bibliographie de la littérature française du seizième siècle,* pp. 100–101. The most accessible detailed discussion of his individual works will be found in Henri Chamard's informative entry devoted to him, in *Dictionnaire des lettres françaises: le seizième siècle.* For a more extensive biographical and literary study, see Augé-Chiquet.

3. Blanchemain (Baïf, *Les Mimes,* I:vii) claims, on the contrary, that this first edition of *Les Mimes* contained two books.

Le Corbeau trouua la Vipere
Qui dormoit: et d'elle veut faire
Son gibier. Du bec la beca.
Elle se reueille bequee:
Et s'eueillant s'est rebequee:
Mord à mort cil qui la pica.

Raven espied the sleeping snake
And sought, by dint of beak, to make
Thereof, thereat, indeed, his dinner.
Bitten awake, snake bit him back,
And bit him dead. Alas, alack:
Raven's the loser; snake, the winner.

Tout l'Esté chanta la Cigale:
Et l'hyuer elle eut la faim vale:
Demande à manger au Fourmi:
"Que fais-tu tout l'Esté?" "Ie chante."
"Il est hyuer: dance faineante."
Appren des bestes mon ami.

Cricket, who sang the summer through,
Come winter, starving, nought could do
Save beg of ant: "Food, I beseech you..."
"What did you, then, all summer?" "Sing..."
"So, dance all winter, you lazy thing!"
Learn from the beasts; much can they teach you.

Le Lyon et l'Ours se liguerent:
Vne proie ensemble questerent:

Lion and bear decide that they
Should hunt by two to take their prey.

La prennent: en sont en debat:
Le Renard leur querelle auise:
A l'emblee emporte leur prise:
La mange durant leur combat.

And so they do; but forthwith fall
To fighting over whose it is.
Along comes fox and makes it his,
Carries it off, and eats it all.

Trois bœufs dedans un pasturage
Paissoient d'accord: et nul outrage
De beste qui fust n'enduroient
Tant qu'ils vesquirent en concorde.
Entre eux se fourre la discorde:
Loups et lions les deuoroient.

Three bulls were grazing peaceably,
Safe in each other's company
From beast of every stripe; for none
Would dare attack all three. But when
Enmity came betwixt them, then
Lions and wolves devoured each one.

Philibert Hégémon (pseud. Philibert Guide)   Fables Morales (1583)

In HIS monumental *Bibliothèque françoise, ou Histoire de la littérature françoise,* the abbé Claude-Pierre Goujet grudgingly accords only "un moment" (and a single paragraph) to Philibert Guide (XIII:410–11), also known, from the Greek translation of his surname, as "Hégémon" (i.e., "leader"). One suspects that the good churchman's scorn may have been less than objective. In discussing the family motto, "Dieu pour Guide," the prelate-historian decries the poet's conversion to Protestantism: "Heureux s'il n'avoit pas démenti cette devise en renonçant à la Religion Catholique!" In 1595 Guide had, in fact, embraced Calvinism—"la Religion prétendue réformée," in Goujet's terms—and died shortly thereafter while returning from Geneva, in the town of Mâcon, on November 29 of that year.

These and a few other biographical details—most probably culled by Goujet from the work of another man of the cloth, père Louis Jacob's *De claris scriptoribus Cabilonensibus*—are all that we know about Guide-Hégémon himself. The other facts, to wit: that he was born in the town of Chalon-sur-Saône on March 22, 1535, into a family with deep aristocratic roots, son of one Philippe Guide and Reine Rougeot; that he succeeded to his father's juridical position as *procureur du roi* ("king's prosecutor") for the bailiwick of Chalon; and that he indulged, when professional duties allowed, in both the pleasures of poetry ("les amusemens de la poësie Françoise") and, especially, the joys of a quiet country life, something of a vogue in the latter years of the century. (See Verdun L. Saulnier's entry on Guide in *Dictionnaire des lettres françaises: le seizième siècle,* pp. 367–68.) Goujet concludes his brief biographical sketch by informing us that Guide had married and had fathered children ("& il a eu postérité"). He does not specify, as does a nineteenth-century source, that the latter numbered seventeen. (See Eugène Haag and Emile Haag, *La France protestante,* V:388.)[1]

To all appearances, Guide was not nearly so prolific a poet as he was a father. Only a single slim volume has come down to us. It was published in Paris, in 1583, by Robert Le Fizelier, and contains, in addition to a lengthy bucolic work, *La Colombière, et maison rustique,* his twenty-two *Fables morales*—dedicated (with both a prose and verse dedication) to his cousin, one Noble Bartolomy Galois, "Bourgeois et Citoyen de Chalon sur Saone")—and "Diverses Poésies," as well as the *Louange de la vie rustique* of Guide's better-known contemporary and coreligionist Guillaume Salluste du Bartas.[2] Besides this volume, Goujet tells us that Guide also wrote French versions—"paraphrases"—of some of the Psalms (which, as with Clément Marot, one might suppose to have been inspired by his Protestant faith), as well as the Song of Solomon, both of which, in manuscript, were destroyed by fire after his death. Haag and Haag (*La France protestante*) quote Jacob as indicating that Guide did a translation of Guillaume Paradin's *De rebus in Belgio gestis* (Paris, 1544), which does not appear to have been published, however. The *Fables morales* are available in two modern editions; originally reproduced in toto by Arthur F. Whittem, in his article "Two Fable Collections," they have been edited again by Laura Rovero, with introduction and notes.[3]

Like those of his sixteenth-century predecessors, Guide's fables, despite their modest number, treat the Aesopic corpus with considerable variety of length, meter, and—especially true in his case—rhyme. His rhyme schemes range, in fact, from the very simple and straightforward to the overly complex, not to say capricious. Without the technical deftness of a Guéroult or the rhythmic inventiveness of a Corrozet, Guide's contributions to the fable literature are engaging in their didacticism without being verbose. They are, on the contrary, undemandingly brief, the longest having only thirty-six lines. One imagines that they must have served him well in the rearing of his considerable progeny.[4]

Translated here are numbers 3, 6, 15, and 19.

1. The authors indicate further that only one of Guide's children, a son named Daniel, survived him; that he, in turn, had a son, Philippe, doctor of medicine in Montpellier and author of a great many unpublished poems in Latin and French, as well as of a medical treatise; and that a great-grandson, also Philippe and also a doctor and author of medical studies (in French and English), was obliged to flee Paris after the revocation of the Edict of Nantes and settled in London, where he died in 1718. (Readers interested in untangling the Guide family genealogy may wish to consult the maze of references to them in Raoul Violot, *Histoire des maisons de Chalon-sur-Saône*, I:82, 141, 317, 426–27, 434, 436, 453–55, 461–62, 469, 524; II:37.)

2. An augmented copy in Harvard University's Houghton Library, also bearing the imprint of Parisian publisher Jamet Mettayer, with no date, adds two other poems of rustic inspiration while eliminating the Du Bartas. This may well be the edition mentioned by Whittem (see below) as being of dubious existence.

3. Two studies on Guide are listed in Alexandre Cioranescu, *Bibli-ographie de la littérature française du seizième siècle*, p. 357, and are cited as well by Rovero (Hégémon, *Fables morales*, p. 81): Jules Guillemin, *Philibert Guide, poète chalonnais (1535–1595)*, and J. Roy-Chevrier, "Philibert Guide, poète chalonnais." They would undoubtedly yield more biographical details, but I have been unable to consult either one. Regarding Guide's possible sources, see also Rovero's convincing article, "Plutarco, fonte delle *Fables morales* di Philibert Guide, favolista del Cinquecento."

4. There is, to my knowledge, no concrete reason to accept the rather categorical assertions by some that they were of immediate inspiration to La Fontaine, though the possibility cannot be discounted. (See Haag and Haag, *La France protestante*; also the entry on Guide in the original edition of the *Biographie universelle, ancienne et moderne*, which proffers the critical judgment that his fables "offrent trop souvent l'emploi des enjambements; mais, en faisant la part du temps où il les composa, on y trouve encore de l'invention et de la verve" [LVI:228].)

De L'Aigle, & du Roitelet

Qui monte plus haut qu'il ne doit,
Descend plus bas qu'il ne voudroit.[1]

Le Roitelet prier si bien s'employe
L'Aigle Royal, qu'icelle luy ottroye
De le porter jusqu'aupres du Soleil,
Pour d'iceluy voir le beau appareil
Ensemblement: Et pource elle l'emporte
Dessus son dos, haut en l'air, & de sorte
Que commençans d'approcher le Soleil,
Le Roitelet (orgueilleux) lors seulet
S'evola haut, laissant l'Aigle derniere,
Et le premier approcha la lumiere.
Dont l'Aigle eust dueil, voyant que devancé
L'avoit celuy qu'elle avoit si haussé.
Parquoy le laisse, & pour voir la vengeance,
Retourne à terre en toute diligence:
Où aussi tost ce brave Roitelet
(Ne se pouvant si haut tenir seulet)
Tomba froissé, en recevant la peine
Que merité a toute orgueil vileine.

MORAL

Plusieurs apres avoir porté & mis
En grans honneurs quelcuns de leurs amis,
Sont aussi tost d'iceux mis à mespris:
Mais tousjours mal (en fin) leur en est pris.

1. Guide introduces all his fables (except the first and the ninth) with a pithy, two-line summary of the ensuing text, usually, but not exclusively, in octosyllables, and often substantially different from the concluding moral. (In the original these couplets are inserted between the number and the title of the fable.)

The Eagle and the Wren

He who climbs higher than climb he should
Falls farther, too, than fall he would.

A wren there was who importuned an eagle
Kindly to let him ride his person regal
Up to the heavens, that both of them might see
The sun in his resplendent majesty.
The eagle acquiesces, takes the wren
Upon his back, lifts him aloft. But when
They reach the precincts of the sun, the latter—
Probity being no overriding matter—
Straightway goes soaring off, in haughty show,
Leaving his host behind, still far below,
To watch the wren, alone, pursue their quest.
"Traitor!" the eagle sighed, "I should have guessed!"
Bested, betrayed by one he had befriended,
Swearing revenge, he eagerly descended.
The wren, abandoned (and too frail to fly
Unaided in those reaches of the sky),
Plummeting helpless, headlong back to earth,
Reaps the reward such perfidy is worth.

MORAL

Many there are of good and generous bent
Who help their friends to glorious ascent,
Only to earn their scorn malevolent.
But woe awaits: in time the rogues repent![2]

2. I have followed the poet's uncharacteristic lead here by using a single rhyme for all four lines of his moral.

Du Soleil, & de la Bise

L'on vient au bout avec raison,
De toute chose en sa saison.

Entre la Bise, & le Soleil luisant,
Contention s'émeut pour leur puissance.
L'un plus que l'autre alloit la sien' prisant.
Mais pour au vray en avoir cognoissance,
L'Homme ils ont pris, taschans le despouiller,
A qui mieux mieux, pour le rendre en chemise.
La Bise doncq' commença de souffler
Impetueuse, & sur l'Homme s'est mise:
Mais lors que plus en ventant s'efforçoit
Oster sa robbe, iceluy s'amassoit,
Et restreignoit en ses habits qu'il serre,
Sans demeurer vaincu de telle guerre.
Apres laquelle, & du vent les effors
Du tout cessez, le clair Soleil dés lors
A eschauffer se mit l'Homme, de sorte
Que son manteau de luy mesme il osta,
Et puis apres le saye aussi qu'il porte:
Finablement la chaleur fut si forte,
Que sa chemise encor ne luy resta.

MORAL

Des femmes sont de naturel si nices,
Que qui voudra avec efforts oster
Leurs affiquets, & superflu's delices,
On ne pourra jamais les surmonter.
Mais au contraire, alors qu'avec raison
On les remonstre, & reprend doucement,
La paix se voit tousjours à la maison
Et tout orgueil laissent patiemment.

The Sun and the Wind

He who pursues his aims with reason
Surely succeeds, all in good season.

Betwixt the blowing wind and blazing sun
Arose a rivalry as to which one,
Indeed, was stronger. Thus, to prove their strength
(With more than simple words), they choose, at length,
An ordinary mortal, and propose
To see who, first, can strip him of his clothes.
And so the wind begins to blast, to bellow,
Trying to rip the garments from his back.
Alack! The more he blows, the more our fellow
Cringes against his blustering attack,
Pulling his mantle tight, and tighter still,
Bowed but unbeaten by the bitter chill.
The wind, for all his bellicose insistence,
Failing to overcome the man's resistance,
Ceases his efforts. Then the sun, in turn,
Begins to shine. The man grows warm (nay, hot!),
Removes his cloak—unbidden, unbesought—
His tunic too; and, as the sun's rays burn,
Strips to his shirt and, shortly, strips to nought.

MORAL

So too it is with woman, addlebrained:
Seek to divest her of her vain excess—
Baubles and all—and, should she feel constrained,
She stands fast, spiteful, in her stubbornness.
But if, contrariwise, you chide her gently—
Mellow your voice and reasoned your reproof—
Quickly she comes around; and, consequently,
Blessèd peace reigns again beneath your roof.[1]

1. Despite the curiously derived moral, the reader will easily recognize an ancient folktale spread over half the world, from the Baltic to Indonesia, and probably originating in India. (See Stith Thompson, *Motif-Index of Folk-Literature*, V:20 [L 351]; also, Murray

B. Emeneau, *Kota Texts*, I:81 ss.) An Aesopic version, "Boreas and Helios," is no. 46 of the "Fabulae Graecae," in Perry, *Aesopica*, p. 339. La Fontaine's adaptation, "Phébus et Borée" (VI, 3), characteristically presents a considerable expansion of the original material.

De la Lune, & d'un Tailleur

On ne peut au fol de nature
Donner aucuns biens par mesure.

La Lune un jour un Tailleur rencontra,
Et le pria de luy faire un surcot,
Lequel joignist au corps, qu'elle monstra,
Fort proprement, & qu'elle, avec l'escot,
(Le contentant) le pay'roit à son dit.
Mais le Tailleur à ce luy respondit:
"Je ne puis pas faire ce que tu veux.
Car maintenant le plain, ronde te monstre,
Tantost croissant apparois à mes yeux,
Et puis soudain en decours te rencontre:
Cela seroit pour abuser les Dieux."

MORAL

A l'homme fol (comme Lune inconstant)
On ne sçauroit faire chose qui serve:
Mesme des biens ne peut estre contant.
Car tantost trop, tantost rien se reserve.

The Moon and the Tailor

One cannot deal in proper wise
With arrant fool, for all one tries.

One day, the Moon (while out to take her leisure)
Happened upon a tailor, and requested
That he prepare a mantle to her measure—
Eager to be more elegantly vested.
"And if it fits," said she, "I'll pay you well."
"Nay, nay," the tailor soberly protested.
"Nought can I sew to please you, truth to tell.
Full are you now, but soon shall I observe you
Waning to but a slip. And then again
I'll watch you wax. And yet again you'll wane.
The gods themselves would be hard put to serve you."

MORAL

The fool is fickle, like the changing Moon,
And he who tries to please him comes a cropper:
One day his purse is full; the next, jejune.
Today he's rich, tomorrow he's a pauper.

Du Regnard, & de l'Herisson

Souvent celuy qui un malheur evite,
En un plus grand bien tost se precipite.

Un vieil Regnard las, & recreu gisoit,
Par la chaleur, dessous un bel ombrage,
Où molesté, & fort piqué estoit
De gros Bourdons luy faisans maint dommage,
Qu'il enduroit a toute extremité.
Dont l'Herisson (present) fut incité
(Meu de pitié) à dechasser à l'heure
Tous ces Frelons: mesme oster luy vouloit
Du vil vermin, qui aussi le mangeoit.
Mais le Regnard luy dit, "Amy demeure,
Bon gré te sçay de cetuy tien vouloir,
Encor qu'il soit pour bien plus me douloir:
Car déchassant ces Bourdons, & vermine
(Qui sont ja saouls du sang de ma ruïne)
Il en viendroit des affamez, & maigres,
Qui me seroient plus dangereux, & aigres."

MORAL

L'homme prudent doit tousjours endurer
Le Tyran saoul, encores qu'il le mine:
Sans pour changer, un autre desirer,
Qui affamé causeroit sa ruïne.

The Fox and the Hedgehog

Avert one fell misfortune, and you will
Fall into yet another, fouler still.

A tired old fox, one sweltering day, was lying
Deep in the shaded wood, while to and fro
A swarm of bumblebees, abuzz, were flying,
Biting him here and there, from head to toe.
A hedgehog (so does kind compassion move him)
Tries to chase off the bees—and, by the way,
Other vile vermin too. "Nay, comrade, nay,"
The fox commences mildly to reprove him.
"I thank you for the kindness you would do.
It's really very generous of you;
But I'll be troubled less if you agree
To let those bees and all the vermin be.
Please, friend, leave well enough alone, unless
You choose to see me treble my distress:
Gorged, glutted on my blood—if they take flight,
Others await with heartier appetite!"[1]

MORAL

Suffer the tyrant whom you know; and who,
Sated at length, wields power attenuated.
Better to keep the old than risk the new,
Whose tyranny still hungers unabated.

---

1. This fable is a rather faithful version of an Aesopic original with a particularly long and distinguished history. The tale of the fox harassed by gadflies, who rejects the hedgehog's well-intentioned help (see Perry, *Aesopica*, "Fabulae Graecae," no. 427, p. 490), is first cited by Aristotle in his *Rhetoric* (II, 20) as a characteristic example of the apologue put to political use. It crops up several centuries later, in slightly altered form, in Flavius Josephus, *Antiquities of the Jews*, (XVIII, vi, 5), also with political reference; and eventually makes its way into the corpus of Western European didactic wisdom, notably in the *Gesta Romanorum* and the fourteenth-century

Spanish chivalric romance, *El libro del Cavallero Zifar,* among numerous other works. (See the *Gesta Romanorum,* ed. Hermann Oesterley, p. 346, and note, p. 741; *Libro de los exenplos por a.b.c.,* ed. John Esten Keller, no. 225 (155), p. 177; *El libro del Cavallero Zifar,* ed. Charles

Philip Wagner, no. 172, pp. 373–75.) In this collection it will appear again in a further-developed seventeenth-century incarnation, Boursault's "Les Sangsues et le Lion" (see p. 52).

Philippe Desprez (?)   Le Théâtre des Animaux (1595)

Virtually nothing seems to be known about the poet who published the one hundred sonnet-fables that form the collection entitled *Le Théâtre des animaux.*[1] Since the "Au lecteur" is signed by one "P. Desprez," it is generally assumed that this shadowy figure is, indeed, the author.

According to Gianni Mombello, the only bibliographical reference to Desprez is to be found in an article on the Flemish fable by L. Scharpé, "Van De Dene tot Vondel." (See Mombello, *Le Raccolte francesi di favole esopiane dal 1480 alla fine del secolo XVI,* p. 149, n. 1.)[2] Scharpé cites Desprez's work, appropriately question-marked, as one of three fable collections whose apparent provenance was Pierre (or Peeter) Heyns's *Esbatiment moral des animaux,* published by P. Galle, the other two being Flemish: "Niet minder dan drij verschillende fabel-versamelingen zijn uit Galle's *Esbatement moral* gesproten, een Fransche, van Desprez (?), en twee Nederlandsche: de eene van Anthoni Smytens, de andere Vondel's bekende *Vorsteliicke Warande.*" For Scharpé, Desprez's—or whoever's—work is, in so many words, a plagiarism: "Op 't eerste zicht schijnt de Fransche zelfs uit *Esbatement moral,*—ja hoe zullen we dat zeggen en beleefd zijn?—... gestolen" (Scharpé, "Van De Dene tot Vondel," p. 47).

Since neither the original edition of the Heyns collection—with illustrations by the publisher, Philippe Galle—nor a modern reprint is readily available, I cannot verify or contest Scharpé's allegation. Be that as it may, questions of originality aside, *Le Théâtre des animaux,*

to whomever it is ultimately attributable, seems to have enjoyed a certain success over the half-century following its original publication, as three reeditions attest. A second and third edition (with minor typographical variations in its title) were published in Paris by Jean Le Clerc, in 1613 and 1620;[3] and a fourth, also in Paris, by Guillaume Le Bé, in 1644.

The hundred Aesopic fables of *Le Théâtre des animaux,* each characteristically (and anonymously) illustrated in sixteenth-century *emblème* style, are introduced, as mentioned, by a brief "Au lecteur," in which the author sets forth both his rather ambitious didactic intent and his rationale for presenting all of the fables in readily remembered sonnet form: "Ce n'est donc point sans profit que ce liure t'est presenté, duquel tu ne peux receuoir que contentement, & principalement la ieunesse à laquelle la lecture sera prompte, chasque histoire ou fable n'estant plus longue qu'vn Sonet, & pource très-aisée à retenir, ce qui les conduira (en ce faisant) sans y penser, & auec plaisir, à receuoir vne prompte resolution en toutes leurs affaires: mais aussi recognoistre en quelle façon ils se doiuent gouuerner auec vn chacun." Each fable is headed by a pithy summary of its moral content, and is preceded by an appropriate biblical quotation, or quotations, intended to buttress its moral lesson.

"Des Colombes, et de l'Esprevier," reproduced here from the 1620 edition, is the sixth fable of the unnumbered collection.

---

1. The entire title is considerably more detailed: *Le Théâtre des animavx, avquel, sovs plvsievrs diverses fables et histoires, est representé la pluspart des actions de la vie humaine: Enrichy de belles sentences tirees de l'Escriture-Sainte et orné de figures pour ceux qui ayment la peinture.*

2. Given the utter dearth of sources regarding our "P. Desprez," one has to wonder how it has been determined that his first name was Philippe. (See Mombello, *Le Raccolte francesi di favole esopiane,* p. 149.)

3. Mombello (p. 149) is correct in noting that Desprez is absent from Alexandre Cioranescu's *Bibliographie de la littérature française du seizième siècle.* The 1620 edition, however, ostensibly the most common, is indeed cited in Cioranescu's three-volume seventeenth-century bibliography, *Bibliographie de la littérature française du dix-septième siècle,* II:746, n° 25737.

Des Colombes, et de l'Esprevier[1]

Le Milan guerroyoit contre les Colombelles
Sans tréfves ny repos: & celles-cy iamais
Ne pouuoient tenir l'air, que cet oyseau mauuais

The Doves and the Sparrowhawk

The doves, in combat with the vicious kite,
Were constant victims of his villainy:
No sooner would they fly aloft, than he

N'allast les desmembrant de ses serres cruelles.
Les pauurettes adonc, prennent aduis entre-elles,
Que c'est qu'il est de faire, & pour rachepter paix
S'en vont à l'Espreuier le prier desormais,
Qu'il vueille estre le Roy de leurs trouppes fidelles.
Cet affamé l'accepte, & tout soudain aprez
Tous ces pauures coulons s'en vont tous massacrez
Dessous la cruauté de l'Espreuier ramage.
On ne doit s'esbahir de voir vn cruel Roy,
Commettre laschement, quand il manque de foy,
Sur ses pauures subjects toutes sortes d'outrage.

Would claw them limb from limb in mortal flight.
Pondering, in their councils, how they might—
Poor beasts—devise some peaceful remedy,
Lo! they invite the sparrowhawk to be
Their king, to save them and put things to right.
Ravenous, he accepts their invitation;
But oh! he sows such savage devastation
That soon a myriad doves lie dead. Just so,
Best we should not be too surprised to find
A cruel and faithless king all too inclined
To wreak his dole and deal his bitter woe.

---

1. The single line of prose used to introduce the present fable, in the manner of predecessors Corrozet and Guéroult (see pp. 12–13 and 20–21), is "Ne requerir ayde aux Tyrans." The biblical passage chosen to characterize its moral is from Isaiah, 36:6 ("Behold, thou trustest upon the staff of this bruised reed, even upon Egypt; whereon if a man lean, it will go into his hand, and pierce it; so is Pharaoh king of Egypt to all that trust on him").

Jean de La Fontaine   Fables (1668–94)

JEAN DE La Fontaine, as a toastmaster might put it, surely needs no introduction. And he will get no lengthy one here.[1] He is, quite simply, the most important fabulist since Aesop; and his name, like that of his classical, semilegendary predecessor and model, has become synonymous with his genre. Born on July 8, 1621, at Château-Thierry, he died almost seventy-four years later, in Paris, on April 13, 1695, having produced—among other poetic works remembered mainly by specialists— some twenty dozen verse fables collected in twelve books and printed over a period of twenty-five years by Parisian publisher Claude Barbin (I–VI, 1668; VII–VIII, 1678; IX–XI, 1679; XII, 1693). It was for these extremely popular *vers libres* apologues, clothing his good-naturedly cynical observations of humankind in an artistic elegance perfectly crafted despite its seeming nonchalance, that he was destined to rank, if not as the creator of the genre, certainly as its modern transformer and undisputed champion.

Any attempt to give a comprehensive La Fontaine bibliography is an exercise in both redundancy and frustration. Redundancy, because there are so many accessible sources that offer so much material; frustration, because the already vast body of books, monographs, and articles devoted to every aspect of his life, works, and literary artistry is constantly proliferating. As his bibliographer the comte de Rochambeau observed almost eight decades ago, "Quand on considère le nombre d'ouvrages consacrés au seul La Fontaine, il semble bien qu'il n'y ait plus grand'chose à en dire; tous les ans, cependant, quelque nouvelle étude se fait jour, tous les ans, quelque nouveau point de vue est mis en valeur et le sujet paraît aussi inépuisable que la verve et l'esprit du conteur." (See René Lacroix de Vimeur, comte de Rochambeau, *Bibliographie des œuvres de J. de La Fontaine*, p. 1.) What was true in 1911 is no less so today, and even a most selective bibliography would be well beyond the scope of these brief remarks. Suffice it to note that the single most useful work remains the eleven-volume critical edition of Henri Regnier, *Œuvres de J. de la Fontaine,* in the series "Les Grands Ecrivains de la France," containing a thorough biography, detailed provenance of the fables and other works, a grammatical study of their style, extensive notes, and a systematic lexicon. An exhaustive listing, through the end of the nineteenth century, of the various editions of his *Fables,* of his pleasantly scabrous *Contes* in verse, as well as of his theater and other disparate writings, is found in Rochambeau's above-mentioned mammoth (nineteen-hundred-page) bibliography. Alexandre Cioranescu's *Bibliographie de la littérature française du dix-septième siècle* expands that listing through the 1960s, along with scholarly and stylistic studies extending over more than seven hundred entries (II:1137–55; nos. 38393–39125). In addition, the two recent works mentioned in note 1, by Jean Orieux and Marie-Odile Sweetser, present usefully selective bibliographies, and I cite them with no intention of slighting the virtual scores of others left unnamed.

The ten fables translated here are the following numbers: I, 1; I, 2; I, 3; I, 10; I, 22; III, 14; V, 10; VI, 17; IX, 4; and X, 2. They are reproduced from my bilingual collection *Fifty Fables of La Fontaine.*

1. Biographical details are not in short supply. In addition to any number of encyclopedia entries, the reader may consult many biographies—in English, French, and a variety of other languages—from Frank Hamel's now venerable *Jean de La Fontaine* to Jean Orieux's more recent *La Fontaine, ou La Vie est un conte* and Marie-Odile Sweetser's *La Fontaine,* to name but three of the many. As for the plethora of more specialized literary studies, several titles come immediately to mind: Jean-Dominique Biard, *The Style of La Fontaine's "Fables"*; Georges Couton, *La Poétique de La Fontaine*; Richard Danner, *Patterns of Irony in the "Fables" of La Fontaine*; Margaret Guiton, *La Fontaine, Poet and Counterpoet*; Renée Kohn, *Le Goût de La Fontaine*; Odette de Mourgues, *"Ô Muse, fuyante proie..." Essai sur la poésie de La Fontaine*. But dozens of others, equally accessible, can be consulted to good advantage.

La Cigale et la Fourmi

La Cigale, ayant chanté
    Tout l'été,
Se trouva fort dépourvue
Quand la bise fut venue:
Pas un seul petit morceau
De mouche ou de vermisseau.
Elle alla crier famine
Chez la Fourmi sa voisine,
La priant de lui prêter
Quelque grain pour subsister
Jusqu'à la saison nouvelle.
"Je vous paierai," lui dit-elle,
"Avant l'oût, foi d'animal,
Intérêt et principal."
La Fourmi n'est pas prêteuse:
C'est là son moindre défaut.
"Que faisiez-vous au temps chaud?"
Dit-elle à cette emprunteuse.
"Nuit et jour à tout venant
Je chantois, ne vous déplaise."
"Vous chantiez? j'en suis fort aise:
Eh bien! dansez maintenant."

The Cricket and the Ant

The cricket, having sung her song
    All summer long,
Found—when the winter winds blew free—
Her cupboard bare as bare could be;
Nothing to greet her hungering eye:
No merest crumb of worm or fly.
She went next door to cry her plight
To neighbor ant, hoping she might
Take pity on her, and befriend her,
Eke out a bit of grain to lend her,
And see her through till spring: "What say you?
On insect's honor, I'll repay you
Well before fall. With interest, too!"
Our ant—no willing lender she!
Least of her faults!—replied: "I see!
Tell me, my friend, what did you do
While it was warm?" "Well... Night and day,
I sang my song for all to hear."
"You sang, you say? How nice, my dear!
Now go and dance your life away!"

Le Corbeau et le Renard

Maître Corbeau, sur un arbre perché,
    Tenoit en son bec un fromage.
Maître Renard, par l'odeur alléché,
    Lui tint à peu près ce langage:
    "Hé! bonjour, Monsieur du Corbeau.
Que vous êtes joli! que vous me semblez beau!
    Sans mentir, si votre ramage
    Se rapporte à votre plumage,
Vous êtes le phénix des hôtes de ces bois."
A ces mots le Corbeau ne se sent pas de joie;
    Et pour montrer sa belle voix,
Il ouvre un large bec, laisse tomber sa proie.
Le Renard s'en saisit, et dit: "Mon bon Monsieur,
    Apprenez que tout flatteur
    Vit aux dépens de celui qui l'écoute:
Cette leçon vaut bien un fromage, sans doute."
    Le Corbeau, honteux et confus,
Jura, mais un peu tard, qu'on ne l'y prendroit plus.

The Crow and the Fox

Perched on a treetop, Master Crow
    Was clutching in his bill a cheese,
When Master Fox, sniffing the fragrant breeze,
Came by and, more or less, addressed him so:
    "Good day to you, Your Ravenhood!
How beautiful you are! How fine! How fair!
Ah! Truly, if your song could but compare
    To all the rest, I'm sure you should
Be dubbed the *rara avis* of the wood!"
The crow, beside himself with joy and pride,
    Begins to caw. He opens wide
    His gawking beak; lets go the cheese; it
Falls to the ground. The fox is there to seize it,
    Saying: "You see? Be edified:
Flatterers thrive on fools' credulity.
The lesson's worth a cheese, don't you agree?"
    The crow skulked off, abashed, and swore—
Too late, however: "Nevermore!"

La Grenouille Qui Se Veut Faire
aussi Grosse que le Bœuf

Une Grenouille vit un Bœuf
Qui lui sembla de belle taille.
Elle, qui n'étoit pas grosse en tout comme un œuf,
Envieuse, s'étend, et s'enfle, et se travaille,
Pour égaler l'animal en grosseur,
Disant: "Regardez bien, ma sœur;
Est-ce assez? dites-moi; n'y suis-je point encore?"
"Nenni." "M'y voici donc?" "Point du tout." "M'y voilà?"
"Vous n'en approchez point." La chétive pécore
S'enfla si bien qu'elle creva.

Le monde est plein de gens qui ne sont pas plus sages:
Tout bourgeois veut bâtir comme les grands seigneurs,
Tout petit prince a des ambassadeurs,
Tout marquis veut avoir des pages.[1]

1. La Fontaine's last line has become proverbial. As for the whole of the final quatrain, a number of critics were to take him to task for unnecessarily appending self-evident morals to many of his fables—a point of view by no means universally shared. Jean-Jacques Rousseau especially—no lover of La Fontaine's moralizings—citing this fable, observes in a well-known passage from Book Four of his pedagogical treatise *Emile* (1762): "Si votre élève n'entend la fable qu'à l'aide de

The Frog Who Would Grow
as Big as the Ox

A frog espies an ox
Of elegant dimension.
Herself no bigger than an egg, she gapes and gawks
In envy at his grandeur. Her intention?
To grow as huge as he. And so,
Huffing and puffing, all a-fuss, a-fret,
She asks: "Friend, have I done it?" "No!"
"And now?" "Nay, nay!" "There! Have I yet?"
"Not even close!" The paltry mite—galled, goaded—
Swelled up so well that she exploded.

This world of ours is full of foolish creatures too:
Commoners want to build chateaus;
Each princeling wants his royal retinue;
Each count, his squires. And so it goes.

l'explication, soyez sûr qu'il ne l'entendra pas même ainsi" (ed. Michel Launay, p. 323). For the present fable at any rate, not to mention all the rest, the reproach is unwarranted on literary grounds if no other. At least one of the several Aesopic originals (Phaedrus, I, 24) begins with a similar explanatory moral: "Inops, potentem dum vult imitari, perit . . ." ("When the poor man wants to ape the powerful, he comes to grief . . .").

Le Loup et l'Agneau

La raison du plus fort est toujours la meilleure:
Nous l'allons montrer tout à l'heure.

Un Agneau se désaltéroit
Dans le courant d'une onde pure.
Un Loup survient à jeun, qui cherchoit aventure,
Et que la faim en ces lieux attiroit.
"Qui te rend si hardi de troubler mon breuvage?"
Dit cet animal plein de rage:
"Tu seras châtié de ta témérité."
"Sire," répond l'Agneau, "que Votre Majesté
Ne se mette pas en colère;
Mais plutôt qu'elle considère
Que je me vas désaltérant
Dans le courant,
Plus de vingt pas au-dessous d'Elle;
Et que par conséquent, en aucune façon,
Je ne puis troubler sa boisson."
"Tu la troubles," reprit cette bête cruelle;
"Et je sais que de moi tu médis l'an passé."
"Comment l'aurois-je fait si je n'étois pas né?"
Reprit l'Agneau; "je tette encor ma mère."
"Si ce n'est toi, c'est donc ton frère."
"Je n'en ai point." "C'est donc quelqu'un des tiens;
Car vous ne m'épargnez guère,
Vous, vos bergers, et vos chiens.
On me l'a dit : il faut que je me venge."
Là-dessus, au fond des forêts

The Wolf and the Lamb

The strongest argue best, and always win.
Read on: you'll find the proof thereof herein.

A certain lamb his thirst was slaking
Next to a crystal stream, when lo!
A hungry wolf drew near, his leisure taking,
Hoping to find a tasty meal or so.
The beast in fearsome tones snarled, snorted:
"How dare you foul my drink! I'll make you pay!"
"Pardon me, sire," meekly the lamb retorted,
"But if Your Majesty, I pray—
With due respect—
Would please consider, in effect,
The facts, I'm sure that he would plainly see
I'm twenty paces farther down than he.
I fail to fathom what he's thinking,
Since in no way can I disturb his drinking."
"Yes, yes! You do!... And that's not all!,"
Replied the wolf. "I'll thank you to recall,
Last year you cursed me!" "Me? But how?
I wasn't even born, sire! Ask my mother!
I'm still a suckling." "Then it was your brother!"
"Brother? I haven't any." "Then, I vow,
It was some other of your scheming kin.
You're all the same, plotting to do me in—
Sheep, shepherds, hounds! Well, tit for tat!"
Wherewith the beast, in all his fury,
Whisked him into the woods; whereat

Le Loup l'emporte, et puis le mange,
Sans autre forme de procès.

He wolfed him down. And that was that—
No judge, no jury.

Le Chêne et le Roseau

Le Chêne un jour dit au Roseau:
"Vous avez bien sujet d'accuser la nature;
Un roitelet pour vous est un pesant fardeau;
    Le moindre vent, qui d'aventure
    Fait rider la face de l'eau,
    Vous oblige à baisser la tête,
Cependant que mon front, au Caucase pareil,
Non content d'arrêter les rayons du soleil,
    Brave l'effort de la tempête.
Tout vous est aquilon, tout me semble zéphyr.
Encor si vous naissiez à l'abri du feuillage
    Dont je couvre le voisinage,
    Vous n'auriez pas tant à souffrir:
    Je vous défendrois de l'orage;
    Mais vous naissez le plus souvent
Sur les humides bords des royaumes du vent.
La nature envers vous me semble bien injuste."
"Votre compassion," lui répondit l'arbuste,
"Part d'un bon naturel; mais quittez ce souci:
    Les vents me sont moins qu'à vous redoutables;
Je plie, et ne romps pas. Vous avez jusqu'ici
    Contre leurs coups épouvantables
    Résisté sans courber le dos;
Mais attendons la fin." Comme il disoit ces mots,
Du bout de l'horizon accourt avec furie
    Le plus terrible des enfants
Que le Nord eût portés jusque-là dans ses flancs.
    L'arbre tient bon; le Roseau plie.
    Le vent redouble ses efforts,
    Et fait si bien qu'il déracine
Celui de qui la tête au ciel étoit voisine,
Et dont les pieds touchoient à l'empire des morts.

The Oak and the Reed

The oak one day spoke to the reed: "I swear,
You have good cause to fret at Nature. Why,
Even a wren weighs more than you can bear.
And when the slightest breeze that, by the by,
Ripples the water's face, down must you bow;
    Whereas my broad and mighty brow,
Caucasus-like against the sun and sky,
    Defies the storm. For you, see how
Each gust is like a northwind blast; for me,
Mere zephyr. Now, had you the luck to be
Born in my shadow, nothing need affect you,
    Safe from the wind's tempestuous whim,
Beneath my overspreading leaf and limb.
For I, the mighty oak, I would protect you!
But no! Denied by Nature's harsh neglect, you
Grow by the dank dominions of the wind.
    Poor wretch!" "Monsieur," replied the reed,
"It's kind of you to be so sore chagrined
On my account. I thank you. But, no need!
I fear the winds far less than you, my friend.
You see, I never break; I only bend.
    Till now, indeed, you have withstood
Their frightful force unbowed. So far so good.
    But wait. We haven't seen the end."
    As thus he spoke, from out beyond
The far horizon, like the crack of doom,
There looms the fiercest offspring ever spawned
    From deep within the Northwind's womb.
Oak holds... Reed bends... Wind blows... Then more
                                    and more,
Till it uproots the one who, just before,
Had risen heavenward with lofty head,
Whose feet had reached the empire of the dead.

Le Lion Devenu Vieux

Le Lion, terreur des forêts,
Chargé d'ans et pleurant son antique prouesse,
Fut enfin attaqué par ses propres sujets,
    Devenus forts par sa foiblesse.
Le Cheval s'approchant lui donne un coup de pied;
Le Loup, un coup de dent; le Bœuf, un coup de corne.
Le malheureux Lion, languissant, triste, et morne,
Peut à peine rugir, par l'âge estropié.
Il attend son destin, sans faire aucunes plaintes;
Quand voyant l'Ane même à son antre accourir:
"Ah! c'est trop," lui dit-il; "je voulois bien mourir;
Mais c'est mourir deux fois que souffrir tes atteintes."

The Lion Grown Old

    The lion, terror of the forest, lies
Laden with years, lamenting feats of prowess past.
    His loyal subjects, grown at last
    More daring at his imminent demise,
    Come and attack him with their newfound strength,
    Each in his own most brutish wise:
Horse kicks, wolf bites, ox butts and gores... At length,
Resigned—crippled, too weak to roar—he spies
The ass approaching! O disgrace unbounded!
    "I don't mind facing death," he sighs,
    Eyeing the ass. "But you!" he cries.
"To suffer your abuse is death compounded!"

La Montagne Qui Accouche

Une Montagne en mal d'enfant
Jetoit une clameur si haute,
Que chacun, au bruit accourant,
Crut qu'elle accoucheroit sans faute
D'une cité plus grosse que Paris:
Elle accoucha d'une Souris.
Quand je songe à cette fable,
Dont le récit est menteur
Et le sens est véritable,
Je me figure un auteur
Qui dit: "Je chanterai la guerre
Que firent les Titans au maître du tonnerre."
C'est promettre beaucoup: mais qu'en sort-il souvent?
Du vent.

The Mountain in Labor

A pregnant mountain, just about
To enter labor, bellows out,
And raises such a monstrous roar
That all who run to watch surmise
She'll bear a city more than Paris' size.
A mouse is what she bore.
When I conceive this fiction,
Empty of fact but full of sense,
It seems to me a true depiction
Of authors' vain grandiloquence.
They promise: "Ah, my lyre will sing
Of Titans' combat with the Thunder's king."
Fine words! And yet, what often comes to pass?
Just gas.

Le Chien Qui Lâche Sa Proie pour l'Ombre

Chacun se trompe ici-bas:
On voit courir après l'ombre
Tant de fous, qu'on n'en sait pas
La plupart du temps le nombre.
Au Chien dont parle Esope il faut les renvoyer.
Ce Chien, voyant sa proie en l'eau représentée,
La quitta pour l'image, et pensa se noyer.
La rivière devint tout d'un coup agitée;
A toute peine il regagna les bords,
Et n'eut ni l'ombre ni le corps.

The Dog Who Drops His Prey for Its Reflection

To err is human. Here below,
Many the folk—or fools—who go
Chasing a shadow; more, indeed,
Than one can count. Best let them read
The tale about a dog that Aesop tells,
Who, by a stream, prey clutched between his teeth,
Eyes its reflection in the waves beneath,
Lunges, falls in. The water swirls and swells.
Near drowned, he struggles back to shore. But oh, the cost:
Shadow and substance both, alas, are lost.

Le Gland et la Citrouille

Dieu fait bien ce qu'il fait. Sans en chercher la preuve
En tout cet univers, et l'aller parcourant,
Dans les citrouilles je la treuve.
Un Villageois, considérant
Combien ce fruit est gros et sa tige menue:
"A quoi songeoit," dit-il, "l'auteur de tout cela?
Il a bien mal placé cette citrouille-là!
Hé parbleu! je l'aurois pendue
A l'un des chênes que voilà;
C'eût été justement l'affaire:
Tel fruit, tel arbre, pour bien faire.
C'est dommage, Garo, que tu n'es point entré
Au conseil de celui que prêche ton curé:
Tout en eût été mieux; car pourquoi, par exemple,
Le Gland, qui n'est pas gros comme mon petit doigt,
Ne pend-il pas en cet endroit?
Dieu s'est mépris: plus je contemple
Ces fruits ainsi placés, plus il semble à Garo
Que l'on a fait un quiproquo."

The Acorn and the Pumpkin

The Lord knows best what He's about.
No need to search for proof throughout
The universe. Look at the pumpkin.
It gives us all the proof we need. To wit:
The story of a village bumpkin—
Garo by name—who found one, gazed at it,
And wondered how so huge a fruit could be
Hung from so slight a stem: "It doesn't fit!
God's done it wrong! If He'd asked me,
He'd hang them from those oaks. Big fruit, big tree.
Too bad someone so smart and strong—
At least that's what the vicar's always saying
With all his preaching and his praying—
Didn't have me to help His work along!
I'd hang the acorn from this vine instead...
No bigger than my nail... It's like I said:
God's got things backwards. It's all wrong...
Well, after all that weighty thought I'd best
Take me a nap. We thinkers need our rest."

Cette réflexion embarrassant notre homme:
"On ne dort point," dit-il, "quand on a tant d'esprit."
Sous un chêne aussitôt il va prendre son somme.
Un Gland tombe: le nez du dormeur en pâtit.
Il s'éveille; et, portant la main sur son visage,
Il trouve encor le Gland pris au poil du menton.
Son nez meurtri le force à changer de langage.
"Oh! oh!" dit-il, "je saigne! et que seroit-ce donc
S'il fût tombé de l'arbre une masse plus lourde,
    Et que ce Gland eût été gourde?
Dieu ne l'a pas voulu: sans doute il eut raison;
    J'en vois bien à présent la cause."
      En louant Dieu de toute chose,
      Garo retourne à la maison.

No sooner said than done. Beneath an oak
Our Garo laid his head in sweet repose.
Next moment, though, he painfully awoke:
An acorn, falling, hit him on the nose.
    Rubbing his face, feeling his bruises,
He finds it still entangled in his beard.
    "A bloody nose from this?" he muses.
"I must say, things aren't quite what they appeared.
    My goodness, if this little nut
Had been a pumpkin or a squash, then what?
God knows His business after all, no question!
It's time I changed my tune!" With that suggestion,
    Garo goes home, singing the praise
    Of God and of His wondrous ways.

La Tortue et les Deux Canards

Une Tortue étoit, à la tête légère,
Qui, lasse de son trou, voulut voir le pays.
Volontiers on fait cas d'une terre étrangère;
Volontiers gens boiteux haïssent le logis.
    Deux Canards, à qui la commère
    Communiqua ce beau dessein,
Lui dirent qu'ils avoient de quoi la satisfaire.
    "Voyez-vous ce large chemin?
Nous vous voiturerons, par l'air, en Amérique:
    Vous verrez mainte république,
Maint royaume, maint peuple; et vous profiterez
Des différentes mœurs que vous remarquerez.
Ulysse en fit autant." On ne s'attendoit guère
    De voir Ulysse en cette affaire.
La Tortue écouta la proposition.
Marché fait, les Oiseaux forgent une machine
    Pour transporter la pèlerine.
Dans la gueule, en travers, on lui passe un bâton.
"Serrez bien," dirent-ils, "gardez de lâcher prise."
Puis chaque Canard prend ce bâton par un bout.
La Tortue enlevée, on s'étonne partout
    De voir aller en cette guise
    L'animal lent et sa maison,
Justement au milieu de l'un et l'autre Oison.
"Miracle!" crioit-on: "venez voir dans les nues
    Passer la reine des tortues."
"La reine! vraiment oui: je la suis en effet;
Ne vous en moquez point." Elle eût beaucoup mieux fait
De passer son chemin sans dire aucune chose;
Car, lâchant le bâton en desserrant les dents,
Elle tombe, elle crève aux pieds des regardants.
Son indiscrétion de sa perte fut cause.

Imprudence, babil, et sotte vanité,
    Et vaine curiosité,
    Ont ensemble étroit parentage.
    Ce sont enfants tous d'un lignage.

The Turtle and the Two Ducks

    A turtle, none too quick of mind,
And tiring of her hole, was quite inclined
To roam the world and visit lands far-flung.
(A common wish, especially among
    The lame, or slow of limb, confined
    To lodgings that they come to hate,
Such as our tortoise friend.) At any rate,
Two ducks she prattled to of her ambition
Assured her they could bring it to fruition:
    "Our highway is the sky, and we
    Can take you where you've never been.
We'll fly you to America! You'll see
Kingdoms, republics, peoples never seen.
    Imagine what you'll learn. You'll be
Just like Ulysses, traveling far and near."
(Ulysses? Who would think to find him here!)
    No sooner does she answer "Yes!"
    Than, there and then, the ducks prepare
    Their transport for our pilgrimess—
A simple stick. Each bites one end: "Now, there!"
They say. "You bite the middle." She complies.
    The ducks advise: "Hold tight! Take care!"
    And up they rise, high in the air,
    Much to the wonder and surprise
Of those below, who see her, house and all,
Hanging between two ducks! "Come look!" they call.
"A miracle! The Turtle Queen is flying
Heavenward!" "Queen!" she boasts. "There's no denying..."
Those words would be her last. Poor fool! She should
    Have kept her big mouth shut! Instead,
She opened it, and now it's shut for good,
As she lies—dashed to pieces—proud, but dead.

A babbling tongue, vain curiosity,
    And witlessness: one family!
    All of a kind, all kith and kin—
And all of them, in time, will do you in.

Pierre de Saint-Glas   Œuvres de Monsieur ***, Contenant Plusieurs Fables d'Esope Mises en Vers (1670)

WITHIN a decade of the publication of his first six books of the *Fables,* several of La Fontaine's contemporaries were to compete with him—briefly—for a place in the genre's sun. The best known, and surely the most notorious, was Antoine Furetière, who would indeed leave his mark, though less as a fabulist than in other areas of French letters. (See pp. 40–42.) Two other close contemporaries, L.-S. Desmay and Pierre de Saint-Glas—as well as a third, the prolific Madame de Villedieu—deserve at least passing mention, for historical reasons if for no other.

Madame de Villedieu will be discussed below (see pp. 37–38). As for Desmay, little of importance is known, and of his fables little need be said. He was the author of *L'Esope du Temps, fables nouvelles,* a collection of twenty-eight fables published in two parts, of fourteen each, with accompanying *pièces liminaires* (Paris: Veuve François Clousier & Pierre Bienfait, 1677), the second part of which was separately printed as *L'Esope françois, fables nouvelles* the following year by the same publishers. Desmay's rather prolix and uninspiring *vers libres* fables are characterized by equally uninspiring morals.[1] The only interest they present, frankly, is the possible influence of one or two on La Fontaine's later books. However, Desmay's reluctant apologist, Daniel Delafarge, in a brief study of the question, can neither prove nor disprove the possibility. He defends the somewhat futile exercise as an additional (if unnecessary) tribute to the early supremacy of La Fontaine: "Resterons-nous sur des résultats aussi incertains ou même aussi négatifs? Non: la lecture de Desmay n'est nullement inutile aux amis de La Fontaine, car elle les aide à mesurer le succès immédiat des *Fables.* Elle les aide, en outre, à comprendre l'art exquis du poète." (See his "Remarques sur les fables de Desmay et celles de La Fontaine," p. 250.)

Pierre de Saint-Glas (or the abbé de Saint-Ussans), while no greater a threat to La Fontaine's hegemony, is a somewhat more substantial literary figure, having several varied works to his credit. In addition to a one-act prose comedy, *Les Bouts-rimez,* dedicated to an appreciative prince de Condé and performed a respectable nine times at the Comédie-Française in 1682 and 1684, Saint-Glas authored an anonymous collection of thirty-six fables (*Œuvres de Monsieur ***, contenant plusieurs fables d'Esope mises en vers*), a volume of twenty-five *Contes nouveaux en*

vers, with a preface invoking the name of La Fontaine, whose *Contes et Nouvelles en vers* had begun appearing in 1665; and a few other minor works, both secular and religious, among them one bearing the intriguing title *Particularités remarquables des sauterelles qui sont venues de Russie,* apparently inspired by a plague of locusts.[2]

Though more is known about this emulator of La Fontaine than about the shadowy Desmay, concrete facts are few and far between. The two-volume *Biographie toulousaine* tells us that Saint-Glas was born in Toulouse "en 16...," that he entered the priesthood at an early age, devoted himself to "l'étude de l'histoire anecdotique et de la Biographie," and that his poetic efforts were recognized in 1669 with a prize at his city's venerable Jeux Floraux (II:380). Among the laudatory comments about an obvious native son, the same entry makes the claim that several of his poetic compositions were praised by Bayle in his monthly review of literary, scientific, and intellectual miscellany, the *Nouvelles de la république des lettres.*[3] The one incontrovertible fact seems to be that he died in Paris on May 11, 1699.

Saint-Glas's fables, like his *contes,* are introduced by a preface, striking in its backhanded admiration of La Fontaine, whose first six books appeared a scant two years before. It is only after he leads us through an explanation and general history of the *vis comica*—beginning with Aesop and coursing through Lucian, Martial, Juvenal, Horace, Plautus, Terence, a spate of Italians and Spaniards, Rabelais, Marot, et al.—that he finally arrives at a defense of his own fables. Although he admits, with a false modesty that would almost be pathetic if it were not presumptuous, that they are not so good as La Fontaine's, he proceeds to assure us that it is only because he had mostly the latter's leftovers to work with: "le rebut de M.r de la Fontaine." As a result, "la sterilité de la matiere ne m'a point permis de donner à mon Ouvrage vne plus grande beauté que celle qu'il a."[4] (Clearly, La Fontaine, who went on to write six more books of fables, was not similarly hampered.)

From the example included here—the thirty-fifth, "L'Homme & l'Asne"—the reader can judge for himself whether it was, in fact, the sterility of the material alone that made the good abbé fall short of his celebrated contemporary.

---

1. One of them, the concluding lines of "Le Lievre, le Cheval, le Cerf, l'Asne, la Taupe," ou "Les Envieux" (II, 14), will serve as an example: "Et c'est ainsi que va le monde. / Jamais contents des biens qu'ils ont, / Les uns portent toûjours envie aux biens des autres. / Toûjours les maux d'autruy sont moindres que les nôtres."

2. Regarding Saint-Glas's comedy, see Henry Carrington Lancaster's detailed discussion in *A History of French Dramatic Literature in the Seventeenth Century,* II:539–42. As for his other works, most of them are listed in Frédéric Lachèvre's *Bibliographie des recueils collectifs de poé-*

sies publiés de 1597 à 1700, III:520–21. Several others are also discussed by "P.-L. Jacob" (one of the pseudonyms of literary antiquarian Paul Lacroix) in his essay "L'Abbé de Saint-Ussans et ses ouvrages," pp. 38–45.

3. None of the numbers that I have been able to consult (Mar. 1684–June 1688, Jan. 1689–Apr. 1689) makes any mention whatever of Saint-Glas. Likewise, the claim in Lacroix's essay that "Pierre Richelet, dans son *Dictionnaire de la langue françoise,* a cité l'abbé de Saint-Ussans presque aussi souvent que La Fontaine" (p. 39), seems hard to confirm. Saint-Glas's (or Saint-Ussan's) name is not listed among the

authors quoted in the original edition of Richelet, or those in the Amsterdam edition of 1732.

4. The citation is taken from the next-to-last page of the unpaginated preface.

L'Homme & L'Asne

Qvand vn mortel souffre quelque malheur,
Afflige-t'en, sois seur de la pareille,
De t'en mocquer seroit d'vn méchant cœur,
Autãt, mon cher, t'en pend à ton oreille,
Voudrois-tu bien qu'vn tel tour il te fist?
A ses dépens tu peux devenir sage:
C'est de bon sens de tourner à profit
De ton prochain la perte & le dommage;
Pour ce coup-cy ne te déplairra pas
D'vn gros Baudet d'apprendre ce beau cas.

Un gros Pourceau ne mangeoit point de son,
Ains au cõtraire on le nourrissoit d'orge,
Non pour son nez, c'estoit pour faire don
A Iupiter, & luy couper la gorge:
Vn jour avint qu'vn Prestre fit l'office
De le tuër, cela fut bien-tost fait,
Puis il en fit vn digne sacrifice,
Le bon Iupin en fut fort satisfait,
Lors le Pourceau plus d'orge ne mangea,
Il en restoit, le maistre de ce reste
De le donner à son Asne songea;
Lors le Baudet, "ce present est funeste,
Monsieur" (dit-il) "je suis vostre valet,
Ie ne suis pas jusqu'à ce point Baudet
Que de vouloir prendre telle pasture,
A d'autres bon, c'est à faire aux Pourceaux,
Pour moy je crains la pointe des coûteaux,
Pour Iupiter ma chair seroit trop dure."

The Man and the Ass[1]

When ill befalls your fellow mortal
Best you be moved to sympathy.
Beware lest you would chaff and chortle:
You can get stung no less than he.
Would you then want him, friend, in turn,
To laugh and make fine sport of you?
Better, from his misfortune, learn
What best to do and not to do.
About an ass I'll tell a tale you
Ought take to heart: may it avail you.[2]

A hog, well-fed and fat, there was,
Who ate no bran but only rice:
Not for his charm; rather because
They raised him for the sacrifice.[3]
Jupiter's priest, at length, came round
And promptly slit his throat;[4] whereat
The god was passing pleased: he found
Our pig most worthy, for all that.
Now, with a store of rice unused—
The farmer had no hog to feed—
"I'll feed it to my ass," he mused.
Replied the latter: "Nay indeed!
Thanks just the same, but not a jot!
An ass I am; a fool I'm not.
For such fare there are swine enough:
To them the woe that it betides!
Myself, I fear the knife... Besides,
For Jupiter I'm much too tough."

1. Saint-Glas's bland title is rather surprising. Given the scenario, one would expect, I think, something more encompassing; perhaps "The Farmer, the Hog, and the Ass," or the like.
2. The ensuing fable is somewhat oblique in its illustration of this moral preamble. But that is only one of the reasons why this fabulist, for all the talent his apologists attribute to him, was clearly no serious rival to La Fontaine.
3. I have taken the modest liberty of changing the hog's distinguished diet from the original *orge* ("barley") to the more rhymable "rice." Note also the expression "pour son (beau) nez," an ephemeral

seventeenth-century equivalent of the more common "pour ses beaux yeux." The poet Mathurin Régnier had popularized it early in the century in one of his *Satyres* (III:135). (See his *Œuvres complètes*, p. 33.)
4. "Jupin" was used for pleasant effect by La Fontaine as a typically irreverent nickname for Jupiter in a half-dozen of his fables. Littré records it as belonging to "l'ancien français," but gives no older source than Rotrou's tragedy *Hercule mourant*, of 1636 (II, ii). (An unfortunate misprint would seem to refer to a nonexistent *"Mercure mourant,"* and compounds the error by citing the wrong scene [II, i].)

Madame de Villedieu   Fables, ou Histoires Allégoriques (1670)

It is ironic, though understandable, that a genre whose first French-language practitioner was a female—Marie de France (see p. 3)—would have to wait five centuries before another of her sex would try her hand at it, albeit rather tentatively, and not without at least a trace of doubt concerning the authenticity of her authorship. The woman who broke through that gender barrier was Marie-Catherine Desjardins, known to literary history as Madame de Villedieu, one of the more colorful, controversial, and even scandalous figures of the French seventeenth century.[1] "Car cette femme étrange, issue d'assez basse condition, eut l'audace géniale de l'aventurière, se glissa dans tous les mondes, à la faveur de la littérature ou du théâtre, apportant partout le souci de ses préoccupations amoureuses, brouillant maints ménages, se brouillant elle-même avec les puissants du jour, se raccommodant avec eux, laissant partout les traces de son audace et de ses passions, pour finir humblement sa vie comme elle l'avait commencée, dans la solitude perdue d'un petit coin de province." (See Alphonse Séché and Jules Bertaut, "Une Aventurière de lettres au XVIIe siècle: Madame de Villedieu," p. 616.)

The "coin de province" where this picturesque adventuress died, on October 20, 1683, was Saint-Rémy-du-Plain, not far from the other provincial "coin" where she was born—Alençon—in the 1630s or 1640.[2] The years between saw her rise from her humble beginnings as daughter of a chambermaid to the duchesse Anne de Montbazon, who would long remain her protectress, to become not only one of the Parisian salon favorites of the age, sought out by the social, intellectual, and artistic celebrities, and notorious among them for her unorthodox marriages and assorted amours, but also one of the first professional French *femmes de lettres,* author of much occasional verse—typical in its precious excesses—several pastoral novels inspired by D'Urfé's *Astrée* and the like, and a number of plays.[3]

A dozen years before her death—which, if we can believe Séché and Bertaut ("Une Aventurière," p. 631), would be precipitated by a growing addiction to alcohol—Madame de Villedieu published her *Fables, ou Histoires allégoriques.* The volume, dedicated to Louis XIV himself, who had granted her a generous pension the previous year, contained eight lengthy fables very similar in subject, dramatis personae, style, and detail to those which La Fontaine, in his first six books, had published only two years before. It was that striking similarity that prompted one later critic, Auguste-Louis Ménard, to put forward the elaborate thesis that the not-yet-famous fabulist was, in effect, Madame de Villedieu's lover, and that the eight fables in question were really his, published under her name—with the collusion, and perhaps at the instigation, of their common publisher Barbin—to take advantage of her social and literary prominence.[4] The thesis, explained in detail by Séché and Bertaut ("Une Aventurière," pp. 620–22, 626–28), is categorically discredited by Morrissette in his discussion of Madame de Villedieu's fables (*Life and Works,* pp. 31–35), but remains a telling tribute, however farfetched, to the prestige, at least passing, of this singular seventeenth-century "courtisane de lettres."[5]

"Le Singe Cupidon" is the second fable in the collection: a typically gallant mini-drama, perhaps a little too précieux for the usually less vaporous La Fontaine; but still, all in all, not wholly unworthy to have been thought to be his work.

---

1. The name "Hortense," which modern observers often add to Mlle Dejardins's "Marie-Catherine," is apparently spurious. See Bruce Morrissette, *The Life and Works of Marie-Catherine Desjardins (Mme de Villedieu), 1632–1683,* p. 2; and Micheline Cuénin, *Madame de Villedieu (Marie-Catherine Desjardins, 1640–1683),* I:25.

2. The exact date is disputed, as evidenced in the titles of the two works cited in the previous note. The date of her death has also been subject to controversy, many sources (including Séché and Bertaut) citing it as 1692, which would seem, rather, to be the year her mother died. (See Morrissette, *Life and Works,* p. 2, and p. 19, n. 67.)

3. Her first novel, *Alcidamie* (1661), an involved adventure tale centering about the fanciful "Isle Délicieuse," interspersed with amorous debate and gallant romance, was among her best-known, if not most successful, works. As for her several theater pieces, the first of substance, and the one which would establish her literary reputation, was *Manlius* (1663), a tragicomedy that brought her, obliquely, into conflict with the declining Corneille, largely through the machinations of her champion (and perhaps coauthor), the abbé d'Aubignac. (See

Henri-E. Chatenet, *Le Roman et les romans d'une femme de lettres au XVIIe siècle. Mme de Villedieu [1632–1683],* pp. 36–53; and Morrissette, *Life and Works,* pp. 45–69.) Regarding others of her works possibly composed, at least in part, by other hands, see Séché and Bertaut, "Une Aventurière," p. 629. A detailed bibliography, including a number of false attributions, is found in Alexandre Cioranescu, *Bibliographie de la littérature française du dix-septième siècle,* III:1975–76. It includes several tragedies and various other titles not mentioned in Morrissette's otherwise authoritative biography and literary study. For more recent bibliographical data, see also Cuénin, *Madame de Villedieu,* II:1–17.

4. See Auguste-Louis Ménard, *La Fontaine et Mme de Villedieu, les Fables galantes présentées à Louis XIV le jour de sa fête, essai de restitution à La Fontaine.*

5. The uncharitable but rather accurate description is Ménard's, quoted by Morrissette (*Life and Works,* p. 35). For a recent study of her fables, see Jean-Pierre Lafouge, "Madame de Villedieu dans ses fables."

Le Singe Cupidon

Vn vieux Singe des plus adrois,
Ayant veu l'Amour plusieurs fois,
Décocher ses fléches mortelles,
Sur les cœurs de maintes Cruelles;
Comme luy, voulut estre Archer,
Et fléches d'Amour décocher.
Il eust donné leçon d'adresse,
A tout maistre en tours de souplesse.

The Monkey Who Played Cupid

A shrewd old monkey, deft and sly,
Often had watched as Cupid would let fly
Those barbs of his—love-dealing darts,
To prick so many heartless damsels' hearts—
And thought that surely he could wield as well
The bended bow. Now, truth to tell,
So artful was the ape that he
Could teach the masters of skulduggery:

Il prend si bien son temps, choisit si bien son lieu,
   Qu'il détrousse le petit Dieu.
   Enrichy d'un butin si rare,
A se cupidonner le Magot se prepare;
Endosse le carquois, s'affuble du bandeau,
En conquerant des cœurs, se rengorge, & se quarre,
   Et se mirant dans un ruisseau,
Se prend pour Cupidon, tant il se trouve beau.
   Ces Animaux pour l'ordinaire,
  Naissent sçavans, en l'art de contrefaire,
   Et dans le langage commun,
   Singe, & Copiste ce n'est qu'un.
  Celuy-cy donc campé dans un boccage,
   Attend une Nymphe au passage,
   Et comme souvent le hazard,
Aux blessures du cœur a la meilleure part,
   Nostre Archer d'espece nouvelle
   Atteint droit au cœur de la Belle.
   Iamais la Nymphe avant ce jour,
  N'avoit senty les fléches de l'amour.
   Si cette blessure cruelle,
   Fut un cas surprenant pour elle;
   I'en fais Iuge le jeune cœur,
   Atteint de pareille douleur.
   Iour, & nuict, la nouvelle Amante
   Soûpire, se plaint, se tourmente,
   Sans sçavoir ce qu'elle sentoit,
   Ny pourquoy tant se lamentoit.
   Maistre Magot darde-sagette,
  Qui mieux instruit du mal de la Pauvrette,
   S'applaudissoit de sa dexterité,
   Se voyant la Divinité,
Pour qui se preparoit l'amoureux Sacrifice,
   Se tenoit fier comme un Narcisse.
   Quand la Belle par ses soûpirs,
   Exprimoit ses tendres desirs;
  Que de ses yeux, la langueur indiscrette,
   A son cœur servoit d'interprete,
   Peu s'en faloit, qu'en ce moment,
   L'indigne Auteur de son tourment,

Lying in wait for Cupid, to undo him,
He chose the proper place and moment; whence
   The little god had no defense,
But had to yield his bow and arrow to him.
   Enriched by such a priceless prize,
   Quiver behind and blindfold tying
About his face, now in the godlet's guise,
   He sets about cupidifying...
   At length, stopping beside a brook—
   Swelling with pride—he goes to look,
And there perceives so fair and fine a sight
   That he, indeed, believes he might
Play Love himself. (For monkeys are such mimes
   That, in the common speech, at times
We say "to ape" and mean "to imitate.")
   This beast of ours, at any rate,
   Among the bushes takes his stance,
Stalking a passing nymph. The counterfeit,
Unwonted bowman shoots... By sheerest chance—
For so it is with love—the sprite is hit,
   Square in the breast. Nor had she ever,
Until that day, suffered the merest whit
   From Cupid's dart; nay, none whatever.
Imagine her surprise: like many a young
And callow heart, to be so cruelly stung!
By day, by night, Love's newest devotee
   Sighs, beats her bosom, sobs and cries,
With never a notion, not the least surmise
Of what the reason for her woes might be.
   Sir Ape the Archer knows, for sure,
   The cause of her discomfiture.
Thanking his godly skill for her new passion,
   Proudly the would-be Cupid waited,
   Pleased with himself, Narcissus-fashion,
   And watched it flourish unabated.
With sighs aplenty our poor nymph expressed
The tender yearning burning in her breast.
And when her eyes, with languid indiscretion,
   Eloquent in their mute confession,
   Revealed her heartsick melancholy,

Ne se crust ce qu'il feignoit d'estre.
Il eust avec l'amour disputé d'agrément,
    Tant l'orgueil nous fait méconnoistre.
    Mais on voit ordinairement,
    Que la Gloire sans fondement,
    Est chimerique, & peu durable.
Du carquois dérobé, le Maistre redoutable,
    Cherchoit plein de ressentiment,
Le sacrilege Auteur, d'un fait si punissable.
    Le sort le guida sur le lieu,
Où le Magot paré des dépoüilles du Dieu,
    Recevoit l'amoureux hommage
    Qu'on devoit à son Equipage.
    Si Cupidon fut offensé;
    Qu'un Magot pour luy se fist prendre,
    Et comme tel fust encensé,
    Il est aisé de le comprendre.
    "Quoy?" dit-il, "ce ridé Museau,
    A la faveur de mon Bandeau,
    Chez les Mortels remplit ma Place?"
    A ces mots Messire l'Amour,
    Détrousse le Singe à son tour,
    Montre a nud sa laide grimace,
    Et tirant la Nymphe d'erreur,
Fit naistre un plus beau feu, dans son aveugle cœur.

    Ainsi l'ame préoccupée,
    Et par l'apparence trompée,
    Eleve aux hommes des Autels,
    Qui ne sont deus qu'aux Immortels.
Le bandeau de l'Amour, fait des Metamorphoses
    Des plus desagreables choses;
    Mais quand un retour de raison,
    Peut enfin trouver sa saison,
  Ou qu'un Amour, d'une plus pure essence,
A nois cœurs prevenus, fait sentir sa puissance,
    Combien trouvons-nous odieux
    Ce qu'avoient admiré nos yeux?

The wretched author of her woe—O Folly!—
    All but believed himself, forsooth,
To be the one he feigned, and fairer truly.
(So much does pride distract us from the truth.
    But glory that we claim unduly
    Is vain illusion, quick to dim.)
Quiver-bereft, but filled with righteous wrath,
The god decides to search the wood for him.
    Fate leads him on the proper path:
There sits the ape, still at his vile charade,
Reveling in the amorous homage paid
His godly trappings. Is it any wonder
    That Cupid takes offense, by thunder!
To see himself by monkey imitated
    And his impostor adulated?
"What?" he exclaims. "That dunderhead! That lout!
An ape, to play at Love? to mimic me,
    Hiding his grizzled, wrinkled snout
Behind my blindfold? And shamefacedly!
    Ye gods, what fools these mortals be!"[1]
That said, he said no more, but ripped the ape's
Disguise away, and left the jackanapes
    To leer his naked leer, stripped bare,
From top to bottom, front to *derrière*.
    Whereupon mistress nymph discovers
That there can be more gallant, gracious lovers.

Too often, in the blindness of the mind,
    Gulled by appearance, we erect
    Gods' altars to mere mortal kind:
Love's blindness makes us less than circumspect,
Transforming ugly cause to fair effect.
But when, in time, our reason, once again
    Returns to grace our wit; or when
New love—of purer essence, therewithal—
    Seizes and holds our hearts in thrall;
Then do we see how hateful was the prize
That once we longed for with adoring eyes.

---

1. The perspicacious reader will, of course, appreciate that this somewhat deformed Shakespearian reminiscence does not occur in the original.

Antoine Furetière   Fables Morales et Nouvelles (1671)

THE ABBÉ Antoine Furetière is one of those figures of French literary history whose name is vaguely familiar to graduate students but whose works precious few have actually read. Those who have, most likely know only his satirical *Roman bourgeois,* remarkable especially for its picturesque use of the popular language of the period, in striking contrast with the elegance of his classical contemporaries and colleagues, Racine, Boileau, et al.[1] It was, indeed, Furetière's concern with language that earned him both his early successes and his eventual cataclysmic fall from literary grace.

Furetière was born in Paris, December 28, 1619, the

son of a petit bourgeois family, according to one source (and not the son of lackeys, as his enemies were later to allege). (See J.-C. Barbier, "Un Exilé de l'Académie," p. 199.) He was educated in the law, civil and canon, and was awarded, in May of 1652, the administrative post of *procureur fiscal* for the abbey of Saint-Germain des Prés;[2] and, subsequently, the abbacy of Chalivoy, among other ecclesiastical charges. Although he was, in the pithy judgment of Emmanuel-Louis-Nicolas Viollet Le Duc, "un esprit ardent, sarcastique, et une très mauvaise tête," he enjoyed the friendship of the likes of Molière, La Fontaine, and most of the other literary and intellectual luminaries of the Age of Louis XIV.[3]

In 1682 Furetière was elected to the Académie Française, largely on the strength of the linguistic talents revealed in his *Nouvelle allégorique, ou Histoire des derniers troubles arrivez au royaume d'éloquence,* as well as for his long satirical poem *Le Voyage de Mercure* and his *Poésies diverses.*[4] It was also generally known at the time of his election that Furetière, the budding lexicographer, was contemplating a comprehensive encyclopedia of terms used in the sciences, arts, and industry. (See Barbier, "Un Exilé de l'Académie," p. 205.) The Académie, almost since its very inception in 1635, had been laboring—slowly—on its own supposedly definitive dictionary of the French tongue; and when a sample of Furetière's *Dictionnaire universel* appeared in 1664, in Amsterdam—the royal permission for publication in France having been revoked—the academicians saw it not only as an encroachment on their jealously guarded linguistic preserve, but, even worse, as an unauthorized and underhanded use of their own scrupulously assembled documentation. In a word, plagiarism. Despite Furetière's protestations of innocence and the support of a few staunch friends, he was duly expelled from the Académie in 1685, the only "immortel" ever to suffer such symbolic mortality, before or since.[5] The embittered author spent the last few years before his actual death, on May 14, 1688, in a war of accusation and counteraccusation, penning satirical pamphlets— "factums"—against his erstwhile colleagues, especially La Fontaine, who would consign him, literally, to artistic nonentity.[6]

Furetière's travails at the hands of the arbiters of literary and linguistic decorum are of particular interest here in that the only one of his close colleagues not to come to his defense was, in fact, his longtime friend La Fontaine. Their friendship may already have begun to waver when Furetière failed to support the fabulist in his own controversial bid for election to the august body. (See Marmier, "La Fontaine et son ami Furetière," pp. 460–61.) Be that as it may, it surely could not have been strengthened by Furetière's publication of his fifty *Fables morales et nouvelles,* appearing three years after La Fontaine's very successful first collection, and composed in the same irregular *vers libres* that La Fontaine had made his hallmark. In his preface Furetière praises the fables of his contemporary with what might well be considered merely polite lip service, pointing out that they are really only translations, despite the "grandes beautez" that La Fontaine "adjoûte aux Originaux"; whereas his own fables, though not graced with "cette belle manière d'écrire que tant de gens ont admirée," are at least all of his own invention: "tous de moy."[7] Whether intended as sincere admiration or sarcastic faint praise, in hindsight at least Furetière's remarks were generally taken as the latter, further evidence of a jealousy that would make his subsequent attacks on his former friend, in the last years of his life, all the more vitriolic and regrettable.[8]

Francis Wey, in his laudable attempt to rehabilitate Furetière's literary reputation after a lengthy eclipse, is understandably exaggerating more than a little in his judgment of the *Fables morales et nouvelles.* While agreeing with Furetière's own modest assessment of his style, he sees the poet's powers of "invention" as being even superior to those of La Fontaine, who, we are told, was responsible for the actual subject mattter of only a dozen or so of his fables. (See Wey, "Antoine Furetière," p. 610.) In any event, unfortunate comparisons aside, a dispassionate reading of Furetière's collection reveals a workmanlike, often lively and colorful contribution to the genre; one that, despite a rather rigid didacticism, is still worthy enough to stand on its own, and certainly not deserving of the obscurity—or, indeed, oblivion—to which, like most of his works, it had long been relegated.

The examples translated here—numbers 1, 24, 27, 28, and 33—are characteristic, in form and content, of Furetière's fables, all of which conclude with an explicitly announced moral reminiscent of the sixteenth-century fabulists rather than of the far less predictable, lighterhanded La Fontaine.

---

1. There have been a number of later editions of the *Roman bourgeois,* notable among them the first critical edition, by Edouard Fournier and Charles Asselineau, discussed at length by critic-novelist Jules Barbey d'Aurévilly in his posthumous *Voyageurs et romanciers,* pp. 35–40.

2. See J. Marmier, "La Fontaine et son ami Furetière," p. 450.

3. Viollet Le Duc, *Catalogue des livres composant la bibliothèque poétique de M. Viollet Le Duc,* p. 589.

4. Charles Bruneau, in his entry on Furetière in *Dictionnaire des lettres françaises: le dix-septième siècle,* p. 442, places the publication of *Le Voyage de Mercure* in 1659. Two editions, however, are cited by Alexandre Cioranescu in his *Bibliographie de la littérature française du dix-septième siècle,* II:934, as dating from 1653 and 1655, the first of which is in the Bibliothèque Nationale.

5. The completed dictionary appeared posthumously in three volumes, with great success and posterity, serving as the basis for the first edition of the Jesuits' *Dictionnaire de Trévoux* (1701), and, through it, extending its influence even into areas of Diderot's celebrated *Encyclopédie.* (See Bruneau, in *Dictionnaire . . . le dix-septième siècle,* pp. 443–44.) For a detailed chronicling of Furetière's tempestuous and often scandalous rift with the Académie, see the following: Augustin-Simon Irailh, *Querelles littéraires, ou Mémoires pour servir à l'histoire des*

révolutions de la République des Lettres, depuis Homère jusqu'à nos jours, IV:260–81; Francis Wey, "Antoine Furetière: sa vie, ses œuvres, ses démêlés avec l'Académie française"; Barbier, "Un Exilé de l'Académie"; and Marmier, "La Fontaine et son ami Furetière"; and, much more recently, Fabienne Gegou, *Antoine Furetière, abbé de Chalivoy ou La Chute d'un immortel.*

6. The "factums" were collected in a single edition with introduction and notes by Charles Asselineau, *Recueil des factums d'Antoine Furetière,* based on an earlier collection (Amsterdam, H. Desbordes, 1694). (For titles and editions of the individual pamphlets, as well as for other bibliographical details, see Cioranescu, *Bibliographie . . . du dix-septième siècle,* II:933–35.)

7. Furetière's "Au lecteur" is unpaginated. The quotations are taken from the sixth and ninth pages respectively.

8. Furetière would not be the only one of our fabulists French to lay claim—with differing dosages of modesty and adulation—to the virtues of originality and inventiveness vis-à-vis the Master, La Fontaine. The reader will hear the same motif intoned in many a *préface, discours, avant-propos,* and such, in several variations, over the ensuing decades.

De Devx Escrevices

Vne jeune Escrevice, & sans experience,
Vid d'un œuil envieux paroistre en un festin,
Quantité de ses Sœurs, en pompeuse apparence,
    Teintes d'un bel incarnadin.
  Elle courut soudain dire à sa mere,
"I'admire de mes sœurs la fortune prospere.
    I'en ay veu trente dans un plat,
    Si magnifiquement vestuës;
    Que je les croyrois parvenuës,
    Aux honneurs du Cardinalat:
Tandis que barbotant dans la boüe & l'ordure,
    Nous sommes couvertes de bure.
Que je souhaiterois un sort si fortuné;
Et d'avoir un habit si bien enluminé."
    La vieille & prudente Escrevice,
A sa fille répond: "Vous estes bien novice.
  Celle qui brille avec plus de splendeur,
Voudroit bien retenir sa premiere couleur;
    Et quoy qu'il semble qu'elle éclatte,
    Soubs une robbe d'écarlatte;
    C'est un funeste acoustrement,
    Qui ne doit pas faire d'envie,
    Puis qu'il est vendu cherement,
    Et qu'Elle en a perdu la vie.

MORALITÉ

    Tel, & Semblable est le sort,
    D'un Heros, couvert de gloire;
    Il vit de vray, dans l'Histoire,
    Mais cependant, il est mort.

The Two Crayfish

A crayfish, young and utterly naive—
    Spying a sumptuous feast, wherein
    Her envious eyes, in awe, perceive
    A scarlet bevy of her kin,
    Lying in elegant array—
Goes running to her mother, sighing: "Ah!
Why are we not so fortunate as they?"
"Who, child?" "My sisters on that plate, mamma...
    Thirty, decked out in fanciest clothes—
    Looking like Cardinals, goodness knows—
    Whilst you and I, in pauper's dress,
    Languish in muck and wretchedness.
Would I could share their honor! Would, as well,
I could be garbed in such resplendent guise!"
    The mother crayfish, worldly-wise,
Replies: "Nay, nay, dear daughter. Truth to tell,
    I fear you know but little. For,
Though you admire their splendor, they would be
Happy to sport their pallid hue once more.
    Don't envy that false finery,
    Symbol of crayfish doom and death!
    Your sisters gave their final breath
    To don that brilliant shade of red:
They're splendid... but alas, they're also dead!"

MORAL

    History tells the selfsame story:
    Heroes in every age abound—
    Honor-bedecked and laurel-crowned—
    But no less dead, for all their glory!

Dv Cigne et dv Corbeau

  Certain Procés fut mis en arbitrage,
    Qu'avoient le Cigne & le Corbeau,
    Sur la beauté de leur plumage.
Le Cigne soûtenoit qu'il estoit le plus beau,
    Et que sa blancheur singuliere,
    Estoit la premiere en valeur,
    Puis qu'elle avoit l'éclat de la lumiere,
Qui donne la naissance à toute autre couleur.
    L'autre soûtenoit au contraire,

The Swan and the Crow

A crow there was, engaged in sharp dispute,
Arguing with a most conceited swan—
    His rival staunch and resolute—
Each fancying himself the paragon
Of feathered comeliness. The swan maintained
That white, in all its brilliance, was the best—
Source of all other colors, he explained.[1]
"Pshaw pshaw!" guffawed the crow, quick to protest.
    "I'll have you know, white hurts the eyes.

Que la blancheur ébloüyssoit les yeux;
  Que ce noir extraordinaire,
  Dont l'avoient honoré les Dieux,
  Estoit plus capable de plaire.
Par le Corbeau, fut arbitre nommé,
Vn More qui de noir avoit deux ou trois doses;
  Et par le Cigne, un beau fils renommé,
  Par son tein de Lys & de Roses.
  Ces arbitres plus d'une fois,
  Sur ce fait tinrent conferance;
  Mais la diversité des voix,
Les empescha de donner leur Sentence.
  Chacun d'eux trop passionné,
Pour le party qu'il tâchoit de défendre;
Dans son advis demeuroit obstiné,
N'en vouloit point démordre, ny se rendre.
  Aprés avoir cherché long-temps,
Pour sur-arbitre, entre les Consultans,
  Quelqu'un d'une vie exemplaire,
  Et qui n'eust point en cette affaire,
  D'interest, ny de passion,
  Ny de preoccupation:
  Il ne fut pas en leur puissance,
De rencontrer ce Iuge indifferend,
  Ce qui leur osta l'esperance,
De voir finir jamais leur different.

MORALITÉ

Pas un mortel ne fut jamais capable,
  De bien juger de la beauté;
On prononce en faveur, toûjours de son semblable,
Et de l'opinion dont on est entesté.

But black, by far the loveliest
Of colors—gift divine—more than the rest,
  Pleases, and soothes, and satisfies."
  "Rubbish!" the swan, in turn, replied.
Wherewith, each picked a judge to help decide.
  The crow chose as his referee
A Blackamoor, as black as black could be;
The swan, a youth renowned the country wide
  For lily skin and blush of rose.
  The arbiters discuss, debate,
  And do their best to mediate
  Betwixt our disputatious beaus.
In vain: amid the contras and the pros,
  Obdurate, each one roundly damns
The other's taste, while singing dithyrambs
Unto his own. And on and on it goes...
At length, the parties realized they ought
Choose one alone, of more objective mind—
One having, as they say, no axe to grind.
  And so, indeed, straightway they sought,
  Looking and looking, high and low,
To find a judge whose taste had not been fashioned,
Of yet unformed opinion, unimpassioned,
Sure to decree impartially... But no!
  Our crow and swan are searching still:
Their spat goes on—and, likely, always will.

MORAL

No mortal, howsoever hard he try,
Can judge of beauty with unbiased eye.
  'Twill ever be, 'twas ever thus:
Beauty we see in what looks most like us.

1. This would seem to be a virtually contemporaneous allusion to Newton's celebrated prism experiments on the refraction of light, believed to have taken place in the late 1660s.

Dv Chien et dv Voleur

  Un Chien fameux, par sa fidelité,
Et par sa vigilance, & par sa hardiesse,
Avoit fait tellement ses preuves de noblesse,
  Que son Seigneur dormant en seureté,
Le laissoit gardien de toute sa richesse.
Il saûtoit au collet du plus hardy voleur,
S'il paroissoit un Loup, c'estoit pour son mal-heur,
Enfin toûjours actif, & toûjours en haleine,
Tantost dans la Maison, & tantost dans la Plaine,
  Il empeschoit qu'on ne fist tort,
  Aux Troupeaux comme au Coffre fort.
  Mais quoy que de servir son Maistre,
  Il ne pust estre détourné,
  Par quelque appas que ce pût estre,
  Certain voleur adroit & rafiné,
Pour suborner ce Chien tant affectioné,

The Dog and the Thief

  A shepherd had a dog, renowned
  Round and about for loyalty,
  Vigilance, strength, and such. The hound
Had shown himself to be so utterly
  Trusty and true that, when night fell
  And all lay dark, his master slept
Sure in the knowledge that his watchdog kept
The vigil of a faithful sentinel,
Guarding his treasure, quick to pounce on any
  Thieving intruder—like the many
Murderous wolves that eyed his sheep... In short,
Ever alert—within, without—to thwart
  All base designs upon his wealth:
  Without the house, his precious flocks;
  Within, his precious money box.
  No thief, by cunning, craft, or stealth,

Meine en laisse une Chienne chaude.
Le Chien poussé d'un instinc naturel,
    Ne se doutant point de la fraude,
    Court apres le plaisir charnel.
    Et sans qu'il jappe, ou qu'il abboye,
Comme un amant discret, n'osant faire de bruit,
    Quitte le logis & la suit.
    Mais cependant qu'il s'en donne au cœur joye,
Le Voleur enfonçant coffres & cabinets,
    Prend le Thresor du Gentilhomme,
    Sans que ny Maistre, ny Valets,
    Qui dormoient tous d'un profond somme,
        Sur la foy de leur Chien,
        S'apperçoivent de rien.

MORALITÉ

    La Fable apprend que les femelles,
Ont l'art de suborner les gens les plus fidelles;
    Et quand on void la liaison,
    Que des Valets ont avec elles,
Il les faut aussi-tost chasser de la maison.

Had swayed our hero from his duty... None,
That is, until a certain canny one
Hit on a scheme. He found a bitch in heat...
    Brought her along... The hound, unwary,
    Prey to his passion temporary,
Follows the call of nature. But, discreet—
Like any worthy lover—and afraid
Lest he reveal their amorous escapade,
He takes care not to make the slightest sound.
    Result? While he pursued his pleasure,
Blithely the malefactor went his round,
    Sacking at will the master's treasure.
Confident, as they slept their sleep profound,
    The household, meanwhile, had no notion
What can, alas, become of dog's devotion.

MORAL

    This fable teaches, yet again,
That woman's wiles seduce the best of men.
    When faithful servant falls before
Her female charms, beware... Right there and then,
Don't wait to be betrayed: show him the door!

Dv Bœuf et dv Crocodile

    Si l'on croit les Historiens,
    On consacroit des Temples, & des Festes,
    Iadis chez les Ægyptiens,
    A toutes les sortes de Bestes.
    Vn jour, entre-deux de leurs Dieux,
L'ancien estoit le Bœuf, l'autre le Crocodile,
    Sur un pretexte specieux,
Naquit un different, à juger difficile.
    Le Bœuf disoit, avoir toûjours esté,
    Vn symbole de patience,
    Que les cornes d'autre costé,
    Estoient celuy de la puissance.
    Qu'un Dieu Bœuf n'estoit pas nouveau,
    Iupiter s'estant fait Taureau.
    Mais que le vilain Crocodile,
    N'estoit qu'un dangereux Reptile,
Le plus affreux de tous les animaux:
Inutile à tout bien, autheur de mille maux,
Implacable ennemy de la nature humaine,
    Et qu'il n'est pas possible qu'on comprenne,
    Par quel motif l'homme adoroit,
    Vn Monstre qui le devoroit.
Le Crocodile ouvrant un gosier effroyable,
    Dit, pour réponse, à ce Dieu tout tremblant,
    "Ce que tu dis est veritable,
Ie suis un Monstre affreux, cruel, & violent,
    Ie mange, détruis & saccage,
    Ce que je trouve en mon passage;
    Mais souvien toy que ma grandeur,

The Ox and the Crocodile

    In Egypt of a bygone day,
    Beasts of all manner of descriptions—
    At least, so the historians say—
    Were deified by the Egyptians.
    Often, betwixt a pair of these
Proud objects of religious veneration,
    There would arise antipathies,
And, sometimes, even open disputation.
    Witness the ox and crocodile,
    Whose argument—at first, for nought—
Soon grew impossible to reconcile.
The ox had simply stated that he thought
    Himself the worthier of the two
("Symbol of patience without parallel...
And, with my horns, symbol of strength as well...");
That bovine deities were nothing new
    ("Did Jupiter, all-powerful,
    Not turn himself into a bull?...");
    Whereas his rival crocodilian
    ("Vicious, vile enemy of man...")
Was nothing but a murderous reptilian,
Scourge of the human race since time began:
    What folly to bow down before
So deadly, dastardly a carnivore!
Replied the crocodile, with gaping jaws
That set the ox atremble (and for cause!):
"Quite so! I'm all the frightful things you say:
    Savage and brutal, drunk with power!
    I ravage, pillage, sack... devour

Vient de sçavoir bien faire peur,
Et que des Dieux, en qui l'homme a croyance,
La crainte en a plus fait que la reconnoissance.
Et si toy-mesme encor, tu veux en murmurer,
Quelque Dieu que tu sois, je vais te devorer."

MORALITÉ

Apres un tel aveuglement,
Peut-on pas jurer hautement,
Que la raison humaine est une folle?
Puis qu'il n'est rien si monstrueux,
Si ridicule, & si defectueux,
Dont elle n'ait fait son idole.

Anyone fool enough to pass my way.
Well, *c'est la vie!* It's fear, not love,
That keeps mankind below, and gods above.
And if that fact offends the likes of you,
God though you be, beware! I might just eat you too!"

MORAL

Blind folly triumphs yet again
Over this mindless race of men,
Bereft of reason—who denies it?
Nothing is too grotesque, absurd—
Even too monstrous, in a word—
But that mankind is quick to idolize it.

D'vn Bvfle

Cent Bourgeois estoient attroupez,
Prés d'un faiseur de Tours de passe passe,
A ses discours, autant qu'à sa grimasse,
Attentivement occupez.
Ce Charlatan leur contoit cent sornettes,
Pour vendre de son baume & de ses Savonettes,
Et les preschoit avec tant d'agrément,
Que ces gens d'esprit imbecille,
Le croyoient aussi fortement,
Que s'il eût dit paroles d'Evangile.
Quand par hazard, on vid vn gros Rustaut,
Qui menoit par le nez vn Bufle dans la place;
Aussi-tost cette populace,
Autour de luy, fit vn cercle badaut,
Iettant de grands éclats de rire,
Sur la sotte façon dont se laissoit conduire,
L'animal des moins raffinez.
Mais il leur sçeut pourtant bien dire,
"Ne soyez point, Messieurs, tant estonnez:
Ie ne suis pas si sot que de merveilles.
Ie me laisse, il est vray, conduire par le nez,
Pour vous, vous vous laissez mener par les oreilles."

MORALITÉ

Tel qui s'estime fort habile,
Se moque d'vn pauvre imbecille,
Aux sentimens d'autruy toûjours abandonné:
Cependant, quand il s'examine,
Il se trouve en effet, luy mesme gouverné,
Par vne personne plus fine.

The Buffalo

A throng of townsfolk, rapt in admiration,
Watched as a juggler, artfully,
Performed his feats of prestidigitation.
Our master of chicanery,
Eager to sell his salves and balms,
Had no great trouble—fewer qualms—
Inventing tales about his merchandise.
The people, hanging on his every word—
However imbecilic and absurd—
Swallowed them with no "wherefores" and no "whys,"
Like preachments from the Holy Writ.
Suddenly, as they watch, a buffalo
Comes lumbering along; preceding it,
Leading it by the nose (for so
One does), a country lad... [1] "Tee hee!... Ha ha!..."
Chortle and chaff our good bourgeois,
Crowding about the servile beast in glee.
"Spare me your barbs," the creature cries. "It's true,
I follow blindly... But then, so do you;
And no less stupid, too, from what I see!
You let yourselves be led, I fear—
Not by the nose, like me, but by the ear!"

MORAL

Easy it is to taunt and twit
A poor fool wanting in his wit,
Who yields, unthinking, to another's will.
Let his tormentors not be so unkind,
Lest they, on self-inspection, find
Themselves the pawns of master shrewder still.

1. It goes without saying that the author is referring to the oxlike animal of Asia and Southern Europe, and not to the American bison, frequently misnamed. As early as the Middle Ages, the buffalo—whose French equivalent, *le buffle*, has undergone several different spellings— had become prototypic of the simpleton, easily led by the nose. The expression "mener par le nez comme un buffle" dates at least from the sixteenth century.

A DECADE after the appearance of La Fontaine's first six books of fables in 1668, his popular contemporary Isaac de Benserade, toward the end of a long career of artistic service to Louis XIV and his court, published one of the more curious (not to say baroque) collections in the French verse-fable literature. His *Fables d'Esope en quatrains* were hardly his crowning literary achievement, however.[1] And yet, as far as the exaggerated brevity of his mini-fables is concerned, Benserade had had at least one celebrated model: the Greek poet Babrius, one of the major transmitters of the Aesopic corpus and a principal source for La Fontaine, had likewise composed his versions in the pithy four-line form. La Fontaine himself, in the brief prologue to his fable "Le Pâtre et le Lion" (VI, 1), had, in fact, called into question—between the lines, at any rate—the appropriateness for his generation of the spare Babrian quatrain, thus leading literary historian Emile Faguet to suggest that Benserade, no bosom friend of La Fontaine, might have expressly picked up the gauntlet in an effort to duel his much-admired rival on the latter's own ground. (See his *Histoire de la poésie française de la Renaissance au Romantisme,* III: 317–20.)[2]

Faguet, in fact, unlike most observers, who had derided Benserade's quatrains, rather admired his "effort épigrammatique" as something of a tour de force (see *Histoire,* III:318). Still, when compared to the easygoing, dramatic, ingratiating versions of La Fontaine, Benserade's fables fade into drabness. (Which may explain why a generation that could admire the pared-down concision of aphorisms the likes of La Rochefoucauld's *Maximes* [1665] could disparage the same quality in these no-frills little verses.) But if read by and for themselves, all comparisons aside, they are not without their charm. With no pretense at being serious art, many of them achieve the unassuming elegance of stylized miniatures. Curios, to be sure, but pleasantly undemanding cameos as well. Furthermore, what Faguet failed to mention is that these uniformly straitjacketed apologues, most of which presuppose some prior acquaintance with their subjects—a kind of "subtext" in today's critical parlance—were originally, like the Ovidian *rondeaux* before them, the result of a "command performance." In the *avertissement* to his collection Benserade explains that Louis XIV had specifically requested four-line inscriptions for the thirty-nine statue-fountains adorning Le Nôtre's lavish Labyrinthe de Versailles, each of which represented one of the Aesopic fables popularized by La Fontaine only a few years before.[3] With more enthusiasm, perhaps, than judgment,

he then proceeded to expand the collection—most likely his own idea and not that of his royal protector, his protestations to the contrary notwithstanding.[4]

If the result did nothing to enhance Benserade's reputation—and if, indeed, he more or less retired from active literary life soon after—neither does it seem to have much tarnished his contemporary prestige as one of the foremost poets at the Sun King's sumptuous court. That reputation had been built essentially on works that, by present-day standards, have little to recommend them as meaningful art: on the one hand, his host of *madrigaux, épigrammes, rondeaux, ballades, élégies,* and such, light verse even at its ostensibly most serious, all examples of his preciosity and undeniable wit; and, on the other, his thirty-years-worth of balletic divertissements provided for the entertainment (and with the frequent participation) of the royal family and its retinue.

There is much confusion surrounding Benserade's birth and genealogy: whether he was born in 1612 or 1613; in a small Normandy town or Paris; of bourgeois or noble parents, who were either Protestant or Catholic at his birth.[5] But if his early years are obscure, the rest of his life is amply documented. He began his artistic career in 1635 with a tragedy, *Cléopâtre,* the first of several moderately successful but undistinguished theater pieces, eventually entering into collaboration with the official court composer Michel Lambert—and even the latter's eminent son-in-law, Jean-Baptiste Lully—producing, between 1651 and 1681, the score of above-mentioned *ballets de cour.*[6] Much admired throughout his lifetime for his quick and clever wit, much lionized and patronized by many a prominent Maecenas, Benserade, who had achieved the "immortality" of the Académie Française in 1674, had every reason to assume that posterity too would treat him with admiration and respect. When he died on October 20, 1691 (of a severe case of medical malpractice, anecdotalists may wish to note), he left a large body of works that has, however, over the years, borne eloquent witness to the mutability of artistic taste.[7]

Of Benserade's 221 Aesopic quatrains, the group of ten translated here are numbers 12, 13, 24, 30, 46, 139, 151, 174, 185, and 193 of the 1678 edition.[8] (It should be noted that, although he intentionally left the originals untitled, affirming in his *avertissement* that they "s'expliquent par elles-mesmes, sans qu'elles ayent besoin de Titre," he—or someone—did give them titles in the table of contents.) Of these, numbers 12, 30, and 46 figure among the original thirty-nine composed for the Labyrinthe de Versailles.

---

1. Nor had been his similarly esoteric rendering of Ovid's *Metamorphoses* into lilting *rondeaux* a few years before. (For a study of Benserade's Ovid in *rondeaux,* as well as of his Aesop in quatrains, see Jean Jehasse, "De la fable aux *Fables:* Benserade et La Fontaine.") One

La Fontaine scholar, scornfully referring, in passing, to Benserade's Aesop, echoes, after two centuries, the bemused reaction of the poet's own contemporaries: "Rien de plus étrange que de parcourir tous ces récits obscurs, étranglés, qui ressemblent à une gageure." (See Prosper

Soullié, *La Fontaine et ses devanciers,* p. 237.) But if Benserade was most likely the first French fabulist to compose in quatrains, he was not the last. The "gageure" was taken up some thirty years later by the semi-anonymous Vaudin (see p. 58). Nor was he the last either, apparently. In his correspondence with Diderot et al., Grimm makes a brief (and nasty) reference to one "M. de La Cour Dumonville," who, in 1756, published a collection of *Fables moralisées en quatrains* intended for children. The author seems even to have out-Benseraded Benserade: "Dédicace, préface, épilogue, envoi, supplication aux critiques, tout est en quatrains." (See Friedrich Melchior von Grimm, *Correspondance littéraire, philosophique et critique,* III:350.) La Cour Dumonville's volume has successfully eluded my research, I suspect with little loss.

2. Faguet's work is a reedition of his Sorbonne lectures. His discussion of Benserade was originally published in the *Revue des cours et conférences* for 1896–97.

3. See Daniel Bellamy, *Ethic Amusements,* pp. 209–10: "No subject was thought more proper to decorate this Spot, than some select Fables of *Æsop* . . . Upon each Fountain is inserted, in a proper place, a large copper-plate, with a black ground, on which there is an inscription of four *French* verses, written in characters of gold." The author presents each of the fables, with his own florid eighteenth-century translations, and an engraving of the respective fountains. See also Pierre de Nolhac, *La Création de Versailles,* pp. 256–62. (Nolhac's work first appeared in 1901 [Versailles, L. Bernard].) Benserade's quatrains, accompanying Sébastien Le Clerc's engravings of the scriptures, along with prose "epitomes" of the fables by Charles Perrault (see pp. 56–57), were published in a number of editions of a work entitled, appropriately, *Le Labyrinte de Versailles.* The earlies edition I can corroborate dates from 1679, though bibliographical descriptions of later printings refer, perhaps in error, to a first edition of 1677. (See the *National Union Catalogue, Pre-1956 Imprints,* CCLXXII:83 and CCCX:322.) It is the 1679 edition that figures in Avenir Tchemerzine, *Bibliographie d'éditions originales et rares d'auteurs français des XVe, XVIe, XVIIe, et XVIIIe siècles,* IX:167.

4. ". . . comme cela s'est trouvé du goust de Sa Majesté, l'on a réduit en Quatrains toutes les autres Fables d'Esope."

5. The indefatigable archivist Auguste Jal, in his *Dictionnaire critique de biographie et d'histoire,* p. 194, citing an unearthed baptismal record, opts for November 5, 1613, and Paris, as date and place of birth, and Catholic aristocracy, as family background. But the question is not so easily resolved. For a thorough discussion see Charles I. Silin, *Benserade and His 'Ballets de Cour,'* pp. 19–27.

6. Typical of the role Benserade was to play in the artistic life of the period is the celebrated quarrel, early in his career—one of those trivial disputes endemic to French letters—between partisans of his sonnet on Job and Voiture's sonnet to one Uranie, pitting so-called "Jobelins" against "Uranistes" throughout the salons of the social luminaries. The quarrel, although eventually "lost" by Benserade and his followers through the machinations of a dedicated "Uraniste," laid the groundwork for both his courtly and literary success. (See Faguet, *Histoire,* III:311–16.)

7. See the bibliography of Benserade's numerous published titles in Alexandre Cioranescu, *Bibliographie de la littérature française du dix-septième siècle,* I:332–34. For an authoritative study of his life and work, especially his *ballets de cour,* see Silin, *Benserade;* and for a representative selection of his occasional verse, see Octave Uzanne's edition, *Poésies de Benserade.*

8. Faguet (*Histoire,* III:303) indicates a prior edition of 1677, which I assume to be the first edition of the illustrated *Le Labyrinte de Versailles* referred to above (see n. 3).

Le Renard & le Corbeau

Le Renard du Corbeau loûa tant le ramage,
Et trouva que sa voix avoit un son si beau,
Qu'enfin il fit chanter le malheureux Corbeau,
Qui de son bec ouvert laissa choir un fromage.

1. A comparison of this straitjacketed version of the fable, and of the next, with their analogues in La Fontaine (see pp. 31 and 33) will let the reader appreciate Benserade's attempts at stylistic concision, ingenious if not always aesthetically appealing.

The Fox and the Crow

The fox approached the foolish crow and told him
He loved his lovely voice; he so cajoled him
That crow, much moved by praises such as these,
Opened his beak to sing, and dropped a cheese.[1]

Le Lion Affoibli de Vieillesse

Contre un Lion caduc la rage se débonde
Des autres Animaux qui luy furent soumis.
  C'est la plus grand' pitié du monde
D'estre vieux, & d'avoir quantité d'ennemis.

The Lion Weak with Age

Grown weak with age, the lion lies, attacked
By former subjects, now emancipated.
  Ah! what a woe—the worst, in fact—
To be so old, and be so roundly hated!

La Truye & le Loup

A la Truye en travail le Loup disoit, "Madame,
Si vous voulez, je puis vous soulager beaucoup":
Elle qui reconnut l'intention du Loup,
  "Peste soit de la Sage-femme."

The Sow and the Wolf

Said wolf to sow in labor: "Pray, madame,
Let me but ease your pain and see you through."
  Answered the sow, sensing his sham:
"A plague on midwives, friend, the likes of you!"

Les Paons & le Geay

"Oses-tu bien cacher tes plumes sous les nostres?"
Dirent les Paons au Geay rempli d'ambition:
Qui s'éleve au dessus de sa condition
Se trouve bien souvent plus bas que tous les autres.

The Peacocks and the Jay

"How dare you wear our feathers!" Thus protest
The peacocks to the overweening jay.
He who would rise above his lot today
Tomorrow may fall far below the rest.

Le Serpent & la Lime

Le Serpent rongeoit la lime;
Elle disoit cependant,
"Quelle fureur vous anime
Vous qui passez pour prudent?"

1. In tribute to the author's obvious aim of concision in composing his Aesopic quatrains, I append two further renditions of this fable, whittling it down progressively (if not artistically) to its Benseradian quintessentials:

> The snake chewed on the file,
>   Who, all the while,
> Chided: "What rash endeavor
>   For one so clever!"

The Snake and the File

The snake was chewing on the file,
    Who, all the while,
Chided: "What foolish, rash endeavor
    For one so clever!"[1]

and:

> Snake chews on file,
> Who, all the while,
> Chides: "Rash endeavor
> For one so clever!"

I hope the reader will agree that, if brevity is the soul of wit, it needn't be the soul of art.

Le Crocodile & le Renard

Le Crocodile noble, & d'une humeur hautaine,
Vantoit de sa maison les titres anciens:
"Pour moy," dit le Renard, "j'ay beaucoup plus de peine
A sçavoir où j'iray, qu'à sçavoir d'où je viens."

The Crocodile and the Fox

Haughty, the crocodile, of high degree,
Was boasting of his genealogy.
"For me," replied the fox, "what's worth the knowing
Is less from where I come than where I'm going."

L'Homme & le More

Un Homme passe & les nuits & les jours
A teindre un More, il y perd sa teinture.

The Man and the Blackamoor

A man who tried to bleach a blackamoor,
All night and day, got nothing for his pain.

Ce qu'une fois nous sommes par Nature L'Art n'y fait rien, nous le sommes toujours.	Let Art do what it might, one thing is sure: What Nature makes of us, so we remain.

La Femme en Travail & Son Mari

De la Femme en travail l'Epoux entend les cris,
Et la voyant par terre en sa douleur cruelle,
Veut qu'on la mette au lit: "Espérez-vous," dit-elle,
"Que le mal que je sens finisse où je l'ay pris?"

The Woman in Labor and Her Husband

A woman, on the ground, in labor lay,
Wailing her pain, for she could scarce endure it.
"Put her to bed!" her husband cried. "Nay, nay,"
Cried she, "how can what caused my torment cure it?"

Les Loups & les Brebis

Aux Brebis une fois disoient les Loups subtils,
"Chassez tous ces Mastins, à quoy vous servent-ils?"
    Les Brebis obéïrent,
    Et les Brebis perirent.

The Wolves and the Ewes

Said wolves to ewes—a wily stratagem!—:
"What good are all your hounds? Get rid of them!"
    Straightway the ewes complied,
    And straightway died.

Le Vieillard Se Mariant

Assez bizarrement un jeune homme en usa
De femme se passant tant qu'il en eût affaire:
    Devenu vieux il s'avisa
    D'en prendre une, & n'en sceût que faire.

The Old Man Who Would Marry

  A strange young man who, all his life,
  Scorned womenfolk and wanted none,
Grown old, took it in mind to take a wife,
But had no notion what to do with one.

Edme Boursault   Esope à la Ville (1690)   Fables, *in* Lettres Nouvelles (1697)
Esope à la Cour (1701)

In 1764 the abbé Claude-Henri de Fusée de Voisenon voiced the categorical opinion that Edme Boursault's posthumous comedy, *Esope à la cour,* would be a "passeport pour l'immortalité."[1] While immortality has a long time to prove itself, it would seem, for the present at least, that Voisenon's prediction was overly sanguine. If Boursault is remembered at all today, it is as an ill-advised adversary of his elder contemporary Molière, having had the youthful temerity, probably at the instigation of the latter's enemies, to take part in the celebrated quarrel occasioned by *L'Ecole des femmes* in 1663. Boursault's entry into the lists was marked, the same year, by the one-act verse comedy *Le Portrait du peintre, ou la Contre-critique de "L'Ecole des femmes,"* for which the aspiring young playwright—he was twenty-five at the time—was promptly and mercilessly ridiculed by Molière in *L'Impromptu de Versailles.* As a corollary to the unfortunate affair, Boursault was to tilt with the eminent poet-satirist Boileau as well—though apparently in justifiable self-defense—and would even take up cudgels for his paternalistic mentor, the venerable Corneille, in the latter's feud with Racine.[2]

Ironically, this writer who "a eu le tort et le malheur d'être l'adversaire de trois des plus grands écrivains de son temps" (Boursault, *Théâtre choisi,* p. xviii; Fournel, *Le Théâtre au XVIIe siècle,* p. 274) was one of the more congenial, witty, gracious, and generally charming literary figures of the age of Louis XIV, and one much admired by his contemporaries—that prestigious trio to the contrary notwithstanding—for both his personal qualities and literary talent. And that talent was quite considerable, especially when one realizes that his native language was not "the king's French," and that he was, for all intents and purposes, by the standards of his time, virtually uneducated.

Born in the Champagne town of Mussy-L'Evêque in October of 1638, Boursault grew up speaking his region's patois and, owing to parental negligence, totally lacking in the classical education generally held to be the sine qua non of any aspiring seventeenth-century man of letters. By the tender age of thirteen he had found his way to Paris, where he soon came under the artistic tutelage of the libertine poet Jacques Vallée Des Barreaux (1599–1673). His native intellect and abilities compensating for his deficient erudition, he spent the next dozen-or-so years dabbling in the comic theater, producing several one-act trifles whose titles tell all—*Le Jaloux endormi, Le Mort vivant, Le Médecin volant,* et al.—and making his winsome way into the social life of the capital, championed by luminaries the likes of Condé, Turenne, and Fouquet, to whom he toadied, albeit with characteristic charm and discretion, dedicating to them his various novels, epistles, and incidental verse. Boursault's literary and worldly successes had early attracted the attention of even the king himself, who subsidized for a time a weekly "gazette" in verse: a kind of anecdotal chronicle of the doings of the social elite, prefiguring the subject of the first of his three major plays, *Le Mercure galant.*[3] By the time that comedy was performed, Boursault had already served as secretary to the duchesse d'Angoulême, declined the king's invitation to become the dauphin's tutor (thanks to his unfortunate ignorance of Latin and Greek), and spent several disillusioning years in the world of provincial finance as tax collector (*receveur de tailles*) in the city of Montluçon.

Le Mercure galant is the prototype of the *comédie à tiroirs,* or episodic comedy: a loosely connected series of independent scenes around a central subject. In this case they revolve about the editor of the social gazette that gives the play its title, and the fauna of every sort that comes parading by, seeking his favors.[4] For Fournel, this very successful comedy, which remained in the repertory for the better part of a century, revealed the playwright as moralist: "Un second Boursault était né, qui, tout en gardant la belle humeur, la vivacité d'esprit, la verve facile et piquante du premier, . . . développait chaque jour davantage les qualités de moraliste qu'il avait en germe." (See "Un Moraliste au théâtre," p. 970.)[5]

Boursault would push that moralistic bent to didactic extremes in his last pair of major five-act plays. *Esope à la ville* (originally entitled simply *Esope,* and often referred to as *Les Fables d'Esope*) was premiered in 1690, and is considered to be the first French comedy to bring the verse fable to the stage.[6] It did so by including Aesop, somewhat anachronistically, as the hero of the comedy, ready and more than willing to illustrate his moral judgments at appropriate moments in the action with fables cast in the now-typical La Fontainesque *vers libres.*[7] While later critics often looked askance at these nondramatic interruptions—Geoffroy, for example, complained that Boursault turned his theater into "un cours complet de morale sur les vertus et les vices" (*Cours de littérature dramatique,* I:467)—*Esope à la ville* was a great contemporary success. Enough of one, in fact, to encourage the author to devote most of his dozen remaining years to composing its equally successful posthumous sequel, *Esope à la cour.* His death in Paris, on September 15, 1701, preceded by three months the first performance of that comedy on December 16 of the same year.[8]

If that play and its predecessor have not conferred on Boursault the immortality predicted by Voisenon, they have all the same added twenty-nine gracefully didactic examples to the French verse fable literature. Some fifteen more were likewise added to the repertory, nestled among the miscellany in one of the several collections of Boursault's letters: *Lettres nouvelles de Monsieur Boursault, Accompagnées de Fables, de Contes, d'Epigrammes, de Remarques, de bons Mots, & d'autres particularités aussi agréables qu'utiles.*

The group of six translated here represent all three sources: *Esope à la ville* (III, iii; III, v), *Lettres nouvelles* (the first and third of the unnumbered collection), and *Esope à la cour* (III, iii; V, iv).

---

1. See his *Anecdotes littéraires,* published by "Le Bibliophile Jacob" (pseudonym of Paul Lacroix), p. 50. (The playwright-academician's manuscript was originally published a century earlier, a half-dozen years after his death, in *Œuvres complettes de Voisenon.*)

2. Boursault's attack on Racine's *Brittanicus* is found in the prologue to his novel *Artémise et Poliante.* For detailed discussion of his confrontations with Racine, Molière, and Boileau, the reader should consult Victor Fournel's biographical sketch of Boursault in his edition of *Théâtre choisi,* pp. xix–xxxvi (or the condensed reproduction of same in his chapter on Boursault in *Le Théâtre au XVIIe siècle: la comédie,* pp. 270–85); and, more specifically, the following: René Des Granges, *La Querelle de Molière et de Boursault,* and Alphonse Pauly, "Boileau et Boursault."

3. Two dates are given for this five- (and sometimes four-) act comedy: March 5, 1679, and March 5, 1683. Fournel appears to resolve the question in favor of the latter. (See his edition of *Théâtre choisi,* p. xxxviii, note.)

4. Boursault, not one to shrink from confrontation, used the name of an acutal gazette of the period, written by third-rate poet, playwright, and critic Jean Donneau de Visé (1638–1710), who, while not especially singled out for ridicule, took umbrage at Boursault's liberty. For that reason the play was, for a time, performed under the sarcastic title *Comédie sans titre.* (See Fournel, in his edition of *Théâtre choisi,* pp. xxxviii–xxxix.)

5. This article presents extracts from Fournel's above-mentioned biographical sketch of Boursault in the *Théâtre choisi.* The passage quoted, however, was added to the article in question.

6. At least one source suggests that credit for the innovation should perhaps be given to Eustache Le Noble. (See Julien-Louis Geoffroy, *Cours de littérature dramatique,* I:467.) His five-act comedy *Esope,* written in *vers libres* for the Théâtre-Italien, was published in Paris by Guillaume de Luynes et al. in April of 1691, and could thus conceivably have predated the Boursault work. (See p. 53.) It is clear, however, that the opposite is the case. In prefatory remarks a supposedly anonymous "Personne de considération" compares Le Noble's Aesop play, at some length, to a successful predecessor—obviously Boursault's—recognizing that "il étoit bien hazardeux d'entreprendre pour un coup d'essai un second *Esope,* aprés le succès qu'avoit eu celui qu'on a joué sur le Théâtre François." Be that as it may, it was surely the success of Boursault's comedy, and of its sequel, *Esope à la cour,* that spawned

several imitations: among them, Louis Fuzelier's one-act prose comedy *Momus fabuliste, ou les Nôces de Vulcain* (1719) (see pp. 72–73), De-launay's *Vérité fabuliste* (1732) (see pp. 73–74), and Charles-Etienne Pes-selier's one-act verse comedy *Esope au Parnasse* (1739) (see pp. 75–76), to name only three of many emulators. (See E. Wesley O'Neill, "A Trend in Fable Literature after La Fontaine: The Fable Play.")

7. In his preface to the comedy Boursault duly recognizes his debt to his model—one literary contemporary with whom he does not seem to have had a falling out—acknowledging the danger of treading in the

footsteps of "l'illustre Monsieur de la Fontaine, qui m'a devancé dans cette route, & que je ne prétens suivre que de très-loin," and protest-ing the futility of doing so: "les soins inutiles que j'ai pris de l'imiter m'ont appris qu'il est inimitable" (see Boursault, *Théâtre*, p. 258). It should also be noted that while most of the fables in *Esope à la ville* do, indeed, duplicate La Fontaine, most of those in *Esope à la cour* do not.

8. A useful bibliography of Boursault's work and studies devoted to it will be found in Alexandre Cioranescu, *Bibliographie de la littéra-ture française du dix-septième siècle,* I:463–64.

L'Alloüette et le Papillon

Autrefois une Alloüette,
Qu'aimoit un riche Coucou,
Epousa par amourette
Un fort beau Papillon qui n'avoit pas un sou.
Outre beaucoup d'indigence
Il avoit tant d'inconstance,
Qu'il muguettoit les Fleurs, & les poussoit à bout.
Rien ne pouvoit fixer ni ses vœux, ni sa flamme;
Cependant sa pauvre femme
Avoit disette de tout.
Elle connut bien-tôt, quoi que trop tard pour elle,
Que lors qu'on veut s'unir pour jusques au tombeau,
Un Epoux inconstant & beau
N'en vaut pas un laid & fidelle.

The Lark and the Butterfly

A lark was being courted by
A cuckoo; but the lady bird,
Despite his riches, much preferred
A handsome, impecunious butterfly.
They wed, much to her woe. For he—
Not only poor, but fickle too—
Had but one thought: to wit, to woo
And wench with every flower, fancy-free.
Meanwhile the lark, unhappiest of creatures—
Impoverished, neglected wife—
Learned from experience, that best of teachers,
That when one takes a spouse for life,
Better an ugly mate and true, 'tis said,
Than handsome rogue who flits from bed to bed.[1]

1. By voicing a moral that thus minimizes ugliness in favor of fidelity, Boursault's protagonist can be said to be acting in obvious self-interest. Aesop's own legendary ugliness is recounted in the several versions of his supposed life, in considerable detail. (See, for exam-ple, Perry, *Aesopica*, pp. 35, 81, and 111.)

L'Ecrevisse et Sa Fille

L'Ecrevisse une fois s'étant mis dans la tête
Que sa Fille avoit tort d'aller à reculons,
Elle en eut sur le champ cette réponse honnête:
"Ma Mere, nous nous ressemblons.
J'ai pris pour façon de vivre
La façon dont vous vivez:
Allez droit si vous pouvez,
Je tâcherai de vous suivre."

The Crayfish and Her Daughter

A mother crayfish took a mind
To criticize her daughter's rearward walk:
"Face forward, love... Backside behind..."
The daughter smiled: "You're one to talk!
I do as I've been taught. I try
To be like you as best I may,
And follow you in every way.
Walk forward—if you can—and so will I."

Le Paisan et l'Asne

Un Baudet de bon sens (supposé qu'il en soit)
Chancelant tous les jours sous des charges trop lourdes,
S'en plaignit plusieurs fois au Manan qu'il servoit,
Qui toûjours à sa plainte eut les oreilles sourdes.
Un jour étant accablé,
Et suant à grosse goute:
"Fuyons," lui dit son Maître, inquiet & troublé,
"J'apperçois des Voleurs sur notre même route:

The Peasant and the Donkey

A donkey blest with most uncommon sense
Staggered beneath his daily loads, complaining
Bitterly to a master never deigning
To listen to his plaintive eloquence.
The beast, hard-pressed one day
(Worse than the rest), and sweating,
Straining, suddenly heard the peasant fretting:
"Misery me! Despair! Dismay!

Gagnons le premier hameau,
Il nous servira d'asile."
"Qu'ai-je à craindre de pis," dit le grison tranquille,
"A moins qu'on ne veüille ma peau?
Porterai-je avec eux une charge plus forte?"
"Non," répondit le Manan.
"Pourquoi donc fuir? Que m'importe
Qui je serve, Pierre ou Jean?
S'il faut avec l'un ou l'autre
Endurer le même mal,
Etre leur Asne ou le vôtre
N'est-ce pas un sort égal?"

What's that I see? A pack of brigands, lurking,
Waiting to pounce... Come, let's fly, you and I,
To some safe haven." "Really? Why?"
Queries the donkey, calmly, smirking.
"What will it matter? Will they flay my hide?
Will they give me a heavier load to bear?"
"I don't suppose..." the lout replied.
"Then what care I? Jean or Pierre,
One master's worth another, no?
Since nought will make my rough lot rougher.
Burden for burden, woe for woe,
Tell me, what matter at whose hands I suffer?"

Les Sangsues et le Lion

Un Lion replet & sanguin
Etant tombé malade, un fameux Médecin,
Après bien des peines perdües,
Lui fit, vaille qui vaille, appliquer les sangsuës.
De gros que le Lion étoit
En douze ou quinze jours il devint presque étique.
"L'admirable remede, & qu'il est spécifique!"
Dit le Docteur qui le traitoit,
"Il faut que de nouveau, demain on en applique."
"Tout beau," lui répondit le Lion langoureux;
"Laissez-moi celles qui sont pleines;
Dans l'état où je suis de nouveaux ventres creux
Du reste de mon sang épuiseroient mes veines."

The Leeches and the Lion

A robust lion, hale and fit,
Had fallen ill. An eminent physician,
Coming to study his indisposition,
Figured how best to treat the beast: to wit,
With leeches. (Harder done than said!
But still, he did.) Two weeks went by. Well bled,
Our lion lay, now frail and gaunt.
The doctor marveled at his cure's success:
"More leeches! New ones! Yes, that's what we want!"
"Please," groaned the lion, in distress.
"Leave me the old ones, much though they chagrin me.
New, empty bellies, in their eagerness,
Will drain what little blood still flows within me."[1]

1. Differences in scenario and characters notwithstanding, this fable, by its moral, clearly belongs to the long tradition of the Aesopic apologue "The Fox and the Hedgehog" (see pp. 28–29).

Le Faucon Malade

Un Faucon qui croyoit les Dieux muets & sourds,
Etant à son heure derniere
D'un lamentable ton sollicita sa mere
D'aller en sa faveur implorer leur secours.
"Mon enfant," lui dit-elle, en mere habile & sage,
"Pendant que tu te portois bien,
Tu disois qu'ils ne pouvoient rien:
Ils ne peuvent pas davantage."

The Sick Falcon

A falcon felt his final hour had come,
So sick was he; and, though he always thought
The gods above were deaf and dumb,
Nevertheless, he piteously besought
His mother to implore their aid. "Ah yes,
My son," the wise old mother nods.
"When you were well you scorned the gods.
Today I fear they'll hear you even less."

L'Homme et la Puce

Par un homme en courroux la Puce un jour surprise,
Touchant, pour ainsi dire, à son moment fatal,
Lui demanda sa grace, & d'une voix soumise,
"Je ne vous ai pas fait," dit-elle, "un fort grand mal."
"Ta morsure, il est vrai, me semble un foible ouvrage,"

The Man and the Flea

One day a man, in anger, caught a flea.
The latter, seeing his moments numbered, pled
In plaintive tones. "Spare me, kind sir," he said.
"In truth, I've done you no great injury."
The man replied: "No quarter in this war!

Dit l'homme. "Cependant n'espere aucun pardon:
Tu m'as fait peu de mal; mais j'en sçai la raison,
C'est que tu ne pouvois m'en faire davantage."

No mercy, mite! No, none! I'll not deny
You did me little harm. But I know why:
Only because you couldn't do me more!"

Eustache Le Noble   Esope (1691)   L'Ecole des Sages (1692)
L'Esprit d'Esope (1694)

THE LIFE of La Fontaine's colorful and rather little known contemporary Eustache Le Noble, baron de Saint-Georges et de Ten(n)elière, reads much like an Alexandre Dumas novel. He was born in Troyes on December 26, 1643, of a family as aristocratic as its name proclaims, and, as a young man, acquired the office of *procureur général* of the parliament of Metz. Before long, however, he fell precipitously into disgrace when, to support a lifestyle that would, over the years, be his undoing, he was guilty of counterfeiting and embezzlement, and was eventually imprisoned in the Conciergerie. It was there that he wrote many of the erudite, polemical, but often witty politico-philosophical pamphlets that are among his most characteristic works. It was there, too, that he began his lengthy romanesque involvement with fellow-prisoner Gabrielle Pereau, alias "la Belle Epicière," whose escape he engineered in properly swashbuckling fashion. The rest of his life was punctuated by amorous escapade, several illegitimate paternities, flights from justice, imprisonment, banishment, and assorted rounds of dissipation and debauch. Although, during his tempestuous lifetime, he had earned a fortune for his numerous publishers, he died a pauper's death in Paris, on January 31, 1711.[1]

The verse fable was obviously one of Le Noble's preferred genres, judging both by the number of them that he sprinkled throughout his heterogeneous literary production, and, in fact, by his own admission: "J'avoüe pour moi qu'en tout tems & en tout âge j'ai pris un plaisir singulier à cette ingenieuse invention, je ne me suis point en cela écarté du goût commun, les Fables spirituelles & naïves m'ont toûjours plû" (see the preface to his *Contes et fables,* cited below, p. viii). One finds them not only in his two discrete (if not always discreet) fable collections but also in his theater, his spate of dialogues, his periodical pamphlets on a vast array of subjects, and his other disparate writings. Just how many he wrote is not easy to determine; primarily because not all of his works come readily to hand, and also because a number of his fables crop up, in various versions, more than once throughout his rather chaotic *œuvre.*[2]

Le Noble's first important use of the genre occurs in his five-act comedy *Esope,* written for the Théâtre-Italien and, like Boursault's successful *Esope à la cour* of the preceding year (see pp. 49–50), turning a Gallicized incarnation of the Greek fabulist—this time betrothed to the prostitute Rodope—into its apologue-spouting protagonist.[3] In a prefatory letter supposedly written by "une Personne de consideration à un de ses Amis qui lui avoit demandé son sentiment touchant cette Comedie," we are told, in an obvious reference to Boursault, that the author was aware of the seeming presumptuousness—and risk—of undertaking as his first theatrical venture "un second Esope, aprés le succès qu'avoit eu celui qu'on a joué sur le Theâtre François." Of the dozen *vers libres* fables that the hero mouths at appropriate moments, much briefer and more to the point than the increasingly verbose and abstruse examples that will later characterize Le Noble's style, about half will appear some six years after *Esope,* in varying degrees of transformation, in his two-volume *Contes et fables.*[4]

It is with considerable pride that he informs us in his prefatory remarks that this collection resulted from the admiration of the public for his fables: "elles on été si bien reçüës que quantité de personnes m'ont témoigné le desir qu'elles avoient d'en voir un recueil" (p. ix). With no less pride he declares that most have been "corrigées, ou augmentées"—the latter verb being, in fact, particularly appropriate—and that, as a personal mark of originality, he has embellished them all with distinctive trappings: a preceding Latin distich, an introductory moral in verse, and another concluding moral, this one in prose. Unfortunately, as with Houdar de La Motte a generation later (see pp. 63–65), Le Noble's quest for originality, in a genre in whose soul of whose wit is its relative brevity, was too often counterproductive. But it is easily explained. The shadow of La Fontaine, only recently deceased, loomed especially large. One does not have to read deeply between the lines of his preface to sense in Le Noble's rather grudging praise of his predecessor an elevated opinion of his own excellence and importance as a fabulist. "Cependant si son ingenieuse naïveté l'emporte sur tout ce qu'on a fait jusqu'ici dans ce genre, je puis dire, sans rien ôter à la juste reputation qu'il s'est aquise, qu'il y a quãtité de personnes d'un jugement tres-solide qui se persuadent que la beauté de celles qu'il nous a données n'ôte rien au goût ce celles-ci, dans lesquelles mêmes ils prétendent trouver en beaucoup d'endroits quelque chose de plus fort, de plus correct, & qui montre plus d'élevation & d'érudition" (p. xi).

In the years between his *Esope* and his *Contes et fables* Le Noble indulged his predilection for the fable in a number of his "entretiens politiques"—or "Pasquinades," as they were dubbed—among them the following: *L'Ecole des sages* (later expanded into *L'Ecole du monde, ou Instruction d'un père à un fils touchant la manière dont il faut vivre dans le monde*); *L'Esprit d'Esope*; and *La Grotte des fables*.[5] As already suggested, many of his most typical fables, especially those contained in these various dialogues and

pamphlets, are long, heavy, often cryptically political allegories referring to complicated contemporary intrigues and requiring explanatory notes to be fully understood.[6] Fortunately, however, not all of them are that ponderous and long-winded, even when the surrounding works are.

The three presented here are examples of his briefer and more approachable inspiration. "De la Grüe et du Renard" is taken from *Esope* (Act IV, scene iii); "Du Serpent et du Laboureur" is the eighth fable of the first dialogue between Esope and Porphyrogenète, in *L'Ecole des sages*; and the outspokenly *gaulois* "De la Puce et de la Pucelle" is the second fable of the first dialogue between Pasquin and Marforio, in *L'Esprit d'Esope*.[7]

1. For picturesque details of Le Noble's life, see the *Annales dramatiques, ou Dictionnaire général des théâtres*, V:346–47.

2. A substantial portion of the author's work appeared under the title *Les Œuvres de M. Le Noble*, in nineteen volumes, the first and most of which were published in Paris (P. Ribou, 1718). Not unexpectedly, however, for an author whose bibliography seems to thrive on confusion, several of the subsequent volumes bear earlier dates and diverse places of publication (and names of publishers).

3. Preceding his *Esope*, several of his monthly pamphlets, printed by a variety of publishers from January 1690 through November 1691, under the collective title *La Pierre de touche politique*, also contain occasional fables. As for his further dramatic endeavors, Alexandre Cioranescu cites only one other, the three-act comedy *Les Deux Arlequins*, produced at the Théâtre-Italien, September 26, 1691. (See his *Bibliographie de la littérature française du dix-septième siècle*, II:1265–67, no. 42562.) Jean Sgard, however, makes mention of three others: an unpublished three-act prose comedy, *Le Fourbe*, dating from 1693; a tragedy, *Talestris, Reine des Amazones*; and, supposedly, the comedy *La Fausse Prude*, unrecorded in other sources, and which, on May 14, 1694, resulted in the expulsion of the Comédiens Italiens owing to its alleged veiled allusions to Madame de Maintenon. (See *Dictionnaire des journalistes [1680–1789]*, pp. 236–37.)

4. This volume contains a total of 105 *contes* and *fables*, though an error in numeration between the two volumes lists them as totaling only one hundred. As for their seemingly capricious double designation, Le Noble takes care to explain in his preface (p. x) that he uses the latter term for those pieces with exclusively animal characters, reserving the former for those in which gods and human beings figure as well. *Contes et fables* should not be confused with another volume similarly entitled, from the end of his career, and which several sources, Cioranescu among them (*Bibliographie . . . du dix-septième siècle*, II:1266, no. 42544), seem to take merely for another edition of the

earlier work. *Contes et fables tirez des entretiens politiques de M' Le Noble*, is, as the title implies and as the "Au lecteur" goes to some pains to explain, a collection of the author's previously published "allégories historiques."

5. For detailed bibliographical references to the almost impenetrable labyrinth of individual works represented in these and other titles, and to the revisions, developments, retitlings, and collections thereof, see Sgard, *Dictionnaire des journalistes*, pp. 236–38. There appears to be no general published study of Le Noble and his writings, but the same entry gives an extensive listing of specific articles and other pertinent material. There is also a University of Colorado thesis by Jeanne Foreman: "Eustache Le Noble (1643–1711), témoin de son temps."

6. One observer's specific remarks concerning a single such fable could well be generalized to apply to most: "Mais cette allégorie est tellement abstruse, qu'il est nécessaire que l'auteur éclaire sa lanterne et donne des explications à ses lecteurs. Il n'est pas facile de comprendre que Junon représente l'Eglise catholique et l'oiseau de paradis, le pape. Et quel effort, de la part du fabuliste, pour soutenir de pareilles calembredaines et tâcher de leur donner vie d'un bout à l'autre de pièces interminables!" (See Jacques Janssens, *La Fable et les fabulistes*, p. 61.) Clearly, fables of such agonizing complexity give the lie to the commonly held misconception that the fable is primarily children's fare. Le Noble himself, in the preface to *L'Ecole des sages*, categorically and rather pompously objects to such a notion: "Les Fables ingenieuses ne sont pas inventées pour faire taire les Enfans ou les endormir au berceau, elles sont faites pour donner aux Grands des Leçons d'une profonde Politique, & aux Particuliers les plus sages instructions de la Morale" (p. v).

7. All three were subsequently included in *Contes et fables*; the first two, significantly reworked (and, of course, lengthened), the third, relatively unchanged. I have, for reasons of artistic if not historic integrity, chosen to retain the original versions in my translation.

De la Grüe & du Renard

La Grüe & le Renard resolurent un jour
    De faire ensemble leur ménage,
    Et se chargerent tour à tour
    Du soin de dresser le potage.
    Quand ce fut le tour au Renard,
    Ce Tricheur d'un coup de sa pate
Ependit le broüet sur une assiette plate,
Et soudain lécha tout, tandis que de sa pars
    Auprés de la soupe ependuë
    Mouroit de faim la pauvre Grüe.
    Mais cet oiseau le lendemain
    Pour se vanger du chagrin de la veille,

The Crane and the Fox

    The crane and fox, one day, decide
    To dwell together and divide
    The cooking chores betwixt the two:
Each one, by turns, will fix the supper stew.
Now, being the first, the fox—fell trickster he!—
Deft-pawed, spreads out the gruel flat on a platter
    And laps it up immediately.
    (For such as fox, a simple matter!)
    Meanwhile, poor helpless crane stands by,
Eyeing the stew, so hungry she could die.
Next day, however, she conceives a plan
To wreak her vengeance on our charlatan.

Entassa le broüet, & la viande & le pain,
    Dans le ventre d'une bouteille.
Et fourant aisément jusqu'au fond son grand cou,
    "Hier," dit-elle, "vous étiez fou,
C'est aujourd'hui mon tour, Compere, à la pareille."

As fox looks on with wondering eye,
Crane stuffs the stew into a jar, straightway
Sticks her long neck down deep, and sups.[1] Whereat,
Says she: "My friend, you glutted yesterday.
    Today it's my turn... Tit for tat!"

1. I have retained the "neck" (*cou*) of Le Noble's original—which he obviously uses for the rhyme—even though it would be more reasonable, anatomically, to assume that what the crane (or stork) sticks into the jar is her beak, as she does in the Aesopic corpus (e.g., Phaedrus, I, 26), as well as in La Fontaine's more elaborate and engaging version, "Le Renard et la Cigogne" (I, 18).

Du Serpent & du Laboureur

Sur un monceau de neige, un Serpent en langueur
Estoit prest d'expirer engourdi de froidure,
Lorsqu'un bon Païsan passant à l'avanture,
Le vit, & de pitié sentit toucher son cœur.
Plus plein de charité que rempli de lumiere,
    Il étendit sur luy sa main,
    Le prit, le serra dans son sein,
    Et le porta dans sa chaumiere,
Où bien-tôt l'Animal couché prés des tisons,
    Sentit reveiller ses poisons.
Alors dressant la teste, & vomissant l'écume,
Par d'aigus sifflemens il marqua sa fureur;
    Et ses yeux que la rage allume,
Porterent jusqu'au sein du triste Laboureur,
    Et la menace & la terreur.
"Ingrat, c'est donc ainsi," s'écria le Bon-homme,
"Que tu pretens payer un signalé bienfait.
Tu mourras." La menace eut bien-tôt son effet.
    Il court, prend sa hache, & l'assomme.

The Snake and the Ploughman

    A snake upon a snowpile lay,
Languishing and benumbed, waiting to die.
By chance, a kindly ploughman happens by,
Sees the poor beast in anguished disarray,
    Stops, reaches out his hand to touch it,
And—being less full of wit than of compassion—
    Proceeds in charitable fashion
To pick it up, and coddle it, and clutch it
    Against his breast, and take it home.
No sooner by the embers than, within it,
The sleeping venom springs to life. Next minute,
    With head erect, and mouth a-foam,
And eyes aflame, it spits its threats against
    Our peasant, quaking by its side.
"So!" cried the ploughman, properly incensed—
    Angered but no less terrified;
"This is how you repay my kindness, eh?
Then die!" Wherewith, he fetched his axe straightway,
    And smote the snake, who straightway died.

De la Puce & de la Pucelle

    Une Pucelle à sa Toilette,
    Et prête à se deshabiller,
    Sentit qu'une Puce indiscrete
    Faisoit pis que la chatoüiller.
Lors en coulant sa main par la poche secrete,
Elle surprend la bête, & la roule en ses doits.
La Puce qui se voit dans les derniers abois,
    "Pardon, jeune & belle Nannette,"
Dit-elle en gémissant, "pardon pour cette fois,
    Pour une piquure legere,
    Quoi faut-il qu'une mort amere
    Tranche mon malheureux destin?
    Ciel qui vois ma triste avanture,
    Pourquoi sur un si doux satin
M'as-tu fait rencontrer une peine si dure?
Pardon jeune Beauté, je n'y retourne plus,
    Encore un coup, pardon," s'écria-t-elle;
    "Foible Bête," dit la Pucelle,

The Mite and the Maiden

    At her toilette a maiden sat,
    About to doff her clothes; whereat
    She felt a flea's untoward attention,
    Tickling her where I dare not mention.
    At which, probing her privatemost recess,
With fingertip and thumb she snatches up the flea,
    Rolls it betwixt. In direst of distress
    The mite cries out: "Misery me!
    Spare me, I prithee, lovely demoiselle!
    What? For the merest bagatelle,
    The slightest bite, must dismal death snuff out
My luckless life? Ah, Heaven, who see my sorry plight,
    How could you let me loll about
    That smooth and satin-soft delight
Only to be undone?... Mercy, O maiden fair!
    Spare me, and gladly will I swear
    Never to bite again!" "You puny mite,"
    Answers the maid, "your tears don't move me.

"Tes pleurs sont ici superflus,
Je te sens avec insolence
D'un temeraire bec insulter à mes Lys,
Ne tient-il qu'à faire une ofense
Puis demander pardon de ses délits?
Non, de ton coup de bec tu porteras la peine,
En vain tu voudrois m'apaiser,
Créve, & de ta mort qu'on aprenne
Qu'il ne faut point piquer qui peut nous écraser."

You dare attack unblushingly
The flower of my virginity,
And arrogantly think it ought behoove me
To listen to your vain excuse?
No, no! Die, bug! And may your prompt demise
Help us and others recognize
The folly of such foul abuse:
Would we be wise, best we be cautious,
Lest we go biting those whose might can squash us!"

Charles Perrault   Traduction des Fables de Faërne (1699)

Just as the name of La Fontaine is inextricably linked to the verse fable, so that of Charles Perrault has long been synonymous with the fairy tale. Years before the Brothers Grimm and Hans Christian Andersen, it was he who created the genre for the Western world. Not that the eminent seventeenth-century intellectual didn't have more serious—even ponderous—works to his credit.[1] But by one of those not-uncommon ironies of artistic history, his only lasting legacy, and the one that would achieve for him undeniable immortality, was one to which he himself, it seems, gave the shortest of shrift. So short, in fact, that the earliest editions of the internationally celebrated *Histoires et contes du temps passé*, known to posterity as *Contes de ma Mère l'Oye* ("Tales of Mother Goose")—with its panoply of heroes and heroines the likes of Cendrillon ("Cinderella"), Le Chat Botté ("Puss-in-Boots"), La Belle au bois dormant ("Sleeping Beauty"), et al.[2]—were attributed to his son, Pierre Perrault D'Armancour (or Darmancour).[3] "Quand Perrault publia . . . son divertissement de bon père de famille, croyait-il que ces contes où il gardait de compromettre son nom feraient plus pour sa gloire que ce poème en six chants et quatre mille vers sur *Saint Paulin de Nole,* orné de tant de magnifiques gravures et que les bibliophiles, mais les bibliophiles seuls, les vrais, ceux qui ne lisent pas, se disputent encore aujourd'hui à prix d'or?" (See Maurice Rat, "Perrault," p. 116.)

More likely than not, Perrault must have assumed that his "gloire" would rest on his role as godfather of what was to become the famous "Querelle des Anciens et des Modernes," a typically French literary feud that would last well into the next century (see p. 64). Born in Paris on January 12, 1628, and admitted to the bar in 1651, he spent his early years engaged in a number of administrative functions for the court of Louis XIV, not the least striking of which was his role in the future Académie des Inscriptions et Belles-Lettres, entrusted with devising the official Latin mottoes for commemorative medals and public monuments. A member of the Académie Française from 1671, after publishing several

works ranging in inspiration from burlesque verse to religious epics, this classical scholar would, ironically, set the intellectual world on its ear by reading before that august body, in 1687, his poem *Le Siècle de Louis le Grand,* in which—a devotee of the idea of progress, and probably to flatter the artistic pretensions of his royal patron—he affirmed the superiority of the modern authors over the ancients. By the time he died, in Paris, on May 16, 1703, Perrault had locked aesthetic horns with antagonists the likes of Boileau, Racine, and La Fontaine (who, in all likelihood, were as much put off by his material successes as a favorite of the Sun King as by his theories), and had defended his thesis in a number of weighty tomes, especially the four volumes of his *Parallèle des anciens et des modernes* and *Les Hommes illustres qui ont paru en France pendant ce siècle.*

Perrault's connection with the fable was twofold. Two years before the appearance of the *Contes de ma Mère l'Oye,* of shadowy attribution, he had published his descriptions of the Aesopically inspired fountains of Versailles for which the court poet Benserade was to provide his famous quatrains (see pp. 46–47). The text of *Le Labyrinte de Versailles* was originally included in a heterogeneous collection entitled *Recueil de divers ouvrages en prose et en vers, dédié à Son Altesse Monseigneur le Prince de Conti,* and was subsequently reprinted a number of times along with Benserade's fables and elegant engravings by Sébastien Le Clerc (see p. 47, n. 3). In the *Recueil* text each terse fable précis is followed by an equally lapidary moral in verse—ostensibly his own—often no more than a couplet and rarely longer than seven lines. The entire group of these thirty-eight "epitomes" is introduced by a short prose fantasy in which Perrault attributes to the divine Amour himself the original choice of fables; in keeping with which fiction he proceeds to provide exaggeratedly gallant *morales,* clearly wrenching them out of their original didactic intent.[4]

Much more authentically—and diversely—moralistic are the little-known apologues in Perrault's *Traduction des fables de Faërne,* verse adaptations, done toward the end of his life, of the hundred concise Latin fables of Gabriello Faerno, which the sixteenth-century Italian poet had composed at the behest of Pope Pius IV for the instruction of the young.[5] Perrault's own aim was equally pedagogical, at least if we can take him at his word. In his dedicatory *épître* to the abbé Louis de Dangeau, "Maistre de l'Ordre de S[aint] Lazare," who had undertaken the education of indigent nobles' offspring, he explains that it was his desire to provide the grammarian abbé's pupils with moral models that encouraged him to complete a project he had originally begun and abandoned some time before: "Il me vint alors en l'esprit, que si j'achevois la Traduction des Fables que j'avois commencée, il pourroit arriver qu'elles entreroient dans le nombre des choses qui doivent servir à leur instruction, & que la moralité de ces Fables pourroit contribuer à former en eux cet esprit de prudence dont vous les animez." Without wholly impugning Perrault's high-sounding intentions, one might be tempted to look somewhat askance. When, concluding his *avertissement,* he modestly contrasts the simplicity of his own fables with the elegance of La Fontaine's, to the admitted advantage of the latter ("les nostres ressemblent à un habit d'une bonne étoffe, bien taillée & bien cousuë, mais simple & toute unie; les siennes ont quelque chose de plus, & il ajoûte une riche & fine broderie qui en releve le prix infiniment"), we can wonder, with Soriano (*Contes de Perrault,* p. 348), whether his compliment is not rather a little left-handed, so to speak; whether, indeed, that stark, unadorned concision, faithfully borrowed from Faerno's originals, was not merely a means of distinguishing himself—by subtly suggesting a greater degree of pedagogical utility—from his illustrious predecessor. Be that as it may, Perrault's fables represent a significant element in the genre. They do not deserve the obscurity into which they, like all of his works—with the prominent exception of his (or his son's) fairy tales—have fallen.

Of the hundred apologues in *Traduction des fables de Faërne,* equally divided into five books, both "La Mouche" and "La Femme noyée et son mari" are taken from Book I, where they are, respectively, numbers II and 13.

---

1. For a listing of his titles and of a lengthy array of studies they have generated, see Alexandre Cioranescu, *Bibliographie de la littérature française du dix-septième siècle,* III:1605–10, nos. 54185–54384. For more recent studies, see the bibliographies in Marc Soriano, *Les Contes de Perrault, culture savante et traditions populaires,* and in Jacques Barchilon and Peter Flinders, *Charles Perrault.*

2. The earliest known version of Perrault's fairy tales in English, establishing most of the now traditional nomenclature of the characters, was the anonymously translated *Histories, or Fables of Past Times,* published in London for J. Potevin in 1729. For recent speculation on the much-discussed yet still unresolved "Goose" connection, see Maria Tatar, *The Hard Facts of the Grimms' Fairy Tales,* pp. 106–14.

3. That attribution has been at the center of a long and spirited controversy. (See, inter alia, Soriano, *Contes de Perrault,* pp. 21–71 and passim; and Barchilon and Flinders, *Charles Perrault,* pp. 83–90.) Some observers claim the work entirely for the son; others, entirely for the father. Still others see it as a familial collaboration. "Son nom pose à l'histoire littéraire un problème qui n'est pas résolu, malgré le brio et l'habileté de ceux qui veulent que les contes donnés sous son nom soient de lui seul (Marty-Laveaux, Funck-Brentano), de ceux qui les lui refusent pour les donner au père seul (abbé Dubos, Walckenaer, A. Hallays) ou de ceux qui croient à une collaboration entre le père et le fils (abbé de Villiers, E. Henriot)." (See Robert Barroux's entry in *Dictionnaire des lettres françaises: le dix-septième siècle,* pp. 797–98.) There is also disagreement regarding the younger Perrault's age at the time of the work's appearance. Barroux, for example (among others), perpetuates the notion that he was a mere lad of ten, though he himself records the date of his birth as 1678, making him, in effect, nineteen in 1697. (See Soriano, *Contes de Perrault,* pp. 23, 40–41.)

4. One example, the eleventh, will suffice to illustrate both the brevity of these Versailles texts and the amorous optic through which Perrault views them all:

Le Singe et ses petits

Un Singe trouva un jour un de ses petits si beau,
qu'il l'étouffa à force de l'embrasser.

***

Mille exemples pareils nous font voir tous les jours,
Qu'il n'est point de laides amours.

Concerning Perrault's contribution to *Le Labyrinte de Versailles,* see Jean Jehasse, "De la fable aux *Fables:* Benserade et La Fontaine," pp. 331–35.

5. So Perrault himself informs us in the opening paragraph of his *avertissement:* "Le Pape Pie IV, persuadé que la lecture des Fables d'Esope estoit d'une très-grande utilité pour former les mœurs des jeunes enfans, ordonna à Gabriel Faërne qu'il connoissoit pour un excellent Poëte, & pour un homme qui avoit le goust de la belle & élegante Latinité de mettre ces Fables en vers Latins, afin que les enfans apprissent en mesme-temps & dans un mesme Livre, la pureté des mœurs & la pureté du langage." Faerno's often-reprinted *Fabulae centum ex antiquis auctoribus delectae* had achieved a certain notoriety owing to unproven accusations that his work had been plagiarized from Phaedrus, accusations that Perrault vigorously denied. (See Soriano, *Contes de Perrault,* p. 349.)

La Mouche

Une Mouche tomba dans une ample marmite,
Où, s'étant bien remplie & de viande & de jus;
"Il faut finir," dit-elle, "en mouche de merite,
Et ne point se repandre en regrets superflus.

   J'ay bû, j'ay mangé comme trente,

The Fly

A fly there was who, falling in a pot,
   Supped herself full on savory stew:
"I'll end my days in dignity, and not
   With vain lament, as others do;
Indeed, I've drunk and dined my fill," cried she.

The Fabulists French / 57

Je meurs satisfaite & contente."
Lorsqu'un malheur ne se peut éviter,
De bonne grace il le faut supporter.

"I die content and satisfied."
When woe cannot be turned aside,
Best we accept it gracefully.

La Femme Noyée & Son Mari

Un Laboureur, le long des bords
    D'une impetueuse riviere,
De sa femme noyée alloit cherchant le corps,
    Et s'y prenoit d'une étrange maniere.
Au lieu d'aller en bas, il remontoit en haut.
    "Vous ne cherchez pas comme il faut,"
Lui dirent ses voisins; "les flots l'ont entraînée,
    Du fleuve elle a suivi le cours."
"Nullement," leur dit-il, "cette vieille obstinée
A fait, & fait encor toute chose à rebours."
Femme contrariante, envieuse & colere,
    Ne quitte point son caractere.

The Drowned Wife and Her Husband

A ploughman's wife had drowned and, curiously,
He sought her body at the torrent's source.
Said friends: "You err. The waters, in their course,
    No doubt have swept her toward the sea.
    The mouth is, logically speaking,
    Where you ought properly be seeking."
"Nay," he replied, "'tis you who err.
She is my wife, and I know her:
That stubborn crone, whether she lives or dies,
    Will always act contrariwise!"
No wife of irksome, contradictious bent
    Has ever changed her temperament.

Vaudin   Fables Diverses, en Quatre Vers (1707)

NEITHER I nor, apparently, anyone else can offer much enlightening information about the author of the *Fables diverses, en quatre vers* other than his naked last name, Vaudin, and the bibliographical details pertaining to his curious little volume published in Paris by Laurent d'Houry in 1707. Curious, not only because of its apparent imitation of Benserade's tightly corseted mini-fables in quatrains (see pp. 46–47) but even for its physical appearance: twice as wide as it is long, with its texts printed only on the front of each page. Its 155 fables, of obvious Aesopic inspiration, are dedicated by "Le tres-humble, tres-obeissant, & tres-soumis Serviteur, VAUDIN," in a brief epistolary paragraph, to a no-less-enigmatic

"Madame la Duchesse," under whose protection the author places his "nouvelles Fables," which, he observes—perhaps somewhat self-defensively—"ont tous des habits uniformes quoi que differens par leur caractere." The only reference I am able to find to the author is the citation of this work in Alexandre Cioranescu, *Bibliographie de la littérature française du dix-septième siècle* (III:1948, no. 65768), and the most passing of mentions in Jacques Janssens, *La Fable et les fabulistes*, p. 72.

"La Puce et la Sangsue" and "Le Porc-épic et le Loup," respectively the sixteenth and eighteenth of the unnumbered collection, are characteristic examples of the mononymous Vaudin's terse talents.

La Puce et la Sangsue

La Puce en se plaignant disoit à la Sangsue:
"Tu te gorges de sang, tu le bois à longs traits,
Moi pour moins d'une goutte on m'écrase, on me tuë."
Mort aux petits voleurs, aux grands honneur & paix.

The Flea and the Leech

Lamented flea to leech, in conversation:
"You gorge yourself on blood; you drink your fill.
Me, for a drop or less, they crush and kill!"
To small thieves, death; to great ones, admiration.[1]

---

1. Since I take the liberty of adding the quotation marks to the original (see note, p. xv), the last line may as logically be considered

the flea's observation as the author's moral, though I assume it to be the latter.

Le Porc-épic et le Loup	The Porcupine and the Wolf
"O Mon cher Porc-épic!" dit un Loup sanguinaire,	Said cutthroat wolf to porcupine: "Dear friend,
"Certes tu serois beau sans tes vilains piquans:	Surely a handsome creature dwells beneath
C'est ta honte, croy moi, tu devrois t'en défaire":	Those ugly quills of yours. I recommend
"Oüi," dit-il, "quand les Loups auront quitté leurs dents."	You shed them..." "Yes. When wolves pull out their teeth."

Le Chevalier de Saint Gilles   Essai de Rondeaux sur Quelques Fables
d'Esope (1709) (posthumous)

Le Chevalier de Saint Gilles—with or without hyphens—has posed a challenge to bibliographers and other researchers, one not always met with signal success. In 1709 a modest little volume appeared, entitled *La Muse mousquetaire,* purporting to be his posthumous collected works.[1] Although he was a very minor literary figure of the period, a number of biographical facts about him have been preserved. Unfortunately, they are confused by the existence of another personage of the same name, also apparently a dabbler in letters.[2] The confusion is compounded by yet a third Chevalier de Saint Gilles, namely our author's elder brother, an artillery officer who, we are told, besides authoring an undistinguished tragedy, *Ariarathe* (1699), was the anonymous compiler of *La Muse mousquetaire.* (See Henry Carrington Lancaster, *A History of French Dramatic Literature in the Seventeenth Century,* part IV, I:401.)[3]

As for our rather shadowy author, Lachèvre assures us that "N. de L'Enfant, Chevalier de Saint-Gilles," was born around 1670 or 1680; that he was an officer in the king's musketeers (hence the title given to his collection); that he quit the service in 1706, after the battle of Ramillies; and that, shortly thereafter, he abandoned the worldly life and retired to a Capuchin monastery, dying at an uncertain date (though obviously before 1709). (See *Bibliographie,* II:459–60 and III:519–20.)[4] All Lachèvre's facts, except the supposed date of Saint Gilles's birth, are to be found in Evrard Titon du Tillet's two-volume literary history, *Le Parnasse françois* (II:567). According to Titon du Tillet, writing at about a generation's distance, Saint Gilles was a taciturn and pensive character, who would often go about composing verse in his head, "qu'il récitoit avec plaisir à ses amis." He was especially known to his contemporaries for his witty and racy *contes,* at least one of which, "Le Contrat," was good enough to be attributed to La Fontaine. (See the entry on Saint Gilles in the *Nouvelle Biographie générale,* XL:30–31.)[5] Another of his probable works, a comedy, *Je vous prends sans verd,* had also been attributed variously to La Fontaine, to the actor Champmeslé (i.e., Charles Chevillet), and indeed to both. (See Ferdinand Gohin, *Les Comédies attribuées à La Fontaine,* pp. 1, 58.)[6]

Besides containing a variety of satirical prose and light verse—among which are "Le Contrat" and other *contes* and playlets—*La Muse mousquetaire* also contains a curious collection of twenty-nine fables in *rondeau* form, entitled "Essai de rondeaux sur quelques Fables d'Esope." They were composed, according to a note (p. 18), while the poet, very young, was serving as a page at the court of Louis XIV. Reminiscent of the *ballade*-fables of Deschamps (see pp. 9–10), though with little of his elegance, they bend the essentials of the various Aesopic originals to the formal demands of the *rondeau,* resulting in usually forced, often obscure, and generally pallid versions, relieved here and there by snatches of pleasant dialogue

and wry humor. They are clearly of more youthful inspiration and less literary interest than Saint Gilles's *contes,* the latter written in the unconstrained La Fontainesque *vers libres,* in which he could give freer rein to a more graceful style and a rather lusty wit.

The three fables presented here in translation, primarily for their curiosity value—and with all their abundance of orthographic (and most of their capricious punctuational) peculiarities left intact—are the second, seventh, and fifteenth of the unnumbered collection.

---

1. The volume, apparently privately printed, was published without printer's name, but bearing rather the names of the four Parisian booksellers at whose stalls it could be purchased for "quarante sols": Guillaume de Luynes, Augustin Hebert, La Veuve F. Mauger, and La Veuve J. Charpentier. In the prefatory "Au lecteur" the anonymous compiler takes pleasure in presenting to the public "les Oeuvres de feu Monsieur le Chevalier de Saint Gilles assemblez," several of which, according to him, had already been published with success. He goes on to suggest that, owing to the late poet's negligence in preserving his work, composed for his own amusement and that of his friends, the pieces published were the only ones saved from eventual oblivion, while holding out the hope that others might eventually be discovered.

2. Saint Gilles's namesake was the "personnage bizarre" whom Molière is said to have had in mind when drawing the verbal portrait of Timante in *Le Misanthrope* (II, 4). (See Frédéric Lachèvre, *Bibliographie des recueils collectifs de poésies publiés de 1597 à 1700,* II:459–60; and Paul d'Estrée, "Molière et les Jocondes.")

3. There is, to my knowledge, no evidence to show that chevaliers two and three were not, indeed, one and the same.

4. This clearly gives the lie to A.-C.-M. Robert's assertion, in his *Fables inédites des XIIe, XIIIe et XIVe siècles, et Fables de La Fontaine,* that "de Saint-Gilles Lenfant" [*sic*], whom he cites briefly

as a contemporary of La Fontaine, wrote his fables before 1677 (see I:cxcix).

5. The entry in this biographical dictionary is more detailed (and more credible) than the one in its rival, the revised *Biographie universelle, ancienne et moderne* ("Biographie Michaud"), XXXVII:325, which categorically gives Saint Gilles's dates as 1680 to 1736. The former is possible, if debatable, but the latter is clearly in error.

6. Given the conditions under which he wrote and his reportedly cavalier attitude—no pun intended—toward his works, it is difficult to establish a reliable and comprehensive bibliography for Le Chevalier de Saint Gilles. The interested reader should consult Lachèvre (*Bibliographie,* II:459–60; III:519–20; and IV:182) for individual poems included in collections, other than those published in *La Muse mousquetaire.* Unfortunately, the entry on "Charles Lenfant [*sic*], chevalier de Saint-Gilles" in the usually authoritative bibliography of Alexandre Cioranescu (*Bibliographie de la littérature française du dix-septième siècle,* III:1801) appears rather suspect. In addition to four scholarly Latin texts of unlikely attribution, recorded in no other sources consulted, it lists as a study of our author a work by one E. C. Jones (*Saint-Gilles; Essai d'histoire littéraire* [Paris, Champion, 1914]) which is actually a thesis on the Catholic saint Aegidius ("Saint Giles"), subject of much popular medieval legend.

La Cigalle et la Fourmy

Le tems n'est plus de la belle saison,
L'hiver approche, & neige à gros flocon
Tombe du ciel. Cigale verdelette
Ne chante plus, autre soin l'inquiete,
C'est de dîner dont il est question.

Mais où dîner? car de provision
Il n'en est point, point de précaution;
D'aller aux champs succer la tendre herbette,
    Le tems n'est plus.

Elle va droit à l'habitation
De la Fourmy: Belle reception,
Mais rien de plus. Il faut faire diette.
Quand on est vieux, c'est trop tard qu'on regrette
Les jours perdus; & de faire moisson
    Le tems n'est plus.

The Cricket and the Ant

Gone are the days that brought the joys to spring.
The winter's snow lays thick its covering
Over the land. And so it comes to pass
That cricket—hale, but now no sprightly lass—
At length stops singing and starts wondering:

Where will she dine? For not a blessèd thing
Has she put by to ease her hungering.
Finished her nibbling on the tender grass:
    Gone are the days.

So off to ant's she goes one evening,
And there receives a proper welcoming,
But nothing more! Soon must she starve, alas!
Vain her regrets: they'll not turn back Time's glass.
Too late! For planting and for harvesting,
    Gone are the days.

Le Voleur et le Chien

La nuit sur tout l'hemisphere à pas lens,
Avoit semé pour assoupir nos sens,

The Thief and the Hound

Night, above all the hemisphere, has spread,
Silently, with her ever-gentle tread,

De ses pavots les douceurs qu'on admire,
Lorsqu'un Larron prés d'un huis tourne & vire;
Mais un mâtin lui montroit grosses dens.

"Quoi de veiller à telle heure est-il tems?"
Dit le Voleur. "Veux-tu du pain? tien! prens!
Faire la garde est un cruel martyre,
          La nuit sur tout."

"Je crains les Grecs, & je crains leurs presens,"
Répond le Chien. "Un Troyen de bons sens,
Fort à propos jadis le sçut bien dire,
J'en dis autant, & vous croi fort bon Sire.
Mais pour du pain on n'entre point ceans,
          La nuit sur tout."

Sowing her poppies and their sweet repose.
Outside, a thief on tiptoe comes and goes,
When, suddenly, a hound growls, rears his head.

"What?" cries the thief. "So late, and not abed?
Standing your guard all day? You must be dead!
Here, take this loaf. You're hungry, goodness knows!
          Night, above all..."

Answers the hound, declining to be fed:
" 'Beware the Greeks with gifts!' the Trojan said.
And rightly so, good sir, as history shows.
Now, though I'm sure you can't be one of those,
Nobody enters here, bread or no bread.
          Night, above all!"

Le Renard et le Chat

"Il n'est rien tel que d'avoir de l'esprit,"
(Dit un Renard) "pour moi, sans contredit,
J'en ai bien plus qu'aucune autre pecore:
Et sans mentir, je puis compter encore
Deux cens bons tours que j'ai mis par écrit."

"Moi," dit le Chat, "j'en sçai pour mon profit
Un merveilleux, que ma mere m'apprit.
Content du mien, tous les autres j'ignore:
          Il n'est rien tel."

Dans cet instant, l'un & l'autre entendit
Un bruit de Chiens: l'un & l'autre partit.
Le Matou grimpe au haut d'un Sycomore;
L'autre est en proye au Chien qui le dévore.
Point de finesse où le bon sens suffit.
          Il n'est rien tel.

The Fox and the Cat

"There's nothing better, really, than to be
Crafty and sly!" said fox. "Just look at me.
No other beast knows more good tricks than I.
I've written down a volume, by the by:
Two hundred of my best, I guarantee."

"I," answered cat, "know only one. You see,
My mother long ago taught it to me.
Just one, no need for any others... Why,
          There's nothing better."

Just then, they hear the hounds, and suddenly
Away they fly. Cat scampers up a tree.
But fox, in but the twinkling of an eye,
Done in, though quick of wit is quick to die.
Good common sense, instead of trickery:
          There's nothing better!

François Gacon   Homère Vengé, ou Réponse à M. de La Motte
sur L'Iliade (1715)

SATIRIST François Gacon will be far more important for his literary skirmishes with Antoine Houdar de La Motte than as a figure in his own right. (See pp. 63–65.) The twenty fables that he included in his *Homère vengé, ou Réponse à M. de La Motte sur l'Iliade,* are, to be sure, not a particularly noteworthy example of the fabulist's art or a significant contribution to the history and development of the genre. Since they do not appear in a collection of the usual "*Fables* de Monsieur..." variety, but are, rather, tucked away, à la Le Noble (see pp. 53–54), in a nonpoetic polemical text, they can easily go unnoticed

and probably have long done so. While they are, on the whole, too pointedly satiric and anti-La Motte to be of general application, and, with few exceptions, too pedestrian in form and expression to distinguish themselves, a few of them, I think, can be read with interest, irrespective of the author's sallies into the "Querelle des Anciens et des Modernes."

Suffice it to add the following details to the facts that will be found below. Gacon was born in Lyon in 1667 and spent his youth studying for the priesthood. In 1691, having failed to complete his theological studies, he abandoned religion for a life in letters. Satire, it seems, was most compatible with his personality, and it is said that he was even employed by the early eighteenth-century playwright Jean-François Regnard to versify scenes in some of his comedies. (See Louis Trenard's entry on Gacon in the *Dictionnaire de biographie française,* XV:8–10.)

Despite his spirited defense of Madame Dacier and her translation of the *Iliad,* Gacon does not appear to have been an especially savory character, attacking with an often-underhanded wit writers past and present, the well-known and the lesser-known: Boileau, Bossuet, Dufresny, Fontenelle, Pradon, and, of course, Houdar de La Motte.[1] His favorite target, however, seems to have been Jean-Baptiste Rousseau, whom he defeated for a poetry prize offered in 1717 by the Académie Française, much to the subsequent chagrin and embarrassment of the forty "immortels," who regretted having awarded it to one so roundly disliked. Toward the end of his life Gacon participated with some success in the monetary speculations of John Law; but he died virtually penniless, on November 15, 1725, reconciled with the Church, at the priory of Baillon, near the Abbaye de Royaumont.

Gacon's best work is said to be his translation, *Les Odes d'Anacréon et de Sapho en vers françois,* though even in his commentary to that straightforward text he was unable to refrain from his usual barbed attacks on a number of literary figures. (For the most authoritative and detailed listing of his considerable writings, see Frédéric Lachèvre, "Bibliographie des ouvrages de Gacon.")

The present pair of Gacon's "fables allégoriques" are translated from the fables and other assorted satiric verse interspersed among the twenty letters of his *Homère vengé.* The first, "La Pie et le Renard," is from the fourteenth letter. With its obvious and engaging allusion to La Fontaine's own famous crow and fox (see p. 31), it purports, in context, to illustrate that Madame Dacier will not fall prey to La Motte's insincere conciliatory blandishments. The second, "La Grenouille et la Cigogne," from the fifteenth, allegorizes Gacon's sarcastic suggestion, immediately preceding, that rather than criticize Homer, La Motte should look to his own inadequacies: "En vérité, Monsieur, il vous sied bien de vous vanter de pouvoir corriger Homere, vous qui auriez tant besoin de correction" (*Homère vengé,* p. 368).

---

1. His scorn for La Motte, and especially for his verse translation of the *Iliad,* is best summed up in his final fable: an adaptation of "Le Pot de Terre et le Pot de Fer"—better remembered in La Fontaine's celebrated version (V, 2)—to which he appends the following moral (with which few, in fact, even partisans of La Motte, would argue):

> La Muse d'Homere virile
> Du Fer a la solidité,

> Celle de La Motte débile
> Du verre a la fragilité:
> Mais aussi de leurs destinées,
> Bien different sera le cours,
> L'un vit depuis trois mille années,
> L'autre ne vivra que trois jours.
> (*Homère vengé,* p. 461)

La Pie et le Renard

Sur un haut donjon acroupie,
Une sage & prudente Pie,
Tenant sous sa pate un lopin
D'un Sassenage vieux & fin:
Le Renard d'une voix flateuse,
Lui dit, agreable chanteuse,
"Quittez ce fromage moisi,
Et venez à trois pas d'ici,
Je vous regalerai d'un Brie
Dont la pâte n'est point pourrie;
Il n'est fait que depuis deux jours.
Le Roy le trouve delectable,
Et veut qu'on en serve toujours
    A sa table."
"Ami Renard, tu n'es qu'un sot,"
Lui repartit Dame Margot,
"Je n'ai garde de lâcher prise:
En vain tu trouves mon chant beau;
Je me souviens de la sotise
De feu compere le Corbeau."

The Magpie and the Fox

Prudently perched as fox passed by,
High on a turret, Mistress Pie
Clutched in her claws a chunk of cheese—
A Sassenage, fine as you please—[1]
Whereupon fox, in flattering wise,
Called up: "Fair songstress of the skies,
That cheese is rotten, can't you see?
Drop it and I'll give you some Brie,
Just two days ripe... No mold upon it...
Come, you can feast your palate on it,
So tasty that His Majesty,
In fact, each time he sits to sup,
Insists that there should always be
    A slice served up."
"Really, friend fox," replied Dame Mag,[2]
"I warrant you're a dotty wag!
Chatter away: the more you flatter,
The less you'll make my claws let go.
I still recall that other matter—
Our foolish friend, late *compère* Crow."

1. *Sassenage* is a hard cheese made from a combination of cow's, goat's, and sheep's milk. It takes its name from a town in the southeast of France, near Grenoble.

2. The noun *margot* had already long been used with the mean-

ing of "magpie," since at least the early fourteenth century, when La Fontaine popularized it as a proper name in his fable "L'Aigle et la Pie" (XII, 11).

La Grenoüille et la Cigogne

Pour se rendre plus importante
Parmi les autres animaux,
Une Grenoüille impertinente
Prétendoit guerir de tous maux.
"Accourez," disoit-elle au Lievre,
"Je ferai passer vôtre fievre:
Approchez Messieurs les Chevaux,
Je gueris malandres claveaux,
Il n'est aucune maladie
Qu'à l'instant je ne congedie:
Venez à moi grands & petits,
Je donne mes conseils gratis."
Tu fais, repartit la Cigogne,
"Bien plus de bruit que de besogne:
Tu jases comme un Medecin;
Mais vû que ta pâleur extrême,
En toi dénote un corps mal sain,
Que ne te gueris-tu toi-mëme?"

The Frog and the Stork

A frog of self-important bent
Among the beasts, with pompous air
Declares herself an eminent
Physician *extraordinaire:*
"Come," she invites the hares, "I'll cure you!
Finished your fevers, I assure you...
Come, Messrs. Horse, you too shall be
Healed of that pus-pox of the knee... [1]
No ills, indeed, my friends, but what
My skills dispatch them on the spot!
Yes, let me cure you, great and small—
And gratis, too!—come one, come all!"
To which the stork replies: " 'Tis true,
You jabber just as doctors do.
But look! Yourself, you look half-dead—
Pale, sickly... So before you tell
The rest how best we might be well,
'Physician, heal thyself,' instead!"[2]

1. A *malandre* ("melander") is a scabby sore or fissure appearing in the crook of a horse's knee. I do not know if the author's apposition of the medical term *claveau*—a purulent discharge characteristic of the sheep pox—makes for an authentic veteri-

nary syndrome, but my translation, at any rate, attempts to convey one.

2. The reference is, of course, to the proverbial admonition found in Luke, 4:23.

Antoine Houdar de La Motte Fables Nouvelles (1719)

Generally considered the most significant successor to La Fontaine before the advent of the fabulist Florian (see pp. 100–101), Antoine Houdar de La Motte was born in Paris on January 17, 1762.[1] The study of law, for which the Jesuits had prepared him, gave way to his overriding interest in the theater; but the failure of his first play, a three-act farce in prose and verse entitled *Les Originaux, ou L'Italien,* performed at the Théâtre-Italien in 1693, discouraged him enough to send him packing briefly to the monastery of La Trappe. While there, however, he composed the libretto for André Campra's opera-ballet *L'Europe galante*—one of the first of the new hybrid genre—which, upon his reemergence into the world, was to score an impressive success in 1697.

From that point on La Motte would provide a long list of innovative librettos to some of the more important

theater composers of the age; among them, François Francœur, Michel de La Barre, and especially André Cardinal Destouches. Of his numerous comic and tragic plays, the most successful, and not the least controversial, was his five-act tragedy *Inés de Castro,* performed at the Théâtre-Français in 1723, at the height of his career. Though blinded at the age of forty-three, he continued writing for the rest of his life, and took an active part in the salon and coffeehouse society of the period, notably as one of the early habitués of the celebrated Café Procope, breeding ground for many an eighteenth-century philosophical debate. By the time of his death, in Paris, on December 26, 1731, his vast quantity of prose and verse—dramatic, occasional, philosophical, theoretical—had surely given him cause to suppose that posterity, whether kindly or not, would at least not lose sight of him.[2]

Like Antoine Furetière before him, however, if Antoine Houdar de La Motte was a prominent and productive literary figure of his own time, he is little remembered by ours; he was, in fact, little remembered even by his immediate followers.[3] A member, like Furetière, of the Académie Française—though without the latter's negative distinction (see p. 41)—he was, like him too, a part-time fabulist; one for whom the fable was a minor source of a major reputation. And, like his predecessor, and numerous fabulist followers as well, he went to some pains to voice his admiration of La Fontaine's supremacy in the genre—one would expect and, indeed, accept no less—while, at the same time, distinguishing himself from him by his humble profession of originality and inventiveness. "Aussi ne me serois-je pas hazardé à écrire des Fables," he protests in the fifty-one-page "Discours sur la fable" that prefaces his *Fables nouvelles*, "si j'avois crû qu'il fallût être absolument aussi bon que lui, pour être souffert après lui: mais j'ai pensé qu'il y avoit des places honorables au dessous de la sienne." And, he continues, with perhaps an excess of humility, "je serois trop heureux d'obtenir cette approbation modérée, qui en me pardonnant de n'avoir pas les mêmes graces que La Fontaine, feroit honneur à ce que je puis avoir d'heureusement original" (p. 10).[4]

That originality in which Houdar de La Motte takes such pride is a function not only of his "véritez nouvelles," original scenarios that he contrasts with La Fontaine's "borrowed" subject matter—after all, he explains, "ce fonds n'est pas à lui" (*Fables*, p. 11)—but also of the lengthy verse prologues that he appends to many or most of his fables, some longer than the texts themselves. For him these innovative introductions were a worthy addition to the fabulist's craft, thanks both to the variety that they introduced to the narration and to the philosophical reflection that they purported to invite: "J'ai orné, ou du moins j'ai prétendu orner de Prologues une grande partie de mes Fables. J'ai cru qu'en interrompant ainsi la continuité des narrations, je jetterois dans l'Ouvrage une variété plus amusante; et qu'on passeroit avec plaisir des simples récits à des réflexions un peu étendues, et quelquefois un peu profondes, selon ma portée" (*Fables*, pp. 55–56).

Not everyone, however, would agree with his judgment. For example, Claude-Joseph Dorat, the "Ovide français" (see pp. 91–93), would complain half a century later that one of the most striking flaws in his predecessor's fables was, precisely, "la pompe sentencieuse et doctorale dont elles sont précédées." And that often-unsuccessful candidate for election to the Académie Française would add, perhaps with more than a trace of professional jealousy: "Une Fable de six lignes a souvent un avant-propos de cinquante. Après les dogmes prolixes de l'Académicien, l'âne, le rat ou le lapin n'ont pas bonne grâce à débiter les leurs."[5] In relatively modern times, even the sympathetically disposed Faguet, while generally admiring La Motte, would admit that his fables tended to be prosaic and single of purpose: "on voit très bien qu'il voudrait faire de la fable une anecdote mathématiquement développée, et propre, avant tout, à servir de support à une vérité morale" (*Histoire*, p. 249).

A number of his own contemporaries too would satirize the philosophical pretensions of La Motte's fables. Probably the first to do so was playwright Louis Fuzelier, himself an aspiring fabulist, who poked rather good-natured fun at them the very year of their publication (see pp. 72–73). Another more persistent—and nastier—*railleur* was a notorious satirist of the period, one François Gacon (see pp. 61–62), known especially by the pseudonym "le P. S. F." or "le Poète Sans Fard," who, a few years after the appearance of the *Fables nouvelles*, would publish a volume the mere title of which makes his parodic intent quite clear: *Les fables de m^r Houdart de La Motte traduittes en vers françois par le P. S. F.*[6] Gacon, to press his point, and not without considerable malice, ostensibly rewrote several of the fables in what he considered more acceptable verse. With more civility but no less rancor he would likewise attack La Motte's popular tragedy, *Inés de Castro*. (See his pamphlet, *Le Secrétaire du Parnasse, au sujet de la tragédie d'Inés de Castro*.) Still another contemporary detractor, the sentimental playwright Pierre-Claude Nivelle de la Chaussée, for all his dramatic moral rectitude, had no scruples at the beginning of his career against penning an anonymous attack against the fables as well. (At least the *Lettres de Mme la marquise de * * * sur les Fables nouvelles* are generally attributed to him.)

By the time he wrote his fables, however, Houdar de La Motte was no stranger to sarcasm and not an unaccustomed object of controversy. And that, despite the fact that he was warmly regarded by most, much appreciated as a wit, and highly thought of for his prose, even if his verse was less admired in many quarters.[7] The reason for that notoriety, and virtually the only reason for which he is remembered at all today, is the central role he played in the revival of the famous "Querelle des Anciens et des Modernes," the century-old debate initiated by Perrault and waged in typical French fashion between the partisans of classical literature, on one side, and contemporary, on the other. (See p. 56.) La Motte had aroused the ire of the "Anciens" by publishing his verse translation of Homer, *L'Iliade, poème, avec un discours sur Homère*, reducing his twenty-four books to twelve, and taking issue with those who would set him up as the perfect poet.[8] Especially outraged was the classical scholar Madame Dacier (née Anne Lefèvre), who, several years earlier, had published her three-volume prose translation, *L'Iliade d'Homère, traduite en françois, avec des remarques*, with extensive erudite commentary, and whose adulation of Homer would brook no discussion.[9] La Motte's seeming temerity evoked not only her 600-odd-page defense of the Greek and attack on the Frenchman, in her treatise *Des causes de la corruption du goust*, but also resulted in his first encounter with the irascible Gacon.[10]

Of all his voluminous writings, La Motte's *Fables nouvelles* were to be the longest to survive his almost-immediate posthumous eclipse. While they failed to attract imitators, for all their innovation, editions continued to be published over the years, the last, to my knowledge (Avignon: Seguin, 1808), appearing almost a century after the first; and individual fables, singly and in groups, were anthologized for some time thereafter.

The collection consists of ninety-nine fables divided almost equally among five books, with an introductory hundredth, placed before the "Discours sur la fable," serving as a dedication to Louis XV.

The examples translated in the present selection are a representative sampling, and are numbered in the original 1719 edition as follows: I, 6; I, 7; II, 3; II, 7; II, 15; II, 17; III, 2; III, 10; and IV, 15.

1. There are probably as many or more variations in the spelling of his surname as in Shakespeare's. Archivist Auguste Jal, in his *Dictionnaire critique de biographie et d'histoire*, cites the following: La Motte Houdart, La Motte-Houdar, Lamotte-Oudart, La Mothe Houdar, and La Mothe-Houdart (pp. 687–88); and one also finds similar permutations—with and without a hyphen—using the spelling "Houdard." In practice, he was usually referred to simply as "La Motte" (or, less frequently, "Lamotte").

2. La Motte's many writings were posthumously collected in the *Œuvres de Monsieur Houdar de La Motte*. For a comprehensive listing of works by and about him, see Alexandre Cioranescu, *Bibliographie de la littérature française du dix-huitième siècle*, II:1017–21; and for an informative and compact biographical and critical account, Emile Faguet's chapter devoted to him in his *Histoire de la poésie française de la Renaissance au Romantisme*. (Faguet's same original lectures can also be found spread over several numbers of the *Revue des cours et conférences* for the years 1898–99 and 1899–1900.)

3. His relative oblivion was not long in coming. "Il avait désiré toutes les gloires littéraires, il les poursuivit toutes avec une persistance que les infirmités ne calmèrent jamais, et, jusqu'au dernier jour, applaudi au théâtre, recherché des salons, honoré de l'amitié des princes, élevé au premier rang par ses amis, vainqueur de ses ennemis qu'il avait lassés par ses répliques spirituelles, ou désarmés par sa douceur et sa bonne foi, il dut croire qu'il laissait après lui une réputation inaltérable. Fontenelle, en effet, lisant son éloge à l'Académie, lui décerna sans hésiter le nom de grand poète. Mais quelques années plus tard, ses œuvres tombaient presque toutes dans l'oubli." (See Jean Morel, in Eugène Crépet, *Les Poètes français*, III:158.)

4. The entire "Discours sur la fable" was summarized in detail, the year after its publication, in the *Journal littéraire*, XI (1720): 41–61. The anonymous author concludes his review with one of his rare (and debatable) personal judgments of La Motte's collection: "La versification en est infiniment plus correcte que celle de *la Fontaine*, & plus proportionnée au sujet que celles des Fables & Contes de *le Noble*. Nous ne doutons point que ce Livre n'ait l'approbation de tous les Lecteurs qui ont du goût; & il est également digne de son Auteur, & du Monarque à qui il est dedié" (p. 61).

5. Dorat's observations are found in his "Réflexions préliminaires," the preface to his own similarly (and not uncommonly) entitled collection, *Fables nouvelles*, p. xiii.

6. Several printings of the volume exist, with minor variations in title and detail, but with significant difference in length, from 136 to 232 pages, if the indications in the catalogue of the Bibliothèque Nationale and the National Union Catalogue of the Library of Congress, respectively, can be believed.

7. Voisenon, in his *Anecdotes littéraires* (see p. 50, n. 1), summed up the situation with his customary terseness: "ses vers étoient foibles et prosaïques, mais en revanche personne n'écrivoit aussi bien en prose. ... Il possédoit toutes les vertus sociales, et n'eut jamais pour ennemi déclaré que Rousseau, qui étoit plus poëte que lui, mais qui avoit bien moins d'esprit, et qui étoit aussi lourd que l'autre étoit aimable" (p. 78). (The Rousseau referred to was the poet Jean-Baptiste Rousseau [1671–1741], who had underhandedly and unsuccessfully opposed La Motte's election to the Académie Française in 1710, coveting the seat for himself.) Regarding his poetic talent, or lack of it, a modern observer quotes one of La Motte's contemporaries, a certain "femme d'esprit," who likened him to the prototypic artistic unsophisticate, hero of Molière's *Le Bourgeois gentilhomme*: "La Motte ressemble à M. Jourdain: il fait de la prose sans le savoir." (See Jacques Janssens, *La Fable et les fabulistes*, p. 70.)

8. Cioranescu (*Bibliographie ... du dix-huitième siècle*, II:1018, no. 36533) lists a translation of the first book dating from a dozen years earlier (Paris, 1701).

9. Louis Pichard, in *Dictionnaire des lettres françaises: le dix-huitième siècle*, II:362, cites a prior four-volume edition dating from 1699, to which I find no other references.

10. See the latter's *Homère vengé, ou Réponse à M. de La Motte sur L'Iliade*, a collection of twenty polemical letters interspersed with as many brief fables (and other assorted verse) ostensibly of Gacon's own composition, taking La Motte to task for his enterprise: "A peine ceux qui connoissent parfaitement Homere en Grec, peuvent ils le reconnoître en François, tant vous l'avez défiguré en l'abregeant, & abregé en le défigurant" (p. 424). La Motte is said not to have deigned a direct reply to Gacon's polemics, stating, with accustomed mild-mannered wit, that "on n'a rien à gagner avec ceux qui n'ont rien à perdre." It was, in fact, this riposte that provoked Gacon to his "rewriting" of La Motte's fables, mentioned above.

Le Mocqueur

La Nature est par tout variée & féconde.
    Dans un païs du nouveau Monde[1]
Qu'habitent mille oyseaux inconnus à nos bois,
    Il en est un de beau plumage;
    Mais qui pour chant n'eut en partage
Que le talent railleur d'imiter d'autres voix.
    Sire Mocqueur (c'est ainsi qu'on l'appelle),
Entendit au lever d'une aurore nouvelle,
    Ses Rivaux saluer le jour.
De brocards fredonnez le railleur les harcelle;
    Rien n'échappe; tout a son tour.

The Mockingbird[3]

    Off in the New World's forests, where
Strange birds abound in Nature's panoply, I've heard
    Of one more wondrous than the rest; a bird
    Like none we know. Not for his plumage rare—
    Though fair he is—but for a curious skill:
    Himself, he has no song, but mocks at will
    The songs of others. Thus it was, one morning,
That he—our mockingbird, so-called—was making fun
    Of all his rivals, up to greet the sun,
      Mimicking, taunting, scorning
Each one in turn, with his sarcastic art.

De l'un il traîne la cadence;
De l'autre il outre le fausset;
Change un amour plaintif en fade doleance,
Un ramage joyeux en importun sifflet;
Donne à tout ce qu'il contrefait
L'air de défaut & d'ignorance.
Tandis que mon Mocqueur par son critique écho
Traitoit ainsi nos Chantres *da poco;*[2]
"Fort bien," dit un d'entre eux, parlant pour tous les autres:
"Nos chants sont imparfaits; mais monstrez-nous
des vôtres."

One, for his languorous, warbling trill;
Another, for his accents shrill...
And still another, pouring out his heart,
Would hear his tender love call made
To sound like doleful, dull lament. In short,
He turned their joyous serenade,
Blithely, to mean, disdainful sport.
At length, one of the bolder birds chirps a retort:
"Our songs are far from perfect, as you've shown.
Now, friend, let's hear you try to sing your own!"

1. The poet, in a note in the original, specifies that he is referring to "la Virginie dans l'Amérique."
2. Another note in the original informs us that *da poco* is a "terme de mépris emprunté de l'italien."

3. Like many of the author's fables, this one is preceded by a lengthy prologue, longer than the fable itself. In some cases, where I find his prologues of interest, I include them in my translation. In others, as here, I omit them.

L'Asne

"Sous quelle étoile suis-je né!"
Disoit certain Baudet couché dans une étable;
"Que de bon cœur je donne au diable
Le Maître ingrat que le Ciel m'a donné!
Combien lui rends-je de services?
Et combien m'en faut-il essuyer d'injustices?
Debout long-temps avant le jour,
Il faut marcher, porter les herbes à la ville;
Courir de porte en porte, & puis à mon retour
Rapporter le fumier qui rend son champ fertile;
Aller chercher au bois ma charge de fagot;
Toûjours sur pied, toûjours le trot.
Vient-il un Dimanche, une Fête?
Je le porte à la foire, en croupe sa Margot,
Et puis en deux paniers Jacqueline & Pierrot.
Son maudit Singe encor se campe sur ma tête.
Si je m'écarte un peu pour un brin de chardon,
Soudain marche martin bâton.
Tandis que son Bertrand, son baladin de Singe,
Franc faineant, maître étourdi,
Sautant, montrant le cul, gâtant habits & linge,
Vit sans soins, mange à table, est surtout applaudi.

The Jackass

"What evil star was I born under?"
Bitterly whined a jackass in his stable.
"Gladly I'd damn my master, were I able!
See how I suffer! Is it any wonder?
Morning to night, how many's the hateful
Burden he makes me bear! And is he grateful?
Up at the crack of dawn, and long before,
Dragging my load of straw from farm to city,
Toiling beneath my pack, from door to door—
No moment's rest, no thanks, no pity—
And back from town, only to sweat some more:
Piles of manure, bundles of wood...
And Sunday? To the fête or fair,
Carrying him and all the blessèd neighborhood—
This one, that one, here, there, and everywhere!
Margot his maid, Jacqueline, Pierrot—
Even his monkey, don't you know,
Squatting—yes, squatting on my head!—and if I stop
To nibble at the thistles, *whish!* his crop
Whistles across my aching back! And yet,
The foolish ape—foul, filthy lout—
Lifts his beshitten chemisette

Peste du mauvais Maître, & que Dieu le confonde!"
"Ami," lui dit un Bœuf de cervelle profonde,
"Le Maître à qui le Sort a voulu t'asservir,
N'est pas pire qu'un autre. Apprends qu'en ce bas monde
    Il vaut mieux plaire que servir."

And shows his arse! How clever! Still, he lolls about,
    Eats with my master, lives without a care!
God damn them both!" An ox heard his lament. "*Compère,*
Your master is no worse than most. You serve,
                        sustain him...
    Better for you if you could entertain him!"

L'Enfant et les Noisettes

    Que j'aime une image naïve
Qui soit en apparence une leçon d'enfant,
    Et qui pour le Sage instructive
    Renferme un précepte important!
Les grandes véritez charment sous cette écorce;
On ne les attend point, & d'abord on les voit;
    Cette surprise y donne de la force.
"Un exemple," dit-on; eh bien, exemple; soit.
Philosophiquement, si je vais dire à l'homme,
    "Contente toi de médiocrité;
Il ne t'en coûtera le repos ni le somme;
    Tu l'auras sans difficulté.
Mais par mille projets je te vois agité;
    Tes désirs n'ont point de limites;
Toutes fortunes sont à ton gré trop petites;
Tu veux tout; tout échape à ton avidité."
    Belles leçons! mais l'homme y bâille.
    Que faire pour le réveiller?
    Or voici comme j'y travaille;
Je lui conte une Fable; il cesse de bâiller.

    Un Jeune Enfant, je le tiens d'Epictete,
    Moitié gourmand & moitié sot,
    Mit un jour sa main dans un pot
Où logeoit mainte figue avec mainte noisette.
Il en emplit sa main tant qu'elle en peut tenir;
Puis veut la retirer; mais l'ouverture étroite
    Ne la laisse point revenir.
Il n'y sçait que pleurer; en plainte il se consomme;
Il vouloit tout avoir & ne le pouvoit pas.
    Quelqu'un lui dit, (& je le dis à l'homme,)
"N'en prends que la moitié, mon enfant; tu l'auras."

The Child and the Nuts

    I love a tale that, in its guise
    Of truth naive and moral gentle,
    Nevertheless still edifies
    The wise with precept fundamental.
The deepest truths, concealed and unsuspected,
    Charm us the more with their unmasking,
When, stripped, to our surprise, they stand detected.
    "Oh? For example?" do I hear you asking?
Fine! An example then!... Suppose I should
    Wax philosophical and, morally,
Commend to you the golden mean. Much would
I say. To wit: "Be satisfied with half. Don't be
    Aflame with limitless ambition, lest,
    A slave to it, you lose your sweet repose.
    Take less; for, coveting the rest,
You risk the half you have..." Such precepts, then, are those
    I would intone, still droning on and on,
    Watching as you began to yawn!
How to prevent such a reaction somnolescent?
    By telling you a fable, like the present.

A tale—in Epictetus, if I recollect—
    Tells of a jar abrim with fig and nut,
And of a foolish child, eager to gorge and glut.
    In goes his hand, just as one might expect,
    Grasping its fill. But when he turns about,
    Behold! The jar is narrow-necked:
    Too full, his fist will not come out!
The child laments his loss. Alas, what can he do?
He sought to get it all. Much less is what he got.
    Someone advised him (just as I would you):
    "Be satisfied with half, it's more than nought."

La Rose et le Papillon

Il étoit une Rose en un jardin fleuri,
Se picquant de regner entre les fleurs nouvelles.
    Papillon aux brillantes aisles,
    Digne d'être son favori,
Au lever du Soleil lui compte son martyre:
    Rose rougit & puis soupire.
Ils n'ont pas comme nous le temps des longs délais;
    Marché fut fait de part & d'autre.
"Je suis à vous," dit-il. "Moi, je suis toute vôtre."

The Rose and the Butterfly[1]

    Once, in a garden, bloomed a rose,
    Reigning with pride among the flowers.
A brilliant butterfly, worthiest of beaus,
    One morning—in the wee, small hours—
Woos her, regales her with his amorous woes,
    Recounts his lover's martyrdom.
    Rose blushes, sighing...
For them, none of our long betrothals. Time's a-flying.
    A week is a millenium.

Ils se jurent tous deux d'être unis à jamais.
Le Papillon content la quitte pour affaire:
    Ne revient que sur le midi.
"Quoi! ce feu soit disant si vif & si sincere,"
    Lui dit la Rose, "est déja réfroidi?
Un siècle s'est passé," (c'étoit trois ou quatre heures)
    "Sans aucun soin que vous m'ayez rendu.
    Je vous ai vû dans ces demeures,
Porter de fleurs en fleurs un amour qui m'est dû.
    Qu'à peine on regarde en ces lieux;
Ingrat, je vous ai vû baiser la Violette,
    Entre les fleurs simple grisette,
Toute noire qu'elle est, elle a charmé vos yeux.
Vous avez caressé la Tulipe insipide,
    La Jonquille aux pâles couleurs,
    La Tubéreuse aux malignes odeurs.
Est-ce assez me trahir? Es-tu content, perfide?"
    Le petit-maître Papillon
    Repliqua sur le même ton.
"Il vous sied bien, coquette que vous êtes,
    De condamner mes petits tours;
    Je ne fais que ce que vous faites;
Car j'observois aussi vos volages amours.
    Avec quel goût je vous voiois sourire
Au souffle caressant de l'amoureux Zephire!
    Je vous passerois celui-là:
    Mais non contente de cela,
    Je vous voyois recevoir à merveille
    Les soins empressez de l'Abeille;
Et puis après l'Abeille arrive le Frelon;
Vous voulez plaire à tous jusques au Moucheron.
    Vous ne réfusez nul hommage;
Ils sont tous bien venus, & chacun à son tour."

    C'est providence de l'amour
    Que Coquette trouve un Volage.

    1. I have omitted the thirty-four-line prologue that accompanies the original.

So, quickly, both
    Pledge, seal their troth:
"I'm yours!" So swears the rose. The butterfly: "Likewise!"
    And, happy, off to work he flies,
Not to return till almost noon. "Well, well! I see!"
Fretted the rose. "That fire! That passion so sincere!
    Grown cold so soon? It's been a century..."
    (Just a few hours, in fact!) "... since you were here
    To pay the slightest mind to me. And yet,
    You flirt with all the flowers, go flitting
    Round and about! My, my! How fitting!
Oh yes! I saw you kiss the violet!
That worthless jade, dark skin and all, still charmed
                    your eye!
And the insipid tulip! Yes, you kissed her too!
    And the pale jonquil..." "But..." "Wait, I'm not through!
You even kissed the stinkweed, though I can't guess why!
Have you betrayed me quite enough, you faithless worm?"
    "Beg pardon, love!" the haughty butterfly
    Replies in accents no less firm.
"You really have your nerve, I must admit,
    To criticize me when I flirt and flit.
I do no less than you, my vain coquette! Ah yes,
    Don't think I haven't watched you carry on!
    Oft and anon,
I've seen you smile beneath the Zephyr's warm caress.
    That much I might forgive. But, not
Content with him, you think you ought let every bee
    Come court you too, make fast and free,
    My fine cocotte!
After the bees, the wasps... Soon the whole buzzing lot—
    Down to the tiniest gnats!—all queuing,
    Waiting in line, my love, to go a-wooing!
And each one gets just what the others got!"

    How providential, Nature's plan:
    To mate coquettish maid with fickle man!

L'Huître

    Deux Voyageurs firent naufrage;
    Et sur le débris du vaisseau
Ils abordent tous deux dans une Isle sauvage,
    Où les suit un danger nouveau:
L'affreuse faim. Nos gens cherchent par tout à vivre;
Mais ils ont beau courir, nuls fruits, nuls animaux;
Sable altéré comme eux. Les voilà près de suivre
    Leurs Compagnons engloutis dans les eaux.
Après deux ou trois jours, sur la rive ils découvrent
    Grand nombre d'Huîtres prenant l'air.
    "Voilà des coquilles qui s'ouvrent,"
Dit l'un, "nous serions bien obligez à la mer,
Si c'étoit quelque proye." Il prend le coquillage,

The Oysters[1]

    A pair of shipwrecked travelers found
Their way—by clinging to their boat's debris—
    To safety and to solid ground:
A desert island, bare as bare could be.
No sooner there, another enemy—
Hunger—pursues the pair. They look around,
Hunt everywhere. In vain! Not a beast, not a tree!
Nothing but sand, as parched as they! In dark despair
They envy their lost comrades, swallowed by the sea.
    One day goes by... Two days... Suddenly, there,
    By water's edge, a multitude
Of oysters, shells agape, taking the air!
One of our travelers, puzzled, stares. "I swear,"

Et l'ouvrant tout-à-fait, voit les mets odieux,
    Effrayant le goût par les yeux.
"Il vaut autant mourir," s'écria le moins sage,
    "Que de manger cela"; disant pour sa raison,
    Que faim n'est pire que poison.
Le cœur lui soûlevoit contre l'affreuse proye.
    Il languit & mourut de faim.
    L'autre à l'extrémité l'employe,
L'avale en grimaçant. "Oh oh!" dit-il soudain,
    "Ce mets est exquis; c'est dommage
Que les humains encor n'en sçachent pas l'usage.
Quel goût! Quelle fraîcheur!" il avaloit toûjours.
Grande exclamation à chaque Huître avalée:
    "Vive," dit-il, "cette eau salée.
Quel delice! A ce prix je passe ici mes jours."
"C'est assez" lui crioit Temperance importune.
Il est sourd à ses cris: encor une, encor une;
    Et d'une en une il arriva
    Que l'imprudent glouton creva.

    Voilà l'humaine extravagance.
    Nous nous perdons par les excès.
    Contre plaisir & répugnance
    Raison perd toujours son procès.

1. I have taken the liberty of pluralizing the original title, in keeping with the story.

Says he, "If that's some kind of food...
Ocean be praised!" He picks one up, eyes with distrust
    The curious beast, and in disgust:
    "I'd rather die than eat that thing!" he cries.
    "Hunger or poison—which is worse?"
And so, indeed, he languishes and dies.
    The other, starving, less averse
To swallowing the slimy creature, tips
    Its shell betwixt grimacing lips,
    Throws back his head... And down it goes...
Surprised, he sighs: "Ah! What a glorious taste!
    Long live the brine, if it bestows
    Delicacies as fine as those!
If only mankind knew... My goodness, what a waste!...
Another... More... More, more... I could eat these forever!"
On and on gluts our friend, with many an "oh" and "ah"...
    "Enough!" wise Temperance warns. However,
    Deaf to her plea, he sneers: "Stop? Bah!"
    Until, at length, he bursts. Voilà!

    Reason is ever powerless:
    She pleads in vain against excess.
    As with disgust, so too with pleasure;
In both, man errs beyond all proper measure.

L'Homme et la Sirène

    Quelle espece est l'humaine engeance!
    Pauvres Mortels où sont donc vos beaux jours?
    Gens de desir & d'esperance,
Vous soûpirez long-temps après la jouïssance;
    Jouïssez-vous? vous vous plaignez toujours.
Mille & mille projets roulent dans vos cervelles.
"Quand ferai-je ceci? Quand aurai-je cela?"
    Jupiter vous dit, "Le voilà,
    Demain dites-m'en des nouvelles,
    Jouïssez! Je vous attends-là."
Ne vous y trompez pas; toute chose a deux faces;
    Moitié défauts & moitié graces.
Que cet objet est beau! Vous en êtes tenté.
    Qu'il sera laid, s'il devient vôtre!
Ce qu'on souhaite est vû du bon côté;
    Ce qu'on posséde est vû de l'autre.

D'une Sirène un homme étoit amoureux fou.
    Il venoit sans cesse au rivage
Offrir à sa Venus le plus ardent hommage;
    Se tenoit là, soupiroit tout son soû.
    La nuit l'en arrachoit à peine,
Les soucis avoient pris la place du sommeil;
Et la nuit se passoit à presser le Soleil
    De revenir lui montrer sa Sirène.
    "Quels yeux! Quels traits! & quel corps fait au tour!"

The Man and the Mermaid

    How curious the ways of men!
Complaining mortals! Never satisfied, they yearn
    To win their heart's desire... They sigh... They burn...
    And when they win it? They complain again.
    Such insincerity is man's!
    His brain teems with a thousand plans,
And dreams: "I want this... I want that..." "Well then,"
    Jupiter says, "I grant it! Let it
    Henceforth be yours, my friend. Tomorrow,
Tell me how fine it was!" Next day: complaints, woe, sorrow!
Man's appetite is such. Little it takes to whet it;
    Little, as well, to dull it. Here below,
Everything has two faces: foul and fair. And so,
You want that tempting object? Well, you may regret it!
We see the beautiful in what we crave. But oh!
    We see the ugly once we get it!

A man adored a certain siren. Every day
    He visited the water's edge to render
Amorous homage to his Venus. He would stay
    Long, long into the night, sighing his tender,
    Desperate sighs, his vigil keeping,
    Waiting and hoping, never sleeping,
    Begging the laggard sun to rise
And let him see his love. "That face! Those breasts!
    Those eyes!

S'écrioit-il: "quelle voix ravissante!
Le Ciel n'enferme pas de beauté si touchante."
    Il languit, séche, meurt d'amour.
Neptune en eut pitié. "Ça," lui dit-il un jour,
"La Sirène est à toi; je l'accorde à ta flame."
L'Himen se fait; il est au comble de ses vœux;
Mais dès le lendemain le pauvre malheureux
    Trouve un monstre au lieu d'une femme.
Pauvre homme! autant l'avoient travaillé ses transports,
    Autant le dégoût le travaille.
Le desirant ne vit que la tête & le corps
Le jouïssant ne vit que la queuë & l'écaille.

And that bewitching voice!" he cries, heart leaping.
    "Her beauty has no peer in heaven above!"
In short, the poor soul languishes with love.
    Neptune looks on. The mortal's plight
Moves him to pity: "If you want her... Well, so be it!
    Take her, she's yours! There! I decree it!"
And so they wed. Next morning, in the cold, hard light,
    Our friend, eyeing his mermaid bride, discovers
    One of the world's more monstrous lovers!
Yesterday, ecstasy; today, disgust!
    Alas, how quickly passion pales!
Wooing, he only saw her head and bust.
Winning, he only sees her fins and scales.

La Montre et le Quadran Solaire

    Un jour la Montre au Quadran insultoit,
        Demandant quelle heure il étoit.
    "Je n'en sçais rien," dit le Greffier Solaire.¹
"Eh! que fais-tu donc là, si tu n'en sçais pas plus?"
"J'attends," répondit-il, "que le Soleil m'éclaire;
        Je ne sçais rien que par Phœbus."
    "Attends-le donc; moi je n'en ai que faire,"
Dit la Montre; "sans lui je vais toûjours mon train.
        Tous les huit jours un tour de main,
C'est autant qu'il m'en faut pour toute ma semaine.
Je chemine sans cesse, & ce n'est point en vain
        Que mon aiguille en ce rond se promene.
Ecoute; voilà l'heure. Elle sonne à l'instant.
Une, deux, trois & quatre. Il en est tout autant,"
Dit-elle; mais, tandis que la Montre décide,
        Phœbus de ses ardents regards,
        Chassant nüages & brouillards,
Regarde le Quadran, que fidele à son guide
        Marque quatre heures & trois quarts.
        "Mon enfant," dit-il à l'Horloge,
        "Va t'en te faire remonter.
        Tu te vantes, sans hésiter,
        De répondre à qui t'interroge:
    Mais qui t'en croit peut bien se mécompter.
Je te conseillerois de suivre mon usage.
Si je ne vois bien clair, je dis: 'Je n'en sçais rien.'
        Je parle peu, mais je dis bien."

    C'est le caractere du Sage.

The Clock and the Sundial

    "Pray tell, what time is it, my friend?"
    A clock, delighting to offend
    A neighboring sundial, asked, insulting.
The sun's recorder answered: "I don't know."
    "Don't know?" echoed the clock, exulting.
"No," said the other, "I can only show
The hour when Phoebus lights my brow." "Ah, so,"
Sneering, the clock replied. "Then wait your fill!
    Myself, you see, I need no sun!
I show the hour for eight full days, at will.
A twist or two of someone's wrist, and off I run,
With no one's help. My hands trot on their endless rounds...
    Listen! Right now I'm just about to strike."
    True to his word, forthwith he sounds:
    One, two, three, four... "You see? That's what it's like!"
    "Do tell," the sundial nods. Just then, Apollo's
    Luminous gaze dispels the clouds and lights
His face. The sun-god shows the way, his minion follows:
Lo and behold! A quarter-hour to five! "By rights,"
    The sundial chides the clock, "you ought not be
        So quick to boast your accuracy
        When someone asks the hour, my child!
        Go get yourself rewound!" he smiled.
        "Take my advice, do as I do,
    Lest he who asks you may be led awry.
When I don't know, I say so. So should you.
I don't talk much, but what I say is true!"

Wise rule indeed! Man would do well to live thereby.²

---

1. We are told in an anonymous "note de l'éditeur" that "on a justement blâmé cette expression, *le greffier solaire;* mais ... à cela près, la fable mérite d'être conservée." (The pithy judgment appears in a brief selection of Houdar de La Motte's fables appended to the works of Florian [see pp. 100–101]: *Fables de Florian, suivies des poèmes de Ruth et de Tobie, et autres poésies, de Galatée et d'Estelle; des idées sur nos auteurs comiques, des lettres et du théâtre; de Myrtil et Chloé, et d'un choix de fables de Lamotte,* p. 549). At least one of those to ridicule the prosaic expression was Louis Fuzelier, in scene xi of his parody of La Motte's fables, *Momus fabuliste, ou les Nôces de Vulcain* (see pp. 72–73).

2. Houdar de La Motte was certainly not the first French fabulist to expand, albeit modestly, the personnel of the fable by adding to its

traditionally natural protagonists—animal, human, even allegorical—the occasional inanimate artifact, as here. La Fontaine, after all, had breathed life into a pair of pots ("Le Pot de Terre et le Pot de Fer"), and even he had had his models. The practice, however, was still much the exception in the eighteenth century, and examples like the present one tend to stand out. (In this collection the reader will see them become progressively more common: evidence of later fabulists' attempts to show their originality by bending their time-honored genre to the technological advances of everyday life.) As for the present fable, specifically, it should be noted that our author, not withstanding his pride in his originality ("pour moi j'ai encore mieux aimé prendre le parti d'inventer" ["Discours sur la fable," in

Fables nouvelles, p. 53]), was not the first to treat the rivalry between the "modern" clock and the traditional sundial, nor would he be the last. The earliest example I find of this obviously non-Aesopic scenario is from the pen of the seventeenth-century Italian fabulist Giulio Cesare Capaccio. His "Horologio da ruote, e da Sole" is the first of his brief fables, *Gli apologi di Giulio Cesare Capaccio*. Each of Capaccio's ninety-four apologues—in verse of irregular line lengths, and unrhymed except for the final couplet—is followed by a one-line prose moral, itself expanded upon in exegetical "Dicerie morali intorno a gli apologi," not unreminiscent, in retrospect, of Houdar de La Motte's own philosophical prologues. Since mechanical clocks had been in existence in Europe since about the tenth century, Capaccio's

example may well not be the first. As for a successor to La Motte's fable, see "L'Horloge et le cadran solaire," by an obscure fabulist with a name inversely proportional to his celebrity, Alexandre-Auguste-Donat-Magloire Coupé de Saint-Donat (1775–1836), anthologized in *Le Fablier du jeune âge*, II:65. (The chevalier, "chef d'escadron, chevalier de l'Ordre royal de la Légion d'honneur, de l'Ordre royal et militaire de Saint-Henri de Saxe," and "de plusieurs académies," was author of at least two collections. A number of his early fables were translated into Italian by one Camillo Ugoni [*Favole...*], but I do not know if—by an appropriate literary turnabout—this one was among them.)

La Brebis et le Buisson

Une Brebis choisit, pour éviter l'orage,
Un Buisson épineux qui lui tendoit les bras.
    La Brebis ne se moüilla pas;
Mais sa laine y resta. La trouvez-vous bien sage?

    Plaideur, commente ici mon sens.
Tu cours aux Tribunaux pour rien, pour peu de chose.
Du temps, des frais, des soins; puis tu gagnes ta cause.
    Le gain valoit-il les dépens?

1. I have omitted the fable's twenty-seven-line prologue.

The Lamb and the Brier[1]

Fleeing a storm, a lamb was quick to find
Shelter beneath a beckoning brier. However,
Dry though she was, she left her fleece behind.
    Really now, was she very clever?

You who would run to law, hear my intent:
You rush to court for little, or for less!
    And, though you win, and gain redress,
Is victory worth the woes, time, money spent?

Les Amis Trop d'Accord

Il étoit quatre Amis qu'assortit la Fortune;
    Gens de goût & d'esprit divers.
L'un étoit pour la Blonde, & l'autre pour la Brune;
Un autre aimoit la Prose, & celui-là les Vers.
L'un prenoit-il l'endroit? l'autre prenoit l'envers.
    Comme toujours quelque dispute
    Assaisonnoit leur entretien,
    Un jour on s'échaufa si bien,
    Que l'entretien devint presque une lutte.
Les poumons l'emportoient; Raison n'y faisoit rien.
    "Messieurs," dit l'un d'eux, "quand on s'aime,
Qu'il seroit doux d'avoir même goût, mêmes yeux!
    Si nous sentions, si nous pensions de même,
Nous nous aimons beaucoup, nous nous aimerions mieux."
Chacun étourdiment fut d'avis du problème,
Et l'on se proposa d'aller prier les Dieux
    De faire en eux ce changement extrême.
      Ils vont au Temple d'Apollon
      Présenter leur humble Requête;
      Et le Dieu sur le champ, dit-on,
      Des quatre ne fit qu'une tête:
      C'est-à-dire, qu'il leur donna
Sentimens tout pareils & pareilles pensées;
    L'un comme l'autre raisonna.
"Bon," dirent-ils, "voilà les disputes chassées."
Oui, mais aussi voilà tout charme évanouï:

The Friends Who Agreed Too Much

    Fortune had fashioned friendship's bonds
About four men of diverse taste and thought.
One favored dark-haired maids; another, blondes.
    One preferred verse; another, prose.
    And when, at times, the four were caught
    In disputatious quid pro quos—
As was, of course, their wont more oft than not—
    One was all "yeas"; another, "noes."
    One day their disagreement grew
Hotter and hotter still, all reason cast aside.
    Lungs bellowed, tongues lashed out, fists all but flew,
Until, "My friends," one of the foursome cried,
    "We love each other far too well to be
So fettered by such individuality.
How much more sweet were all our tastes to coincide,
Were you to think and feel like me, and I like you!"
    They all agreed, and so it was suggested
      That they go pray Apollo, who
      Forthwith granted what they requested,
    Giving the four a single head. (That is,
      Each man, in fact, held onto his,
      But—so to speak—they shared one view:
      Four heads with but a single mind.
What each one thought, so thought the others too.)
    "How wonderful!" our friends opined.
"No more disputes, no fights, no bitterness..."

Plus d'entretien qui les amuse.	True. But the charm had fled as well! No more
Si quelqu'un parle, ils répondent tous, "Oui."	The joys of conversation for our four.
C'est desormais entr'eux le seul mot dont on use.	To every question, just one answer: "yes"!
L'ennui vint: l'amitié s'en sentit alterer.	Boredom ensues. Soon friendship is its victim.
Pour être trop d'accord nos gens se désunissent.	The bonds grow thin... The friends are barely speaking...
Ils chercherent enfin, n'y pouvant plus durer,	Desperate, at length, each one goes seeking
Des amis qui les contredissent.	Somebody—anybody—who will contradict him.
C'est un grand agrèment que la diversité.	Diversity gives life its spice.
Nous sommes bien comme nous sommes.	Each one is as he is; that should suffice.
Donnez le même esprit aux hommes;	Let you be you and me be me.
Vous ôtez tout le sel de la société.	Make everyone the same? Too high the price:
L'ennui nâquit un jour de l'Uniformité.	Society condemned to sheer ennui!

Louis Fuzelier   Momus Fabuliste, ou les Nôces de Vulcain (1719)

Hardly one of the better-known French playwrights of the eighteenth century, Louis Fuzelier was, nonetheless, one of the more prolific, if not, indeed, the most.[1] "Sa carrière dramatique s'étend sur cinquante ans, et l'on peut considérer sa production comme la plus féconde du siècle." (See Michel Gilot's entry on him in Jean Sgard, *Dictionnaire des journalistes (1600–1789)*, p. 164.)[2] To be sure, little of this impressive production was devoted to serious and weighty subjects or to the "noble" genres. While a number of Fuzelier's works were performed at the Opéra, the Théâtre des Italiens, and the Théâtre-Français—including an undistinguished five-act tragedy, *Cornélie, vestale* (1713) (ostensibly a reworking of a youthful opus by academician-historian Charles-Jean-François Hénault), the majority of his ballets, parodies, and divertissements of all kinds were staged at the Opéra Comique and—his numerous marionette playlets especially—at the more popular, not to say proletarian, *théâtres de la foire* in and around Saint-Germain. Many of the latter were written in collaboration with his far more illustrious colleague René Lesage, with whom Fuzelier had a particularly close association, and with the semi-anonymous but very productive playwright known only as "d'Orneval," while he counted among his musical collaborators some of the more prominent composers of the day.[3]

Fuzelier was born in Paris in either 1672 or 1674.[4] In addition to his copious theatrical works, he wrote a large number of articles for the *Mercure de France* and served as the editor of that journal from 1744 until shortly before his death in Paris, on September 19, 1752. While not primarily a fable writer, he is of interest in this collection for one of his more fanciful theater pieces, *Momus fabuliste, ou les Nôces de Vulcain*. The one-act comedy, in the tradition of Boursault's Aesop plays (see pp. 49–50), puts on stage the mythological Momus, personification of ridicule, who spouts fables in *vers libres* to accompany and enliven his prose dialogue. Unlike Boursault's Aesop, however, he does so as a practical expedient. Jupiter, it seems, has forbidden him to express his satiric wit in "discours," and so he will invent the fable: "Inventons des fables... Ne nommons pas les Dieux, mais empruntons hardiment pour eux les noms des animaux, des hommes, tout cela est égal.... Oüi, devenons *Fabuliste* puisqu'on me contraint de l'être; je n'ai que cet expedient pour soulager ma bile & pour frauder impunément la loi qu'on vient de me faire" (sc. iv). Fuzelier turns his fiction to his own satiric purpose, namely to parody the often pretentiously philosophical fables of rival Houdar de La Motte, published the same year (see pp. 63–65), making fun of those fabulists who would "servir de la métaphysique dans une fable" (sc. xv).[5]

The plot of the comedy is summarized in detail, along with its specific parodic elements, in the *Journal literaire*, XI (1720): 62–70. The anonymous critic lets himself get carried away a little when he likens the author's public sport of La Motte to Aristophanes' ridicule of Socrates before the Athenians (p. 62); but one would have to agree with his judgment that, while Fuzelier's pointed satire is amusing, his own fables are less well crafted that those of his victim, for all their philosophizing: "Nous croions... qu'il devoit faire les siennes avec plus de soin" (p. 69).

The text of *Momus fabuliste* contains ten fables. The one translated here is not part of the text itself, but concludes the author's preface (which contains also two other brief fables) as proof to the fickle public, as he says, "que j'ai l'honneur de le connoître & par consequent que ses bontez ne m'empêcheront pas de le craindre."

1. Like that of many of his contemporaries, the author's name appears in a number of incarnations; among them: Fuselier, Fusellier, and Fusillier.

2. The assertion is corroborated by Gilot's detailed listing of his works, as well as by the 206 titles under his name in Clarence Brenner, *A Bibliographical List of Plays in the French Language (1700–1789)*.

3. The most celebrated was Jean-Philippe Rameau, who composed the music for *Les Indes galantes*, one of Fuzelier's many *ballets héroïques*, originally performed in 1735 and one of the author's more enduring works, thanks no doubt in large part to that music. For a selection of the collaborations with Lesage and d'Orneval, see their *Théâtre de la*

foire. Fuzelier's contributions appear in volumes II, III, VI, VII, and VIII, where they are identified, in typical eighteenth-century fashion, simply as the work of "Monsieur F***."

4. Sources differ. See Gilot's entry in Sgard, *Dictionnaire des journalistes*.

5. Though by no means the only butt of Fuzelier's satire, La Motte was one of his favorites. Gilot cites several other examples (Sgard, *Dictionnaire des journalistes*, p. 166). To them should be added his *Discours à l'occasion d'un discours de M. D. L. M. sur les parodies*, whose initials thinly veil "Monsieur de La Motte."

Le Chat & les Sapajous

Un Matou tricolor avoit à son service
Deux ou trois Sapajous voüez à ses plaisirs:
 Le soin d'occuper ses loisirs
 Leur fournissoit de l'exercice.
Par mille jeux badins qu'ils changent tous les jours
 Chacun à l'envi s'étudie
 De lui donner la Comedie.
 Lorsqu'il est content de leurs tours
Le Rominagrobis fait pate de velours:
 Mais si l'un de nos Pantomimes
Se dément une fois, l'impatient Matou
 Etend la griffe & prend pour ses victimes
 Les oreilles du Sapajou.

 Poëtes, vous qui sur la Scene
 Suivez Thalie & Melpomene,
Des faveurs du Public ne vous targuez jamais:
 Il aplaudit tant qu'on l'amuse,
Vient-on à l'ennuier, près de lui rien n'excuse,
Aujourd'hui de l'encens & demain des siflets.

The Cat and the Monkeys

 A tomcat, colored calico,
Kept monkeys—two or three—to do his pleasure.
 Their task: to entertain his leisure
 With playful trick and artful show
Culled daily from their endless repertory,
 Each minion bent—so goes the story—
On pleasing him with comical distraction.
Now, when they did so to his satisfaction,
Sire Puss would tender velvet paw, content.[1]
 But let one of our simian mimes
 Fail to provoke his merriment—
 As might, indeed, occur betimes—
And cat's claw wrought its wrath on monkey's ear!

My message, Poets of the stage, is clear:
You who serve Thalia and Melpomene,
Trust in the Public's favor to your sorrow:[2]
 Amuse, and be admired; but be
 A trifle tiresome, and... *fini!*
Today, applause; whistles and hoots tomorrow.

1. Spelling variant (or error) notwithstanding, Fuzelier's allusion is to Rabelais's pompous old cat, Raminagrobis (*Pantagruel*, Book 3, chapter 21), whose name was later used by La Fontaine in three of his *Fables* ("Le Chat, la Belette et le petit Lapin," "Le vieux Chat et la jeune Souris," and "La Ligue des Rats"). The picturesque ex-

pression "faire patte (here: 'pate') de velours," which I have rendered rather literally, is still a common idiom meaning to draw in one's claws.

2. Two of the nine mythological Muses, Thalia and Melpomene presided, respectively, over comedy and tragedy.

Delaunay Recueil de Fables (1732)

Information is hard to come by concerning the writer known simply as "Delaunay"—or "De Launay"—with or without the title of "M(onsieur)." Even, apparently, the good gentleman's first name. Though well enough known in his own time and after to have been modestly performed, published, and even occasionally republished, he remains no less an enigma. Especially puzzling is the fact that, despite this semianonymity, the dates of his life—1695 to 1751—seem, indeed, to be a matter of record.[1] It is also known that he served for a time as secretary to Philippe de Bourbon, the Prieur de Vendôme, a position previously held by another dramatist, Jean Palaprat.[2]

The only other specific facts I can offer are those concerning the author's three extant comedies: *La Vérité fabuliste*, one act, in prose; *Le Paresseux*, three acts, in verse; and *Le Complaisant*, five acts, in prose.[3] A fourth comedy, *L'un pour l'autre*, one act, in verse, first performed on June 18, 1805, is incorrectly attributed to Delaunay in volume 8 of the *Fin du Répertoire du Théâtre*

Français.[4] In addition, the catalogue of the Bibliothèque Nationale lists under the works of our dramatist an apparently posthumous volume of verse, *Poésies diverses de société,* by "M. de L∗∗∗"(London: La Compagnie, 1767), but I cannot vouch for its authenticity.[5]

The most significant of Delaunay's three plays from our point of view is *La Vérité fabuliste,* a semi-allegorical comedy superficially reminiscent of the two Aesop plays of Boursault (see p. 50, n. 6), in which Truth—La Vérité—intervening in human affairs, recites a number of illustrative fables at appropriate moments in the action. As a kind of sequel to the comedy in its several editions is the author's *Recueil de fables,* apparently intended—according to La Vérité's final speech—to be recited after the play itself. The collection contains fifty short fables, whose main interest is that, like many eighteenth-century predecessors and followers, Delaunay seems intent on avoiding any thematic debt to La Fontaine, though the formal similarity is obvious and perhaps inevitable. The pair translated here are numbers 17 and 20. The former is typical of the conventional wisdom found in many another animal fable, while the latter gives a brief, sardonic glimpse into the world of the theater.

1. These facts are provided by M. Lepeintre, editor of the *Fin du Répertoire du Théâtre Français,* VI:259–60, in a few brief paragraphs on Delaunay. He does not indicate his source, however.
2. Palaprat (1650–1721) was a minor playwright, best known for his several collaborations with David-Augustin de Brueys, theologian and comic author much admired by Voltaire. (I assume it is only a coincidence that a collection of Brueys's plays, *Le Œuvres de théâtre* [Paris, 1735], contains an introduction to the author's life by one Abbé C.-M. de Launay.)
3. Of these three plays, the first, according to the *Fin du Répertoire du Théâtre Français* (VI:259–60), was performed at the Théâtre des Italiens in 1731, with success; the second, at the Théâtre-Français, on April 25, 1733. The third, supposedly performed in the year of its publication, is of dubious attribution. It bears no author's name in the cited edition of 1733, and was originally thought to be the work of Antoine de Ferriol, comte de Pont-de-Veyle, comic author of some celebrity. It is included, however, in the posthumous collection *Œuvres de théâtre de De Launay.*
4. This play cannot possibly have been written by our author. The first edition was published a half-century after his death (Paris, Masson, 1805) under the name "A. J. Delaunay." A copy of that edition, in the Harvard College Library, bears the author's autograph, thus obviously precluding the possibility that both Delaunays are one and the same.
5. The anonymous collection is ascribed, by the authoritative bibliographer Antoine-Alexandre Barbier, to one "M. de Launay." (See J.-M. Quérard, ed., *Les Supercheries littéraires dévoilées* [augmented edition of Barbier's *Dictionnaire des ouvrages anonymes*], II:467.) There is no indication, however, that he is the Delaunay in question.

Le Mouton, et le Loup

Un Mouton qu'élevoit la fille d'un Fermier,
    De la fenêtre d'un grenier
Voyoit passer un Loup, l'effroi de la contrée:
    "Bonjour donc, Monsieur le Boucher,
    Vous irez à jeun vous coucher,
Si vous comptez de moi ce soir faire curée;
Je me mocque de vous, grincez-moi bien les dents.
    Porte-toison vous fait la nique."
(C'étoit pour un Mouton des discours bien fendants.)
Aussi le Loup lui dit: "Si j'étois là-dedans,
Je te ferois chanter toute une autre musique.
Adieu, conserve-toi, tien-toi gras & dispos,
Tu sortiras peut-être un jour du domicile."

    Etre fier dans un sûr azile,
    C'est être fier mal à propos.

The Lamb and the Wolf

A lamb there was, raised by a farmer's daughter.
    One day, secure within his loft,
He watched the wolf go by. "What ho!" he scoffed,
"Scourge of the countryside! So! Off to slaughter?
    Well now, my butchering knave, what say you?
Whom will you sup on, sire, tonight, I pray you?"
Boldly he twits: "You'll starve if I'm your pleasure!
Snarl, gnash your fangs at this poor woolly lamb;
    For though, forsooth, that's all I am,
Pish tush and pshaw! I mock you at my leisure!"
The wolf: "You'd sing a different tune, I bet you,
Were I within! Well, friend, stay nice and fat:
One day you'll leave... and I'll be there to get you!"

    How vain to boast, "I this... I that..."
    Smug in our safe, snug habitat.

Le Roi de Théâtre, et l'Ecolier

    Un Ecolier avoit dans un Spectacle,
Goûté par-dessus tout un Acteur renommé,
Qui se croyoit lui même un prodige, un miracle
S'estimant beaucoup plus qu'il n'étoit estimé.
    Notre jeune homme en étoit si charmé,
Qu'il donnoit à l'Acteur le mérite & la gloire,
Des vers, des sentimens récités de mémoire,

His Thespian Majesty and the Schoolboy

    A schoolboy, at the theater, much admired
A certain player, known the country round—
An actor, competent but uninspired,
Yet one who thought himself far more renowned
(O prodigy! O genius laurel-crowned!),
    More glorious than, indeed, he was.
The child was charmed, and lavished his applause.

En un mot, il croyoit l'Histrion un Héros,
    C'étoit assurément bien croire!
Voilà comme toujours nous donnons dans le faux.
    Notre Ecolier opiniâtre
    Dans son erreur, dans ses desirs,
Epargna quelque tems sur ses menus plaisirs,
De quoi traiter un jour l'Acteur qu'il idolâtre;
Il l'invite à dîner; le Monarque s'y rend;
    Mais qu'il fut trouvé different!
    Soit qu'il raisonne, ou qu'il folâtre,
Ce Roi n'avoit plus rien, ni de fin, ni de grand,
    Il n'étoit plus sur son Théâtre.
L'Ecolier en rougit... Combien est-il d'objets,
    Qu'il ne faut jamais voir de près.
On riroit bien souvent du plus grand Personnage,
    S'il découvroit ses propres traits;
Le masque heureusement est pris pour le visage.

For him, those sentiments, those noble lines recited
Sprang from the actor's soul. No simple histrion he!
Nay nay! A hero! (Ah, how our idolatry
    Leads us astray!) At length, the lad, delighted—
    Scrimping his modest pleasures—has invited
Monsieur to dine... Monsieur accepts... But oh,
How different, now, His Majesty! Ah, woe!
    Gone are the wisdom and the wit;
Gone are the grace, the grandeur, the bons mots!
What? Can it be that they were counterfeit,
    Mere products of the stage? Our youth
Blushes to think how foolish he has been.
    Would he had known this simple truth:
Some things look best when not too closely seen.
    How many's the fine seigneur, forsooth,
    Of form and feature commonplace!
But, happily, we see the mask and not the face.[1]

1. One is tempted to conjecture that Delaunay, himself a playwright, is here complaining of the public's adulation of the actor, at the expense of the author whose glorious lines he mouths.

Charles-Etienne Pesselier   Esope au Parnasse (1739)   Fables Nouvelles (1748)

LITERARY historian Emile Faguet seems to be aware of the curious contradiction inherent in his finding Charles-Etienne Pesselier "parfaitement inconnu" and, indeed, "sans doute digne de l'être," on the one hand, and yet, on the other, devoting to him one of his Sorbonne lectures, which would become a chapter in his posthumous eleven-volume *Histoire de la poésie française de la Renaissance au Romantisme*.[1] He explains the apparent anomaly by suggesting at the outset that Pesselier, author of a substantial collection of *Fables nouvelles*, has a certain historical importance as the only writer of his time to have devoted himself exclusively to that genre: "Pesselier a ceci d'intéressant qu'il est un fabuliste exclusivement. Or vous savez qu'ils sont rares à l'époque que nous étudions. Qui trouvons-nous, en effet, comme fabulistes, de Lamotte à Florian? Pesselier, et c'est tout" (*Histoire*, p. 195).

Without proposing the even lesser known Jacques Péras as significant proof to the contrary (see pp. 78–79), we may, however, properly take issue with the eminent historian's assertion on the grounds that Pesselier did, in fact, cultivate other literary interests. While acknowledging (and dismissing) three other works—his *Nouveaux dialogues des morts* (1752), his *Lettres sur l'éducation* (1762), and an ephemeral journal, *Le Glaneur françois*, of which he was coeditor—Faguet seems to have ignored (or, uncharacteristically, not to have known) some two dozen

others;[2] especially three one-act verse plays, one of which, *Esope au Parnasse*, was first performed at the then Comédie Françoise, with some success, on October 14, 1739.[3] More surprisingly, in his brief biographical sketch he fails to mention that Pesselier, a minor official in Louis XV's *ferme*, or tax administration, was the author of the two articles "Ferme" and "Financier" in the *Encyclopédie*; a fact soundly ridiculed by Diderot's celebrated correspondent Friedrich Melchior von Grimm. (See his letter of May 15, 1761, in the *Correspondance littéraire, philosophique et critique*, IV:404 ff.) Pesselier had been selected by the enemies of the comte de Mirabeau to refute the latter's economic theories, and had attempted to do so—with little effect, according to Grimm—in his *Doutes proposés à l'auteur de la "Théorie de l'impôt"* of 1761. Grimm's lengthy discussion centers about these economic questions rather than about Pesselier's literary accomplishments, which he dispatches summarily in his opening paragraph: "Autrefois, M. Pesselier faisait des fables et des dialogues des morts dont il n'est point resté de souvenirs."[4]

Faguet's seventeen-page essay offers little more in the way of actual fact than the dates of Pesselier's birth and death: July 9, 1712, and April 24, 1763.[5] Biographical inadequacies and discrepancies aside, however, it certainly presents the most readily available sampling of his none-too-accessible fables, and surely the most literarily informative. In the dozen examples that he includes from among the 106 of the *Fables nouvelles*—divided into five books, with epilogue—virtually all of which, Faguet assures us, are of Pesselier's own invention, he analyses the fabulist's philosophical leanings (as a follower of Houdar de La Motte), his frequent sentimentalism, typical of the period, and his pleasant, if somewhat long-winded, wit: "Il a du talent; mais il lui manque l'élégance de la concision" (*Histoire*, p. 200). As for Pesselier's subject matter, Faguet calls attention to his frequent use of human characters—in some two dozen fables, by my count—and especially to his affinity for the "fable végétale," a variety for which La Fontaine, in his "Contre ceux qui ont le goût difficile" (*Fables*, II, 1), had assumed appropriate credit: "J'ai passé plus avant: les arbres et les plantes / Sont devenus chez moi créatures parlantes."[6]

The *Fables nouvelles* were neither Pesselier's first nor only venture into the world of the apologue. A decade before, one of his plays, *Esope au Parnasse*, continued the vogue, introduced by Boursault and imitated by Le Noble, Fuzelier, Delaunay, and no doubt others (see p. 50, n. 6), of incorporating fables into the dramatic dialogue, in the mouth of a fictional Aesop or the like. The comedy contains nine such examples. In addition, its predecessor, *L'Ecole du tems*, substitutes a fable, "Le petit

Oranger & son Maître," for the more conventional prologue.[7] In it, the author compares himself to a young orange tree, promising but not yet ready to bear the fruits of maturity, and begs the audience's indulgence for what he seems to indicate is, indeed, his first composed, if not first performed, comedy: "Daignez donc m'accorder un regard favorable / Pour le nouvel Auteur & pour son coup d'essai."[8]

The two fables translated here are samples of Pesselier's briefer muse. The first is taken from *Esope au Parnasse*, scene i, in which Aesop, tipping his hat anachronistically to La Fontaine, temporarily declines Apollo's request that he remain on Parnassus to continue spreading the salutary influence of the fable:

> Moi, rester au Parnasse!
> Ah! Seigneur, ma franchise auroit pour ennemis
> Presque tous les Auteurs à vos ordres soumis.
> Exempt du vain désir d'une gloire incertaine,
> Celui d'entretenir l'ingénu *La Fontaine*
> Dans le sçavant Empire, a seul guidé mes pas:
> Je retourne content.

The second, from *Fables nouvelles* (I, 7), if not artistically unflawed, touches a subject of interest to modern readers.

---

1. See Faguet, *Histoire*, IX, "Les Poètes secondaires du XVIIIe siècle (1750–1789)," chap. 8. (The quotation is from p. 198.) The lecture was originally published in the *Revue des cours et conférences* for 1904–5.

2. The *Catalogue collectif des périodiques* of the Bibliothèque Nationale (II:752) lists the journal in question as consisting of seventeen numbers in four volumes, from 1734 to 1737, somewhat at odds with the citation in Alexandre Cioranescu, *Bibliographie de la littérature française du dix-huitième siècle*, II:1377, no. 49613. (in Cioranescu's listing, Pesselier's titles are numbered from 49609 to 49642.) It is also of interest that the author edited the works of two prolific, if little remembered, playwrights: Jacques Autreau (1657–1745) and Christophe-Barthélémy Fagan (1702–58): the former's *Œuvres* and the latter's *Théâtre*, for which he also provided an "Eloge historique de M. Fagan" (I:i–xvi) and an "Analyse des Œuvres de M. Fagan" (I:xvii–lvii).

3. The two other plays are *La Mascarade du Parnasse* and *L'Ecole du tems*, in *vers libres*, first published, according to Cioranescu (*Bibliographie . . . du dix-huitieme siecle*, II:1377, no. 49615), in 1738, though probably actually written before its published predecessor (see below). Of the three, a brief entry in the *Annales dramatiques, ou Dictionnaire général des théâtres* informs us that *La Mascarade du Parnasse*, being an allegorical play, is "conséquemment sans intérêt"; that *L'Ecole du tems*, despite a lack of unity and "des longueurs," presents a sprightly style and pleasant versification; and that *Esope au Parnasse*, "représentée aux Français, . . . y réussit le jour même que deux autres pièces venaient de tomber" (VII:300).

4. Pesselier was a member of the Académies of Amiens (1749), Anvers (1761), and Nancy, though whether for his economic or literary endeavors is open to conjecture.

5. While there seems to be no question regarding these dates, the places are somewhat controversial. The entry in the *Annales dramatiques* cites Paris in both instances; Cioranescu gives the village of La Ferté-sous-Jouarre as his birthplace; whereas *Dictionnaire des lettres françaises: le dix-huitième siècle* suggests the possibility that it may have been Château-Thierry (II:365). (For that matter, the same source indicates that the author's middle name may have been "Joseph," rather than "Etienne," though that seems unlikely, given the many other references.) For more colorful personal insights the reader might consult the brief paragraph on Pesselier in Voisenon's *Anecdotes littéraires* (see pp. 49; 50, n. 1), in which we are told the following about our author: "C'étoit un homme d'une probité irréprochable, excellent ami et très-bon mari. Ayant obtenu une place qui le mettoit fort à son aise, il attira chez lui toute la famille de sa femme, qu'il adopta. . . . Il est mort jeune, et a laissé une veuve trop peu jolie pour ne pas le regretter longtemps" (pp. 75–76).

6. The fable with plants as characters would be especially exploited a half-century later by Madame de Genlis (see pp. 116–17).

7. This prologue-fable appears on pages 4 and 5 of the 1739 edition of the comedy. It was subsequently included in *Fables nouvelles* (I, 4).

8. Besides all the cited examples, Cioranescu ascribes another fable collection to Pesselier—unmentioned by Faguet or, indeed, by any other sources—one ostensibly published in 1743, in the first volume of a journal entitled *Recueil du Parnasse*. (See Cioranescu, *Bibliographie . . . du dix-huitième siècle*, II:1377, no. 49622.) I have been unable to locate the journal or otherwise corroborate the reference, but suspect that, in all likelihood, such a collection would have contained some of the fables to be published five years later in *Fables nouvelles*.

Le Mouton Réformateur

> Quelque part j'ai lû qu'un Mouton
> Sincere, simple & bonne bête,
> Choqué des mœurs du tems, se mit un jour en tête

The Sheep-Reformer

> I've read about a sheep somewhere—
> A simple beast, sincere and debonair,
> Shocked by the tenor of the times—who had a mind

D'exposer, moderne Caton,
Aux autres Animaux les Dogmes de Platon.
Un Mouton Orateur n'étoit chose ordinaire;
Car on n'ignore pas que malheureusement
L'esprit & le sçavoir habitent rarement
    Avec une humeur débonnaire.
    On affiche donc en tous lieux
    Ce Phénoméne curieux:
    Dans tel Pré, tel jour, à telle heure,
Maître Robin Mouton en public parlera.
Pas un des Animaux ne fut pris en demeure.
Lions, Ours & Renards, Singes, & cætera.
Notre Réformateur, à ce que dit l'Histoire,
    Eut un fort nombreux Auditoire.
    Il tança de chaque Animal,
    Ou le redicule, ou le vice,
    Et même il ne parla pas mal
    Pour un Orateur si novice.
Mais quel fut le succès? Le Malin Auditeur,
Sans songer aux discours, critiqua l'Orateur.
    L'un, c'est la voix, l'autre le geste,
    D'autres le stile, ainsi du reste:
    En un mot, tant fut procedé,
Que le pauvre Mouton, de fatigue excedé,
Regrettant, mais trop tard, l'inutile dépense
    De ses preceptes superflus,
S'en fut, & n'emporta pour toute recompense
    Que des Ridicules de plus.

To play the modern Cato, and reveal
Platonic dogma to the commonweal.
    Now, since it's rather rare to find
Wisdom, and wit, and gentle disposition
Dwelling together—as, alas, you know—
The prospect of a sheep as rhetorician
    Seemed all the more malapropos.
And so, when it was aired from south to north
That such and such a day, and hour, and place,
Good Master Robin Mutton would hold forth,
    Animals all, of every race,
Thronged there to hear—according to the story—
    Our sheep-reformer's oratory.
Bears, lions, foxes, apes, et al., heard him deride
    Their foibles and their faults, and chide
    Sinner and sin, with much to-do.
(And rather well, for a beginner yet untried.)
    But nothing he would say hit true:
The way he spoke was all they listened to.
They judged the speaker and ignored the speech:
Some mocked his gestures; some, his voice, his style;
    And all the rest. In short, by each
Was our poor sheep reviled. After a while,
    Regretting—but too late!—his vain,
Useless attempt, he leaves, never to preach again,
    Fatigue now weighing heavy on him,
    With little to show for all his pain
Save foibles of his own now heaped upon him.

L'Homme & le Lion

    L'Homme eut un jour occasion
De parler librement à sire le lion:
Leur entretien tomba sur la dame lionne.
    "Seigneur," dit l'homme, "en vérité,
Si je puis, sur ce point, m'ouvrir en liberté,
La reine est, selon moi, bien hardie ou bien bonne
    De coucher à votre côté.
Je suis assurément, je suis plus que personne,
Très-humble serviteur de votre majesté;
Mais dans votre ménage, entre nous, je soupçonne
Que vous êtes bien moins aimé que redouté.

"N'est-ce pas devant vous que tout animal tremble?
    Vous êtes un si puissant roi,
    Que vos caresses, ce me semble,
Doivent remplir un cœur moins d'amour que d'effroi:
J'ai peine à concevoir, & comment & pourquoi
La reine a pû former le nœud qui vous rassemble?
Encore si c'étoit pour vivre sous la loi
Que suivent dans Paris tant d'époux que je voi?
Mais quoi, toujours parler, manger, coucher ensemble,
    Et tout cela, de bonne foi;
Je ne puis revenir d'une juste surprise;
Si j'étois votre épouse, ah! Sire, franchement,

Man and the Lion

It happened, once upon a time, that Man
    Engaged King Lion in conversation.
    Eventually the subject ran
To lioness, the queen. "Sire," he began,
"If I may speak without equivocation...
How can milady share her bed with you?
It seems a rather risky situation!
Now, surely I respect, as others do,
    Your Majesty's administration.
    But I suspect, sire, *entre nous*,
That she acts less through love than trepidation.[1]

    "Are you not so omnipotent
That beasts of every stripe cower before you?
Can your caress, however gently meant,
Not make her fear you rather than adore you?
Indeed, I find it odd that she consent,
Of her free will, to live connubially
    With one so rash and truculent.
    If you were wed—milord and she—
Parisian-style: footloose and fancy-free...
But no. Awake, asleep, days, nights—all spent
    Each in the other's company...
Why, if I were your wife, Your Majesty,

Je craindrois éternellement
Que votre majesté, d'un vif amour éprise,
　Ne se trompât d'embrassement,
　Et ne m'étranglât par méprise."

　"Pitoyable raisonnement,"
Répondit le lion; "me prens-tu pour un homme?
　Tu conclurois plus sagement
Que ma femme doit craindre un mauvais traitement."

　Oui, cet être dont on renomme
　Le bon goût & le jugement;
　L'homme, en un mot, que l'on appelle
L'animal raisonnable, est le seul assez vain,
　Assez lâche, assez inhumain,
Pour oser méconnoître & frapper sa femelle.

I fear, whenever you would make
Husbandly love, in proper fashion,
　You well might lose your head with passion
And strangle me, albeit by mistake!"

Lion replied: "Poor reasoning!
What? Am I human? No, but if I were,
　My wife might fear just such a thing:
As Man, what harm would I not do to her!"

　Ah yes, alas and welladay!
That model of good taste, epitome
Of reason: Man... Yes, he and only he,
The "thinking animal"—or so they say—
Is beast enough to scorn his mate, mistreat her...
　Coward enough to dare to beat her.[2]

1. The reader will appreciate, I hope, that my apparent overuse of certain rhymes here and throughout this fable is an attempt to reproduce the effect of the original, which many might consider a weakness rather than a tour de force.

2. The author, more concerned with sentimentality than with scientific fact, paints the animal kingdom here with rather a broad brush.

Many monogamous male primates are certainly seen to cuff their females from time to time. And vice versa. Fortunately, too, for Pesselier's thesis, he does not postulate its converse. Examples abound of females mistreating their mates, especially at the lower end of the zoological scale, in the insect world, where the male, after mating, is distinctly expendable.

Jacques Péras　　Fables Nouvelles (1751)

JACQUES Péras is one of our fabulists about whom virtually no solid biographical information is available, other than what can be deduced from his bibliography. As he himself informs us in "La Nature et la Fortune," the opening fable of his collection: "Un Frontispice, par usage. / D'un nom fameux doit être décoré, . . . / Mais moi qui suis presqu'ignoré, / Le mien n'a pas cet avantage."

Péras was the author of a slim volume of *Fables nouvelles,* completed (according to the date of the royal imprimatur) before October of 1748 and first published three years later. Apparently the little collection enjoyed enough success to warrant two subsequent editions in 1769, if not more.[1] Prior to the publication of his fables, Péras had collaborated with the dramatist François Nau (born ca. 1715), on a brief work entitled *Les Dieux protecteurs de la France,* described as "scènes épisodiques; divertissement pour le retour de la campagne du roi." In all likelihood this was a *pièce de circonstance,* like others of similar actuality,[2] in honor of Louis XV's return to Paris from a victorious campaign in Alsace, during the War of the Austrian Succession. Péras's collaboration with Nau is of interest—even if its significance cannot be documented—in that, among his number of popular theatrical and musical pieces, the latter was author of two works obviously inspired by the contemporary vogue of the fable: a one-act comic opera entitled *Esope au vil-*

lage—whose title, at least, recalls Boursault's pair of Aesop plays (see pp. 49–51)—and *Les Fables de La Fontaine mises en chansons, vaudevilles et pots-pourris.* The frustrating lack of dates on these works, however, makes any question of direct influence on Péras strictly conjectural.

Evidence points to the possibility that Péras, if not himself a scholar, in all likelihood frequented scholarly circles. Among a few generally anonymous dedications—"Mademoiselle C✶✶✶," "Madame L✶✶✶," etc.—one finds the names of three eminent contemporary sinologists. The fable "Le Strass et les Pierres Fines" (II, 2)—an apologue that owes its subject to the recent development of artificial gems by a German jeweler named Strass (or Strasser)—is dedicated to "Messieurs Deguignes et Deshautesrayes" (i.e., Joseph de Guignes [1721–1800] and Michel-Ange-André Le Roux Deshautesrayes [1724–95]), "élèves de feu M. Fourmont" (i.e., Etienne Fourmont [1685–1745]), whose death shortly before moved Péras to note that the teacher was already achieving immortality through the distinguished work of his two students. More substantive "proof" of Péras's own erudition is a *Dictionnaire anatomique latin-français,* cited in the *Dictionnaire des lettres françaises* as dating from 1753, but whose existence I cannot otherwise corroborate.

Among his eighteenth-century fabulist confrères, Péras distinguishes himself by the brevity and directness of most of his fables. As he himself observes, he is more concerned with the truth of his message—usually quite cynical—than with the medium that clothes it. "Les Vers," he protests, "ne sont pas ma manie" (Epilogue, Livre Premier). He stands out, too—like more celebrated predecessors Furetière and Houdar de La Motte (see pp. 40–42, 63–65), to whom he seems to make less-than-sympathetic veiled allusions in his verse prologue—by his lack of specific indebtedness to La Fontaine for choice of subjects. In a not-too-original metaphor Péras describes himself as a "gleaner," who comes to pick up the last few grains left after the envious "foragers" have made off with most of La Fontaine's leavings.[3]

Fables nouvelles is composed of forty-seven animal and allegorical fables divided into three books of quite uneven lengths. Besides the prologue, and the epilogue of the first book already cited, the entire collection contains a second brief epilogue, in which the author, addressing his Muse, and adducing the difficulty of the fable genre, warns her not to be disheartened by the critics, but—moralist that he is—to be spurred on by their "esprit caustique." Succeeding editions of his work, mentioned above, would seem to indicate that his pessimism was unfounded.

The following numbers, from the 1751 edition, are translated here: I, 11; I, 19; I, 20; II, 16; and III, 8.

1. The Bibliothèque Nationale has two copies dating from that year, apparently separate editions, given the differing number of pages and other details. (A copy of one of these editions is also in the British Museum, with ten manuscript pages of "Fables diverses" appended to it.) In addition, a standard eighteenth-century French bibliography cites the work with the dates 1754–61 and 1768 (see *Dictionnaire des lettres françaises: le dix-huitième siècle*, II:362), but I have been unable to verify the citation.

2. For example, the *Ballade au roi à son retour triomphant*, of the same date, by Alexis Piron (see pp. 97–98).

3. The metaphor would continue to be a favorite among La Fontaine's followers. It provides the basis, for example, of "Le Glaneur et le Moissonneur" of Anatole de Ségur (see pp. 151–52), the first fable in the third book of the Hetzel edition of 1864.

Le Rossignol

   Un Rossignol depuis long-tems
    Avoit contracté l'habitude
De vivre seul, & dans sa solitude
Chaque saison lui sembloit un Printems.
Pour son malheur il vit une fémelle,
Elle lui plut; les soupirs, les soucis
   Vinrent lui troubler la cervelle.
Ce n'est pas tout. Il épousa la Belle,
Et quelque tems après, nâquirent des petits.
Le pauvre Rossignol ne fut plus connoissable,
   Du soin des siens il se vit tourmenté,
   Et par l'apas d'un plaisir peu durable
    Il perdit sa tranquillité.

The Nightingale

   A nightingale, for many a moon,
    Had lived contented with his state
    Of solitary celibate.
Each year was but one endless spring. But soon
He met a maiden nightingale—ah, woe!—
And fell in love. What torments racked his breast,
   Muddled his brain! What's worse, our Beau
Married the Belle, and... Well, you know the rest:
Little ones don't take long! Soon one, two, three...
   No more the gleeful songster he!
How to support his brood? No peace, no leisure...
Gone now the easy life, the fancy free...
Gone, for the fleeting joys of fleshly pleasure.

Les Deux Chats & la Souris

   Une Souris trotoit dans un Grenier,
    L'Imprudente l'échappa belle;
    Deux Chats y faisoient sentinelle.
    Un d'eux l'apperçut le premier,
Mais il en étoit loin & ne pouvoit l'atteindre.
Voyant son Compagnon prêt à sauter dessus,
"Tu crois donc la tenir," dit-il, "c'est un abus."
   Il miaule, moins pour se plaindre,
    Que pour avertir la Souris
Qui sçut agilement profiter de l'avis.
   Ici je vous trace l'esquisse
   D'un envieux difficile à guérir;

The Two Cats and the Mouse

   A brazen mouse was scurrying about—
In, out, here, there—atop a grain loft, where
There dwelt as well two sentinels: a pair
   Of cats! The mouse was not without
Good luck: one cat caught sight of him, but being
   Rather too far, had to renounce
Her prey. However, in a moment, seeing
   Her neighbor readying to pounce,
She squeals: "Nay, nay! He's not for you!" And
             with a "meow"
Alerts the mouse, who, happily, knows how
   To take the hint. And off he scampers.

Le bien d'autrui fait son supplice,
Il ne veut pas que son voisin jouisse
D'un bonheur dont lui-même il ne sauroit jouir.

This fable shows how envy hampers
Human affairs. Some jealous souls, I vow,
Feel it's their bounden duty to refuse
To let their friends enjoy what they can't use.

La Tourterelle Qui A Perdu Sa Compagne

Une Tourterelle,
Le vrai symbole de l'Amour,
Avoit perdu sa Compagne fidèle;
Elle en gémissoit nuit & jour.
Pour adoucir son Etat déplorable,
Ses voisins, ses amis vinrent la supplier
De se choisir parti sortable,
Tous prétendoient l'associer;
Mais la Tourterelle plus sage
Leur dit: "L'Amour ne doit plus m'enflamer;
Ce seroit folie à mon âge,
Si je me laissois charmer;
Je ne suis plus au tems d'aimer,
Je dois rester dans le veuvage."
La Tourterelle avoit bien du bon sens.
Les femmes aujourd'hui ne pensent pas de même;
Et l'on en voit plus d'une à soixante & dix ans
Réfuter son systême.

The Turtledove That Lost Her Mate

A certain turtledove—
Symbol, if ever one there was,
Of long-enduring human love—
Moaned, groaned, lamented night and day. The cause?
Her faithful spouse had died. To calm her state,
Her friends came round and pleaded, for her good,
That she accept another mate
And put aside the woes of widowhood.
But she, far wiser, said: "Don't be absurd!
The joys of love are for a younger bird.
I'll do what aging widows should:
At my age it's a little late
To burn with passion—even if I could!
And so I'll just accept my fate."
Our dove's reply made sense, no doubt about it,
Though women of today would seem to doubt it!
Many of threescore years and ten, before our eyes,
Behave quite otherwise.

L'Enfant & le Serpent

Un jeune Enfant
Vit un Serpent,
Il s'en saisit le croyant une Anguille.
Qui se méprend
Légérement
Doit-il subir le moindre châtiment?
L'Animal vénimeux se plie & se tortille,
Et méchamment pique l'Enfant au bras,
Qui lors sans défense & sans armes
N'eut d'autre recours qu'à ses larmes;
Il fuit tout effrayé, mais n'a pas fait vingt pas
Qu'il tombe & trouve le trépas.

The Child and the Snake

A youngster caught
Sight of a snake,
And picked it up because he thought
It was, in fact,
An eel. Now, ought
One suffer for so simple a mistake?
The creature coiled... uncoiled... attacked,
And bit his arm... The venom spread...
Frightened and quite without defense—
Save for his tears—the poor tot turned and fled.
The consequence?
In less than twenty paces he fell dead.

Quoi! punir ainsi l'innocence!	Shame! Must it be that innocence
Je suis irrité de ce trait.	Pay dear for mishap thus ensuing?
La Nature avec sa prudence	Nature, for all her providence,
Néglige trop ce qu'elle a fait.	Blindly abandons man to his undoing.

Le Papillon & l'Araignée

Pour suppléer aux besoins de sa vie
Une Araignée assidument filoit:
Un Papillon la taxoit de folie
    En lui disant qu'il suffisoit
      D'avoir chaque jour sa pitance,
        Et que demain
      Améneroit son pain:
"Accumuler est une extravagance,
Jouissons du présent, cela seul est certain;
    L'avenir peut ne jamais être,
    A quoi bon tant se tourmenter?"
    Le Papillon parloit en maître;
Mais ne je sçais si l'on doit l'imiter.

The Butterfly and the Spider

A butterfly approached a certain spider,
    Busily spinning all day long,
      And, nastily, to chide her,
Told her she must be mad, that it was wrong
    To work so hard: "Life is too tough...
    Something will always come along...
      Enough's enough!
      Live for today!
    Tomorrow? Bah! Let come what may!
Why hoard more than you use if you don't need it?..."
Such was the butterfly's advice. Perhaps he knew
    Whereof he spoke. Yet I would caution you
    Please to think twice before you heed it.

Jean-Louis Aubert   Fables Nouvelles (1756–73)   Fables et Œuvres Diverses (1774)

WHEN THE winds of enlightenment blew over the eighteenth century, not everyone bent to the breeze. The philosophical liberalism of the Encyclopédistes had many opponents; some, mere fatuous naysayers of the type caricatured in Beaumarchais's Bartholo; others, more implacable enemies for whom philosophy was not to be the exclusive domain of the philosophes.[1] Not a few of both types—and especially of the latter—were to be found, understandably, in the ranks of the Church. One of the more antagonistic was the abbé Jean-Louis Aubert. Little remembered today, Aubert enjoyed an importance in his own time disproportionate to his talents, and owed it primarily to two things: his journalistic accomplishments and his fables. A self-styled literary critic, he held positions of importance on a variety of prominent journals of the period, from which he was able to snipe at the Encyclopédistes, in general and in particular, counting among his many adversaries the celebrated novelist-playwright-memorialist Marmontel, the prolific critic La Harpe, the intellectually ubiquitous Grimm, and even, in time, Voltaire himself. As a fabulist he gave vent to a rather overinflated creative ego, producing several editions of quite acceptable, if not exceptional, fables which, for all their pedestrianism, enjoyed a considerable popularity in the France of his day, and were, in fact, translated into a number of European languages.[2]

Aubert was born in Paris on February 15, 1731, son of a noted violinist and composer, Jacques Aubert.[3] After studies at the Collège de Navarre he took orders, probably as much for social as for religious reasons, if not more, since a clerical collar was, for those without aristocratic birth or personal fortune, often a passport to worldly success. In 1751 the twenty-year-old Aubert, while gaining a modest reputation with occasional verse published in the Mercure de France, began his journalistic career by authoring a regular column of literary criticism in the then-new Affiches, Annonces et Avis divers (also known as the Affiches de Paris), a basically commercial publication to which he contributed erudite and frequently truculent articles over the next several decades.[4]

Of greater importance, journalistically, was Aubert's association with the so-called Journal de Trévoux, the highly visible Jesuit-run organ that often found itself in more or less violent opposition to the Encyclopédie and its philosophes. Thanks to the influence of one of his many protectors, the comte de Vergennes, Aubert succeeded to the directorship of that important reactionary journal in 1768, and held the strategically useful post until 1775.[5] He reached the pinnacle of his journalistic career, however, when, in 1774, much to the stupefaction of Voltaire and his cohorts, he was named director of the venerable and most prestigious Gazette de France, the semiofficial governmental organ founded in 1631 by Théophraste Renaudot. He would serve in that capacity until 1786, and again briefly from 1791 to 1792.

In addition to fulfilling his various journalistic obligations, Aubert occupied a chair in French literature at the Collège Royal, created especially for him in 1773 by another of his influential patrons, the duc de la Vrillière, through whose intercession he was also named to the powerful position of *censeur royal*. Toward the end of his life he gradually divested himself of his several professional posts. Opportunistic royalist that he was, he had great difficulty in adjusting to the last revolutionary years of his life, and died in Paris on November 10, 1814.

One of Aubert's earliest efforts to earn a literary reputation was a somewhat-impetuous youthful attempt to lock theoretical horns with Rousseau, in the musical squabble known as the "Querelle des Bouffons," that pitted partisans of French and Italian opera against one another during the early 1750s. His pro-French *Réfutation suivie, détaillée des principes de M. Rousseau, de Genève, touchant la musique françoise* was, more than likely, not a little indebted to his musician-father's reflections on the subject.[6] The work, however, failed to win him the desired recognition, and the ambitious young abbé turned to the ever-popular genre which could almost always be counted on to confer at least passing celebrity: the fable.[7] Since Aubert's fables were quite popular in their day—with the public, if not always with the critics, some of whom, at least, probably had their personal axes to grind—they were published in a number of editions. Cioranescu (*Bibliographie ... du dix-huitième siècle,* I:254) lists only three editions in the author's lifetime: *Fables nouvelles* (1756); a "nouvelle édition" of the same, "augmentée de plusieurs pièces" (1764); and *Fables et œuvres diverses,* also a "nouvelle édition" (1774), including his eight-canto poem *Psyché* and "le discours de l'auteur pour l'ouverture de ses leçons au Collège Royal."[8] There are, besides, at least two others, both in the catalogue of the Bibliothèque Nationale: a *Fables nouvelles* of 1761, reviewed in the *Mercure de France* (February 1762); and another of 1773, reviewed in the same journal (August 1773), where it is identified as a "quatrième édition, considérablement augmentée."

Of particular interest are the two above-mentioned reviews. Separated by a decade, they offer widely differing perspectives onto Aubert's talents as a fabulist. The first (1762), sounding almost as if it could have been written by the author himself, suggests his position as a rival of La Fontaine, and gives a lengthy apologia of his self-justificatory *avant-propos,* in which he affirms that "quelque réputation qu'un Auteur ait acquise dans un genre, on doit avoir le courage, quand on s'y sent appellé [*sic*] par la Nature, de courir à son tour la même carrière" (p. 63). The second (1773), sounding more as if it had been written by Grimm—or any other of Aubert's many enemies—gives his fables the shortest of shrift. Its anonymous author declares, pointedly, that multiplicity of editions is no proof of literary worth, and that, in effect, most of the abbé's fables "n'ont aucun sens" (p. 75). He goes on to dissect a number of them to disprove Aubert's own rather fatuous assertion that, unlike La Fontaine, a mere copier, he, at least, had invented the subjects of all his fables. Even so, the acidulous critic is obliged to concede that a half-dozen or so are "assez agréables," including among these chosen few "Le Livre de la Raison," one of the three translated here, about which he says, with unequivocal praise: "Il n'y a personne qui ne voulût avoir fait cette fable," and wishing that there were more like them (p. 87).

Of the several editions of Aubert's fables I have been able to consult the first (1756), numbering 50; the third (1764), containing 122, divided into six books; the fourth (1773), containing 160, divided into eight books; and the last (1774), with a total of 163 (along with eleven "imitations" of the Latin fables of his older contemporary, the fabulist-prelate François-Joseph Desbillons). None of the three translated in the present collection is included in the original 1756 edition of *Fables nouvelles.* "Le Chardonneret," "L'Ane et Son Maître," and "Le Livre de la Raison" all appear in the six books of the 1764 edition, numbered I, 18; II, 6; and III, 4, respectively. (They also figure in the two remaining editions, with different numeration; I cannot, however, say if any or all of them appear in the edition of 1761.)

---

1. Bartholo voices his reactionary *profession de foi* in *Le Barbier de Séville* (1775), in his dyspeptic exchange with his ward Rosine:

> ROSINE: Vous injuriez toujours notre pauvre siècle.
> BARTHOLO: Pardon de la liberté: qu'a-t-il produit pour qu'on le loue? Sottises de toute espèce: la liberté de penser, l'attraction, l'électricité, le tolérantisme, l'inoculation, le quinquina, l'Encyclopédie et les drames... (I, iii)

2. See Béatrice Fournel's entry on Aubert in Jean Sgard, *Dictionnaire des journalistes (1680–1789),* p. 17.

3. Aubert senior (1689–1753) was "premier musicien" of the Académie Royale de Musique and "protégé" of Louis Henri, duc de Bourbon and prince de Condé, Louis XV's prime minister. If one source can be believed, young Aubert himself may also have been a composer of sorts (see below, n. 6). At any rate, the father's connections at court would certainly serve the son well during his career, affording him the protection of several important figures.

4. In 1752 he also founded a provincial counterpart of the same journal, the *Annonces et Affiches de province,* which had less literary ambition, however.

5. The official name of the *Journal de Trévoux,* founded in 1701, had been *Mémoires pour servir à l'histoire des sciences et des arts.* Under his direction, Aubert, in an effort to enhance and expand its appeal, renamed it the *Journal des sciences et des beaux arts.*

6. The young Aubert, however, may have been a passably proficient musician himself, and may even have composed music for a pair of his own works: a three-act verse drama, *La Mort d'Abel,* and a dramatic poem, *Le Vœu de Jephté.* (See the *New Grove Dictionary of Music and Musicians,* I:683. The entry, however, not rigorously accurate in some of its other details, may be suspect.)

7. Besides the several works mentioned, Aubert also authored or coauthored a half-dozen others of varied form and inspiration. (See Alexandre Cioranescu, *Bibliographie de la littérature française du dix-huitième siècle,* I:254.)

8. Aubert had already published his *Psyché* (or *Psiché*) previously, "pour servir de suite à son recueil de fables." That publication would give Grimm a much-relished opportunity to savage one of his bêtes noires: "Je défie le lecteur le plus intrépide de lire plus d'un chant de cette misérable *Psyché*; s'il le tente, je le tiens pour suffoqué d'ennui et de dégoût." What annoyed Grimm most—and not without justification—was Aubert's self-comparison to La Fontaine: "Il faut voir en-core avec quelle fausse modestie il se compare à La Fontaine . . . Il nous observe aussi que la gloire de mettre en vers le roman de *Psyché* lui était réservée, La Fontaine n'ayant osé l'écrire qu'en prose." And Grimm concludes with a typical coup de grâce: "Il ne manque à l'abbé Aubert que d'être un homme considérable pour être complètement ridicule." (See Friedrich Melchior von Grimm, *Correspondance littéraire, philosphique et critique*, VIII:408–9.)

Le Chardonneret

Un chardonneret jeune et beau,
Leste, brillant, adroit, mais un peu trop volage,
    Fut esclave dès le berceau.
    Une belle, au printemps de l'âge,
    Etoit folle de cet oiseau.
    Il n'en aimoit pas plus la cage.
    Il demandoit pour quel forfait
    On l'avoit chargé d'une chaîne?
Et pourquoi, dans deux seaux qu'on suspendit exprès,
Il falloit, achetant ses repas de sa peine,
Que lui, chardonneret, puisât soir et matin?
    Tandis que l'oiseau son voisin,
Un pinson, disoit-il, qui ne le valoit guère,
Exempt de tout travail, libre de tout lien,
Mangeoit, sans le gagner, et se donnoit carrière
    Dans un logis plus vaste que le sien;
Il ne demandoit pas liberté toute entière,
    Mais qu'on adoucît sa prison.
On le fit; on brisa cette chaîne cruelle;
En un brillant palais on changea sa maison.
De joie il composa sur l'heure une chanson;
    On n'en fit jamais de plus belle!
    Le voilà comme le pinson,
Allant, venant, sautant de bâton en bâton,
    Pour ses repas, n'ayant qu'à prendre.
Il n'y fut pas deux jours, qu'il ne put se défendre
    De désirer d'être plus libre encor.
    "Si je pouvois prendre l'essor!
Pourquoi n'a-t-on pas fait cette cage plus haute?
Moineaux qui fendez l'air, que vous êtes heureux!
    Je voudrois voyager comme eux;
Content, à la maison je reviendrois sans faute."
    Il perdit cette fois son temps.
Les vœux de cet oiseau sont ceux de bien des gens.

The Goldfinch

A goldfinch—lovely, brilliant-hued,
    Young, sprightly, but a bit inclined to flit—
    Was bound since birth in servitude:
He was, in fact, the feathered favorite
    Of certain lovely demoiselle
    Still in the springtime of her age.
"What frightful crime did I commit, pray tell?"
Complained the pet, who loathed, withal, his cage,
    Wondering why he had to dwell
Behind its bars, and why he had to sup,
Day in day out, from little pail and cup;
    And why his neighbor-bird was free
To fly about the house—to, fro, down, up—
Though finch of far more vulgar pedigree,
And take his meals in utter liberty.
It wasn't freedom unalloyed he sought;
    Just that he really thought they ought
To make more pleasant his imprisonment.
    And so, indeed, they did. They built
A finer cage to house our prisoner pent,
    A palace-cage all brightly gilt.
At last, like neighbor-finch, gaily he came and went,
    Twittering out his happiness in song—
    Fairer than any he had sung before—
Flitting from stick to stick, gorging on feed galore...
    His joy, alas, was less than two days long;
    For soon he craved his freedom all the more.
    "They should have built the cage high as the sky!
    Then, like the happy sparrows, I would soar,
Splitting the clouds..." And, quickly adding: "By the by,
    Needless to say, I'd come back home again!"
    This time, I fear, our goldfinch said
Too much!... Wasted his breath!... Like many men
Who would do best to stop while they're ahead.

L'Ane et Son Maître

Un âne des plus sots prétendoit faire accroire
Que sa cervelle étoit un trésor de bon sens;
    On en parleroit dans l'histoire:
    Les dieux avoient sué vingt ans
Pour former les ressorts qui jouoient là-dedans.
    Raison, sagesse, esprit, mémoire,
    Il avoit tout en un degré parfait.

The Ass and His Master

An ass, as foolish as an ass can be,
    Boasted to have between the ears
    Such wealth of intellect that he
Was destined to go down in history.
    Surely the gods had sweated twenty years
    To form the workings of so exquisite
A brain as his: memory, reason, wisdom, wit...

Si l'avenir regrette un Socrate baudet,
La race des baudets lui devra cette gloire.
Le galant, enivré de cet orgueil si vain,
    Résistant un jour à son maître,
    Refusa d'aller au moulin:
    Cet emploi dégradoit son être:
    Le beau métier pour un Caton!
    "Ah! je trouve celui-là bon,"
Dit Gros-Jean le meûnier. "Et que prétends-tu faire?"
    "Penser," reprit l'aliboron:
    "Je ne veux plus désormais d'autre affaire.
Faites porter vos sacs à quelque âne vulgaire,
    Et respectez un sage comme moi."
Le bonhomme se tut. "Quelle mouche le pique?"
Disoit-il en lui-même; "il est fou sur ma foi:
Gros-Jean, la tête tourne à ta pauvre bourrique.
    Ce mal lui vient je ne sais d'où.
    Laissons-la penser tout son soûl;
    Et cependant retranchons sa pitance."
Ce parti n'étoit pas trop sot pour un meûnier,
    L'âne bientôt se lassa d'un métier
    Qui ne remplissoit point sa panse.
    Il se plaignit. Gros-Jean tout aussitôt
    Lui dit: "Impertinente bête,
    Me prends-tu pour un idiot?
Quel fruit me revient-il des rêves de ta tête?
Porte ton bât, travaille, et l'on te nourrira."
    Tout en iroit mieux sur la terre
    Si chacun se bornoit à faire
Le métier pour lequel Jupiter l'appela.

He had them all in such profusion that, indeed,
    If future years heap eulogies
Upon some late lamented jackass Socrates,
    This creature will have sired the wondrous breed!
Now then, one day, indulging his vainglorious whim,
    The fop, unbending to his master's will,
    Refused to take him to the mill.
Degrading task! Not for a Cato! Not for him!...
Gros Jean, the miller, took a dim and jaundiced view:
    "Oh? Tell me, then. What do you plan to do?"
"Think!" answered our Aliboron, our philosophe.[1]
    "Go find some common ass to slave for you,
    To haul your sacks and all. I'm through!
My mind deserves respect!" "He must be off
    His feed!" the miller mused. "Soft in the head...
    Daft... Touched... What other explanation...?
    Well, one thing's clear: no work, no daily ration!
Fine! Let him think a bellyful! He won't get fed!"
    Rather well reasoned for a miller, what?
    At any rate, our haughty sot,
    Soon tiring of a trade that fails to fill
    His gut, bewails his hungry lot.
    The miller snaps: "What tommyrot!
    Am I some kind of imbecile?
Impudent clod! Remember what you are!
    It's not to think great thoughts I need you!
So, here's your saddle... Work! And then I'll feed you!"
This world would be a better place by far
If everyone would do—no less, no more—
The task that Jupiter designed him for.

---

1. The author uses traditional names for both his characters. "Gros Jean," literally "Big John," is a typical name for a peasant, dating back at least to the mid-sixteenth century—though popularized by La Fontaine's use of it in his fable "La Laitière et le Pot au Lait" (VII, 10)—and usually attributed to rustics less intellectually astute than Aubert's miller. "Maître Aliboron," used as a nickname for the ass in La Fontaine's "Les Voleurs et l'Ane" (I, 13), may have an even lengthier history. Derived from the hellebore (in Latin, *elleborum*), a powerful medicinal plant known since ancient times, the name came to be commonly used by medieval and Renaissance French writers—Rabelais among them—to indicate a pretentious charlatan. An etymological connection with the name of the Arabian mathematician-philosopher Al-Birouni has also been suggested. (See Jacqueline Picoche, *Nouveau Dictionnaire étymologique du français*, p. 18)

Le Livre de la Raison

    Lorsque le ciel, prodigue en ses présents,
    Combla de biens tant d'êtres différents,
Ouvrages merveilleux de son pouvoir suprême,
    De Jupiter l'homme reçut, dit-on,
    Un livre écrit par Minerve elle-même,
        Ayant pour titre: *La Raison*.
    Ce livre, ouvert aux yeux de tous les âges,
    Les devoit tous conduire à la vertu;
    Mais d'aucun d'eux il ne fut entendu,
    Quoiqu'il contînt les leçons les plus sages.
    L'enfance y vit des mots et rien de plus;
        La jeunesse beaucoup d'abus;
    L'âge suivant des regrets superflus,
    Et la vieillesse en déchira les pages.

The Book of Reason

    Many long years ago, when generous heaven
    Bestowed its wondrous gifts on one and all—
        On creatures great and creatures small—
    They say a truly precious one was given
    By Jupiter to man, a special gift:
A book entitled *Reason*, that Minerva wrote—
        At least, so goes the anecdote.
    But we, in turn, gave it the shortest shrift,
    Each generation spurning, through the ages,
    Lessons that might have made us saints and sages:
    For childhood it was words, and nothing more;
        Youth saw in it a tiresome bore;
    Maturity sighed: "Reason? Ah! What for... ?"
    And old age simply ripped up all the pages.

Jean-Baptiste-Joseph Willart de Grécourt   Fables (1761) (posthumous)

THE ABBÉ de Grécourt was one of those worldly ecclesiastics, not uncommon in French history, who honored their vows more in the breach than in the observance. As a literary figure his less-than-austere demeanor seems mirrored in his extensive output of light, satiric verse, very little of which was published during his lifetime, and even less under his name.[1] Notwithstanding a laudatory obituary in Evrard Titon du Tillet's two-volume *Le Parnasse françois,* appreciating his "assez bon nombre de jolis *Contes* & de *Fables* très-amusantes & d'un excellent goût" (II:785–86), subsequent observers were not usually so generous with their approval, especially of his taste. For N.-L.-M. Désessarts and the compilers of *Les Siècles littéraires de la France, ou Nouveau Dictionnaire historique, critique, et bibliographique,* Grécourt's *contes* were to be singled out as "quelquefois plaisans, mais toujours obscènes," while his epigrams, *chansons,* and fables, although occasionally displaying "de la douceur," were in general "assez médiocres, et d'une poésie faible" (III:329). A century after his death, an entry in the twenty-two-volume *Encyclopédie des gens du monde,* ostensibly penned by comic dramatist E.-T. Maurice Ourry, tarred his work with an even more unequivocal brush: "Ses contes sont souvent plus orduriers que plaisants, et il n'a même su respecter la chaste muse de la fable, dont La Fontaine et tous ses disciples n'avaient jamais outragé la pudeur" (XIII:47). None of which appears especially to have diminished his popularity either throughout his life or, indeed, for several decades thereafter.

According to most sources, Jean-Baptiste-Joseph Willart de Grécourt, descendant of a once well-to-do (and possibly noble) family of Scottish émigrés, was born in Tours in 1683, the youngest of several children.[2] After a solid classical education in Paris, he returned to his native city, where, as nephew of a distinguished churchman and through his widowed mother's intervention, he was awarded a *canonicat* in the church of Saint-Martin de Tours at the tender age of thirteen, first step in what his family intended to be his ecclesiastical career. But, although he was duly ordained, and although he is said to have enjoyed a certain notoriety for some rather indiscreet early sermons, the adolescent abbé showed little inclination for the priestly calling. As Taschereau remarks in what sounds like an understatement, "Son vrai lot était la liberté et le plaisir" ("Poètes du clergé," p. 211).

He was, nonetheless, more than willing to enjoy the material advantages of his sinecure. His modest appointments, as well as the protection of several influential patrons and friends—the duc d'Estrées, the duc d'Agénois, and especially, in his later years, the duc d'Aiguillon, at whose chateau in Véretz he was a semipermanent guest—permitted Grécourt to indulge his penchants for both poetry and the worldly pleasures of Parisian and provincial society.

Both had early earned him a reputation as a free-spirited bon vivant and a facile, irreverant rhymester, though Ourry's characterization of him as "l'un des abbés et des poëtes les plus licencieux du XVIIIe siècle" (*Encyclopédie des gens du monde,* XIII:46) clearly smacks of the bluenose. Closer to the truth is the opinion of no less a kindred spirit than Apollinaire, who, with the perspective of two centuries saw in him rather "un fils spirituel de Béroalde de Verville, de La Fontaine et de Voltaire," admiring, as one might suspect, his "gaîté discrète, sensibilité tempérée, [et] scepticisme aimable" (Grécourt, *L'Œuvre badine,* ed. Apollinaire, p. 6). It was that combination of gaiety, sensitivity, and skepticism that would inform the controversial abbé's life and work, until his death on April 2, 1743.

Unfortunately for bibliographers and scholars, the precise extent of that work has never been easy to determine. Largely owing to Grécourt's refreshingly cavalier attitude toward his own production, much of his verse has been attributed to others, and vice versa. Even the authorship of his best-known poem, the anti-Jesuit satire *Philotanus,* first published in 1720, has not been free from question, though he is generally accepted as its author.[3] The first edition of his *Œuvres diverses* was published in Paris in 1747, with a number of succeeding editions purporting to correct errors and omissions. It is likely that even the so-called *Œuvres complettes de Grécourt,* also supposedly "soigneusement corrigée," is not wholly accurate any more than were its predecessors.

It is in the first volume of that edition that there appears a collection of 118 fables attributed to Grécourt. Twenty-one of them, previously printed in Pesselier's four-volume journal, *Le Glaneur françois* (II:325–47) (see p. 75), constitute, to the best of my knowledge, the only work published under his name during his lifetime. All in all his fables are considerably less racy than his *contes* (Ourry's accusation of *outrage à la pudeur* notwithstanding), and also less varied metrically than the latter, many of which are composed in La Fontainesque *vers libres.* Faguet devotes a brief discussion to the fables (*Histoire,* pp. 294–300), finding them typical of the work of eighteenth-century fabulists, for whom, in his opinion, the body of the fable is usually merely an anecdotal pretext to a philosophical or epigrammatic conclusion. Be that as it may, the eminent historian of French letters agrees that they are "gracieuses, aimables, [et] spirituelles." He might have added that they are also notably original in their dramatis personae, presenting an unorthodox array of characters—animate, vegetal, inanimate, allegorical—many of whom are quite unfamiliar to the La Fontaine repertory.

The pair of examples translated here, neither of which was included in the sampling in *Le Glaneur françois,* are the fortieth and ninety-ninth of the unnumbered fables in volume I of the *Œuvres complettes de Grécourt.*

1. The cleric-poet appears to have had little desire—uncharacteristically, for a man of letters—to see his work in print. Guillaume Apollinaire quotes one of Grécourt's editors in this regard: "Tous ceux qui ont connu particulièrement l'abbé de Grécourt savent combien il était peu entiché du goût favori de nos beaux esprits et de nos savants. Le plaisir d'être relié en veau n'a jamais été le sien." (See Apollinaire's edition, *L'Œuvre badine de l'Abbé de Grécourt*, p. 1.) Still, much of Grécourt's verse came to be known through his own spirited and widely admired recitations, and through manuscripts passed from hand to hand and collected by his friends.

2. Like a number of our fabulists and other literati of the period, his name apparently had a variety of spellings, among them Villart, Veillard, and Vuillart. Apollinaire (Grécourt, *L'Œuvre badine*, ed.

Apollinaire, p. 4) categorically places his birth in 1684, contrary to other sources. As for his background, the family was either "peut-être noble, en tout cas assez aisée" or "très-noble et non moins pauvre," depending on whom one wishes to believe. (See, respectively, Emile Faguet, *Histoire de la poésie française de la Renaissance au Romantisme*, VIII:284; and Jules Taschereau, "Poètes du clergé au siècle de Louis XV," p. 211.)

3. The reader should consult both Alexandre Cioranescu, *Bibliographie de la littérature française du dix-huitième siècle*, II:889, and the "Essai bibliographique" in Apollinaire's volume, which supplement one another, though neither is, in fact, complete. Neither, for example, lists the anonymously edited *Œuvres complettes de Grécourt* cited below.

La Chenille et la Femme

"Chenille, vilain animal,
Qui dans ces bois nous importune,
Qu'à nos arbres tu fais de mal!
Ah, Dieux! je crois en sentir une."
La Chenille ayant entendu
Ce qu'une femme disoit d'elle,
Sans se fâcher, a répondu:
"Ma laideur n'est pas éternelle.
Bien-tôt changée en Papillon,
J'aurai des couleurs admirables,
Du bleu, du blanc, du vermillon,
Et je serai des plus aimables.
Plus d'une Femme, à ce qu'on dit,
Est de moi l'image parfaite,
Chenille au sortir de son lit,
Papillon après sa toilette."

The Caterpillar and the Woman

"Vile beast! Foul caterpillar, you!
See how you harm our trees, and how
You bother and annoy us too...
Ye gods! I think I feel one now!"
The caterpillar, vilified,
Heard what the woman said. However,
Calm and unruffled, she replied:
"I'll not be vile, Madame, forever.
Soon, as a butterfly, my wings
Will be bedecked in liveliest hues;
And, loveliest of Nature's things,
I'll sport my scarlets, whites and blues.
Many's the woman who, 'tis said,
Looks much as I do, by the by:
A caterpillar, from her bed;
From her toilette, a butterfly."

Le Morpion et L'Eléphant[1]

L'Insecte ennemi du grand jour,
Qui sur le mont d'une Déesse,
Osant même avoir son séjour,
Y mord, & pullule sans cesse;
Ce tyran des plus secrets lieux,
Qui dans moins d'une heure est grand-pere,
Et, sans le messager des Dieux,
Tourmenteroit la vie entiere;
Ce petit bourreau, triomphant
De sa qualité prolifique,
Au gros & robuste Eléphant
Insolemment faisoit la nique.
"Quoi donc! il faut un jour entier
Pour préparer ta jouissance!
Je suis amoureux sans quartier;
Si-tôt fini, je recommence."
"Vilain, point de comparaison;
De l'amour apprends les mystères:
Esprit, goût, nouveauté, raison
N'est que dans les préliminaires."

The Crab Louse and the Elephant

Enemy of the sunlight, this
Audacious nit, who dares reside
In goddess-dubbed Mount Veneris,
In numbers ever multiplied;
This itching scourge—anathema—
Tyrant of parts most private, who
Becomes a proper grandpapa
Even before an hour is through;
Who, but for cure Mercuric, would
Torment our being;[2] this pest horrific,
Proud of his virile insecthood
And prowess, in a word, prolific,
Taunted a robust pachyderm:
"Sluggard in love! They say you need
A day to bring your lust to term!
Why, in one day I sow my seed
Dozens of times!" "Listen, you twit,"
Replied the elephant, "the waiting
Gives love its reason, spice, and wit:
The joy's in the anticipating."

Charles-François Panard   Fables *in* Théâtre et Œuvres Diverses (1763)

Reputed author of some eighty comedies, parodies, and comic operas, alone or in collaboration, Charles-François (or François-Charles) Panard (or, indeed, Pannard) was dubbed by the prominent Encyclopédiste, playwright, and academician Jean-François Marmontel, "le La Fontaine du vaudeville, et le père du vaudeville moral."[1] In a verse self-portrait Panard himself admits, with perhaps a touch of false modesty, that he is, in effect, a "passable coupletteur"; and he takes a certain pride in the assertion that, unlike those of his contemporaries, neither his *couplets* nor his satirical barbs have anything immoral about them ("Jamais dans mes chansons on n'a rien vû d'immonde, / . . . Jamais contre quelqu'un ma muse n'a vomi / Rien dont la décence ait gémi") (*Théâtre et œuvres diverses,* I:i-ii).

Panard appears to have been born between the years 1689 and 1694, either in Courville or Nogent-le-Roi, near Chartres.[2] He died—less controversially—in Paris, on January 13, 1765. During his seventy-plus years, besides gaining fame for his comedies and *vaudevilles,* he was a well-known, rather Bohemian frequenter of the various Parisian literary cafés and *sociétés bachiques,* among them

Le Caveau, originally founded by Piron in 1729 and the celebrated haunt of the most appreciated chansonniers of the age. Of his vast array of drinking songs, many of which are included in the *Théâtre et œuvres diverses,* he is especially remembered for a pair of amusingly typical examples of what has come to be called "pattern poetry" (or, more impressively, *carmina figurata*): texts arranged typographically in the shape of what they are supposed to represent. Panard's examples, with which his name is frequently associated, are two wine glasses, the first right side up, the second upside down (see *Théâtre et œuvres diverses,* III:434–35).

Panard's generally brief fables, numbering thirty-six in all—along with numerous *pièces anacréontiques, allégories, contes et maximes, épigrammes et madrigaux,* etc.—are among the "œuvres diverses" in the above-mentioned collection (IV:73–104). "Le Neuf de Chiffre et le Zéro," number 7, is the most amusingly abstract of the group, all the others presenting traditional (though not directly Aesopic) heroes from the animal, vegetal, allegorical, and occasionally human realms.

Le Neuf de Chiffre et le Zéro

Un jour le Neuf de Chiffre au Zéro fit querelle;
"Palsambleu," lui dit-il, "vous nous la baillez belle,
Et vous êtes plaisant, Monsieur le Galfretier,
De vouloir avec nous entrer en parallele,
Vous qui ne valez pas ce qu'on nomme un denier?"
"Cesse," répond Zéro, "cet injuste langage;
 Je me connois, & je sçais bien
 Qu'étant tout seul, je ne suis rien;

The Number Nine and the Zero

One day the zero and the number nine
Were met in quarrelsome debate. "Gadzooks
 And zounds!" the latter mocks, rebukes...
"I say, my good-for-nothing friend! How fine
You are! To dare compare your worth to mine!
 You nought! You utter nullity!"
Zero replies: "Cease your snide calumny!
 I may be worthless, I confess,

Mais les autres de moi tirent grand avantage;
Toi-même qui prétends me faire ici la loi,
 N'est-il pas vrai, dis-moi,
 Que tu vaux neuf fois davantage,
 Quand on me place auprès de toi?"

1. Although, when added to nine, nine times more ("davantage")—i.e., eighty-one—does indeed total ninety, I have taken an obvious liberty, as much with Panard's grammar as with his somewhat-convoluted arithmetic. His conceit, hardly original, recalls several previous incarnations. The most striking is found among the gallant quatrains of Isaac de Benserade (see pp. 46–47). In his *stances* "Sur l'Amour d'Uranie avec Philis" (*Poésies de Benserade*, pp. 165–73), he not only criticizes the apparently lesbian affection of "Uranie" for the beautiful "Philis" but also uses the conceit to express his unabashed sexism:

 Vous estes nos moitiez, avec nous assorties
 Vous formez un beau tout;

When left alone. But, nonetheless,
All of you seem to profit from my touch!
 Why, even you, who twit and chide me,
 Have to admit, you're worth ten times as much
  Standing beside me.'"

 Séparez-vous de nous, vous n'estes que parties,
  Vous n'estes rien du tout.

 Séparez-vous de nous, vous n'estes que des ombres
  Sans force et sans pouvoir.
 Vous estes les zéros, et nous sommes les nombres
  Qui vous faisons valoir.

More prosaic, Richelieu is said to have likened himself—in a moment of false modesty—to a zero, protesting that his only value lay in his proximity to Louis XIII. The exact citation, however, eludes me.

Jean-Jacques-François-Marin Boisard Fables (1773–79)

POSTERITY has not treated Jean-Jacques-François-Marin Boisard—surely one of the more prolific of fabulists if not one of the best remembered—as kindly as the considerable literary success he enjoyed during much of his long life might have led him to expect. Born in the Normandy town of Caen on June 4, 1744, he soon abandoned the legal career that his family had chosen for him, to devote himself to letters.[1] His early efforts were crowned with local laurels in the traditional annual poetry competitions—Palinods—of Caen and Rouen. (See Joseph-André Guiot, *Les Trois siècles palinodiques, ou Histoire générale des Palinods de Rouen, Dieppe, etc.*, I:115–16.) It was this youthful celebrity that earned for Boisard the attention and eventual protection of François-Jean d'Orceau, baron de Fontette, influential member of the Caen aristocracy—*intendant de la Généralité de Caen*—and subsequently chancellor to the comte de Provence, the future Louis XVIII. Thanks to Fontette, with whose family he was to enjoy a lifelong friendship, Boisard, in or about the year 1768, was awarded a post in that prince's retinue, that of *secrétaire du conseil et des finances*. He proceeded to sell that position soon after for a handsome sum, we are told, retaining for a time the honorary title of *secrétaire de Monsieur*, which he shared with the poet-playwright Jean-François Ducis, early French adapter of Shakespeare.[2]

Youthful efforts aside, Boisard was to owe his reputation to several collections of *Fables*. The first appeared in 1773 and consisted of 120 fables equally divided among four books, with four prologues and a final epilogue. It helped earn him election to the Académie des Belles Lettres de Caen—no doubt through the good offices of the *intendant* Fontette, the society's *vice-protecteur*—and,

more significantly, attracted the attention and admiration of no lesser literary lights than Diderot and Voltaire. (See Porquet, "Le Fabuliste Boisard," pp. 13–17.) The latter, in a letter to Boisard (April 20, 1773), praised his "fables . . . pleines d'invention et d'esprit," and made special mention of the young poet's originality and notable lack of direct debt to La Fontaine: "vous n'avez rien imité de personne et c'est un grand mérite après tous les ouvrages que nous avons en ce genre." If Diderot too, was especially laudatory, his celebrated correspondent Grimm was somewhat less so. "Ces Fables n'ont pas fait beaucoup de sensation," he announced to Diderot in his correspondence of April 1777, "d'abord parce que le talent de ce jeune poète laisse encore beaucoup de choses à désirer." But even he felt moved to acknowledge that Boisard, in his choice of subjects at least, was perhaps "de tous nos fabulistes, celui qui a le moins imité son maître," and, at the same time, a worthy stylistic disciple, "celui qui en est le moins éloigné, s'il est vrai qu'une narration aisée et naïve soit le premier mérite de ce genre de poésie." (See Friedrich Melchior von Grimm, *Correspondance littéraire, philosophique et critique*, X:226–27.)

Yet another eminent, albeit dogmatic, critic and journalist of the period, Jean-François de La Harpe, presenting a sampling of Boisard's first collection of fables in the *Mercure de France* (April 1773), echoed Grimm's ambivalence: "Plusieurs fables de M. Boisard peuvent figurer à côté des meilleures qu'on ait faites depuis La Fontaine. On y trouve du naturel, de la précision, un très grand sens, & jamais d'affectation; mais le défaut du plus grand nombre est une moralité vague & trop commune" (pp. 119–20). La Harpe would voice no such reservations, however, when commenting on Boisard's second collection (1777), a reedition of the first four books and a second volume containing four more. "M. Boisard est certainement un des Fabulistes qui ont marché avec le plus de succès sur les traces de l'inimitable La Fontaine. Ses Fables ont le style naturel & facile, & la naïveté propre à ce genre aimable." (See the *Mercure de France* [July 1777].) This 1777 edition, dedicated to the two sons of his protector Fontette, was reprinted in 1779. It was followed a quarter-century later by three additional collections in rapid succession (1803, 1804, 1805), proof, at least, of his continuing popularity. Boisard's entire fable corpus, thirty-three books in all—along with several translations from Horace and assorted light verse—was published in four volumes under the evocative title *Mille et une fables;* a few years later his literary career seems to have come to an abrupt halt.[3]

This facile fabulist—in the opinion of some, perhaps too facile and unselective—had been keenly distressed by the Revolution of 1789 and its results. After his many years of intense productivity and almost-exclusive devo-

tion to a single genre, Boisard retired to a virtually reclusive obscurity in his native Caen, living with his protectors, the family Fontette, until his death on October 10, 1833. For all his former celebrity, the event, we are told by his cynical descendant, passed quite unnoticed. (See François Boisard, *Notices biographiques,* p. 55.)

Many of Boisard's fables—and some of those most preferred by his contemporaries, who enjoyed hearing him recite them at length—tend to be rather wordy and long-winded. The six translated here, however, are representative of a more fleeting and, I think, more attractive inspiration. The first five are taken from the 1773 collection, where they are numbered as follows: II, 6; II, 10; II, 19; III, 23; and IV, 15. The last, "Le Chêne et le Roseau," is not found in that collection or, in fact, in any of the others. It appeared in the 1805 number of the *Almanach des Muses* (p. 161), a popular annual verse anthology published without interruption from 1765 to 1833, where it was ascribed to Boisard, possibly in error.

1. Some sources incorrectly give the year of Boisard's birth as 1743. As a further posthumous ignominy, his name too has not come down unscathed, several bibliographical references citing the fourth of his forenames as "Marius"; and even his contemporary, the feisty pamphleteer Antoine de Rivarol, in a typically sarcastic entry, misspells his surname as "Boizard." (See *Le Petit Almanach de nos grands hommes, pour l'année 1788,* p. 42.)

2. These and other biographical and bibliographical details are related by his descendant, one François Boisard, in his *Notices*

biographiques, littéraires et critiques sur les hommes du Calvados, pp. 28–35. They are amplified by Charles Porquet in his article "Le Fabuliste Boisard."

3. Our Boisard should not be confused with another fabulist of the same name, the painter Jean-François Boisard (whose surname is misspelled in the catalogue of the Bibliothèque Nationale as "Boissard"), who was in fact his nephew, author of two collections of *Fables,* both dedicated to Louis XVIII.

Le Paon et le Rossignol

La Paon de son plumage étalant les rubis,
Fixoit par leur éclat les regards éblouis.
On admiroit encor sa superbe attitude.
    A quatre pas de là
    Le Rossignol chanta;
La cour du Paon se change en solitude.

The Peacock and the Nightingale

The peacock, cynosure of every eye,
Spreads out his tail as one and all stand by,
Bedazzled by his splendor, ruby-hued.
    But let the nightingale begin
    To sing, and lo! to his chagrin
The peacock stands in sudden solitude.

La Cigale et la Fourmi

"Chante, chante, ma belle amie,
Etourdis-toi; voltige avec légéreté;

The Cricket and the Ant

"Sing! Sing, my friend! Go idly flitting!
Fritter away your summertime! Make hay

Profite bien de ton Eté,
Et vîte hâte-toi de jouir de la vie;
   L'Hiver approche..." Ainsi parloit un jour
      La Fourmi thésauriseuse
   A la Cigale, à son gré trop joyeuse;
   "Avez-vous dit, radoteuse m'amour,"
      Lui repliqua la chanteuse?
"L'Hiver approche! Hé bien, nous mourrons toutes deux:
Vos greniers seront pleins, & les miens seront vides;
   Or donc, en maudissant les Dieux,
Vous quitterez bientôt vos épargnes sordides...
Moi, je veux en chantant aller voir mes ayeux.
Aussi je n'ai jamais retenu qu'un adage:
Amasser est d'un fol, & jouir est d'un sage."

While yet you can. It's only fitting.
   Winter is coming, come what may..."
So jeered the frugal ant—sarcastic—twitting
Her friend, the playful cricket, sneering at her.
"Are you quite through, my dear?" queried the latter.
   "True, winter's coming... No denying...
And so, for all your prattling chatter,
   Both of us, love, will soon be dying—
You, oh so rich; and I, without a sou!
You'll curse the gods; I'll sing my life away.
   You'll bid your sordid wealth adieu;
I'll greet my forebears with a roundelay...
My friend, I have a rule, and you should too:
'Don't hoard for your tomorrows: live today!'"

1. The carpe diem theme, no rarity in Western literature, is of special interest here in that the author chooses it as a contradictory counterpoise to the Aesopic confrontation between the grasshopper (or cricket) and the ant, best known in La Fontaine's celebrated ver-

sion, "La Cigale et la Fourmi" (I, 1) (see p. 31). We have also seen a similar—though morally opposite—example in the butterfly's advice to the spider in a fable by Jacques Péras (see p. 81).

La Brebis et l'Agneau

Un Loup mourut. Les Moutons en liesse
Remplissoient l'air de leurs cris d'allégresse.
Une Brebis rêvant seule à l'écart,
A ces transports ne prenoit nulle part:
"Quoi!" lui dit un Agneau, dans la publique joie,
"Bonne mère, au chagrin vous paroissez en proie!
   N'entendez-vous pas qu'il est mort?...
Il est mort l'ennemi!... l'ignorez-vous encor?..."
   "Eh! non, mon fils," répondit-elle;
"Mais c'est aux Bergers seuls qu'importe la nouvelle."

The Ewe and the Lamb

A wolf had died. As one might guess,
   The sheep's delight was limitless:
They bleated out their joy with common voice.
All but one ewe, that is, loath to rejoice.
   Her lamb exclaimed: "But mother dear,
Why do you look so sad? Didn't you hear?
Our enemy, the wolf, is dead!... He's dead,
   I tell you... Dead!" "Yes, so you said,"
   The ewe replied. "But why the fuss?
It's good news for the shepherd, child, but not for us!"

Le Bonze et le Chien

Un Bonze fut mordu d'un Chien.
Il pouvoit riposter par un coup de massue;
   Il se vengea par un autre moyen:
"Ma loi ne permet pas," dit-il, "que je te tue;
Je ne te tuerai pas, mais tu n'y perdras rien;
Et je vais te donner mauvaise renommée."
   Il tient parole, & dans l'instant
Crie: "*au Chien enragé*"; le peuple en fait autant;
Estafiers d'accourir, la bête est assommée.

The Buddhist Monk and the Hound

A hound, they tell us, bit a priest
(A Buddhist monk, that is, come from the East),
Who would have countered with a cudgel-blow.
But no. "My law lets me not kill," he said.
"I'll take revenge by speaking ill instead."
And so he cries: "Mad dog! Mad dog!" "Oh, oh!"
   Echo the folk, in fear and dread,
Beating to death our quadruped, who, lo!
Lies no less cudgeled now, and no less dead.[1]

1. Boisard's monk is merely heeding the advice of an old French proverb: "Qui veut noyer son chien l'accuse de la rage." Its medieval equivalent is traceable at least as far back as the thirteenth century: "Qui bon chien veut tuer, la raige li met seure"—that is, if you want an excuse to kill your dog, just say that he's rabid. (See Antoine-Jean-

Victor Le Roux de Lincy, *Le Livre des proverbes français*, I:109.) The proverb also provides the moral for one of the Aesopic fables in the medieval collection *Isopet I de Paris*. (See "The Wolf and the Lamb," in my *Fables from Old French: Aesop's Beasts and Bumpkins*, p. 55.)

La Flèche

"Hôtes des airs, voyez mon vol audacieux,"
    Disoit la Flèche au haut des cieux,
"J'habite comme vous la région suprême!..."
      Un Oiseau reprit: "oui;
    Mais tu t'élevois par autrui,
    Et tu retombes par toi-même."

1. I suspect that this fable may well be one of Boisard's earliest. It first appeared in the 1768 number of the *Almanach des Muses* (p. 96). It is probably significant, given the early stage of the fabulist's career, that the fable bears no attribution of authorship and is listed

The Arrow

An arrow boasted, from its lofty height:
"Denizens of the heavens, see my dauntless flight!
    I too can fly the firmament!"
    "True," said a bird, "but not alone:
    You need Man's hand for your ascent...
Only your fall, my friend, is all your own!"[1]

in the table of contents among the "anonymes." Later, once he had established something of a reputation, he would shed his timidity—and anonymity—and become a frequent contributor, especially between 1804 and 1810.

Le Chêne et le Roseau

"De mes rameaux brisés la vallée est couverte,"
Disait au vent du Nord le chêne du coteau:
"Dans ton courroux barbare, as-tu juré ma perte,
Tandis que je te vois caresser le roseau?"
"J'ai juré," dit le vent, "d'abattre le superbe
    Qui me résiste comme toi,
    Et de caresser le brin d'herbe
    Qui se prosterne devant moi.
Avise à l'instant même à désarmer ma haine,
Ou j'achève à l'instant de te déraciner."
    "Je puis tomber," reprit le chêne;
    "Mais je ne puis me prosterner."

1. The poet's spare but effective treatment of this popular subject invites comparison, inevitably, with La Fontaine's classic rendition, and even with Anouilh's latter-day sequel (see pp. 33 and 199–200). Were it not for his celebrated literary antecedent, and considering the scenario, Boisard—or whoever the author may have been (see p. 111)—might rather have entitled his version "Le Chêne et le Vent du Nord." One literary historian suggests that this fable has a spe-

The Oak and the Reed

The oak addressed the Northwind thus:
"My twig and bough bestrew the hill and plain.
    Have I no reason to complain
    Of your intentions barbarous?
What? Do you vow to blow me down? Indeed!
Even as you caress the lowly reed?"
"I topple those who, haughty, stand before me,
And coddle those who bow low, and adore me!
    So, here and now, take heed: allay
My wrath, or be uprooted, here and now, forever!"
    Replies the oak: "Fall down, I may...
    But bow down? Never!"[1]

cific historical reference. The confrontation between the Northwind and the oak would presumably be an allusion to Napoleon's demands to the future Louis XVIII, during the Consulat, to renounce for himself and his descendants all claim to the French throne, thereby eliciting Louis's noble response. (See Bernard Jullien, *Histoire de la poésie française à l'époque impériale,* II:163, n. 2.)

Claude-Joseph Dorat   Fables Nouvelles (1773–75)

IF FURETIÈRE holds the dubious honor of being the only academician ever to be expelled from the august ranks of the Académie Française (see p. 41), Claude-Joseph Dorat surely has the distinction of being the most—or at least one of the most—persistent aspirants to membership in that body, having tried some twenty times over a relatively brief career to join the "immortels." Unsuccessfully, it should be noted, despite an extensive and varied literary production that had earned him, during his lifetime, a considerable reputation. Not that he was without his detractors. On the contrary, he seems to have had more

than his due, especially among the Encyclopédistes, for whose aspirations to all-encompassing erudition he had little sympathy; and thanks especially to a minor literary skirmish with Voltaire. (See Emile Faguet, *Histoire de la poésie française de la Renaissance au Romantisme,* VIII: 241–46.) It was, in all likelihood, his tiff with the great philosophe that repeatedly barred the doors of the Académie to him; a fact that bears witness in a subtle way to Dorat's prestige among his contemporaries. "Voltaire l'a estimé, a été vivement touché par ses attaques, si fines, si spirituelles, toutes empreintes de l'esprit, du talent de

Voltaire lui-même" (Faguet, *Histoire,* p. 246). If virtually unknown today, the poet dubbed by some "l'Ovide français," if not universally and unreservedly admired in his own time, was, by the extent and variety of his work alone, a figure to be reckoned with.[1]

Dorat was born in Paris on December 31, 1734, possibly a descendent of the Jean Dorat (or Daurat) of Pléiade fame. Abandoning a traditional legal career which his father, a member of the royal retinue ("conseiller du Roi et auditeur à la Chambre des Comptes"), had intended him to pursue, the future poet entered the first company of the king's musketeers in April of 1757 and began what would be a lifelong existence of the classic *galant,* cutting a dashing figure in many of the fashionable salons of the period. His military career lasted less than a year, however, when, to allay the prudish concerns of a wealthy aunt of Jansenist persuasion—his closest relative after the death of his parents—he left what she considered the licentious life of the soldier to devote himself to letters. Ironically, despite the good lady's pure intentions, when the musketeer-turned-poet gave up the sword for the pen he relinquished none of the social perquisites of his uniform (even numbering among his several mistresses the likes of the countess Fanny de Beauharnais, aunt of the future empress Joséphine), and remained very much the social butterfly—albeit an impoverished one in his later years—until his dying day, on April 29, 1780.[2]

In two decades of literary life Dorat, in his seemingly boundless quest for artistic celebrity, produced a steady stream of tragedies and comedies, a prerequisite for any aspiring French *littérateur* of the postclassical era, as well as tales in verse and prose, letters, epistolary novels, heroic verse epistles or "héroïdes" (imagined correspondence between pairs of historical figures, great and small), didactic poetry, and light verse of every kind—odes, epigrams, pastorals, erotica, and such—inspired by and dedicated to his numerous admirers and admirees.[3] And, of course, a lengthy collection of fables. As Faguet observes somewhat exaggeratedly, and as the reader has already had occasion to observe, eighteenth-century French letters were particularly rich in followers of La Fontaine, at however great a distance. "Il est peu de poètes au XVIIIᵉ siècle qui n'aient écrit des fables ... Il était, du reste, aussi nécessaire à un écrivain, pour se faire classer parmi les hommes de talent, d'avoir fait des fables que d'avoir écrit des tragédies. De sorte que, si l'on voulait faire sa carrière dans les lettres, on commençait par faire une tragédie; puis, si l'on échouait, on composait des poésies légères, et, parmi celles-ci, des fables" (*Histoire,* p. 270).[4]

Faguet sees Dorat's hundred-odd published fables as typical of the post–La Fontaine apologue as practiced by the cohort of eighteenth-century fabulists; pretexts, that is,

for a clever concluding epigram: "Depuis Lamotte [i.e., Houdar de La Motte], cette sorte de fables épigrammatiques était à la mode, et c'est ce genre de fables que pratique Dorat" (*Histoire,* p. 253). Overly categorical, his observation applies to some but not to others. Readers will see for themselves in the sampling translated here, and will likewise have the opportunity to judge the harsh indictment by the celebrated and rather tradition-bound critic-playwright Jean-François de La Harpe—no admirer of Dorat, or indeed of any antagonist of Voltaire's—who found his fables to be "peut-être le plus mauvais de ce qu'il a écrit." (See his *Lycée, ou Cours de littérature ancienne et moderne,* VIII:299.) La Harpe to the contrary notwithstanding, Dorat's fables do no dishonor to their obvious French stylistic model; nor, for that matter, to the several German fabulists, Lessing foremost among them, who provided many of his subjects. Properly cut from the La Fontaine cloth, if they lack the Master's offhand bonhomie and intimate collusion with the reader, they are nonetheless pleasant and skillfully crafted little dramas, "peopled" with both the traditional animal and human characters and a number of far less usual ones, though less esoteric than those of the contemporary abbé de Grécourt, for example (see pp. 85–86). Modestly philosophical, they have the advantage of being rarely pretentious in their allusions or long-winded in their developments. In short, they are always quite respectable—and, on occasion, quite elegant—examples of the genre as practiced by La Fontaine's many eighteenth-century emulators.

First published under the title *Fables ou allégories philosophiques,* Dorat's collection originally contained eighty-four fables divided into four books. It was preceded in that and a successive edition by his introductory "Réflexions préliminaires," in which he not only intones the praises of La Fontaine and his intuitive talent as a fabulist ("Le Ver à soie file, l'Abeille fait du miel; La Fontaine compose des Fables" [p. v]), comparing him to the distinguished but prolix Houdar de La Motte and others, but also self-defensively dedicates his work to "ce Public qui m'a défendu contre l'adresse de la malignité, l'effronterie de la satyre, les préventions de quelques Hommes célèbres" (p. xxi). The collection of four books, now numbering ninety-nine fables after deletions and additions, revised and reordered, was republished, in parts, over the next three years as *Fables nouvelles.*[5]

The present six fables are translated from the second edition, where they bear the following numbers: I, 16; III, 19; III, 21; IV, 21; IV, 22; and IV, 24. (The fourth, "Le Singe et le Renard," and the fifth, "La Goutte d'Eau," do not appear in the edition of 1772, in which the remaining four are numbered, respectively, as follows: IV, 2; III, 14; IV, 6; and I, 20.)

---

1. Faguet is not faint in his praise of "ce poète aimable, spirituel, au génie si souple et si attrayant, qui réunit merveilleusement en lui tous les caractères de l'écrivain du XVIIIᵉ siècle" (*Histoire,* p. 283).

2. Owing to his extravagant tastes, and especially to his self-indulgent habit of spending handsomely to insure the success of his ventures, theatrical and literary, Dorat would be obliged, a few years

before his death, to turn to journalism, as editor of the ill-fated *Journal des dames*. With the failure of that publication it was only the generosity of the playwright Beaumarchais, through the countess Fanny's intercession, that saved him from complete disaster.

3. Among Dorat's plays still occasionally read are the three-act verse comedy *La Feinte par amour*, performed at the Comédie-Française, July 31, 1773, and the five-act verse comedy *Le Célibataire*, performed at the same theater, September 20, 1775. Another work of theatrical inspiration is of special interest to historians and scholars of stagecraft. His *Essai sur la déclamation tragique* of 1758, subsequently republished in final expanded form as *La Déclamation théâtrale*, is a four-canto *ars dramatica* devoted to tragedy, comedy, opera, and dance, that owes much to Dorat's practical association with many of the actors (and, especially actresses) of his day. (See Anna Raitière, *L'Art de l'acteur selon Dorat et Samson*.)

4. For a detailed study of Dorat's life and—secondarily—his work, the reader should consult Gustave Desnoiresterres, *Le Chevalier Dorat et les poètes légers au XVIIIᵉ siècle*. That volume, unfortunately, contains no bibliography. For such a listing see Alexandre Cioranescu, *Bibliographie de la littérature française du dix-huitième siècle*, I:697–700.

The latter, however, may not be wholly accurate. It is somewhat at odds, in number, with literary historian Bernard Jullien, who attributes to Dorat at least a dozen more "héroïdes" than are listed by Cioranescu. (See *Histoire de la poésie française à l'époque impériale*, II:2.)

5. Both editions are lavishly illustrated by the prominent contemporary engraver Clément-Pierre Marillier, who, among other well-known artists, sumptuously adorned many of Dorat's works. Not without considerable adverse comment, apparently. In a brief prefatory *avis* to the second edition, the author defends himself against "ceux qui critiquent la pompe typographique de cet Ouvrage" by citing a passage from Locke's essay *Some Thoughts Concerning Education*, which praises the utility of the fable in teaching a child to read, and especially when pleasantly illustrated, to "l'encourager à poursuivre sa lecture" (p. ii). Many of Dorat's volumes, in fact—and both editions of his fables among them—early became collectors' items, more sought after for their illustrations than for their text. "Bibliophilists," we are told, "have long competed for the possession of illustrated copies of 'Les Baisers' and 'Les Fables,' the original editions of which nowadays command almost prohibitive prices." (See *The Kisses*, H. G. Keene's translation of Dorat's *Les Baisers*, pp. v–vi.)

Le Jet-d'eau et le Réservoir

Dans un Parc dessiné d'après les meilleurs plans,
Un Jet-d'eau dans les airs s'élevoit sous l'ombrage,
   Et retomboit à travers le feuillage,
En perles, en rubis, en globules roulans:
Notre Jet-d'eau s'oublie, ainsi que c'est l'usage;
(On a vu de tout tems les sots se prévaloir)
     Il insulte, dans son langage,
     L'onde obscure du Réservoir,
   Qui fournissoit à tout son étalage.

   "Voi," lui dit-il, "ce pompeux appareil,
   Si jusqu'à moi peut arriver ta vue:
Voi ces gerbes d'argent dont s'enrichit la nue,
   Et que j'oppose aux raïons du Soleil.
   A quoi sers-tu, misérable eau dormante?
Quand je m'élève aux cieux, dans l'ombre tu croupis:
     Ton voisinage me tourmente,
Et gâte bien souvent les lieux que j'embellis."

   Comme il parloit, un des canaux se brise.
Au fond du Réservoir il s'entr'ouvre un chemin,
     Et soudain,
   L'onde sourdit, décroît, coule & s'épuise.
   Vous eussiez vu les rubis s'exhaler,
     Toutes les gerbes disparoître,
     Et les perles dégringoler.
Notre orgueilleux commence à se connoître:
Il baisse, il tombe, il ne peut plus aller,
Il est à sec. Vous devinez peut-être,
     De ma Fable quel est le sens:
Appauvrissez le Peuple; adieu l'éclat des Grands.

The Fountain and the Pool

A fountain in a stately park shot high
   Its column through the leafy shade,
   Reaching its waters toward the sky
And raining down in shimmering cascade
   Of rubies, pearls... But by and by
The jet grows vain—like many a pompous fool—
     And in their common tongue
     Insults the humble pool
From whence his elegant self has sprung:

   "Behold my beauteous display,"
He jeers. "That is, if you can see this far!
See how the clouds embrace my silvered spray,
And tell me, if you can, what good you are—
You and your stagnant waters! Look, I rise
   Among the sun's bright rays, but all
The while you cower, cast your dismal pall
On everything my grandeur glorifies."

And so the fountain pressed his proud harangue,
   Exulting in his majesty.
     But suddenly,
Within the pool one of the gutters sprang
(Alas!) a leak... The waters drain... Our jet
   Spurts, sputters, gurgles, gasps... Ah, me!
Pearls, rubies, every silvered globulet,
Blown to the wind! More chastened now, our fount
Dries up and dies, with one last pirouette.
Clear is the moral I would here recount:
Deprive the Common People of its due;
The Court, with all its pomp, will perish too.[1]

1. Emile Faguet appropriately calls attention to the epigrammatic conclusion of this fable as an example of contemporary prerevolutionary social musings: "'Le Jet d'eau et le Réservoir' a une allure politique et économique . . . C'était le temps où les sages . . . et les autres devisaient de la richesse, de la production et de l'échange" (*Histoire*, p. 273). Compare with Alexis Piron's even more daringly pointed warning in "La Tour et le Rocher" (p. 99), published a few years after Dorat's collection, though composed many years earlier.

Le Chesne et le Gland

Un Chêne altier s'indignoit de son fruit.
"De mon ombre," dit-il, "je protége la terre;
Je suis l'arbre du Dieu qui lance le tonnerre,
    Et voilà ce que j'ai produit!"
"Ingrat," reprit le Gland, "qui parloit comme un Sage,
    D'où te vient tant de vanité?
Dans tes vastes rameaux reconnois mon ouvrage;
    Sans moi tu n'aurois pas été:
J'enfermois dans mon sein ton superbe feuillage.
    Toujours sublime, en ses moindres décrets,
      La nature qui me destine
A te perpétuer dans le fond des forêts,
      Sur ta cime m'éleve exprès,
Pour mieux te rappeller à ton humble origine."

The Oak and the Acorn

An oak, disdainful of the fruit he bore,
Complained: "Me! Me, whose shade protects the
               land! Me! Me,
    The thunder-bearer Zeus's favorite tree!
    Yet I spawn acorns, nothing more!"
An acorn, chiding, wisely took the oak to task:
    "Arrogant creature! Where, I ask,
Where would you be today if not for me? I bore you
    Deep in my nurturing breast before you
Sprouted to lavish leaf! Here, as in all the rest,
    It's clear enough that Nature still knows best:
She chose an acorn as your procreator, set it
    High on your august crest for all to see,
      Sign of your lowly pedigree,
        Lest you forget it!"

La Martre, le Renard, et le Loup

    La Martre, dans certain détour,
    Etrangla le Coq de Bruyere,
Compere le Renard, friand de bonne chere,
    Dévora la Martre à son tour,
    Et Sire Loup déjeûna du compere.
    Ma Fable est le tableau du jour.
Du jour? De tous les tems. L'Apologue a beau faire.

The Marten, the Fox, and the Wolf

    A marten meets a woodcock, lays him low.
      Enter the fox, with one endeavor:
    To tuck away a delicate *morceau!*
And so the marten's fate is like the cock's. However,
    The wolf, in turn, devours the fox... Ah, woe!...
So goes the world today... Today? Forever!
Fables, I fear, have done no good whatever.[1]

1. Dorat, in his 1772 edition, *Fables ou allégories philosophiques,* cites the German fabulist Friedrich von Hagedorn (1708–54) as the source for this fable. In turn, the index notes to Hagedorn's two-couplet fable "Der Marder, der Fuchs und der Wolf," in his *Fabeln und Erzehlungen,* I, 30—part of his *Sämmtliche Poetische Werke*—refer to a still-earlier version: that of Antoine-Louis Lebrun (1680–1748) in his *Fables de Monsieur Lebrun,* IV, 26. The immediate trail appears to end with Lebrun, who fails to tell us if he too had a predecessor for his no-less-pithy seven-line original, "La Fouine, le Renard, et le Loup," though a classical antecedent is certainly not unlikely. Another rendering, contemporary to Dorat's, is the equally terse five-line fable by Simon-Pierre Mérard de Saint-Just, "La Martre, le Renard, et le Loup" (III, 17), dated 1766 in his *Fables et contes mis en vers.* It would seem, however, not especially to have influenced Dorat's version.

Le Singe et le Renard

    Un trône étoit demeuré vuide;
    Un Singe y saute & s'y campe soudain.
Le costume royal n'a rien qui l'intimide;

The Monkey and the Fox

    A land there was that lost its king.
    One day an ape, seeing the empty throne,
      The crown, robes, scepter—everything—

Il ceint le diadème, il prend le sceptre en main,
Et le voilà qui regne: à sa mine hardie,
    A son air, noblement altier,
    On eût juré que de sa vie,
    Il n'avoit fait d'autre métier.
    Invités par le Chat sauvage,
    Qu'il nomme son Ambassadeur,
Les autres animaux viennent lui rendre hommage,
  Et sont frappés de son air de grandeur.
    Le seul Renard examine le Sire,
    Se moque de la dignité
    Que la foule imbécille admire,
    Et par un tour que je vais dire,
    Il déroute sa Majesté.
  Il va chercher régal de toute espèce,
Des oranges, des noix, des raisins bien dorés;
    Puis vient offrir, fendant la presse,
    Les tributs qu'il a préparés.
Gille premier soudain s'élance hors du trône
    Aux yeux des courtisans surpris,
  Et, délivré du poids de la couronne,
Capriole à son aise, & va gruger les fruits.

    Qu'importe une frivole marque?
Affublez un Bouffon de l'attirail des Cours,
    Le Singe percera toujours,
    A travers l'habit du Monarque.

Dauntless, decides to make them all his own.
    So up he jumps and takes possession;
And thus begins his reign... Noble his air,
    Bold, haughty his expression...
  One look, and one and all would swear
That surely this must be his life's profession.
The wildcat—minister plenipotentiary—
  At length, convokes the other beasts, who come
To pay their homage, heap encomium
Upon His Majesty extraordinary.
    The fox alone is unimpressed
  (Unlike the imbecilic sycophantics),
    Viewing our monkey, richly dressed,
    Doing his would-be regal antics.
Vowing to bring him down with foxy strategem,
  Off he goes, gathering luscious fruits galore—
    Oranges, walnuts, grapes, and more—
Then, pressing through the crowd, he offers them
As tribute to the royal diadem.
King Ape the First,[1] before his courtiers' eyes
    (And very much to their surprise),
  Leaps from his throne, jumps up and down,
  And, quick to doff his weighty crown,
Runs off with but one thought: to gluttonize.

Clothes never made a monarch of a flunky:
An ape dressed like a king is still a monkey.

---

1. By Dorat's time the name "Gille" had come to imply simplicity (from the name of a popular seventeenth-century clown, Gilles le Niais), perhaps with the additional suggestion of roguishness inherited from the Old French *gilain* 'trickster' (used to personify fraud and deceit as early as the twelfth- and thirteenth-century *Roman de Renart*). La Fontaine had already used "(Maître) Gille" as a characteristic appellation for the monkey in two of his fables: "Le Singe et le Léopard" (IX, 3) and "L'Eléphant et le Singe de Jupiter" (XII, 21), though without especially pejorative connotations. Ironically, he did not use the name in "Le Renard, le Singe, et les Animaux" (VI, 6). The latter, or its Aesopic original, "The Fox and the Monkey" (Perry, *Aesopica*, "Fabulae Graecae," no. 81, p. 353), appears to have inspired Dorat's fable, at least in its broad lines.

La Goutte d'Eau

    Dans la crise d'une tourmente
    Qui bouleversoit l'océan,
Tout-à-coup enlevée à la vague écumante,
    Parmi la foudre & l'ouragan,
    Une Goutte de l'onde amere
    Réjaillit sur un roc voisin.
    "D'ici je vais voir tout le train,"
Dit-elle; "qu'il est doux de vivre solitaire!
N'existons que pour nous, & respirons enfin.
Sans dépendre toujours de quelque flot mutin,
  Des élémens j'observerai la guerre;
    Et l'océan aura beau faire,
    Il ne m'aura plus dans son sein."
Le Dieu du jour alors s'échappe de la nue,
    Et sur le roc voilà soudain
    Ma raisonneuse disparue.

The Drop of Water

    A storm was lashing at the sea,
    Howling its winds, its lightning flashing.
Suddenly, from the churning foam, tossed free,
    A single drop of brine went splashing
    Onto a nearby rock protruding
    Out of the deep. "Ah, fine!" he cried,[1]
    "From here I'll watch the raging tide
In solitary splendor!" And, concluding:
"At last my life's my own. No longer need I be
    Slave to the ocean's slightest whim,
    Submerged in anonymity!
    Let nature wage her war on him,
    It matters not one whit to me!"
Just then the sun appears... Dries up the rock...
    Well, so much for our *bel-esprit*
    And all his talk.

Mêlée avec les flots, elle suivoit leur cours,
    Des vents affrontoit la furie,
Et dans les vastes mers eût roulé pour toujours;
    Seule un instant, elle est tarie.

Part of the sea, he might roll on forever,
    Safe in the multitude. However,
    Free and alone, he pays the price:
      Gone in a trice!

1. As elsewhere in this collection, when it has seemed appropriate, I have disregarded the grammatical gender of the noun—*la goutte,* feminine—in favor of the suggested gender of the pompous character personified.

Le Serpent et la Colonne

    Un Serpent des plus étourdis,
Sous les parvis d'un Temple insulte une Colonne;
    Et le voilà qui l'environne
    De ses innombrables replis.
    "Il est tems," dit-il, "qu'on t'abatte,
Que de ton faste antique on délivre les airs."
    En même tems jaillissent les éclairs
    De sa prunelle d'écarlate.
Il s'enfle, il se courrouce, il vomit son poison;
    Et, dans l'accès de sa rage inutile,
    Va contre le Marbre immobile
Dardant les traits aigus de son triple aiguillon.

Un Passant qui survient coupe en deux le reptile,
    Qui, dans l'instant, détaché du fronton,
    Ensanglante le Péristile,
S'agite, & rampe encor sur son double tronçon:
Mais, malgré ses efforts, la force l'abandonne;
Sa crête, qui pâlit, veut en vain se dresser;
    Il meurt au bas de la Colonne
    Qu'il s'efforçoit de renverser.

The Serpent and the Column

A mindless serpent, lodged in precincts solemn
(Beneath an ancient temple portico),
    Took umbrage at a certain column,
    Deeming him, in a word, *de trop.*
    "It's time we brought you down," he hissed—
    Twining his arch antagonist
    Within his endless coils—"time we
Were rid of you and your pomposity!"
And so the serpent, in his fury, plies
His venomous attacks: bites, spits, stings, scores him—
Baring his fangs, fire darting from his eyes...
    Stolid, the column quite ignores him.

Shortly, a passerby with trusty axe
    Comes on the scene and, forthwith, hacks
    In twain the obstinate reptilian.
    Blood stains the peristyle vermilion.
Vainly the snake—now halved and doubled—tries
To raise his head, rear up and strike. But no!
    Too weak, the foolish beast, laid low,
Writhes at his would-be victim's feet... and dies.[1]

1. The anonymous chronicler of the *Almanach des Muses* of 1773 (pp. 204–5), giving a thumbnail appreciation of Dorat's *Fables ou allégories philosophiques* published the preceding year, used a variety of adjectives to characterize several of his fables: "touchante," "plaisante," "gracieuse," "ironique," and even "naïve." The present fable, however, elicited a "sublime."

Alexis Piron   Fables (1776) (posthumous)

WIDELY admired in his own day but little read in ours, Alexis Piron exemplifies the wit of eighteenth-century France rather than its wisdom, its "élégant badinage," to borrow a celebrated phrase, rather than its philosophical enlightenment. It was, in fact, his brilliant, often merciless wit that made him notorious—fancied by most and feared by many—in the social world of Parisian letters, and that led him to cross verbal rapiers with dozens of prominent antagonists.[1] Not least among the latter was the great Voltaire himself, for whom Piron had an especially implacable—and reciprocal—dislike. Indeed, if he is remembered today by more than the occasional specialist, it is largely because of that bitter rivalry in which even the acerbic Voltaire, no novice in the art of repartee, often came out the loser.[2]

Piron was born in Dijon on July 9, 1689, and studied law in Besançon.[3] Financial difficulties prevented him from practicing the profession, however; and after a youth marked by the composition of light and licentious verse—notably a celebrated *Ode à Priape,* which was to come back to haunt him later in life—he moved to Paris at the age of thirty, soon gaining among the literati of the capital a reputation for his satires, epigrams, and barbed bons mots cast in every direction. His first professional writing took the form of brief comedies for the popular Théâtre de la Foire, followed by more serious endeavors for the official Théâtre-Français, largely at the urging of the talented soubrette Jeanne-Françoise Quinault, who was to be his friend and confidante throughout his long life, even after his marriage. His most successful play, the comedy *La Métromanie* (1738), was considered by many to be a masterpiece.[4] It was sufficient, at any rate, along with other works of lesser stature, to earn him nomination to the Académie Française in 1753.

His enemies, however—and by now they were legion—objected to the honor, citing his youthful *Ode à Priape* as reason enough to exclude him from the august company. Louis XV was obliged to concur, granting him nonetheless a handsome *pension* equal to an academician's stipend, probably thanks to the coaxing of Madame de Pompadour. Piron's resentment, like Furetière's before him (see pp. 40–42), produced an unrelenting stream of satiric verse directed against the Académie in general and his antagonists in particular, for the rest of his days.[5] One couplet, which he proposed as his own sarcastic epitaph, summed up his feeling: "Ci-gît Piron, qui ne fut rien, / Pas même académicien." In his later years, widowered and virtually blind, he turned to the writing of religious verse, though hardly as a conventional penitent seeking forgiveness for literary or other indiscretion.[6] He died in Paris on January 21, 1773, having produced a large body of works in a variety of genres.[7]

Piron's fables, numbering only fifteen, do not represent a particularly important part of that *œuvre.* They were published in the sixth volume of the posthumous Rigoley de Juvigny edition of 1776, and had not appeared in the editions of his work during his lifetime (*Œuvres,* 1758 and 1763). No doubt because they were not printed as a separate collection, the fables do not contain the expected prefatory praise of La Fontaine or disclaimers of his influence.[8] As for the dates of composition, a few can be determined rather accurately, since they allude pointedly to specific incidents in Piron's life: his exclusion from the Académie ("Le Lion et la Fourmi," dedicated to Louis XV), his brief falling-out with Mademoiselle Quinault ("L'Ours et l'Hermine"), et al. Most, however, seem more general in their application. Chapponière gives them all rather short shrift.[9] (See *Piron,* pp. 332–33.) But while they are not, certainly, the most colorful examples of Piron's talent or of his most persuasive verse, neither are they without their charm. To wit, the three translated here. "Le Roitelet" is the most La Fontainesque, both in form and minidramatic scenario; "La Neige" is a conventional allegory, but more graceful than most; and "La Tour" is especially striking in its Enlightenment tone: an almost-prophetic warning to a soon-to-be-toppled monarchy not to disdain "the people," from whom it derives its legitimacy.

The three appear, unnumbered, as the second, thirteenth, and twelfth, respectively.

---

1. In the words of the francophile German critic Grimm, he was, "dans ce genre de combats à coups de langue, l'athlète le plus fort qui eût jamais existé nulle part." (See Friedrich Melchior von Grimm, *Correspondance littéraire, philosophique et critique,* X:161.)

2. "Voilà pourquoi," Grimm assures us, "M. de Voltaire craignait toujours la rencontre avec Piron, parce que tout son brillant n'était pas à l'épreuve des traits de ce combattant redoutable" (*Correspondance,* X:161–62). In his posthumous *Anecdotes littéraires* (see pp. 49; 50, n. 1) a contemporary observer, the abbé Claude-Henri de Fusée de Voisenon, relates a typical encounter between the two. After the first performance of his less-than-successful play *Adélaïde du Guesclin* (1734), Voltaire met Piron and asked what he thought of it. "Je pense, Monsieur," the latter replied, "que vous voudriez que je l'eusse fait" (p. 63).

3. There is no dearth of sources for biographical information. The most extensive study is Paul Chapponière, *Piron, sa vie et son œuvre.* Most collections of his works also provide details; among them, the less-objective study in the first volume of his posthumous seven-volume *Œuvres complettes,* edited by his friend and admirer Rigoley de Juvigny, but not as complete as the title indicates; and the introduction to Honoré Bonhomme's edition, *Poésies choisies et pièces inédites de Alexis Piron,* pp. i–xlvii.

4. For Grimm it was "un chef-d'œuvre dans son genre, et le seul que nous ayons peut-être depuis la mort du sublime Molière" (*Correspondance,* II:261).

5. And even beyond, if we can believe the report that he left behind a number of epigrams to reply to any insults that Voltaire might address to his memory. (See Grimm, *Correspondance,* X:165.)

6. A translation of the *De profundis* was not particularly admired. One commentator, with a wit worthy of Piron himself, noted that, if those in the afterworld knew anything about poetry, the work would keep him out of heaven just as his infamous ode had kept him out of the Académie. (See Voisenon, *Anecdotes,* pp. 63–64.)

7. For a full bibliography, see Chapponière, *Piron,* pp. 408–36, and Alexandre Cioranescu, *Bibliographie de la littérature française du dix-huitième siècle,* II:1397–1401.

8. The illustrious predecessor is not absent, however. In the fourth fable, "La Lyre d'Orphée et les Singes," written "au sujet des nombreux Fabulistes de ce temps," Piron not only acknowledges La Fontaine's supremacy in the genre, but, undercutting even his own modest efforts, takes a typical jab at La Fontaine's many contemporary followers: "O pauvre Orphée! Et qui lit / Les Fables nouvelles, dit: / O pauvre Jean LAFONTAINE [*sic*]!"

9. He prefers to all fifteen a single twenty-three-line fable written in Piron's youth and addressed in a letter to an ecclesiastic relative, one "Monsieur M∗∗∗," of Dijon. The fable represents a bull—Piron—at odds with a swarm of gnats—his provincial detractors—numerous, apparently, even before his arrival in Paris. (It was printed the year after Piron's death in Fréron's *L'Année littéraire,* année 1774, II:21–24.) The concluding lines sound a note that he would repeat often in later life: "Cher Abbé, j'ai des ennemis / En si grand nombre & si petits, / Que je n'en puis tirer vengeance."

Le Roitelet

Il parut aux Oiseaux qu'ils vivroient plus à l'aise,
S'ils en choisissoient un qui regnât sur eux tous.
   Les Bêtes, ne leur en déplaise,
N'ont pas eu quelquefois plus de raison que nous.
Restoit à convenir, qui, d'entre eux, seroit digne
   De donner aux autres la loi:
C'est le nœud gordien; chaque Oiseau dit: "c'est moi."
   S'il ne se nomme, il se désigne.
   L'Aigle adjuge le sceptre au vol:
"Moi, je le donne au chant," disoit le Rossignol:
Le Merle royalise à hauts cris la finesse:
Le Vautour l'appétit: le Corbeau la vieillesse.
   Et le Duc les airs insolens.
Le Moineau-franc enfin vante aussi des talens,
   Assez rares dans leur espèce.
   C'est comme ici bas, bonnes gens:
   Chacun définit le mérite,
Par sa qualité propre, ou du moins favorite.
Le Petit le dispute au Grand, & n'a pas tort:
Car les Grands ont toujours la rapine en partage.
Mais il fallut se rendre à l'avis du plus fort.
   Si ce n'est l'ordre, c'est l'usage.
   L'Aigle opina donc en ces mots:
   "C'est l'aile qui nous fait Oiseaux:
   Déployons la mienne & les vôtres!
   Voyons qui vole le plus haut!
   Celui-là sera Roi des autres."
   Il dit: tout s'envole aussitôt.
   L'Aigle fend l'air, perce la nue;

The Wren

The birds convened, and planned, from that day hence,
To find a king, for their felicity.
   (Animals—meaning no offense—
Often have no more common sense than we!)
They set about to choose the one to be
   Their ruler: Ah! the Gordian Knot!
Each bird proclaimed his excellence, and sought
   The signal honor: "Me!... Choose me!"
   More subtle, some were quick to cite
Some quality—their own!—that ought prevail:
The eagle, flight; music, the nightingale;
Old age, the crow; the vulture, appetite;
   The owl, his pride; the blackbird, stealth.
Even the common sparrow boasts a wealth
   Of talents rare and recondite.
   (So too in human intercourse,
   Dear, gentle reader: each defines
Merit according to his own designs.
The small defy the great, who use their force
To pillage and to plunder, as they may:
Might still makes right, no matter what we say.
   It's sad but so...) At any rate,
   The eagle took the floor to state:
   "Wings are what make us birds, correct?
   Let's spread them and see who can fly
   The highest. One of you, or I!
   Whoever does is king-elect!"
   The eagle spoke. The flock took flight.
   Cleaving the clouds, he soars on high,

Et les voyant loin dessous soi,
Il brave la foible cohue:
"Qui maintenant," dit-il, "doit être votre Roi?"
Le Roitelet caché sous l'aile appesantie
De l'Aigle, s'élance & s'écrie:
"C'est moi."

Force, talens, vertu, sagesse
Ne servent guère, il en faut convenir.
Du prix qu'il devroit obtenir,
Le mérite est exclus sans cesse.
Joindre l'impudence à l'adresse,
Est le moyen d'y parvenir.

Leaving his rivals out of sight.
"Well now, my friends," he sneers, "who should be king?"
"Who?" chirps the wren, hidden beneath his wing,
Flying aloft with piping cry:
"Who?... I!"

Strength, talent, virtue, wisdom—these
Are not, alas, man's winning qualities.
Little will they achieve, or less!
True merit knows no victories.
You who would meet with sweet success,
Join impudence to artfulness.

La Tour et le Rocher

Du sommet d'un Rocher une superbe Tour
    Alloit se cacher dans la nue,
    Et, de tous les lieux d'alentour
    Dominoit la vaste étendue.
L'orgueil aveugle tout: elle ôsa s'oublier.
Le Rocher éprouva sa fierté criminelle.
    "Abaisse-toi," lui disoit-elle:
"Et sous mon noble poids gémis tout le premier."
    "Eh, qui t'a si mal informée,"
Répondit le Rocher, "de tes droits & des miens?
    N'est-ce pas moi qui t'ai formée,
    Qui t'élève & qui te soutiens?
    Le Ciel en approchant ton faîte
    Des régions de la tempête,
Te favorisa moins qu'il ne te menaça.
    Puisse-t-il un jour te détruire!"
    Un coup de foudre l'exauça.
    Rois, voilà qui doit vous instruire.

The Tower and the Rock

Atop a rock a lofty tower was standing—
    Head in the clouds, above the plain—
    Proudly and haughtily commanding,
    Round and about, the vast domain.
Alas, the proud are blind. Our mighty tower
Waxed arrogant, much to the rock's distress.
    "Bow down before my lordliness,"
Said he, "and be the first to moan my power."
    "Ah," sighed the rock, "who filled your head
With lies about your rights and mine? Do I
    Not form your very being," he said,
    "And lift you up, and hold you high?
    Head in the storm, you were not graced
    By heaven to be so proudly placed.
Rather, its wrath more easily may reach you:
    I pray one day it take your measure!"
    A lightning bolt obliged with pleasure.
    Kings, here's a tale with much to teach you.

La Neige

Ce qu'en trop peu de temps l'œil étonné voit naître,
    En peu de temps s'évanouit;
    Et tout ce qui nous éblouit,
    N'est pas long-temps à disparoître.
La Neige par les airs tomboit à gros flocons;
Elle eut bientôt blanchi la plaine, les montagnes,
    Les prés, les bois, & les vallons.
La voilà qui se croit la Reine des campagnes.
Flore n'étoit plus rien: sa plus vive couleur
N'eut jamais un éclat pareil à sa blancheur:
    Jamais Palès n'eut un si vaste empire:
Faune & Bacchus étoient des Dieux à dédaigner;
Et les fiers Aquilons qui la faisoient régner,
Ne devoient plus jamais laisser régner Zéphyre.
Elle pensoit ainsi, quand les vents appaisés,

The Snow

What is too quickly born, to our surprise,
    Dies just as fast. Yes, it is clear
    That those things straightway disappear,
    That burst before our dazzled eyes.
Snow, once upon a time, with giant flakes
Blanketed hills, woods, valleys, plains. The ground
    Lay white. But soon proud Snow mistakes
Herself for queen of all the country round.
Then Flora counts for nought: "What hues has she
To match my white of brilliant purity?
    Fauna and Bacchus?... How can they
    Compare!... And Pales?... Even less!..." [1]
No more let Zephyr waft his warm caress,
Let blustering Aquilon alone hold sway!"
Such were her thoughts when, as the storm subsided,

Le Soleil perça le nuage,
Et la fondit, à l'avantage
De ceux qu'elle avoit méprisés.

1. Less familiar than the other divinities and semidivinities referred to, Pales, in Roman mythology, was the god who protected
shepherds and their flocks.

The sun shone through. Snow quickly thaws.
Again the land is as it was:
Ruled by the gods whom she derided.

Jean-Pierre Claris de Florian   Fables (1792)

WHILE it is true that, if you say "fables" to practically any Frenchman, literate or not, he will reply: "La Fontaine," it is equally true that, if you press him to continue with an "Et encore?" he might be hard put to name another fabulist off the top of his head. Those who can, however, will surely come up with "Florian." It has long been the fate of Jean-Pierre Claris, chevalier de Florian, to play second fiddle, as it were; but certainly there is no shame in that when the first fiddle is La Fontaine.

That honor to flourish in the master's shadow was early bestowed. No more than two years after the first appearance of Florian's *Fables,* the *Almanach des Muses* of 1794 (coincidentally the year of his death), in a brief mention, described the volume as "l'un des meilleurs recueils de ce genre qui aient paru depuis La Fontaine" (p. 218). The opinion was to be echoed later by critics of consequence. Traditionalist Jean-François de La Harpe, for example, would write at the turn of the century, calling attention to Florian's preeminence in a crowded field: "Des nombreux recueils de fables qui ont paru dans ce siècle, celui-ci me paraît le meilleur; c'est celui où il me semble que l'on a le mieux saisi le véritable esprit de la Fable." (See his *Lycée, ou Cours de littérature ancienne et moderne,* XIII:374.) Apparently the lay public shared that professional opinion. La Harpe's contemporary, Jean-Joseph Dussault, noted in the *Journal des Débats* of February 1812 that "le goût du public place M. de Florian à la tête de tous ceux de nos écrivains qui ont osé faire des fables après La Fontaine"; and, the usually crusty critic continued, "je crois qu'il ne se trompe pas."[1] That popularity, lasting for well over a century, is confirmed by a score of editions, more than of any other of Florian's works, all of which enjoyed numerous printings.[2] A hundred years ago, latter-day apologist Léo Claretie would still feel justified in comparing him to La Fontaine: "Si les deux fabulistes ne sont pas égaux, ils se suivent de si près, que le second est assuré de toujours passer à la faveur et à l'ombre du premier." (See his volume *Florian* [p. vii].)

"Toujours," however, is a long time. Today Florian's popularity has certainly waned.[3] The homespun *bon sens*

of his "Golden Mean" morals, and the *sensibilité* of many of his dramatic little scenarios, were qualities consonant with his own age but not very fashionable in ours. "On a cru longtemps," wrote Marcel Thiébaut in the fifties, "qu'il survivrait comme fabuliste. Cela paraît peu probable aujourd'hui. Ouvrez le recueil de ses fables . . . vous y trouverez quelques tableaux aimables, maintes platitudes, mille résonances de pastiches et très peu de poésie." (See "Parmi les livres," p. 145.)[4] Still, such negativity notwithstanding, the literary commonplace remains more or less intact: Florian the fabulist, in the perception of those who judge such matters (and those who defer to their judgments), continues to rank as the honorable first runner-up.

But as for Florian the man behind the fables, today we know more, perhaps, than did his admiring contemporaries and immediate followers, and we might form a somewhat different opinion. If Dussault could suggest, perceptively but rather tentatively, that "elles ont une certaine fleur de naïveté, pour ainsi dire artificielle, qui n'est qu'un calcul, mais qui ne ressemble pas trop à un calcul" (*Annales littéraires,* III:455 and V:191), we know now that our author's moral stance and sentimental style were, indeed, largely affectation designed to strike a responsive chord in his public and to please his very straitlaced protector, Louis de Bourbon, duc de Penthièvre. The image projected by his fables, as well as by his pastoral novels, verse and prose comedies, biblical eclogues, and other assorted writings, is not quite the image of the flesh-and-blood Florian.[5] A collection of letters written to his uncle, *Lettres au marquis A. de Florian, 1779–1793,* unpublished until 1957 and previously unknown to scholars, reveals, in fact, something of a calculating poseur ready to pander to contemporary taste; very different from the kindly, high-principled moralist, characterized by Sainte-Beuve as "modeste, naturel, sincère," whose gentle image takes shape behind the pages of his *Fables.*[6] In short, a literary—and social—opportunist, albeit a thoroughly charming, witty, and talented one.

There is no dearth of information regarding Florian's biography, and it is hardly necessary to relate it here in detail.[7] Suffice it to say that he was born into an aristocratic but debt-ridden family in Languedoc, in the village of Anduze (or Sauve, depending on sources), on March 6, 1755; that he enjoyed the affection and encouragement of Voltaire, a distant relative by marriage, and the lifelong patronage of the duc de Penthièvre, one of the grandest of the *grands seigneurs* of the time; that he was elected to the Académie Française in 1788 (not in 1778, as Cioranescu indicates); and that, suffering from an almost month-long imprisonment at the hands of the Revolutionary authorities, he died a few weeks after his release, at Sceaux, on September 13, 1794, at the still-young age of thirty-nine.

We may not share nineteenth-century polymath Charles Nodier's opinion that Florian's fables are "un des chefs-d'œuvre du dix-huitième siècle, et un des meilleurs livres de tous les temps." (See his prefatory "Notice sur Florian et sur ses Fables," in *Fables de Flo-*

rian, p. xii.) But if we tend today to be too sophisticated to be moved by their underlying moral tone—sincere or not—we can nonetheless appreciate the skill and facile finesse with which they were written, and the good-natured rectitude and subdued, sometimes mischievous, humor that unploddingly runs through them. We can also appreciate their apparent originality. Apparent, because, while he borrows his subjects liberally from a variety of models—especially his contemporary, the Spanish fabulist Tomás de Iriarte (or Yriarte)—he seems intent on avoiding any direct debt to La Fontaine. There is, as a result, little if any *déjà entendu;* or, for that matter, any *déjà presque entendu,* so to speak.

Translated here, of Florian's five books of 110 fables—preceded by a lengthy, imaginative essay, "De la fable"—are the following numbers: I, 1; I, 4; I, 7; I, 19; II, 11; II, 14; II, 20; II, 21; III, 4; III, 16; IV, 16; V, 11; V, 18; and V, 22.

1. The review was reprinted in Dussault's *Annales littéraires,* III:452–58; and, for some obscure reason, repeated in toto (V:188–94).

2. As early as 1827 the compilers of the *Biographie nouvelle des contemporains*—one of whom was the fabulist Arnault (see pp. 124–125), who pays a personal tribute to his elder—could write with authority, if somewhat hyperbolically: "Ses œuvres complètes ont été réimprimées souvent dans tous les formats, et chacun de ses ouvrages séparément a eu un nombre presque incalculable d'éditions. Peu d'auteurs sont aussi répandus" (VII:186). As for the *Fables,* Alexandre Cioranescu, in his *Bibliographie de la littérature française du dix-huitième siècle,* cites twenty editions between 1792 and 1938, but there are certainly others. He does not, for example, include the edition reproduced in this collection (Paris: Mame, 1811). (Although Cioranescu mistakenly gives Florian's first name as Louis, his bibliographical data are usually reliable.)

3. For one of the rather few recent studies of his fables, see Hinrich Hudde, "Florians Fabeln: Regression angesichts der Revolution."

4. Even during his lifetime, and at the height of his career, Florian was not universally admired. He was, for example, a frequent and favorite target for the barbed wit of the maverick essayist Rivarol. The two following anecdotes are typical. "Un jour il [i.e., Rivarol] rencontra Florian, qui marchait devant lui, avec un manuscrit qui sortait de sa poche, il l'aborda, et lui dit: Ah! monsieur, si l'on ne vous connaissait pas, on vous volerait. . . . Il disait d'un écrit de Florian: Il y a la

moitié de l'ouvrage en blanc, et c'est ce qu'il y a de mieux." (See the anonymous *Esprit de Rivarol,* pp. 164, 176.)

5. See Cioranescu (*Bibliographie . . . du dix-huitième siècle,* I:800–804) for a detailed listing of his numerous titles, as well as a substantial number of studies devoted to his life and works.

6. See the "lundi" of December 30, 1850, in his *Causeries du lundi,* III:179.

7. In addition to the entries in a whole spate of biographical dictionaries, there are numerous works of interest, not the least engaging of which are his own very romanticized posthumous memoirs, *La Jeunesse de Florian, ou Mémoires d'un jeune Espagnol*—jauntily picaresque in flavor—a more modern edition of which, prefaced by André Bouis, bears the simple title *Mémoires d'un jeune Espagnol.* (Florian, who knew Spanish quite well, betrayed his affection for things Hispanic in many of his writings; especially in his controversial free, and abridged, translation of *Don Quijote:* the posthumous six-volume *Don Quichotte de la Manche.* Many nineteenth-century critics—Sainte-Beuve, Anatole France, and Emile Faguet among them—have taken their turn at recounting his life and works. For a detailed biography see Gustave Saillard, *Florian, sa vie, son œuvre.* (The preface to Alfred Dupont's above-mentioned edition of letters presents a particularly concise and well-documented biographical sketch.)

La Fable et la Vérité

    La Vérité toute nue
    Sortit un jour de son puits.
Ses attraits par le temps étoient un peu détruits.
    Jeunes et vieux fuyoient sa vue.
La pauvre Vérité restoit là morfondue,
Sans trouver un asile où pouvoir habiter.
    A ses yeux vient se présenter
    La Fable richement vêtue,
    Portant plumes et diamants,
    La plupart faux, mais très brillants.
"Eh! vous voilà, bon jour," dit-elle:
"Que faites-vous ici seule sur un chemin?"
La Vérité répond: "Vous le voyez, je gèle:
    Aux passants je demande en vain
    De me donner une retraite,

Truth and Fable

    Up from her well,
  One day, climbed naked Truth.[1]
    Now, truth to tell,
Time had not spared the beauty of her youth.
  At her approach, both young and old
Took flight and left her standing in the cold.
While thus she stood, abandoned and distressed,
    Fable appeared, sumptuously dressed—
    Feathers galore, diamonds a-glitter
    (Most of the latter false, forsooth!)—
    And tweaked her with a little twitter:
"Whatever are you doing there?" And Truth
    Replied: "I'm freezing! Can't you see?
I beg a lodging of the passersby,
    But when they take one look at me

Je leur fais peur à tous. Hélas! je le vois bien,
    Vieille femme n'obtient plus rien."
    "Vous êtes pourtant ma cadette,"
    Dit la Fable, "et, sans vanité,
    Partout je suis fort bien reçue.
    Mais aussi, dame Vérité,
    Pourquoi vous montrer toute nue?
Cela n'est pas adroit. Tenez, arrangeons-nous;
    Qu'un même intérêt nous rassemble:
Venez sous mon manteau, nous marcherons ensemble.
    Chez le sage, à cause de vous,
    Je ne serai point rebutée;
    A cause de moi, chez les fous
    Vous ne serez point maltraitée.
Servant par ce moyen chacun selon son goût,
Grâce à votre raison et grâce à ma folie,
    Vous verrez, ma sœur, que partout
    Nous passerons de compagnie."

1. Truth's proverbial residence at the bottom of a well—or pit, or abyss—is commonly attributed to the Greek philosopher Democritus, who is said to have stated: "Of a truth we know nothing, for truth is in a well." (See Diogenes Laertius, *Lives of Eminent Philosophers*, IX, 72, trans. R. D. Hicks, vol. 2, p. 485.) It would not be surprising to learn, however, that it antedates him, and is part of the wisdom of the ages. There is, for example, apparently a Scandinavian legend suggesting the same notion (see James S. Reid's edition of Cicero's *Academica* [Hildesheim: Georg Olms Verlagsbuchhandlung,

They quake with fright. And I know why.
An old hag begs in vain: they all refuse!"
"Old? Nonsense! You're much younger, dear, than I!
    Yet I go anywhere I choose.
    Besides, if you weren't standing there
    Without a stitch, completely bare,
I'm sure..." She paused. An idea crossed her mind.
"Dame Truth, it strikes me that we two could share
A common purpose, if you're so inclined.
Here, take my cloak. It's big enough for two.
    Then off we'll go... Because of you
    The wise will welcome me, whereas
    Because of me the fools will do
    No harm to you. Each of us has
    Her special style, her special skill.
Each with the other we'll go where we will.
Your wisdom and my folly: I doubt whether
There's anything that they can't do together!"[2]

1966], p. 216, n. 1); though even that legend may have been borrowed from Greco-Roman learned tradition. For other examples of the same theme, see the *Oxford Dictionary of English Proverbs*, p. 844.
2. Florian, knowingly or not, introduces his collection with an appropriate fiction already used in French fable literature by Claude-Joseph Dorat (see pp. 91–93), as the opening fable in his collections of 1772 and 1773–75. Dorat's "La Fable et la Vérité" recounts essentially the same cooperation between the two allegorical heroines.

Les Deux Voyageurs

Le compère Thomas et son ami Lubin
Alloient à pied tous deux à la ville prochaine.
    Thomas trouve sur son chemin
    Une bourse de louis pleine;
Il l'empoche aussitôt. Lubin, d'un air content,
    Lui dit: "pour nous la bonne aubaine!"
    "Non," répond Thomas froidement,
"Pour nous n'est pas bien dit, *pour moi* c'est différent."
Lubin ne souffle plus; mais, en quittant la plaine,
Ils trouvent des voleurs cachés au bois voisin.
    Thomas tremblant, et non sans cause,
Dit: "nous sommes perdus!" "Non," lui répond Lubin,
"Nous n'est pas le vrai mot; mais *toi* c'est autre chose."
Cela dit, il s'échappe à travers les taillis.
Immobile de peur, Thomas est bientôt pris:
    Il tire la bourse et la donne.

Qui ne songe qu'à soi quand sa fortune est bonne,
    Dans le malheur n'a point d'amis.

The Two Travelers

    Two friends—two peasants—one fine day,
    Loping along their merry way,
    Are going to town when, suddenly,
The first, Thomas by name, looks down. What does he see?
    A gold-filled purse! He pockets it straightway.
The other one—Lubin—beside himself with glee,
    Chortles: "What luck for us, my friend!"
"For *us?*" Thomas retorts. "No, not for *us*... For *me!*"
    Lubin keeps still. But as they round the bend,
A band of highwaymen jump from behind a tree!
    Thomas, in terror, shakes from head to toe.
    "We're done for!" he bewails. Lubin says: "Oh?
    Not *we*, my friend! No, no... Not *we*, but *you!*"
So saying, he turns, leaps through the bushes, runs, escapes...
    And leaves the other jackanapes,
    Frozen with fright, to bid his gold adieu.

He who forgets his friends when fortune smiles, may find
    No friends at all should fortune change her mind.

La Carpe et les Carpillons

"Prenez garde, mes fils, côtoyez moins le bord,
    Suivez le fond de la rivière;

The Mother Carp and Her Little Ones

    "Avoid the shallows, children dear.
    Beware the deadly line, and, deadlier yet,

Craignez la ligne meurtrière,
   Ou l'épervier plus dangereux encor."
C'est ainsi que parloit une carpe de Seine
A de jeunes poissons qui l'écoutoient à peine.
C'étoit au mois d'avril: les neiges, les glaçons,
Fondus par les zéphyrs, descendoient des montagnes;
Le fleuve enflé par eux s'élève à gros bouillons,
   Et déborde dans les campagnes.
      "Ah! ah!" crioient les carpillons,
      "Qu'en dis-tu, carpe radoteuse?
      Crains-tu pour nous les hameçons?
Nous voilà citoyens de la mer orageuse;
Regarde: on ne voit plus que les eaux et le ciel,
      Les arbres sont cachés sous l'onde,
      Nous sommes les maîtres du monde,
      C'est le déluge universel."
"Ne croyez pas cela," répond la vieille mère;
"Pour que l'eau se retire il ne faut qu'un instant:
Ne vous éloignez point, et, de peur d'accident,
Suivez, suivez toujours le fond de la rivière."
"Bah!" disent les poissons, "tu répètes toujours
      Mêmes discours.
Adieu, nous allons voir notre nouveau domaine."
      Parlant ainsi, nos étourdis
      Sortent tous du lit de la Seine,
Et s'en vont dans les eaux qui couvrent le pays.
      Qu'arriva-t-il? Les eaux se retirèrent,
      Et les carpillons demeurèrent;
         Bientôt ils furent pris
            Et frits.

      Pourquoi quittoient-ils la rivière?
      Pourquoi? Je le sais trop, hélas!
C'est qu'on se croit toujours plus sage que sa mère,
      C'est qu'on veut sortir de sa sphère,
C'est que... c'est que... Je ne finirois pas.

The leaded net!
   Swim deep... Swim deep, and never fear."
Such was the wisdom that a carp who called the Seine
Her home offered her young. They scarcely lent an ear.
      The month was April. Once again
      Spring zephyrs thaw the winter ice and snow,
Gushing in torrents, rushing down the mountainside.
   The river's waters, swollen, overflow.
      "Ha, ha!" the carplets cried,
      "Babbling old carp! A lot you know!
      Lines? Hooks? Nets? Bah! The mighty seas.
   Are now our home. We can swim where we please
   Even the trees have disappeared. Wherever
   You look—high, low—there's only sea and sky.
And this new world is ours! Not just some simple river!"
   "Tut tut," the mother cautions in reply.
"Don't be too sure, my little ones. However high
      The water rises, it can sink
         In but a wink.
Swim deep... Swim deep, I tell you, and stay close by me!"
   "Bah, bah!" they jeer. "We've heard that song before!
   And now, bye-bye! We think we'll go explore
   Our vast domain, and see what we can see."
      With that, they leave the Seine
         And, stubbornly,
   Swim through the flood that overspreads the plain.
What happened? Yes, the waters sank—you guessed,
                                    no doubt—
And left our carplets floundering about.
      In no time they were hooked,
            And cooked.

   Why? Why? I'll tell you why... Because
   There is no child, nor ever was,
Who takes his mother's word, or thinks himself less clever;
   Because man never knows his place, wherever;
Because... Because... Alas, I could go on forever.

Le Rossignol et le Prince

   Un jeune prince, avec son gouverneur,
      Se promenoit dans un bocage,
      Et s'ennuyoit, suivant l'usage;
      C'est le profit de la grandeur.
   Un rossignol chantoit sous le feuillage:
Le prince l'aperçoit, et le trouve charmant;
Et, comme il étoit prince, il veut dans le moment
      L'attraper et le mettre en cage.
      Mais pour le prendre il fait du bruit,
         Et l'oiseau fuit.
"Pourquoi donc," dit alors son altesse en colère,
      "Le plus aimable des oiseaux
Se tient-il dans les bois, farouche et solitaire,
Tandis que mon palais est rempli de moineaux?"
"C'est," lui dit le Mentor, "afin de vous instruire

The Nightingale and the Prince

   A prince was walking through the wood,
   His tutor by his side. The young patrician,
      True to His Highness's condition,
Found himself bored, as any proper young prince should!
   Just then, he saw a nightingale, and stood
In admiration. "Ah! I'll capture it," thought he.
   (Being a prince, he saw no reason not to.)
         But, as he sought to,
   Reaching, he made a sound, and instantly
         Off the bird flew.
      "Damnation!" cries His Majesty.
"Why must the fairest bird of all, concealed from view,
      Live in a savage wilderness,
      While, in my palace, sparrows swarm?" "Ah yes,"
Replies his mentor. "Yes, the nightingale keeps hidden—

De ce qu'un jour vous devez éprouver:
    Les sots savent tous se produire;
Le mérite se cache, il faut l'aller trouver."

A situation with a moral, sire, behind it:
    Folly will flock about your throne, unbidden;
True worth will hide. You'll have to seek to find it."

Le Grillon

    Un pauvre petit grillon
    Caché dans l'herbe fleurie
    Regardoit un papillon
    Voltigeant dans la prairie.
L'insecte ailé brilloit des plus vives couleurs;
L'azur, le pourpre et l'or éclatoient sur ses ailes;
Jeune, beau, petit-maître, il court de fleurs en fleurs,
    Prenant et quittant les plus belles.
"Ah!" disoit le grillon, "que son sort et le mien
    Sont différents! Dame nature
    Pour lui fit tout, et pour moi rien.
Je n'ai point de talent, encor moins de figure;
Nul ne prend garde à moi, l'on m'ignore ici bas:
    Autant vaudroit n'exister pas."
    Comme il parloit, dans la prairie
    Arrive une troupe d'enfants:
    Aussitôt les voilà courants
Après ce papillon dont ils ont tous envie.
Chapeaux, mouchoirs, bonnets, servent à l'attraper.
L'insecte vainement cherche à leur échapper,
    Il devient bientôt leur conquête.
L'un le saisait par l'aile, un autre par le corps;
Un troisième survient, et le prend par la tête:
    Il ne falloit pas tant d'efforts
    Pour déchirer la pauvre bête.
"Oh! oh!" dit le grillon, "je ne suis plus fâché;
Il en coûte trop cher pour briller dans le monde.
Combien je vais aimer ma retraite profonde!"
    Pour vivre heureux vivons caché.

The Cricket

    Hidden within a flowering thicket,
    A poor, pathetic cricket
    Espied a butterfly
Spreading its hues against the meadow sky.
Flitting from lovely flower to flower, the wingèd bug
    Shone in a blaze of azure, purple, gold.
    Beautiful, young—and, if the truth be told,
    Rather a trifle smug—
He lit, wooed, made his conquest, loved... and left.
    "Ah me!" the cricket sighed. "Why? Why
    Was I, by Lady Nature, so bereft?
    For him all goes aright, for me awry!
Talent? She gave me none! And beauty? Even less!
    Unknown, unloved... My life is emptiness.
    Why go on living?" Just as he
    Bemoans his dismal fate, a band
    Of children comes along. They see
The butterfly, admire, desire it, and
Give chase. Hats, bonnets, handkerchiefs... The eager troop
Puts everything to use: they swat, they swing, they swoop...
    Until the butterfly is caught at last.
    One holds the captive's body fast;
    Another pulls it by the wing;
    Another still grasps at his head...
    No need to try: the fragile thing
    Comes all undone... Dismembered... Dead.
    "Alas!" the cricket sighs, aghast, deciding
To flee the world and cherish his retreat instead:
    To live content, best live in hiding!'

1. The last line of Florian's moral has become proverbial.

La Pie et la Colombe

    Une colombe avoit son nid
    Tout auprès du nid d'une pie.
Cela s'appelle voir mauvaise compagnie,
D'accord; mais de ce point pour l'heure il ne s'agit.
    Au logis de la tourterelle
    Ce n'étoit qu'amour et bonheur;
    Dans l'autre nid toujours querelle,
    Œufs cassés, tapage et rumeur.
Lorsque par son époux la pie étoit battue,
    Chez sa voisine elle venoit,
    Là jasoit, crioit, se plaignoit,
    Et faisoit la longue revue
    Des défauts de son cher époux;

The Magpie and the Dove

    A dove had nested by a tree
    That housed a magpie. (I doubt whether
One could consider that good company—
But that's another matter altogether.)
    Nought but tranquillity and love
    Abounded where the turtledove
Abode with all her brood;' not like the pie,
Whose nest was fraught with constant hue and cry—
    Noise, broken eggs, and such. And when
Her mate would thrash her, time and time again,
She would come cackling to the dove, next door,
    Jabbering endless litanies
    About friend spouse's faults galore:²

"Il est fier, exigeant, dur, emporté, jaloux;
De plus, je sais fort bien qu'il va voir des corneilles";
    Et cent autres choses pareilles
    Qu'elle disoit dans son courroux.
    "Mais vous," répond la tourterelle,
"Etes-vous sans défauts?" "Non, j'en ai," lui dit-elle;
    "Je vous le confie entre nous:
En conduite, en propos, je suis assez légère,
Coquette comme on l'est, parfois un peu colère,
Et me plaisant souvent à le faire enrager:
Mais qu'est-ce que cela?" "C'est beaucoup trop, ma chère;
    Commencez par vous corriger;
Votre humeur peut l'aigrir..." "Qu'appelez-vous, mamie?"
    Interrompt aussitôt la pie:
"Moi de l'humeur! Comment! je vous conte mes maux,
Et vous m'injuriez! Je vous trouve plaisante.
    Adieu, petite impertinente:
    Mêlez-vous de vos tourtereaux."

    Nous convenons de nos défauts,
    Mais c'est pour que l'on nous démente.

1. Though purists—and ornithologists—would argue that there is a difference, Florian refers to his heroine as both *colombe* 'dove' and *tourterelle* 'turtledove'. I have followed him in this liberty.

"Arrogant... jealous... mean... And these
    Are only half the tale. There's more!
    The cad goes wenching night and day
With every cawing daw that struts his way!
Oh yes, I know! But that's not all..." "I see,"
    The dove retorts. "And you, I gather,
    Are free of every flaw?" "Who, me?"
She answers. "No, I have a few. I'm rather
Frivolous, you might say... Coquettish too...
And cross... And hard to live with, I suppose..."
"Good gracious," sighs the dove, "with faults like those
    I'd mend my ways if I were you!"
    "Faults? Faults? What faults, my friend? You dare to
Tell me I've got the flaws the flesh is heir to?"
"But... but..." "I came to you for sympathy,
    Not insults!" "But I thought you said..."
"I did. But did I say you should agree?
Bah! Go and tend your brood, you dunderhead!"

Yes, we admit our faults—indeed, decry them—
But only so that others may deny them.

2. This apparent disdain for the wife-beating magpie is more than a little ironic, considering that Florian himself had the unpleasant reputation of having manhandled, on occasion, at least one of his numerous mistresses. (See Thiébaut, "Parmi les livres," pp. 140–41.)

Le Chat et le Moineau

    La prudence est bonne de soi;
Mais la pousser trop loin est une duperie:
    L'exemple suivant en fait foi.
Des moineaux habitoient dans une métairie.
Un beau champ de millet, voisin de la maison,
    Leur donnoit du grain à foison.
Ces moineaux dans le champ passoient toute leur vie
Occupés de gruger les épis de millet.
Le vieux chat du logis les guettoit d'ordinaire,
Tournoit et retournoit; mais il avoit beau faire,
Sitôt qu'il paroissoit, la bande s'envoloit.
Comment les attraper? Notre vieux chat y songe,
    Médite, fouille en son cerveau,
Et trouve un tour tout neuf. Il va tremper dans l'eau
    Sa patte dont il fait éponge.
Dans du millet en grain aussitôt il la plonge;
    Le grain s'attache tout autour.
Alors à cloche-pied, sans bruit, par un détour,
    Il va gagner le champ, s'y couche
    La patte en l'air et sur le dos,
    Ne bougeant non plus qu'une souche.
Sa patte ressembloit à l'épi le plus gros:
L'oiseau s'y méprenoit, il approchoit sans crainte,
Venoit pour becqueter, de l'autre patte: Crac!
    Voilà mon oiseau dans le sac.
    Il en prit vingt par cette feinte.

The Cat and the Sparrow

    Caution is wise, there's no denying.
    Nevertheless, too much can do you harm.
    This fable should prove edifying.
A flock of sparrows, living on a farm,
    Next to a field of millet, spent
Day in day out among the ears of grain,
Eating and eating to their hearts' content,
And only stopping to begin again.
The household cat—an old and crafty beast—
Ogled the sparrows at their daily feast,
Trying his best to catch them, but in vain:
As soon as he crept close, the flock took flight.
    He pondered, thought, mused, wracked his brain...
At length he hits upon a stratagem that might,
    Indeed, succeed: he soaks one of his paws,
    Spongelike, and plunges it into a batch
        Of millet grain... Pauses... Withdraws...
    Success! As planned, the grains attach
Themselves about his paw. Now, off without a sound,
    He limps into the field, the long way round,
    Lies on his back among the stalks, stock-still,
    Paw in the air, content to wait until
    The birds arrive... One does, and sets about—
    Lured by the millet-paw—to peck her fill.
    Voilà! The other paw comes flying out...
    One bird, then two, then three... Into the sack!

Un moineau s'aperçoit du piège scélérat,
    Et prudemment fuit la machine;
      Mais dès ce jour il s'imagine
Que chaque épi de grain étoit patte de chat.
      Au fond de son trou solitaire
      Il se retire, et plus n'en sort,
      Supporte la faim, la misère,
      Et meurt pour éviter la mort.

Twenty in all, that day, fell prey to his attack.
But one, too clever, spied the trick and kept her distance.
    Henceforth, however, every time she saw
    An ear of grain, she feared it was a paw!
Result? Our sparrow leads a miserable existence,
Imagining, at every turn, that lurking claw!
    Starving, in time, she gasps her final breath,
Done in, not by the cat, but by the fear of death.

Le Roi de Perse

    Un roi de Perse certain jour
    Chassoit avec toute sa cour.
    Il eut soif, et dans cette plaine
    On ne trouvoit point de fontaine.
Près de là seulement étoit un grand jardin
Rempli de beaux cédras, d'oranges, de raisin:
    "A Dieu ne plaise que j'en mange!"
Dit le roi, "ce jardin courroit trop de danger:
Si je me permettois d'y cueillir une orange,
Mes visirs aussitôt mangeroient le verger."

The Persian King

    A Persian king, and retinue,
Were hunting, when, at length, His Highness grew
    Quite thirsty. But the plain traversed
Offered no spring to slake the royal thirst.
    Close by, there stood an orchard, though,
Laden with rich and luscious fruit. "Ah no,
It's best I not partake," the king professed.
    "No, not one orange, heaven forbid!
Farewell fair garden if I ever did!
Soon my viziers would come devour the rest!"

Le Rhinocéros et le Dromadaire

    Un rhinocéros jeune et fort
    Disoit un jour au dromadaire:
    "Expliquez-moi, s'il vous plaît, mon cher frère,
D'où peut venir pour nous l'injustice du sort.
L'homme, cet animal puissant par son adresse,
Vous recherche avec soin, vous loge, vous chérit,
    De son pain même vous nourrit,
    Et croit augmenter sa richesse
    En multipliant votre espèce.
    Je sais bien que sur votre dos
Vous portez ses enfants, sa femme, ses fardeaux;
Que vous êtes léger, doux, sobre, infatigable;
J'en conviens franchement: mais le rhinocéros
    Des mêmes vertus est capable;
Je crois même, soit dit sans vous mettre en courroux,

The Rhinoceros and the Dromedary

    Two beasts—rhinoceros and dromedary—
    Were having a discussion. "Why,"
    Queried the former, young and robust—very!—
"Why is it that you have more luck with man than I?
    Man... Man, that animal extraordinary!
    Fate isn't fair! He cherishes you, brother,
    Whereas with me, it's quite another
    Matter indeed! He houses you, he feeds you...
Handsomely, too!... In fact, he even breeds you,
Much to his own advantage monetary.
    Oh, I know all you do. I know
All of those things—wives, children, loads—you carry.
I know your docile temper, and your legendary
    Love of hard work. But, even so,
    I'm sure that a rhinoceros could do

Que tout l'avantage est pour nous:
Notre corne et notre cuirasse
Dans les combats pourroient servir;
Et cependant l'homme nous chasse,
Nous méprise, nous hait, et nous force à le fuir."
   "Ami," répond le dromadaire,
   "De notre sort ne soyez point jaloux;
C'est peu de servir l'homme, il faut encor lui plaire.
Vous êtes étonné qu'il nous préfère à vous:
Mais de cette faveur voici tout le mystère,
   Nous savons plier les genoux."

All of those things as well as you,
And some things even better—no offense!
In war, for instance, with our horn and hide,
We could help fight his battles. Why, it's common sense!
   But no! He scornfully casts us aside,
   And even hunts us with his blunderbuss!"
   "You needn't be so envious,"
The dromedary soberly replied.
"We serve. But, more, we please. That's why he honors us.
   And what's the secret? How? How do we please?
   Simple, my friend. We've learned to bend our knees."

Le Paon, les Deux Oisons et le Plongeon

Un paon faisoit la roue, et les autres oiseaux
   Admiroient son brillant plumage.
Deux oisons nasillards du fond d'un marécage
   Ne remarquoient que ses défauts.
"Regarde," disoit l'un, "comme sa jambe est faite,
   Comme ses pieds sont plats, hideux."
"Et son cri," disoit l'autre, "est si mélodieux,
   Qu'il fait fuir jusqu'à la chouette."
Chacun rioit alors du mot qu'il avoit dit.
   Tout à coup un plongeon sortit:
"Messieurs," leur cria-t-il, "vous voyez d'une lieue
Ce qui manque à ce paon: c'est bien voir, j'en conviens;
Mais votre chant, vos pieds, sont plus laids que les siens,
   Et vous n'aurez jamais sa queue."

The Peacock, the Two Goslings, and the Loon

A peacock, tail outspread—his pose of predilection—
   Was deemed by fellow birds the loveliest;
Except, that is, a pair of goslings, unimpressed.
   "Bah!" honked the first. "Such imperfection!
   Those legs, so ugly! And those feet, so flat!"
   "Ha!" squawked the second. "True! And that
Sweet voice" (he smirked) "that even makes the owl
                  take flight!"
   Just then, a loon, appearing from the marsh,
   Rebukes our goslings: "Friends, don't be so harsh.
   You're right. His legs, and feet, and voice are quite
Inelegant indeed! But oh, you silly birds,
   Your own are even more so, mark my words!
   Messieurs, the only difference is
You'll never, never have a tail like his!"

Les Deux Chauves

   Un jour deux chauves dans un coin
   Virent briller certain morceau d'ivoire:
Chacun d'eux veut l'avoir; dispute et coups de poing.
Le vainqueur y perdit, comme vous pouvez croire,
Le peu de cheveux gris qui lui restoient encor.
   Un peigne étoit le beau trésor
   Qu'il eut pour prix de sa victoire.

The Two Bald Men

   One day, two bald men spy a bit
   Of precious ivory shining on the floor.
   Each one, of course, lays claim to it.
Dispute... Words... Fists... The victor profits not a whit,
   Loses what few grey hairs he had before.
   His treasure? Price of all his pains?
   A comb, to comb the nothing that remains!

Le Crocodile et l'Esturgeon

Sur la rive du Nil un jour deux beaux enfants
   S'amusoient à faire sur l'onde,
Avec des cailloux plats, ronds, légers et tranchants,
   Les plus beaux ricochets du monde.
Un crocodile affreux arrive entre deux eaux,
S'élance tout à coup, happe l'un des marmots,
Qui crie, et disparoît dans sa gueule profonde.
L'autre fuit, en pleurant son pauvre compagnon.
   Un honnête et digne esturgeon,

The Crocodile and the Sturgeon

   One day, two fine Egyptian lads, at play,
      Along the river Nile,
   Were skimming stones in wondrous ricochet,
         When lo! a crocodile
      Appeared and reared its ugly jaws,
      And, one two three—no hems, no haws—
      Snapped up one of the children, who
   Went disappearing with a shriek into
The gaping gullet, as the other fled, lamenting.

Témoin de cette tragédie,
S'éloigne avec horreur, se cache au fond des flots;
Mais bientôt il entend le coupable amphibie
    Gémir et pousser des sanglots:
"Le monstre a des remords," dit-il: "ô providence!
    Tu venges souvent l'innocence;
    Pourquoi ne la sauves-tu pas?
Ce scélérat du moins pleure ses attentats;
    L'instant est propice, je pense,
    Pour lui prêcher la pénitence:
Je m'en vais lui parler." Plein de compassion,
    Notre saint homme d'esturgeon
    Vers le crocodile s'avance:
"Pleurez," lui cria-t-il, "pleurez votre forfait;
    Livrez votre âme impitoyable
Au remords, qui des dieux est le dernier bienfait,
Le seul médiateur entre eux et le coupable.
    Malheureux, manger un enfant!
Mon cœur en a frémi; j'entends gémir le vôtre..."
"Oui," répond l'assassin, "je pleure en ce moment
    De regret d'avoir manqué l'autre."

    Tel est le remords du méchant.

A righteous sturgeon, powerless, viewed the affair,
And fled as well. But when the reptile, in his lair,
Began to sob, thought he: "Aha! The cad's repenting!
    Strange are your ways, O Providence!
    Thus you avenge the innocent, although
    You might, instead, have taken his defense
    And spared him his travail! Well, even so,
At least the beast repents!... I'll teach him pentinence.
    Methinks the time is right..."
Compassionate, our pious sturgeon swims abreast.
    "Weep, sinner, weep! Repent with all your might!
Of all the gifts the gods bestow, forsooth the best—
    Better by far than all the rest—
    Is sweet remorse!
    The only road to heaven for the sinner!
    Alas! To eat a child... Oh, wretched dinner!
    I watched and shuddered at the sight, perforce.
    Ah, but you weep. Yes, now you weep..." "Of course
I weep," replies the crocodile, impenitent.
    "I weep, my friend, and so would you:
I only ate one child. I should have eaten two."

    Such is the way the villainous repent.

Le Milan et le Pigeon

    Un milan plumoit un pigeon,
    Et lui disoit: "méchante bête,
   Je te connois, je sais l'aversion
Qu'ont pour moi tes pareils; te voilà ma conquête!
Il est des dieux vengeurs." "Hélas! je le voudrois,"
Répondit le pigeon. "O comble des forfaits!"
S'écria le milan, "quoi! ton audace impie
    Ose douter qu'il soit des dieux?
J'allois te pardonner; mais, pour ce doute affreux,
    Scélérat, je te sacrifie."

The Falcon and the Pigeon

    A falcon caught a pigeon, with a mind
To pluck its feathers, gloating: "See? I've won, vile beast!
    I know how you and all your kind
    Loathe me and mine. But there are gods, at least—
Just and avenging gods!" "Alas!" the pigeon sighed,
"I wish there were!" "What did you say?" the falcon cried.
    "You doubt the gods exist? You don't believe...?
    What blasphemy! What heresy! What sin!
    Well, I was going to grant you a reprieve,
But now, to teach you piety, I'll do you in!"

Le Poisson Volant

Certain poisson volant, mécontent de son sort,
    Disoit à sa vieille grand'mère:
    "Je ne sais comment je dois faire
    Pour me préserver de la mort.
De nos aigles marins je redoute la serre
    Quand je m'élève dans les airs;
    Et les requins me font la guerre
    Quand je me plonge au fond des mers."
La vieille lui répond: "mon enfant, dans ce monde,
    Lorsqu'on n'est pas aigle ou requin,
Il faut tout doucement suivre un petit chemin,
En nageant près de l'air, et volant près de l'onde."

The Flying Fish

    A flying fish, unhappy with his state,
Was seeking some grandmotherly advice. He said:
"I fear, grandmamma dear, I'm like to end up dead!
    I wish I knew how to avoid that fate!
    Each time I fly up through the air,
    I worry that the eagles' claws will snatch me;
And when I plunge deep, deep beneath the waves,
                    that's where
    My enemies, the sharks, are sure to catch me."
    The elder fish replied: " 'Twas ever thus.
We who are neither sharks nor eagles... Woe to us,
    Unless we learn this rule and live thereby:
    Don't swim too deep, my child, or fly too high!"

Auguste Tandon   Fables et Contes en Vers Patois (1800)

[ANDRÉ-] Auguste Tandon was one of the important immediate predecessors of the Félibrige. When Joseph Roumanille and his colleagues initiated the neo-Provençal linguistic and artistic renaissance by founding that organization in 1854, the new school did not spring full-blown from their brows. Their endeavors merely crystallized and gave structure to a movement that had produced its sporadic champions for several hundred years. From the sixteenth century on, neo-Provençal writers like Louis Bellaud de la Bellaudière (1532–88) and Claude Brueys (1570–1636), among others, had already been taking determined—if less-organized—steps in the same direction. (See E. Portal, *La Letteratura provensala moderna*, pp. 68–69.) By the late 1700s the forerunners were legion.

For a variety of reasons the verse fable had early become one of their preferred genres and would continue to enjoy favored status throughout the nineteenth century, producing scores of works in a spectrum of southern dialects spreading from Gascony to Provence. (See Emile Ruben, *De quelques imitations patoises des Fables de La Fontaine*, pp. 4–7;[1] F. Roustan, *Pichoto Istòri de la Literaturo d'O: o prouvençalo despièi sis óurigino enjusquo à noste tèms*, p. 183.)[2] Most of them, indeed, would be inspired to some degree by La Fontaine; but they would be no less imbued with a flavor very much their own, typical of the Midi and all its earthy wisdom and wit.[3]

Known as "le troubadour de Montpellier," Tandon was born in that city on July 15, 1759, into a family long respected for its scientific and cultural achievements. (See Frédéric Donnadieu, *Les Précurseurs des Félibres: 1800–1855*, pp. 64–66; and the entry on Tandon in the revised *Biographie universelle, ancienne et moderne* ("Biographie Michaud"), XI:671–72.)[4] After studying mathematics, for which he showed an exceptional aptitude even as a child, he entered the banking house of an uncle, eventually rising to a director's position in one of the most important banks in the south of France at the time. During the Revolution he resisted the invitation to play an active role in the economic reorganization of the government. He did, however, fill a number of important municipal posts in Montpellier—though not without running afoul, temporarily, of local revolutionary zealots—turning to his poetry and dialectal studies as a diversion from his weightier occupations. He died suddenly in his native city on November 27, 1824.

Tandon's poetry in the Montpellier dialect enjoyed considerable success, both during his lifetime and beyond. His collection *Fables et contes en vers patois* was well enough received to warrant an enlarged edition a dozen years later, as well as a contemplated third edition, projected by the Montpellier bookseller and publisher Virenque, announced in 1842, almost two decades after his death, but apparently never realized. Tandon also left a number of works in French unpublished, including two linguistic studies: "Traité sur les lettres, les diphthongues, les différents sons et l'orthographe du patois" and "Observations grammaticales sur le patois du Languedoc"; two collections of tales: "Contes en vers français" and "Recueil d'historiettes en prose"; a group of theater pieces, among them a one-act verse comedy, "Le Dénouement imprévu," and fragments of two tragedies; and several others. (There is no indication in the sources consulted what became of the manuscripts in question.)

As might be expected, Tandon's fables are largely Provençalized versions of the works of other fabulists, ancient and modern; foremost among them, La Fontaine. Some—for example, "Lou Guindou et lou Diaman," in this collection—are almost literal renderings. Others stray farther afield from their models and exhibit more of the poet's individuality and local color. Still others are wholly original creations. All of them display "la verve, l'esprit," and "le naturel" that earned for them Donnadieu's judgment that "aucun recueil dans ce genre et dans cette langue n'est supérieur à celui d'Auguste Tandon" (pp. 63–64).

The first edition of *Fables et contes en vers patois* contains seventy-seven fables and an epilogue, as well as six tales (though the distinction between the two genres is not always obvious) and a brief Anacreontic imitation, all divided into three parts. The second edition contains one hundred and four. The five fables translated here are taken from the first edition, where they are numbered as follows: I, 11; I, 23; I, 27; II, 27; and II, 28.

---

1. Among the earliest examples, overlooked by Ruben, would seem to be the thirteen fables of the Marseille poet François-Toussaint Gros (1698–1748), in his *Recueil de pouesiés prouvençalos*.

2. Foremost among the reasons is probably the down-to-earthiness of the fable; its applicability to the lives of a basically rural population, for whom the fable's typical domain, with all its simplicity of subject and language, was unaffected by what Ruben calls "la prétention d'être une littérature" (p. 85).

3. Not all the Provençal fabulists would choose to write in patois, however. The celebrated Marseillais, Louis Jauffret (see pp. 131–32), would write in French, as would a number of other lesser-known southern predecessors and contemporaries. (See Robert Reboul, *Fabulistes provençaux*.)

4. The original edition (1811–62) includes no entry on Tandon. The one cited, however, contains considerable biographical and anecdotal information.

(after Goya)

Lou Mulét Sé Vantan dé Sa Généalogia

Lou Mulét d'un Ampérur,
Fier d'avédre un parèl mèstre,
Tranchava dâou grand Ségnur,
Et s'imaginava d'èstre
Aoutan noble qué dégus;
Dé sa mayre la Cavala
Fasiè mila contes blus,
D'Alphana ou dé Bucéphala
Disiè qu'èra décéndut.
Vouïe per él, dis l'histoira,
Plaça âou Témple dé mémoira;
Et sé sériè créségut
Déshounourat, misèrable,
Sé y'aviè fâougut servi
Un Ministre, un Conétable.
Quand séguèt vièl, âou mouli,
Triste ét capot l'énmandèrou;
Sa Noubléssa s'ésclipsèt,
Sous Ancètras s'oublidèrou;
Et Moussu sé rapélèt,
San soungeâ pus à sa mayre,
Qu'un Ase èra éstat soun payre.

The Mule Who Boasted of His Family Tree[1]

An emperor's mule was so impressed
At being regally indentured
That, *à la grand seigneur,* he ventured
To think himself best of the best.
Ah! What fine tales preposterous
He would recount, puffed up with pride:
Those stallions on his mother's side—
Alfana and Bucephalus—[2]
Ancestors all, to hear him tell!
Why, history owed him a place
In glory's lofty citadel!
And it would be a vile disgrace—
Indelible escutcheon smutch!—
Were he obliged to serve a mere
Marshal, or minister, or such!...
Well, he grew old, our chevalier,
And got packed off to work the mill.
Broken of body, heart, and will,
He fast forgot his airs, alas!
As sadly he recalled, perforce,
That mother, true, had been a horse,
But father, just a lowly ass.

1. Tandon's obvious model is La Fontaine's "Le Mulet Se Vantant de Sa Généalogie" (VI, 7), although the latter's mule labored for a priest and would have thought himself dishonored in the service of a doctor. But Tandon, all in all, takes fewer liberties with his model than did La Fontaine with the Aesopic original (Babrius, 62). (See Perry, *Aesopica,* "Fabulae Latinae" no. 315, p. 446.)

2. Alfana—King Gradasso's horse in Ludovico Ariosto's Renaissance epic of the Roland legend, *Orlando Furioso* (1516)—is less well known than Alexander the Great's "ox-headed" charger Bucephalus; but he served his master, "the bravest of the Pagan knights," with no less panache.

Lou Lioun Amourous

Un Lioun d'alura superba,
En traversan un certèn prat,

The Lion in Love[1]

A lion strode with noble air
Across a grassy field, and spied

Végèt foulatrégeâ su l'herba
Fiïa qu'èra for à soun grat;
La démandèt vite én mariage.
Démanda dé Lioun és couma qué diriè
Absolumén fàou qu'aco siè.
Lou Péra, home d'ésprit, rusat âoutan qué sage,
Et qué saviè qu'és aco qu'un Lioun,
May qu'agèsse vougut un géndre
Et mén tèrrible ét d'una âoutra façoun,
Embé plési paréy l'énténdre:
Lou prèga dé fayre aténsioun
Qué sa Fiïa èra délicata;
Qué, quand voudriè la caréssâ,
Sas grifas poudrièn la blassâ:
"Permétès doun qu'à chaqua pata,
Vous las râougnén." "Râougna-mé lâs."
"Aco's pa tout" (ajusta alor lou Pèra)
"Ma Fiïa vôou... Ma Fiïa éspèra
Qué vostras déns sé limou." "Lima-lâs,"
Dis lou Lioun qué s'impassiénta,
Et qué l'amour aviè privat dé soun bon sén.
Alor una man diligénta
Râougnèt, limèt ét désarmèt tan bén
Nostre amourous, qu'un soul gros dogue
Lou tuèt san gayre susâ.

On véy per aquél apologue
Qu'émbé l'Amour Prudénça habita pâ.

A maiden frolicsome and fair.
"Ah me, just to my taste!" he sighed.
And he decided then and there
To seek to make the winsome belle his bride.
Now, what a lion wants a lion gets.
Her father, quick of wit and no less clever,
Knows well a lion's ways, but lets
Our suitor ply his suit. However,
He would prefer, in simple truth,
A different sort of son-in-law,
Rather less powerful of paw
And not so well endowed of tooth.
"Listen," says he, "my daughter's flesh is tender.
One hug, and you... Well, in a word, you'll rend her
Delicate body, limb from limb!
Of course, if we could cut your claws..." "Cut! Cut!"
The lion answers him.
"Well, if you're sure," replies the father, "but
That's not quite all. Your teeth, you see...
She'll find them rather sharp!" "Tut tut!"
"If we could file them..." "File! File!" eagerly
Echoes the lion, love-benighted.
And so they did as he invited—
Teeth, claws, and all—until one single hound
Attacked him, hacked him, and he meekly died.

It's clear that, as our lion found,
Love and good sense live seldom side by side.

---

1. Tandon's rendering of this Aesopic original (Babrius, 98), was clearly inspired by La Fontaine's "Le Lion Amoureux" (IV, 1). The latter is a much more elaborate version, however, including a dedica- tory prologue to Madame de Sévigné's daughter, to whom she was to write her famous letters that would become the model of seventeenth-century epistolary style.

Lou Guindou ét Lou Diaman

Un jour un Guindou trouvèt
Un Diaman, ét lou pourtèt
Aou pu proche lapidayre:
"Disou bé, s'ou dis, qu'és fin;
Mès un pâouquét dé réprin
Fariè miïou moun afayre."

Un ignara qu'héritèt
D'un manuscrit, lou pourtèt
A soun vési lou Librayre:
"Disou bé qu'és éxcélén,
S'ou dis, mès un pâou d'argén
Fariè miïou moun afayre."

The Turkey and the Diamond[1]

A turkey found a diamond, and
Went to the jeweler close at hand,
Complaining: "Yes, I know... *On dit*...
It's fine... But it won't feed me, will it?
I'd rather find a pile of millet.
That would be much more use to me!"[2]

A fool inherited a book—
A manuscript, in fact—and took
The heirloom to the bookman. "See?
They say it's rare. Who cares? Not I, sir!
A little money would be nicer!
That would be much more use to me!"[3]

---

1. The reader will recognize a variation of the often-treated theme of the precious gem discovered by the unappreciative cock. (In this volume, see, for example, p. 4. For another medieval rendering, see my *Fables from Old French: Aesop's Beasts and Bumpkins*, pp. 50–51.) The Aesopic original ("Pullus ad margari- tam" [Phaedrus, III, 12], cited as no. 503 of the "Fabulae Latinae" in Perry, *Aesopica*, p. 573) suggests no comparison between the cock and an oafish bibliophobe. The idea, however, was not Tan- don's. With minor differences his version is an almost literal trans- lation of La Fontaine's "Le Coq et la Perle" (I, 20). Tandon's *guindou* is dialectal for *dindon* (or *coq d'Inde* 'turkey-cock'). In France the turkey has long enjoyed—so to speak—the same

reputation for stupidity as in America, from which it had been introduced soon after its discovery in Mexico early in the sixteenth century.

2. I take liberties here with the turkey's fancied diet. While La Fontaine's cock does, indeed, yearn for millet (*grain de mil*), the *réprin* of Tandon's Montpellier dialect refers to bran; specifically,

to the bran left after milling, but still containing grain. (See Pierre-Augustin Boissier de Sauvages, *Dictionnaire languedocien-françois*, II:227. This dictionary was originally published in Nîmes in 1756 and revised in 1785.)

3. I follow the author here, who in turn followed La Fontaine in his effective—if unusual—use of a single line to end both verses.

Lou Cat ét lou Chi

Un Cat, qué toumbèt dins un pous,
  Cridava couma un malhérous:
"Misèricorda! assisténça! mé nègue."
  Un certèn Chi dé sous amis,
  Qu'èra pa sourd, mès qu'èra bègue,
  Anèt d'ounte végnèn lous cris:
"T'ou disièy bé, moun pâoure Camarada,
  Qu'un jour malhur t'arivariè:
Touta la gnoch ét touta la journada
  Trépes dé la cava âou gragnè;
Mès, diga-mé, couma as fach ta fatiga
  Per toumba aval? Aco m'éntriga."
"Hé! moun Amic," yé réspoundèt lou Cat,
  "S'as un pâou dé misèricorda,
Jita mé vite quâouqua corda;
Té diray pioy couma tout s'és passat."

1. It will be obvious that I have taken the liberty—justified, I think—of incorporating into the dialogue the dog's stammer, to which the author merely alludes.

The Cat and the Dog

A cat fell down a well. "Help! Help!
Save me, I'm drowning!" he began to yammer.
  His friend the dog—a pleasant whelp—
Quite sound of ear, but speaking with a stammer,
  Rushes to where he hears the cries
  And caterwauls, looks down, and sighs:
  "D-d-dear me, d-d-dear me!...
I t-t-told you you were going to be
In t-t-trouble, traipsing night and day,
Upstairs and d-d-down... Well, anyway,
  How did you f-f-fall, I wonder?...
Tell me, I'm really f-f-fascinated."[1]
  "Not now, not now!" the cat berated.
  "Throw me a rope, or I'll go under!
I'll tell you later how it came about.
But first, good God in heaven, just get me out!"

Lou Roussignôou

Annuïat dé soun ramage,
Un Roussignôou fort voulage,
Vouguèt, un jour, né changeâ;
Et, vési d'una Linota,
Qué juste ét nota per nota,
Cantava un er d'Opèrâ,
Moussu qué crésiè facille
Dé cantâ dins aquél gous,
Sé créséguèt fort habille
Après sèpt ou yoch liçous:
Mès aquél Pâoure imbicille
Moustrèt bé soun pâou dé sén;
Car d'aquél événémén
Perdèt soun ancièn ramage;
Et, bousigan lou nouvèl,
Soun sort dévénguèt cruèl.
Lous Aoussèls dâou vésinage,
Quand couménçava à cantâ,
Fugissièn san l'éscoutâ.

The Nightingale

A nightingale much given to whim,
Tired of his song, found it unfit,
In fact, for one the likes of him,
And had a mind to better it.
A linnet in the neighborhood
Knew note for note an opera air.
"Easy!" monsieur opined: he could
Learn just as well and sound as good.
And so our misinclined *compère*,
After some lessons—seven or eight—
Decided it was time to bare
His talents. But the dunder-pate,
Because he thought himself so clever,
Suffered a most unhappy fate:
Lost was the old sweet song forever.
What's more, so mucked up was the new,
That now, whenever he would sing,
Birds round about would all take wing
And leave him there, unlistened to.

Antoine-Pierre Dutramblay   Apologues (1801–22)

I F LA FONTAINE seems originally to have intended his *Fables* for the entertaining edification of the young, he soon expanded his horizon to embrace the more intellectually sophisticated. While some of his followers maintained the fiction of writing for a youthful audience, it is clear that most hoped to be read and appreciated by the more mature. Some, nevertheless, truly did compose their apologues with children in mind.[1] One of the most straightforward of purpose was Antoine-Pierre Dutramblay, family man par excellence—father, grandfather, great-grandfather—who wrote his fables, in fact, for his own grandchildren.[2]

Dutramblay was born in Paris, on April 27, 1745, of landed aristocracy from the village of Rubelles, near Melun. Though not of sufficient stature to have warranted a full-length study, he does appear in many of the standard nineteenth-century biographical dictionaries, and his life is sketched in some detail—though none too objectively—in the *notice* to the posthumous edition of his *Apologues*.[3] After finishing his studies at the celebrated Collège de Juilly, Dutramblay, following a two-century-old family tradition, prepared for a career in the law. He subsequently spent his long professional life in public service, placidly weathering the revolutionary storms and going on to fill a number of administrative posts—principally in the *Chambre des comptes* and *Caisse d'amortissement*—under kings, consul, and emperor. Throughout his career he enjoyed an unblemished reputation for integrity, moral judgment, and personal benevolence, qualities that will come as no surprise to readers of his fables. Dutramblay's devotion to duty was rewarded with the cross of the Légion d'honneur and the title of baron, conferred by Louis XVIII upon his retirement in 1817, after fifty-four years of service. He died at Rubelles on October 24, 1819.

Besides compiling two substantial technical works relating to law and finance, Dutramblay collaborated on several theater pieces, the most significant of which would appear to have been a three-act opera entitled *Henri de Bavière*, performed at the Opéra-Comique in 1804.[4] As for his principal, albeit modest, claim to literary laurels,

biographers have pointed out the appropriateness of the fable as his preferred genre: he was, in fact, related to the great La Fontaine. The latter's influence is, of course, clear, as it is with most of his successors; but it would be a wild exaggeration to claim, with some overly enthusiastic partisans, any but a superficial formal resemblance. On the other hand, readers of Dutramblay's fables may find a little harsh and uncharitable the observations of nineteenth-century literary historian Bernard Jullien, who, while acknowledging "l'expression d'une âme honnête et candide," criticizes "la morale et la disposition communes, le style plat et lâche." (See *Histoire de la poésie française à l'époque impériale,* II:172.)

Dutramblay's fables were published under the title *Apologues* in five editions: 1801, 1806, 1810, 1818, and 1822.[5] Of the first two, both published anonymously, I have been able to locate only the latter. Its 120 fables, evenly divided into six books, are preceded by a dedicatory *épître,* in verse, to his grandchildren; an epilogue is placed after the first three books.[6] Of the third and fourth editions, the former is a reprinting of the first two, but including the author's name; the latter, an augmented collection of 133. The fifth, posthumous, edition was privately printed as a memorial to Dutramblay by his grandchildren, and was intended only for family and friends. Besides the lengthy biographical sketch (see above), it contains 127 fables, distributed as before over six books, reproducing in different order most of those in the 1806 (and presumably 1801) edition, as well as a few previously unpublished and discovered among the author's papers. (Characteristically, the dedicatory *épître,* apparently modified in one of the two intervening editions, includes the name of an additional grandchild.)

The group of fables translated here from the 1822 edition—I, 14; III, 2; III, 3; V, 12; and VI, 11—are examples of Dutramblay's uncomplicated homespun morality and unabashed didacticism, naively charming nonetheless, and relieved here and there by an occasional dramatic flash and unexpected insight. Of the five, all but the first and last had also appeared in the edition of 1806.

---

1. Or at least so some of their later editors assumed. See, for example, the many fables collected in *Le Fablier du jeune âge.* This volume contains the work of scores of seventeenth-, eighteenth- and nineteenth-century fabulists—well-known, lesser-known, little-known, and unknown.

2. There is considerable variety in the ways that Dutramblay's name is misspelled and miscited: Dutremblay, Du Tremblay, Du Tramblay de Rubelle(s), etc. I have to assume that the spelling used by his family in the posthumous edition of his *Apologues* (see below) is authoritative. Ironically, it is not the one used by the compilers of a current biographical dictionary, who, while cautioning against error, cite him as Du Tramblay. (See the *Dictionnaire de biographie française,* XII:929–30.)

3. See, among others, the entry in the *Biographie universelle et por-*

tative des contemporains, II:1544–45. Dating from two decades after Dutramblay's death, it served as an obvious basis for others that followed.

4. The catalogue of the Bibliothèque Nationale lists this title as being the work of "M. Léger... et M. D✳✳✳y [Dutramblay]." The "M. Léger" in question is undoubtedly François-Pierre-Auguste Léger (1766–1823), who wrote numerous light comedies at the turn of the century. Dutramblay also collaborated in at least three recorded *comédies-vaudevilles* presented at the Théâtre des Troubadours: *A bas les diables, Le Bureau d'adresse des mariages,* and *Deux et deux font quatre.* Sources indicate that the first two were written with one "Lefèvre" (whom I suspect to be Joseph Lefèbvre [1761–ca. 1822], composer of comic operas for the Comédie-Italienne); the last, with two collaborators referred to variously as "Gassicourt et Bonnin" and

"Cadet-Gassicourt et Bonin." (I can offer no information concerning the latter; the former, however, was obviously Charles-Louis-Félix Cadet de Gassicourt [1769–1821], chemist, gastronomer, and satirist of the period.)

5. His seemingly intentional avoidance of the term "fable" may reflect his frequent use of human rather than animal characters. The distinction, however, was honored by his predecessors—La Fontaine included—more in the breach than in the observance.

6. The opening lines of the *épître* leave no doubt as to the author's intended audience: "Oui, mes enfans [*sic*]: oui, mes petits amis, / Laure, Hippolyte, Adèle, et toi cher Alexis; / Oui! c'est pour vous que j'ai fait cet ouvrage . . ." (p. 5). In the midpoint epilogue he justifies his devotion to a seemingly juvenile genre, not only on the grounds of personal predilection, but also with the pretext of furnishing his descendants with a moral self-portrait: "dans ce travail si léger, / On a tant de plaisir, avec si peu de peine! / Je suis le penchant qui m'entraîne: / Sans y penser, je vous fais mon portrait" (p. 137).

La Bonbonnière

Sur sa table, une bonne mère
Avait laissé sa Bonbonnière.
Doit-on ainsi tenter les gens?
Un marmot l'aperçoit; les marmots sont friands;
    Il s'en empare sans scrupule,
    Et de croquer à belles dents;
    Mais qu'a-t-il pris?... une pillule.
    Bientôt un léger mal de cœur...
    Le larcin est clair, tout l'annonce;
    Le lit, la diète et la semonce
    Vont punir le petit voleur.
  La friandise est souvent corrigée.
    Gardons-nous de l'esprit malin;
    Il nous présente la dragée
    Et nous donne du chicotin.

The Bonbonnière

A mother left her bonbonnière
Out on a table. Don't you think
She might have taken greater care?
Sweet-toothed, a tot espies it. In a wink,
Untroubled by his childish indiscretion,
    Gluttonously he takes possession...
    Digs in... Begins to chew his fill,
    Until... Good heaven! What's that he's got?
    A pill! An awful pill, that's what!
    In no time, not a little ill,
    His crime is clear, and drear his lot:
    Off to bed... Scolded... Supperless!
Moral: beware the mind's maliciousness:
    Often that crafty counterfeiter
    Promises sweet, and gives us bitter!

L'Esprit et le Cœur

    Bouffi d'orgueil et d'arrogance,
    L'esprit voulut un jour, au cœur,
    Disputer la prééminence.
"Comme on jouit de moi! comme on me fait honneur!"
  S'écriait-il. "Je consens qu'on t'admire,"
  Reprit le Cœur, "j'aime à voir tes succès:
    Mais un instant tu peux séduire,
    Et moi j'attache pour jamais."

The Mind and the Heart

    The mind and heart were in dispute,
    Protesting their respective value.
"What," cried the former—haughty, pompous—"shall you
Dare to deny that I reign absolute?"
    The heart was quick in repartee:
"Indeed, you're much admired. That's understood.
Yes, you seduce... But oh, so fleetingly!
With me, what once I charm, I charm for good."

Le Tigre et le Serpent

    "Quand tu piques, moi je dévore,"
    Disait au Serpent venimeux,
    Un Tigre au regard furieux.
    "On peut bien te valoir encore,"
    Dit le reptile... "inaperçu,
    J'empoisonne sans être vu."

    Qu'on calomnie ou qu'on médise,
    On est cruel profondément;
Mais qu'on soit Tigre au moins, et qu'on ait la franchise
    De déchirer ouvertement.

The Tiger and the Snake

    "You sting, but I devour my victim,"
    Tiger taunts snake. To contradict him,
    Snidely the latter sneers: "Pooh pooh!
    I sting, yet I'm no less pernicious.
    I can kill quite as well as you...
    My poison's just more surreptitious."

    Insult is cruel; slander, malicious.
    Still, if you must indulge such passion,
At least attack like tiger, in straightforward fashion:
    Be forthright even if you must be vicious.

Le Vieillard et le Chêne

"Tu n'es qu'un embryon, cher homme, en vérité,"
Disait un Chêne, fier de sa haute stature,
    A celui qui l'avait planté:
"Qu'auprès de moi tu fais triste figure!
Je puis bien me permettre un peu de vanité:
Le ciel touche mon front, et l'enfer ma racine."
    Le Vieillard piqué, lui dit: "Tiens,
    Dans ce gland, vois ton origine;
    Tu sauras du moins d'où tu viens:
    En t'arrosant, je t'ai fait naître;
Pour soutenir, pour agrandir ton être,
    Je n'ai cessé de te choyer:
Devenu grand, tu veux me méconnaître;
    Tu ne seras pas le premier."

The Old Man and the Oak Tree

    "Poor dwarf!" an oak tree shouted, flaunting
    Proudly his stature—tall and stout of limb.
    "How small you are," he twitted, taunting
The very man who, years before, had planted him.
    "I know I'm vain. But then, why not? You
See how I reach my head to heaven, my roots to hell."[1]
    The old man, vexed, replied: "Well, well,
    My haughty one, look what begot you:
Nought but an acorn, small as small can be.
And me? I nurtured you from sprout to tree...
    I fed your hunger, slaked your thirst...
I cared for you... 'Cared?' No, say 'coddled,' 'nursed'...
    And now, grown great, you scoff at me!
Alas, my friend, I fear you're not the first."[2]

1. It is not unlikely that the author is here echoing La Fontaine's description of his more celebrated oak tree at the end of "Le Chêne et le Roseau" (I, 22): "Celui de qui la tête au ciel était voisine, / Et dont les pieds touchaient à l'empire des morts" (see p. 33).

2. It should not be assumed that this cynical moral was directed at the author's own children. In a similar fable on the evils of filial ingratitude, "Les Deux Vieillards" (V, 1), he takes pains to explain in a note that such reflections are strictly secondhand, based on his observation of "le tableau souvent douloureux de la société," and that he, on the contrary, is blessed with "bons enfants, qui ne m'ont jamais donné que de la satisfaction." (The reader may also note the probably accidental similarity to Dorat's "Le Chêne et le Gland" [p. 94].)

Le Château de Cartes

    Un jeune enfant avait fait un château,
    Château de cartes, mais fort beau.
    Il avait jusqu'à triple étage,
    Salon, boudoir, *et cætera*:
    On s'extasiait sur l'ouvrage,
    Tout allait au mieux jusques-là.
    Un succès nous rend téméraire.
    Le marmot prétend ajouter:
    Sagement on veut l'arrêter,
    Il se fâche, il est en colère.
    "Le Château va se renverser,"
Lui dit-on, "gardez-vous de passer la mesure,
    Le moindre poids va l'affaisser."
Vain conseil, il est sourd, il tente l'aventure.
    Sa carte pose, adieu le beau Château;
    Tout l'édifice est à vau-l'eau.

The House of Cards

    A youngster built a house... That is,
    A house of cards, three stories high!
With "ohs" and "ahs," and many a "my oh my,"
Everyone much admired this house of his—
This castle, with its halls, boudoirs, and such.
    But what can rise in turn may fall:
    Success can make us risk our all.
Indeed, the lad would add one final touch...
    "No, no! Leave well enough alone!"
    Wisely the others warn. "Tut tut,"
    The tot replies in surly tone;
    "Why don't you mind your business!" "But...
But can't you see... One breath and down it tumbles!"
Deaf to their plea, despite their admonition,
    Deftly he makes one last addition...
    And, sure enough, his castle crumbles.

Bon avis aux faiseurs d'affaires.	Such is the price of vain ambition.
—Quelle soif affreuse de gain!	Be satisfied with sweet, don't look for sweeter!
—Les destins furent si prospères!	Good lesson for our young entrepreneurs,
—Encore celle-ci.—Celle-ci, puis demain	When greed eggs on and speculation spurs.
Une autre encore, et jamais la dernière.	Fortune's a fickle-hearted cheater.
Tu veux fixer la fortune légère,	She lets you think you're going to beat her,
Mon bon ami, gare la fin.	But in the end the victory is hers!

Madame de Genlis   Herbier Moral, ou Recueil de Fables Nouvelles (1801)

Almost a century would pass after the publication of Madame de Villedieu's brief collection of lengthy fables (see pp. 37–38) before the genre would again inspire female writers to put moralizing pen to paper. The honor should probably be shared more or less *ex aequa* by three lady fabulists: the marquise de La Férandière, of the late eighteenth century, and, give or take a few years, both Madame de Genlis and Madame Joliveau de Segrais, who wrote in the early nineteenth; the former for being the first in more modern times to write and publish fables at all, and the second two for publishing actual collections of them, within a year or so of each other.

The fables of Marie-Amable Petitau (1736–1817), marquise de La (or "la") Férandière (or "Laférandière," or even "La Ferrandière"), began appearing in the *Almanach des Muses* of 1780 and continued to be published in that anthology of *pièces fugitives* through 1798, most often attributed, for whatever coy reasons, simply to "Madame la marquise de La Fér∗∗∗." (The "marquise" was noticeably absent in the numbers printed during the height of the Revolution.)[1] Those that I have been able to lay my hands on, not without their period charm, are very traditional in form and sentimentally saccharine in their moralistic content, and offer little to distinguish themselves other than the sex of their author.[2] They are not represented here. On the other hand, the work of her fabulist *consœurs*, Madame de Genlis and, especially, Madame Joliveau de Segrais (see pp. 118–19), do, I think, deserve more than passing mention.

The comtesse de Genlis was, without question, one of the more imposing and productive female French writers of the years straddling the Revolution, characterized by one historian of the fable, unflatteringly, as "l'incorrigible écrivailleuse."[3] Born Caroline-Stéphanie-Félicité Du Crest (or "Ducrest") de Saint-Aubin, near Autun, on January 26, 1846, she devoted most of her life, almost single-mindedly, to the education and would-be edification of the young, both as governess to the children of the duchesse de Chartres—notable among them the future king Louis-Philippe—and in her truly voluminous literary production: theater, essays, verse, memoirs, and moral tales of didactic inspiration and intent.[4] This

did not prevent her from having a notorious affair with the libertine Louis-Philippe-Joseph, duc d'Orléans, father of her royal charges, whose ultraliberal views would earn him the nickname "Philippe-Egalité." Nor did it prevent her from being an active participant in the aristocratic political and social life of that troubled time; a time that saw both her husband and Philippe-Egalité sent to the guillotine in 1793, the latter despite his liberal politics.

Madame de Genlis, who had emigrated in 1791, spent the following years in England, Switzerland, and Germany, continuing to mine the vein of her seemingly inexhaustible, if rather lackluster, inspiration. Allowed to return to France in 1802, she enjoyed the favor and largesse of Napoleon for a time, which permitted her to continue exploiting it further, thanks to an annual pension and lodgings at the Bibliothèque de l'Arsenal. She lived on long enough to see her former pupil, Louis-Philippe, on the throne of France, and died in Paris on December 31, 1830.[5]

One of the more modest, though original, products of the countess's decade of expatriation was her *Herbier moral, ou Recueil de fables nouvelles, et autres poésies fugitives.*[6] The originality of the eighteen fables in her collection lies neither in their already-traditional *vers libres* form, nor in the good-sense message of their morals, but rather in the relative novelty of their characters: "Vous savez," she writes in the dedicatory *épître* to Lady Edward FitzGerald—reputed to be her daughter by Philippe-Egalité—"que depuis long-temps j'avois le désir de composer des fables, et qu'en même temps je n'avois pas assez de présomption ni assez d'humilité pour entreprendre de faire parler *messire loup, maître renard*, et *la gent'-trotte-menu*, après l'inimitable La Fontaine." Furthermore, echoing Rousseau, she finds that La Fontaine's fables, with their frequent scenes of animal treachery and skulduggery, "présentent nécessairement des tableaux révoltans, qu'on doit éviter de mettre sous les yeux de la première jeunesse." Her novel solution? To "people" her fables, as the title of her collection indicates, with characters drawn only from the vegetable kingdom: "Les apologues puisés dans le règne végétal ne fournissent que des sujets dans lesquels de telles peintures ne peuvent se trouver" (pp. 11–15). Plants, after all, she argues, have their distinctive characteristics too, and have given rise to a whole symbolism that can be put to use by the moralizing fabulist: "Leur genre d'utilité ou de beauté, leur aspect, leur port, les lieux où elles paroissent se plaire, les fictions consacrées par la poésie, les vertus dont elles sont les symboles, leur ont fait attribuer une multitude de caractères emblématiques, dont il n'est pas permis de les dépouiller" (p. 18).[7]

In point of fact, her solution was not all that novel. The fabulist Pesselier, a half-century before, while not motivated by the same concerns, made plants the heroes (and villains) of a number of his fables; and even La

Fontaine, and surely others, had done so sporadically (see p. 76). To Madame de Genlis, however, belongs the credit, such as it is, of doing so to the intentional exclusion—or almost—of the usual sacrosanct animal hierarchy. The result is a collection that stands out not only as, apparently, the first (albeit slim) volume of fables produced by a French woman writer since Marie de France, but also one that is not a mere echo of those of her legion of male predecessors and contemporaries.[8]

"Le Papyrus," translated here, is number 8 of the collection. The venerable papyrus's verbose self-importance is typical of the author's attempt to fit her dialogue to the perceived characteristics of her vegetal dramatis personae.

1. Her literary career had begun in 1766 when a song she had composed for her ten-year-old daughter was surreptitiously submitted to the *Mercure de France*. There followed a variety of *poèmes de circonstance* in Dorat's *Journal des dames* and the contributions to the *Almanach des Muses*. Her disparate writings were subsequently collected in two editions under the title *Œuvres de madame de la Fér***. Apparently the collection of her fables was eventually published in toto (see the revised *Biographie universelle, ancienne et moderne* ["Biographie Michaud"], XXI:113); presumably in the *Œuvres*, though bibliographical precision is difficult to come by. A number of the fables, on which her reputation rested, were also anthologized in *Le Fablier du jeune âge*. One would suppose that they appeared in other similar collections as well.

2. And that, notwithstanding the rather pallid praise of bibliographer A.-J.-Q. Beuchot, whose brief entry on her in the above-mentioned *Biographie universelle, ancienne et moderne* (XXII:473–74) concludes: "La grâce, la facilité, l'élégance qu'on remarque dans les écrits de madame de la Férandière font honneur à son sexe et à la littérature française."

3. See Jacques Janssens, *La Fable et les fabulistes*, p. 84.

4. For an authoritative chronological bibliography, see Jean Harmand, *Madame de Genlis, sa vie intime et politique, 1746–1830*, pp. 533–37. Works by and about her are also catalogued in Alexandre Cioranescu, *Bibliographie de la littérature française du dix-huitième siècle*, II:851–57, nos. 30600–30853. (The catalogue of the Bibliothèque Nationale contains over four hundred entries under her name—ample indication of her productivity—albeit several editions, of course, of various titles.)

5. A more recent detailed study of her life and work is found in Alice M. Laborde, *L'Œuvre de Madame de Genlis*.

6. In her *avertissement* to this edition Madame de Genlis notes that the collection had already appeared eighteen months earlier in Germany, and that the present edition contains "quelques morceaux nouveaux" (p. 5). (Whether the latter were added to the fables or to the *pièces fugitives* is a matter of conjecture.) Cioranescu (*Bibliographie . . . du dix-huitième siècle*, no. 30625) refers to an 1800 edition published in Paris (probably the copy in the catalogue of the Bibliothèque Nationale [Paris: Moutardier, n.d.]); and Harmand, to confuse the bibliographical detail still further, gives the date as 1799, with no place of publication (*Madame de Genlis,* p. 534).

7. Even so, principle notwithstanding, Madame de Genlis does relent a few times and allows an occasional nonbotanical character—animal, mineral, and even human—to stray into her scenarios. (See numbers 7 ["L'Oiseau, le Prunier et l'Amandier"]; 10 ["La Fleur Commune et le Beau Vase"]; 11 ["Le Voyageur, l'Orme et le Mancenilier"]; 5 ["L'Enfant, le Pédagogue et la Figue"]; and, especially, the last fable, "Le Sassafras et la Vigne," a curious strophic ode to America and the unspoiled nobility of Nature, inspired in part by the Franco-American Saint-John de Crèvecoeur's *Letters from an American Farmer* [1782], and set "Loin des murs de Philadelphie, / Au milieu des vastes forêts.")

8. Madame de Genlis indicates that the fables in her volume represent only a small portion of her intended botanically inspired work. Without the press of other literary obligations, the collection would have been considerably larger: "Il me reste une centaine de fables de ce genre, écrites en prose, et que je n'aurai peut-être jamais le temps de mettre en vers" (p. 10).

Le Papyrus

Devenu misanthrope, et sauvage et frondeur,
   Le papyrus, fort mécontent des hommes,
     Exhaloit ainsi son humeur:
"Quel maudit temps, grand Dieu, que le siècle où
              nous sommes!
     Et qui pourra nous rendre, hélas!
     Ces jours de bonheur et de gloire,
   Dont le récit nous charme dans l'histoire!
     Mais il n'est plus d'Agésilas!
De ces gens qui savoient discerner le mérite,
Et dont chaque discours et toute la conduite,
     Et les goûts et l'opinion,
     Excitoient l'admiration
     Du sage ainsi que du vulgaire.

The Papyrus-Plant

   Grown mean, dyspeptic, dour and misanthropic,
     Venting his spleen against the human race,
       Papyrus-plant holds forth apace;
       And, ranting on his favorite topic,
Complains: "What times are these! Ye gods! Shame
              and disgrace!"
   Gone are the days of heroes and their glory—
Heroes in deed and word, masters of oratory—
     Moral exemplars gone before.
The great Agesilaos and his like: no more![1]
     Today it's quite another story:
No more those souls whose merest thought could
              move the nation—
     Sages and proles—to admiration.

Aujourd'hui, sur toute la terre,
Le bon sens n'est plus de saison,
On a su le bannir; combien d'arts inutiles!
Combien d'inventions futiles!
L'esprit, les mœurs, tout est perdu,
On s'éloigne de la nature,
Et s'écarter d'une source si pure,
C'est renoncer à la vertu."
"Oui, je comprends," dit un arbuste,
"Le sujet de ce grand courroux:
On fait du beau papier, et tout vous semble injuste,
Depuis qu'on a cessé de recourir à vous."

Alas, today... Today, good sense
Knows not the slightest recompense:
Futile and useless art, vain innovation,
Have cast it out, driven it hence
With meaningless inventions. And the cost?
Spirit, mind, morals... All is lost.
Nature no longer sets the tone, and thus
Is virtue vanished. Woe is us!"
Nodded a bush: "The interesting thing about you,
My angry friend, is that no doubt you
Look at the world with jaundiced eye.
And, if I may, I'll tell you why:
Man makes fine paper now, and he can do without you!"

1. Citing the first-century Greek historian Diodorus Siculus as her source, the author specifies in a note that, to understand her fable, it is necessary to recall that Agesilaos, king of Sparta, prized most highly the gift of papyrus bestowed on him by the Egyptian pharaoh.

Madame Joliveau de Segrais   Fables Nouvelles en Vers, Suivies
de Quelques Poèmes (1801)

IF MADAME de Genlis is, technically speaking, the first French woman writer of relatively modern times to produce an entire collection of fables, Madame Joliveau de Segrais is surely the most important. Far less consequential a historical and social figure, and far less varied and prolific a writer, she was, in the fabulist's modest realm, much more productive and, in her own way, quite as distinctive.

The *femme de lettres* known to her intimates, affectionately, as "Adine" Joliveau—née Marie-Madeleine-Nicole-Alexandrine Gehier—was drawn to the fable not only because of her literary interest in general and a taste for well-turned verse in particular but also for reasons of practical expediency. Born to a well-to-do family on November 10, 1756, in the Champagne town of Bar-sur-Aube, she married early, had five children, and dutifully spent her early years as wife and mother. Before long, however, the ravages suffered by the schools during the Revolution posed a problem for her children's education, and she decided to undertake it herself, learning Latin, Italian, and English to facilitate her task. Weaned, like so many of her compatriots before and since, on the fables of La Fontaine, and, we are told, having early given proof of a natural gift for verse, she soon began composing her own as well, as aids in her instruction. (See H. Audiffret's entry on her in the revised *Biographie universelle, ancienne et moderne* ["Biographie Michaud"], XXI:113.) Supposedly it was the encouragement of several other contemporary fabulists—among them the abbé

Aubert and the venerable Dutramblay (see pp. 81–83 and 113–114)—that persuaded the reluctant poet to publish the six books of her *Fables nouvelles en vers, suivies de quelques poèmes*.[1] There followed a second edition, composed of 175 fables divided into nine books (1807), and a third (1814), extensively revised, in which a large number of earlier fables were omitted in favor of new ones. Many of her fables were also published over a twenty-five-year period in the *Almanach des Muses,* from 1803 to 1828, and, according to Audiffret, in other similar journals.[2] Several also appeared in *Le Fablier du jeune âge.*

Madame Joliveau, in addition to disparate *poésies fugitives,* also published a four-canto poem, *Suzanne* (whose allegedly "scabreux" subject was treated, according to Audiffret, "avec la grâce, la décence et la délicatesse qu'une femme seule pouvait y mettre"), followed by the two-canto *Repentir.* But a variety of personal and familial misfortunes—the premature deaths of her husband and four of her children—prevented a long-announced fourth and definitive edition of her fables; an edition that was also to include imitations of the Russian fabulist Krilov, whose work had appeared in French translation in 1825. At her death, in Paris, on December 27, 1830, she also left unfinished a projected fifteen-canto prose and verse poem on the English king Alfred the Great; a happily coincidental link with her medieval artistic ancestor, Marie de France (see p. 3).[3]

As a fabulist, Madame Joliveau, by the time the third edition of her collection was published, had established a substantial reputation for the high moral tone and sentimentality of her fables, which, in the words of the anonymous chronicler of the *Almanach des Muses* of 1816, "décèlent un cœur excellent, et où se montre tout bonnement celui de la plus tendre des mères" (p. 285). A half-century later, intending no doubt to be complimentary, Audiffret would emphasize their suitability for "l'éducation des jeunes filles" (*Biographie universelle, ancienne et moderne,* XXI:113). But the reader should not be put off by what sounds like an overpowering dose of virtue. True, maternal concerns and undisguised didacticism do seem to dominate her inspiration. Many of her fables, borrowing the La Fontainesque form, are, in fact, slightly less maudlin echoes of the good marquise de La Férandière. But a number of others—and certainly the most distinctive and, to my mind, the most attractive—without forgoing their moral message, mute it in a charmingly epigrammatic style that owes little or nothing

to La Fontaine: brief scenes, whose tersely concluding dialogues suggest their moral without explicitly stating it. In these lapidary fables Madame Joliveau calls to mind the style with which her much better known contemporary, prolific fabulist Antoine-Vincent Arnault, would distinguish himself in the development of the genre (see pp. 124–25).[4]

The four fables translated in the present collection are typical of Madame Joliveau's duality: epigrammatic in "Le Peintre et la Pudeur" and "Le Ver Luisant et le Crapaud," more traditional in "Le Porc et les Abeilles." In the nine books of the 1814 edition these three are numbered, respectively, I, 6; III, 9; and IX, 7. As for the delightful ne plus ultra of the epigrammatic fable, "L'Aigle et le Ver," it does not, curiously, figure in that final edition at all, although it is probably her most widely known, quoted as a characteristic example of her art in several sources.[5]

1. The volume is so listed in the catalogue of the Bibliothèque Nationale, although Audiffret and other sources cite the date of publication as 1802.

2. Audiffret seems to imply that her works had appeared in the *Almanach des Muses* before she first published her *Fables nouvelles en vers.* As far as I can determine, however, the contrary seems to be the case.

3. Enthusiasts of the anecdotal may find their curiosity piqued by Audiffret's starchily euphemistic account of her demise: "Une affection d'estomac, occasionnée par l'ancien abus de boissons rafraîchissantes,

lui causa des attaques de paralysie, dont la dernière l'emporta" (revised *Biographie universelle, ancienne et moderne,* XXI:114).

4. Because the two fabulists overlap chronologically, and because—given the virtual unavailability of Madame Joliveau's earliest editions—precedence of composition is impossible to establish, the question remains open, for those concerned with such matters, as to which of the two may have "influenced" the other.

5. Among them, the *Nouvelle Biographie générale,* XXVI:847, and the *Dictionnaire des lettres françaises: le dix-neuvième siècle,* I:538. It was also anthologized in *Le Fablier du jeune âge* (I:162).

Le Peintre et la Pudeur

L'amour nu paraissait respirer sur la toile;
La Pudeur l'aperçoit, rougit, baisse les yeux.
"Quel défaut trouves-tu, belle, au plus beau des Dieux?"
Dit le peintre alarmé; "que lui faut-il?" "Un voile."

Modesty and the Painter

Cupid stood painted on a canvas, bare.
Modesty looked, blushed, turned... "What? You, so fair..."
The painter cried, "you scorn this god of lovers?
What does he lack, this peerless beauty?" "Covers."

Le Ver Luisant et le Crapaud

Un ver luisant brillait des feux du diamant;
Un crapaud lui lança son venin malfaisant.
"Quel tort," lui dit le ver, "ai-je donc pu te faire
Pour me traiter ainsi?" "Tu répands la lumière."[1]

The Glowworm and the Toad

A glowworm's diamond sparks brightened the night;
Spiteful, a toad spat out his venom at her.
"Why?" asked the worm. "Whatever is the matter?
What harm do I do you?" "You spread the light."

1. Imitation being the sincerest form of flattery, Madame Joliveau would indeed have had reason to be pleased at another fable for which this one appears to have served as the obvious model. G. Illberg, in his little collection *Les plus belles fables des 50 meilleurs fabulistes* (p. 52), cites the following quatrain, attributed simply to one "Layet":

Le Ver Luisant et le Serpent

Un ver luisant errait sous de vertes charmilles;
Un serpent s'en approche et lui perce le sein.

"Que t'ai-je fait?" dit-il au perfide assassin.
"Tu brilles."

The author referred to was the abbé Layet, author of *Le Fablier chrétien, ou Allégories nouvelles sur l'existence de Dieu, la Trinité, . . . ,* originally published in 1851 and apparently popular enough to support several enlarged editions over the next few years. The quatrain in question is included in the first and subsequent editions.

Le Porc et les Abeilles

Après dîner, seigneur pourceau
Dormait près d'une ruche: une petite abeille
De son faible aiguillon perce sa tendre peau:
    Lors en fureur l'adolescent s'éveille;
Il s'en prend à la troupe, attaque son palais,
        Et de son grouin le renverse.
Mais sur lui tout-à-coup l'essaim fond et s'exerce,
Le poursuit, et l'accable enfin de mille traits.
Qui cherche à se venger d'une légère offense
S'attire bien souvent plus de mal qu'il ne pense.[1]

---

1. Interestingly, Madame Joliveau's contemporary, the fabulist Guichard (see pp. 120–21), treated precisely the same subject as that of the present fable in his "Le Pourceau et les Abeilles" (I, 13); proof, perhaps, that, as he admits in the *avant-propos* to his own collection

The Pig and the Bees

Proud piglet, after dinner, lay beside
    A beehive, sleeping. All at once, a bee—
One of the smallest—rather inoffensively
    Pricks at the adolescent's tender hide,
Waking him with a start. Furious, he lashes out
Against the lot, pokes with his snout against the hive
        And knocks it down. Swarm comes alive,
As pig, pursued, gets soundly stung, round and about.
    He who, in rage, would settle a modest score
    Often gets more than what he bargained for.

---

of fables (p. vii), "lorsque parmi les écrivains français j'ai rencontré des traits de morale qui m'inspiraient le désir de les mettre en action, je me suis permis de m'en emparer."

L'Aigle et le Ver

L'Aigle disait au Ver, sur un arbre attrapé:
"Pour t'élever si haut, qu'as-tu fait?" "J'ai rampé."

---

1. At the risk of writing a note longer than the fable itself, I should point out that the verb "ramper," of the original, suggests the idea of groveling that "crawling" only hints at. Still, inadequacies aside, I can't resist including this fable here. It is surely one of the

The Eagle and the Worm

Eagle spied worm atop a tree and, calling,
"How did you climb so high?" he asked. "By crawling."[1]

---

shortest bona fide examples in the literature, if not the shortest. It makes the pithy Benserade seem veritably verbose by comparison (see pp. 46–47).

Jean-François Guichard   Fables et Autres Poésies (1802)

Facts concerning the life of Jean-François Guichard are few and far between. As one biographical dictionary informs us, "il mena une vie obscure" (see the *Nouvelle Biographie générale,* XXII:524). Not so obscure, however, as to prevent our learning that he was born in the village of Chartrette, near Melun, on May 5, 1730, where, after a long and largely undocumented life, he would die, on February 23, 1811, leaving a list of works—theater-pieces mostly—a good deal longer than his biography.

During the decade from about 1757 to 1768, while employed in a variety of governmental functions primarily associated with the navy, he had, either alone or in collaboration, written a half-dozen brief comedies and comic opera libretti, from *Les Apprêts de noces* through his operettic adaptation of Voltaire's philosophical tale *Memnon.* The most successful of these productions was *Le Bûcheron, ou Les Trois souhaits,* a one-act comedy based on a tale by Perrault, written with one Monsieur Castet (about whom virtually nothing else is known), and with music by the popular composer François-André Danican,

known as Philidor. It was performed at the Comédie-Italienne on February 28, 1763, and subsequently before the court, at Versailles, on March 15 of the same year, and its many printings—and even translations—attest to its popularity.[1] Guichard, who considered himself a disciple of the sharp-tongued, sharp-penned Piron (see pp. 97–98), had also composed a substantial body of occasional and satirical verse and prose.[2] It was no doubt in recognition of those combined theatrical and literary efforts that the revolutionary government, through the Ministère de l'Intérieur, in 1790, awarded him one of the modest annual stipends bestowed on worthy and needy men of letters.[3]

Under the Empire Guichard went on to publish his fables, his *contes*—many of which, typical of the genre, were thought at the time to exceed the bounds of good taste—and an anonymously printed collection of twenty-seven *Epigrammes faites dans un bon dessein.* (The "bon dessein" in question was their satire directed against the traditionalist drama critic Julien-Louis Geoffroy, notorious for "cette critique *acerbe* qu'on lui a reprochée contre ses contemporains.")[4] Both his fables and his *contes* were first published in 1802 in two separate collections: *Fables et autres poésies, suivies de quelques morceaux de prose,* consisting of 196 fables divided into eight books, and *Contes et autres poésies, suivis de quelques mots de Piron,* both printed in Paris by Suret (An X). A second edition, bringing together both collections under one title—*Contes et fables, suivis de quelques mots de Piron*—was apparently unauthorized, not to say pirated, if we can believe the author of the entry in the revised *Biographie universelle, ancienne et moderne,* who claims to have heard Guichard himself complain of "cette ruse de libraire" (XVIII:93).

Guichard's fables are little remembered, nor were they universally admired even before they fell into relative oblivion. The testy literary historian Bernard Jullien, for one, seemed to take an almost perverse pleasure in meticulously dissecting a number of them and holding up their supposed shortcomings to view. (See his *Histoire*

de la poésie française à l'époque impériale, II:167–72.) Rather unjustly, in my opinion. Seeming to demand nothing less than the artistry and casual elegance of a La Fontaine, Jullien fails to appreciate the pleasingly direct, no-nonsense brevity of many of Guichard's apologues, less concisely epigrammatic than the best of those of his contemporary, Madame Joliveau de Segrais (see pp. 118–19), but frequently quite as effective.[5]

Of the trio of characteristic fables translated here, the first two, "Le Singe et le Renard" and "Le Lézard et la Tortue," are numbered, respectively, I, 7 and IV, 17. The third, "Le Cygne et les Canards," presents something of a minor mystery. It does not appear among the 196 fables of the unauthorized, so-called *deuxième édition* of 1808; and since the latter purports to reproduce all the fables of the original edition, I have to assume—that edition being unavailable—that it does not appear there either. It was included in *Le Fablier du jeune âge* (II:41), ascribed to Guichard, along with a number of others.

---

1. Philidor, one of the more prolific of a prominent family of French musicians, supposedly also collaborated on the music for Guichard and Antoine-Alexandre-Henri Poinsinet's one-act prose *opéra-bouffon, La Bagarre,* presented at the Théâtre-Italien, February 10, 1763. (See the *New Grove Dictionary of Music and Musicians,* XIV:629.) Translations of *Le Bûcheron* exist in German, Danish, and Italian: respectively, *Der Holzhauer, oder die drey Wünsche,* trans. J. H. Faber (Frankfurt am Mayn, 1773); *Skovhuggeren, eller de tre Ønsker,* trans. Lars Knudsen (Kiobenhavn [Copenhagen]: M. Hallager, 1783); and *I Tre desideri,* trans. Giuseppe Brunati (Venezia [Venice]: A. Rosa, 1805).

2. For a bibliography of Guichard's works the reader should supplement the listing in Alexandre Cioranescu, *Bibliographie de la littérature française du dix-huitième siècle,* II:918, with those referred to in both the revised *Biographie universelle, ancienne et moderne* ("Biographie Michaud"), XVIII:93, and the *Dictionnaire de biographie française,* fasc. 1 of vol. XVII:63.

3. We are told that, at his death, Guichard left a valuable collection of rare books and art works, which would have fetched a handsome price, but which he could not part with despite his straitened circumstances. (See the *Nouvelle Biographie générale,* XXII:524.)

4. See the preface, signed "H. M.," to Julien-Louis Geoffroy's *Cours de littérature dramatique,* I:vii. The author justifies the critic's alleged hostility on the grounds that, "dévoré du zèle de la science, il avait l'intention de ramener à l'étude et à l'imitation des grands modèles de la scène française, des écrivains qui semblaient s'en éloigner à plaisir." I find no indication that Guichard had any personal axe to grind with Geoffroy, who would doubtless not have deigned to assess his minor works. The critic did, however, have unpleasant things to say about the comedy *La Métromanie,* by Guichard's idol, Piron, which would have been sufficient to elicit the satirical response of his *Epigrammes.* (See *Cours de littérature dramatique,* II: 499–504.)

5. Nowhere is this concision better illustrated, perhaps, than in a couplet—a "Distique pour mettre en bas du portrait de La Fontaine"—appearing in the *Almanach des Muses* of 1770. Guichard says more to glorify La Fontaine in two lines than many an adulating admirer in their often verbose prefatory tributes: "Dans la Fable & le Conte il n'eut point de rivaux; / Il peignit la nature & garda ses pinceaux."

Le Singe et le Renard

"On connaît mes talents; de tous les animaux
J'imite," dit le singe, "au mieux le caractère."
Le renard l'écoutait: "Tu seras sans rivaux,
L'ami; car nul de nous ne veut te contrefaire."

The Ape and the Fox

"Mimic supreme," boasts ape, "I have no peer.
Beasts one and all, see how I duplicate you!"
"True," replies fox, "and you need have no fear:
None of us, friend, would want to imitate you!"

Le Lézard et la Tortue

"Pauvre tortue, hélas!" s'écriait le lézard.
    "Pourquoi pauvre?" "Oui, quelle misère!
Sans porter ta maison tu ne vas nulle part."
    "Charge utile devient légère."

The Lizard and the Turtle

    "Poor turtle!" sighed the lizard. "What?
Why 'poor'?" "Your house... You drag it everywhere!"
    "Indeed," replied the turtle, "but
No useful load is burdensome to bear."

Le Cygne et les Canards

Jaloux de la blancheur d'un majestueux cygne,
　　De canards une troupe indigne,
Sur les bords d'un étang loin de lui barbottait,
　　Et dans sa criailleuse rage
　　Faisait jaillir la bourbe, et l'en couvrait.
"Qu'il étale à présent," dirent-ils, "son plumage!"
Le magnifique oiseau plonge, puis, se dressant,
A leurs regards trompés se montre éblouissant.
Cette fable, je crois, s'applique avec justesse
　　A certains canards d'autre espèce.
Malgré tous leurs efforts, cygnes, pour vous noircir,
Ces petits insolents ne font que se salir.

The Swan and the Ducks

　　Mucking about beside a pond,
　A pack of paltry ducks, quacking their spite—
　Jealous to see a swan of dazzling white,
　Majestic, ply the waters just beyond—
Spatter the glorious bird with mud, from head to claw.
　"So much for that fine plumage now!" they caw.
　The swan submerges for a time, and then
Rises before their eyes, resplendent once again.
　This fable ought, I think, put us in mind
　　Of other ducks—the human kind:
Swans, though they blacken you from claw to head,
Those petty prigs besmirch themselves instead.

Pierre-Louis Ginguené　　Fables Nouvelles (1810)

STRADDLING the years from Revolution to Empire, Pierre-Louis Ginguené was one of the minor, albeit prolific and many-faceted, artistic figures of that troubled time. A Breton, and a distant relative of Chateaubriand, he was born in Rennes on April 25, 1748, and received his early education at the hands of the Jesuits, until their suppression in 1764. Proficient in several languages, ancient and modern, and especially in music, he arrived in Paris in 1772, where he soon began to contribute occasional verse, as well as literary and musical criticism, to a number of journals—the *Mercure de France,* the *Almanach des Muses,* the *Gazette nationale,* and the *Journal de Paris,* among them—while supporting himself both as a private tutor and as a minor civil servant attached to the finance ministry.

In the early 1780s Ginguené took an active part in one of those artistic quarrels for which the French are famous: the virtual "war" between the partisans of the then-emerging Italian composer Niccolò Piccinni (1728–1800) and those of the more traditional Christophe Willibald Gluck (1714–87), pitting against the "Gluckistes" such formidable intellectual adversaries as Marmontel and La Harpe, as well as the newcomer Ginguené, who had, however—unlike most of his co-"Piccinnistes"—"l'avantage de savoir parfaitement la musique."[1] A decade later, for none-too-clear reasons, and despite a staunch republicanism, he apparently offended the Revolutionary powers and was imprisoned for several months in 1794, during the Terror, along with his friend, the well-known moralist-playwright Sébastien-Roch-Nicolas de Chamfort. Ginguené, luckier than Chamfort—who, in despair, was driven to suicide—survived his imprisonment. Upon his release he was named to the Commission de l'instruction publique, rising to its directorship shortly thereafter.

His commitment to public education took a more active turn when, in 1803—after several political appointments that included an ambassadorship to the Italian city-state of Turin, and brief membership in the Consulat's deliberative Tribunat—he undertook a course of lectures in Italian literature at the Athénée de Paris, much of which resulted in his *Histoire littéraire d'Italie,* and which he continued to give almost until his death, in Paris, on November 16, 1816.

In addition to that historico-literary magnum opus, and besides his extensive journal writings on philosophical, musical, and literary subjects (see Roussel, in Sgard, *Dictionnaire des journalistes*) and his continuous production of occasional verse, Ginguené published a number of substantial literary studies.[2] One might cite among them his *Lettres sur "Les Confessions" de Jean-Jacques Rousseau* and his *Coup d'œil rapide sur "Le Génie du christianisme,"* a less-than-sympathetic view of Chateaubriand's defense of Catholicism, despite Ginguené's own early education among the Jesuits.[3]

He also, to be sure, wrote a body of fables. If length were the measure of excellence, then no doubt Ginguené's fables would place him far above most of the French practitioners of the genre: predecessors, contemporaries, and successors alike. Confirmed Italophile that he was, and borrowing most of his subjects from seventeenth- and eighteenth-century Italian fabulists—Capaccio, Bertola, Pignotti, et al.—he elaborated and developed the originals with overly generous digression and detail that led him to spread the fifty texts of his *Fables nouvelles* over some 230 pages. "Toutes ces fables de Ginguené," observes Bernard Jullien somewhat cynically, "n'ont rien qui les distingue de celles que font tous les poètes qui se mettent à en composer, si ce n'est peut-être leur longueur."[4] (See his *Histoire de la poésie française à l'époque impériale,* II:180.) One might be tempted to imagine as the reason for this rather leisurely treatment the excuse that, for him, the writing of fables—a common enough pastime among literati of the period—was little more than a form of self-indulgent relaxation. As his very favorably disposed biographer Daunou notes, "il n'avait cherché que son propre amusement dans ces compositions ingénieuses" ("Notice," in Ginguené, *Histoire littéraire d'Italie,* I:xxii).

Even if we believe Daunou, however, it would be naive to assume that Ginguené was wholly indifferent to public approval. Daunou himself seems to suggest this when, explaining his predilection for the adaptation of Italian models, the sympathetic biographer, somewhat self-contradictingly, attributes it to a desire on the author's part to avoid the ever-present pitfall of comparison with La Fontaine: "En ce genre difficile, la plus grande témérité est d'imiter Lafontaine [*sic*]; il est moins périlleux et plus modeste d'essayer de faire autrement que lui, et c'est ce qu'a tenté Ginguené" (I:xxii). Although Daunou admits, rather reluctantly, that the success of these fables was "peu éclatant," he claims that it was nonetheless substantial, and, at any rate, greater than what the author had aspired to with their modest composition. A far-less-sympathetic critic, Jean-Joseph Dussault, in reviewing Ginguené's above-mentioned *Fables inédites,* is less sanguine about his success as a fabulist: "les apologues que l'auteur a mis au jour, il y a quelques années, n'ont presque pas fait de sensation, et sont déjà presque oubliées" (see his *Annales littéraires,* IV:560).[5]

Whether we choose to believe Daunou or Dussault, and whatever the reception of Ginguené's fables at the time, no one will deny that today they have become little more than a footnote to the history of the genre. One of them, however, much shorter than the rest, seems to me to deserve rescue from artistic oblivion, and it is translated here. "La Machine Hydraulique et l'Eau," number 20 of the *Fables nouvelles,* is a striking example, I think, of what one might call the "technological fable" (see pp. 70–71, n. 2); even more striking in that its Italian original, dating from the first decade of the seventeenth century, must itself surely be one of the earliest such examples.

---

1. See Pierre-Claude Daunou, "Notice sur la vie et les ouvrages de M. Ginguené," in the second edition of the author's monumental *Histoire littéraire d'Italie,* I:viii-ix. (Daunou's twenty-seven-page introduction is, to my knowledge, the only detailed biographical account of Ginguené's life and work; also informative, however, is the summary entry by Jean Roussel, in Jean Sgard, *Dictionnaire des journalistes (1600–1789),* pp. 173–74.) Many of Ginguené's articles of music criticism were signed with the pseudonym "Mélophile."

2. As for his occasional verse, the first and probably most successful example was his youthfully précieux and slightly erotic poem in *vers libres,* "La Confession de Zulmé" (first published in the *Almanach des Muses,* 1779, pp. 129–32), which brought him a certain celebrity and even considerable notoriety.

3. For a bibliographical listing of works by and about the author, see Alexandre Cioranescu, *Bibliographie de la littérature française du dix-huitième siècle,* II:867–68. Cioranescu, however, makes no mention of Ginguené's several prefaces to, and even editions of, the works of others: inter alia, his essay regarding the bardic hoaxes of "Ossian," translated from English by Pierre Le Tourneur (in *Ossian, fils de Fingal* [Paris: Dentu, 1810]), and which Ginguené thought to be authentic; his four-volume edition of the *Œuvres* of his erstwhile fellow prisoner, Chamfort; and the likewise four-volume *Œuvres* of his friend, the poet Ponce-Denis Ecouchard, known as Le Brun.

4. Four years after publication of his collection, Ginguené brought out a supplement of sorts: *Fables inédites.* In addition to a variety of other *poésies diverses,* it contained ten lengthy fables intended to compensate for approximately that number that had, for unclear political reasons, been stricken from the original volume. (See Daunou, "Notice," in Ginguené, *Histoire littéraire d'Italie,* I:xxii-xxiii.)

5. Dussault's critique was originally published in the *Journal des débats,* October 5, 1814.

La Machine Hydraulique et l'Eau

Au détour que formait le lit d'une rivière,
    Un mécanisme ingénieux
Arrêtait, enfermait, tenait l'eau prisonnière,
    Et la portait en de hauts lieux
Où d'arides canaux et des bassins pierreux
Attendaient le bienfait de la nymphe étrangère.
    L'onde captive murmurait
    De ce long et triste voyage:
Qui la délivrerait d'un pénible esclavage?
    Pour l'affranchir qui briserait
    Et les ressorts et le rouage?
Qui la rendrait au sable, aux roseaux de son lit?
L'orgueilleuse machine en ces mots répondit:
"Eau bavarde, tais-toi; ta sottise est extrême,
    Et tu te plains injustement:

The Hydraulic Machine and the Water[1]

A mechanism of ingenious kind,
Built at the turning of a riverbed,
Dammed up the water, held it there, confined,
    And lifted it high overhead,
Where parched canals and stone-dry pools awaited
The blessing of the distant watersprite.
Captive, the billow grumbled, unabated,
    Against her headlong, homesick flight:
Who would deliver her from bondage? Who
Would smash those wheels and springs forevermore,
    And free her to return, anew,
Home to her sandy bed and reed-lined shore?
The proud machine gave ear and answered thus:
    "Be still, you babbling brook! Your fuss
Makes precious little sense. True, I presume

Si je te mène rudement,
Ne reçois-je pas de toi-même
Et la force et le mouvement?"

You suffer from my deeds, and rue them.
But is it not yourself from whom
I get the strength, in fact, to do them?"[2]

1. Ginguené, in this uncharacteristically brief fable, was clearly inspired by the even-sparer apologue, "Machina & Acqua," by the early seventeenth-century fabulist Giulio Cesare Capaccio (see pp. 70–71, n. 2): "Nel letto ove correa l'Acqua d'un Fiume / Era da mano industre / Fabricata una Machina che l'onda / Per forza rimovea dal proprio corso..."

2. One may suppose that the author's depiction of the powerful machine deriving its strength from its very victim was intended, in some respect, to be a political allegory, superficially reminiscent of Piron's "La Tour" (see p. 99). The precise allusion, however, and its applicability to the imperial regime during which the fable was published, remain rather obscure. (See Jullien, *Histoire de la poésie française à l'époque impériale*, II:180–82.)

Antoine-Vincent Arnault   Fables (1812–25)

IN THE words of one biographer, Antoine-Vincent Arnault was "l'un des hommes les plus distingués de cette période littéraire qu'on appelle 'la littérature de l'empire.'" (See Charles Durozoir's entry on Arnault in the revised *Biographie universelle, ancienne et moderne* ["Biographie Michaud"], II:255.) Writing from the eve of the First Empire through the Revolution of 1830, at a time when French classical tragedy, temporarily rebounding from the assaults of bourgeois sentimentality, had not yet been challenged by the avant-garde romantic drama of Hugo, Dumas, Vigny, and company, poet-playwright Arnault considered himself destined, early in his career, for theatrical celebrity. Furthermore, his youthful expectations were fostered by royal and imperial patronage, not a little contemporary success, and even his share of notoriety. But like many artists, unrealistic judges of their own best talents, if he still commands the attention of the occasional specialist and researcher into pre- and post-Napoleonic French letters, it is not as a serious dramatist but as the author of a body of highly original fables composed over the years as a progressively more cynical descant above the often tempestuous events of his personal and public life.[1]

Arnault was born in Paris on January 22, 1766, into a family of the *haute bourgeoisie*.[2] After traditional schooling at the hands of the reverend fathers of the Collège de Juilly, during which he stood out for both his sharp mind and sharper tongue, he was able, through family connections, at age nineteen, to enter the service of the comtesse de Provence as an honorary *secrétaire de cabinet*, subsequently buying his way into the entourage of her husband, the future king Louis XVIII. In 1791, in the midst of the revolutionary upheaval, the first of his dozen-odd classical tragedies, *Marius à Minturnes*—notable for its daring absence of female roles—was performed with success at the official Théâtre-Français, a typical example of the painter David's starkly neo-Roman aesthetic, as applied to the theater. After a second trag-

edy, *Lucrèce* (1792), the excesses of the Terror and Arnault's associations with the royal household prompted him to follow the lead of the future king and emigrate for a time to England and Belgium. Upon his return, he was arrested as an émigré; it was only his prestige as a dramatist that saved him from a lengthy imprisonment. He would spend the next few years mining the same dramatic vein, one which he was to exploit through the first half of his literary career.[3]

In 1797, during Bonaparte's Italian campaign, the young Arnault was introduced to the general. Hitching his wagon to Napoleon's rising star, he quickly became his protégé and trusted confidant, carrying out a number of official missions, foremost among them the organization of the government and administration of the newly annexed Ionian Islands. After the Egyptian campaign and the coup d'état of the eighteenth of Brumaire, to which he was privy, the poet and now part-time administrator was named to Napoleon's ministry of the interior in charge of the arts and public education. This and other governmental functions, for which he was named to the Institut de France in 1799, gradually brought Arnault's dramatic career to a halt. Napoleon's fall and eventual exile put an end to his public career as well.[4]

With the return of Louis XVIII and the restoration of the Bourbons, Arnault, in his own precipitous fall from grace, was exiled by his former royal protector, and once again found refuge in Belgium. He spent the next four years there, writing often satirical articles for various newspapers and journals, and, of particular interest, several books of fables, a genre he had begun to practice in the last years of the Empire and to which he would devote much of the rest of his literary life.[5] Allowed to return to France in 1819, Arnault eventually returned to grace as well, being named to the Académie Française some ten years later, and becoming its *secrétaire perpétuel* in 1833. He spent his last years, before his death, on

September 16, 1834, writing the four volumes of his incomplete memoirs, *Souvenirs d'un sexagénaire*.[6]

The eight books of Arnault's fables were published at various times over the latter half of his life. Bibliographical sources are not rigorously consistent in detail. The first four books, containing seventy-two pieces, including prologue and epilogue, were published as *Fables* (1812). The poet himself, in the preface to the complete collection in volume IV of his *Œuvres* (see above, n. 1), indicates that a second edition containing two more books had appeared in Brussels in 1817.[7] Several sources list two more collections: *Fables et poèmes* (1826), which I have been unable to consult, but which I assume to be a reedition of volume IV of the *Œuvres*, published the preceding year; and *Fables nouvelles*, dating from the year of Arnault's death, whose contents I cannot determine. The eight books in his *Œuvres* contain 142 fables. They are preceded by an essay, "De l'apologue," a prologue with the usual evocation of La Fontaine (both of which are also part of the 1813 edition), and contain also the epilogues in the previous collection, various dedications, and a final epilogue dated "A Bruxelles, en février 1819." In the latter Arnault announces that he has finally finished with the genre, begun under happier times: "Mon pays rayonnait alors / De l'éclat de toutes les gloires; / Et les chants de mille victoires / Se mariaient à mes accords" (*Œuvres*, IV:299).

Bibliographical minutiae aside, Arnault stands out among the followers of La Fontaine, not only because his subjects are of his own invention—many predecessors had prided themselves no less on their originality—but especially for the unique style that he introduced into the genre. While many of his fables are written in the traditional mode and peopled (so to speak) with or without appropriate animal characters, others are really fables in name only. Many of the most striking are really brief, trenchant epigrams of sorts, so pithy that often the very subjects would remain obscure if not clarified by their titles. "L'apologue," Arnault himself observed, "a pris peut-être sous ma plume un caractère plus épigrammatique, mais par cela, du moins, une physionomie particulière" (pp. xvii–xviii).[8]

The fables in the present collection are examples of both Arnault's traditional and innovative styles. They are taken from the eight books in volume IV of his *Œuvres*, where they are numbered as follows: I, 6; II, 10; II, 11; II, 16; III, 14; IV, 7; IV, 13; V, 10; V, 11; V, 14; and VIII, 2.

---

1. "J'ai cherché dans les lettres," he tells us unequivocally, speaking of his fables, "des distractions à mes malheurs." (See the preface to his complete collection, in his *Œuvres*, p. ii.)

2. The date January 1, given by Alexandre Cioranescu in his bibliography of Arnault, is clearly in error. (See *Bibliographie de la littérature française du dix-huitième siècle*, I:249.)

3. "Arnault, dans un aveuglement d'ambition louable, se crut alors destiné à succéder à Voltaire sur la scène tragique, comme Racine avait succédé à Corneille." (See Eugène Crépet, *Les Poètes français*, III:371.) For a list of Arnault's published tragedies, as well as several left unpublished, see Hugo P. Thieme, *Bibliographie de la littérature française de 1800 à 1930*, I:50. For a more nearly complete bibliography of his work and related studies, see also Cioranescu, *Bibliographie . . . du dix-huitième siècle*, I:249–51.

4. Arnault, who never lost his admiration for the emperor, would chronicle the imperial years in his massive two-volume *Vie politique et militaire de Napoléon*. His devotion was rewarded by a substantial bequest left to him by Napoleon in his will.

5. The author's diverse Belgian writings, especially those from the *Vrai-Libéral*, were published in the two-volume *Les Loisirs d'un banni*, edited by Auguste Imbert. During his exile the Théâtre-Français performed his tragedy *Germanicus* (February 22, 1817), whose veiled political allusions provoked among the pro- and anti-Bonapartists in the audience one of those tumultuous and bloody *batailles* for which the French theater is famous.

6. Arnault's biography, unlike that of some of the fabulists in this volume, is more than amply documented. Besides his own abovementioned detailed memoirs, the reader can consult Auguste Dietrich's introduction to the second edition of the *Souvenirs*, I:i–lxxi, or, indeed, most of the biographical dictionairies of the period, especially the *Biographie universelle, ancienne et moderne* (see above, p. 13, n. 3), where he is discussed at great length. For a briefer account of his personal and literary life, see especially Charles-Augustin Sainte-Beuve, *Causeries du lundi*, VII:394–411.

7. There is some confusion regarding this date. Some sources, including Arnault's own twenty-volume *Biographie nouvelle des contemporains*, I:257–60, give it as 1815. Cioranescu, on the other hand, cites it as 1816.

8. Arnault's originality was appreciated from the outset. A brief note on the first edition of his fables, in the *Almanach des Muses* of 1814 (p. 285), refers to his "manière absolument originale" and optimistically praises his collection "dont le succès est à jamais assuré." (Regarding the striking resemblance between his epigrammatic style and that of his contemporary Madame Joliveau de Segrais, see p. 119.)

Les Cygnes et les Dindons

On nous raconte que Léda,
Par le diable autrefois tentée,
D'un amant à l'aile argentée,
Un beau matin s'accommoda.
Hélas! ces caprices insignes
Sont encor les jeux des Amours;
Si ce n'est qu'on voit de nos jours
Les dindons remplacer les cygnes.

The Swans and the Turkeys

We're told that Leda, long ago—
Because the devil tempted her!—
Engaged in an *affaire de cœur*
With silver-winged lothario.
Today the same phenomenon
Mirrors our dalliance amorous.
One difference, though, 'twixt them and us:
The turkey has replaced the swan.

L'Ours, le Sansonnet, le Singe et le Serpent

    Naguère un ours encor sauvage,
    Ours sans esprit et sans usage,
    Mais non pas sans ambition,
Disait: "Je veux aller à la cour du lion.
Pour plaire en entrant là comment faut-il que j'entre?"
    Le singe dit, "C'est en sautant";
    Le sansonnet, "C'est en chantant";
"Ou bien," dit le serpent, "en marchant sur ton ventre."

Le Mulot et l'Eléphant

    Un jour, tout en philosophant,
    Tout en promenant ses pensées,
    Une bête des plus sensées...
    Un homme?... non, un éléphant,
D'un mulot sous ses pieds rencontra la retraite.
    La voûte ici n'était pas faite
Pour porter un tel poids: comme on l'a deviné,
Maître et maison, d'un pas, tout fut exterminé.
    Et puis après que l'on prétende
Que pour notre bien seul les grands penseurs sont nés.
Bref, la petite bête échappait, si la grande
Eût pu voir une fois jusqu'au bout de son nez.
"Barbare," s'écriait, en sa douleur amère,
Du malheureux défunt l'inconsolable mère,
    "Le ciel punisse ton forfait!
    Hélas! quel mal t'avait-il fait,
    Mon pauvre enfant?" "Aucun, sans doute;
    Mais faut-il vous en prendre à moi?"
    Dit le rêve-creux, "et pourquoi
    S'est-il rencontré sur ma route?"

Monseigneur passe; amis, rangeons-nous de côté.
Sous ses pas, croyez-moi, bien fou qui se hasarde:
    S'il ne vous fait du mal par volonté,
    Il vous en fera par mégarde.

The Bear, the Starling, the Ape, and the Snake

    A bear, fresh from his habitat—
    Wit, social grace were not his forte;
    No less ambitious, for all that—
Announced: "I'd like to visit at King Lion's court.
I want to be admired. What entrance should I make?"
    "Jump in!" the ape was quick to say.
    "Sing!" said the starling. "That's the way!"
"Go crawling on your belly," said the snake.

The Field Mouse and the Elephant

    Musing his way in thoughtful mood
    And philosophic attitude,
    A creature gifted with the liveliest
    Of intellect... ("A man?" you say?
Hardly! An elephant!) Well, anyway...
    Our beast chanced on a mouse's nest—
Field mouse, that is—and, as you may have guessed,
    One careless step, and welladay!
    (Still, there are those who will protest
    That thinkers great and ponderous
    Were born for purpose philanthropic:
To be a boon, and not a bane, to us!)
In short, two creatures; one, all too myopic,
Much to the dire misfortune of the other...
    "Murderer!" moaned the mouse's mother.
    "Heaven repay the ill you do!
    What harm did my child do to you?"
"None, ma'am. But still, despite your grief parental,
Surely the fault was his, for all your talk:
Why did he choose to live where I might walk?"[1]

A fool will scorn this precept fundamental:
    His lordship comes? Well, let him pass,
Lest, with his power, he do you ill, alas!...
    Intentional or accidental.

1. The author informs us in a note (*Œuvres*, IV:345–46) that this fable was inspired by an actual event at the Jardin des Plantes, where the victim was a newly imported South African wombat that had chosen the elephant's yard for its burrow.

La Statue Renversée

Je ne sais quel despote aperçoit sa statue
Le nez sur le carreau, dans la fange abattue.
Jeune et prince, à juger il était un peu prompt.
    "La mort, la mort au téméraire
    Qui m'ose faire un tel affront!
Qu'il périsse à l'instant!" "Sire, c'est le tonnerre."

1. In another note (*Œuvres*, I: 348) Arnault indicates that he found the subject of this fable in a prose collection entitled *Apologues modernes*, published in Brussels in 1789. The reference is to the eleventh "leçon" in Pierre-Sylvain Maréchal's *Apologues modernes, à l'usage du Dauphin: premières leçons du fils aîné d'un roi* (p. 15), itself no less concise than Arnault's verse adaptation:

En ce tems-là; un prince ombrageux se promenant dans une place publique de sa capitale, aperçut sa statue renversée.
    "Quel est le téméraire qui m'a fait cet outrage? Qu'il meure!"
    "Prince," lui répondit-on, "c'est le tonnerre."

Maréchal (1750–1803) was a noted scholar, philosopher, social critic,

The Statue Overturned

A certain despot—young, impetuous—
Happens upon his royal statue, cast
Down in the muck and mire. Gazing aghast,
    "Who dares insult my person thus?"
    Bellows the prince in accents frightening.
"Off with his head!" "But sire, it was the lightning."[1]

and poet, best known for his anticlerical *Almanach des honnêtes gens* (1788), for which he was briefly imprisoned, and for his equally controversial *Dictionnaire des athées anciens et modernes* (1800). Arnault's fable is significant in that it is, as he tells us (p. 324), one of only three whose subjects he did not invent himself, unlike many followers of La Fontaine; the other two being imitations of the Russian fabulist Krilov, done at the behest of one comtesse Orloff. The same subject was also treated by the fabulist Agniel, under Arnault's title but without his characteristic brevity. (See *Le Fablier du jeune âge*, II:17.) There is no indication whether the latter was inspired by Maréchal or Arnault, however.

Le Zèbre

    Le zèbre débarque en Europe;
Les ânes d'admirer, et les savants aussi.
    "Le beau cheval que celui-ci!"
Disent nos connaisseurs qu'éblouit l'enveloppe.
    Le cheval, lui seul étonné,
Prétend qu'à son espèce on ose faire injure.
"Un cheval! lui, messieurs, un cheval! je le jure,
    Ce n'est qu'un âne galonné."

The Zebra

The zebra comes to Europe, and, in awe,
    Asses—and scholars too, of course—
Ogle, agog. Our connoisseurs hee-haw
Their admiration for "that fancy horse!"
    In pique, the horse gives vent to his
    Dissent: "That thing, a horse? You dare
Call that a horse? That creature? That... I swear,
    An ass with stripes, that's all it is!"

L'Arbre Exotique et l'Arbre Indigène

"Tandis qu'en vain cet arbre utile
Attend l'eau dont il a besoin,
Pourquoi prenez-vous tant de soin
De cet arbre ingrat et stérile?"
"Mon ami, c'est qu'il vient de loin."

The Exotic Tree and the Native Tree

"Why do you parch that fruitful tree,
While watering so lavishly
And tending with tender persistence
This other, barren as can be?"
"This one, my friend, comes from a distance."

Le Chien et les Puces

    A-t-on des puces, mes amis,
    Il faut songer à s'en défaire.
    Mais loin qu'il fût de cet avis,
Certain barbet jadis faisait tout le contraire,
    Et du ton d'un riche, ou d'un grand

The Dog and the Fleas

    If one has fleas, it's best to find
    A remedy. And yet, a hound
    There was of quite a different mind,
Who, flea-infested, never scratched, but used to sound
    Like grand protector—royal host—

Qui s'enorgueillirait des amis de tout rang,
Dont toute bonne table en tout pays foisonne,
    Disait, au lieu de se gratter:
    "Que de gens je puis me flatter
    D'avoir autour de ma personne!
Un peuple tout entier accompagne mes pas."
    "Rien de plus vrai," dit une puce;
    "Mais, crois-moi, ne t'en prévaux pas:
    S'il tient à toi, c'est qu'il te suce."

One of that self-deluding kind, eager to boast
The guests (or parasites) happy to share his board.
    Our friend would say: "How proud am I
    To be surrounded daily by
    Such an admiring, loyal horde,
Who follow me, do what I do, go where I go!"
    "Quite so," replied a flea, "but sire, you
    Err if you think that they admire you.
    'Feed on you' would be much more *à propos!*"

L'Arbre et le Jardinier

"Lève une tête un peu moins haute,
Toi qui n'es bon qu'à me chauffer.
Tes fruits sont affreux." "C'est ta faute.
Ne devais-tu pas me greffer?"

The Tree and the Gardener

"Don't stand so proud, you wretched tree,
You're only fit for firewood!
Your fruit is vile!" "Well, don't blame me!
Why didn't you graft me while you could?"

L'Huître et la Perle

Après n'avoir rien pris de toute la semaine,
Un pêcheur trouve une huître au fond de son filet:
"Rien qu'une huître! voyez," dit-il, "la bonne aubaine,"
    En la jetant sur le galet.
    Comme il s'en allait, l'huître bâille,
    Et découvre à ses yeux surpris
    Une perle du plus grand prix
    Que recélait sa double écaille.
Patience, au milieu du discours le plus sot
    Ou du plus ennuyeux chapitre,
    On peut rencontrer un bon mot,
    Comme une perle dans une huître.

The Oyster and the Pearl

A fisherman, after a week without success,
Looks in his net and finds an oyster. "Well! I say...,"
He smirks, "what luck! An oyster! Lovely catch, no less!"
    And flings the irksome thing away.
    But, as he does, it opens wide:
    What do his startled eyes perceive?
    "No! Can it be?... I don't believe..."
    Yes, there's a precious pearl inside!
Patience! Amid a chapter dull or speech absurd,
    Who knows what hidden treasure dwells?
    Well may you find a witty word,
    Like pearl betwixt the oyster's shells.

Le Cachet

Sur la cire brûlante imprimons une image;
Elle s'y fixera d'autant plus fortement
Que le cachet si mou dans le premier moment,
En se refroidissant se durcit davantage.
    Leçon pour nous: par un outrage
    Avons-nous blessé notre ami,
    Et du mal dont il a gémi
Voulons-nous effacer jusqu'à la cicatrice;
    Qu'au plus tôt il soit réparé,
    Avant qu'en son cœur ulcéré
    L'amitié se refroidisse.

The Seal

    In molten wax we press our seal
    And watch as it solidifies,
To let our crest take shape before our eyes.
Beware! So can affection, too, congeal
    Betwixt distressed, dissenting friends.
    When thoughtless deed or word offends,
Take care! While yet the hurt can be redressed,
    Make your amends; lay bare your breast:
    Before the wound becomes too old—
    Before it scars—repair it, lest
    Friendship, like wax, grow hard and cold.

La Châtaigne

"Que l'étude est chose maussade!
A quoi sert de tant travailler?"

The Chestnut

"Of all the irksome, boring tasks,
Studying is the worst! What good

Disait, et non pas sans bâiller,
Un enfant que menait son maître en promenade.
Que répondait l'abbé? Rien. L'enfant sous ses pas
Rencontre cependant une cosse fermée,
Et de dards menaçants de toutes parts armée.
      Pour la prendre il étend le bras.
    "Mon pauvre enfant, n'y touchez pas!"
"Eh! pourquoi?" "Voyez-vous mainte épine cruelle
Toute prête à punir vos doigts trop imprudents."
"Un fruit exquis, monsieur, est caché là-dedans."
"Sans se piquer peut-on l'en tirer?" "Bagatelle!
      Vous voulez rire, je le crois.
Pour profiter d'une aussi bonne aubaine,
      On peut bien prendre un peu de peine,
      Et se faire piquer les doigts."
"Oui, mon fils: mais de plus que cela vous enseigne
     A vaincre les petits dégoûts
     Qu'à présent l'étude a pour vous.
Ces épines aussi cachent une châtaigne."

Is all that work?" a youngster asks
   (With many a yawn), while, through the wood,
   He strolls beside his tutor—an abbé.
The master gives no answer to his protégé...
    The pair walked on, as was their wont.
But suddenly the child spied something round
And small and spiny lying on the ground.
Stooping, he goes to pick it up. "No, don't!...
No, no, my child! Don't touch!" "Why not? I found it!"
"But don't you see those prickly spines around it?"
"Yes, but *mon père*... Inside... A tasty nut..."
    "Ah, but the spines will hurt!" "So what?
I'd risk a little pain for such a prize!"
    "And rightly so! By the same token,
    Perhaps you'll come to realize
That all that studying you so despise
Is just a prickly pod; but once it's broken,
    Nettlesome though the task has been,
A tasty chestnut always waits within."[1]

---

1. This fable, one of Arnault's most widely anthologized, is followed in his collection by an eight-line poem dedicated, during one of his two exiles, to his children, Louis and Gabrielle, from whom he was separated and for whom the message was especially intended: "De mon errant exil, c'est à vous que j'adresse / Ces conseils qui pour vous surtout sont de saison" (*Œuvres*, IV:261).

Stanislas-Jean de Boufflers   Œuvres (1813)

THE NAME of Stanislas-Jean de Boufflers—deeply rooted aristocrat, chevalier de Malte, member of the Académie Française, the Légion d'honneur, and other honorable and honorific institutions—is one of those names that crop up from time to time in eighteenth-century French studies in a variety of contexts: social and political, as well as literary. I should hasten to add that the literary context does not, properly speaking, extend to the fable, and that Boufflers specialists, such as there may be—and even the good marquis himself—would no doubt be surprised to see him figure in a collection devoted to that genre.

As a *littérateur* Boufflers probably owes whatever reputation he has retained over the generations to his ten-year correspondence with the comtesse de Sabran, his longtime ladyfriend and, eventually, wife (see the *Correspondance inédite de la comtesse de Sabran et du chevalier de Boufflers, 1778–1788*). In his own day, however, this *galant* of many a fashionable pre- and post-Revolutionary salon was much admired for his charm and wit by some of the more prominent literary lights, Voltaire himself not the least luminous and enthusiastic among them.[1] Rousseau, on the other hand, no doubt put off by Boufflers's social ease and success, and convinced that the young chevalier, like so many others, bore him no good will, was to damn with faint praise his talents—musical, painterly, and literary—in an often-misquoted passage: "Avec autant d'esprit, il eût pu réussir à tout; mais l'impossibilité de s'appliquer et le goût de la dissipation ne lui ont permis d'acquérir que des demi-talents en tout genre. En revanche, il en a beaucoup, et c'est tout ce qu'il faut dans le grand monde où il veut briller. Il fait très bien de petits vers, écrit très bien de petites lettres, va jouaillant un peu du cistre [i.e., "lute"] et barbouillant un peu de peinture au pastel." (See *Les Confessions*, Part II, Book 11, p. 652.)[2] Known to his contemporaries primarily for his occasional verse, and especially for his often exotic and sometimes erotic verse and prose *contes*—some of which had proven rather an embarrassment to the Church, in which he was nominally an abbé during a less-than-sacerdotal youth—Boufflers was to spend his artistic life on the fringes of literary celebrity, and would assure himself an important position among the second-rank eighteenth-century men of letters.[3]

Boufflers was born May 31, 1738, to Catherine de Beauvau, marquise de Boufflers, one of the more celebrated beauties of the age, literally "en route" between Nancy and Lunéville.[4] With his mother, he spent his childhood in the latter town at the elegant and artistic court of his godfather (and Louis XV's father-in-law), Stanislaus, semiexiled king of Poland, and duke of Lorraine; an environment well suited to foster the talents that were to mark his social and literary careers.[5] Like many youngest sons of noble families, Boufflers was destined for the Church, and spent a number of halfhearted years in a calling to which he was, clearly, not called at all. "Il a commencé par être abbé," Voisenon quips (*Anecdotes*, p. 157), "et s'il avoit eu autant de goût pour l'honneur que pour les plaisirs, il seroit peut-être devenu cardinal." Abandoning the cassock for the hussar's uniform, he swashbuckled his way up the ranks, seeing service in a few of the skirmishes of the period, and eventually finishing his military career at the rank of *maréchal de camp* ("brigadier") in 1784.

The following year Boufflers was appointed governor of the then newly acquired colony of Senegal, which he administered through 1787, apparently with considerable governmental skill and an enlightened humanitarianism—enlightened, that is, by comparison with other regimes.[6] Upon his return he was elected to the Académie Française in 1788 and to the Etats Généraux in 1789, but was to fulfill his functions in those bodies only briefly. The Revolution made it prudent for him to join the ranks of aristocratic émigrés, and he spent most of his self-imposed exile in Switzerland and Germany. After the accession of Napoleon, and with the latter's indulgence, the marquis—claiming that he would prefer to starve to death in France than to live in Prussia, and having finally married the comtesse de Sabran—returned to Paris in 1800. He lived out the remaining years before his death in the capital, on January 18, 1815, supporting the imperial cause, continuing to write—his *contes*, especially—and still a frequenter of the social salons, though growing more and more acerbic with the deterioration of both his physical and financial health. In 1814, the year before his death, he was named by the newly restored monarchy to the largely honorary curatorship of the Bibliothèque Mazarine.

As noted above, Boufflers is not usually thought of as a fabulist, as a perusal of his bibliography will show. (See Alexandre Cioranescu, *Bibliographie de la littérature française du dix-huitième siècle*, II:374–77.) One finds, however, among the various epigrams, madrigals, couplets, quatrains, classical translations, odes, and the like that fill many of the pages of his two-volume *Œuvres*, a total of five fables: three rather lengthy, quite traditional examples (I:88–90, "Le Singe et l'Amour"; 90–93, "Les Deux Pinçons"; 93–96, "Le Rat Bibliothécaire") and two shorter, more apparently personal ones, composed in the guise of a mother, a cryptic "Madame de✱✱✱," for the romantic edification, respectively, of her daughter (II:365) and her son (II:368–69). The first of the latter pair, translated here, is especially attractive in that it seems to suggest a self-portrait—and even something of a self-justification—of our physically and sentimentally peripatetic marquis, who penned as his own epitaph a tribute to his unwillingness, like that of Cupid's butterfly in his fable, to "se fixer":

> Ci-gît un chevalier qui sans cesse courut;
> Qui sur les grands chemins naquit, vécut, mourut,
>   Pour prouver ce qu'a dit le sage,
>   Que notre vie est un voyage.[7]

---

1. In his frequent travels Boufflers was to pay Voltaire several visits, between 1764 and 1766, at the patriarch's Swiss retreat at Ferney. (See Octave Uzanne's bio-bibliographical preface to his edition, *Poésies diverses du chevalier de Boufflers*, pp. xxi–xxix.)

2. Rousseau to the contrary nothwithstanding, Boufflers was actually quite an accomplished portraitist. Regarding some of his pastels, painted in Switzerland, see W. Deonna, "Quelques portraitistes genevois du XVIIIe siècle." The author also quotes a few lines of Voltaire's that serve as a pleasant counterpoise to Rousseau's remarks:

> "C'est à vous ô jeune Boufflers,
> A vous dont notre Suisse admire
> Les crayons, la prose et les vers,
> Et les petits contes pour rire." (p. 149)

3. It is as such that he was the subject of two of Emile Faguet's Sorbonne lectures on "Les Poètes secondaires du XVIIIe siècle (1750–1789)," subsequently printed as part of his posthumous *Histoire de la poésie française de la Renaissance au Romantisme*, vol. IX, chap. 3. The lectures were originally published in the *Revue des cours et conférences* for 1903–4.

4. Many sources, even the usually authoritative Faguet (*Histoire*, p. 35), mistakenly give the year as 1737. (See Uzanne's edition of *Poésies diverses*, pp. iii–iv.) As for the circumstances surrounding his birth, they would prove appropriate for one whose "goût dominant," to quote Claude-Henri de Fusée de Voisenon, was "celui d'être toujours ambulant . . ." Voisenon illustrates his observation with a typical quip from his *Anecdotes littéraires* (see pp. 49; 50, n. 1): "Quelqu'un l'ayant rencontré sur les grands chemins, lui dit: 'Monsieur le Chevalier, je suis charmé de vous trouver chez vous!'" (p. 157).

5. For detailed studies of Stanislaus's court and the involvement of the marquise and her son in it, see the several historical volumes by Gaston Maugras: *La Cour de Lunéville au dix-huitième siècle; Dernières années de la cour de Lunéville: Mme de Boufflers, ses enfants et ses amis* (originally published as *Dernières années du roi Stanislas*); and *La Marquise de Boufflers et son fils le chevalier de Boufflers*. Boufflers has also been the subject of a more recent study: Nicole Vaget-Grangeat, *Le Chevalier de Boufflers et son temps: étude d'un échec*.

6. Rumor had it, at the time, that he was actually being "banished" to that remote outpost as punishment for an indiscreet epigram directed against Louis XVI's aunt, Christine de Saxe. P. Leguay, however, in his entry on Boufflers in the *Dictionnaire de biographie française*, claims that the heavily debt-ridden marquis had actively sought the post for financial reasons (VI:1284).

7. *Œuvres*, I:26. (The epitaph is also quoted in Jean Ravennes, "Les petits écrits du chevalier de Boufflers," p. 468.)

Fable de Madame De✱✱✱ à Sa Fille,

Qui lui avait envoyé un camée d'un Amour qui voulait attraper un Papillon pour lui couper les ailes.

Fable by Madame De✱✱✱ to Her Daughter,

Who had sent her a cameo of a Cupid trying to catch a Butterfly and cut off its wings.

L'Amour, voyant un papillon
   Voltiger sur des fleurs nouvelles,
Prétendit corriger cet insigne frelon,
   Et le fixer en lui coupant les ailes.
      Aussitôt dit, aussitôt fait:
Le papillon, perdant le charme dont il brille,
De léger devient lourd, de joli devient laid,
      Il ne reste qu'une chenille.

Quand l'Amour par hasard fixe certains amans,
   On rit de la métamorphose:
Va, ma fille, crois-moi, des papillons constans
   Fatigueraient bientôt les roses.

Cupid, one day, watched as a butterfly
   Flitted from flower to flower, and thought that he
Ought clip the wings of that resplendent moth, thereby
   To cure him of his infidelity.[1]
No sooner said than done. Now dull and wearisome,
   Beauty-bereft, our sometime wayward swain,
      No more a-flitting, has become
      A caterpillar once again.

When Love makes fickle lovers faithful beaus,
We laugh, my dear, to see their transformation:
The butterfly's unflagging adoration,
I fear, in time, must even tire the rose.

1. I have taken the liberty of changing the author's *frelon* 'hornet', which he seems to use only for the rhyme, to a no less disparaging but rather more logical "moth."

Louis-François Jauffret   Fables Nouvelles (1814)

IF VOLUME, variety, and sincerity of purpose were guar-
antors of literary renown and posterity's admiration, the
"méridional" Louis-François Jauffret would today be
counted among the more famous of nineteenth-century
French men of letters. His published works number
some four dozen (not to mention numerous journal articles and an assortment of editorial enterprises) and range
over the arts and sciences in subject matter from ancient
history to zoology.[1] As for his purpose, it was almost exclusively and unabashedly didactic. The majority of his
writing was, in fact, composed for the moral and intellectual edification of the young.[2] If much or most of it is,
by today's standards, rather on the maudlin and prudish
side, it should be noted that his own less-sophisticated
age was apparently of a different mind, judging by a contemporary encyclopedia entry: "Les nombreux ouvrages
de M. Jauffret offrent tous de l'intérêt, contiennent une
morale pure, et présentent l'instruction sous des formes
qui éloignent ce qu'elle a de plus répugnant pour la jeunesse" (*Biographie nouvelle des contemporains*, IX:383).

It should come as no surprise, then, that among
Jauffret's many publications are found an edition of the
posthumous works of his friend and adviser, the homey
fabulist Florian (see pp. 100–101): *Œuvres posthumes de
Florian;* the complete works of another then prominent
mentor of youth, the lyrical moralist Arnaud Berquin:
Œuvres complètes de Berquin;[3] and, especially, a lengthy
collection of fables. Jauffret's two-volume *Fables nouvelles*
were originally published in 1814. A second, enlarged
edition, also in two volumes and containing 442 fables
divided into fifteen books, attests to their success, at least
among his contemporaries.[4]

One of the more outspoken of those contemporaries
in his admiration for Jauffret's fables was the well-known
literary critic Jean-Joseph Dussault, whose reviews appeared in the *Journal des débats* from 1800 to 1817. Dussault was categorical in his praise, according Jauffret
third place among the fabulists French, after Florian
himself, distant runner-up to the untouchable La Fontaine. "...je pense que les *Fables* de M. Jauffret doivent
être rangées parmi celles qui se soutiennent le mieux à
côté des agréables apologues que nous devons à l'auteur
d'*Estelle* et de *Galatée*..." He goes on, in his enthusiasm,
to suggest that perhaps even Florian might need look to
his laurels.[5] Dussault could be suspected of collegial non-
objectivity, having been a fellow student of Jauffret's at
the Collège de Saint-Barbe, in Paris. (See Reboul,
Jauffret, p. 4.) Be that as it may, at least one observer, the
literary historian Bernard Jullien, would take serious issue with his generous assessment. (See his *Histoire de la
poésie française à l'époque impériale,* II:178–79). But if many
of Jauffret's fables do tend toward the overblown and
long-winded, Jullien's negativity is, I think, exaggerated
and rather suspect, since he tars them all with the same
dour—indeed, dyspeptic—brush. Even the more charming among them; namely, his "sequels" to some of the
better-known fables of La Fontaine, in which, instead of
rewriting the Aesopic original, he takes up where his
predecessor leaves off, continuing the scenario and developing it along his own imaginative lines and, of course,
to his own didactic purpose.

This little-studied figure was born on October 4, 1770,
in the southern French village of La Roque-Brussane,
one of six children.[6] An early classical, religious, and

legal education in Aix-en-Provence and Paris resulted, at the unusually tender age of twenty, in a *licence en droit* and admission into the Parlement de Paris. Shortly after, however, that body was abolished by the Revolution of 1789, thus ending Jauffret's career in the law, which he abandoned in favor of a life in letters, science, and education. He was fortunate enough, in those early years, to enjoy the friendship and encouragement of Florian, who, with Berquin and others, fostered his literary ambitions and endeavors. Those endeavors lasted over a productive period of four decades, including the stormy years of two revolutions, the Terror, and their aftermaths; decades that saw him devote his efforts not only to literature, but—as a typical, albeit late, product of eighteenth-century encyclopedism—to the popularization of the sciences, natural and social, as well. By the time of his death, in Marseille, on December 11, 1840, he had been a member of literally three dozen academic and learned societies (see Reboul, *Jauffret,* pp. 102–3), had taught natural history for a time at the Ecole Centrale de Versailles, had served as headmaster of the *collèges* of Montbrison and Saint-Etienne, and as *secrétaire perpétuel* of the Académie des Sciences, Belles Lettres et Arts de Marseille, and had been curator, from 1818 to 1830, of that city's municipal library, to note only a few of his civic and pedagogical functions and accomplishments.

Jauffret's devotion to the fable as an ideal vehicle for his didactic preoccupations produced not only his *Fables nouvelles* but also several other works, both creative and descriptive.[7] The six characteristic fables presented in translation are taken from the fifteen books of the 1826 edition, in which they are numbered as follows: II, 17; VI, 13; VII, 17; X, 16; XI, 19; and XIV, 18.

1. The reader interested in Jauffret will find the most authoritative (and only complete) bibliography of his works, published and unpublished, in Robert-Marie Reboul's homage-biography, *Louis-François Jauffret: sa vie et ses œuvres.* The compatriot-biographer may well be accused of biased exaggeration when, in his preface, he presents Jauffret as "l'une des figures les plus intéressantes qui aient illustré à la fois les lettres et les sciences de ce siècle" (p. x). Still, mention of only a few titles will bear out the polymathic scope of his interests: *Voyage au Jardin des Plantes, contenant la description des galeries d'histoire naturelle* . . . ; *Dictionnaire étymologique de la langue française, à l'usage de la jeunesse; Les Veillées de pensionnat, contenant des dialogues destinés à être représentés dans les maisons d'éducation et des comédies propres à instruire et à amuser la jeunesse.* Interestingly, his prolific output and Reboul's adulation notwithstanding, he is ignored by such standard latter-day encyclopedias and bibliographies as *Dictionnaire des lettres françaises: le dix-neuvième siècle* and Hugo P. Thieme, *Bibliographie de la littérature française de 1800 à 1930.*

2. A few more of his titles will suffice as illustrations: *Petit théâtre des familles: drames à l'usage de la jeunesse; La Gymnastique de la jeunesse; La petite école des arts et métiers.*

3. Spiritually a descendant of Rousseau and an ancestor of the comtesse de Ségur (see pp. 151–52), Berquin (1749–91) was the author of poetic idylls and romances, and of edifying prose tales and playlets for children—the extremely popular collection *L'Ami des enfans,* for exam-ple—which, later dubbed "berquinades," were to become synonymous with the period's mawkish sentimentality. Several editions of Berquin's complete works, beside Jauffret's, are proof of his popularity.

4. The collection, dedicated to the dauphine, is preceded by a fanciful essay, "L'Elysée des fabulistes," in which a number of fabulists come together in the Great Beyond to discuss the ancient and modern luminaries of their genre.

5. The review was originally published in the *Journal des débats,* December 28, 1814, and was reprinted in Dussault's *Annales littéraires,* IV:400–401. A substantial portion was also quoted in the *avis des éditeurs* prefacing the 1826 edition of the *Fables nouvelles* (pp. ii–xi).

6. An elder brother, Gaspard-Jean-André-Joseph Jauffret (1759–1823), was a distinguished churchman: bishop of Metz and author of a large number of works of religious interest.

7. Reboul's bibliography cites the following published works: *Trois fables sur la girafe; Lettres sur les fabulistes anciens et modernes; Quelques fables inédites, lues aux séances publiques de l'Académie Royale des Sciences, Belles-Lettres et Arts de Marseille.* Three others remain in manuscript: "Notices biographiques et bibliographiques sur les fabulistes Fumars, de Marseille, Vitalis, d'Aix, et Guichard"; "Dissertations sur Phèdre le fabuliste et sur le poëte Saadi, auteur de 'Gulistan, ou le Jardin des Roses'"; "Dissertations sur quelques fabulistes modernes." (See Reboul, *Jauffret,* pp. 114, 115, 121, and 122.)

La Corneille

    Une corneille au noir plumage
      (Elle était parente, je crois,
Du corbeau qu'un renard cajola sur sa voix,
Et qui voulant chanter laissa choir son fromage),
Une corneille, dis-je, errant dès le matin,
      Vit sur un terrein purgé d'herbes,
Certain agriculteur éparpillant ses gerbes
Pour les battre en plein air, et récolter son grain.
"Quel froment!" disait-elle, "et qu'il a bonne mine;
      L'hiver vient; je devrais songer
A faire une cachette, où je puisse gruger
      Quelque chose en cas de famine.
      Procédons à l'enlèvement.
Accrochons ces épis, dont la terre est couverte;
Et, les ongles chargés, sauvons-nous promptement

The Raven

A raven, black of feather (and who well might be
    A cousin to that overweening crow
    Whose cheese went falling to the fox below
    When he—the latter—worked his flattery
In praise of his—the former's—voice)...[1] Well, anyway...
    A raven, since the break of day,
Fluttering to and fro above a grassless plain,
    Watched as a farmer spread his sheaves of grain.
    "What gorgeous wheat!" she mused. "I'd better lay
      Myself away a proper store,
      Something to nibble on, before
The winter's chill. Who knows when I may need a meal?
    So let's proceed to steal what we can steal:
      Let's fill our talons chockablock
      With all those stalks aplenty, lying

Dans le creux ignoré d'une roche déserte."
Jusque-là, c'était bien; mais il advient parfois
 Qu'on fait pis en voulant mieux faire.
La corneille de loin, les yeux fixés sur l'aire,
 Considérait le villageois.
"Que fait-il?" disait-elle; "il s'agite, il travaille
A séparer, je crois le froment de la paille.
 Bon! le travail sera tout fait.
Attendons, et j'aurai le froment pur et net."
La corneille attendit; et quand, de son haleine,
Eurus eut fait voler la paille dans la plaine,
Quand le fermier, tout prêt à serrer son trésor,
Eut mis en un seul tas le froment couleur d'or,
 La commère, du haut des nues,
 Regardant déjà tout ce bien
 Comme sien,
Tombe sur le monceau les deux griffes tendues.
On la vit de ses doigts, s'escrimer bel et bien.
Mais, hélas! vains efforts! espérances déçues!
La griffe eut beau jouer, elle n'emporta rien.

 La fortune est comme les belles;
Acceptons ses faveurs, tant légères soient-elles.
Qui veut attendre mieux, et montre du dégoût,
 Le plus souvent n'a rien du tout.

Here, there and everywhere! Then let's go flying
 Off to the hollow of some hidden rock..."
So far, so good. But oftentimes we ought
 Leave well enough alone. Our raven, viewing
The farmer from afar, watched as he threshed, and thought:
 "My goodness me! Now what's he doing... ?
I know! He's separating out the chaff!... Well then,
 Let's wait and let him do my work. And when
 He's done, I'll have myself my wheat,
 All nice and neat."
And wait she did. But while the Eastwind, at his leisure,
 Blusters and blows the chaff about; and while
The farmer, set to gather in the gold-hued treasure,
 Collects it all into one heavy pile,
 Our cawing crone,
 Soaring aloft and confidently staring
Down at the precious trove, already now her own!
 Swoops—talons ready, poised—preparing
To seize her prize... Stabs, lunges, grabs... Oh, vain
 endeavor!...
Unable to make off with anything whatever.

Fortune is like a lady fair: he who would get her
Had best be thankful for her boons, however small:
 If he turns up his nose and waits for better,
 He may well come away with none at all.

1. The reference is, of course, to La Fontaine's celebrated "Maître Corbeau," victim of the fox's blandishments in "Le Corbeau et le Renard" (I, 2) (see p. 31). (For Benserade's pithy rendition, see p. 47.)

Le Tambour et la Rose

Après avoir gaîment, jusqu'au milieu du jour,
Assourdi les voisins en battant son tambour,
Petit Paul, las lui-même, interrompt son vacarme,
 Réfléchit, et cherche à savoir
Si son tambour percé pourra lui laisser voir
 D'où provient le bruit qui le charme.
 Non loin de lui, le jeune Albin
S'emparait d'une fleur. "La rose que tu cueilles,"

The Drum and the Rose

 All morning, little Paul has been
Beating his drum, raising a deafening thunder,
 Much to his neighbors' great chagrin.
At length he stops, reflects, begins to wonder
 Whether the drumhead, slashed asunder,
Will show the source of his belovèd din.
Same time, another lad, not far away—
Albin by name—has picked a splendid rose,

Se disait-il tout bas, "est la rose à cent feuilles,
    La plus belle de ce jardin.
Cent feuilles!... c'est beaucoup... Mais en est-on certain?
Peut-être à l'assurer ma langue est un peu prompte.
Examinons d'abord si l'on m'aurait trompé."
Voilà mon curieux du calcul occupé;
Il effeuille la fleur, pour mieux trouver son compte.
    Qu'arriva-t-il aux deux enfans?
La curiosité de leur malheur fut cause.
De leur joujou tous deux privés en même temps,
Paul n'eut plus de tambour, Albin n'eut plus de rose.

Humains, désirez-vous être heureux ici-bas?
Jouissez du plaisir, ne l'analysez pas.

Muttering: "My! How beautiful! They say
It's got a hundred petals!... But, who knows?
A hundred? That's a lot! How can they tell?
    Maybe I spoke too soon!... Oh well,
    Let's count and see!..." And so, engrossed
    In calculation, then and there,
He plucks, counts, plucks... Down to the innermost
Of petals, till he's plucked the flower bare.
    Result? Too curious, our pair
    Lose what they love the most. In sum,
Albin has no more rose; Paul, no more drum.

You who seek happiness, best be advised:
Pleasure should be enjoyed, not analyzed.

Le Chat et le Rat

Un rat tout jeune encor, au sortir de son trou,
Jeunesse est aisément confiante et crédule,
    Fit rencontre d'un vieux matou,
Qui vous allait soudain le croquer sans scrupule.
"Un mot," lui dit le rat, "quand vous me connaîtrez,
Seigneur, ou je me trompe, ou vous m'épargnerez.
    N'êtes-vous pas Grippe-Fromage?"
"Oui. Qui t'a dit mon nom?" "Ne vous souvient-il pas
Qu'étant un certain jour tombé dans certains lacs,
    Vous déploriez votre esclavage,
    Et n'attendiez que le trépas,
Quand Rongemaille vint vous tirer d'embarras?"
    "J'en ai quelque réminiscence."
"Il est mort depuis peu, le pauvre infortuné,
Et je dois le pleurer, je suis son fils puîné.
    Avec lui, par reconnaissance,
Ne jurâtes-vous pas éternelle alliance?"
    "Oui, mon ami, rien n'est plus vrai."
"Ne lui dîtes-vous pas: 'Va, sois en assurance;
Envers et contre tous je te protégerai,
    Et la belette mangerai,
    Avec l'époux de la chouette?'"
    "Oui, jaloux d'acquitter ma dette,
Je promis, en prenant tout l'Olympe à témoin,
De défendre ce rat et les siens, au besoin."
"Eh bien! protégez donc le fils de Rongemaille":
"C'est mon dessein. Les fils de mon libérateur
    Sont tous adoptés par mon cœur,
Pour eux, je me battrais et d'estoc et de taille.
    A-t-il laissé beaucoup d'enfants?"
    "Douze." "Intéressante jeunesse!
Innocents orphelins! comptez sur ma promesse;
    Reposez vous sur mes serments!
Ne pourrai-je point voir ma famille adoptive!
Je voudrais prodiguer à ces ratons charmants
    Mes soins et mes embrassements!
Cours vite, cours chercher cette troupe craintive;
    En priant les dieux, je t'attends."

The Cat and the Rat

A rat of tender years—as trusting and naive
    As callow youth is apt to be—
    Had blithely just begun to leave
His hole when, there before him, suddenly,
    He happened on a tough old cat,
    Who gladly would have munched him just like that
Had not the rat implored: "Wait, sire! A word!
    I'm sure you'll spare me once you've heard...
Your name is Seize-Cheese, right?" "Who told you
                                    so?" The rat
    Replied: "Don't you recall, not long ago
    You fell into a net, and spent
    Long hours in whimper and lament,
    Waiting to die, wailing your woe,
Until a rat named Sawtooth came and gnawed you free?"[1]
Answered the cat: "I seem to recollect... And so?"
"Well, Sawtooth was my father, rest his soul. You see,
    I was his youngest... Anyway, he died,
    Poor thing! But I remember how you swore,
    In gratitude, to be forevermore
His ally and his friend. Isn't that true?" Replied
    The cat: "Indeed it is!" "And didn't you
    Assure him he could live in peace... ?" "I did."
    "Secure and safe, even amid
    The weasel and the hoot owl too,
Because you promised to protect him?" "True.
Before Olympus' gods I swore a solemn oath
    To be a staunch defender, both
    To him and all his rodent kin."
    "Then prithee, sire, why not begin
    With me, his son?" "For sure, for sure...
In fact, his whole precious progeniture
Shall be more dear to me than my own young have been!
    Trust in my strength, child of my heart! With tooth
    And nail I'll succor you... You and the others...
Oh, by the way, how many are you: sisters, brothers...?"
    We're twelve in all." "Ah! Charming youth!
    Sweet orphans mine!... Well now, go run and fetch

Le rat obéissant court, vole et les amène.
Le saint homme de chat, roulant des yeux malins,
Tombe alors sans pitié sur tous ces orphelins;
Au lieu d'en croquer un, il croqua la douzaine.
L'avare, le buveur, peuvent se corriger;
L'égoïste, à la fin, peut devenir sensible;
Mais l'hypocrite a beau promettre de changer,
    Je tiens qu'il est incorrigible.

My new adopted family. I yearn
    To hug each poor, dear, trembling wretch!
    Hurry! I'll wait in prayer till you return..."
Off runs the rat, gullible as a country cousin,
    And brings back all the blessèd orphan troupe.
Our saintly cat leers, lunges; and, in one fell swoop,
    Instead of croaking one, he croaks the dozen!
Some sinners—miser, drunkard, selfish sot—can quit
    Their wicked ways; but not the hypocrite.

1. The proper names "Grippe-Fromage" and "Rongemaille," used for the cat and the rat, are borrowed from La Fontaine's fable "Le Chat et le Rat" (VIII, 22). "Rongemaille," literally "Gnaw-Stitch," is also used for the rat in the latter's "Le Corbeau, la Gazelle, la Tortue, et le Rat" (XII, 15).

Le Chêne et les Animaux

Un Chêne fort âgé, patriarche des bois,
Sentant tomber ses glands et languir son feuillage,
    Appela, d'une faible voix,
    Les animaux du voisinage.
    "Venez partager mes faveurs,"
Leur dit-il, "profitez de ma munificence.
Ma facile bonté n'exige de vos cœurs
Que le simple tribut de la reconnaissance."
"De la reconnaissance! en dois-tu demander?"
Lui dit un Marcassin; "franchement, tu m'étonnes!
    Semblable à ces vieilles personnes,
Qui, volontairement, ne peuvent rien céder,
    Tes faveurs sont belles et bonnes;
    Mais si tu nous les abandonnes,
    C'est que tu ne peux les garder."

The Oak and the Animals

Patriarch of the woods, an agèd oak,
Losing his leaves, watching his acorns fall,
With failing voice, summons the forest folk:
    "Animal friends, come, one and all!
    Look at the generous gifts I spread
    Before you! Help yourselves!" he said.
"Share in my bounty. All I ask of you
Is simple gratitude, and nothing more."
"Your bounty? Ha!" replied a brash young boar.
    "You make me laugh! You really do!
    You want our gratitude? What for?
You're like those human misers—old and cheap—
    Who let go nothing willingly.
Your gifts are fine, but friend, they don't fool me:
You only give what you're too weak to keep."

Le Lion et le Loup

Un Lion, au milieu d'une forêt sauvage,
Ayant surpris un Loup, lui dit: "Je te cherchais.
Ne viens-tu pas tantôt, sans forme de procès,
De manger un agneau vers le prochain rivage?"
"Sire," répond le Loup justement alarmé,
    "Cet agneau troublait mon breuvage."
"Il ne le troublait pas: je m'en suis informé."
"Un an auparavant, personne ne l'ignore,
Sur mon compte il avait jasé dans le hameau."
    "Tu mens, le malheureux agneau,
Un mois auparavant, n'existait pas encore."
"Mais, sire, ce fut donc son frère..." "Il n'en a point,
Et tu voudrais en vain m'abuser sur ce point.
    Meurs! je dois venger l'innocence..."
    "Vous êtes clément." " Je suis roi.
    Un vil assassin comme toi
    Est indigne de ma clémence."

The Lion and the Wolf[1]

A lion, in the forest wilderness,
Happening on a wolf, exclaimed: "Ah, yes!
    You're just the one I'm looking for!
    Wasn't that you, there, by the shore,
Who just dispatched a lamb... No judge, no jury?"
    The wolf, alarmed—and rightly so—
    Replied: "Indeed, milord. For sure, he
Sullied my drink!" "He couldn't have done! I know..."
    "Well, last year he besmirched my name.
    Ask anyone..." "More lies! For shame!
He wasn't born even a month ago!"
"Maybe his brother..." "Nonsense! He has none!...
No! No excuse! You'll die for what you've done!
Innocence be avenged! No controversy!...
    Enough deceitful jabbering!..."
    "But sire, you're merciful!..." "I'm king!
    For murderers like you, no mercy!"

1. In characteristic fashion, Jauffret provides not a simple reworking of the famous La Fontaine fable "Le Loup et l'Agneau" (I, 10) (see pp. 32–33), but rather a sequel that might well be subtitled "The Lamb's Posthumous Revenge."

La Grenouille Qui A Peur de Grossir

La Grenouille d'Esope et du bon La Fontaine,
Celle qui fut jadis assez folle, assez vaine,
    Pour s'enfler aux yeux de sa sœur,
S'imaginant d'un bœuf égaler la grosseur,
Creva, comme l'on sait. Au bruit de sa rupture,
Les Grenouilles, témoins de sa mésaventure,
Plongèrent dans l'étang. Au fond de leur réduit,
Elles disaient: "Voyez où l'orgueil nous conduit!
L'exemple est effrayant. Toutes, tant que nous sommes,
    Tirons-en du moins quelque fruit:
Donnons, par cela même, une leçon aux hommes!"
La sœur de la défunte, isolée en son coin,
De se rapetisser sent dès-lors le besoin,
    Perd la voix, se met à la diète,
    Et n'avale morceau ni miette.
Sa voisine lui dit: "Crois-tu donc aller loin,
En te nourrissant d'air? Va, si tu n'es plus sage,
    Avant deux jours le marécage
    De ton trépas sera témoin:
    Tu descendras au noir rivage."

Que du juste milieu l'on ne sorte jamais!
La sagesse consiste à fuir tous les excès.

    1 The reference is to La Fontaine's "La Grenouille Qui Se Veut Faire aussi Grosse que le Bœuf" (I, 3) (see p. 32), inspired by several Aesopic sources: among them, Babrius, 28; Phaedrus, I, 24; Horace, *Satires,* II, 13, vv. 314–20. The popular subject was taken up

The Frog Who Is Afraid of Growing Fat

    We all recall what happened when
That frog that Aesop tells about—and La Fontaine—
    Tried, in her foolish vanity, to show
    Her sister that, no question, she could grow
    Fat as an ox... Remember?... Right, she burst.[1]
        The noise of her explosive ending
        Sent all the other frogs attending
    Diving into the swamp to hide, head first.
"Ah!" sighed the lot. "See what a sin is pride!
        Well, let's at least be edified
    By her example; let Man, too, learn by it!"
        Alone, off brooding in her corner,
        Our late frog's sister, silent mourner,
        Immediately goes on a diet,
        Bent and intent on staying small,
    And eating not a crumb... No food at all...
"Don't be so dumb! You can't eat air!" her neighbors warn.
    "A day or two, and, dying, you'll be borne
        Over the dark divide—that shore
        Of no return—forevermore!"

    Good counsel, too. The golden mean, it seems,
Is still the wise man's course between extremes.

by many of La Fontaine's successors. (For another version in the present collection, see p. 178.) It is typical of Jauffret that his treatment does not merely reproduce the original tale, but elaborates, somewhat whimsically, on its consequences.

Jacques-François Roger   Fables Sénégalaises Recueillies de l'Ouolof et Mises en Vers Français (1828)

Baron Jacques-François Roger,[1] born in Longjumeau, south of Paris, in 1787, was a man of many parts and impressive culture: lawyer, classical scholar, philologist of no mean erudition, agronomist, government administrator, and writer of prose and verse. In a lyrical passage reminiscent of Chateaubriand, he recounts his youthful flight from the excesses of "civilization" into the tropical and unspoiled wilds of Senegal. (See *Recherches philosophiques sur la langue ouolofe,* pp. 6–7.) Soon after, however—"par un étrange caprice du destin"—he was to be appointed governor of those French territories on the west coast of Africa, newly retrieved from Great Britain with the Treaty of Paris in 1814.

    This "strange caprice of destiny" was, in reality, the result of considerable politicking, both by Roger himself

and by various influential protectors. (See Georges Hardy, *La Mise en valeur du Sénégal de 1817 à 1854,* pp. 117–19.) Originally assigned in 1819, after numerous solicitations, to oversee a model farm set up by royal decree, he was named to the post of governor two years later, in July of 1821, despite his lack of the usual military credentials, compensated for, to some extent, by his admission into the Légion d'honneur shortly after his appointment. Roger assumed his official duties early in the following year. (See G.-G. Beslier, *Le Sénégal,* p. 104.) His personal and professional qualities, as well as the accomplishments of his enlightened five-year tenure—the longest and most productive in a rapid succession of short-lived administrations—are described in detail in Hardy's account of this outstanding figure in the early history of French involvement in Senegal (pp. 115–249 and passim). The picture that emerges is one of a strong-willed, somewhat visionary official, sympathetic to the culture and sensibilities of the indigenous inhabitants, though not wholly without personal ambitions. Suffice it to say that his major contribution as "Commandeur et administrateur du Sénégal et dépendances"—and, judging by his own reflections, one of his proudest achievements—was in the area of agronomy. (See *Recherches philosophiques sur la langue ouolofe,* p. 125.) It was under his direction that a vast program was initiated, introducing into Senegal a wide variety of previously uncultivated crops—cotton, indigo, grains, fruits of all kinds, and the like—that would have a lasting effect on the economic life of the area.

Despite the demands of his official duties, by the end of his administration in 1827 Roger had found time not only to learn the Wolof language well enough to write the exceptional scholarly treatise cited above but also to write a lengthy story of African life and customs, *Kelédor, histoire africaine,* whose apparent popularity had earned it ten reprintings within two years of its publication. His fascination with Wolof language and folk culture had also prompted him to collect and translate into French verse, à la La Fontaine, a volume of local fables, his *Fables sénégalaises, recueillies de l'ouolof et mises en vers français.* In his preface, like most of the legion of La Fontaine's followers, he excuses the seeming temerity of imitating the master fabulist by invoking the exotic nature of his subject matter (pp. 6–7), and goes on to justify, on similar grounds, his voluminous notes. It is, in fact, these notes, often longer than the fables themselves, that make his work a mine of information on the flora, fauna, customs, and life of the country he would come to refer to as "mon Sénégal," in addition to being a strikingly original example of the post–La Fontaine fable.

In 1827, Roger, having been promoted to the grade of officer in the Légion d'honneur, resigned his position, claiming ill health and vague "personal reasons." (See *Recherches philosophiques sur la langue ouolofe,* p. 125, n. 2.)[2]

In 1831 we find him serving in the new government of Louis-Philippe, in the Chambre des Députés, representing Le Loiret.[3] He would remain in that body—and, with the Revolution of 1848, its successor, the Assemblée Nationale Constituante—until his death, still a legitimist, albeit a most enlightened one. Roger, monarchist though he was, was too much the philosophical heir of the Enlightenment to subscribe to archaic Ancien Régime views on innate social or ethnic inferiority. His liberal opinions on slavery, for example, fostered by his sympathetic personal experiences in Senegal, and passionately enunciated in his Ouolof grammar (pp. 104–5)—in the midst of a chapter on adverbs, no less—placed him among the ranks of those favoring its abolition when that question divided French opinion in the 1840s. (See André-Jean Tudesq, *Les Grands notables en France, 1840–1849,* II:840.) He died in 1849, a year after the demise of the July Monarchy.

Besides authoring the several works mentioned, Roger was coeditor, with the prolific jurist François-Xavier-Paul Garnier (1793–1879), of the *Annales universelles de la législation et de la jurisprudence commerciales,* and also published several other minor writings and technical papers. In addition, he makes mention in his early *Recherches philosophiques sur la langue ouolofe* (pp. 7, 9) of two intended works: one, on the customs of the Wolofs, to be entitled "La Sénégambie, ou Mémoires descriptifs, philosophiques et politiques sur cette contrée," and the other on the exploits of the intrepid Senegalese sailors known as *laptots.* I find no indication that either one was ever actually completed.

The *Fables sénégalaises* consist of thirty-six translations from the Wolof, followed by eight fables of Roger's own invention, written, as he tell us, as distractions "dans les ennuis de l'absence, dans les fatigues de continuels voyages, dans les inquiétudes, les contrariétés d'une entreprise difficile" (p. 252). The collection also includes a prologue dedicated to the "Esope africain," and an epilogue. My translations are numbers 10, 15, 17, and 38.

---

1. Roger's title was less than venerable, dating from 1824. It should be pointed out, however, that he doesn't seem to have been overly impressed by nobility. Two of his original fables, numbers 39 and 40 in the collection cited below, make obvious fun of the pretensions of both the old and new aristocracy, a fact to which he himself calls attention in his notes.

2. Hardy suggests a more specific cause, namely the disappointing results of some of his programs (*La Mise en Valeur du Sénégal,* pp. 231 ff.).

3. A two-page document of Roger's authorship, "Amendemens au projet de résolution tendant au rétablissement du divorce," from the 1831 session of the Chambre des Députés, obviously establishes his membership in that body well before the year 1838, the date given by Hardy (p. 231, n. 2). For some reason, the *Almanach Royal et National* fails to list him as a *député* until 1832, but confirms his service between that year and 1848–49.

Les Deux Maures et le Cheval

Biram venait de vendre à Moktar son Cheval.
    Ils voyageaient de compagnie.
L'acheteur cheminait monté sur l'animal;
L'autre suivait à pied, triste et séchant d'envie.
Vint l'heure du repos. Nul abri, nul couvert

The Two Moors and the Horse

One day Biram sells friend Moktar his horse.[1]
    The two, together, then proceed
    Along their way; Moktar, of course,
    Riding astride his new-bought steed,
    With poor Biram stumbling behind,

Ne défendait nos gens du soleil du désert;
Le vendeur se couchait à l'ombre raccourcie
De son ancien coursier. L'acheteur réclamait:
"Ce Cheval m'appartient," disait-il en colère;
   "J'ai seul droit à l'ombre qu'il fait."
La mobile *oasis* fut un sujet de guerre.
On s'est battu pour moins. Le vendeur répondait:
   "Souviens-toi mieux de notre affaire.
   Oui, je t'ai vendu l'animal,
   Mais je ne t'ai pas vendu l'ombre."
"C'est vrai," dit l'acheteur, "la ruse n'est pas mal.
Hé bien! chacun son lot: reste au frais sans encombre."
Et puis, au grand galop, il partit à cheval.

Grumbling: "What have I done! What have I done!"
   Comes time to rest... Trying to find
   Some shelter from the sweltering desert sun,
   Biram lies in the horse's scanty shade.
   Moktar objects, with not a little pique:
"The horse is mine! His shadow too! All bought and paid!"
In short, the quadruped "oasis"—so to speak—[2]
Soon has the buyer and the seller jaw to jaw.
   "You see," explains the latter, "there's one flaw.
   If you remember... Yes, it's true,
   I sold the beast. But not his shadow too!"
"Oh? Well then, keep it!" shouts Moktar. And, with a scoff,
He jumps up on the horse and gallops off.[3]

1. As mentioned above (p. 137), Roger delights in supplying copious notes with his fables, and I would not attempt to reproduce them all in their entirety. The reader will appreciate some, however; for example, the observation that "Biram" and "Moktar" are common given names among the Moors.
2. Although, by Roger's time, the word *oasis* had already had a long history in French, he apparently considered it still exotic enough to justify italics, and—characteristically—an explanation.

3. In another note Roger expresses his pleasure and surprise at finding, among the Senegalese, "une fable si semblable à celle que Démosthène racontait un jour aux Athéniens" (p. 92); a reference to the Aesopic fable of "The Ass's Shadow," no. 460 of the "Fabulae Graecae," in Perry, *Aesopica*, p. 503. (See also Stith Thompson, *Motif-Index of Folk-Literature*, IV:82 [J 1169.7].)

Le Loup, le Bœuf et l'Eléphant

Un Loup se laissa choir, la nuit, au fond d'un trou;
   S'en tirer n'était pas facile:
Il grimpait, retombait, s'agitait comme un fou;
Vains travaux, vains efforts; c'était peine inutile.
Epuisé, tout honteux, quand le jour fut venu:
"A mon aide! au secours!" criait la pauvre bête.
   Certain Bœuf, personnage honnête,
   S'approchant, par les cris ému,
   Vers le trou présenta sa tête.
"Au nom de Mahomet, Marabout généreux,"
Lui dit le pauvre Loup d'une voix souterraine,
   "Viens secourir un malheureux.
Permets que par la queue un moment je te tienne,
   Et de ce trou malencontreux
   Tu pourras me tirer sans peine."
Le Bœuf lui répondit: "Je voudrais t'obliger,
   Mais aussitôt hors de danger,
Tu suivrais, contre moi, ton instinct sanguinaire,
   Et la mort serait mon salaire."
"Je te respecterai, j'en jure par ma mère,"
   Reprit le Loup: "un tel serment
   T'assure ma reconnaissance;
   Prends donc pitié de mon tourment."
   Le Bœuf, touché de sa souffrance,
Tendit au Loup sa queue au fond de la prison,
Et le tira du trou comme on pêche un poisson.
   Il voulait suivre son voyage;
Mais le perfide Loup lui barra le passage.
   L'Eléphant, par hasard, vint là;
Il fallut se soumettre à son haut arbitrage.
   Voici ce qu'il imagina:
   "Ce procès," dit-il, "m'embarrasse;

The Wolf, the Ox, and the Elephant

   A careless wolf, one night, fell with a clatter
      Into a deep hole, dark and gaping.
Madly he struggled, clambered, climbed... In vain.
                           Escaping
      Turned out to be no easy matter.
At length, come dawn, the poor beast, tired and mortified,
      Had no recourse. "Help! Help!" he cried.
A certain ox—a decent gent—comes by and hears
      The desperate wolf's lament. "Oh my,"
      He thinks, as he approaches, peers
Over the top. "By Mahomet the Prophet, I
   Entreat you," whines the wolf from down below.
"Get me out of this blasted hole! Please, I beseech you!
   Lower your tail. I'm sure that I can reach you..."
"Well now," the ox replies, demurring, "I don't know...
   It's not that I don't want to help you out.
      It's just that... Well, I have a doubt
      Or two about what you might do
      When all is said and done, and when
   You're free to be your nasty self again.
      I guess I'm worried—*entre nous*—
   That if I pull you out you'll do me in."
   "Perish the thought," retorts the wolf. "I'll be
Your friend for life. I swear by all my kith and kin—
      Even my mother!... [1] There! You see?
How can you doubt me now?" The ox relents: "Fine, fine..."
   And, like an angler dropping hook and line,
   Dangles his tail, pulls up the wolf... "That's that's"
   Says he, and starts to lumber off. Alas,
      Without the slightest caveat,
The wolf, true to his nature, snarls, won't let him pass...
An elephant, who happens to be standing near,

Que chacun se remette en place,
Je verrai mieux comment la scène se passa."
Le Loup fut, dans son trou, forcé de redescendre.
"Que chacun maintenant fasse comme il voudra,"
Dit alors l'Eléphant;—et puis il s'en alla.
 Le Bœuf, ne s'y laissant plus prendre,
 S'enfuit, et le Loup resta là.

 L'ingrat en vain croit pouvoir s'en défendre;
Un juste châtiment tôt ou tard l'atteindra.

1. This oath, the author assures us, is one of the strongest that an African can utter. ("En général, ils ont beaucoup d'attachement de famille, et poussent extrêmement loin leur piété filiale, surtout envers

Offers to arbitrate the case.
"But first... ," he tells the pair, "I'm not quite clear...
 Could each of you please take your place,
 Just as you were before, and show me... ?"
And so they do. "Here's where I was," the ox replies.
"And he, as you can see, was in the hole, below me."
"Aha... Tsk tsk!... Well, so it goes..." The judge nods, sighs...
 And promptly leaves. The ox, likewise.

 The wolf is left to learn—like any traitor—
That treachery brings punishment, sooner or later.

les mères" [p. 124].) I assume it to be a bowdlerized rendition of an oath he discusses, invoking the maternal genitals, in *Recherches philosophiques sur la langue ouolofe*, p. 128.

La Boule de Beurre et la Motte de Terre

Une Boule de beurre, une Motte de terre,
 N'ayant un jour ni feu ni lieu,
 Roulaient en contrée étrangère.
 Un voyage n'est pas un jeu.
Pour vivre, en tout pays, il faut de l'eau, du feu.
Besoin s'en fit sentir à nos Boules errantes.
 La Terre alla puiser de l'eau;
Et la Boule de beurre à des flammes brillantes
 S'en fut allumer un flambeau.
 Toujours la sotte imprévoyance
 Produit des résultats fâcheux.
 Qu'advint-il de leur imprudence?
 Elles fondirent toutes deux.

The Ball of Butter and the Clump of Earth

 A ball of butter and a clump of earth—
  Two homeless vagabonds—one day,
  Were rolling on their aimless way
 Far from the country of their birth.
Now, travelers, just like people everywhere, require
 Necessities of life—like water, fire—
 And our wayfaring pair soon felt their need.
  The earth went to the well; the butter
Went to the hearth to fetch a torch... Alas, the utter
 Thoughtlessness of their acts! Indeed!
  A splash... A splutter...
 What misery their folly dealt!
 What happens to our pair?... They melt.

Le Laboureur, le Dormeur et les Petits Oiseaux

Autour d'un Laboureur, tout près de ses chevaux,
 Un jour quelques petits Oiseaux
 Sautaient, jouaient sans défiance.
Le mouvement, le bruit, rien ne les effrayait.
 Non loin de là, dans un bosquet,
Couché sur le gazon, un Fainéant dormait.
 Malgré le calme et le silence,
Tous les petits Oiseaux fuyaient en le voyant.
Un Enfant s'étonnait d'un contraste si grand.
 Pour lui c'était une merveille.
Craindre celui qui dort et non celui qui veille!
L'instinct les trompait donc! "Voici ce qu'il apprend,"
 Repartit aussitôt son père:
"Sur l'homme qui travaille on peut toujours compter;
 Il n'a pas le temps de mal faire;
 Mais le paresseux, au contraire,
Il peut songer au mal; il est à redouter."

1. Unlike his preceding fables, adapted from native originals, this is one of the fables of Roger's own inspiration.

The Ploughman, the Idler, and the Birds[1]

 A ploughman on his plough was sitting,
Busy, behind his team; and all the while a brood
 Of little birds kept fluttering, flitting,
 Round and around, in carefree mood,
 Undaunted by the noise and agitation.
 Hard by, in calm and silent solitude—
 Picture of perfect relaxation—
Out on the grass, a lazy churl was lying.
Spying him there, the birds take care not to go flying
 Anywhere near. "Strange!" thinks a child who views them.
 "Nature gone topsy-turvy? Some mistake?
They shun the one asleep, yet seek the one awake,
 The one who could so easily abuse them!"
 "Those birds," his father says, "know what they're doing!"
Trust the industrious man: his leisure hours are few,
Too few to plot and scheme—unlike the idler, who
 Always has time to get his mischief brewing."

Jean-Joseph-Marius Diouloufet   Fablos, Contes, Epitros et Autros Pouesios Prouvençalos (1829)

Like Auguste Tandon (see p. 109), Jean-Joseph-Marius Diouloufet was one of the important precursors of the neo-Provençal renaissance, and one of the many for whom the verse fable seems to have held a special attraction. If his name is not exactly a household word today—even in the households of his native Midi—he was nonetheless, in his time, one of the most respected practitioners of the latter-day Provençal muse, to some extent a theoretician as well as an artist, and especially one of its most eminent fabulists. (See Mary-Lafon [pseud. Jean-Bernard Lafon], *Histoire littéraire du Midi de la France*, p. 413.)

Diouloufet's importance is reflected in the comparative ease with which one finds accounts of his life and work.[1] All give almost the same essential facts, in greater or lesser detail. Son of a schoolmaster, he was born in the town of Eguilles, close to Aix-en-Provence, on September 19, 1771.[2] The Revolution cut short his budding ecclesiastical career when, as a seminarian of distinctly royalist family leanings, he was obliged to leave France and emigrate to Italy for a number of years. He put his exile to good use learning Italian and developing his already aroused interest in the classics. On his return, having put aside all thoughts of the priesthood, he married a local beauty—"l'estello de soun vilagi" ("the star of his village")—and settled down to a rustic life in the relative peace and quiet of the Restauration. His first major work, *Leis Magnans* ("The Silkworms"), is a "pouèmo didactique en quatre chants," product of both his classical erudition and his contemporary concerns, bucolic and linguistic. It is no less than a four-canto Virgilian treatise on the art and craft of sericulture, decked out in Provençal decasyllables, duly annotated for the uninitiated with explanatory footnotes in French.[3] But Diouloufet's reputation and importance would not rest on his patois would-be Georgics, nor on his subsequent overly ambitious *Epître en vers provençaux*.[4] It was, rather, in his collection of fables and other verse—*Fablos, contes, epitros et autros pouesios prouvençalos*—that Diouloufet, like so many colleagues, found the ideal lyre for his Provençal inspiration.[5]

With the Revolution of 1830 this easygoing monarchist once again ran afoul of history. For several years he had enjoyed the post of librarian in the Bibliothèque Municipale d'Aix, and was a member of the learned societies of that city and of Marseille. The upheaval in regimes not only deprived him of his librarianship, but in the bargain sapped him, for a time, of his enthusiasm for erudition and creativity. As a result, a long-projected Provençal-French/French-Provençal dictionary was never finished. (See Ripert, *La Renaissance provençale*, p. 248.)[6] In the last two years of his life, however, he did produce both a much-admired biblical poem, "Le Voyage d'Eliézer" (apparently unpublished), and a four-volume work, in French, entitled *Le Don Quichotte philosophe, ou Histoire de l'avocat Hablard*.[7] He died in the Vaucluse village of Cucuron—of apoplexy, his biographers tell us—in May of 1840.[8]

Diouloufet's fables are clearly and inevitably imbued with the spirit of La Fontaine, to whose memory he dedicates his forty-four-line prologue, composed, like the succeeding fables, in characteristic *vers libres*. But if "bouen La Fontaine" is evoked in yet another metaphor of the "gleaner" (see p. 79), it is precisely for the loan of his form and inspiration rather than for very much of his actual subject matter. And even where Diouloufet owes an intertextual debt to La Fontaine, his fables bear the unmistakable mark of their own rustic Provençal origins. As one observer noted, lamenting—even then—the leveling power of Paris over the provinces: "elles semblent être l'expression intime d'un peuple sur lequel le funeste niveau d'une centralisation exagérée n'avait point encore passée." (See Louis de Laincel, *Des troubadours aux Félibres: études sur la poésie provençale*, pp. 363–64.) (The same observer, unaware of the unintentional contradiction, went on to suggest that Diouloufet's well-deserved fame would have been even greater had he composed his "jolis apologues dans la langue de La Fontaine.") Be that as it may, Diouloufet's fables offer a charming perspective on a picturesque corner of French literary history, and one too seldom visited.

In addition to eighteen "contes," ten "epitros," and ten "melangi" on assorted subjects, *Fablos, contes, epitros et autros pouesios prouvençalos* presents ninety-eight fables of varying lengths, of which I have translated numbers 46, 54, and 95.

---

1. The following are especially useful: Emile Ruben, *De quelques imitations patoises des Fables de La Fontaine*, pp. 47–62; Frédéric Donnadieu, *Les Précurseurs des Félibres: 1800–1855*, pp. 181–202; Emile Ripert, *La Renaissance provençale, 1800–1860*, pp. 240–49; Robert Lafont and Christian Anatole, *Nouvelle histoire de la littérature occitane*, II:547–48.

2. This is one of the details on which there is less than unanimity. Several sources cite the date as 1785, but Donnadieu (*Les Précurseurs*, p. 182) authoritatively puts the matter to rights.

3. Perhaps the work's chief claim to fame is the fact that it earned for Diouloufet the encouragement of an eminent academician, the Provençal linguist, dramatist, and scholar François Raynouard (1761–1836), one of the early—if inexact—pioneers in Romance philology.

4. The latter, the text proper of which bears the added Provençal title *Epitro sus l'atheisme, a Moussu l'Abbé de La Mennais* [sic], is a rather turgid apologia addressed to the religious thinker and writer Robert Lamennais (1782–1854), attempting to prove the existence of

God in Provençal alexandrines, and to show thereby, as Diouloufet tells us in his *avant-propos,* that his language, like the lyrical Provençal of the troubadours, can sing to more than one string: "Notre objet est d'essayer de prouver ici que ce langage se prête encore au ton élevé et peut reproduire toutes les preuves de notre religion, sans les affaiblir ou les dégrader" (p. i). (Diouloufet goes on to acknowledge his gratitude to Lamennais, "un des plus célèbres écrivains de notre temps . . . que j'ai l'avantage de connaître personnellement." He might have been less sanguine had he written his "epitro" a few years later, when Lamennais's revolutionary doctrines were officially condemned by the pope.)

5. Among the "epitros" included in the volume is the previously published *Epitro sus l'atheisme* addressed to Lamennais. The collection includes also, among its "autros pouesios prouvençalos," a number of trifles, both pre- and postdating the early *Leis Magnans.*

6. The thirty-odd pages of "Observations préliminaires" that serve as a preface to his collection of fables (pp. ix–xxxix) give a good idea, however, of the considerable extent of Diouloufet's scholarly and, especially, linguistic interests.

7. It is evident that the latter—which, like Donnadieu (*Les Précurseurs,* p. 201), I must admit to not having read, but which one might suspect to be the fruit of his personal misfortunes—must have been quite well received. It was republished in successive editions of 1841, 1854, 1863, and 1872, all of which are in the Bibliothèque Nationale.

8. The exact date seems open to speculation. One hopes, for Diouloufet's sake, that the dates given by Ruben—May 24, corrected in an *erratum* to May 19 (*De quelques imitations,* pp. 47, 86)—are in error, since Donnadieu (*Les Précurseurs,* p. 201) assures that he was, in fact, buried on May 14 of the year in question.

Lou Chambre et la Granouilho

Lou Chambre et la Granouilho agueroun fantesié
    De faire ensèm pelerinagi,
    Partem, anem de coumpagnié
Se digueroun, quittem un pau lou marescagi,
    Leissem lou fanguas et lou joun,
    Anem prendre l'air doou bouscagi;
Mais pousqueroun jamais s'accourdar en vouyagi:
La Granouilho camino et per saut et per boun,
    Lou Chambre va de recouloun,
Eroun jamais ensèm, la Granouilho trimavo,
    Soun coumpagnoun jamais venié,
Car au luech d'avançar eou toujours reculavo;
    Vegueroun qu'èro uno foulié
De vouilher s'acoublar per faire mémo cavo,
L'un poou pas se tenir toujours de recular,
    L'autre en avant de sautrilhar,
Renounçoun au proujet de faire ensèm la routo,
    Vian que degun se changeara.
    Uno margot qu'èro à l'escouto:
"Qu'es nach pounchut," cridet, "poou pas mourir cara."[1]

The Crayfish and the Frog

One day a frog and crayfish had a mind
To take a trip and leave their swamp behind:
    "Reeds, marshes, murky bog, adieu!"
    So cried the frog; the crayfish, too.
"Off to the forest for a change of air!"
    Just one thing wrong: our would-be pair
Couldn't agree on how they should pursue
Their partnership. It quickly came a-cropper,
    As it, indeed, was bound to do:
    The frog, by nature, is a hopper,
    Always jumping about; whereas
The crayfish—quite a different creature—has
    A rather slow (and backward!) crawl.
    Surely not too well matched at all!
    As one sprang forward, with a leap,
The other fell retreating, at a creep...
Soon they renounce their folly, realizing
    That there can be no compromising.
Up in her tree, a magpie cackles: "I'm afraid you
    Never can be what Nature hasn't made you!"

1. The use of a local proverb to provide the concluding moral to most of his fables is an original and distinguishing feature of Diouloufet's style. While the French fabulists had difficulty in finding new subjects for their morals, "je crois," he is quoted as saying, "avoir trouvé du neuf dans nos proverbes qui sont, comme on dit, la sagesse et l'expérience de nos anciens." (See Ripert, *La Renaissance provençale,* pp. 245–46.) The proverb in the present fable means literally "He who is born pointed cannot die square," and is cited (with minor dialectal spelling differences) as "Qu es neiçu pounchu poou pas mouri carra," in A.-M. de La Tour-Keyrié, *Recueil de proverbes, maximes, sentences et dictons provençaux,* p. 84.

La Limasso sus uno Piboulo

A forço d'escalar, la Limasso un matin,
 De se tirassar sus sa bavo,
Au d'aut d'uno Piboulo ello arribo à la fin;
 Epiey d'amoun la terro regardavo,
  Et s'admiravo,
 En se truffant deis oousselouns.
"Me vaqui," se disié, "tant qu'eleis anaussado,
Cresien pousquer soulets planar sus leis vallouns;
Coumo eleis dins leis airs tambèn me siou quilhado,
Aro tout me parei d'eici de limaçouns:
  Ma gran sara bèn estounado
  Se poou me veire de soun trau."
 Mais au moument que resounavo,
   Que se gounflavo,
   Que banegeavo,
  Uno bouffado de mistrau
Faguet brandar lou brout oute s'èro quarrado,
  Patafloou eissavau
   Lou Cacalau.
   "Qu trop s'en hausso,
   Diou lou debausso."[1]

The Snail on a Poplar Tree

A snail went slithering up a poplar tree
One day, leaving his sticky trail behind him.
  In time we find him
 Perched at the top, in victory,
Surveying everything beneath, content
To mock the birds with his accomplishment.
"See? Here I am," he thought, conceitedly,
 "As high as they! They think that they're
 The only ones to own the skies!
 Well, look at me! I'm in midair!
 And there, below, all snaildom lies!
 If grandmamma could see me now,
 Down in her hole... What a surprise!"
 As thus he rants and speechifies,
The mistral gives a gust and shakes his bough.[2]
  Horns outstretched wide,
  And puffed with pride,
Our slug goes falling with a little *pluk,*
  Back to his muck.
  'Twas ever so:
We rise too high? God lays us low.

1. I do not find this proverb in print in exactly this form, although a similar one, minus the reference to divine intervention ("Qu s'enausso se debausso," "He who rises high gets thrown down"), is recorded in Pau Roman, *Lei Mount-Joio: voucabulàri dei prouverbi e loucucien proverbialo de la Lengo Prouvençalo,* vol. 1, p. 412. (No subsequent volumes were, in fact, published.)

2. *Mistral* is the name of the violent wind that blows down the Rhône valley and over much of southern France. It is also—by one of those especially appropriate coincidences—the name of the leading poet of the Félibrige, the nineteenth-century neo-Provençal cultural movement (see p. 109). Frédéric Mistral (1830–1914), best known for his epic poem *Mirèio* (1859), was colaureate of the Nobel Prize for literature in 1904.

Lou Tigre et lou Chin

Un Tigre mangeo un cerf, piey accuso lou Chin;
Aquo dins la forest faguet bruech et grand trin;
Qu va cres, va cres pas, et la cavo es pourtado
  Davant leis assisos doou lien,
  Et l'y fouguet que trop prouvado
Que lou Tigre a coumes esto marrido actien.
 De groupatas qu'avien vis lou carnagi
Fougueroun leis temoins que leis cerfs prouduisien;
Mais lou Tigre a d'amis et quauque parentagi;
  Entre leis jugis fan partit,
  Voueloun sauvar aquestou persounnagi,
  De la hounto d'aqueou delit;
Et coumo l'un deis dous fau que siegue punit,
La cour dit qu'es lou Chin qu'a coumes lou dooumagi,
  L'arrest est clar coumo lou jour,
  Fouguet jugear senso appel, ni retour,
  A subir lou darnier supplici.
  Eiço, deou certo! faire hourrour;

The Tiger and the Hound

A tiger ate a stag, but claimed a hound
Was guilty of the crime. The woods around
 Resounded with the accusation;
But when the case comes up for litigation,
The victim's kin, in court, produce some crows,
Witnesses to the vile abomination,
 Whose testimony clearly shows
The tiger to have done the deed. No matter:
 Among his friends and family
Are several judges; and, of course, the latter
Decide that such a personage as he,
Perforce, should suffer no disgrace. And yet
 Since someone must be guilty, let
The hound be punished for the crime committed.
And so he was. The tiger was acquitted;
The hound, condemned, despite his innocence,
 Sentenced to die!—O horrid fate!—
With no appeal, no recourse, no defense...

Mais es que troou verai: "qu'uno ounço de favour,
    Vau mai qu'un quintau de justici."[1]

1 Roman (*Lei Mount-Joio,* p. 601) cites a somewhat less hyper-
bolic version of the same proverb, substituting a *liéuro* ("pound")

Justice, it seems, though by the hundred-weight,
Weighs less than just one ounce of influence!

for the poet's *quintau:* "Uno ounço de favour vau mai qu'une liéuro
de justici."

Jean-Jacques Porchat   Glanures d'Esope (1840)   Fables et Paraboles (1854)

WHILE some of our fabulists spent a number of their
productive years in Switzerland—the chevalier de Boufflers and Madame de Genlis, for example (see pp. 129–30
and 116–17)—Jean-Joseph Porchat, the only Swiss national
to figure in this collection, spent much of his literary life
as an expatriate in France, establishing a reputation as one
of the more appreciated Francophone Swiss authors of
his generation: indeed, "le plus délicat, le plus vif, le plus
varié" of the *vaudois* poets. (See Virgile Rossel, *Histoire littéraire de la Suisse romande, des origines à nos jours,* II:466.)

Born on May 20, 1800, in the village of Crète, near
Geneva, Porchat (who also published under the name
"Porchat-Bressenel" and the pseudonym "Valamont")
spent his early years teaching Roman law and Latin literature in the Académie de Lausanne. Following a period of political unrest in the canton of Vaud, in 1845, an
academic coup brought him into disfavor, and he left for
Paris, where he remained for over a decade.[1] Returning
to Switzerland in 1857, he died three years later, leaving a
goodly number of writings in several genres: dramatic, narrative, and poetic. He was also an accomplished translator
from Latin and German, having translated, among others, much of Tibullus and Horace and most of Goethe.[2]

Porchat owes whatever reputation briefly survived
him to his large number of prose works written for the
young, and to his verse fables.[3] The latter, much admired
by no less an arbiter of nineteenth-century literary taste
than the prolific and ubiquitous Philarète Chasles (see
Rossel, *Histoire littéraire de la Suisse romande,* I:467), were
collected in four editions. The first three, ranging in length
from 40 to 144 fables, were published in the same year—

testimony to their popularity—under the apt (if not
overly original) title *Glanures d'Esope,* divided, respectively, into three, ten, and twelve books. The fourth, augmented and revised, abandoning "cette division, qui est
assez inutile," appeared during Porchat's Parisian "exile,"
retitled simply *Fables et paraboles,* and dedicated—like the
third edition of over a dozen years earlier—to the French
queen Marie-Amélie, "objet de la vénération universelle,"
wife of the deposed Louis-Philippe, in recognition of the
"intérêt que la Suisse lui inspire." As the author explains
in his brief preface (pp. vii-viii), this definitive edition contains rather few "Aesopic gleanings," most of the fables
stemming from other sources. However, despite the superficial changes, Porchat, in a wistful reference to the political upheavals of his age, is quick to insist that the moral
content of his fables has remained constant: "L'état de
l'Europe a changé plusieurs fois pendant que ces apologues naissaient à l'écart... mais, après tant de révolutions, l'auteur ne voit rien qu'il doive effacer ou changer
dans l'expression de ses sentiments et de ses vœux."[4]

Porchat's fables are, formally, of two basic types. The
traditional, virtually sacrosanct, *vers libres,* which dominate, are intermixed with less derivative, brief compositions, usually in eight- or six-syllable quatrains. "La
Feuille de Chêne," representative of the latter, stands as
the forty-seventh of the 176 unnumbered fables in the definitive *Fables et paraboles.* It had earlier appeared in the
third edition of *Glanures d'Esope* (V, 4), though I cannot
say for sure if it had also figured in either or both of its
previous editions.

---

1. One source dates his academic dismissal a half-dozen years earlier, and attributes it to his digression from the orthodox, stodgily
philological teaching of the Latin poets. (See Philippe Godet, *Histoire
littéraire de la Suisse française,* p. 517.)

2. Neither of Porchat's two five-act verse dramas seems to have enjoyed great success. One, *La Mission de Jeanne d'Arc,* was published;
the other, *Winkelried,* glorifying one of Switzerland's semilegendary
national heroes, appears not to have been, but is discussed briefly by
Rossel (*Histoire littéraire de la Suisse romande,* II:466–67). Most of his
works and translations, which are not included in the standard bibliographies, are listed in the catalogue of the Bibliothèque Nationale.

3. Among the most widely read and often republished of the
former were his *Trois mois sous la neige, journal d'un jeune habitant du
Jura,* "couronné" by the Académie Française and immensely popular,
judging by its numerous editions and translations; *Les Colons du rivage,
La Sagesse du hameau, Le Berger et le proscrit,* and *Contes merveilleux.*

4. Besides the four editions cited, Porchat also published a brief
early fable collection, *Recueil de fables,* under the pseudonym "J.-J. Valamont," whose contents I cannot determine, as well as an anthology of
the French fable for students, *Le Fablier des écoles, ou choix de fables des
fabulistes français.*

La Feuille de Chêne	The Oak Leaf
Une feuille de chêne Volait au gré du vent, Et, dédaignant la plaine, Disait en s'élevant:	Breeze-blown—now to, now fro— An oak leaf, borne aloft, Sneered at the plain below And, rising skyward, scoffed:
"Oh! que loin de la terre J'ai pris un noble essor! Au séjour du tonnerre Qui peut me suivre encor?"	"Far from the earth, flown free, I take my noble flight. Ah! Who can follow me Up to the thundering height?"
Elle fut aussi vaine Tant que Zéphir l'aida; Il retint son haleine, Et la feuille tomba.	Indeed, she flew. But oh, How vain our demoiselle! For Zephyr ceased to blow, And back to earth she fell.
Vous tomberez comme elle, Célébrités d'un jour, Quand la vogue infidèle Aura changé d'amour.	Today's celebrities: You too will be displaced When fickle fortune's breeze Blows us a change of taste.

Jean-Pons-Guillaume Viennet   Fables (1843)

JEAN-PONS-GUILLAUME Viennet (1777–1868) was one of that elite band of forty French intellectuals endowed with a self-conferred "immortality." But like many (if not most) of the members of the august Académie Française, his immortality was to be short-lived. If he is remembered at all today, it is perhaps by the historian of the troubled post-Revolution years, during which he served a succession of monarchs as soldier, *député,* and peer; or, more likely, by the occasional specialist in the Romantic movement, who will recall him dimly as a staunch defender and practitioner of a rigid latter-day classicism in the face of the new school's vigorous and, at the time, outrageous reforms.

Viennet, indefatigable author in a variety of genres—epigram, epistle, satire, fable, historical novel, opera libretto, tragedy, comedy, drama, and even epic—was anathema to the likes of Victor Hugo and his colleagues.[1] In a scathing anecdotal sketch of the academician's public and literary career, written some dozen years before his death, the pseudonymous scandalmonger Eugène de Mirecourt (né Charles Jacquot), dubbing him the "Napoléon du ridicule," delights in venting his sardonic spleen, at every turn, on the prolific archconservative (and, nonetheless, eventual champion of the bourgeois king Louis-Philippe), mocking his seeming political opportunism on the one hand, and his personal and artistic pomposity on the other. (See Eugène de Mirecourt, *Viennet,* number 68 in his hundred-volume series *Les Contemporains.*)[2] The aversion was mutual, as can be seen especially from Viennet's *Epître aux Muses sur le Romantisme.*

Needless to say, Viennet also had many an old-guard, anti-Romantic admirer, impressed by his fidelity to both the spirit and style of Corneille, Racine, and Voltaire. He himself is said to have considered that he would stride to immortality on his "two crutches," as he called them: his *Mémoires*—a detailed recollection of Parisian life under Louis XVIII, Charles X, and Louis-Philippe—and, of more interest here, his *Fables.* "J'ai deux béquilles pour marcher devant la postérité," he is quoted as stating, "mes *Fables* et mes *Mémoires.*" (See the article on Viennet by Le Duc de La Force, in *Dictionnaire des lettres françaises: le dix-neuvième siècle,* II:497.) The *Mémoires* were not published until long after Viennet's death, and then in abridged form. (See *Journal de Viennet, pair de France, témoin de trois règnes, 1817–1848,* preface and postface by Le Duc de La Force.) As for the fables, Viennet apparently composed them off and on throughout the latter half of his long life, using them as a favorite vehicle for casting satiric barbs at his adversaries of the moment.[3] The first volume, entitled simply *Fables*, consists of eighty-four fables equally divided into four books. It is introduced by a preface—a kind of self-portrait and artistic profession of faith—in which Viennet attempts rather touchingly to parry the often-vicious attacks of his detractors, and in which he credits fabulist Dutramblay (see pp. 113–14) with having first suggested that he try his hand at the fable. A second collection, *Fables nouvelles,* appeared eight years later. Both collections were grouped in a third combined edition, published in 1855, augmented with sixty-three fables previously unpublished.

The three translated here are taken from the first edition, where they are numbers I, 15; II, 4; and II, 16. Although they allude, in all probablity, to specific contemporary events, it is difficult at this distance to determine the precise targets of their satire. At any rate, their probable specificity does not make them any the less applicable to the generality of human nature. "Le Huron et le Baromètre" is of particular interest for its unusual New World setting.

1. A bibliographical listing of his numerous writings in verse and prose is given in Hugo P. Thieme, *Bibliographie de la littérature française de 1800 à 1930.* It is not complete, however. The catalogue of the Bibliothèque Nationale devotes eight full pages to Viennet, including some titles left unrecorded by Thieme. Among his better-known (or less little-known) works are the classical-style tragedy *Clovis* performed at the Comédie-Française—a triumphant success or utter failure, depending on whose account we accept—and subsequently published; and *La Franciade,* a ten-canto epic poem, glowingly prefaced by critic Jules Janin, that calls to mind the similarly titled unfinished Renaissance epic of Ronsard. The manuscript of *Clovis,* propitiously placed, is reputed to have stopped a bullet and saved the author's life at the battle of Leipzig in 1813. (Mirecourt [see below], recounting the same anecdote [pp. 50–51], attributes the author's good fortune to a manuscript entitled *La Mort de César,* a title unattested elsewhere in Viennet's bibliography, however.)

2. Mirecourt would seem to have a point, judging by Viennet's profusion of occasional verse in toadying homage to various patrons in power.

3. "Il y a de la politique dans mes apologues," Viennet admits in the preface to his *Fables* (see below), "c'est peut-être fâcheux." Mirecourt, characteristically, paints a snide picture of the author, at the annual sessions of the Académie, regaling his colleagues with some of his latest fables: "Régulièrement, aux séances annuelles, après les interminables discours, . . . M. Viennet lit deux ou trois fables, que l'auditoire, assommé par les léthargiques morceaux qu'il vient d'entendre, trouve charmantes par comparaison" (p. 85). Even Mirecourt, however, goes on to admit, grudgingly, that some of his fables "ont de l'esprit et du mordant." A far more admiring Jules Janin, in his introduction to *La Franciade* (pp. x–xi), has only praise for the *Fables,* "le digne ornement de toutes les bibliothèques modernes," painting a more sympathetic picture: "Infatigable et d'une espérance aussi vaste que la pensée, il écrit sans cesse et toujours; à la ville, à la campagne, et malade, et bien portant, toujours patient et convaincu."

Le Nid d'Hirondelles

Possesseur d'un nid d'hirondelles,
    Un enfant gâté
Veut leur donner la liberté.
Et les pauvres petits ont à peine des ailes.
"Soyez libres," dit-il; "tout l'est dans l'univers."
    Et la nichée est dans les airs.
    Chaque oisillon, enchanté de lui-même,
Encouragé par un premier essor,
En essaie un second, et reprenant encor,
    Fait, hélas! naufrage au troisième.
L'un s'écrase en tombant, un autre meurt de faim,
    L'autre est croqué par le chat du voisin;
    Tant qu'à la fin, de la couvée
    Aucune tête n'est sauvée.

Laissons faire le temps; tout arrive à son point.
    L'à-propos est une science
    Que les hommes n'entendent point.
On perd son avenir par trop d'impatience.
Sur un pareil sujet je crains de trop parler;
Un mot en dira plus que cent mille volumes:
    Les oiseaux sont faits pour voler,
    Mais attendez qu'ils aient des plumes.

The Swallows' Nest

A youngster has a swallows' nest,
    But, none too wise,
Decides to loose the birds. "Fly off!" he cries.
    "Why shouldn't you be like the rest
Of Nature's creatures, fetterless and free?"
    Unwittingly,
    The birds, unfledged and weak of wing,
    At first take flight
With eager, confident delight...
But all too soon, alack, go plummeting.
    One breaks his neck. Another lies
    Unfed and dead. A luckless third
Provides the neighbor's cat a meal of bird.
And so it goes, until the whole brood dies.

Everything in its time, all in good season.
    Man has to learn this rule, alas!
    Woeful impatience is the reason
Why many a future never comes to pass.
    All things considered, I doubt whether
    More need be said, so I'll be brief:
Unless they wait till wings grow firm of feather,
Birds, born to fly, will no less come to grief.

Le Huron et le Baromètre

Ignorant héritier d'un docte voyageur,
    Qui, sachant l'Europe par cœur,
    Etait allé, par-delà l'Acadie,
Finir chez les Hurons ses courses et sa vie,
Un d'eux avait choisi, pour sa part du butin,
    Un baromètre de voyage.
    Il n'en savait pas trop l'usage;
Mais il avait longtemps, autour du lac Champlain,
    Du voyageur transporté le bagage;
Il avait à part lui raisonné longuement
Sur cette invention qu'il tenait pour magie,
Interrogé le maître, et son raisonnement
Avait enfin logé dans sa tête applatie
    Que le merveilleux instrument
    Faisait le beau temps et la pluie.

Le baromètre alors devint pour mon Huron
Le plus puissant des dieux, le Manitou suprême.
    Son respect fut d'abord extrême.
C'est ainsi qu'on débute en toute passion.
Soit qu'il voulût chasser le daim ou le faucon,
Ou lancer sur le lac sa pirogue légère,
    Si son oracle était contraire,
Il suspendait son arc et posait l'aviron.
Ce fut bon pour un temps; la servitude ennuie;
L'esclave le plus doux s'en est parfois lassé.
    Un jour que par sa fantaisie,
Vers un pays lointain plus fortement poussé,
    D'une bourrasque il se vit menacé,
Il perdit patience, et d'un peu de colère
    Mélangeant d'abord sa prière:
"Fais du beau temps," dit-il, "j'en ai besoin; je pars."
    Mais le dieu, sourd à la requête,
    Annonçait toujours la tempête,
Et déjà sur le lac s'amassaient les brouillards.

"C'est ainsi," répond-il, "que tu me contraries!
Tu fais un ouragan quand je veux un zéphir!
    J'affranchirai mon bon plaisir
    De tes folles intempéries."
Mon Huron, à ces mots, croyant tout applanir,
    Met son baromètre en cannelle,
S'embarque, et la bourrasque emportant la nacelle,
    Dans les flots il va s'engloutir.

J'ai vu des rois, hélas! qui n'étaient pas plus sages,
    Des ministres pis que des rois.
D'un conseiller prudent ils étouffent la voix,
Quand pour les arrêter il prédit des orages:
C'est au prophète seul que s'en prend leur ennui.
    S'ils se perdent, c'est encor lui
    Qu'ils accusent de leurs naufrages;
    Et les honnêtes courtisans
    Qui leur servent de baromètre,
    Pour être bien venus du maître,
    Prédisent toujours le beau temps.

The Huron Brave and the Weatherglass

A wise old traveler, who had had his fill
    Of European climes, had gone
    Off to the New World, whereupon
He lived among the savages, until,
    In time, he died.
At length, his hosts divide the spoils. His guide—
A Huron brave[1]—is quick to claim as his
    A weatherglass, although, in truth,
    The simple youth
Hasn't the faintest notion what it is;
Albeit in many a trek round Lake Champlain
    He marveled, time and time again,
Wondering what this curious thing might be,
    Convinced that, by some sorcery,
It turned the weather fair or brought the rain.

For him it soon becomes a deity—
All powerful, almighty Manitou.[2]
He worships it with awe, as zealots do
When new the object of their veneration.
    Are bow and arrow set to stalk
    The doe or stag, or hunt the hawk?
Or is canoe poised in anticipation,
    Ready to glide upon the lake?
Let his god but say no: make no mistake,
The bow is set aside, the oar put by.
    And so it goes for many a moon.
But slaves who dance to someone else's tune
In time grow tired. One day, the threatening sky
Portends a squall. Alas, plans all awry!
    Our brave, heart bent on distant travels,
Prays to his god... Prays? No... Commands, whines, cavils:
"Give me fair weather! Fair, you hear? And dry!..."
    But as the clouds begin to form,
The glass, unmoved, continues to say "Storm."

    "So," the brave bellows, "you defy me!
I ask for breeze, you give me hurricane!
Well, I'll no longer take what you ordain:
No more will you be blindly worshiped by me!...
There!..." And he breaks his god to bits... Next minute,
    Down pours the rain, up blows the squall...
The frail canoe, caught unprotected in it,
Sinks to the bottom, Huron brave and all.

Many the kings I've seen, alas, no wiser
    (And ministers still less than kings),
Who turn deaf ear to prudent underlings.
    In vain, I fear, the wise adviser
    Warns them: "My lord, a storm is brewing."
    His recompense? His own undoing.
    Let his prediction come to pass:
    He gets the blame for their disaster.
    Our kings despise the doom-forecaster.
    Wise courtier—faithful weatherglass—
Foretells fair skies if he would please his master.

1. The name "Huron," supposedly derived from the archaic French adjective *huré* 'bristle-headed', was derisively applied to certain Iroquois tribes by early Canadian settlers. It dates at least as far back as 1684. (See Louis-Armand de Lom d'Arce de Lahontan, *Nouveaux voyages de Mr. le baron de Lahontan dans l'Amérique Septentrionale*, pp. 19–20.) By Viennet's time the figure of the Huron was an already well established French literary commonplace. Its best-known incarnation is no doubt in Voltaire's philosophical tale *L'Ingénu* (1767), whose hero, a young and innocent Frenchman born in Canada and raised by the Hurons—typical "noble savages" of the period—returns to France, where he is educated in the evils of a corrupt society.

2. The word *manitou*, of Algonquin origin, was first recorded by Champlain in his *Voyages* (1619), to describe a kind of native medicine man. (See *The Works of Samuel de Champlain*, III:144.) It was subsequently applied to a personal divinity or fetish, as described by Chateaubriand in a passage that might well have directly inspired Viennet's fable: "C'est une chose effrayante que de voir les Indiens s'aventurer dans des nacelles d'écorce sur ce lac où les tempêtes sont terribles. Ils suspendent leurs Manitous à la poupe des canots, et s'élancent au milieu des tourbillons de neige, entre les vagues soulevées" ("Lacs du Canada," in *Voyage en Amérique* [1827]). (See Chateaubriand, *Œuvres romanesques et voyages*, I:698.) The term eventually came to be used for the "Grand Manitou," or Great Spirit. Viennet's Huron seems to regard his weatherglass as both personal fetish and Supreme Being at one and the same time.

La Chute d'un Gland

Au pied d'un chêne et sur un vert gazon,
   Se reposait une belette;
Quand un gland, détaché par le froid aquilon,
   Vint tomber à plomb sur sa tête.
   Elle s'éveille, et, tremblante d'effroi,
De ce lieu dangereux s'enfuit à perdre haleine,
Criant au rat des champs qu'elle regarde à peine:
   "Là-bas, là-bas vient de tomber sur moi
   La branche énorme d'un gros chêne."
   Le rat n'eut garde d'aller voir.
Il dit à deux lapins broutant sur la colline,
   Qu'un gros chêne venait de choir
   Sur la belette sa voisine;
   Les lapins, en le racontant,
Y mêlent des éclairs et le feu du tonnerre;
   Un écureuil, qui les entend,
   Y joint un tremblement de terre.
Bref, les faits, les détails, l'un par l'autre appuyés,
S'étaient le lendemain si bien multipliés,
   Qu'à trente milles à la ronde,
   Tous les animaux effrayés
Dans la chute d'un gland voyaient la fin du monde.

L'animal raisonnable a-t-il plus de raison,
Moins de crédulité? l'histoire dit que non.
Il a même de plus la malice et l'envie.
   S'occupe-t-on d'un accident fatal,
   D'un crime ou d'une calomnie;
Par nature, à plaisir, il grossira le mal.
Mais citez un beau trait, osez louer la gloire
D'un homme de mérite ou d'un homme de bien:
   Il la rabaisse, il refuse d'y croire;
   Et mieux vaudrait qu'il n'en dît rien.

The Acorn That Fell from the Oak

   Beneath an oak reposing
  Amid the grassy greenery,
   A weasel lies a-dozing.
Suddenly, in the northwind's blast, blown free,
An acorn falls and hits her on the head.
  The weasel wakes, jumps up in dread,
And dashes off, as fast as fast can be.
Passing a field mouse in her flight, she shouts,
  With little more than sidelong glance
   Cast hastily askance:
  "Just now... An oak... Back thereabouts...
  A giant branch... Broke all asunder
And smashed my head..." The mouse, undoubting, meets
  Two rabbits, grazing, and repeats:
An oak tree felled his friend... The pair add thunder,
  Lightning, and such... Taking his leisure,
A squirrel overhears them, gapes in wonder,
  Throws in an earthquake for good measure...
In short, an acorn falls: from mouth to mouth
  The news spreads, grows—east, west, north, south.
  Next day, the forest—heaven forfend—
Learns that the world is coming to an end.[1]

For all his wit, not one whit less naive,
Man, like our beasts, is ready to believe
The worst. Tell him a tale of woes pernicious—
Accident, scandal, crime—he'll magnify it.
  What's more, he's often mean, malicious.
Tell him a tale of virtue; he'll deny it,
  Though goodness shine before his eyes:
  "Pooh pooh! Impossible!" he sighs,
  Quick to decry it... Ah, if ill
Is all a man can speak, best he be still!

1. It is tempting, if fruitless, to speculate whether this fable might have been inspired by the character of Chicken Little, whose dire exclamation, "The sky is falling!" has made her name a symbol for paranoid hyperbole. The sources of the well-known nursery tale are lost in obscurity, and details differ from country to country. In some versions—as in Viennet's fable—an acorn falling on the head is the original culprit; in others, a pea; while in the first published American version, appearing in 1840, the cause of Chicken Little's apocalyptic panic is, more poetically, a rose leaf falling on her tail feathers. (See John Greene Chandler, *The Remarkable History of Chicken Little*.)

Marc-Louis de Tardy   Fables et Tragédies (1847)

TYPICAL of the, literally, scores of provincial fabulists that flourished throughout the nineteenth century, the marquis Marc-Louis de Tardy was one of the more distinguished citizens in his corner of France: member of the gentry, government official, agronomist, and dilettante *littérateur*. From August 6, 1817, to September 2, 1830, this respected aristocrat served a term of unprecedented length as mayor of the city of Roanne, near Lyon. (See J. Prajoux, *Roanne autrefois et aujourd'hui*, p. 141.) For several years, from 1828 to 1831, he was also a *député* from his native *département* of La Loire. (See the *Almanach Royal* and, subsequently, the *Almanach Royal et National* for the years in question.) By the end of his long life we find him holding such positions, appropriate to a venerable landowner and longtime agronomist, as honorary president of the Société d'Agriculture de Roanne.[1] (See the *Annuaire administratif et statistique du département de la Loire*, p. 165.)

As a young engineering student in 1790, Tardy, who had been preparing for a career in the military, wrote a five-act tragedy in verse, *Cromwel* [*sic*], anticipating Victor Hugo's celebrated romantic drama by almost four decades. Many years later, in an afterword to a revised edition of the play (in his *Fables et tragédies*, pp. 123–28), he tells of his trip to Paris in an unsuccessful effort to have it performed by the Théâtre-Français, attributing the refusal—perhaps more than a little self-deceptively—to its inflammatory subject matter, inappropriate to the troubled revolutionary times. He also recounts, in passing, his participation in some of the military campaigns following the proclamation of the Republic, and takes the opportunity to comment on contemporary matters political, leaving little doubt as to his archconservative, nationalistic, ultra-Catholic persuasion. It is safe to assume that it was his military activities, as well as his subsequent membership in the Conseil Général de la Loire—not to mention his family background—that earned him, in 1814, the ribbon of the chevalier of the Légion d'honneur. (See the *Annuaire de l'Ordre Impérial de la Légion d'honneur*, année 1852, p. 633.)[2]

In addition to *Cromwel,* Tardy wrote a second classical tragedy, *Sylla,* also dating from his "première jeunesse," as he tells us in *Fables et tragédies* (p. iii). It is not clear, however, whether most or any of the fables that follow the two plays in that volume—as a kind of comic relief, he suggests (pp. 318–19)—are likewise of youthful composition.[3] Nor is it clear why the author chooses to enshroud his volume in a thin veil of mystery: the title page does not bear his name, but rather, in the best style of eighteenth-century novels, identifies him merely as "M. le Mis [i.e., Monsieur le Marquis] de T. . . ." The semianonymity would be easily pierced by his Roannais countrymen.[4] Perhaps this half-hidden pose is indicative of an aristocratic aversion to the flaunting of literary aspirations. More obviously indicative of an aristocratic stance is the fact that the profits from the sale of his *Fables et tragédies* were donated to charity.[5]

In his prefatory remarks (p. ii) our somewhat reticent marquis refers to a prior publication of his work, intended only for the enjoyment and edification of his friends, and including, besides the fables and tragedies, a collection of *odes, épîtres,* and the like. (That volume did, in fact, appear eight years before, under the authorship of "M. L.-M. de T^{+++}," and entitled *Tragédies, fables et pièces de vers.* He also promises to bring out still another edition if public reception and advanced age permit; but, for whichever negative reason, he seems not to have done so.

The 1847 edition of *Fables et tragédies,* minus the occasional verse, contains a total of thirty-six fables, preceded by a de rigueur bow in La Fontaine's direction, and followed by a brief poem dedicated to Tardy's nephew, "mon neveu de R . . ."—characteristically semi-anonymous—"en lui donnant les *Fables* de La Fontaine." The ones translated here—numbers 17, 25, and 28 in that edition—are typical of a collection that reflects traditional moral values with a large dose of contemporary social and political observation.

---

1. An article in the Roanne newspaper *Le Conciliateur* (Sept. 25, 1847), on the occasion of an annual agricultural fair presided over by Tardy, informs us that the marquis had devoted much of his life to important agricultural innovations.

2. It is difficult to believe that our marquis, still a student in 1790, could be the same Tardy who, already active in public life before the Revolution, was named *officier municipal* of the Loire town of Saint-Rambert from that year to 1793. (See Colin Lucas, *The Structure of the Terror: The Example of Javogues and the Loire*, p. 321.) The family apparently had deep roots in the region, and it would not be surprising to find others of the same name prominent in local affairs.

3. It is obvious that at least three—numbers 18, 19, and 20—are not, since they are dedicated to his grandsons.

4. And, ironically, no less so by the reading public at large, since the author does indeed sign his name to a somewhat obsequious dedication to Pope Pius IX, immediately preceding *Sylla* and dated July 16, 1846, a month after the latter's election. In it he calls attention to the similarity between the subject of his play and an event in the new pope's reign.

5. A handwritten leaf, pasted inside the cover of the copy in the Harvard College Library, indicates that the beneficiary of all sales was the Maison de la Providence du Côteau de Roanne, a hospice for orphans and the infirm, operated by the Sœurs de Saint Vincent de Paul.

L'Ane Orateur

 C'était le mois où, sortis du cocon,
Mille insectes sont fiers de leur métamorphose.
 C'était le mois où le frêle bouton
 S'épanouit pour se changer en rose.
 Les animaux, qui tenaient leurs états,
Allaient au mois de mai nommer leurs magistrats.
La médiocrité, qui toujours vit d'intrigue,
 Là comme ailleurs avait formé sa brigue.
 L'âne, pensif, était seul en un coin;
Nul ne pensait à lui, lorsque certaine ânesse,
 Avec laquelle il était en promesse,
Arriva sur sa piste et lui cria de loin:
 "Hé! l'ami, vous savez que l'écharpe et la toge
 Ont à mes yeux de souverains appas;
 Songez-y bien, car je n'épouse pas,
Si le futur n'est point maire, échevin ou doge;
Triomphez ou crevez." "Soit," dit l'âne, excité
Par le printemps bien plus que par la vanité;
 "Rassurez-vous, je réponds de l'affaire."
Sur un tertre il se juche, et puis se met à braire;
  Mais avec tant d'action,
 D'éclat, de force et de profusion,
  Que, par un trait comique,
Un tas de bonnes gens ébahis, demi-sourds,
Crurent que l'orateur avait fait un discours.
  Pour prix de sa rhétorique,
Le baudet fut pourvu d'une charge publique.

C'est ainsi que souvent la force des poumons
En plus d'un lieu supplée à celle des raisons;
Et c'est connaître bien des auditeurs frivoles
Que joindre à peu de sens un grand flux de paroles.

The Jackass Orator

 It was the month when, from the chrysalis,
 Thousands of insects quit their dark repose
 To sport with pride their metamorphosis;
 The month when fragile bud becomes the rose;
When beasts, in body politic, await the day
To choose their magistrates—in short, the month of May—
A choice wherein, no less than everywhere, intrigue
 And mediocrity consort, in league.
 Now then, off in a corner, pensively,
 Dawdled the jackass. Clearly no one thought
 Much serious consideration ought
 Be given to the likes of such as he;
Until his she-ass fiancée strode up and cried:
 "Listen! The robe and sash would suit me fine!
 And any jackass fiancé of mine
 Can go and find himself another bride
Unless he's mayor, magistrate... Or doge, at least!
 Win or go hang!" "Indeed!" whinnied the beast,
 Excited more by spring than vain ambition,
"I'll do my best!" Whereat our would-be politician
 Perched on a hillock and began to bray.
 But with such force and such éclat
That soon a crowd of openmouthed—half-deaf!—
      bourgeois
 Assume that all his hee-haw and his neigh
  Have been a fine harangue, and they
 Promptly elect our comic rhetorician—
Our simple ass—to fill some public, high position.

 A pair of lusty lungs, in proper season,
 Does more to win your cause than all your reason.
 Spout floods of words... and precious little sense:
 The witless throng repays your eloquence.

Le Rat des Champs

"Que je suis malheureux!" disait le rat des champs.
"Il me faut des pourceaux partager la pâture,
  Et je n'ai pour nourriture
  Que des vers ou des glands.
  Dans ma triste solitude,
 Je suis rongé d'inquiétude.
  J'ai bien la liberté;
 Mais à quoi bon sans la sécurité!
  Quand les chiens sont en quête,
Ils laissent le gibier pour fouiller chaque trou;
S'ils attrapent un rat, c'est pour eux une fête
  De lui serrer le cou.
Si je sors, le milan me déclare la guerre,
Et le hibou, la nuit, me fait rester sous terre.
  Je n'y tiens plus... il faut ailleurs
  Chercher des destins meilleurs.
Le sort en est jeté; mettons-nous en campagne;
J'aborderai peut-être au pays de Cocagne."

The Country Rat

Exclaimed a country rat: "Ah! What a life of woe!
 My food? Worms, acorns... Fit for pigs!
  And for my digs?
 A solitary hole, below!...
 Sad solitude! Alone and free!...
 But what's the use of liberty
  Where fear abounds?
  Those blessèd hounds...
 When they come coursing round about,
 They leave their prey and poke their snout
 Down every hole. And if, by chance,
 They catch a rat, what do they do?
  Oh, happy circumstance!
 What joy to snap his neck in two!
And if, by day, I leave my lair, the kite
 Is there to swoop and pounce! By night,
 The owl!... It's more than I can bear!
I've had enough! I'm leaving!... Anywhere!...

Il dit, et plantant là ses lares ébahis
　　De sa brusque incartade,
Le voilà qui se met à courir le pays,
　　Sans bagage et sans camarade,
　　　Comme fait un pèlerin,
Le bourdon au côté, le bâton blanc en main.
　　　La fortune lui fut propice.
　　　　Parvenu, sur le soir,
　　Au pied des murs d'un rustique manoir,
Il grimpe avec adresse, et bientôt il se glisse
　　　Jusque dans un grenier,
　　　Où la femme du fermier
　　Avait serré, pour y prendre à toute heure,
Ses fromages, ses œufs, son lard, ses pots de beurre,
Comme aussi ses jambons; jambons de carnaval,
　　Qu'on tenait là faute d'autre local.
Le fermier ne sut pas quel ennemi vorace
Venait de pénétrer jusqu'au cœur de la place.
　　De ses méfaits il souffrit peu de temps.
　　　Le rat, devenu carnivore,
　　Agit si fort des pattes et des dents,
　　　Et comme une pécore,
Il se rua si bien sur la provision,
　　Qu'il creva d'indigestion.

C'est un piège tendu qu'une trop bonne table,
Et de l'intempérant la fin est misérable.

Perhaps I'll find some fairer, happier land!"[1]
　　With that, ending his monologue,
　　He leaves his household gods agog
At such a sudden turn; and, staff in hand,
Pilgrimlike—unprovisioned, unbefriended—
Wanders off. But before the day had ended,
　　Fortune, in fact, had smiled. Our rat
Had come upon a rustic habitat.
Scurrying up the walls, he deftly slipped inside
And happened on a loft, most copiously supplied:
　　Eggs, butter, cheeses... Cheese galore!...
　　Whole loins of pork!... Hams by the score,
For Shrovetide feast, and which the farmer's wife
Stored there for lack of space... The farmer never
Suspects the slightest treachery whatever,
Has no idea what danger threatens, rife;
　　What enemy prepares to gnaw
　　And nibble to his tongue's content...
Well, actually, he hardly makes a dent:
Oh yes, the rat attacks with tooth and claw—
　　Like any proper carnivore—
But so uncouth, devouring more and more,
　　That, gorging on his gain ill-got,
An indigestion croaks him on the spot.

Beware the trap of table too well-spread.
The glutton's lot? Well fed and fat... But dead.

1. The *pays de Cocagne* referred to in the original is an imaginary land of joy and plenty. The allusion, traced back to the twelfth century, is of uncertain origin, though the etymology of the name is thought to be Provençal.

La Révolution des Chiens

　　　Après de grands débats,
　　Des pourparlers et de longs dialogues,
　　Entremêlés d'émeute et de combats,
　　Le peuple chien resta soumis aux dogues;
　　Et le pays, par eux bien gouverné,
　　Reçut le roi qu'il avait couronné.
Tout allait bien, mais grâce aux faiseurs d'épilogues,
Les chiens trouvaient leurs chefs taciturnes et rogues.
　　　Messieurs les mâtins,
　　　Tracassiers et mutins,
　　Provocateurs de mauvaises querelles,
　　Firent si bien pour brouiller les cervelles,
　　　Que cette sotte nation
　　Se mit encore en révolution.
Les roquets, gens hargneux, tenant du prolétaire,
Amateurs du désordre, en firent leur affaire.
　　　Pendant la paix et son loisir,
　　　　Ils avaient à plaisir
　　Exercé leur talent pour la progéniture;
　　Le nombre les servant dans cette conjoncture,
　　Les dogues et leur roi, surpris et désarmés,
　　Furent sous les verrous par décret enfermés.

The Revolution of the Dogs

　　　With much debate and dialogue,
　　　As well as angry demonstration
　　And not a little strife, the people Dog
Finally submitted to the bulldogs' domination.
　　　The country, governed well by them,
　　　Bestowed the royal diadem
　　Upon its king, in fitting celebration.
　　The nation prospered; would have done so longer
　　　If not for many a scandalmonger
　　　Who, at the mastiffs' instigation
　　(Mastiffs are masters at such provocation!),
　　Spread far and wide the word that those in power
　　　　Were haughty, dour,
　　　　Mean and officious.
　　Minds muddled by such obloquy seditious,
　　The foolish folk, swayed by their elocution,
Decide to have themselves another revolution:
The mongrels, mutts of proletarian temperament,
　　Will do the job. In peace their time was spent
　　　Indulging their proclivity
　　　For an excess of progeny.
　　Hence now, by force of numbers, they surprise

Voilà donc les mâtins, les bassets, la canaille,
    Faisant ripaille,
Se déchirant parfois pour contenter leurs goûts.
Ce bonheur dura peu. L'ost menaçant des loups
  Un beau matin parut sur la frontière.
  Nos fédérés avaient l'âme guerrière,
Mais n'étaient pas de taille à lutter un moment;[1]
  Et des roquets la race tout entière
    Périssait misérablement,
Si les mieux avisés n'eussent ouvert la porte
  Et fait sortir les dogues promptement.
    On vit alors combien est forte
  L'affection qu'à la patrie on porte,
  Quand de l'honneur on a le sentiment.
Les dogues et leur roi, chargeant de bonne sorte,
Sur les loups tout surpris firent un tel houra,
  Que la victoire aux canins demeura.
      Après un tel service,
La concorde régna comme elle règne en Suisse.
    Le roi, l'épée au côté,
    Reprit la main de justice;
Et ce peuple de chiens sut que l'autorité
Est un moyen de gloire et de sécurité.

Bulldogs and king, who, by decree,
  In none-too-ceremonious wise
Find themselves prisoners under lock and key.
Ah! Then what revelry! Hounds, bassets, mastiffs... Curs
    All of one stripe: frondeurs
  Venting their revolutionary passion—
  And, often, not in very selfless fashion...
  At any rate, the joy was not to last:
  One morning, Wolfdom's fearsome host stood massed,
Ready to strike! Our confrere commoners, despite
Soldierly zeal, were little match, and would have been
    Promptly done in,
Each canine mother's son, had not some seen the light
  And freed the king and bulldogs, who displayed
That love of country of which patriots are made.
  Attack the wolves they did, and with such might
  That, in the end, the dogs had won the day.
    Thanks to their feat, calm reigns once more
(That harmony our friends the Swiss are famous for!):[2]
    The king, sword by his side, holds sway,
Again dispensing justice in a kingly way.
  And thus his subjects learn an age-old story:
Monarchy is the surest road to strength and glory.

---

1. The noun *fédéré*, in specific revolutionary context, refers to the deputies to the Fête de la Fédération of 1790. It was used in Tardy's lifetime during other periods of French political upheaval—the Hundred Days, the Revolution of 1830—and would be used again, a generation later, during the Commune of 1871. Inviting speculation notwithstanding, it is difficult to say to which of the several revolutionary episodes he witnessed the author may be alluding. Then too, this may not be a *fable à clef*, but merely a generally promonarchic apologia.

2. In defending the monarchy, our aristocratic fabulist seems unbothered by the contradiction that Switzerland, to whose harmony he refers—for rhyme, apparently—had long been a republic.

Anatole de Ségur   Fables (1847–64)

MEMBER of a French family illustrious since the seventeenth century for its statesmen, prelates, and men—and, especially, one woman—of letters, the count (and eventually marquis) Anatole-Henri de Ségur was one of its most prolific authors, albeit not the best known to the general readership. That honor goes, uncontestedly, to his mother, Sophie Rostopchine, comtesse de Ségur, daughter of the celebrated governor-general of Moscow responsible for the defensive burning of the city before the Napoleonic advance in 1812. The good countess, surrounded in middle age by her many grandchildren, and committing her impromptu rainy-day tales to paper, was the author of some two dozen sentimental, impeccably moral, and wildly successful little novels familiar to generations of French youth. (See Paul Guérande, *Le petit monde de la comtesse de Ségur*, pp. 7–9; René Gobillot, *La Comtesse de Ségur: sa vie, son œuvre*, pp. 13–19.)[1]

The countess's second of eight children, son Anatole, was born in 1823. He became heir to the paternal title when his elder brother, Louis-Gaston, entered the priesthood, to become one of the most distinguished churchmen of the period, an influential Catholic apologist and prolific author in his own right. On his father's side Ségur was the great-grandson of Louis-Philippe de Ségur, who had fought in the American Revolution under Rochambeau and gone on to play an important role in French diplomacy and government under Napoleon, serving as ambassador to the court of Catherine the Great and eventually being elected to the Académie Française for his numerous historical, political, and poetic works. With such a family tradition it is not surprising that Anatole de Ségur would also devote his long life to government service and writing. He served, in fact, for a quarter-century in the administrative Conseil d'Etat, first under the Second Empire, as one of the body of *maîtres des requêtes,* and subsequently, despite his strong legitimist leanings, under the Third Republic, as a *conseiller d'état en service ordinaire* for internal affairs. He retired from service in 1879, having been decorated as a chevalier of the Légion d'honneur in 1858, and promoted to the rank of *officier* in 1873, and died in 1902.[2]

As might well be expected from his aristocratic and religious background, Ségur's many writings reflect, throughout his career, an unswerving allegiance to the traditional principles of Throne and Altar, and, corollary to them, of Family. Cases in point, among his host of works: *Témoignages et souvenirs; Les Congrégations religieuses et le peuple; Histoire de Saint-François de Sales; Grandes questions du jour, de la veille et du lendemain;* his nostalgic recollections of a trip to Rome and papal audience in 1864, *Un Hiver à Rome* (reprinted, with minor alterations, as *La Rome de Pie IX*); as well as his monuments of familial devotion: *Vie du comte Rostopchine* and *Monseigneur de Ségur: souvenirs et récits d'un frère.*[3]

The same traditionalism, as well as the same high-toned moralizing of his mother's saccharine little tales, informs many of Ségur's fables, the genre with which he initiated his long career and in which he continued to publish at intervals throughout it.[4] Although biographical sources differ in detail, it appears that his first collection, entitled simply *Fables,* was published in 1847,

followed by a second, *Fables et poésies diverses* (1853) and a third, *Nouvelles fables et contes* (1863). According to Ségur himself, portions of the first and third volumes were reprinted in a fourth, again under the title *Fables* (published by Hetzel in 1864), containing sixty-one poems divided into four books. (A prefatory note specifies that Books I and II contain fables from the 1847 collection; Books III and IV, from that of 1863.) The catalogue of the Bibliothèque Nationale also cites a collection, appearing in several editions, entitled *Premières fables,* and another, *Fables complètes.* While their titles appear to speak for themselves, I cannot vouch for the exact content of either. At any rate, precise bibliographical details aside, it is clear that the author was devoted to the genre.

If Ségur's fables (at least the ones I have been able to consult) are, on the whole, somewhat pompous and "preachy" in their traditional dramatization of human frailty and divine wisdom, these pallid reflections of an appropriately adulated La Fontaine are nonetheless relieved on occasion by pleasantly wry humor, as in "L'Oison et le Cuisinier"—a charming slap at the arrogance of aristocracy by an undisputed aristocrat—and, especially, in the very uncharacteristically "modern" "L'Homme Qui Cherche un Fiacre." Both are translated here from the Hetzel edition of 1864: I, 12 and IV, 2, respectively.

---

1. For a more detailed biography of the countess, see Marthe de Hedouville, *La Comtesse de Ségur et les siens.* Among her best-known novels of the "Bibliothèque Rose" are the following: *Les petites filles modèles* (1857), *Les Malheurs de Sophie* (1858), *Les bons enfants* (1863), *Un bon diable* (1865), and *Après la pluie le beau temps* (1871).

2. The even briefer biographical sketch of Ségur in *Dictionnaire des lettres françaises: le dix-neuvième siècle,* II:391–92, states that he began his governmental career as a *préfet* under the Second Empire; but I find no corroborative mention of him in the lists of *préfets* or *sous-préfets,* actual or honorary, printed annually in the *Almanach Impérial* for the years in question.

3. See Hugo P. Thieme, *Bibliographie de la littérature française de 1800 à 1930,* II:766–67. The reader should be aware, however, that most of Thieme's references to studies of the author's work are erroneous, referring rather to others of his relatives.

4. Fables, it would seem, ran in the family. One of his illustrious great-grandfather's lighter works was, precisely, a collection of *Contes, fables, chansons et vers.*

L'Oison et le Cuisinier

    Certain oison de basse-cour,
Bête autant qu'un oison, ou que maint homme est bête,
Un jour fut désigné (chaque chose a son tour!)
Pour servir de rôti dans un repas de fête.
Il aurait volontiers décliné cet honneur:
"Comment," s'écria-t-il avec un cri d'horreur,
    "C'est moi que l'on destine
      Au couteau de cuisine!
    Assurément l'on fait erreur!
    Qu'on réserve pour cet usage
Poules, dindons, canards, tous gens de bas étage,
Rien de mieux; Dieu les fit à cette intention!
Mais pour moi, je croyais, sans grande ambition,
Devoir être à l'abri d'un si cruel outrage!"
"Et pourquoi, s'il vous plaît," lui dit le cuisinier,
"Au lieu de vous manger, faut-il qu'on vous admire?
Quels exploits inconnus avez-vous faits, beau sire,

The Gosling and the Cook

    A barnyard gosling, foolish bird—
As silly a goose as many a human—heard
That it was he, one day, who'd been selected
    To be that evening's festive roast.
    (Each in his turn!) But, as expected,
The honor notwithstanding, he was most
    Chagrined to be so designated.
    "It can't be!" he expostulated.
"Me? For the kitchen knife? Nay! Say not so!
There's some mistake! It's just not *à propos!*
Take vulgar turkeys, chickens, ducks, or such...
That's what they're for. God made them for as much.
    But me? It's not that I'm ambitious...
Just that I've always thought I ought to be
    Safe from a fate so inauspicious."
"And why," queried the cook, sarcastically,
"Instead of eating you, should we admire you?

Qui vous donnent sujet de tant vous récrier?"
"Inconnus," fit l'oison, "cela vous plaît à dire!
Mes exploits sont connus de l'univers entier."
"Et quels sont-ils?" "Monsieur," dit l'oison d'un ton fier,
"Mes aïeux ont jadis sauvé le Capitole!"
    "Le conte est bon, sur ma parole!
Vos aïeux, c'est fort bien; j'admire vos aïeux,
    Et Rome, par reconnaissance,
    Fit bien d'honorer leur vaillance:
Mais vous, qu'avez-vous fait?" "Moi?" "Vous?" "Je
                  descends d'eux!
    Le sang qui coule dans mes veines
    Coula dans ces cœurs généreux
Qui sauvèrent jadis les légions romaines."
"Voilà tous vos exploits? Vous vous êtes borné
A naître, et puis à dire: 'O peuples, je suis né:
Me voici, regardez, je suis né, c'est moi-même!'
Oison, mon cher ami, mon chagrin est extrême
    De vous causer du déplaisir;
Mais je ne vois rien là qui doive garantir
    De la broche ou de la marmite.
    Vos aïeux avaient du mérite;
    Au lieu de faire l'orgueilleux,
    Vous auriez dû vivre comme eux.
Vous ne l'avez pas fait, malgré votre origine
    Vous finirez à la cuisine.
    Ce trépas n'est point des plus beaux,
Mais en le subissant, quoi qu'en disent les sots,
Vous ne dérogez pas, que cela vous console;
Car sachez que, malgré vos airs ambitieux,
Vous êtes aussi loin de vos nobles aïeux
    Que ma cuisine est loin du Capitole."

What feats have you performed, you noble sire, you?
What unknown deeds of valor have you done,
That give you cause to be so horrified?"
" 'Unknown?' 'Famous,' you mean! Ask anyone..."
"Really? Pray tell!" The gosling, full of pride,
Replied: "My forebears once saved Rome!"' "Quite true!"
Countered the cook. "Bravo for them! Their act
    Of dauntlessness and derring-do
    Earned Rome's respect, and rightly too.
    But you, poor sot, in point of fact,
Tell me what *you* have done." "Who, me?" "Yes, you!"
"Why, I... I'm of their race; my blood was theirs!
It filled the veins of those fair heroes who
    Saved all those Roman legionnaires!"
"That's it? That's all you've done? You merely took
The trouble to be born, proclaiming: 'Look!
It's me! It's me!...'? Well, meaning no offense,
    There's not one spot of evidence—
    I'm sorry, friend, but not one whit—
To spare you from the pot or from the spit.
    Your forebears, true, were valiant birds;
But—unlike you—in deeds, not just in words.
You should have lived like them, my overweening,
Arrogant fowl, so proudly pedigreed!
    For all your puffing and your preening,
You'll end up on the table! Yes, indeed,
    It's an inglorious death; but still,
    A fitting fate, say what you will:
Your ancestors were of a noble breed;
But you're as far from them—poor imbecile!—
As is my kitchen from their Roman hill!"

---

1. This is an obvious reference to the sacred geese that, according to tradition, cackled a warning that alerted the Roman garrison to the stealthy ascent of the Capitol by the invading Gauls in 390 B.C. The event is celebrated in many artistic and literary works, among them the seventeenth-century poet Samuel Butler's *Hudibras:* "Those consecrated geese in orders, / That to the capitol were warders, / And being then upon patrol, / With noise alone beat off the Gaul" (II, 3).

L'Homme Qui Cherche un Fiacre	The Man Who Tries to Find a Cab

<table>
<tr><td>

Il pleuvait à torrents. Un bourgeois tout crotté
Cherchait partout un fiacre avec anxiété,
Et ne le trouvait point. "Vous perdez votre peine,"
    Lui dit à la fin un passant
    Touché de son air innocent.
    "Si la journée était sereine,
Pour un que vous cherchez, vous en trouveriez dix;
Mais, par le temps qu'il fait, votre recherche est vaine.
Vous ne trouverez rien, c'est moi qui vous le dis!"

Les fiacres sont pareils à ces amis du monde
    Sur lesquels à tort on se fonde,
Tout prêts à vous servir quand le péril est loin,
Mais qu'on ne trouve plus dès qu'on en a besoin.

</td><td>

The rain was coming down in sheets.
Muddied and wet, a burgher roamed the streets,
    Desperately, vainly looking high
And low to find himself a cabriolet.
"Don't waste your time," advised a passerby,
    Touched by his air of naiveté.
    "If this were just a nicer day—
    Sunny and dry—believe me, cousin,
Instead of one, you'd find yourself a dozen!"

Cabs are like friends: they can be counted on
    When woe's afar and times are fair.
    But when you need their help... Anon!...
    Look where you will; they're never there.

</td></tr>
</table>

Paul Stevens   Fables (1857)

Wʜɪʟᴇ certainly not one of the "names" in the literature of French Canada, Paul Stevens (1830–82) did enjoy several decades of relative celebrity. It is an overly enthusiastic exaggeration to call him "le Lafontaine [*sic*] du Canada," as the first historian of French Canadian literature generously did. (See Edouard Lareau, *Histoire de la littérature canadienne*, pp. 92–93.) The praise is understandable, however, since, as the same observer indicated, he was the only fabulist of substance that French Canada had produced up to that time. A few disparate fables had, in fact, appeared here and there, especially in the fledgling press. (See Camille Roy, *Nos origines littéraires*, pp. 77–81.) But the genre had hardly been a flourishing one.

Stevens, a native of Belgium, had emigrated early in his life to Montréal, where he edited, successively, the newspaper *La Patrie* and the journal *L'Artiste*. He also taught literature at the Collège de Chambly, and served as a private tutor in a Montréal family.

To the best of my knowledge, Stevens published only two works. His *Fables*—which he may, indeed, have put to practical use in his tutoring duties, like many a mentor of the young—are a collection of sixty-four generally brief and witty apologues, only occasionally marred by a somewhat sententious moralizing, and very much in the free-flowing style of La Fontaine, of whom he was an obvious admirer, judging not only from his derivative style but also from his frequent textual references. Other allusions point to a certain classical erudition on Stevens's part. He appears, also, to have been familiar with the fables of his recent predecessor Arnault (see pp. 124–25), a quotation from whose work serves as an epigraph to his collection. The volume is dedicated, not without the obsequiousness typical of such documents, to the prominent Canadian statesman and would-be poet Denis-Benjamin Viger.

Some ten years after the *Fables,* Stevens published his *Contes populaires*, twelve prose tales on Canadian themes, and four in verse reminiscent of his previous collection. In the preface he attacks the principle of Art for Art's Sake, and subscribes to the time-honored aim of instructing as well as pleasing. The tales, in which the hand of the fabulist is frequently in evidence, bear out his aim. The *Contes populaires* would seem to have enjoyed continuous success, given at least two republications (in part, though with the same title) after the author's death. An especially telling proof is the inclusion of one of the tales, "Fortuné Bellehumeur," as a companion piece to "Les Lutins," a story by one of Canada's most eminent men of letters, Louis-Honoré Fréchette, published under the latter title in a volume of "contes canadiens."

The fables translated here—numbers 43 and 59—are typical, respectively, of Stevens's traditional La Fontainesque inspiration and his use of the fable to reflect playfully the technology of his time.

Le Chat et la Chauve-souris

S'agit-il de rompre un serment
Ou de commettre un maléfice,
Les fourbes savent aisément
Trouver un subtil argument
Pour motiver leur injustice.

Témoin l'exemple de ce chat:
On l'avait pris au piége. Un rat
Sain et sauf l'en sortit; pour payer ce service
Maître Mitis ayant promis
De respecter toute sa vie
La nation rateuse et la gent son amie.[1]
Or, il prit un matin une chauve-souris:
"Je t'épargnerais rat, mais oiseau je te croque,"
Grommela le rusé matou.
Tout en faisant ce soliloque
Le traître lui tordit le cou.

1. The author's reference to "Maître Mitis" is a typical borrowing from La Fontaine, who gives the name to his feline hero in the fable "Le Chat et un Vieux Rat" (III, 18). The name—from the Latin *mitis* 'soft'—is apparently a reference to the cat's coat. It may have been suggested to La Fontaine by a passage in one of the tales (no. XXI) of the *Nouvelles Récréations et joyeux devis* (1558) attributed to the intellectual heir of Boccaccio, Bonaventure Des Périers. (See *Œuvres françoises de Bonaventure Des Périers*, II:97.)

The Cat and the Bat

The traitorous rogue impenitent,
Eager to break his word, or bent
On fouler villainy, will use
Any excuse or wily ruse
To justify his infamy.

For instance, take a certain cat,
Whose life was saved because a rat
Once nibbled on a net to set him free.
In gratitude Sir Tom had sworn
That any beast of rodent nation born
No longer had to fear his enmity.
Now then, one day it came to pass that he
Had got his clutches on a hapless bat.
"I'd spare you as a rat,"—so meowed our crafty sinner—
"But as a bird you're going to be my dinner!"
So saying, he wrung his neck. And that was that.

La Boîte aux Lettres et le Télégraphe

"Bon Dieu! que l'homme est inconstant!"
S'écriait en se dépitant
Cette humble boîte où l'on va mettre
Soit un paquet, soit une lettre.
"Chaque jour mon culte décroît,
Je le sens, ma gloire est passée,
Pourquoi suis-je ainsi délaissée,
Hélas! qui me dira pourquoi?"
"Pourquoi? la réponse est aisée,"
Lui répondit en badinant
Le télégraphe. "Ecoutez bien, ma chère,
L'homme, je l'avoue, est changeant.
La nouveauté lui plaît et pour se satisfaire
Il n'est rien qu'il n'invente. Aussi le voyons-nous
Me prêter le tonnerre
Afin de le servir plus promptement que vous.
Vous vous traînez, ma pauvre amie
Et le progrès veut de grands pas;
Ainsi ne vous étonnez pas
De n'être plus si bien garnie."

The Postbox and the Telegraph

"Good God, but man's a fickle lot!" So cried
A humble postbox, mortified
To find herself abandoned, by degrees,
Losing those faithful devotees
Who long had trusted packages and letters to her:
"Each day," she sighed, "they're growing fewer and fewer.
I feel my glory fading fast;
Relic, already, of an age now past!
But why?..." "Why? Easy!" answered, with a laugh,
The telegraph.
"Listen, my love. They're fickle, true...
Always in search of something new...
Nothing they won't invent... Why, look at me!
They tamed the thunder so that I could be
Their messenger, to do what you can do.
But faster! In the twinkling of an eye!...
Much as I hate to disabuse you,
That's progress, friend. You crawl, I fly!
And so, poor soul, now you know why
You shouldn't be surprised if they don't use you."

Henri Burgaud des Marets   Recueil de Fables et Contes en Patois Saintongeais (1859)

THE NINETEENTH century, age of nationalistic awareness and ethnic self-affirmation, saw not only the phenomenon of a neo-Provençal renaissance (see pp. 109 and 140) but also a revival of pride and interest in a variety of other French provincial dialects and the cultures they reflected. One of the first areas to take formal self-conscious stock of its regional identity was the west, the country around Charente and Saintonge; and this, owing mainly to the pioneering studies of one of the earliest of the serious French linguistic folklorists, and one of the region's leading intellectuals: scholar, philologist, bibliophile, and patois poet, [Jean-] Henri Burgaud des Marets.[1]

Born in the Saintonge town of Jarnac on November 2, 1806, into a middle-class merchant family long established in the region, Burgaud des Marets began his career with brilliant studies at the Collège de Bordeaux, after which he was sent to Paris to be educated in the law—albeit reluctantly, we are told.[2] Receiving his *licence* in 1829, he was admitted to the bar the following year. Although he halfheartedly continued to pursue the legal profession, even receiving his *doctorat* in 1837, he pursued it, one might say, at a distance. Other interests monopolized the passions and talents of "notre grand jarnacois . . . notre curieux érudit patoisant," who resisted parental pressure to return to Jarnac and the family business—the "anémiante sécurité d'un bon négoce." (See Comandon, "Burgaud des Marets," pp. 65–67.) A talented linguist, proficient in Latin, Greek, Old French, and a number of modern languages—English, Spanish, Italian, Portuguese, German—he was especially fascinated by Polish, mastering it well enough—no small feat!— to translate the work of famous patriot-poet Adam Mickiewicz. His anonymous version of the latter's historical epic *Konrad Wallenrud* was, in fact, the first of Mickiewicz's work to be translated into French. Several years later, thanks to his enthusiasm for the Polish cause and his contacts among the growing expatriate community in Paris, he met the poet himself, who, driven by a charismatic Byronesque zeal, became for him something of a personal idol.[3]

Burgaud des Marets's studies in Old French led him to a related interest in dialectology, and especially in the patois of his native region, which had preserved many elements of the ancient tongue. A devoted bibliophile, he collected over the years a vast library of works in and about the dialects of France and other European countries.[4] More directly, we are told that, as an avid field-worker *avant la lettre,* he would spend long hours, whenever back home on a visit, listening to and chatting with the local peasantry—who viewed this curious observer, "cet homme étrange, qu'on disait parisien," not without a little distrust—in the hope of recording their dialect for posterity. (See Delamain, *Jarnac,* p. 274.)

The first result of his dialectal studies was a slim volume of four brief pieces, *Fables en patois charentais* (1849), in the idiom of his native town, followed several years later by a *Noveau fabeulier jarnacoès* ("New Jarnac Fable-Book," 1852), almost as slim, containing only six. Succeeding years, however, saw the steady production of a variety of publications—some serious, some less so—including, in addition to numerous miscellanea, a patois translation of the *Parabole de l'enfant prodigue, en dialecte saintongeais,* several comedies and other theater pieces, an augmented collection of fables in 1857, and his definitive *Recueil de fables et contes en patois saintongeais* (1859), containing fifteen fables (including those previous published), two tales, a version of Virgil's first *Eclogue,* and a trio of lighthearted introductory verses.

But if we can believe his biographers, Burgaud des Marets's patois occupations, for all his time and devotion, were merely a *délassement* in his serious scholarly studies of the great provincial Renaissance figures Montaigne and Rabelais. (See Beaulieu, *Vie et travaux,* pp. 130 ff.) His work on the former was never to bear fruit. Of the latter, however, he produced a much-acclaimed critical edition, after two decades of research, in collaboration with Edme-Jacques-Benoît Rathery, curator of the Bibliothèque du Louvre.[5] When, during the Commune riots of 1871, that library was burned, Burgaud des Marets was chosen, with two other scholars, to begin the rebuilding of its collection. Ironically, not long after, in failing health and straitened circumstances, he was obliged to sell his personal library for the proverbial song.[6] No less ironically (and perhaps even symbolically), during a fit of despair uncharacteristic of this congenial scholar, he was to burn much of his own unpublished writing, throwing into the fire sheaves of manuscripts and notes, among them what was to have been his volume on Montaigne. Burgaud des Marets died penniless on October 6, 1873, in circumstances worthy of a Romantic opera, attended *in extremis* only by one last faithful domestic. But he left behind a solid reputation among his respectful, admiring, and affectionate Jarnac compatriots. Their descendants paid him public tribute with a centenary commemoration of his death, in 1973. (See Comandon, "Burgaud des Marets," p. 76.)

The fables "La Cigale et l'Feurmit" and "La Fumelle et le Seugret" are typical examples of his chatty, down-to-earth adaptations. Originally appearing in the collections of 1852 and 1849, respectively, they were subsequently included in the *Recueil de fables et contes en patois saintongeais,* where they figure, unnumbered, as the second and the eleventh.

1. In the words of anthologist Adolphe Van Bever, "il prit une place à peu près unique parmi les écrivains de terroir, devançant d'un demi-siècle nos modernes folk-loristes" (*Poètes du terroir*, IV:238).

2. See Camille Beaulieu's extensively detailed and meticulously documented homage-biography, *Vie et travaux de Burgaud des Marets*, pp. 21 ff. For thumbnail biographical sketches, see Robert Delamain, *Jarnac à travers les âges*, pp. 273–78; and Odette Comandon, "Burgaud des Marets."

3. Burgaud des Marets's Polish associations in general, and the influence of Mickiewicz in particular, are thoroughly discussed in Beaulieu, *Vie et travaux*, chaps. 1 and 2.

4. His personal library was probably the most extensive ever assembled on the subject by a private individual, containing a total of 2275 items covering a wide range of specialized topics. (See *Bibliothèque patoise de M. Burgaud des Marets: livres rares et précieux*.)

5. The two-volume *Œuvres de Rabelais, collationnées pour la première fois sur les éditions originales* appeared in a second edition (1870–73), as well as in a revised posthumous third and fourth, in numerous reprintings. (See Beaulieu, *Vie et travaux*, p. 246.)

6. The volume cited in n. 4 is, in fact, a catalogue of that sale, in May of 1873.

La Cigale et l' Feurmit

> Peurq' tié cigale et tieû feurmit
> Se voyissian meû, més amit,
> Mon sieu Garnier m'a fait in paire de lunette.
> A sont bein boune foutiquette!
> Saquez-lés donc d'sus voût' nazot,
> Vous voérez tieû feurmit aussi groû qu'in barbot.
> Et vous voérez b'n otout lés ale
> De tié mâtine de cigale,
> Qui s'épiraye en tieûl ourmiâ.
> Diâb' m'essarte, a sembian à tielles d'in osiâ.
>
> Le quate jein dârié ('l è sûr qu'o fasait biâ)
> Ine feugnante de cigale,
> De poûr' que le soulail l'achale,
> S'était b' déparpassée au mitan d'in ourmiâ.
> A silait keume cent fumelle,
> Menait dau brut bein pu groû qu'elle,
> Et se fourchait, poin à demit,
> D'in paure diâbe de feurmit,
> Qui treinait dés agrain deveurs sa feurmigère.
> (Oh! tiellés beite sont bein boune ménagère!)
> Venit l'hivar. Fazit in frét
> Que reun que d'y songé me fait sabé lés dét.
> Toute grape et catise en in creux, tié cigale
> Se fourçan d'éparé sés ale,
> Cheû le feurmit, boun'gen! volit keume a poyut.
> "Mon vieux," qu'a li dissit, "n'ai de més jôr oyut
> Ine faim keume aneut; ol é la vrai' fringale.
> Peûris-tu me preité tan set peu d'gigourit,
> De la mique, dau pain ratit,
> O beun dés beurnuzon de tourtiâ chaumenit?
> O n'arat reun que je n'avale,
> Qu'o set dés poume chope, o b' dés coudin cotit."
> "Ma mignoune, fait poin," que le feurmit dissit.
> "Tiet été tu chantis; s'o te chausse, en tielle aire,
> Astoure de dansé ton petit rigaudon,
> M'en vas q'ri tout comptan Beurnard le vioulounaire."
>
> Sauv' qu'il arait poyut avoér le kieur pu bon,
> Tieû feurmit, m'é-t-avis, avait b'n' in p'tit rason.

The Cricket and the Ant

> To make these two—this ant and cricket—
> Easier for the eye to see,
> Monsieur Garnier, my friends, went and made up for me
> This damned fine pair of specs. Just stick it
> Onto your nose; and there, before your eyes,
> The ant grows fat—dung beetle size!
> As for the cricket, mark my words:
> Look at her in that elm tree rub her wings...
> The Devil take me if those things
> Don't look as big as any proper bird's![1]
>
> The fourth of June last year—a lovely day,
> As I recall[2]—a lazy cricket, fearing lest
> The sun's rays do her in, had shamelessly undressed
> Up in an elm tree, up about half way;
> And, screeching like a hundred women strong—
> A lot of noise for one her size!—
> Watched as a poor ant—wretched creature—dragged along
> Some paltry grains of wheat. The cricket sneered:
> "How wise!
> My, my! Aren't we the provident householder!..."
> Well, winter came, and it grew cold... And colder...
> So cold that at the very thought I shiver.
> The cricket, numb, and cowering in her nest,
> Trying to spread her wings, could barely quiver,
> But made her painful way, as best
> She could, to neighbor ant, to see what she might give her:
> "I've never seen such awful famine, friend!
> Perhaps you would be good enough to lend
> The likes of me a spot of gruel," the cricket said.
> "A crumb of corn?... A rotten apple?... Crust of bread,
> However stale and rat-infested?...
> A slice of rancid quince?... A smidge of moldy cake?...
> Anything?... For our friendship's sake?..."
> The ant was quite uninterested.
> "My dear," she answered, "not a chance!
> Last summer all you cared to do was dance.
> I'll call Bernard the fiddler: you can do your jig!"
>
> Our ant was something of a heartless prig;
> But not so wrong, given the circumstance.

La Fumelle et le Seugret

Reun n'é mein seurge qu'in seugret:
Su dés épale de fumelle
Pas putoû qu'in quéquin zou met,
   O chet.
O y' a b' dés mâle otout dièr' pû vaillan que zelle.
Mais que j'ou dis, faut beu qu'o set.

Jacquot ébaudissan ine neut sa borjoêse:
Li luchit: "Léve-te, boune, je seu fichut!"
"Qu'é-t-ou, stelle, qu'ol é? qu'é-tou que tu dégoèse?"
"Ah! boune, o me fait zir, sti, qu'ei-ji donc sentut?
J'ai pounut... j'ai pounut... j'ai pounut in œu d'oèe.
I me baran le châf' de fumelle dau jar:
N'ouserais poin saillî d'oère de to l'hivar.
Si tu zou dis, t'aras l'air d'ine grande coèe.
   Et quant' j'iron
   Vende au canton,
I-z-allan s'ébeuglé tretous: 'Piron! piron!
   Pire! pire!
   Faut lés confire!'"

De se teizé la fumelle jurit;
   Mais dés que le jor treleusit,
A s'enfut vîteman zou dire à sa cousine,
   Qui zou dissit à sa voésine.
   La voésine allit au canton,
Contit qu'il en avait pounut mais d'in quartron,
Et quant tieû brut oyut corut de goule en goule,
I passit p'r avoèr pon cent-z-œu d'oèe et de poule.

   Des gens qu'o y at
   Dedan Jarnat,
Peur feire aq'neûte ine nouvelle,
La fasan batte peur Ballet.
J'amris meû la conté tansman à deux fumelle,
   En leû disan qu'ol é seugret.
Peut beun que leû marit jacasserian keum' zelle.

   Peur que le monde sachan reun...
O n' faut, ma fi! conté sés seugret qu'à son cheun.

Women and Secrets

Nothing weighs more than secrets. Lay one on
A woman's shoulders: in a wink it's gone
      A-tumbling
   Down to the ground. (Though I admit
There are some men as well, forever stumbling
Under their weight. That's true; I'll vouch for it.)[1]

At any rate, a certain burgher, Jacques, one night
   Got up and, shouting, shook his wife awake:
"Woman, get out of bed, for goodness' sake!"
"What's wrong?" "I've laid... I've laid a goose egg!"
      "What?" "That's right!
It's terrible!... Oh! What a belly ache!...
Imagine what my friends are going to say!
They'll tell me I'm a mother goose! I'll have to stay
   Indoors and hide all winter! As for you,
   One word, and you'll be jeered and laughed at too!
      Come market day,
      Think what abuse!
      'Goose! Goose!
Let's make them into nice pâté!'"

The wife swore not to tell a soul. No, never!...
Next morning, as the sun comes up, however,
   She runs and tells her cousin; who
Runs to her neighbor; who, without ado,
Runs to the marketplace to spread the word
That Jacques has laid a brood, bird upon bird.
By time the news has run its course, poor Jacques
Has laid a hundred goose eggs!... And some hen's as well!

   Now, in Jarnac,
   When people have some news to tell
They let Ballet the crier drum it out.[2]
   Frankly, I think it's just as good
   To tell two women—if it's understood
   That mum's the word! (And, little doubt,
   Their husbands too will noise the news about!)

In short, unless you want your secrets bruited round,
   Tell nobody... Except, perhaps, your hound!

1. Burgaud des Marets follows his La Fontaine model "La Femme et le Secret" (VIII, 6) in not restricting loose tongues to women alone. He will stray from it, however, by not explaining the husband's motivation—namely, to test his wife's ability to keep a secret—and by failing to tell us if he actually shows her an egg to prove his story. The latter details occur in both La Fontaine and his source, a Renaissance Latin prose fable by Abstemius. (See Prosper Soullié, *La Fontaine et ses devanciers,* pp. 136–38.)

2. The author, characteristically, assures us in a footnote that the "Ballet" referred to was, indeed, the actual town crier in the town of Jarnac.

J. Héré   Fables et Poésies (1860)

ALTHOUGH a mathematics professor by vocation, J[ean] Héré owed his local celebrity in the northern city of Saint-Quentin more to his lifelong pursuits as poet and translator than to his profession. Born in 1795 in Château-sur-Loing, and orphaned at the age of ten, he was brought up by a curé whom his family had protected during the Terror, and who, out of gratitude, saw to his early education at the seminary of Orléans. (See Héré's obituary, by his colleague Charles Daudville, in the *Mémoires de la Société Académique des Sciences, Arts, Belles-lettres, Agriculture et Industrie de Saint-Quentin,* for these and other biographical details.)

Once finished with his studies, Héré was assigned to teach mathematics in a series of schools, among them the Institution Morin, in Paris, finally arriving at Saint-Quentin early in 1822, where he was to remain for the rest of his life. Within a few years of his arrival, he and a number of other local literati founded what was to become, three years later, the Société Académique de Saint-Quentin, one of the earliest of the provincial learned societies in France. Throughout his life Héré continued to take an active part in its deliberations and publications, appearing frequently in the pages of its *Mémoires* with a variety of both scholarly articles and verse—especially his fables and translations from the *Odes* of Horace—as well as in the publications of other provincial *académies* of which he was a correspondent.

In 1846 Héré was elected to the town council of Saint-Quentin, on which he devoted much time to questions of public education, serving on that body until his death in 1864. His pedagogical concerns were also reflected in a volume on French composition, *Leçons de rhétorique et de littérature française,* a portion of which appeared two decades before its publication, in the *Mémoires* of the Société Académique (1831–33, pp. 268–304), and which was intended to serve better the needs of his students—especially the young ladies, we are told—than the outmoded materials then in use.

Héré's fables, many of which likewise first appeared in the *Mémoires,* are all samples of good, staunch bourgeois morality, obviously and not unexpectedly cast in the La Fontaine form. A number of them are rather faithful translations from the Italian fabulists, especially Aurelio Bertola, for whom he seems to have had a particular fondness. A brief, forty-page collection, *Fables,* was published with philanthropic motives ("au profit des indigens") early in his career. A more comprehensive volume, *Fables et poésies,* appeared a few years before his death. Its verse introduction, ostensibly an extract of a longer "épître sur la fable," offers the usual excuse for following in La Fontaine's footsteps, though more original than most such disclaimers: "Quand, par un destin favorable, / L'homme entend de divins concerts, / D'irrévérance est-il coupable / S'il fredonne, après, quelques airs?" The volume contains fifty fables, divided arbitrarily into two books. A third book, entitled "Les Lapins," is composed of five lengthier poems, dated from 1855 to 1860, in which, in the venerable tradition of the political fable, a variety of rabbit characters allegorize specific events in the Crimean War. A fourth and final book presents four miscellaneous poems, among them a curious tribute to Parmentier, the celebrated agronomist.

My translations are of the following numbers in *Fables et poésies:* I, 26; II, 5; II, 6; II, 11; and II, 16.

La Ménagère et la Souris

Certaine ménagère, à la recherche sûre,
Un jour croit reconnaître à quelque égratignure
    Qu'une souris a mis la dent
Sur un morceau de lard en son fournil pendant.
    "Ah! ah! la belle délicate,
Il paraît qu'il vous faut du lard pour vos repas!
      C'est très-bien, ne vous gênez pas;
      Mais je vous enverrai ma chatte,
      Qui vous fera sentir sa patte;
      Oui, pas plus tard que cette nuit,
      Elle vous croquera sans bruit."
      La chose ainsi fut arrangée
      Et n'a que trop bien réussi;
   Non-seulement la souris fut mangée,
      Mais tout le lard le fut aussi.

The Housewife and the Mouse

A certain housewife, of discerning eye,
Notices that a mouse has happened by,
    And that he's taken
More than one nibble in a chunk of bacon
    Hanging there by the fire. "My, my,"
She sneers, "you've got expensive taste, I see!
    Well, don't be shy! Oh, don't mind me!
    But watch your step: tonight I'll send
    My cat to do you in, my friend!
    One swat, one swipe... He'll knock you flat,
    And that, quite simply, will be that!"
    And so it was. At night, her feline,
    True to his nature—ah, too true!—
    Gobbles the mouse... then makes a beeline
Right for the bacon, and devours that too.

Pour éviter un mal, nous tombons dans un pire;
    C'est ce que ma fable veut dire.

Parry one problem... Fume and fret...
You'll only find another, graver yet.[1]

1. The danger of falling "from the frying-pan into the fire" is not uncommon to fable literature. In the present collection, see, for example, Philibert Guide, "The Fox and the Hedgehog" (p. 37). Specifically, however, this fable is a variation on the exemplum of the cat who is employed to guard a cheese from a rat and ends up devouring them both. The author does not acknowledge an immediate model, though the apologue had been extant since at least the thirteenth century. It seems to have originated in Latin, either with Cardinal Jacques de Vitry (1178?–1240?) or as one of the moralistic parables of his contemporary, the English Cistercian, Odo of Cheriton (d. 1247), and appears to have entered the fable literature of the western vernaculars through the translation of Odo's work into Spanish, under the title *Libro de los gatos*. (See *Libro de los gatos*, ed.

Bernard Darbord, no. 16, pp. 77–78; *El libro de los gatos: A Text with Introduction and Notes*, ed. G. T. Northup, p. 40; Thomas Frederick Crane, *The Exempla of Jacques de Vitry*, pp. 4, 138; and Léopold Hervieux, *Les Fabulistes latins depuis le siècle d'Auguste jusqu'à la fin du moyen âge*, IV [1884]: 194, 304, 450.) The fable surfaces in a sixteenth-century incarnation in the work of the German moralist Johannes Pauli, whose part-humorous, part-serious religious anecdotes, *Schimpf und Ernst*, appeared in 1522. (See the edition of Johannes Bolte, I:28–9, no. 35.) It is not impossible that any of these versions, recondite though they are, could have been known to our author, who seems to have been familiar with the literature. Nor is it impossible, of course, that he thought he was original.

L'Autruche

"Gare, gare," criait une autruche massive,
"Place, je vais voler, m'élever dans les airs."
Se rangeant aussitôt, de mille oiseaux divers
    La troupe demeure attentive.
"Holà! regardez-moi, voyez ma course vive,
Apprenez à voler, suivez-moi du regard,
    Si vous le pouvez par hasard."
De la part des oiseaux, cette jactance énorme
Attire de sifflets un concert uniforme.
L'autruche n'y prend garde et ne les entend pas.
Elle va s'envoler, mais ses ailes débiles
Font pour la soulever des efforts inutiles;
Son aile maigre en vain s'agite avec fracas;
Quand elle croit planer au-dessus de la nue,
Par son poids sur le sol l'autruche est retenue;
Elle a beau s'agiter, elle pose toujours
    Sur la terre par ses pieds lourds.

Messieurs les beaux-esprits, vous que je vois sourire
D'un oiseau trop pesant, pourriez-vous bien nous dire
Si, lorsque vous rêvez vous élever aux cieux
    Dans vos accents mélodieux,
Quelques coups de sifflet échappés du parterre,
Ne vous ont pas parfois réveillés sur la terre?

The Ostrich[1]

"Avast! Make way!" a massive ostrich cries,
Amid a thousand birds of every feather.
"Watch me! I'm taking off! Up to the skies..."
    The birds look on, uncertain whether
They should believe their ears and trust their eyes.
    "Now then, poor creatures, all together...
Watch—if you can—and learn what flying is!"
Mortified by this arrogance of his,
    They whistle, hiss, raise quite a fuss...
The ostrich, utterly oblivious,
Flutters and flails, unwieldy and ungainly,
Trying to raise his clumsy bulk. But no...
    The hulking beast endeavors vainly:
Flapping his feeble wings fortissimo,
Dream though he may of heavenward ascent,
Our would-be traveler to the firmament
Stands planted, all too firmly, here below.

Well now, my fine, fair literary wits,
You read this tale and smile... "Ah yes, it's... it's
So droll... That bird..." you say, forgetting quite
That you, yourselves, will soar in lyric flight—
    Until the public's hoots resound,
And let you know you've never left the ground!

1. Scrupulous—though vague—in acknowledging sources, the author here cites the work of the celebrated Italian fabulist Lorenzo Pignotti (1739–1812), possibly unaware that an even earlier source of this fable was Lessing's "Der Strauss" (*Fabeln* [1759], I, 18). Pignotti was probably unaware as well. In the preface to his *Favole e novelle* (1782) he does acknowledge substantial borrowings "d'Inglesi e Francesi scrittori"; but since he credits no German antecedents it is

safe to assume that Lessing's prose fable was not his inspiration. "Lo Struzzo" (no. 27 or 28, depending on the edition) may, in fact, have been modeled after the fable "L'Autruche," by Claude-Joseph Dorat (see pp. 91–93), who, in his *Fables ou allégories philosophiques* (1772), does give Lessing as his source. In any event, these four ostrich fables—Lessing's, Dorat's, Pignotti's, and, ultimately, Héré's—are remarkably similar in detail and moral.

Le Pin et le Grenadier[1]

"La nature envers vous fut prévoyante et sage
En vous faisant ainsi naître sous mon ombrage";[2]
A l'humble grenadier dit le pin orgueilleux.
    "Lorsque l'orage éclate dans les cieux,

The Pine and the Pomegranate Tree

The lofty pine presumptuously addressed
    The humble pomegranate tree:
"Nature, my poor, pathetic friend, knew best
When thus she planted you so close to me.

Que la vent siffle et que tombe l'averse,
Sous mon feuillage épais et que rien ne traverse,
　　Vous vous riez de leur fureur;
Je vous mets à l'abri sous mon toit protecteur."

"C'est vrai," répond l'arbuste, "et votre épais feuillage
　　Me défend, je le reconnais,
　　Contre la fureur des vents, mais
Ne me prive-t-il pas d'un plus grand avantage?
Votre dôme touffu qui m'invite au sommeil,
　　S'il me garantit de l'orage,
　　Me prive aussi de mon soleil."

Let lightning rend the heavens in twain;
Let tempests roar, and torrents rain:
　　Beneath my majesty erect, you
Weather the worst, for I—yes, I—protect you."

"Truly," replies the bush, "I quite agree.
　　I prize the succor of your shade,
　　And face the torment unafraid,
Thanks to your gracious magnanimity.
　　But are you not, as well, the one—
　　Proud benefactor though you be—
Who, all the while, deprives me of the sun?"

1. No less scrupulous (or vague) than in the preceding fable, the author acknowledges his debt to another fabulist, Aurelio Bertola (1753–98), for the subject of this one. Héré's version is a rather faithful imitation of "Il Pino e il Melogranato," no. 30 in Bertola's *Cento favole* (1785): "Fausta ti fu la sorte, / Che sotto l'ombra mia nascer ti feo; / Diceva un ampio [ed] orgoglioso Pino / Ad un Melogranato

suo vicino . . ." The same fable is no. 105 in an expanded collection, *Favole dell' abate Bertola* (1834).
2. The reader will notice, also, a no-doubt-intentional reminiscence from La Fontaine's dialogue between his celebrated antagonists in "Le Chêne et le Roseau" (I, 22): "La nature envers vous me semble bien injuste." (See p. 33.)

Le Portrait Vu de Trop Près

　　Un enfant disait à son père:
　　"Papa, comment se peut-il faire
　　Que ce portrait de grand seigneur
　　Que j'admirais à certaine hauteur,
　　Maintenant qu'il repose à terre,
　　Me paraisse avoir maint défaut?
　　Les traits sont durs, à chaque place
　　On voit crévasse sur crévasse.
Il faut, pour qu'il soit bien, qu'il soit vu de fort haut."
Le père lui répond: "Cette toile est fidèle,
　　Mon cher enfant; à son modèle
　　Ce portrait ressemble en tout point:
　　Il faut ne le voir que de loin."

The Portrait Seen Too Close

　　"Papa," a youngster asked, "how can
　　It be? That picture of the man—
　　The nobleman—I used to see
　　Hanging up on the wall, up high...
How fine, how beautiful it used to be!
　　But now, instead, I see it lie
　　Here on the floor, up close, and find
　　Harsh features, blemishes of every kind,
　　The canvas full of cracks... Why, papa? Why?"
"You see the noble's flaws, son, as they really are,"
　　Replied the father. "That's the way he is.
　　The faults the portrait paints are his.
　　He too, I fear, is best seen from afar."[1]

1. The reader will recall a virtually identical moral in Delaunay's fable, "His Thespian Majesty and the Schoolboy" (see pp. 74–75).

Le Cerf-Volant

> Poussé par un vent favorable,
>> Un cerf-volant montait, montait!...
> De s'élever on est insatiable.
> Tout en montant, il s'impatientait
> Contre la main, à ses désirs rebelle,
>> Qui lentement lui lâchait la ficelle
>> Pour éviter tout accident.

> "Vraiment, ma sottise est extrême
> De me laisser conduire ainsi par un enfant!
>> Ne puis-je pas me diriger moi-même?
> Faut-il comme un captif me laisser retenir?
>> Cela m'ennuie, et je veux en finir."

> Il dit, s'agite, et, par un coup de tête,
>> Rompt la ficelle qui l'arrête.
>> Mais, au lieu de monter plus haut,
>> Soudain il fait un soubresaut,
>> Puis tourbillonne à l'aventure,
> Et tombe en se faisant plus d'une déchirure.

> Quand le vent du bonheur, rapide et continu,
> Nous entraîne, il est bon que l'on soit retenu.

---

1. The author gives no indication that this fable was inspired by Antoine-Vincent Arnault (see pp. 124–25), although it bears a close

The Kite

> Borne on the breeze, a kite was rising
>> High in the sky... and higher... still higher...
> (For kites, like men—insatiable—aspire
> To heights unbounded!) and, soliloquizing
>> Crossly against the cautious hands
> Holding the twine that checked his vain desire:

> "Folly! A little child commands
>> My heavenward flights! What kind of fool...
> What kind of slave am I, that I obey,
>> And meekly let another rule
>> My life! I've had enough! No more!
>> Into the blue!... Up and away!..."

> With that, our headstrong popinjay
> Tugs, snaps the string, breaks free!... Alas, before
>> He can begin to soar, go vaulting
> Up to the great beyond, he's somersaulting,
>> Head over tail—back, forth, up, over, under—
> And falling in a twisted heap, torn all asunder.

> When blow the giddying winds of wild ambition,
> Best we resist, lest we be blown to our perdition.[1]

---

resemblance to the latter's "Le Cerf-Volant" (VI, 9), at least in its basic theme.

Hippolyte de Thierry-Faletans   Fables et Contes (1871)

HIPPOLYTE de Thierry-Faletans (or [de] Thierry de Faletans) is a shadowy figure at best. A count, and member of an aristocratic family whose nobility dates from the first decade of the seventeenth century, he appears to have considered himself enough of an intimate of Napoleon III to have taken the liberty of dedicating his *Fables et contes* to the ill-starred imperial prince Eugène on the occasion of the latter's fifteenth birthday, in March of 1871.[1] He states, with an appropriate show of modesty in the dedication of the second edition, published nine months later in Genoa—and with the now-customary allusion to La Fontaine—that "l'approbation que l'Empereur, votre auguste père, a daigné accorder à ce mince ouvrage... et l'accueil encourageant qu'un certain nombre de lecteurs fait à ce livre dont l'impression a été fort restreinte, m'ont décidé à en faire paraître une seconde édition." The work thus takes its place among the many collections of fables and other didactica ostensibly written for the edification of royal youth; albeit, in

this case, of erstwhile royalty, given the bloodless deposition of the monarch the year before.

Thierry-Faletans may also have been a minor diplomat of sorts. It is clear, at any rate, that he spent time in Italy, involved—at least theoretically—in Risorgimento politicking. Of his two other extant writings, one, *Le Nord et le Sud de l'Italie,* is a pamphlet advocating the resolution of the conflict between the papacy and the temporal powers by the division of Italy into two sovereign states, one north and one south, with the latter under the pope. The paucity of available biographical details notwithstanding, our author's conservative sympathies— "reactionary," in a word—are clear in his tract, and no less so in his *Fables et contes,* most of which beat the drum of traditionalism—political, social, moral, religious—in the face of the incursions of change and alleged Progress. A third work, *Théâtre de société,* a collection of five one-act salon comedies, is of interest in that it includes one of our fables, "L'Ane et la Locomotive," apparently inserted as an *intermède* to be recited as a monologue.

The six typical fables here translated—numbers 1, 6, 12, 13, 15, and 18—are from the above-mentioned second edition of *Fables et contes,* with illustrations by Rodolphe

Bresdin and others. The volume contains a total of twenty-three fables and thirteen tales, the latter inspired by a wide variety of national folklores: Spanish, Russian, Persian, and American, among others.

1. The prince would be killed eight years later, while in the British army, fighting the Zulus.

L'Ane et la Locomotive

Un Ane d'âge mûr, cheminait lentement;
Il portait sur l'échine un lourd sac de froment;
Certain bâton noueux avait, sur la surface
De son rude epiderme, imprimé mainte trace...
L'Ane suivait pensif la route du moulin,
Semblant compter ses pas tout le long du chemin;
Mais voilà qu'il s'arrête auprès d'un bloc énorme,
Moitié fer, moitié cuivre et d'un aspect informe;
C'est la Locomotive au ton brusque et criard,
Qui voyant l'embarras de notre campagnard,
Lui fait un beau discours boursouflé d'éloquence,
Pour démontrer au mieux son extrême importance.
L'Orateur tout entier aux lyriques excès
Sans cesse lui vantait l'universel progrès,
Les aises de la vie et l'immense avantage
Qu'aujourd'hui la vapeur offre aux gens en voyage.
L'Ane branle l'oreille et poursuit son chemin;
L'autre, plein de dépit reprend d'un air hautain:
"Quand tu fais quatre pas tu regrettes l'étable.
Moi, j'avance toujours, toujours infatigable...
De la vapeur le souffle emporte les fardeaux
Bien au loin sur les mers et par monts et par vaux:
Une heure et l'on franchit espace sur espace,
Tandis que sur ta maigre et vilaine carcasse
On t'applique à tout pas, ô mon pauvre baudet,
Quelque vigoureux coup de trique ou de fouet."
L'orgueilleux monstre veut qu'à l'instant on l'admire:
Ses naseaux sont en feu, mugissant, en délire,
Il glisse et s'en va, tout fumant, parader
En criant au grison: "Tu n'as qu'à regarder!"
    Mais soudain, à toute vitesse,
    Lançant un aigu sifflement,
    Survient un long train en détresse
    Et tout cède au choc foudroyant:
Voyageurs et colis, et vagons et chaudière
Se heurtant, s'écrasant, roulent dans la poussière;
Enfin bientôt après on n'eut sous les regards
Que des blessés, des morts, et maints débris épars!
Bien que fort peu subtil et de faible sagesse
L'Aliboron se dit, non sans quelque justesse:
"Où diantre est le profit de si fort se hâter,
Pour qu'à moitié chemin tout aille culbuter?

The Jackass and the Locomotive

A jackass, long in tooth and wracked with pain—
Back bowed beneath a heavy sack of grain,
Striped with the welt of many a cudgel-blow
Against his doughty hide—with head hung low,
Heavy of hoof, was trudging toward the mill;
When suddenly he stops, agape, stock-still:
There, in his path, there stands a monstrous mass—
A shapeless block of iron, copper, brass...
A raucous locomotive, who, on seeing
Our rustic ass perplexed at such a being,
Regales him with his own preeminence,
Praising with lyrical grandiloquence
The progress of the age, *ad tedium;*
Heaping his flatulent encomium
Upon that godsend, steam: that splendidest
Of boons to man the traveler! Unimpressed,
The jackass gives his ear a twitch, moves on
About his arduous business... Whereupon
The locomotive, piqued at his disdain,
In haughtiest tones, addresses him again:
"You feeble beast! Best never leave your stable!
You tire so soon. Yet, clearly, I am able,
Ever undaunted, to pursue my course.
The breath of steam, poor ninny, is the force
That moves man's burdens far and wide. One hour,
And space—vast space—is conquered, while you cower,
Toiling, beneath the whip, vile skin and bones!"
Nostrils aflame, our braggart snorts, grunts, groans...
And, huffing, puffing clouds of smoke: "Heave ho! You
Want to see proof, my friend? Well, watch! I'll show you!"
    And off he hove. Next moment, lo!
    A train comes hurtling toward him... Faster...
    Out of control... Shrill whistles blow,
    To no avail... Result? Disaster!
Metal rips into metal. Flashing thunder
Peels from the clash of monsters rent asunder
Spewing the dead, the dying, the debris
Before the ass's eyes. "Dear me, dear me,"
He sighs, simply but to the point. "Who needs to
Trifle with speed if this is what it leads to?
Let them make fun of me. Progress, my hoof!
I may be slow, but I'm disasterproof.

Chacun se rit de moi; mais tout en broutant l'herbe,
Je rumine souvent ce fort ancien proverbe:

    'Chi va piano va sano.
    Chi va sano va lontano.' "

Often, as I graze peaceably, I hear
A wise old saying ringing in my ear:

    'Steady, steady, pace by pace...
    Slow and easy wins the race.' "[1]

1. The moral of the original is a well-known Italian proverb. As for the subject of the fable, Thierry-Faletans is by no means the first French man of letters to decry the supposed technological progess represented by the locomotive. A curious parenthesis in Alfred de Vigny's romantic poem, "La Maison du berger," originally published in 1844, was inspired by the first major French train wreck, two years before, in Versailles. Subsequent disasters continued to fuel the reactionary fires of those who saw in the innovation an infernal, untamed monster, an intruder into the pastoral serenity of the pre–Industrial Revolution landscape. (The subject has been perceptively studied in an unpublished paper by Lillian Bulwa, "Creative Ingenuity and the Engine: Esthetic Applications of the Invention of the Locomotive," the abstract of which appears in the *Journal for the Humanities and Technology*. In American letters the corresponding theme is developed in detail by Leo Marx in *The Machine in the Garden: Technology and the Pastoral Ideal in America*. The present fable has at least one immediate antecedent in the literature: the much less dramatic and picturesque "La Locomotive et le Cheval" of the popular fabulist and follower of Saint-Simon, Pierre Lachambeaudie. It is found in his *Œuvres de P. Lachambeaudie. Fables et poèsies*, though I cannot say for certain in which of his half-dozen-or-so previous fable collections, dating from 1839, it first appeared.

Le Chou et les Limaçons

    Au pied d'un Chou de fort belle venue,
(Ils ont quelque renom en la Franche-Comté)
Un limaçon disait: "J'ai faim!... la charité!
    J'ai froid! ma peau, voyez, est nue!"
    Les Choux ont partout le cœur bon,
    C'est connu, le nôtre répond:
    "Montez donc que je vous recueille,
Mettez-vous à l'abri sous ma plus large feuille."
Le fainéant, sans plus se plaindre ou criailler,
    Quitte le sol et monte s'installer,
D'abord modestement sous un pli du feuillage...
    Puis compagnes et compagnons,
      Limaces et Limaçons,
Y viennent gentiment établir leur ménage.
    Enfin par l'exemple alléchés,
D'autres se sont du Chou tout autour accrochés,
Au point, qu'en peu de temps, sous leur poids il succombe,
Troué comme un vieux crible il se dessèche et tombe.

    Le monde est plein de gens
Pareils aux limaçons, mendiants pleins d'audace,
    L'un vous cajole, un autre vous tracasse,
    Pour ne vivre qu'à vos dépens.
    Il faut être bon, non bonasse!

The Cabbage and the Snails

Beneath a cabbage of fine shape and size—
    The kind they grow in Franche-Comté—
A snail bewails his fate: "Pity, I pray,
    My grievous state! I agonize...
I starve... I freeze... Look! See? My skin is bare..."
Now, cabbages have hearts. That piteous prayer
So moves our generous friend that he replies:
    "Come up, poor slug, and let me share
The ample shelter of my leaves." And so
    The snail, ceasing his tale of woe,
Climbs up and settles in. First, modestly,
Indeed... But soon, lo! kith and kin—friends, brothers—
    Follow his lead. Our refugee
      Attracts still others...
      Snails, snails galore...
      And more... And more...
Until our cabbage, nibbled half to death,
Falls in a heap and gasps his final breath.

Beggars abound. Some beg with bonhomie,
    Some brashly importune instead.
Be charitable, yes, but not misled:
    With parasites, better to be
A little hard of heart than soft of head.

Le Ballon Captif

Au-dessus de Paris planait un gros ballon
Suspendu dans les airs, ainsi qu'un acrobate,
Et sur terre attaché, tout comme un hanneton
    Au fil qui le tient par la patte.
    Fier d'un semblant de liberté,
Il oscillait sur place au bon gré de la brise.
    Sans se douter de sa sottisé,
   (Tant il était gonflé de vanité),
Il croyait dominer et la terre et les ondes
Prétendant, de ce point, régenter les Deux-Mondes.
Ainsi que ce ballon maint bourgeois de Paris
Voudrait nous imposer ses pensers, ses écrits!

1. Tying a string to a May bug and playing with its freedom was a favorite pastime among French children of the nineteenth century. That it continued well into the twentieth is evidenced by a detailed description in one of the whimsical *Fables* of Franc-Nohain (see pp. 188–90), "Le Hanneton" (II, 21): "Par sa patte est lié notre coléop-tère, / Par la patte ou bien par le col; / On l'invite à prendre son vol; / Puis, pour le ramener au sol, / On tire sur le fil: — Hop! terre!... — / (Est-ce de là que vient le nom 'coléoptère'?)" The practice would seem to have died out with the advent of more techno-logically sophisticated playthings.

Vieux et Jeunes Castors

Quelques bons vieux castors, le long d'une eau rapide,
Reparaient une digue, œuvre du temps jadis,
Un travail à la fois pittoresque et solide;
    D'autres castors, jeunes, grands étourdis,
     Parcourant le pays,
Critiquaient, à qui mieux, cet ancien édifice
Exigeant que soudain on le leur démolisse.
Parmi la jeune bande, un moderne pédant,
    Sourd au Divin Commandement,
     Qui prescrit à tous les êtres
     De respecter leurs ancêtres,
S'écrie: "Est-il permis en ce temps de progrès
   D'échafauder des travaux ainsi faits!
Allons qu'on jette à bas cette vieille masure
Sans ornement doré, sans la moindre moulure."
Aussitôt fait que dit... Quelques anciens castors,
Par les jeunes séduits, secondent les efforts
De ceux-ci. Puis, l'on dresse une digue nouvelle,
    Du dernier goût un pur modèle:
    Chacun, sans être né malin,
    Eut pu juger l'œuvre d'avance,
     Car elle avait l'apparence,
     Et surtout la consistance
     D'un beau mur en biscotin.
     Aussi, lors d'un gros orage,
    Ce travail, à peine achevé,
    Fut par les courants enlevé
     Comme un léger coquillage!

    En ce Temps de démolisseurs,
  Nos monuments, nos principes, nos mœurs,
Tout enfin est léger, factice et rien n'est stable;
    Aussi les nouveaux bâtisseurs
Par trop souvent, je crains, travaillent sur le sable!

The Captive Balloon

In midair over Paris, hovering,
A great balloon—huge vehicle pneumatic—
    Flutters in posture acrobatic,
    Tethered like May bug on a string.[1]
Proud of his liberty illusory,
He wafts with every billow, to and fro.
    Puffed up with pompous vanity
    And vapid braggadocio,
He thinks he lords it over sea and land—
Old World and New bowing to his command...
So too our bourgeoisie—vain, fatuous—
That dares to dictate to the likes of us!

The Old and Young Beavers

A band of beavers, venerable-aged,
    But no less worthy souls, perforce,
By river's edge were busily engaged
Mending a dam athwart the rapid course—
A fine old dam, well made and well maintained.
    Meanwhile, another beaver-band,
     Roaming the land—
    Modern young critics, scatterbrained—
Stood by, demanding that it be straightway
Destroyed, this "relic of a bygone day."
One of our dandies, clearly unaffected
    By the commandment specifying
    That ancestors should be respected,
    Brashly harangues his elders, crying:
"What? In this age of progress you permit
A wreck like that to stand? Down! Down with it!
How dull! How bland! How graceless, utterly!"
Alas, they listen to his rash decree—
Even some elders, easily beguiled—
And down it comes, only to be replaced
    By quite another, modern-styled:
    A tribute to the current taste—
Or lack thereof, as any eye can tell—
    And, even worse, ill built as well.
     At length, one stormy day,
     The waters rise and swell,
     And sweep the dam away
     Like fragile cockleshell.

    O empty age of base excess!
Destruction reigns. Nothing is left to stand:
Monuments, morals, man's highmindedness...
    And those who build anew? Ah, yes,
They build their bastions in the shifting sand!

L'Enfant Curieux

Un Enfant de savoir avide,
Voulant trouver l'âme de son tambour,
Le crêve et le met tout à jour;
Qu'y trouva-t-il?... Le vide!

Que de savants chercheurs, en voulant sonder Dieu,
Y perdent grec, latin et leur dernier cheveu!

1. While much pithier, and characteristically religious in its implications, Thierry-Faletans's fable recalls at least half the scenario of

The Curious Child

A youngster, in his eagerness
To find the soul that gave his drum its sound,
Slashed it... broke it apart... and found?
Nothing!... Nothing. No more, no less.

Let scholars who would plumb God's ways beware:
They'll wrack their brains... and only lose their hair![1]

Jauffret's "The Drum and the Rose" (pp. 133–34), though there is no
evidence of direct influence.

L'Eléphant et le Ciron

Un Ciron, qui vivait aux pieds d'un Eléphant,
Eut voulu pour le moins égaler le géant;
Que fait-il? Il gravit tant et si bien au faîte
De l'énorme occiput, sans que rien ne l'arrête,
Qu'il se croit bientôt
Du sage et fin colosse un pareil en puissance.
N'était-ce pas de la démence?
En effet le voilà tout-à-coup bien penaud:
L'Eléphant contre un mur, s'étant frotté la tête,
Fit choir à son insu, l'imperceptible bête!

De même rampe, arrive et tombe plus d'un sot!

The Elephant and the Mite

An elephant has, living at his feet,
A mite with one ambition: to compete
In grandeur with the pachyderm. And so,
Dauntless, he scales his host; and, lo!
Arrives, at length, atop his occiput,
Perching aloft—aswagger and astrut—
Convinced that height makes might. But all in vain:
The elephant, against the wall,
Rubbing his head—unwittingly, withal—
Tumbles the foolish mite to earth again.

Such is the tale of folly's rise... and fall.

Anonymous ("Un ingénieur en chef honoraire des mines") Fables d'Amérique (1880–81)

FABLES D'AMERIQUE is an intriguing collection. Not only because it presents an almost uniquely American fauna as its dramatis personae—or, rather "dramatis animalia";[1] and not only because it does so in a style, spirit, and form uncharacteristically free of any of that La Fontaine influence so pervasive among the master's many followers. It is especially intriguing—and frustrating for the literary researcher—because of the seemingly determined anonymity of its author, who identifies himself on the title page merely as "un ingénieur en chef honoraire des mines," and who indicates, if we are to believe him, that his fables were composed in the years 1880 and 1881, on location: "là-bas, dans les deux Amériques," according to a six-line dedication to a no-more-easily identifiable "petit Paul."[2] To compound the enigma, even the identity of the illustrator is nowhere acknowledged, although scrutiny reveals the witty pen-and-ink sketches to be the work of Auguste Vimar, distinguished sculptor and painter of the period, who was to gain considerable celebrity as an animal illustrator.[3]

If we look to Vimar's collaborators for clues, we find at least three who, for a variety of reasons, suggest themselves as possible candidates for authorship of our collection: Eugène Mouton (1823–1902), Léo Claretie (1862–1924), and one Paul Guigou (1865–96).[4] But no one of them stands out as a really likely prospect. Several of Mouton's works do reveal a fascination with both distant adventure and exotic fauna. (See, for example, *Voyages et aventures du capitaine Marius Cougourdan,* among others.) And animals are at the heart of his capriciously philosophical *Zoölogie morale.* If he was, however, a writer of elegant prose, Mouton does not seem, as far as

I can determine, to have written any significant verse. A more persuasive case might, at first glance, be made for the multitalented and prolific Claretie—nephew of the even more prolific Jules Claretie—who was not only an admirer and commentator of the eighteenth-century fabulist Florian and coauthor of a play in verse, but who also traveled extensively throughout the American West.[5] Persuasive, that is, save for the fact that in 1880 and 1881, years when these fables were supposedly being composed, Claretie was still a mere schoolboy. (See Petrus Durel, *Léo Claretie, biographie critique*, p. 9.) As for Guigou, the only authentic poet of the three, it is, indeed, tempting to see striking similarities between the many animal verses that punctuate *L'Arche de Noë* and some of the fables in our anonymous collection, published at about the same time as both of Vimar's collaborations with him. Unfortunately, the consumptive poet, who was to die a premature death, was even younger than Claretie during the years in question.[6] In short, none of Vimar's three collaborators mentioned would seem to be our retiring author.[7] And of course, no one of them appears to have been a mining engineer, "honoraire" or otherwise.

Now, at this point, if we are to believe that self-description, we might be led to an admittedly farfetched fourth conjecture; to wit, that the epithet "ingénieur en chef des mines," conferred honorarily, is in fact a humorously self-serving play on words. Besides being mineral deposits, *mines,* in French, are also pencil leads. Could it be that Vimar was not only the anonymous illustrator but the anonymous author as well? The importance of his role in the collection is, in fact, underscored by a sketch on the volume's half-title page representing a pipe-smoking chimpanzee loping along with a large book under his arm, entitled *Etudes sur l'homme* and signed with a barely decipherable "A. Vimar";[8] an A. Vimar, however, who, for some curious reason, would take no formal credit for his artwork. Furthermore, *Fables d'Amérique* would not be the only volume of his illustrations to which Vimar the artist would also provide text.[9] Unfortunately for the hypothesis, however, none of the others I have been able to consult is in verse. Vimar's prose, all the same, is elegant and subtle enough not to preclude poetic talent. But what of the supposed yearlong sojourn in the Americas? And who was "le petit Paul" of the dedication? Might there be any connection between him and one Paul Pouvillon, to whom Guigou and Vimar's *L'Arche de Noë* would subsequently be dedicated? Could "le petit Paul" even be the childlike Guigou himself, fourteen years Vimar's junior?... Many questions, but few definite answers. Available details of Vimar's career are too slim to yield firm conclusions.[10]

And so the enigma remains, teasing us with partial hints and dead-end suggestions, but obstinately protecting the author's anonymity. Was he really no more than some obscure mining engineer who, years after a stay in the Americas, published a collection of original fables, probably for the delectation of none but friends and family, and to which the up-and-coming Auguste Vimar lent—or, possibly, sold—his participation?"[11] Perhaps. Be that as it may, the most tantalizing question of all is why the author, whoever he was—even a literary nobody—was so zealously self-effacing. The twenty-four colorful, gracefully turned, and technically impeccable fables, arranged in four groups of six, or *sixains,* would do any professional man of letters proud. They surely deserve a better fate than the obscurity to which their reticent author and almost as reticent illustrator seem to have wanted to consign them.

The three fables translated here are numbers 2, 3, and 5 of the first *sixain.*

1. The American landscape and typically American animals do figure from time to time in earlier fable literature. In addition to a few passing references in La Fontaine, see, for example, in this volume, Houdar de La Motte's "Le Mocqueur" (pp. 65–66) and Viennet's "Le Huron et le Baromètre" (pp. 146–47). To my knowledge, however, this collection is the first to devote itself almost exclusively to them.

2. The work is published too late to figure in Gustave Brunet's reedition of A.-A. Barbier's comprehensive *Dictionnaire des ouvrages anonymes* or J.-M. Quérard's *Supercheries littéraires dévoilées,* including his supplement to both works. It does not appear either in Enrico Celani's "Additions et corrections au *Dictionnaire des anonymes* de Barbier." Furthermore, there is no reference whatever to the work in D. Jordell's continuation of the Otto Lorenz trade catalogue, *Catalogue général de la librairie française,* nor is it registered for copyright in the Library of Congress. (If it were, the name of the assignee might at least offer a clue to the author's identity.)

3. Nicolas-Stanislas-Auguste Vimar (1851–1916), besides contributing to many journals of the period, was the illustrator of numerous collections, among them the fables of La Fontaine and Florian.

4. In the years surrounding publication of *Fables d'Amérique* Vimar illustrated the following works by these authors: Mouton, *Les Vertus et les grâces des bêtes;* Claretie, *L'Oie du Capitole;* Guigou, *L'Arche de Noë* and *L'Illustre dompteur.*

5. Claretie devoted an early study to Florian's work, entitled simply *Florian.* His play, *Le Prêcheur converti,* one act, written with Henri Potez for the annual Molière celebration, was performed at the Théâtre de l'Odéon and subsequently published. His travels were to produce a number of documentary and fictional works about the Far West, among them *Feuilles de route aux Etats-Unis, La Vallée fumante,* and *Les Héros de la Yellowstone.*

6. See the posthumous collection of Guigou's work, *Interrupta,* preface by François Coppée.

7. Another collaborator, Henri Signoret, published two animal works with Vimar. But *Le Mardi Gras des animaux* and *La Légende des bêtes,* as well as his own earlier work *Les Noces fantastiques,* were all in prose.

8. Vimar seems to have had a particular liking for the smoking-ape motif. For another example, see *Le Boy de Marius Bouillabès* (cited below), p. 3. It was apparently inspired by an actual trained chimpanzee named "Consul," celebrated for his tricks in turn-of-the-century Paris.

9. Others include the following: *L'Automobile Vimar; A, B, C, D. La Ménagerie de Bébé; La Poule à poils; Les Maris de Mlle Nounouche: histoire de chats; Le Boy de Marius Bouillabès; Clown.*

10. Vimar himself had three sons. None of them, however, was named "Paul." (See *Qui êtes-vous? Annuaire des contemporains,* vol. 1908, pp. 480–81. Further important biographical details would certainly be available in J. Silbert, *Auguste Vimar, artiste, peintre,* cited in

the encyclopedic Thieme-Becker *Künstler Lexikon,* vol. 34, but which I have been unable to locate.

II. The volume of *Fables d'Amérique* which I have consulted, owned by the Library of Congress, states in its front matter that two hundred numbered copies were printed and not intended for sale. It does not indicate, however, whether these were the only copies printed, or whether they were printed in addition to a regular commercial press run. I suspect the former, since, as I have said, there is no record of publication in the *Catalogue Général de la librairie française.*

Le Chien du Bord et le Racoun

A bord d'un paquebot revenant d'Amérique
    Se lièrent deux animaux:
L'un n'était qu'un vulgaire animal domestique,
    L'ami choyé des matelots,
Un Chien terrier faisant aux rats du bord la chasse,
    L'autre un Racoun, singe ou renard,
Je ne sais pas au juste en quel genre on le classe,
    Mais en tout cas un fier roublard.[1]
"Fi! que c'est laid!" disait à son ami vorace,
    Le Racoun, gourmet délicat;
"Vous vous précipitez sur n'importe qui passe,
    Quêtant la desserte des plats:
Gâteaux, rosbif, poisson, et les plus sales choses
    Disparaissent d'un coup de dent.
Je suis plus raffiné; tout ne sent pas les roses
    A votre bord, et franchement
Si je n'avais pour moi ce beau baquet d'eau claire,
    Pour laver tous mes aliments
Avant de les goûter, je ferais maigre chère!"
    "Parfait! à votre aise, l'ami!
Pour un enfant des bois vous êtes difficile;
    Vous ne faites rien à demi
Trempez! lavez! vous êtes plus tranquille,
    Mais vous perdez beaucoup de temps.
Moi, j'aime mieux bâfrer! Justement voici l'heure
    Où passagers du bâtiment
Sortent de leur repas, et ce n'est pas un leurre
    Que d'espérer bon coup de dent."

La troupe des dîneurs s'amusait d'habitude
    Des façons de maître renard,
Quand de ses mains de singe il commençait l'étude
    Des morceaux jetés au hasard,
Tournant et retournant, et lavant à l'eau claire
    Ces mets la plupart inconnus,
Pendant que le terrier, connaissant son affaire,
    Goulûment se jetait dessus.
Or ce jour-là, parmi toute la victuaille,
    Les deux amis prirent d'assaut.
Racoun un peu de sucre, et Chien, vaille que vaille
    Pour sa part un os de gigot:

Dans l'eau fondit le sucre en faisant la baignade,
Dans le gosier du chien l'os en travers se mit,
Et vous voyez comment, pour chaque camarade,
    Sa gourmandise le punit.

The Ship's Dog and the Raccoon

A pair of animals on board a ship
    Bound from America became
The fastest friends during their lengthy trip.
    One was a pet—domestic, tame—
A terrier who kept the ship rat-free.
    The other, a "raccoon" by name—
Part fox, part monkey, seemingly.
    (Although I wouldn't make that claim
For sure...) At any rate, a crafty cuss.
    What's more, a delicate gourmet.
"For shame!" he teased the dog. "How gluttonous!
    You eat whatever comes your way.
Any old slop from anybody's dish
    Gets grabbed and grubbed and gobbled up,
No matter what! Roast beef, sweetmeats, cakes, fish...
    Frankly, my none-too-fragrant pup,
My tastes are far less crass, far more refined.
    I wash my food before I sup.[2]
If not, it's clear: I fear I'd be inclined
    To eat a rather meager diet!"
"That's well and good, my friend," the dog opined.
    "You're elegant... I don't deny it...
Perhaps too much so, I might add, for one
    Born in the wild. Well, wash, fuss, fret...
Myself, I'll eat my fill. It's lots more fun
    Than all your proper etiquette!
Listen! I think their dinner's almost done...
    Just wait and see the meal I get!"

In fact, each day, with giggle and guffaw,
    The diners throw their scraps and bits,
Watching as the raccoon, with foxlike paw
    And monkeylike attention, sagely sits
Studying, eyeing every morsel fine,
    Washing it first before he eats,
While, less fastidious, our bold canine
    Gorges and gluts on tasty treats.
Now then, what sumptuous victuals will our pair
    Pounce on today to make their own?
Raccoon, a sugar-lump *extraordinaire;*[3]
    And terrier, a mutton-bone.

The sugar, washed with care, melts in a trice.
The bone sticks in the terrier's throat. And thus
Each in his own way has to pay the price
    That gluttony demands of us.

1. Rather than call the unfamiliar animal by its French designation, *raton laveur* (literally "washing rat"), the author opts for local color and uses a transliteration of its English name. As early as the 1750s, the famous French naturalist Buffon had compared the indigenous American mammal not to the monkey but, like our author, to the fox (as well as to the badger and wildcat): "Le raton... était à peu près de la grosseur du blaireau, et même il ressemblait en quelque façon à cet animal par la forme du corps, mais il en différait en ce qu'il avait le museau mince et effilé comme celui du renard... La tête était de la même grosseur que celle du renard... la queue ressemblait à celle du chat sauvage." (Georges-Louis Leclerc, comte de Buffon, *Œuvres complètes*, XX:387.)

2. Romanticized popular belief notwithstanding, Buffon observes that the raccoon's habit of "washing"—or rather "soaking"—its food has little to do with hygiene (p. 388).

3. Buffon also attests to the raccoon's fondness for sugar: "il était fort avide de lait, de crême, de sucre, et de tout ce qui était confit au sucre" (p. 389).

La Baleine et le Poisson-Volant

Sur les flots bleus de la mer du Tropique
On voit filer une flèche d'argent,
Petit Poisson qui dans la vague pique
En s'élevant hors de son élément.

Parfois aussi sur cette mer profonde,
Une Baleine, un vrai léviathan,
D'un jet brillant raye l'azur de l'onde,
En soufflant l'eau par son énorme évent.

Petit Poisson à l'écaille bleutée
Qui follement t'aventures dans l'air.
En agitant ta nageoire argentée
Où le soleil met des rayons d'or clair,

Tu te moquais de cette grosse mère,
Noire et pesante, à l'énorme museau,
Flottante épave, en lui disant: "Ma chère!
Vraiment ton sort ne me semble pas beau.

Je suis poisson, mais quelquefois je vole,
Pour mon plaisir faisant ainsi l'oiseau,
En freluquet, et je change de rôle,
Tu n'es toujours qu'un gros poisson dans l'eau!"

Et ce disant le petit téméraire
Passait et repassait au ras de l'eau,

The Whale and the Flying Fish

Up from the waters of the southern sea,
Piercing the calm blue in a sudden flash,
Dartlike, a flying fish, effortlessly,
Leaps from its habitat with silver splash.

Another beast, a whale—or rather say
"Leviathan"—coursing the deeps as well,
At times will spout his jet of sparkling spray
Over the azure of the ocean's swell.

Ah! Little fish, you of the silvery scale...
What folly for the likes of you to try
To fly on trembling fin and fluttering tail,
A-glint against the sun-resplendent sky!

You mock the huge black hulk, snub-snouted mass
Of mighty flotsam, twitting her: "Madame,
Fate dealt a dreary lot to you, alas!
Most ill-begotten beast that ever swam!

"Myself, I'm just a foolish fish. That's true...
But I can vie with birds, at times, and fly,
To my delight. That's more than you can do.
A fish you are, and fish you'll live and die."

With that, our featherbrain, his talent vaunting,
Leaping, vaults in and out, and round about

Tout en narguant la grosse débonnaire
Et lui frôlant de très près le museau.

Elle bâilla, décrochant sa mâchoire,
L'étourneau fut gobé par son fanon:
C'est souvent le sort que garde l'histoire
A celui qui n'est ni chair ni poisson.

La Grive et le Faucon Se Rencontrant
en Pleine Mer

Pauvre petit oiseau battu par la tempête,
Tu ne peux d'un coup d'aile ainsi que la mouette
    Lutter contre le vent,
Ni sur les flots comme elle aller à la dérive,
Et ton vol est heurté, pauvre petite Grive,
    Jouet de l'ouragan!

Et la terre est bien loin, et la mer est immense!
Mais tu voles plus fort, reprise d'espérance:
    Tu vois un bâtiment;
Tu t'abats, pantelante, aux vergues de misaine,
Espérant que l'esquif vers le port te ramène,
    Poussé par un bon vent.

Mais, ô terreur! déjà la place est envahie;
Un féroce ennemi longtemps l'a poursuivie;
    Un Faucon pèlerin
Erre aussi sur la mer, effrayante vigie,
Porté par la bourrasque, et du sort l'ironie
    En a fait ton voisin.

Cependant, ne crains rien, sa serre frémissante
Sur le bois du vaisseau s'incruste d'épouvante,
    Et son bec de chasseur,
Son bec crochu, dompté par l'effet de la houle,
N'a plus de cris affreux, mais tendrement roucoule:
    "Faisons la paix, ma sœur?"

Spectacle curieux! Le bourreau, la victime,
Aile à aile serrés, paraissent deux intimes.
    Telle était leur frayeur
Qu'un mousse put grimper jusques à leur refuge
Sans les faire envoler; il les prit, et l'on juge
    S'il fut content, cet oiseleur!

La même cage alors abrita ces deux hôtes,
Et pendant quelques jours vécurent côte à côte
    La Grive et le Faucon;
Mais arrivant au port, à peine sur la terre
Le Faucon au gros bec, à la puissante serre,
    Croqua son compagnon:

Un instant le péril fait taire la rancune,
    Faibles et forts peuvent paraître unis,
Mais c'est avec les dents vouloir prendre la lune
    Que croire aux serments de nos ennemis.

The easygoing giant, tweaking, taunting...
Closer and closer to her monstrous snout.

One yawn, and suddenly our friend—the late!—
Is gobbled up in gaping jaw and jowl.
History tells us that's a common fate
For creatures that are neither fish nor fowl.

The Thrush and the Falcon
Who Met at Sea

Poor little bird, gust-swept aloft despite
Your struggling wings! I watch your fruitless flight
    And muse: "Indeed, no seagull he!
Poor little thrush! The wind makes sport of him,
And turns his every effort to its whim,
    Helpless above the stormy sea."

How vast the waters and how far the shore!
Now, flying as no thrush has flown before,
    Spying salvation near at hand—
A boat!—breathless, heart high, battling the gale,
You ply the air and light upon a sail,
    Hoping she'll lead you straight to land.

But oh!... In sudden fright you gaze aghast:
There, lookout-like, perched on that very mast,
    A peregrine! A merciless,
Fierce falcon, tempest-tossed and lost, like you!...
What irony, that fate should make you two
    Companions in the same distress!

And yet, you're safe. The falcon's frantic claw,
Quivering on the mast, inspires no awe,
    Dug in the wood, clutching it fast;
And from his hook-sharp beak, storm-tamed with fear,
You'll only hear him coo and sigh: "My dear,
    Time you and I made friends at last."

A curious sight! There, wing by wing, two foes—
Predator and his prey—caught in the throes
    Of panic, such that, wily-wise,
A sailor climbs the rigging, unsuspected,
Pounces, captures the couple, unprotected,
    And makes off, happy with his prize.

He puts them in a single cage together.
For days they live in peace, feather to feather,
    Little thrush, giant peregrine...
But boats reach port, and tempests pass their peak:
On land, our falcon, cruel of claw and beak,
    Turns on his "friend" and does him in.

    A common danger, for a spell,
May quell the fray betwixt the weak and strong;
    But it's a freezing day in hell
When you can trust your enemy for long.

Pamphile LeMay   Fables Canadiennes (1881–1903)

[Léon-] Pamphile LeMay[1] (1837–1918)—poet, novelist, playwright, translator—while not accorded unqualified admiration by present-day historians of French-Canadian literature, was nonetheless admired during his lifetime as a major figure in the literary life of Québec. For one critic he ranked with Octave Crémazie (1827–79) and Louis-Honoré Fréchette (1839–1908) in the triumvirate of leading Victorian poets. (See Berthelot Brunet, *Histoire de la littérature canadienne-française,* p. 72.) While some critics are less sanguine, most acknowledge in his work—especially in his last collection of sonnets, *Les Gouttelettes*—a simple sincerity and rustic emotion that lighten the predominantly didactic and religious character of his writings.

Born in Lotbinière, Québec, LeMay studied for the priesthood at the seminary of the University of Ottawa, but was obliged by fragile health to abandon the religious calling. With a degree in law, and admitted to the bar in 1865, he worked as a parliamentary translator in the federal capital, and was subsequently appointed librarian of the Québec legislature. LeMay was a founding member of the Royal Society of Canada, and was recognized for his contribution to French-Canadian letters with an honorary degree from Université Laval. He was also decorated by the French government as an Officier de L'Instruction Publique.

Most of LeMay's writing reflects not only his staunch morality but also his patriotic inspiration, from his early *Essais poétiques*—including a translation of Longfellow's *Evangeline*[2]—to his best-known prose work, the collection of popular pseudohistorical tales, *Contes vrais.* LeMay spent most of his latter years in semiretirement, far removed from the mainstream of Québec literary life, scrupulously revising many of his earlier works and, especially, devoting himself to his family of fifteen children and many grandchildren.[3]

One can suppose, indeed, that—perhaps like his distant predecessor Philibert Guide (see pp. 25–26)—it was his rather demanding role as a parent that prompted LeMay to try his hand at the writing of fables; moral exempla useful in rearing his numerous offspring. His *Fables canadiennes* (1881)[4] were immensely popular with readers of their day, if not always with the critics;[5] but their often humorless didacticism, and especially their sometimes ponderous religiosity, deprive them of the subtlety that most readers today expect to find in the genre. Characteristically, LeMay performed an extensive revision on his fables, bringing out a second edition a decade after the first (1891), radically altering many, rearranging their order completely, and reducing their number from an original 105 (equally divided into five books) to 100. A third edition was also published (1903), as well as a posthumous fourth (1925), substantially reedited by the publishers.

Less turgid and more engaging than many of the fables in LeMay's collection, the ones translated here are the following numbers in the edition of 1881 (and 1882): II, 17; III, 13; and IV, 21.

---

1. There is considerable variety in the way the author's name is presented. He is frequently referred to as "L. Pamphile LeMay," and his surname is often spelled "Lemay" or "Le May."

2. A revision of this translation was later published separately (1870), and appeared again in *Evangéline et autres poèmes de Longfellow.*

3. For a discussion of LeMay and his work, see the article by Barbara Godard in William Toye, ed., *The Oxford Companion to Canadian Literature,* pp. 444–45. For a detailed bibliographical study, see John Ellis Hare, "A Bibliography of the Works of Léon Pamphile Lemay (1837–1918)."

4. A second identical printing of the same edition, from the following year, is incorrectly cited by many sources as the first.

5. Charles ab der Halden, for example, while admiring LeMay's "courage" in composing fables after La Fontaine, and recognizing their "bon sens pratique," gives the *Fables canadiennes* rather short shrift in his *Nouvelles Etudes de littérature canadienne-française,* lamenting that "la naïveté du premier âge n'habite plus, hélas, dans nos cœurs" (p. 271).

Le Singe Monté sur des Echasses

Un singe de courte stature,
Mais de grandes prétentions,
Gardait rancune à la nature
De son manque d'attentions
Et cherchait toujours dans sa tête
Le bon moyen de s'élever.

"Je l'ai!" dit-il un jour, "je l'ai! que je suis bête
    De si longtemps rêver!...
C'est bien simple: je vais monter sur des échasses.

The Ape on Stilts[1]

An ape of rather modest size,
But no less grandiose pretensions,
Scores nature for his small dimensions—
Rankling at her neglect—and tries
Unceasingly to find some way
In which he might, indeed, look tall.

At length he cries "Eureka!" one fine day.
    "I'll get a pair of stilts, that's all!
How stupid that I had to think so long!...

Mais il est un danger, je crois:
Sous mes petites jambes grasses
On verra mes jambes de bois.
Bah! j'ai de bons amis qui, moyennant salaire,
Pour cacher ce beau truc se tiendront près de moi.
Ils vanteront ma taille et mon bras musculaire,
    Et moi je me tiendrai bien coi."

    L'idée était originale
Et le singe orgueilleux en sut tirer profit.
    Il trouva l'amitié vénale
      Qui le bouffit.

Lorsque l'on vous dira qu'un homme vous surpasse
Et que devant son nom tout nom s'anéantit,
Regardez avec soin au tour de passe-passe,
Car tel qui paraît grand est parfois bien petit.

Of course, there's only one thing wrong:
If someone looks, they're bound to see
I'm perching on two sticks of wood!...
Oh well, no problem! I've got friends... My money's good...
I'll pay them well to come press close to me,
And hide the hoax—and praise my strength!—while I,
Majestically, stand idly by."

    Novel idea, you must admit!
Our pompous ape would make the most of it:
    Friends puffed his praises, as he thought...
      Dearly bought.

When one extols some mortal's claim to fame,
As if all names must fade before his name,
Beware a subterfuge: as you've surmised,
Often the great are just the small disguised.

1. Nothwithstanding the author's probable preference, I have chosen to translate the version in the original edition of 1881 (and 1882), rather than the substantially shortened version in the edition of 1891.

The latter sacrifices picturesqueness to brevity, to the detriment of the fable.

La Limace et le Rosier

Traînant avec lenteur sa glutineuse masse,
    Une limace
    Vient se coller sur un rosier,
    Et, dans sa turpitude,
    Prenant une fière attitude,
    Lui crie à plein gosier:

"Un beau rosier, vraiment, qui n'a que des épines
    Et quelques feuilles sans couleurs!
Dis donc, l'ami, quand on est sans fruits et sans fleurs
    On ne craint guère les rapines;
    On fait l'important néanmoins...
Tu ne veux point parler? Ne vois-tu pas, au moins,
    Que je te souille?
    Allons! grouille;
    N'as-tu pas de souci?
    Chasse-moi, si tu l'oses,
    Ou demande merci."

    Le rosier, entr'ouvrant ses roses,
    Lui dit:

    "Tes insolents discours
Ne nous empêchent pas, moi de fleurir toujours
    Et toi, pauvre grossière,
    De te traîner dans la poussière."

    Derrière le nuage épais
    Souvent un beau soleil se joue...
L'envie à la vertu jette parfois la boue,
La vertu cependant plane sur elle en paix.

The Slug and the Rosebush[1]

Slowly dragging along his slimy mass,
    A slug
    Clings to a rosebush. There, the crass
    And vile invader, in his smug
And proudest tone, lets loose a diatribe
    Of jeer and jibe:

"My, my! Aren't you the fancy bush! How sick you
Look, with a few drab leaves... All thorns... So bare...
No danger any thieving hand will pick you!
No flowers, no fruits... Yet, still, that haughty air!...
    What? No reply?...
    How can you bear to be
    Fouled by the likes of me!...
    My, my!
    Go on! Go on!
    Try to get rid of me, I dare you!
    Or beg me... Yes, beg me to spare you!"

    Whereupon
The bush, beginning now to flower, replies:

    "Mock and despise
    Me all you like. In time—you must
Admit—my person blooms and beautifies,
While yours, poor wretch, goes groveling in the dust."

The sun is still the sun, despite the cloud.
Let envy sling its mud at virtue: teased and taunted,
    Virtue is virtue—calm, unbowed—
And looks down from on high, proud and undaunted.

1. As in the preceding fable, I have opted for the earlier of LeMay's two versions, and for the same reason.

L'Oiseau-Mouche et le Chêne

Un petit oiseau-mouche aux deux ailes d'ébène,
    A la gorge de pourpre et d'or,
    Prenant dans les airs son essor,
Vint s'abattre, joyeux, sur la cime d'un chêne.
Dans le même moment un grand souffle passa,
    Précurseur de l'orage,
    Qui saisit avec rage
L'arbre superbe et le cassa.
L'oiseau, tout étonné, rouvrit son aile vive
    Avec un gai bourdonnement,
    Et s'écria naïvement:

"Je regrette, crois-moi, le malheur qui t'arrive
    Un peu par ma témérité...
    Je sais qu'il n'est pas mérité.
Avant que de venir me percher sur ta cime
        Qui s'abîme,
    J'aurais dû me douter
    Que tu ne pouvais me porter."

    Plus d'un, comme cet oiseau-mouche,
    Pense écraser tout ce qu'il touche
    Qui n'a de grand, en vérité,
    Que son extrême vanité.

The Hummingbird and the Oak

A hummingbird of gold and crimson breast
        And jet-black wing
    Flew skyward, gaily flittering,
        And came to rest
Upon an oak, just as a mighty gust
Attacked the tree, tearing him limb from limb,
        And toppling him
        Down in the dust.
    The hummingbird, astonished, spread
        His wings, abuzz,
    And then, naively, said:

"Apologies for what my daring does!
    You don't deserve this fate. Perhaps
    I should have found a stronger tree,
    One that could bear the likes of me
        And not collapse.
    I never should have landed on you
    And pressed my heavy weight upon you."

Many there are, possessed of an absurd
Opinion of their power, much like our bird.
In point of fact, their only greatness lies
In vanity of an uncommon size.

Paul Palvadeau   *from* Comptes-rendus de l'Athénée Louisianais (1885)

In recent years the French linguistic and cultural heritage of Louisiana has been undergoing something of a renaissance. Not that it was ever dead, to be sure; only sightly moribund and generally ignored, if not disdained, by those not a part of it. That tradition—a *pot pourri* of original pre–Louisiana Purchase French influence and that of the migrating Acadians ("Cajuns") from Canada, appropriately peppered with francophone Black folklore from the Caribbean—was stubbornly and vigorously kept alive by devoted individuals and organizations. Foremost among the latter has been the Athénée Louisianais, founded in New Orleans in 1876 and fostered by such prominent literati as Alcée Fortier, Edgar Grima, and Jules Choppin, to name only a trio of the many. For over a century it has remained the focal point of that culture, as reflected in the pages of its *Comptes-rendus,* presenting not only the organization's proceedings, but, more importantly, a diverse variety of articles, plays, and poetry of both "French French" and local French inspiration and interest.

Sprinkled among the pages of these *Comptes-rendus de l'Athénée Louisianais* are, not surprisingly, a good many verse fables, traditional in form, and in both the literary language and the Creole patois.[1] The number for May 1, 1885, offers a pair by an otherwise-unknown poet, one Paul Palvadeau (pp. 164–65), the first of which, the picturesque "Le Chêne et Sa Mousse," is translated here.

---

1. Several of these have been collected, along with other relevant material, by Gérard Labarre St. Martin and Jacqueline Voorhies, in their volume *Ecrits louisianais du dix-neuvième siècle.*

Le Chêne et Sa Mousse

    Un enfant, au pied d'un gros chêne
Dont la barbe flottante environnait le tronc,
      Dit à son père: "Pourquoi donc
      Cet arbre a-t-il cette vilaine
          Laine?"
Son papa répondit, pour le tirer de peine:
"C'est par un sol humide et chargé de vapeurs,
      Vois-tu! mon fils, que cette mousse
          Pousse.
      Il n'en vient point sur les hauteurs."

Ainsi la basse Envie acharnée au Mérite,
Toujours s'y cramponnant, cherche à l'embarrasser,
        Le rabaisser,
        Le terrasser.
Souvent l'arbre grandit malgré son parasite.

     1. The reader will no doubt appreciate that the moss evoked in Palvadeau's tableau is the so-called Spanish moss so characteristic of the bayou country.

The Oak and Its Moss

    Beside an oak of towering size,
Whose trunk stood under billowing beards of moss,
    A child looked up with wondering eyes
      And asked, quite at a loss:
    "Papa, why is this tree so full
      Of ugly wool?"[1]
"That 'wool,'" Papa replied, to ease his mind,
    "Grows low, amid the dank morasses'
      Noxious gases.
The higher the tree, my child, the less you find."

So too does lowly Envy, clinging tight,
Beleaguer Merit, try to humble him,
      To tumble him,
      To crumble him...
The oak grows tall, and scorns his parasite.

A. Maltrait   *from* Comptes-rendus de l'Athénée Louisianais (1899)

ANOTHER of the fabulists of the *Comptes-rendus de l'Athénée Louisianais,* A. Maltrait, seems shrouded in rather less biographical uncertainty than his predecessor Paul Palvadeau (see p. 173). Appearing a few times in its pages, he is identified as a "membre correspondant" of the cultural organization; and, assuming that he was, in all likelihood, the same as one "Rév. A. J. Maltrait," he was also the 1897 laureate of its annual writing competition, for an essay entitled "Louis XIV et son siècle." (See the *Comptes-rendus,* May 1, 1898, pp. 278–90.) According to documents provided by Gérard Labarre St. Martin, the prelate-author (whose full name is recorded as Joseph-Auguste-André Maltrait) was born in Brittany on November 30, 1865, served as curé in the southern Louisiana city of Lafayette from 1896 to 1908, and subsequently in the neighboring town of Kaplan, in Vermilion parish, until his retirement in 1921. He died in France, in the town of Saint-Lunaire, near Saint-Malo, on March 20, 1937.

Maltrait's fable "Le Melon" was originally printed in the *Comptes-rendus,* January 1, 1899, p. 403, and is reproduced in St. Martin and Voorhies (*Ecrits louisianais du dix-neuvième siècle,* pp. 203–4). Like Palvadeau's poem, it is really more a brief *conte* than a traditional fable as such, the melon in question being only a "prop" in a human drama rather than a personified actor in it. As St. Martin and Voorhies observe in their introduction, its biting racial theme makes it a work of authentically local inspiration, "une des rares fables originales de Louisiane" (p. xl), as opposed to the many folktales inherited from the Caribbean, originally from Africa and, indeed, probably beyond.

Le Melon

    "Souvent notre méchanceté
      N'est, tout bien compté,
      Qu'une erreur grossière."
    Démontrons cette vérité:
    Un créole avait une melonière
Si belle et riche en fruits, que messieurs ses cochons

The Melon

    The proverb tells us that "our sin
    Is often blunder in disguise."[1]
    There is, I fear, much truth therein,
      As this, our fable, testifies.
A Creole had a melon patch,[2] wherein
So many a melon grew, in such great store,

N'étaient nourris que de melons.
En faisant un matin sa tournée ordinaire,
    Il remarqua par terre
Quelques morceaux d'écorce et des traces de pas.
    Le voilà dans tous ses états,
    Qui s'écrie: "Il faut qu'il périsse,
Le criminel qui vient, au mépris de la loi,
    Me faire l'injustice
    D'entrer la nuit chez moi
Pour gaspiller mon bien!" Alors, suivant l'usage,
    Il soupçonna quelqu'un du voisinage:
    "C'est ce nègre et ses négrillons,"
    Dit-il, "qui mangent mes melons!"
    Et n'écoutant que sa colère,
    Il court de céans chez l'apothicaire
    Acheter du poison;
    (C'était, je crois, de la strichnine,)
    Dont il pique un melon
    De fort belle mine.
    Puis, il se retire en disant:
"Mon gourmand de noiraud peut venir à présent:
    Je lui promets la plus belle colique."
Le voleur vint. Sur lui, le poison fut très fort;
Le faiseur de melons au jour le trouva mort.
    C'était son fils unique!

That monsieur's swine—a fancy lot, indeed—
    For all their feed,
    Feasted on melons, nothing more.
Now, one day, as he makes his morning round,
Monsieur looks down and, scattered on the ground,
    He sees some bits of rind,
    And someone's tracks—before, behind,
    And all about.
"Foul criminal!" our Creole lashes out.
    "Of all the vilest ignominies!...
What? Plunder me by night?... I'll see him hang!...
For sure, it's that old nigger and his gang
    Of pickaninnies!"[3]
(So he suspected, as was customary.)
    Then, furious, off he goes
    Straightway to the apothecary
To buy some poison—strychnine, I suppose...
    He picks a melon, firm and fat,
    And pricks it full. "Well now, that's that!
My darky can come eat his fill!" he crows.
"He'll have himself a proper bellyache,
    My melon thief, make no mistake!"
The felon came. When all was said and done,
Next day, no sooner does monsieur awake,
Than, there... He finds him dead... His only son!

---

1. Although, as the author seems to indicate, his opening lines have a proverbial ring about them—and hence my translation—I find no corroborating proverb in the literature. Perhaps the good prelate is quoting from the Bible. Or, an individual of some poetic culture, he could even be recalling Baudelaire's observation, at the end of his prose poem "La Fausse monnaie," that "le plus irréparable des vices est de faire le mal par bêtise." (Baudelaire's work had first appeared in 1869 and was subsequently incorporated into *Les petits poèmes en prose* [*Le Spleen de Paris*].)

2. Contrary to frequent misconception (and unlike its English equivalent, which often indicates mixed blood), the word "créole" in French, when applied to individuals, always refers, not to Blacks or mulattoes, but to white descendants of Europeans, born in the colony or ex-colony in question. To compound the confusion, the same word applied to language refers to the hybridized patois spoken usually by nonwhites.

3. Until about the middle of the present century, when it was adopted almost as a badge of pride, the French "nègre" was a term of opprobrium.

Rodolphine Young   Fables de La Fontaine Traduites en Créole
Seychellois (ca. 1900)

Though not as well known as the Creole patois of Haiti and the Antilles (see pp. 177–78), the French-based popular language of the island *département* of Réunion, and of France's former Indian Ocean colonies of Ile Maurice (today Mauritius) and the Seychelles, has also produced a vigorous literature. Among its earliest products there figures, not too surprisingly, a slim body of fables, especially those of one L. Héry, whose *Fables créoles* of 1828 (revised and augmented in several editions over the next half-century) was the first work printed on Réunion. (See Alain Armand and Gérard Chopinet, *La Littérature réunionnaise d'expression créole (1828–1982)*, pp.

19–81.) Héry's fables, and those of later compatriot A. Vinson, though in Creole, betray the ever-present canonical mark of La Fontaine, composed in a rather more sophisticated verse than one might expect—metered and rhymed—and seem to have been the result more of folkloric interest than of authentic inspiration.[1]

Quite different in style and spirit is the collection of forty-nine fables composed toward the end of the century by one Rodolphine Young, descendant of the first French settler of the Seychelles, Pierre Hangard, and the first writer of record from that archipelago.[2] Seemingly very freely adapted from La Fontaine into their indigenous environment with all its local color, they are wholly unpretentious. More prosaic than poetic, they lay no claim whatever to literary sophistication, but are no less charming for that in their earthy directness and their disarmingly naive moral intent. A recent study proves quite convincingly, however, that they are, in fact, themselves very close translations of the more literarily felicitous adaptations of the above-mentioned Marbot. (See Robert Chaudenson and Guy Hazaël-Massieux, "Marbot, Sylvain, Young et les autres.") The author's obvious target, whatever her originality (or lack of it), is the native of her islands; and her aim, quite simply, to offer him instruction. She so informs her readers (or listeners?) in her prologue, likewise closely inspired by that of Marbot: "Zott tous, noirs mon bouzois, vini; moin na zistoï pou raconte zott. / Si zott oulé évite çagrin, acoute moi bien." ("Come, all you black bourgeois of mine; I'm going to tell you some stories. / If you want to spare yourself heartache, listen carefully.") The result of learning the lessons well will, quite simply, be Salvation: "Si nous faire ça magnière là, nous capab sîre, / Nous alle dans Paradis l'hère nous a môrt." ("If we act in this way, surely we'll be able / To go to Heaven when we die.")[3]

Rodolphine Young's religious didacticism is not surprising. When she died in 1932 at the age of seventy-two, in the town of Baie Sainte-Anne on Ile Praslin, she had spent most of her long life as a dedicated schoolmistress—one of "cette phalange d'anciennes institutrices, aujourd'hui oubliées, qui au temps où la profession d'institutrice était peu considérée, donc peu rétribuée, se dévouèrent sans compter à la formation des générations de jeunes seychellois" (Young, *Fables de La Fontaine traduites en créole seychellois*, p. 5). Besides her fables, she is known to have composed, typically, a Creole catechism, the manuscript of which, however, is lost.

"La Fille," number 45 of her fables, is based on the second half of La Fontaine's duo of "Le Héron" and "La Fille" (VII, 4 and 5).

---

1. For a discussion of Héry's fables as well as those of a Mauritian predecessor, François Chrestien (*Les Essais d'un bobre africain*), along with comparisons of their work with that of La Fontaine's Antillean adapters Marbot and Sylvain (see pp. 177–78), see Jean-Pierre Jardel, "Des quelques emprunts et analogies dans les fables créoles inspirées de La Fontaine: contribution à l'étude des parlers créoles du XIXe siècle." The author, in his bibliography, also cites several more recent adaptations of La Fontaine into various Creole patois, as well as a number of the more venerable.

2. The manuscript of her collection, saved from oblivion by Annegret Bollée and Guy Lionnet, is published as Band 4 of the "Kreolische Bibliothek" under the title *Fables de La Fontaine traduites en créole seychellois*.

3. For a specific detailed study of the language in Rodolphine Young's fables, see Chris Corne, "Remarques sur la langue des *Fables* de Rodolphine Young."

La Fille

Ein M'sié bien rice tian na ein fiye bon pou mâié.
Plein gâçons y vine tire coude çapeau divant son la
pôte. Fiye là y dî zot:
"Eh! laisse-moi tanquil." Y pas ti trouve ein assez zoli
ni assez grand M'sié
Pou mâié èque li. Ein ti ana trop bel li pié, l'aute ti
trop vié.
Eine ti mette linette, l'aute ti trop béte. Eine son
canneçon ti mal tayé,
L'aute paltot ti trop grand. Ça eine là ti trop gros, ça
l'aute là ti trop maigue.
Ein ti trop grand, l'aute ti trop p'tit. Enfin y pas ti
trouve eine. Mo couâ
Y ti après espè gâçon ler rouâ. Y pas ti ouâ qui li après
monte en graine.
A fôce réfisé, y pas gangne pèsonne aprésent. Tout son
camarades y mâié,
Li, li resté comme çan memme. Y ouâ li après vié, y
commence çagrin.
(Pas na nâien qui femme haïé, coma pas gangne mâié.)
Y ti rogrette son bétise.
Quand y ti ouâ y pas gangne pèsonne, y ti oblizé mâié
èque ein faye zhomme,

The Daughter

A rich monsieur he have a daughter once, ready to marry.
Lots of young men they come to the door, they tip their
hats. But the daughter she tell them:
"Oh! Leave me alone!" For her nobody be pretty enough,
nobody be fine monsieur enough
To marry with her. This one he got feet they be too big,
that one he be too old.
This one he got spectacles, that one he be stupid. This one
he got pants they not be cut right,
That one he got a coat it be too long. One too fat, the
other too thin.
One too tall, the other too short. Anyway, nobody she
find at all.
Maybe, I think, she be looking for some prince. And she
never see how fast she be going to seed!
So she keep saying no, and she wind up with nobody. Her
friends they all be married,
But she stay single. And then she see how soon she be old,
and she get to feeling bad.
(A woman she hate nothing like not being married!) Now
she feel sorry she be such a fool.
And when she see how she got nobody at all, she have to
get married with some terrible man,

Ein vacabond, eine nâien di tout... Ça y oulé dî quand	A bum, a real no-good-for-nothing... This story it show
memme ou rice,	you how, even if you be rich,
Ou pas doite méprise les autes. Anh!	Better you not go stick up your nose at folks. Uh-uh!

Georges Sylvain   Cric? Crac! Fables de La Fontaine Racontées par un Montagnard Haïtien et Transcrites en Vers Créoles (1901)

LIKE MANY French Caribbean men of letters—the list includes such notables as Jean-F. Brierre, Aimé Césaire, Léon Laleau, among others—Georges Sylvain combined his literary life with a life of public and government service. In his case, even more than most, it is hard to know whether to characterize him as a writer-cum-statesman or vice versa. Born April 2, 1866, in Puerto-Plata, Dominican Republic, he did his early schooling in Port-de-Paix and Port-au-Prince, Haiti, and subsequently in Paris, at the Collège Stanislas. After receiving a degree in law from the University of Paris, Sylvain returned to Port-au-Prince, where he practiced and taught. Throughout the rest of his life he held a variety of governmental and judicial positions; among them, division chief in the Department of Public Education, judge in the Appeals Court, and, from 1909 to 1911, minister plenipotentiary to Paris and the Vatican. Two years before his death he was appointed president of the Port-au-Prince bar. The French government had recognized his services by decorating him as an officer in the Légion d'honneur.

With the occupation of Haiti by American marines in 1915, Sylvain became especially vocal in his reaction to the loss of Haitian independence, and was the prime mover in establishing the Union Patriotique, founded the same year to resist, at least intellectually, the American incursion. His polemical and nationalistic writings—letters, speeches, bulletins, and the like—are collected in *Dix années de lutte pour la liberté, 1915–1925*. The introduction to this work (I:vii–xviii) also chronicles the elaborate funeral accorded Sylvain in honor of his patriotic efforts. He died on August 2, 1925, nine years before the occupation was to come to an end.

Sylvain contributed to a number of literary and political journals—especially *La Ronde,* founded in 1896—and was coeditor of an anthology of Haitian poetry and prose, *Auteurs haïtiens: morceaux choisis,* officially honored by the Académie Française. But his literary reputation was made, primarily, on one slim but very successful volume of verse, *Confidences et mélancolies.* The disparity between quantity and importance prompted Louis Mori-peau, historian of Haitian letters, to compare him to the influential early Haitian poet Coriolan Ardouin. (See *Anthologie d'un siècle de poésie haïtienne, 1817–1925,* p. 152.) *Confidences et mélancolies* is a collection of refined and rather mannered lyrics written between 1885 and 1898, in both Haiti and France, in a style reminiscent, for at least one critic, of Sully Prudhomme and Théophile Gautier. (See Henock Trouillot, *Les Origines sociales de la littérature haïtienne,* p. 350.) Despite their Gallic elegance, the occasional flashes of patriotic and racial fervor—curiously less obtrusive in his poetry than in his political life—placed Sylvain in that ambivalent artistic limbo typical of so many Haitian poets of his period, neither thoroughly Haitian nor thoroughly French.

But if his lyrics are cultural hybrids, the verses in his other published collection, dating from the same year, leave no doubt as to their ethnicity. Although supposedly "imitations" of La Fontaine, the Creole fables in *Cric? Crac!: Fables de La Fontaine racontées par un montagnard haïtien et transcrites en vers créoles* owe little but their skeletal plots to the French fabulist. More clearly indebted, in their conception and in frequent specifics, to the fifty Creole fables in François-Achille Marbot's collection *Les Bambous: Fables de La Fontaine travesties en patois créole par un vieux commandeur,*[1] Sylvain's versions are picturesque elaborations, seen through the supposed optic of a peasant, and recounted with none of the pseudofolkloric condescension that one might expect from a sophisticated intellectual. (Even the title bespeaks the work's earthy character: the traditional exchange between narrator and audience at the beginning of a storytelling session, roughly the equivalent of "Ready?" "Let's go!")[2] The entry on Sylvain in *Caribbean Writers: A Bio-Bibliographical Critical Encyclopedia* (p. 509) notes that Sylvain's modest volume has been the subject of a doctoral dissertation by Perry A. Williams.[3]

A second edition of *Cric? Crac!* appeared four years after the poet's death, simultaneously in France and Haiti. The two fables translated here are the first and twenty-second in the collection, which contains thirty-one fables and a verse prologue.

1. A second edition of *Les Bambous* appeared during Sylvain's lifetime; and a third, still more recently (1931), including a translation into French and a commentary by Louis Jaham-Desrivaus.

2. The formula may well be the remnant of a similar Wolof exchange used to introduce a story, and described in detail by Roger in the preface to his *Fables sénégalaises* (see pp. 136–137), pp. 9–10.

3. "La Fontaine in Haitian Creole: A Study of *Cric? Crac!* by Georges Sylvain." See also Douglas Parmée's article, "'Cric? Crac!': Fables of La Fontaine in Haitian Creole: A Literary Ethno-Socio-Linguistic Curiosity"; and Robert Chaudenson and Guy Hazaël-Massieux, "Marbot, Sylvain, Young et les autres."

Téta Qui Couè Li Capab
Gros con Bef

Gnou Téta qui té bò d'leau,
Gnou jou, ouè gnou gros Taureau.
Li rhélé canmarad-li:
"Gadé, parié m'a vini
Gros tancou bef cila-là!"
Yo toutt prend ri: "Coua! coua! coua!
Ou pas gros con gnou zégué;
Conment pou t'a fait gonflé
Ti cò ou, jouq' temps ou t'a
Capab vini grossè ça?"
Li dit: "Eh ben, main! Gadé!
Zott va ouè si cé pas vré!
Moin va rivé mainm pi loin,
Calalou-crab' tranglé moin!"
Li commencé enflé cò:
Pésé! pésé! Et pi: "Dit, atò,
Si moin pas gros tancou li
Press'! Gadé moin ben!" "Bichi!
Ou trò coutt! Ou té doué tann
Ou mangé in pé bannann!"
"Malgré tout ça zott va dit,
Moin gangnin tròpp lesprit, pou
Moin pas ouè m'apé grossi..."
Là-mainm ventt le pété: bôouh!
—Respé m'doué la compagni!—
Toutt tripp li soti dèrhò,
Et pi, lé zott ba li tô.

Nèg' sott qui vlé fait dòctè,
Apr' allé chaché doulè...
Si bottin'-là trò jiss, frè,
Pito-ou rété pié-à-tè!

1. For the La Fontaine model of this unconventional adaptation, and for Jauffret's "sequel," see pp. 32 and 136.

2. *Calalou* 'okra' (or 'gumbo') is a staple of the Haitian diet. It is commonly invoked in Creole, as in the tadpole's picturesque oath, to

The Tadpole Who Thinks He Can
Grow as Big as a Bull[1]

Tadpole, one day, saw a bull
By the shore... Big, powerful...
Called his friends and said: "I bet
You don't think that I can get
Big as that!" Friends looked and saw
Giant bull... Laughed: "Haw haw haw!
You're so tiny! Look at you.
Puny runt! What can you do?
Even if you huff and puff,
How can you stretch big enough?"
"Watch! I can!" was his reply;
"Even bigger, if I try...
If I'm wrong, may I go tangle
In the gumbo-stew, and strangle!"[2]
So he tries to swell: "All set!...
Tell me, have I done it yet?"
"Not quite..." "Now?..." "No, not at all!
You can't make it. You're too small.
Eat a few bananas. Then
Fatten up and try again!"
"Tease me all you please. No matter!
I'm not stupid anyhow!...
There! I'm sure I'm getting fatter..."
Just then, tadpole bursts... Goes *pow!*...
Tripes go flying, splitter-splatter...
(No offense!) Give friends a turn...
"Maybe now," they say, "he'll learn!"

Fool invites a sorry plight
When he plays the smart monsieur:
If your fine shoes pinch too tight,
Best go barefoot, like you were.

attest to the speaker's veracity. The same oath is uttered by the ambitious frog in the earlier Martinican Creole version of the fable by Marbot (*Les Bambous*, p. 5), who, in a note, specifies the ingredients for a *calalou* soup. (Marbot's influence is especially noticeable in this fable.)

Chien Qui Couè l'Ombraj', Cé Viann

Toutt chien gangnin piç',
Main, toutt pas gangnin lesprit.

Gnou chien-mòn', qui té plein toutt viç',
Main qui té sott, tancou Bouqui,

The Dog Who Takes a Reflection for a Chunk of Meat

All dogs have fleas,
But some don't have much wit.

A mountain hound—a stupid twit,
As dumb as Bouqui, if you please,

Gnou bon matin, t'apé couri
Avec moceau viann nan guiol li.
　　Rivé bò la-riviè,
Li ouè nan d'leau-là, qui té clè,
Gnou lott chien, laidd, vòlè, gros gé,
　　Avec moceau mangé
Pi gros, pi gout, passé pa li.
Ça selment mété di fé nan
Sang boug-là. Li prend grondé: "Houan!"
Gnou fois, dé fois. Lott pas pati.
Li vancé; lott-là vancé tou.
Li quioulé; lott fait con li...
　　　　　　　　　Fou,
Con gnou dévorant, li sauté
Nan colett ti insolent-là;
En mainm temps, li mété jappé...
Aguio viann! Ni pa li, ni pa
L'ennmi li, toutt plongé nan d'leau.
Con li t'apé fann dèyè yo,
Li pèdi pié... Ça fait con ça,
Quand Mouché soti là bien frett,
Sans sac ni crab, li ouè lott-là
Cété li-mainm, qui té gnou bett!

Cé ça qu'a toujou rivé
Moun' trò saf, qui fait métié
Quitté cay' Madanm yo, pou
Y' allé couri cascannett.
Lò yo fini bouqué nett
Chaché lanmou tout patout,
Bò Madanm yo, yo vini,
Mandé li: "Côté lanmou?"
Madanm dit: "Lanmou pati!"

And full of nasty qualities—[1]
With chunk of meat between his chops,
　　Suddenly stops
At water's edge. There, down below:
Another hound! A wide-eyed cur!
An ugly, thieving so-and-so,
With bigger chunk, and tastier!
　　More than enough
To make him growl—once, twice—"Ruff!... Ruff!..."
The other, stubborn, stood his ground.
One lunged... Retreated... Other too,
Mimicking every move!
　　　　　"Confound
That blasted beast!" Enraged, he threw
Himself against his rival hound...
Started to bark... Both chunks, adieu!
Down in the drink! Our hero rears,
Set to retrieve... Slips... Disappears...
When he comes up with neither prize,
Freezing, Monsieur will realize—
Still stupid, but a lot more wary—
That he was his own adversary!

Same thing happens when a man
Bites off more than he can chew...
Leaves his house, and woman too,
Gallivants like fancy Dan...
Looks for better... When he's through,
Back home comes our gay romancer,
Weary from so much to-do...
Asks Madame: "Where's love?" Her answer:
"Love, you ask?... It left... Like you!"[2]

1. Bouqui (or Bouki) the hyena and the trickster Malice are popular figures in Haitian folklore. Direct imports from West Africa—where Bouqui's wily antagonist originated as Leuk the hare—they appear in various guises throughout the Caribbean; for example, as Zamba and Compère Lapin in Guadeloupe. Their adventures constitute a virtual narrative cycle reminiscent of the medieval tales of Reynard the Fox—of which they are no doubt at least distant descendants—and recall the Br'er Rabbit stories, which, to a large extent, they inspired.

2. As one might expect, Sylvain's rather curious moral has nothing to do with either La Fontaine's version of this traditional Aesopic fable, "Le Chien Qui Lâche Sa Proie pour l'Ombre" (VI, 17) (see p. 34), or with that of any of the seventeenth-century fabulist's predecessors.

Emile Couteau　Fables et Apologues (1910)　Fables du Vingtième Siècle (1929)

LIKE A number of other fabulists in this volume, Emile Couteau was not a professional man of letters. He was, in fact, already into his seventies before he published his first collection of fables, having turned to the writing of verse as an avocation during a long and distinguished career as a jurist.

Couteau was born in Paris in 1837 of a family native to the town of Blois. After receiving his *licence* in law in 1857 and his doctorate in 1861, he was attached to the Paris appellate court, where he pleaded numerous celebrated cases, especially of a financial nature. Involved for a time in the politics of his ancestral *département* of

Loir-et-Cher, he served in its *conseil général* from 1871 to 1880, as well as in other local bodies, but was an unsuccessful conservative candidate in the legislative elections of 1885. (See Georges Dupeux, *Aspects de l'histoire sociale et politique du Loir-et-Cher, 1848–1914,* pp. 450–53.) Couteau, remarkably, remained professionally active until his retirement in 1924. He died in Paris in 1931 at the age of ninety-four. (See the entries on Couteau in the *Dictionnaire illustré des contemporains* by Emile Saint-Lanne, fasc. 1, p. 306; and *Dictionnaire de biographie française,* IX:1107.)

In addition to a number of works of a technical legal nature, especially regarding probate and insurance law, Couteau published five recorded volumes of fables.[1] He would seem to have come by his interest in the genre naturally, albeit late: his father, also named Emile Couteau, a literary amateur, had achieved a modest local celebrity with his own fables, apologues, and *contes* in verse.[2] Of the first two of the younger Couteau's volumes, we have only the attribution of one Pierre Dufay, who cites them, both under the title *Fables,* as 36- and 33-page collections, respectively, in his "Esquisse d'une bibliographie du Loir-et-Cher (1900–1908)" (p. 248). I can find no other record of these two volumes' publication, nor, needless to say, the works themselves. It seems reasonable to assume, however, that some of their contents may have been reproduced in Couteau's subsequent *Fables et apologues,* in the preface to which he gives 1906 to 1909 as the dates of composition, describing himself candidly as a "nouveau venu dans le monde des lettres, qui n'a même pas l'excuse d'être un jeune'" (p. i). Officially honored by the Académie Française, this collection of the then-septuagenarian contains forty-six

pieces divided into six sections, entitled: "Les Fables de Médor," "Dame Pie," "Suite de fables," "Au temps passé," "Au temps présent," and "Apologues." A fourth collection, *Fables du temps de guerre* (1917), is attributed to Couteau in the *Dictionnaire de biographie française* (see above), but I can find no other reference to its existence, although several of the fables in his final collection bear the obvious marks of World War I. That volume, *Fables du vingtième siècle* (1929), was distinguished not only by a preface by Couteau's compatriot from Blois, Gabriel Hanotaux—prolific historian, *académicien,* and diplomat, who praised its "poésie franche, ferme et sans détours" (p. 3)—but also by the awarding of the Académie's Prix La Fontaine. It is, in effect, an augmented, revised edition of *Fables et apologues,* numbering eighty-three pieces divided into five sections, with epilogue.

Couteau's fables are of two types. To the traditional animal variety he brings a charming personal dimension, especially in those that have as their hero his faithful and very "personable" dog, Médor. (See below, p. 181, n. 1.) But by far the most impressive are the many that, as the title of his final collection suggests, are of specifically twentieth-century inspiration, especially in its technological aspects. Without subscribing to Hanotaux's laudatory superlatives, dictated perhaps more by the venerable author's age than by his literary talent, readers of Couteau's fables will appreciate not only his attachment to the values of his past but also his confrontation with the innovations—social and technological—of his present.

The four fables translated here, representing the range of Couteau's inspiration, are from *Fables et apologues* (I, 4; III, 2; and V, 1) and *Fables du vingtième siècle* (IV, 3).

---

1. Besides his two theses, *De la distribution des biens* and *Des Rapports à succession,* principal among his legal writings are the following: *Lettres sur l'Algérie: De l'administration de la justice; Du Bénéfice de l'assurance sur la vie; Traité des assurances sur la vie;* and *Le Centenaire de 1789 et l'impôt foncier.*

2. The elder Couteau, mayor of Blois from 1835 to 1837, had been a prominent member of the Société des Sciences et Lettres de Loir-et-Cher (originally the Société des Sciences et Lettres de la Ville de Blois), and its president in 1877–78. Selections of his verse appeared in two volumes of that organization's *Mémoires,* (1867 and 1875), and in its *Bulletin* of July 1873. The younger Couteau became a corresponding member of the Société in 1857, after receiving his *licence* in Paris.

L'Automobile

Sur les coussins capitonnés
D'une voiture automobile,
Le caniche Médor, digne, fier, immobile,
Trônait, les lunettes au nez.
La vitesse était sa marotte.

Pataud, pauvre chien qui trotte
Dans la crotte,
Dont les ébats par l'auto sont gênés,
Jappe à Médor ses abois indignés:
"Quel plaisir trouves-tu sur cette mécanique,
Qui répand partout la panique?

The Automobile

Astride his cushions, puffed with pride,
Médor the poodle sits, genteel,
Delighting in the swift automobile
That speeds him through the countryside,
Begoggled, poised, and oh so dignified.[1]

Another pup—mongrel Pataud—trotting among
The muck and dung,
Distraught, unable to abide
Having his canine playground occupied
By the mechanical invader,
Barks at Médor: "For shame, my fancy promenader!

Est-ce digne d'un chien? N'as-tu pas de remords
    En songeant que, pour te distraire,
    Tu risques d'écraser un frère?
Combien de nous déjà par les autos sont morts!
    Crois-moi, descends; notre mère Nature
    Nous a donné des pattes pour marcher.
Quatre pattes! quand l'homme, infime créature,
    N'en a que deux! C'est pour cacher
    Cette infirmité de structure
    Qu'il prit le cheval pour monture,
    Qu'il se fit chauffeur ou cocher.
    Tout n'est en lui que ruse et qu'imposture,
    Dur égoïsme ou vanité.
Nous avons trop longtemps subi sa dictature.
Il nous faut affranchir d'un engin redouté
    Par sa malice inventé.
    Quoique tu sois un chien de qualité,
    Viens avec nous, chiens de roture;
J'en appelle à ton cœur honnête et délicat.
    Nous formerons un syndicat
Pour empêcher qu'aucun auto ne s'aventure
Sur tous chemins par nous, libres chiens, fréquentés!
    Ainsi le veut l'égalité,
Ainsi s'établira pour la race future
Le règne du progrès et de la liberté!"

"Je craindrais," dit Médor, "une mésavanture
    Si j'écoutais votre ressentiment.
Selon qu'on est en bonne ou mauvaise posture,
    On voit les choses autrement.
    Vous parleriez, je crois, différemment,
    Si vous étiez dans la voiture."

Médor avait raison de n'être pas la dupe
    Des plaintes de son concurrent.
    Tout prend un aspect différent
    Suivant la place qu'on occupe.

    Is that what proper dogs should do?
    You go cavorting on that metal giant,
    Spreading his panic—cynical,[2] defiant—
    Trampling on fellow creatures just like you!
How many a brother dog lies lifeless in the street?
    Alas, I fear not just a few!...
    Come now, Nature knew best. She gave us feet
    To walk with... All four paws... A set... Complete...
    Unlike mere Man, with but his paltry two!
    (It was, in fact—and *entre nous*—
    To hide his structural deficiency
    And make up for the two he lacked, that he
Saddled and reined the horse, poor servant tried and true.)
    Man, that self-centered master who,
    By wile and ruse and treachery
    Has ruled too long! Dog's day is overdue!
    Rise up! Down with the auto! Help us free
    Our streets from fear. Forget your pedigree,
    Aristocratic through and through.
    Come, join our cause, commoners though we be.
We'll form a union and we'll rout the enemy.
Be true and stout of heart. It's time we overthrew
    Man the oppressor; time that we
    Stood up to him and struck a coup
    For progress, dogdom... and for liberty!"[3]

Médor replied: "Your dire complaints unending
    Strike me as so much ballyhoo.
Truth is, we find things fair or foul, depending
    Simply upon our point of view.
I fear your attitude would be far less unbending
    Were you, my friend, here in the auto too."

    Médor was right. It's only fitting
    Not to be fooled by such invective.
    Opinion is a matter of perspective:
    It all depends on where you're sitting.[4]

---

1. Médor is the hero of the first fifteen of Couteau's fables, subtitled "Les Fables de Médor." He gets his name, commonly given to French dogs of the more elegant breeds, from that of the Saracen knight Medoro, in Ariosto's *Orlando furioso.* The young Moorish hero was renowned for his grace, beauty, and—especially appropriate to his canine namesakes—for his unflagging fidelity. (See Thomas Bulfinch, *Legends of Charlemagne*, pp. 153–65.) Médor's pedestrian antagonist, Pataud, has a far less aristocratic (albeit no less venerable) name, dating from at least as far back as the late fifteenth century. It is derived, simply, from *la patte* ("paw") and is traditionally given to awkward little puppies with especially big ones. Couteau, however, chose the name for a more pointedly topical reason. (See n. 3.)

2. Lest the philologically astute reader, in a burst of enthusiastic exegesis, be led astray by the etymology of the adjective "cynical" (from the Greek *kynikos* 'doglike'), let me hasten to point out that the corresponding *cynique* does not occur in the French original.

3. The proletarian Pataud's exhortation to join in forming a union might be considered merely as a tongue-in-cheek reference to the flourishing French syndicalist movement of the early 1900s. (The Confédération Générale du Travail, founded in 1895, had become an especially active force after winning out over its rival, the Fédération des Bourses du Travail, in a labor congress at Montpellier in 1902.) Much more specifically, however, it is a clearly sarcastic allusion to Emile Pataud, prominent leftist syndicalist of the period, author of *Comment nous ferons la révolution.* In the months preceding the publication of Couteau's first collection, the labor leader had been the subject of a miniscandal and the butt of considerable journalistic criticism and ridicule, which called into question the sincerity of his proletarian principles. (See *Le Figaro*, Aug. 4, 1909, p. 3, and subsequent issues.)

4. Couteau revised this fable in the 1929 collection. Besides deleting the pleasantly pithy four-line moral and making several minor changes, he substantially shortened Pataud's "Workers of the World" harangue, no doubt because the pointed allusion was no longer topical. In so doing he not only weakened its parodic impact but also did away with the rather striking repeated rhymes of lines 16 through 37. As in the case of LeMay (see pp. 171–72), I have chosen to retain the original version (except for punctuation here and there). It is by far the more attractive, for both its rhetorical and historical qualities. Authors are not always the best judges of their work.

La Mouche

Un jeune enfant mangeait une belle tartine
Enduite d'un miel doux, savoureux, parfumé.
Une mouche survient qui voltige et butine,
Toute heureuse de vivre au beau soleil de mai:
    "Prends garde que ce miel englue
    Ta patte ou ta bouche goulue,"
Dit l'enfant prévoyant; inutile bonté.
L'insecte n'a souci de l'avis qu'il méprise,
Et meurt, malgré son aile et son agilité,
Enlisé dans le miel que le soleil irise.

    Qui se laisse prendre aux douceurs
    De la vie, au malheur s'expose.
    Dans tout plaisir, la prudence s'impose:
    Joie et peine, ici-bas, sont sœurs.

The Fly

A child was nibbling on a tasty bun
Spread thick with honey, savory and sweet.
Happily flitting in the warm May sun,
A fly comes buzzing by, eyeing the treat...
    "Careful, it's sticky!" warns the lad.
    "One greedy bite and you've been had—
Mouth, feet, stuck tight..." Sound, generous advice.
But roundly scorned: our stubbornest of flies,
Though deft and swift of wing, in but a trice
Lights on the sun-lit honey, sticks, and dies.

    Even the sweetest joys are rife
    With hidden woe; and so, beware
    When foul would masquerade as fair:
Pleasure and pain are sisters in this life.

L'Aéroplane

    Une bande d'oiseaux sauvages
    Allait vers de lointains rivages
    Chercher de plus doux climats.
En traversant les mers, l'un d'eux se sentait las,
Quand il vit quelque chose en l'air, étrange, énorme,
    Une sorte de plate-forme,
    Blanche, bruyante, difforme,
    Qui volait, sans qu'on pût voir
    Ce qui la faisait mouvoir
    D'une incompréhensible allure.
    L'oiseau s'y pose et croit ainsi pouvoir
    Finir le voyage en voiture.
"Qu'est-ce donc?" disait-il, "est-ce un oiseau géant,
D'une espèce inconnue et bizarre, qui plane
Et plus vite que moi traverse l'Océan?"
Une voix répondit: "C'est un aéroplane!
C'est moi, l'homme, qui fais la conquête des airs!
    Cela seul manquait à ma gloire,
    Ce jour fait date dans l'histoire,
    Je suis le roi de l'univers!
Mon génie a vaincu la nature rebelle,
    Victoire! Hurrah! la vie est belle!"
    Un coup de vent finit la ritournelle
De ce chant triomphal et brise le moteur
    Du grand appareil migrateur.
L'homme tombe et périt. L'oiseau, d'un seul coup d'aile,
S'envole. Il était né pour être aviateur.

    Ici-bas la sage nature
De chaque être a marqué la place et les emplois,
    Et c'est périlleuse aventure
Que vouloir transgresser ses immuables lois.
    Depuis les ailes d'Icare,
    Combien de projets divers
    Qu'un souffle, un rien contrecarre,
    Que de chutes, de revers!

The Aeroplane

    It was the annual migration—
    Birds flocking off in distant flight,
    Bound for a warmer destination—
When one, mid-voyage, weak and tired, caught sight
Of something in the air—strange, huge—some sort
    Of long, flat object, shining white.
    He saw it flying, heard it snort,
    But didn't have the slightest notion
    How it held up above the ocean,
Moving at speed he never knew existed.
Then, lighting on its back: "Oh well," he sighed,
    "Why finish up the journey unassisted
    When I can have myself a ride?"
    Next moment, he was wondering:
    "Heavens indeed, what is this thing?
Some rare, weird bird of giant breed, that flies
Faster than I across the sea?" A voice replies:
    "No, it's an aeroplane! Three cheers for me!
    Me... Man... At last, the master of the skies!
    My glory is complete. Today's a day
    Sure to go down in history:
Man conquers Nature! Victory! Hip, hip, hooray!..."
Just then a gust ends his triumphal roundelay,
    Destroys the engine—one two three—
    Of our mechanical migrator.
Man plummets, dies... Bird flies away. For he
Was born to be the proper aviator.

    Nature has wisely put each earthly creature
    Into its fit and proper place.
    Pity the eager overreacher,
    Courting defeat, disaster, or disgrace.
    Since Icarus of waxen wing
    Took to the air, how many's the fall—
    For modest cause or none at all—
    That crowns Man's rash endeavoring!

Mais la science humaine inlassable et féconde
Sera sans doute un jour la maîtresse du monde;
Alors les grands chemins des cieux seront ouverts.

And yet, one day, his tireless brain will set the pace
    For Nature, brought to heel, mere underling.
Then, finally, Man will open wide the realms of space.[1]

1. In the 1910 collection, this fable, first of a trio grouped under the subtitle "Au temps présent," is dated September 1909. On July 25 of the same year, Louis Blériot had become the hero of the day and had thrown France into instant euphoria with his Channel flight from Calais to Dover, beating out his British rival, Count Hubert Latham. (The event had moved the academician Jean Aicard to wax lyrical in his poem "La Conquête de l'air," one of many such ephemeral odes: "Hurrah! l'air indigné frémit—mais le supporte; / Dans les hauteurs du ciel où la gloire l'escorte, / Il va tout droit, d'un vol plané" [*Le Figaro,* Supplément littéraire, July 31, 1909, p. 1].) In the ensuing weeks, however, several fatal accidents tended somewhat to tarnish the enthusiasm for the infant field of aviation. One, especially, which took the life of a young aviator by the name of Lefebvre, was the result of an unexplained plunge as precipitous as that of Couteau's hero. (See *Le Figaro,* Sept. 8, 1909, pp. 1–2.) It would be tempting to see in this disaster, or others similar, the source of the present fable, especially given the ambivalent concluding lines, at once skeptical and optimistic. Unfortunately for the hypothesis, Couteau himself muddied the waters two decades later by including the poem in the 1929 collection. There, in addition to upgrading a tenuous "peut-être," in the next-to-last line, to a more affirmative "sans doute," he also changed the date of composition to April 1909, or three months before the Calais-Dover crossing. A brief note explains that the reference was to a flight by Lapham at a competition in Nice, in which the Englishman broke the altitude record. I suppose we must take Couteau at his word, odd though it be for a Frenchman to panegyrize a Briton. It is also just possible that the then-nonagenarian's recollection of specifics had become a little dim.

L'Avion

Quand la science humaine enfin fut parvenue
A trouver le moyen de planer dans la nue,
    Quand l'avion fut inventé,
    Des airs de joie et de fierté
    Saluèrent sa bienvenue;
    On disait: "Pour l'humanité
    Quelle ère de prospérité!
Du progrès pacifique enfin l'heure est venue!
    Les peuples épars et divers
N'auront plus désormais l'existence isolée,
Voici les grands chemins des cieux qui sont ouverts,
Toute frontière est vaine, impuissante, annulée.
Le rapide avion, dans sa course au travers
De l'espace infini, sous la voûte étoilée,
    Par-dessus mont, plaine, vallée,
Est le trait d'union béni de l'univers!"

Ce beau rêve de paix en l'an dix-neuf cent treize
    Avait bercé l'âme française
    Des plus douces illusions;
Mais à peine une année était-elle écoulée,
    Survint la guerre, et nous voyons
    Se transformer les avions
En terribles engins de mort, et la mêlée
    Gronde et monte au sein des cieux clairs,
    Et sa meurtrière envolée,
Par de rouges sillons, ensanglante les airs.

    Bienfaitrice décevante,
    La science que l'on vante
    Ne fait-elle qu'un présent
    Redoutable, en instruisant
    L'humanité trop savante?
Il semble qu'un génie occulte et malfaisant
Détourne ses bienfaits vers le mal et qu'en somme
Quelque danger nouveau suit d'un pas complaisant
    Chaque progrès de l'homme.

The Airplane[1]

When human science finally found a way
    To scale the clouds; when, one fine day,
    The airplane was at last invented,
Many's the joyous tune and proud "hooray"
That rang to greet the feat unprecedented.
    And as it soared against the sky,
    "Dawn of an era!" was the cry.
    "Prosperity is near at hand.
Now progress can begin its peaceful reign.
The airplane, spanning mountain, valley, plain,
Will bind the peoples of each far-flung land—
All boundaries gone, meaningless now and vain—
    Into a single human race.
For Man has opened wide the realms of space![2]
Coursing the stars, the airplane, blessèd tether,
Will join a peaceful universe together!"

Then nineteen thirteen came. That hopeful dream
Still lulled the souls of Frenchmen as before.
    But all was not as it would seem:
Next year, the world goes plunging into war.
    And suddenly, before their eyes,
    The airplane dons a different guise,
Transformed into a death-machine... The drone
    Of motors, pell-mell, as they rise
    Aloft in murderous monotone,
Streaks trails of blood across the furrowed skies.

    Ah, science! Two-faced hypocrite!
    Science, whom men so praise and prize...
    First she bestows a boon; then it
    Becomes a bane, for all their wit.
    It seems some vicious spirit lurks
In wait, to foul the finest of their works;
    Some deadly opposite,
Dread counterpart, that takes malicious pride
In dogging Mankind's every forward stride.

1. The decade intervening between the preceding poem and this one brought about not only a change in nomenclature, from *aéroplane* to *avion*—as in their English equivalents—but also a development of the author's attitude toward the advancing technology. The contrast is made all the clearer by the juxtaposition, obviously intentional, of the two poems in the 1929 collection. (See p. 183, note.)

2. I think one has to assume that Couteau is here consciously echoing the last line of "L'Aéroplane," validating, as it were, his prediction of nine years earlier. (At least I am certain that my repetition is intentional.)

Philippe Mercier   Fables Modernes et Poésies Diverses (1912)

I HAVE no biographical (and little bibliographical) information to offer about the fabulist Philippe Mercier, other than the fact that he was the author of the 175-page *Fables modernes et poésies diverses,* published in Paris by A. Jeande (1912). Who he was, when and where he was born, where he lived, when and where (in all likelihood) he died, and what else he may have written—everything remains a mystery, except for his name and the volume in question.[1]

That collection consists of forty-eight fables, almost all of them in La Fontaine-style *vers libres,* along with twelve other poems which, in fact, are very similar in subject and style to the fables, only longer. It would appear that the author was a man of more-than-average erudition, given a large number of classical allusions in his work, often styled in elegant periphrases a little reminiscent of Lamartine and the like. The fables are actually less "modernes" and more traditional than Mercier's title would imply; certainly much less inspired by latter-day technology than some of those by his contemporary Emile Couteau, and with none of the whimsy—in dramatis personae and morals—typical of his possible contemporary (or, at least, close successor) Franc-Nohain. (See pp. 179–80 and 188–89.) Still, they are workmanlike if not virtuosic, agreeable to read if not compelling, and, though not among the most memorable representatives of the genre, certainly worth at least passing recognition in any sampling of La Fontaine's twentieth-century would-be heirs. Only a cynic would insist that their utter obscurity is well deserved.

"Le Paysan et la Sauterelle" and "Le Perroquet Voulant Imiter le Rossignol," among the more sprightly of Mercier's fables, are, respectively, numbers 23 and 42.

Le Paysan et la Sauterelle

    Un jour certain paysan,
    Qui travaillait à son champ,
    Avise une sauterelle,

The Peasant and the Locust

    There was a certain peasant, who—
    Tilling his field, as peasants do—
    Finding a locust, had a mind

Et va se venger sur elle
De maints dégâts d'autre temps:
"Grâce!" lui dit la locuste,
"Si vous n'êtes pas injuste,
Je vins au monde au printemps;
Dois-je payer pour les autres?"

"Oui-dà!" fait l'homme des champs:
"Mais, lorsque toutes les vôtres
Reviendront par légions
S'abattre sur mes sillons
Pour dévorer mes moissons,
Vous n'en serez pas, la belle!"

    Cela disant,
    Le paysan
Ecrasa la sauterelle.

Chacun défend son bien, personne n'y redit:
En ce monde il vaut mieux être grand que petit.

To wreak revenge for what her kind
Had done to him in former times.
"Mercy!" the insect pled. "I fear
I wasn't born till spring this year.
Be fair! Why make me pay for crimes
Of others, long before? What reason..."

"Bah!" sneered the peasant. "Maybe so.
But I don't care; I only know
Your hordes will come again some season,
Wasting my crops, row after row.
Well, when they do, my pretty pet, you
Won't be among them, I can bet you!"

    That said,
    Our peasant went ahead
    And squashed her dead.

Man fights to keep what's his. So, all in all,
It's better, clearly, to be big than small.[1]

---

1. Mercier's moral—as well as his locust's logical argument in self-defense—is reminiscent of La Fontaine's celebrated fable "Le Loup et l'Agneau" (I, 10). As with La Fontaine, the moral is obviously a cynical observation, not an expression of approval.

Le Perroquet Voulant Imiter le Rossignol

Le chant d'un rossignol en un voisin bosquet
Eut le don de charmer un certain perroquet:
Jacquot n'avait jamais ouï chose pareille;
Oncques si doux accents flattèrent son oreille.
Aussi s'appliquait-il sans cesse à répéter
Ce que du rossignol il entendait chanter.
Vocalisant, roulant, de façon assidue,
    De la note grave à l'aiguë,
    Jacquot souvent changeait de ton,
De la basse au ténor passant en baryton.
De son gosier tirant des sons les plus baroques,
Il emplit le logis de ses cris les plus rauques.

    Tout à son thème favori,
    Il dédaignait toute caresse.
    Au point qu'à la fin sa maîtresse
Lui dit: "Cessez, Jacquot, tout ce charivari;
S'agit-il de siffler, le moindre canari
    Mieux que vous remplirait ce rôle.
N'avez-vous pas reçu le don de la parole?
    Dès qu'il vous suffit d'en user,
Qui vous prend de jouer un autre personnage,
    Et de nous ridiculiser
    Aux yeux de tout le voisinage?"
A l'ouïr ce sermon, d'abord, le perroquet
    Demeura fort interloqué.
    Mais, comme Jacquot était sage,
Il se le tint pour dit: reprenant son caquet,
    Son babil, sa routine,
    Il ne siffla plus qu'en sourdine.

The Parrot Who Would Sing like the Nightingale

A nightingale was warbling in the wood,
While in his cage a certain parrot stood
In utter awe. His ears had never heard
Such flawless notes; never had any bird
Sung sweeter sounds than those. And so our Poll,
As best he could, would try to sing them all—
Runs, trills, arpeggios up and down the scale:
Low, high, high, low—just like the nightingale.
    Or so, at least, the parrot thought.
But no. Each time he opened wide his beak,
    Try though he might, he tried for nought:
His gullet filled the house with squawk and shriek.

    The bird persisted nonetheless
    With singleness of purpose, still
    Squawking his run, shrieking his trill,
Resisting even mistress's caress;
Until, "Cease and desist!" chided the latter.
    "If chirping were the only matter,
Any canary would be quite enough!
    But you, who have the gift of speech,
You should be pleased to talk instead of screech,
To be yourself and not a blessèd bluff.
Why, we're the laughingstock all round about!"
Taken aback at first, and gaping at her,
Poll listened to her sermon, heard her out,
    And, being a cagey bird no doubt,
    Resumed his customary chatter.
As for his song, whenever he would try it,
    He kept it quiet.

Nous nous croyons capables en tout, nous avons tort;
Il vaut mieux essayer, par certaines études,
    Si nous pouvons mettre d'accord
    Nos goûts avec nos aptitudes.

We think there's nothing we can't do. Not so.
    But lest we learn it to our woe,
    Best study how, with application,
To match our talent to our inclination.

Kaddour-Mermet   Fables et Contes en Sabir (1916)

I CAN offer little solid information about Kaddour-Mermet (or, simply, Kaddour) except that he lived in Algiers and was author of the volume *Fables et contes en sabir*. His work is a collection, in North African patois, of twenty-eight briskly styled fables (all but one announced as imitations of La Fontaine, though with appropriate local coloration), followed by a variety of native-inspired pieces: seven verse tales, two humorous songs, a monologue in verse, and two tales in prose. The only extant copies I have been able to locate are a second (1916) and a third edition (n.d.).[1]

Kaddour would appear to have been an Arab frequenter of certain French social and cultural circles in the turn-of-the-century colonial capital. The brief preface to his collection, by one Georges Moussat—French Algerian author of two published volumes of verse and one play[2]—refers to the much appreciated recitations by "le

bon camarade Kaddour" himself, as well as by Alfred Letellier, during "nos joyeuses réunions algériennes" (p. 5). The latter was a prominent Algérois who served as one of the *députés* from the colony between 1882 and 1893. According to Moussat, Letellier and Kaddour, among other bons vivants, were renowned for entertaining their colleagues with spirited—and sometimes salacious—tales in the local pidgin. Moussat likens Kaddour's contribution to the popular literature in *sabir* to the more-celebrated adventures of Cagayous, the swaggering street urchin and antihero created by Auguste Robinet (under the pseudonym "Musette"), and famous throughout the area for his earthy and often scabrous exploits recounted in the same colorful idiom.[3]

The fables of Kaddour that I have translated are the fifteenth and sixteenth in the third edition of *Fables et contes en sabir*.

---

1. The National Union Catalogue suggests a date of 1947(?) for this edition. This is clearly in error, however, since the copy I have consulted, in the Harvard College Library—illustrated by an even more enigmatic figure by the name of Drack-Oub—bears the autograph and indication of place and date of purchase: "Tlemcen, 24 juin 1932."

2. *Les Trois intérieurs, Sonnets*, and *A bon chat bon rat!* The last-named, a one-act prose comedy, was performed on February 29, 1896, at the Lyre

Algérienne, a social and artistic organization where, it is not unreasonable to assume, Kaddour's own recitations may have taken place.

3. The historian Emile-Félix Gautier devotes a chapter to the Cagayous phenomenon and its social implications in *Un Siècle de colonisation*, pp. 117–22. A selection of Cagayous tales, with introduction, notes, and glossary, edited by French Algerian author Gabriel Audisio (see pp. 202–3), appeared under the title *Cagayous, ses meilleures histoires*.

La Zitoun y la Bastique

    Li mon Diou quisqui fir
    Jami ti po fasir.
Y coni blous qui toi, pas bizouan di blagui;
Tojor y son rison, jami y sa trompi.
    Ji pense à cit zaffir
    Barc' qu'on jor on Kabyle,
    Y rigardi bar tire,
    Y son voir one bastique
    Tot à fi manifique.
"Y tiann afic la tirre ji crois bor on ficèle?
    (Qui son dire cit Kabyle),
      Li mon Diou,
    Bor cit fois ji crois, cit on coillon.
Borquoi sor cit zeboudj ni pas mettir çoui là?
Ji crois cit comme y faut? Cit zitoun qui sont là

The Olive and the Watermelon[1]

Don't worry, Allah he know what he do,
    Better than you.
No kidding, he do right. He never make
    No big mistake.
So why I tell you this? So why I say?
Because I think of story... One fine day,
    Certain Kabyle he look around
      And see on ground
    Big watermelon.[2] Really big!
Kabyle he think: "How come such melon grow
      On tiny twig?
    Maybe this time, Allah he go
      Be stupid dunce
        For once!
How come he not use nice big olive tree?

Y son millor bar tirre.
La bastique bor là-haut, y fir bon blizir,
    Cit zitoun bor en bas
    Y son tri biann comme ça."
Y pense por son tite li mon Diou son malade
  Le jour qui son fir cit grann coillonnade.
Por en bas di zeboudj li Kabyle y si coche,
Pas moyen di dormir barc' qu'yana di moche.
Comme y rigarde en l'ir, on zitoun son tombi,
    Qui loui cassi son nez!!
"Ah!! Sacornon di Diou, ji crois y ma cassi
    Ma barol ji saigné.
Aulior di cit zitoun!! Si mi tombe on bastique?
Mon tite y son cassi!!! Bojor, Salamalèque!!
    Ji soui crivi comme mort.
Ji voir bor cit affir, mon Diou nit pas coillon
    Y cit moi j'ana tort."
	Let tiny olives grow on ground, below?
	    Much better, no?
	Big high and little low, like it should be..."
	He say: "Allah he screw up bad, I think,
	Day when he first make melon, olive too."
	Then he lie down, by tree, try catch a wink.
	But flies go "buzz" all round, not let him do.
	So Kabyle he just lie, look up at sky...
	    All of a sudden, down through air,
	    Olive come falling. Hit him square,
	And give him bloody nose! "Oh my! Oh my!
	    Son-of-a-bitch!" Kabyle he cry.
	"Instead of olive, what if melon fall?
	    It break my neck!!
	    Salamaleck!!!
	Me only one who make mistake!" he bawl.
	"Allah he never go screw up at all!"

MORALE	*MORAL*
"Ça qui fir la mon Diou, Ji voir qu'il it tri bon; Quand ji blague?—Ji soui bite!! Y mi fit voir tot suite."	Kabyle he finally know for true: "Allah he know best what he do. Fool who make fun of him not know him. Kabyle he tease: Allah he show him!"

1. Aside from his botanical legerdemain, turning acorn and pumpkin to olive and watermelon, Kaddour-Mermet's folkloric adaptation remains quite close to La Fontaine's fable "Le Gland et la Citrouille (IX, 4; see pp. 34–35); much closer, indeed, than is the latter to La Fontaine's own probable non-Aesopic model. (See Henri Regnier, ed., *Œuvres de J. de la Fontaine*, II:374–75.)	2. The Kabyles are a Berber people living mainly in the mountains of northeast Algeria. Since they are predominantly farmers, it is understandable that the poet chose one of their number to portray the peasant of La Fontaine's scenario.

Li Chacail Qui Yana Pas Sa Queue	The Jackal Who Has No Tail

On vio chacail, ma tot a fi digordi
Qui coni quisqui ci por trapi les poli
Por mangi li lapin y li pitit moton,
On chacail qui ji souis canaille por di bon:
On jor por sa queue, on zarabe (sans sabatte)
    Il attrape cit chacail;
    Comi la por ji m'en aille,
    Y tire mon zami:
	Old jackal—old, but plenty clever yet—
	    Crafty old jackal, not forget
	    How to trap hen, not lose bad habit
	How to be bastard, eat poor lamb and rabbit...
	Come barefoot Arab, catch him one fine day.
	    Grab him by tail, hold nice and tight,
	    Afraid maybe he run away.
	    Jackal he pull with all his might:

Tout d'un coup y si sauve, y cor afic son patte
 Ma sa queue son fini,
Y vian à son mison, tot à fi coilloné.
Sa femme quand il y voir, y sa fouti di loui.
Li chacail son pensi: "Bas bisoan di bloré,
 Ji va sarché quiqu' soge y poui
 Ji ti fir voir quisqui fir on chacail
Qui yana one blissour qui viann dans one bataille."
Li jor qui li chacails y viannent bor la Djemmâa,
Y dimande la barole à mosiou présidann,
 Y voilà quisqui dire:
"Ji si pas borquoi fir, li mon Dio y nos a
Douni cit micanique, por ji traine por tirre.
 Borquoi fir qui j'en a cit queue
Qui son lourd, qui s'accroche, quand ji marche la brosaille
Qui tojor ji son cause, ji peu pas ji m'en aille.
 Si ti yana bon tite
Vos fir quisqui ji di, tos vo copi la queue."
 "Por sûr ti n'y pas bite,
 Ji crois ti a rison,
(Qui son barli por loui, Mosiou li présidann)
Ma fit voir vot darrière, ji dira s'il y a bon;
 Si la queue pas bisoann."
Quand misio li chacails, y son voir cit kouffa
 La queue j'yana pas
Y son crivi por rire, di loui y son fouti.
Pas moyann bor barli, tot suite y son barti
Afic la queue droite, y fir gran fantasia.
Li vio chacail y rage, por quoi y n'en a pas.

MORALE

Ji voir qui li zami, cit tos di saloperi:
Si on jor one poli d'on zarabe ti a pri,
Tot souite la Djemmâa, y vos donne one mardaille,
Y moi qui ja perdu, mon queue dans one bataille
 Y sa fouti di moi
Y parc' qui son bocoup, par force y fir la loi.

1. Added moral aside, this fable, like the preceding, is a faithful imitation of La Fontaine, transposed into a different cultural key. Unlike "Le Gland et la Citrouille," however, "Le Renard Ayant la

Run good with paws but leave poor tail behind!
 Feel like damn fool. Go home. Wife take
One look, and oh! what bloody fun she make!
 Jackal he think: "Never you mind,
 No need you fret and bellyache!
Jackal go fix up battle-wound right now.
 You wait a little, show you how..."
That day big meeting-day. Town Council meet.
 Jackal he ask to "have the floor,"
 He want to speak. He rise to feet
And say: "M'sieu le Président, what for
Allah he give us stupid thing like tail?
 Big heavy business. Always trail
On ground, behind. Get tangled up in thicket,
 Hold jackal back just when, instead,
 He try go run full speed ahead!
If you all smart, better you snick it,
 Snip it clean off, if you ask me."
M'sieu le Président he answer: "Friend,
 You make good sense, for sure. Maybe
 We go do like you recommend.
 But first, turn round. Show rump. Let's see
If tail so necessary, yes or no."
 Old jackal he turn round and show
Bare ugly ass... No tail!!... You so-and-so!!!
Jackals all point and laugh. Make fun: "Ha ha!"
All up and leave. No talk. Meeting all through.
Lift tails in air, march out with tra-la-la...
Old jackal furious... Wished he had one too.

MORAL

Friends bunch of no-good scum, this jackal say!
You go steal hen from Arab? Right away
Council they give you medal! But go fight?
 Go lose your tail, like me today?
 Laugh... Cheer... "Ha ha! Hooray! Hooray!"
Trouble is, them so many, always right.[1]

Queue Coupée" (V, 5) is of Aesopic inspiration. (See no. 17 of the "Fabulae Graecae," in Perry, *Aesopica*, pp. 328–29.)

Franc-Nohain (pseud. Maurice-Etienne Legrand)   Fables (1921)
Fables Nouvelles (1927)

IT IS no exaggeration to say that, if the twentieth century has produced an artistic and spiritual heir to La Fontaine—not only in sheer volume but in form, style, and, generational differences aside, even in tone—that heir is Maurice-Etienne Legrand, known to French letters under the pseudonym "Franc-Nohain."[1] While it is probably mere coincidence that, like his prototypic predecessor, he wrote twelve books of fables, and that his first collection appeared, precisely, the year of La Fontaine's tercentenary, the important resemblances are surely more compelling: results of both a scholarly admiration and an obvious personal affinity.[2]

Obvious, indeed, on even the most superficial reading. It is difficult not to be struck by Franc-Nohain's conscious espousal of the La Fontaine form, albeit a delightfully whimsical handling of it. Throughout his fables, with their exuberant rhythms and capricious—often outrageous—rhymes, one discovers, however exaggerated, the unmistakable "griffe ancienne du Maître, de l'incomparable Bonhomme." (See François Porché, "Franc-Nohain poète, ou l'Esprit des choses," p. 38). A "griffe" marked by those characteristic asides to the reader and generous disgressions that are among the charms of the La Fontaine genius; a narrative that "ne se hâte point, s'avance nonchalamment en tunique légère et lâche, butinant à toutes les pentes de la pensée ou du rêve," leading eventually, but none too hurriedly, to its moralistic conclusion.[3] And, on further reading, an even more telling resemblance: the self-consciously allusive play between certain La Fontaine protagonists and Franc-Nohain's latter-day incarnations of them, in adventures—sequels or, indeed, deformations—reminiscent of Jauffret at his best and foreshadowing some of the fables of Anouilh.[4]

But for all the inspiration tapped directly from La Fontaine, these are no mere exercises in adaptation, "à la manière de..." If Franc-Nohain appropriates the Master's spirit, form, and style, it is his own originality that sets these fables apart. Not content with the "personnel" of the time-honored fable (La Fontaine's, pre- and post-), he adds to its traditional animal, human, and occasionally vegetal characters a whole unlikely panoply of inanimate creatures, bringing to life even the most unexpected objects—like the elevators and soccer ball in our selection—and pushing to a delightfully fanciful extreme that progressive "Industrial Revolutionization" of the fable that the reader cannot have failed to notice developing over the centuries, and to which we have already alluded (see pp. 70–71, n. 2). "Donc, voici les 'choses' lâchées! Dans cette ridicule imitation de l'homme, tous les traits qui marquent nos défauts s'accusent étrangement. La naïveté, la prétention, la sottise prennent, sous cet éclairage fantastique, un relief saisissant." The result is "un rêve qui, parfois, confine au cauchemar, mais un cauchemar-bouffe, qui ne dure que le temps d'un éclat de rire" (Porché, "Franc-Nohain poète," p. 48).

Although Franc-Nohain did not become a fabulist, in the specific sense of the term, until he was almost fifty, the same verbal legerdemain and bizarre humor were evident from his beginnings, although usually without morals attached, in collections such as *Les Inattentions et Sollicitudes, Flûtes*—in which he even characterizes as "fables" some of his so-called *poèmes amorphes*—and *Les Chansons des trains et des gares,* as well as in early

verse comedies like *L'Heure espagnole.*[5] "Le ton enjoué et quasiment cordial, la souplesse et la gouaillerie, . . . tout est, là-dedans, d'un fabuliste qui s'ignore ou qui se prépare, mais qui ne tardera pas à s'affirmer." (See Vandérem, *Le Miroir des lettres,* p. 159.) The same qualities would continue to be his hallmark throughout the rest of his long and productive life.[6]

Maurice-Etienne Legrand was born on October 25, 1873, in the town of Corbigny, in the Loire valley. Despite (or, perhaps, because of) two academic degrees, in both law and history, Legrand, becoming Franc-Nohain, abandoned a promising career in administration, even having served for a time as a provincial *sous-préfet,* in favor of a life in letters. Attracted to the capital, and especially to the artistic atmosphere of Montmartre, he became a habitué of the celebrated cabaret Le Chat Noir, in its waning days, and counted among his friends and associates not only such comic luminaries as Alfred Jarry and Alphonse Allais but also serious writers the likes of popular playwright Maurice Donnay, André Gide, and Pierre Louÿs. Settling in Paris after his marriage, he quickly entered into its literary life, writing criticism and articles for a variety of journals, among them the *Revue Blanche* and the *Echo de Paris.* It was to the latter that he returned as *secrétaire général* after serving with distinction in World War I, during which he was decorated with the cross of the Légion d'honneur. Toward the end of his life he was promoted to the rank of *commandeur* in that elite body. He was further honored, in 1932—two years before his death, in Paris, on October 18, 1934—as recipient of the annual Grand Prix de Littérature of the Académie Française, for the totality of his *œuvre,* but especially for his crowning achievement, his fables.[7] From the first, critic André Fontainas had recognized them as "des manières de chefs-d'œuvre." (See "Revue de la quinzaine," p. 177.) And, writing a decade later, Porché would confidently predict: "A notre époque pédante, il y a beaucoup d'œuvres plus ambitieuses; il y en a peu, selon nous, qui aient plus de chances de durée" ("Franc-Nohain poète," p. 49).

Following a few early and brief periodical inclusions, Franc-Nohain's entire corpus of twelve books of fables was published in four successive volumes over a period of a dozen years: Books I through III, in *Fables* (1921); Books IV through VI, in *Fables nouvelles* (1927); Books VII through IX, together with the preceding six, in *Fables* (1931); and Books X through XII, in *Fables nouvelles* (1933).[8]

The five fables translated here, typical of the author's unmistakable style and unconventional wit, are numbered as follows: I, 3; III, 10; V, 11; V, 16; and VI, 5.

---

1. One also occasionally finds the spelling "Le Grand." As for his pseudonym, the author took it from the name of a river that runs through his native province, the Nohain, adding "Franc" supposedly in assonantal deference to author Jean Lorrain, one of the literary heroes of his youth. (See Georges Suarez, "Franc-Nohain," p. 425.)

2. Franc-Nohain the scholar produced two studies of La Fontaine: a brief article during his tercentenary, "Les Fables de La Fontaine"; and, several years later, a full-length study, *La Vie amoureuse de Jean de La Fontaine.*

3. See Prologue, n. 5 (p. xv). The passage quoted is from Fernand Vandérem's commentary on Franc-Nohain and the La Fontaine tercentenary (*Le Miroir des lettres*). Vandérem was more than a casual admirer, having collaborated with the poet on a three-act play, *La Victime*, originally presented at the Comédie des Champs-Elysées, March 4, 1913.

4. For examples from Jauffret and Anouilh, see pp. 135–36 and 199–200.

5. This *comédie bouffe*, originally presented at the Odéon, October 28, 1904, was subsequently set to music as a successful one-act opera by Maurice Ravel.

6. For a thorough bibliography of Franc-Nohain's verse, theater, and essays, and of his numerous periodical contributions, as well as a copious listing of studies devoted to him, the reader should consult Hector Talvart and Joseph Place, *Bibliographie des auteurs modernes de langue française*, VI:125–32. Also useful, though less extensive and not wholly accurate, is Hugo P. Thieme, *Bibliographie de la littérature française de 1800 à 1930*, I:769. See also the latter's two supplements: S. Dreher and M. Rolli, *Bibliographie de la littérature française, 1930–1939*, pp. 158–59, and Marguerite L. Drevet, *Bibliographie de la littérature française, 1940–49*, p. 235.

7. For general biographical details see the above-mentioned article by Georges Suarez, pp. 420–31.

8. Several other special editions and selections of his fables, in volumes and periodicals, published both during his lifetime and posthumously, attest to their popularity. (See the bibliographies of Talvart and Place, Thieme, Dreher and Rolli, and Drevet.) One, also entitled simply *Fables* (1923), intended for children, is of particular interest in that it was illustrated by his wife, Madeleine Franc-Nohain, daughter of musician-poet Léopold Dauphin.

Le Trompeur Imprudent et les Escargots

Un industriel sans vergogne
        Avait, dit-on, imaginé,
Avec du caoutchouc de confectionner
        Des escargots de Bourgogne.
Comme l'escroquerie, ainsi qu'il apparaît,
    Est, trop souvent, la rançon du progrès,
        Pour son peu scrupuleux négoce,
        Notre homme acquérait, à la grosse,
        De vieux pneumatiques d'autos,
        Qu'il coupait en petits morceaux:
Et c'était ça, dans les banquets, festins et noces,
        Qu'il appelait des escargots.
Cette application imprévue et subtile
        De l'industrie automobile
        Ne faisait aucun mécontent:
        Les gens jugent, de notre temps,
        Les escargots sur la coquille,
            Non sur ce qu'il
            Y a dedans.
        Il arrive que, cependant,
        Le triomphe d'une entreprise
                Nous grise
        Et nous rend imprudents:
        Sans plus vérifier la sorte
        De caoutchouc qu'on lui apporte,
            Toute enveloppe
            Lui semble propre
            A servir chaud
            Comme escargots...
    Mais un jour vint qu'à des convives
Que notre homme traitait dans sa propre maison,
Il présenta des mollusques de sa façon
        En guise de colimaçons.
        Malgré toutes les tentatives,
        Le pneumatique déguisé
        S'arrête au milieu du gosier
        Des dégustateurs angoissés:
D'abord le fabricant, — mais qu'est-ce qui arrive?—
        S'inquiète;

The Complacent Fraud and His Escargots

        A big industrialist we know,
        Unscrupulous in the extreme,
        Had hit upon a novel scheme:
    To manufacture rubber escargots—
        And "de Bourgogne," if you please!
        (Such fraudulent atrocities
        Are just, it seems, the price we're paying
These days for progress!...) Well, as I was saying,
    Our ersatz-escargot inventor got
                Himself a lot
            Of auto tires—old, secondhand,
                And wholesale, you can bet!—
    Cut them up into little pieces, and
    Would pass them off as snails at banquets, fêtes,
        Weddings and such: a new and subtle
Twist to the automotive industry... ("Now what'll
They think of next!..."), with nary a dissatisfied
    Escargot connoisseur; because today,
    The shell's what sells the snail, not what's inside...
            Well, be that as it may,
        It often happens that too much success
            Goes to our head, and makes us less
        Than wary of the pitfalls on our way.
    In time, our cuisinier-cum-money-grubber
        Stopped bothering to check his rubber:
            Any old shoe would do,
            Cooked up as escargots.
                But no, not so!...
    One night, it happened that he had a few
    Friends to his home for dinner. But when he
    Served up his pseudomollusk recipe,
            Try though they might,
        The guests, in dire distress, were quite
Unable to negotiate—swallow, that is—
        Those masquerading tires of his,
        That firmly, resolutely stuck,
            Inglorious,
        Halfway down their esophagus...
"Damn!" thought our sham-gastropodist. "That's just
                    my luck!

Puis, se frappant
Le front: "Je comprends, tout s'explique
J'ai dû utiliser un stock de pneumatiques
　　Munis d'antidérapants."

Parfois un remède identique
Produit des effets inégaux:
Ce qui est excellent pour certains pneumatiques
　Ne vaut rien pour les escargots;
　Le même exemple nous assure
　Qu'en tout l'excès est un défaut:
　Quand on trompe les gens, il faut
Du moins le faire avec soin et mesure.

And, clapping hand to forehead, he opined:
　　"Oh dear! I fear
　　It's all too clear:
They must have gone and sent the nonskid kind!"

Sometime one selfsame remedy, although
Good for the gander, isn't for the goose:
What's fine for certain tires may well produce
Quite negative effects for escargots.
　　Another moral, too: excess
　　Is bad, whatever your profession.
If you're a fraud... Well, that's all right, I guess,
So long as you take care and use discretion.

La Révolte des Ascenseurs

　Un jour, dit-on, les Ascenseurs,
　Las d'accomplir une besogne
　Fastidieuse et monotone,—
Toujours monter, et puis descendre, cela donne
A la longue, en dépit qu'on en ait, mal au cœur,—
　　Las de ce constant esclavage
　　Où les réduisaient sans pitié
　　Le monsieur du cinquième étage,
　　La vieille dame du premier,
Las enfin d'obéir à toute heure au portier,
　　Qui les tient nuit et jour en cage,
　　Les Ascenseurs ayant brisé
　　Leurs cordes (par quel sortilège?)
　　Et, du même coup, écrasé
La concierge, et les filles de la concierge,—
　　"La concierge est dans l'escalier,
　　　Mais elle y est
　　Le crâne tout écrabouillé,
　　Le crâne, et le reste, que sais-je?
　　Dans un état qui fait pitié!..."—
　　Très fiers de cette indépendance,
(Sur leur chemin pourtant tout est ruine et deuil),
　　Hors de la maison ils s'élancent,
　　Ils veulent en franchir le seuil.
　　Mais l'étrange déconvenue,
　　A peine arrivés dans la rue!...
　　Il est possible qu'autrefois,
　　Quand ils vivaient dans les grands bois,
　　A l'état de bêtes sauvages,
　Avant d'avoir été apprivoisés
　　Par quelque concierge rusé,
　　Et soumis à l'apprentissage
　　Et à la domesticité,
　　Les Ascenseurs, c'est bien possible,
　　Tout comme d'autres ont été,
　　　D'aller, venir
　　　Marcher, courir,
　　Tout comme d'autres susceptibles...

The Revolt of the Elevators

　One day, the Elevators, so they say,
　Tired of their vertical peregrinating,
　　　Dull and frustrating,
　(Say what you will: up, down, down, up, all day...
　After a while it can get nauseating...);
　Tired of a life so slavishly dependent
On their "Monsieur from Six," their old "Madame
　　　　　　from Two,"
　And all the apartmental retinue;
　Above all, fed up with the superintendent—
　　That man whose word was law, and who
　Kept them forever caged... Well, as I said,
The Elevators, with a mind to turn the tables,
　Managing (don't ask how!) to snap their cables
(And thereby also crushing the concierge's head...
　　Her daughters' too... "You'll never guess!
　　Madame... She's out there in the hall!...
　　　Her skull is all
　Bashed in!... And maybe more!... My, what a mess!")...
　　At any rate, now shackleless,
　　Our ex-"ascendants and descendants,"
　Reveling in their newfound independence
　(And sowing carnage in their wake), make for
　　　The door.
　But scarcely are they past the threshold, when
　Their bubble bursts... Perhaps, long years ago—
　Before they came to serve the needs of men,
　Roaming the wilds, like untamed beasts, with no
　　Scheming concierge domesticators,
　　　Malapropos,
　　To snatch them from their primal state—
Perhaps the primitive ancestral Elevators
　Were free to come and go, to circulate
　　To, fro, exactly as they chose:
　　　To walk, to run
　　　Like anyone...
　　If so, no longer! So it goes:
　　Habit can change the temperament.

Mais ils ont tant monté depuis, et descendu,
  Les malheureux ne savent plus,
  Car l'habitude est une autre nature,
  Sur un trottoir marcher au pas,
      A plat,
Se glisser dans la rue au milieu des voitures;
  Sur le seuil ils sont demeurés,
  Inquiets et désemparés,
  Puis, sans insister davantage,
Ecraseurs craignant d'être écrasés à leur tour,
  Ils n'ont plus eu d'autre recours
  Que de rentrer, tout piteux, dans leurs cages.

      La liberté, la liberté!...
  La liberté: sans elle on désespère,
    On veut à tout prix l'emporter;
    Mais cette liberté si chère,
  Encor faut-il pouvoir s'y adapter,
    Et, quand on l'a, savoir qu'en faire!...

Since then, because their time's been spent
  In moving perpendicularly,
  They've lost the knack; the poor things now
  Haven't the faintest notion how
      To walk about—
      Particularly
With all those autos weaving in and out...
The erstwhile crushers cower at the door
  Lest they be crushed in turn. No more
Their horizontal grandiose ambition!
Perplexed, with no recourse, and eating crow,
  Back to their cages now they go,
And reassume their vertical position.

Liberty! Liberty! Ah, liberty!
  That priceless quality! Without it,
  How you complain: "Oh, to be free..."
  Well, if you're going to have it, you
Had best know all you need to know about it,
And just what use you're going to put it to!...

Le Ballon de Football, ou le Moyen de Parvenir

    Par un magistral coup de pié
        Envoyé
      Sous la traverse
      Du camp adverse,
Le ballon de football Association,
    Plein d'une morgue ostentatoire,
    Voudrait-il pas nous faire croire
    Que, grâce à ce suprême bond,
    Dont il prétend s'attribuer la gloire,
Sa valeur personnelle emporta la victoire?
      Ton orgueil est hors de raison,
      Sans le pied vaillant qui te pousse
      Au milieu des joueurs alertes,
Tu demeurerais là, immobile et inerte,
        Ballon, sur la verte
        Pelouse!
      Quand tu réclames des bravos,
      Sache un peu mieux ce qui les vaut:
      C'est par une détente brusque
      De solides muscles cruraux,
      Que tu fus précipité jusques
      Entre et par delà les poteaux,—
Et c'est toi, maintenant, qui te crois un héros?
      Ballon, ballon, as-tu des jambes?
        Pour bondir à travers
          Les airs,
      Est-ce que vraiment il te semble
      Que bel et bien tu y atteins,
      Rien que par tes propres moyens,
      Ton agilité sans seconde?
      Et c'est de l'air supérieur
        Du vainqueur

The Soccer Ball, or How to Succeed in Life

Sent flying into the opponent's net,
      A soccer ball
        Has the gall—
O grand and glorious *vedette!*—
To think that he's the one who did it all,
  By dint of personal endeavor—
  Just one gigantic leap—with never
A thought about the kicking foot behind him.
      And so we find him
Taking full credit for *his* victory—
Yes, his and his alone... My friend, your pride
Is rather on the inappropriate side:
  Without that foot, what would you be—
The one that kicked you through the opposition?
      Just a round mass
    Lifelessly lying on the grass,
        Alas!
Please, when you clamor for our recognition,
  Try to remember who's the one
  Who really got the scoring done;
And realize it was a robust pair
Of calves and thighs that sent you through the air,
Soaring between the posts to make that point!
  So, you're a hero, are you? Well,
Your reasoning's a little out of joint:
  Do you have legs? Can you propel
  Yourself, my overweening sphere,
      From there to here?
  Really, can you believe that you
Are such an acrobat that you can do
  A feat like that—that leap, that bound—
      Unaided? Well, you

Que tu regardes tout le monde,
  Tout satisfait,
    Et tout gonflé,
      En effet,
Avec ta grosse balle ronde...

D'aucuns ainsi, — ils exagèrent,—
Volontiers imagineraient
Que le secret de tout succès,
      C'est
Pour avancer dans la carrière,
Comme ce ballon, d'encaisser,
Avec un sourire empressé,
Tous les coups de pied au derrière.

Can't, let me tell you!
And yet you sit there, looking proudly round—
    Self-overrated,
      Ego-inflated—
And full of your victorious air...

Some folks there are who, like our ball
(And just as wrong), assume that all
You have to do if you'd advance
In life, is to adopt a stance:
That is, complacently to stand,
      And,
With toadying smile, let yourself be
Kicked in the butt repeatedly...

Le Chef d'Orchestre, ou les Vocations

Quand, ayant pour cela fait certaines études,
Dans telle ou telle voie on s'était engagé,
  Quand on a pris des habitudes,
  C'est le diable pour en changer.

  Un chef d'orchestre avait eu des déboires;
    Bien qu'il fût un ancien sujet
    Fort brillant du Conservatoire,
Cela ne suffit pas toujours à ménager
De quoi boire et de quoi manger; bref, à chercher
Des moyens d'existence un peu moins illusoires,
    Il avait été obligé.
    N'attendez pas que je vous dise
    Par quel caprice du destin
    Il s'était donc, un beau matin,
    Réveillé agent de police.
Peut-être le préfet, ou bien quelque employé,
    Etait-il son compatriote,
    Qui lui avait ouvert la porte,
    Et mis le pied à l'étrier?
Un jour dans la police il s'était réveillé.
    Il n'y a pas de sot métier.
      Voilà notre homme
      En uniforme,
    Et peu à peu initié
    A un ensemble de pratiques
    Qui n'avaient, pourquoi le nier,
    Nul rapport avec la musique;
    Mais tout allait tant mal que bien
    Jusques au jour où notre ancien
      Musicien
    Fut placé dans un carrefour
      Pour,—
    Au milieu de ce va-et-vient
    Restant immobile lui-même,—
    Apporter son attention
Au difficile, au délicat problème
    De la circulation:

The Orchestra Conductor,
  or When You've Got the Calling

  When you've done all your studies in
  Only a single discipline,
It's tough to change. Make no mistake,
A habit is a damn hard thing to break.

An orchestra conductor, who had been
One of the stars of the Conservatory,
Found out that talent isn't, a priori,
  Certain to feed a hungry belly.
  In point of fact, our hero... Well, he
Fell on hard times, let's say, and had to find
Subsistence of a less illusive kind.
Through quirks of fate I won't attempt to tell, he
Woke up one day a traffic cop. (Perhaps
  The prefect, or one of the chaps
  He knew from home, had helped him put
    His foot—
Figuratively speaking—in the door.)
No matter. Work is work. So, as I say,
    One day
He woke up as a flic, new to the corps,
With uniform and all; and bit by bit,
Learned lots of things he'd never known before;
  Things that, I must admit,
Had absolutely nothing—not a whit—
  To do with music. Anyway,
Nevertheless, and be that as it may,
  He tried to make the best of it,
    Our ex-musician—
    The best he could—
Until the day he took up his position
    And stood
  Stolidly in his intersection,
Charged with his awesome mission: the direction
Of traffic—hustling, bustling back and forth,
  And forth and back: east, west, south, north...
    Now then,
They give our friend a stick—on introspection,

Même eut-on l'imprudence extrême
De lui donner, pour ce faire, un bâton.
　　Dérision, dérision!
　　Aussi bien le bruit des klaxons,
　　Ces cris, ces cloches et ces trompes,
　　Il est naturel qu'il s'y trompe,
　　　　Et qu'il se croie
　　　　Comme autrefois
Chargé de diriger le nouveau concerto
　D'un de nos plus modernes maestros;
Le bâton à la main, il retrouve les gestes,
　Tous ses gestes de chef d'orchestre,—
　　Et c'est tant pis pour les autos,
　　Et les piétons, s'il en reste...

Folly galore! given his predilection—
　　　　And when
He hears those horns, shouts, squeaks, cacophonies,
It's only natural to think that he's
　　Back in the concert hall again,
　　　　On the stand,
　　　　In command,
　　Conducting some new, nonharmonic
Masterpiece from a modern pen symphonic.
　　　　Baton in hand,
　　　　With gestures deft,
Blithely our maestro leads his blaring band,
Oblivious quite to all the autos, and
Pedestrians too... If there are any left...

Les Petits Pois

　　　　Tel, chez soi
　　　　Se trouve à l'étroit,
　Rongeant son frein avec rage, et s'indigne
　Contre les vieilles disciplines:
"Qui donc nous aidera à secouer ce joug?"
Quand l'émancipateur apparaît, magnanime,
　　Tu lui embrasses les genoux,
　En son honneur tu entonnes des hymnes;
　　Prends garde que, sept fois sur huit,
La générosité n'est pas ce qui l'anime,
　　Seul l'égoïsme le conduit:
　　Il t'émancipe à son profit
　Et tu seras sa dupe et sa victime.

　　"Faut-il," disaient ces petits pois,
　　"Emprisonnés dès la naissance,
De la captivité subir les dures lois
　　Tout le long de notre existence?
Aucun contact avec le monde extérieur;
　　Pareils au pire malfaiteur,
　　Au fond d'un cul de basse-fosse,
　　　　Dans cette cosse,
　　　　Nous subissons
　　　　La peine atroce
　　　　De la prison;
　　Quel crime ont commis nos ancêtres,
　　Que si chèrement nous payons?
La chaleur du soleil, il est vrai, nous pénètre,
　　Nous ne voyons pas ses rayons.
　　En vain nos plaintes retentissent,
　　Personne n'y veut faire écho;
　　Les griffes de l'obscurantisme
　　Sur nous, hélas! s'appesantissent,
　　　　Et comme un étau
　　　　Se resserrent:
　　Nous étouffons! de l'air!... de la lumière!..."
　　Enfin le libérateur vient,
Et brisera pour eux les portes de la geôle...

The Peas

　　　There are, I think it's safe
　　To say, some who will champ and chafe
　　　Against the imposition
Of their "old fashioned" family tradition...
　　"Please! Won't someone deliver us
　　　From our submission?..."
And when your merciful, magnanimous
　　Deliverer appears, at last,
You sing his praise and kiss his feet. Well, not so fast,
　Poor dupe! Most times—eight out of nine, to wit—[1]
His generosity is counterfeit:
He'll free you, yes, but only for the profit
　That he and he alone makes off it.

　　A pod of peas sigh, moan: "Ah me!
　　Why must we be confined, since birth,
Condemned to suffer, all our days on earth,
　　The torments of captivity?
　　No contact with the world outside us...
　　Worse than some criminal, they hide us
Down in the bowels of this blasted ditch!
What foul crime did our ancestors commit,
　　That we should have to pay for it,
Imprisoned in our pod, as black as pitch,
　　　　To languish
　　　　And lie
　　　　In anguish!
　　　Why? Oh why?
　It's true, we feel the warm rays of the sun,
　　But still, it's hidden from our eye!
　　And so we mourn, and so we sigh...
　　But all in vain! Won't anyone
Come free us from obscurantism's clutches?[2]
Light! Light!... Air! Give us air!... We're suffocating!..."
　　　　Such is
The peas' lament. In time, when comes the liberating,
　The long-awaited pea-emancipator
　Will smash their prison walls without ado.

Les petits pois bénissent cette main
Qui, dès ce soir, ou au plus tard demain,
    Les mettra dans la casserole.

Our peas will bless their hero's hand; their savior, who,
    Tonight—perhaps tomorrow, but no later—
      Is going to toss them in the stew.

1. The minor liberty I have taken with the poet's arithmetic is dictated by exigencies of meter, much as his own choice of fraction is called for by his rhyme. (For that matter, the observant reader will notice that Franc-Nohain himself is less than rigorous as to the purity of some of the rhymes he chooses.)

2. While the author surely knows the difference between *obscurantisme* and *obscurité*, one has to assume that his peas do not. I respect his malapropism.

Louis Mirault   Roses d'Automne: Recueil de Fables, Chansons et Elégies (1928)

Between 1896 and 1939 there appeared some ten collections of sentimental, patriotic, religious, and folkloric verse and theater by one Louis Mirault, published variously under that name, the compound name "Louis Mirault-Fromont," and the pseudonym "Fanchy," several in collaboration with illustrators of the period: Pierre Chambon, Henry Bar, and Henri Foreau.[1] Biographical details are conspicuously lacking, but it is apparent from a reading of his homey volume *Roses d'automne: recueil de fables, chansons et élégies*—prefaced by World War I memorialist Jacques Péricard, and one of Mirault's two fable collections—that he was a native of Touraine, a devoted father and grandfather, a poet of traditional tastes and style; and that he was already, by his own admission, in the "automne de la vie" when he published his aptly titled work, one which bears as its appropriate epigraph Agrippa d'Aubigné's celebrated line, "Une rose d'automne est plus qu'une autre exquise" ("Aux lecteurs," p. 11).

Of the ninety-three brief poems that constitute Mirault's collection—each one dedicated with a disarming fidelity to some friend, colleague, or family member—about half are, as the subtitle indicates, *chansons* and *élégies,* all of rather saccharine inspiration and expression. The rest are fables, cast in the sacrosanct *vers libres* mold, with equally time-honored didactic purpose. Many, indeed, present characters drawn from a flora and fauna no less traditional, or at least traditional-sounding: "La Chauve-souris et le Papa Crapaud," "Le Champignon et le Petit Lapin," "Le Peuplier et le Sapin," "Le Lapin et le Mulot," et al. A number, however—and clearly the most engaging—offer a more contemporary, and even capricious, personnel that commends them to our attention. The likes of "Le Vieillard et les Automobilistes," "La Sucette et le Hochet," "Le Radiateur et la Cheminée," "La Cravate et les Bretelles," and such, are modern departures from the venerable corpus: pleasant and unpretentious variations within the time-honored form.

Among the latter group, "La Mousse," translated here, is the forty-third poem in Mirault's unnumbered collection; a striking mini-drama typical of his talent when left unencumbered by excessive sentimentality.

1. Mirault has escaped the notice of the standard bibliographies. The list of his work, however, insofar as I can determine it, in addition to *Roses d'automne,* is as follows: *Le Calvaire,* one act in verse; *Fleurs de Touraine,* poems, preface by Edmond Porcher; *Jeanne d'Arc* ("poème héroïque couronné par la ville de Beauvais"); *La Terre qui chante,* poems and theater; *Brindilles: recueil de fables et contes en vers; Molène aux champs; Au pas d'nos bœufs: patoiseries nivernaises, poésies et contes,* preface by Claude Aveline; and *Théâtre nivernais,* three plays by Mirault ("Fanchy"), three by the illustrator Pierre Chambon, and two in collaboration, preface by Simonne Ratel. To the list should be added a volume of verse entitled *Le Sonnailler,* published before 1928, but for which I have no further bibliographical details.

La Mousse

Toute fraîche tirée et débordant du verre,
Demoiselle la mousse, un jour, dit à la bière:
"Que vous devez, madame, au Très-Haut vous louer
Sur votre flot épais de me voir surnager!
    Du houblon lourde fille,
Que seriez-vous sans moi qui foisonne et pétille?

The Foam

Straight from the spigot, freshly poured,
Fairly brimming over the glass,
A head of foam—a bubbling lass—
Said to the beer: "You well might praise the Lord,
    Madame, to have me floating here
Above your dull and sluggish brew.

Jusqu'à votre fraîcheur, tout votre charme enfin
      Est inclus dans mon sein;
Tel au front d'une belle une aimable coiffure,
      Je suis votre parure;
      Et lorsque, les yeux clos,
      Le buveur à grands flots
      D'un seul trait nous avale,
Et puis se pourléchant, sur son siège s'étale
      Et songe tout béat,
A coup sûr c'est de moi qu'il tient ce doux état!"
      D'une race tranquille,
      A troubler peu facile,
      L'autre se recueillit
      Et doucement lui fit:
"Oh! que tu parles bien, que de brio, ma chère!
Pour t'instruire à ce point, qu'a dépensé ton père!
Mais attendons, veux-tu, quelques instants encor,
      Nous verrons, beau trésor,
      En faisant de la sorte,
Comment ton haut talent dans le fond se comporte,
Car enfin si briller est bien pour certains yeux,
M'est avis que durer, ô mousse, est encor mieux."
Elle accepte, on attend, et notre mijaurée
      S'affaisse évaporée.

MORALE

Il est beaucoup d'enfants, et des plus grands aussi,
Qui pourront méditer sur ce simple récit,
Car plus d'un sot bavard en tous lieux qui se pousse,
N'a pour pseudo-talent et que brigue et que mousse.

You dismal daughter of the hops! Why, dear,
      Without my froth to liven you,
          What would you do?
          I am your gem—
          Your diadem—
Like lady's elegant coiffure, your crown!
And when, eyes dimmed, our drinker quaffs us down,
      Sits back, and licks his lips in bliss,
I, madame, I take credit for all that!"
      On hearing this,
The beer decides to give her tit for tat.
      After a moment's hesitation,
Unruffled, she replies: "How eloquent!
My dear, I'm sure your father must have spent
      A fortune on your education!
      But let's just wait a bit, my treasure.
          Let's see, my sweet,
          How time may treat
Your talents; how it takes their measure.
For some, what shines and glitters gives much pleasure;
For me, what lasts gives more and better, surely."
The foam agreed to wait. And so they waited...
Until our precious demoiselle, demurely,
      Evaporated.

MORAL

This simple fable drives its message home.
Children, and grown-ups too, may well take heed:
Many's the foolish chatterbox, indeed,
Whose would-be talents are all fuss and foam.

Jacques Prévert   Histoires (1946)

Jacques Prévert was born in Neuilly-sur-Seine on February 4, 1900, and died on April 12, 1977, in the Channel village of Omonville-la-Petite. Most English-speaking readers who know his name probably remember it dimly from having read one or more of his linguistically straightforward—though deceptively so—little poems in some early French course, in which they have been standard fare since soon after the appearance of his first collection, *Paroles,* in 1946.[1] Fewer, probably, will know him as the lyricist of such favorite French songs as "Les Feuilles mortes," set to music by Joseph Kosma and popularized by singer-actor Yves Montand, or the many others performed by stars Juliette Greco, Mouloudji, Les Frères Jacques, et al.; or for his work on the screenplays of well-known films the likes of *Drôle de drame* (1937), *Quai des brumes* (1938), and *Les Enfants du paradis* (1943), to name only three of many.[2] Fewer still will be aware of

his early ties with the Surrealists—though more for reasons of personal friendship than through much deep stylistic or philosophical affinity—or of the intellectual and artistic prestige he enjoyed as one of the most prominent literary figures of mid-century France. But even French readers, to whom his name is far more familiar, will not think of him as a fabulist. At least not in the traditional sense.

And for good reason. True, it is not difficult to extract an often-irreverent message or a nonconformist *morale* of sorts from much of his wide array of characteristic free verse: messages and morals born of the poet's confrontation with the realities of everyday life, especially the life of the Parisian landscape and its popular fauna, and expressed in a style ranging from the self-consciously simple to the verbally acrobatic. True as well, animals—and birds in particular—are not uncommon or unimportant elements of his poetic palette.[3] But in all his published works, to my knowledge at least, there is only a single traditional fable, even if it is not formally called such; namely, the brief poem "Le Chat et l'Oiseau," dating from early among his publications but already typical of the ironic twist and the spare but compelling style that were to mark much of his later verse.[4] Ironic enough in its moral, and compelling enough in its style, despite its simplicity, to prompt one perceptive scholar to devote an entire article to its apparent parodic intent, analyzing this superbly understated little *reductio ad maleficium,* in

which "Das Böse ist in seinem Element," and whose wit "liegt in der Verbindung von bewahrter Form und pervertierten Geist." (See Hinrich Hudde, "Jacques Préverts Fabelparodie 'Le Chat et l'Oiseau': Über den besondern Nutzen der Fabeln in den Schulen," pp. 246–47.)

In spite of—or, perhaps, because of—its uniqueness among Prévert's works, I offer "Le Chat et l'Oiseau" as a twentieth-century fable very much a product of its own time—not wholly disdainful of traditional French prosody, but almost!—but no less obviously aware of its literary roots.[5]

---

1. *Paroles,* which brought together a number of already-popular poems, and which has gone through several editions, remains, along with *La Pluie et le beau temps,* among Prévert's most widely read work.

2. The lyric of "Les Feuilles mortes" has been published in the posthumous volume *Soleil de nuit,* a collection of disparate texts written from 1936 until his death. For documentation on Prévert's significant work in film, see, inter alia: Jean Queval, *Jacques Prévert,* pp. 245–49; Gérard Guillot, *Les Prévert;* and Michel Rachline, *Jacques Prévert, drôle de vie.*

3. See for example the group of eight deliciously wry *Contes pour enfants pas sages*—prose poems if one wants to see them as such—originally published, with illustrations by Elsa Henriquez, in 1947, and

later included in *Histoires et d'autres histoires.* On Prévert's animal inspiration in general, see Queval, *Jacques Prévert,* pp. 147–55.

4. The fable first appeared in *Histoires: 30 poèmes de Jacques Prévert, 30 poèmes d'André Verdet, 31 dessins de Mayo,* and was subsequently reprinted, along with Prévert's other poems of that collection, with minor typographical alteration, in *Histoires et d'autres histoires.* Like many of his early poems, it too was set to music by Kosma and interpreted by Montand.

5. For other studies of Prévert, and for bibliographies, see especially the following: William Baker, *Jacques Prévert;* Georges Bataille, "De l'âge de pierre à Jacques Prévert"; Andrée Bergens, *Jacques Prévert;* and Verena Weber, *Form und Funktion von Sprachspielen, dargestellt anhand des poetischen Werkes von Jacques Prévert.*

Le Chat et l'Oiseau

Un village écoute désolé
Le chant d'un oiseau blessé
C'est le seul oiseau du village
Et c'est le seul chat du village
Qui l'a à moitié dévoré
Et l'oiseau cesse de chanter
Le chat cesse de ronronner
Et de se lécher le museau
Et le village fait à l'oiseau
De merveilleuses funérailles
Et le chat qui est invité
Marche derrière le petit cercueil de paille
Où l'oiseau mort est allongé
Porté par une petite fille
Qui n'arrête pas de pleurer
Si j'avais su que cela te fasse tant de peine
Lui dit le chat
Je l'aurais mangé tout entier
Et puis je t'aurais raconté
Que je l'avais vu s'envoler
S'envoler jusqu'au bout du monde
Là-bas où c'est tellement loin
Que jamais on n'en revient
Tu aurais eu moins de chagrin
Simplement de la tristesse et des regrets

Il ne faut jamais faire les choses à moitié.

The Cat and the Bird

A village sadly listened and heard
The singing of a wounded bird
The one and only bird in town
And it's the only cat in town
That half-devoured him down at that
But all at once bird's singing stops
And cat stops purring and licking his chops
And the town makes a funeral second to none
As for the cat
Invited along with everyone
He follows behind the little straw coffin
They're carrying the bird's corpse off in
Held in the hands of a little miss
Weeping her eyes out sobbing crying
Well now what's this
The cat surprised queries the tot
If I had known you would be so chagrined
I would have eaten him on the spot
And told you I had seen him flying
Flying aloft off on the wind
Off to some land so far that never
Will he return but stay forever
You'd miss him for a while I guess
But it could well have spared you much distress

We ought not ever leave what we've begun
Half done.

Jean Anouilh   Fables (1962)

DRAMATIST Jean Anouilh is too well known, and his production too well documented and studied, to need extensive elaboration in these pages.[1] When he died at his Swiss retreat near Lausanne on October 3, 1987, he had earned a reputation as, probably, one of the most significant and, unquestionably, one of the most widely staged of modern playwrights, especially beyond the borders of his native France.

Anouilh was born in Bordeaux on June 23, 1910. Early abandoning the study of law in Paris, he began his long theatrical career—sparked no doubt in childhood by his violinist mother's performances in local operettas—as secretary to the renowned actor Louis Jouvet at the age of eighteen. Four years later he produced his first important play, *L'Ermine,* initiating his series of so-called *pièces noires.*[2] It was, curiously, not until relatively late in life, after he had written most of the forty-odd plays of his repertory—dramas, comedies, modern adaptations of classical themes—that his importance was recognized by Parisian theatrical officialdom with a production at the Comédie-Française: a revival of his historical drama *Becket,* premiered a dozen years earlier.

Much admired for his serious plays, philosophical but mercifully free of doctrinaire or ideological attitudinizing, Anouilh characteristically pits his pure and uncompromisingly moral heroes and heroines against an impure and hostile social order. *Antigone,* his reworking of the Sophoclean tragedy, dating from 1944 during the Nazi occupation, is perhaps the best-known example. The same cynical, pessimistic view of the human condition, to some extent at least, and with a variety of dramatic devices, runs through his comedies as well, among the most widely produced of which are *Le Bal des voleurs* (1938) and *La Valse des toréadors* (1952). "If in [his] 'black plays' society triumphs over the absolute ideal and compels the heroes to seek a tragic form of escape, in the 'pink plays' Anouilh's characters escape black reality through fantasy, illusion, and changing personality. It is as if the author felt that the world, with its fiendish problems, lacked and needed the sense of humor that he attempted to provide in 'pink' situations." (See Della Fazia, *Jean Anouilh,* p. 68.)

Many theatergoers and scholars who know Anouilh's theater well probably do not suspect that the dramatist was also a fabulist, though admittedly only as a summer diversion. In 1962 one of his Parisian publishers, La Table Ronde, brought out his collection of forty-seven La Fontainesque *Fables,* "le plaisir d'un été," according to his brief prefatory note. "Je voudrais," he specifies, "qu'on les lise aussi vite et aussi facilement que je les ai faites" (p. 7). These disarmingly offhand mini-dramas were clearly inspired by much the same cynicism as his "pièces noires" and "pièces grinçantes," and the same wry humor that informs his comedies, albeit in different degree and dosage.

"L'Enterrement," "Le Chêne et le Roseau," "L'Oiseau Rare," and "Napoléon et la Puce"—respectively the third, fifth, twelfth, and forty-second of the unnumbered fables in his volume—are typical examples of the qualities that make Anouilh's collection an engaging and indispensable twentieth-century contribution to the genre.

---

1. In addition to chapters in many general and specialized works on the modern theater, a number of studies, in French and English—not to mention other European languages—have been devoted to his career, throughout its progressive stages; among them, the following: Jean Didier, *A la rencontre de Jean Anouilh;* Hubert Gignoux, *Jean Anouilh;* Jean-Pierre Lassalle, *Jean Anouilh, ou La vaine révolte;* Robert de Luppé, *Jean Anouilh;* Leonard C. Pronko, *The World of Jean Anouilh;* Philippe Jolivet, *Le Théâtre de Jean Anouilh;* John Harvey, *Anouilh: A Study in Theatrics;* Pol Vandromme, *Jean Anouilh: un au-teur et ses personnages;* Philip Thody, *Anouilh;* Paul Ginestier, *Jean Anouilh;* Alba Della Fazia, *Jean Anouilh;* Marguerite Archer, *Jean Anouilh;* and Branko Alan Lanski, *Jean Anouilh: Stages in Rebellion.* For a detailed bibliography the reader should consult Kathleen White Kelly, *Jean Anouilh: An Annotated Bibliography.*

2. Anouilh divided most of his plays into several categories: "pièces noires," "pièces roses," "pièces grinçantes," "pièces costumées," et al., although in some cases the division appears rather more arbitrary than those phrases might imply.

L'Enterrement

Le chien suivait l'enterrement du maître.
Il pensait aux caresses;
Et il pensait aux coups.
Les caresses étaient plus fortes...

Dans le cortège, on s'indignait beaucoup.
On excusait la veuve—elle était comme morte.
On pardonnait à la maîtresse
(Elle était morte aussi).

The Funeral

Trotting behind the funeral procession,
The master's dog
Remembers both his cuff and his caress—
Especially the latter...

All monsieur's mourners march agog
At such an untoward indiscretion...
Madame, poor thing, is blameless in the matter,
Utterly prostrate with distress.[1]

Mais, qu'en la présence du prêtre,
La bonne ait pu laisser vagabonder ainsi
Ce chien au milieu du cortège!
Ah! Ces filles vraiment ne se font nul souci.
Quelqu'un, l'ordonnateur, la famille, que sais-je?
Aurait dû l'obliger à attacher le chien!
Elle-même, voyons! C'est une propre à rien
Qui n'avait même pas l'excuse du chagrin.
Pourquoi la gardaient-ils? Un ménage d'artistes...
De véritables bohémiens.
Ce monde-là vivait d'une étrange manière...
De coup de pied en coup de pied dans le derrière,
Rejeté à la queue du cortège, le chien
Songeait que seule la bonne était triste;
La bonne qui ne disait rien,
Et à qui ne parlait personne.
Il suivit jusqu'au bout aux côtés de la bonne.
Au cimetière, tous les deux au dernier rang
Ils écoutèrent le discours du président
De la Société des Auteurs Dramatiques.
A la fin, las du pathétique,
Le chien s'avança posément
Et, pour venger un peu la bonne,
Il pissa sur une couronne.

So too the mistress of the dear deceased
(Laid low, half dead!)... But not the maid.
No!... "She's to blame, the thoughtless jade!..."
"Scandalous! Just imagine!..." "And the priest
Is here to boot! What must he think? To let that beast
Follow the bier!..." "What? No one thought to
Tell her that dogs don't just run loose?..."
"Really, they ought to
Teach her a thing or two!..." "What's her excuse?
Surely not grief!..." "Grief? Her? A maid?..." "Odd family...
Artistes... Bohemians, you know..."
And so they chatter as they go,
Kicking the dog from heel to heel... Back... Back...
Till he
Falls far behind,
He and the maid; but, in his mind,
The thought that she alone—silent, ignored—
Is truly sad, the one real mourner...
And, as monsieur is sent to his reward,
Maid and dog, side by side, off in a corner,
Hear the oration of the chairman of the board
Of the Société des Auteurs Dramatiques...
At length, the dog, fed up with all their mawkishness—
And to avenge the maid, I guess—
Squats on a wreath and calmly takes a leak.

1. I have preserved the curious capriciousness, if not the exact disposition, of Anouilh's opening rhyme (and, for that matter, have taken as much liberty with my rhymes, throughout, as does he with his). The reader will also notice in these translations that I have not, however, preserved Anouilh's rather unorthodox line arrangement; unorthodox, because most French fabulists—indeed, most French poets of any traditional genre—prefer grouping lines according to syllable-count rather than with an eye for visual symmetry. Anouilh opts for the latter arrangement, perhaps because, in fact, a number of his lines do not scan in the usual manner.

Le Chêne et le Roseau

Le chêne un jour dit au roseau:
"N'êtes-vous pas lassé d'écouter cette fable?
La morale en est détestable;
Les hommes bien légers de l'apprendre aux marmots.
Plier, plier toujours, n'est-ce pas déjà trop,
Le pli de l'humaine nature?"
"Voire," dit le roseau, "il ne fait pas trop beau;
Le vent qui secoue vos ramures
(Si je puis en juger à niveau de roseau)
Pourrait vous prouver, d'aventure,
Que nous autres, petites gens,
Si faibles, si chétifs, si humbles, si prudents,
Dont la petite vie est le souci constant,
Résistons pourtant mieux aux tempêtes du monde,
Que certains orgueilleux qui s'imaginent grands."

Le vent se lève sur ses mots, l'orage gronde.
Et le souffle profond qui dévaste les bois,
Tout comme la première fois,
Jette le chêne fier qui le narguait par terre.
"Hé bien," dit le roseau, le cyclone passé—
Il se tenait courbé par un reste de vent—

The Oak Tree and the Reed

One day the oak tree asked the reed:
"That foolish fable, don't you just despise it,
Moral and all? How daft indeed
Of Man, to make his youngsters memorize it![1]
'Bend! Bend!' it preaches!... Bah! As though
Bowing and scraping weren't his normal bent!"
The reed replied: "My friend, quite so...
But, for the sake of argument,
What if the wind that blows your branches to and fro,
That takes your measure, and defies it—
Or so it seems from here below,
From reed's-eye view... What if, likewise, it
Proved that we little folk—weak, wary, humble—
Better resist the storm than those who crow
Their grandeur pompously, only in time to tumble!"

No sooner had he said his say than, with a roar
And thunderous rumble,
There rose one of those gusts that rip the woods asunder,
Toppling the haughty oak, just as before.
"Well now, what do you know! I wonder... ,"
Smirking, the pliant reed derided—

"Qu'en dites-vous donc mon compère?"
(Il ne se fût jamais permis ce mot avant)
"Ce que j'avais prédit n'est-il pas arrivé?"
On sentait dans sa voix sa haine
Satisfaite. Son morne regard allumé.
Le géant, qui souffrait, blessé,
De mille morts, de mille peines,
Eut un sourire triste et beau;
Et, avant de mourir, regardant le roseau,
Lui dit: "Je suis encore un chêne."

Still gently bowing as the gale subsided—
"I wonder, *cher compère,*" he twitted
(Sarcasm seeming now to be permitted),
"What? Can it be that I was right?" His tone betrayed
A longtime loathing, suddenly defiant.
Suffering, dying, but still undismayed,
Smiling a soulful smile, our wounded giant
Chided: "Quite so... You bent, I broke... [2]
Indeed, my friend. But I'm afraid
You're still a reed... And I'm no less an oak!"

1. The allusion to La Fontaine's fable "Le Chêne et le Roseau" (I, 22) is obvious (see p. 33). The moral, however, is not so unambiguous. If Anouilh's oak maintains his pride despite his downfall—as he also does in Boisard's version (see p. 91)—it is a pride not untainted by hubris. The reed, on the other hand, though vindicated and victorious, is not a particularly sympathetic hero either.

2. I have taken the intertextual liberty of having Anouilh's oak refer explicitly to the celebrated assertion of La Fontaine's reed: "Je plie, et ne romps pas."

L'Oiseau Rare

Des canards vexés, des oies satisfaites,
Au bord d'un étang, regardaient passer
Un oiseau royal dont la fière aigrette
Les faisait glousser.
"Mais regardez donc, quelle outrecuidance,
S'en venir ici narguer le fermier!"
"Vraiment, vous trouvez, c'est de l'élégance?
Si c'est ça le goût des grands couturiers!"
"Une robe grise, une robe blanche,
Voilà ce qu'il faut aux bêtes honnêtes!"
"Pour rien au monde je ne porterais d'aigrettes!"
Gémit avec effroi
Une oie,
A qui jamais quelqu'un n'en aurait proposé.
"Et c'est un mâle!" criaient les canards courroucés.
"S'il devait travailler pour vivre, tout crotté,
Il aurait bien le temps de les lisser, ses plumes!"

Un rayon de soleil, qui sortit de la brume,
Les fit taire un instant, inondant l'inconnu
D'or et de pourpre au milieu de l'étang.
Ils se reprirent vite et ils crièrent tant
Que l'homme, enfin prévenu,
Sortit fusil en main et, du seuil de la ferme,
Tira. L'oiseau blessé gagna la terre ferme,
Se coucha et mourut sans un regard
A la basse-cour caquetante.
"Un peu plus tôt, un peu plus tard,
Ça devait arriver!" dirent les oies contentes.
"Il n'a que ce qu'il est venu chercher!
Que gagne-t-on à se faire remarquer?"
"Nous n'avons pas, sur notre tête, une couronne,
Mais du moins nous vivons, et la vie est bien bonne,"
Conclurent-ils tous, satisfaits.

Le fermier prit l'oiseau et pour sa fiancée
Avec ses plumes d'or fit un chapeau de fée.

The Rare Bird

His head all tuft and plume, taking his leisure
Pondside, a royal bird comes strutting by,
As goose and duck—with smug and jaundiced eye,
A-cackle and a-cluck—voice their displeasure.
"The nerve! To come here to impress us!
Vulgar display!..."
"If that's your *grands couturiers,*
Thank heaven they don't dress us!
Good honest folk wear white or grey..."
"I'd never wear such fancy filigree!... For shame,
For shame!" lets loose
A goose
Unlikely ever to be offered same!...
The ducks, vexed by our popinjay,
Heap their abuse:
"Let monsieur work... Dirty his hands... Then we'll
see whether
He has the time to be so fine of feather!

A shaft of sunlight pierced the mist
That hung above the pond. Ducks and geese suddenly
Fell silent, as their elegant antagonist
Stood swathed in gold and purple finery.
But not for long... Next moment, once again
They raise such hue and cry that, there and then,
Out runs the farmer, gun in hand...
Fires... Hits the bird,
Who, struggling to reach land,
Lies down and dies without a word,
Without deigning a glance at all the gaggling band.[1]
"Sooner or later..." sneered the geese. "He should
Have understood!
It's best not to be so conspicuous.
No haughty airs, no tufted crowns for us!
But we still have our life, at least, and life is good."

The farmer took the bird, and, for his fiancée—
Most generous of grooms—

Aux fiançailles, qui eurent lieu deux jours plus tard,
L'oiseau d'or fit rosir de joie la jeune fille
Qui se sentit belle et aimée...
Pour le reste de la famille
Et pour le gros des invités
—Ne se nourrissant pas seulement de beauté—
Dans une bonne fricassée,
Chacun devant, un peu plus tôt, un peu plus tard,
Jouer son rôle,
Mesdames les oies et Messieurs les canards
Passèrent à la casserole.

Fashioned a hat fit for a fairy tale. Next day,
    The couple being duly feted,
Mademoiselle, *la belle* (admired—nay, adulated)
    Blushed in her gilded plumes...
    And for the rest—friends, family—
Since beauty satisfies the spirit, but
    Does precious little for the gut,
    A tasty fricassee...
As everyone, "sooner or later," has to do,
    Our ducks and geese played out their destiny:
        Where?... In the stew![2]

1. Anouilh's scenario is reminiscent of at least two literary antecedents. The farmer's crass, unthinking destruction of a *rara avis*
recalls, if only superficially, the action of Auguste de Villiers de
l'Isle-Adam's antihero Tribulat Bonhomet, in *Le Tueur de cygnes*
(1887). Likewise, the bird's disdainful acceptance of his fate brings to
mind the wolf's stoic death at the hands of the hunters in Alfred de

Vigny's celebrated poem "La Mort du loup" (1838): "Et, sans daigner
savoir comment il a péri, / Refermant ses grands yeux, meurt sans
jeter un cri."
    2. The last line is more than literally true. *Passer à la casserole* has
a variety of figurative slang connotations, from the innocuous "get it
in the neck" to the more physical "get screwed."

Napoléon et la Puce

"Que voulez-vous que cela fasse
A un homme comme moi," dit Napoléon,
        Les regardant
Qui l'acclamaient sous le balcon
"La vie d'un million d'imbéciles?"

(Il dit un mot plus court que Metternich, galant,
    N'osait pas répéter aux dames.)
Au lieu de rétorquer: "Mais, Sire, ils ont une âme..."
    (C'était la réplique facile)
    Metternich demeura de glace,
Sourit dans sa cravate et ne dit rien.
Le mot était lâché, il serait historique;
    Le fin renard se doutait bien
Que le Corse, par lui, aggraverait son cas.
Lui Metternich, bien sûr aussi, dans la pratique...
    Mais lui, il ne le disait pas.

A ce moment, sournoise et rancunière,
    La puce qu'il avait déjà chassée
De son gilet, par tant de sans-gêne agacée,
    Piqua Napoléon au derrière...
        On a beau être Napoléon
On ne peut pas se le gratter dans un salon.
    Le masque du maître du monde
        Se durcit une seconde;
Et Metternich, sans cesser d'être souriant,
Sentit l'Europe soudain jetée sur la table
Comme un quartier de bœuf saignant.
    Tranchant, Napoléon dit: "Non."
Dès lors, la guerre était inévitable;
    La parole était au canon.

L'histoire n'a pas retenu le nom
        De cette puce.
Elle l'aurait pourtant piqué ailleurs, ne fût-ce
Qu'un peu plus haut, un peu plus bas,

Napoleon and the Flea

    "Considering who I am,"
Napoleon mused, as underneath his balcony
    The crowd cheered on, "why should a man like me
        Give a good damn
        About a million stupid scum?"

(He'd used a cruder term; but Metternich, reporting,
        Found it too nettlesome
For ladies' tender ears.) And rather than retorting
        The obvious reply
("Yes, but they all have souls..."), the wily fox had stood
    In icy silence, with a wry
    Vest-pocket smile. The Corsican had spoken.
    His mot, no doubt historic by and by,
        Would surely do him little good
            As little as it would
Do silent Metternich, in time, by the same token.

Just then a flea, chased from his undershirt, and much
        Offended by the cavalier,
    Insouciant scratch, bit at the royal rear...
    Napoleon or not, one doesn't touch
            One's rump in the salon.
    The master of the universe grew grim;
            And thereupon,
    Metternich, still all smiles, observing him,
    Sensed that the Continent had just been hurled
Upon the table, like a bloody side of beef.
        Napoleon's response was brief:
        A cutting "No!" And so the world
            Would soon be plunged in war.
Once more the cannon was to take the floor.[1]

History doesn't give the name of this
            Vindictive flea.
        Still, in the last analysis,
    If it had bitten up or down a bit,

L'Empereur détendu renonçait au combat.
A quoi cela tient tout de même!
Gémit le philosophe blême:
Le nez de Cléopâtre il eût... et cætera.
Changeant—hélas! trop tard pour la France—de place
La puce, sans marquer d'émoi,
Poursuivit son exploration
De l'impérial caleçon
Et dit: "Que voulez-vous que cela fasse
A une puce comme moi
Le derrière de Napoléon?"

The Emperor would have seen fit
To keep the peace. Ah, the absurdity
Of causes and effects! "If Cleopatra's nose..."
Groaned the philosopher... But you know how it goes.[2]
The flea—too late, alas, for France—
Pursuing quite impassively
Its exploration of the royal underpants,
Pressed on and on, exclaiming: "What?
Considering who I am,
Why should a flea like me give a good damn
About Napoleon's blessèd butt?"

1. The fictionalized scenario would seem to have been inspired, in its broad lines, by Napoleon's celebrated meeting with Metternich at the Marcolini Palace in Dresden, on June 26, 1813, during the six-week armistice following the battle of Lützen. The intriguing Austrian diplomat was attempting—at least ostensibly—to negotiate peace between the Emperor and the Allies. Napoleon was ultimately to reject the proposed conditions, though not with the dramatic decisiveness here suggested. (See, inter alia, Louis-François-Joseph de Bausset, *Mémoires anecdotiques sur l'intérieur du palais et sur quelques événemens de l'Empire depuis 1805 jusqu'au premier mai 1814 pour servir à*

l'histoire de Napoléon, II:200–202; and *Mémoires, documents et écrits divers laissés par le prince de Metternich*, II:461–63.) Austria promptly declared war, and the ensuing resumption of hostilities led to the disastrous battle of Leipzig, and to Napoleon's eventual short-lived abdication and exile to Elba.

2. The reference is to Blaise Pascal, who, in his *Pensées* (published posthumously in 1670), made his famous observation on the length of Cleopatra's nose and its influence on world history: "Le nez de Cléopâtre s'il eût été plus court toute la face de la terre aurait changé" (no. 413).

Gabriel Audisio   Fables (1966)

Overshadowed by the towering figure of his younger compatriot Albert Camus, Gabriel Audisio was, nonetheless, among the most prolific and widely respected of pre-Independence French North African writers, and one of the prime movers and pervasive forces of the so-called Ecole d'Alger, a group of literati of the thirties and forties "determined to open the way for the 'new Algerian culture.'" (See Germaine Brée, *Twentieth-Century French Literature*, p. 277.)[1] This loosely knit "school," linked together more by accident of geography and history than by any compelling ideology, included such diverse men of letters as Max-Pol Fouchet, Emmanuel Roblès, Mohammed Dib, Jean Amrouche, Camus himself for a time, and the outspoken historian of Algeria's bloody separation from France, Jules Roy. It is Roy who, in a lyrical preface to Audisio's no-less-lyrical memoirs, *L'Opéra fabuleux*, recalls nostalgically the one element that truly bound them all together: "Notre vraie patrie était pour nous tous le soleil" (p. 12). And he goes on to apostrophize the then-sexagenarian Audisio, spiritual leader of the group, as a latter-day Ulysses: "Toi, Audisio, tu as été Ulysse errant en Méditerranée. Tu... as chanté la mer, le ciel, Jonas et les poissons, la majesté de Salammbô sous les étoiles, les anges qui veillent sur les hommes" (pp. 14–15). It is, indeed, Audisio's passion for the Mediterranean culture in general, and for his adopted Algeria in particular, that informs most of his voluminous *œuvre*.[2]

This influential poet, novelist, and essayist was born in Marseille on July 27, 1900.[3] At the age of ten he arrived in Algiers, where his father, Victor Audisio, was director of the Opéra d'Alger, and spent his childhood in that fabled city which was to provide so much of his inspiration. His schooling, pursued in both Algiers and Aix-en-Provence, eventually led to a degree in Oriental studies and Moslem civilization.[4] After volunteering for military service in 1918, Audisio returned to Algiers two years later to combine a career in public administration with his productive artistic and journalistic life. Settling for a time in Paris in the early thirties, he came under the influence of Jules Romains and his movement of fraternalistic communalism popular during that decade under the name of Unanimism. But Audisio remained unfettered by any identifiable allegiances—especially to that of the Surrealists, so dominant during his generation—leaving him free to express throughout his work what René Lalou has called his "humanisme méditerranéen." (See his *Histoire de la littérature française contemporaine, de 1870 à nos jours*, II:713.)

Audisio's contribution to French letters was twice honored by literary awards among the most prestigious offered: the Grand Prix de la Société des Gens de Lettres, in 1953, and the Grand Prix de Poésie of the Académie Française, in 1975. He died at Issy-les-Moulineaux, near Paris, on January 26, 1978. Among his most appreciated works, besides those cited above, are the poetry collections

Hommes au soleil, his first, and *Feuilles de Fresnes,* the latter inspired by his imprisonment at the hands of the Gestapo; the early novel *Héliotrope;* and the essays in *Jeunesse de la Méditerranée* and *Ulysse ou l'intelligence.*[5]

The very untraditional *Fables* are a charmingly heterogeneous collection of brief, rather wispy pieces grouped under a number of headings. Uncharacteristically "un-Mediterranean" in inspiration, but no less typical, on the other hand, in their deftly crafted style and often sybilline brevity, they are fables in name only. Audisio warns us in a short introduction, "Sur le genre de la fable," not to expect yet another imitation of the inimitable La Fontaine: "si la perfection de La Fontaine est inimitable, il ne faut pas l'imiter." Hence his decision to use the freest of free verse: to "prendre le parti de renoncer à l'art poétique" and express himself in what he, no doubt too self-deprecatorily, refers to as "prose commune" (p. 7).

He proceeds to defend himself, as if defense were necessary, on the grounds that all speech is, etymologically at least, fable. If he alerts us to his work's pleasant diversity of tone, "qui ne craint pas le disparate," he assures us that, nevertheless, the moralist is, as in all proper fables, traditional or otherwise, lurking somewhere behind that "diversité volontaire, . . . allant de l'ironie au tragique, de la concision aphoristique à de claires prophéties, en passant par des adages, des sentences, des apologues, des caractères et même de vieux proverbes" (p. 9).

It should be clear from the three examples translated here—respectively the tenth in a group entitled "Histoires naturelles," and the eighth and fifteenth in a group entitled "Apologues"—that if Audisio the moralist is, indeed, present, his is a presence at once subtly unobtrusive and most delicately suggested.

1. The reader has already encountered Audisio's name in reference to the patois of Kaddour-Mermet's *Fables et contes en sabir* (see p. 186).

2. Audisio was, however, far from subscribing to artistic parochialism. For him there was only a single French literature, one which "prend son bien où elle le trouve," geography notwithstanding. "Le jour où nous viendrait d'Algérie un nouveau *Discours de la méthode,* nous ne nous soucierons pas plus de le tenir pour algérien que l'autre pour hollandais." (Quoted in Pierre Grenaud, *Notre Algérie littéraire,* II:43.)

3. Several sources incorrectly give his birthplace as Algiers, among them the usually authoritative Henri Clouard. (See his *Histoire de la littérature française du symbolisme à nos jours,* II:161.)

4. This lifelong interest produced his earliest novel, *Trois hommes et un minaret,* recipient of the Prix Littéraire de l'Algérie, and his romanticized biography, *La Vie de Haroun-al-Raschid,* as well as many of his succeeding works of poetry and prose.

5. It is difficult to establish a complete bibliography of Audisio's work. S. Dreher and M. Rolli's *Bibliographie de la littérature française, 1930–1939* and Marguerite L. Drevet's *Bibliographie de la littérature française, 1940–1949*—both supplements to Hugo P. Thieme's *Bibliographie de la littérature française de 1800 à 1930,* in which Audisio does not appear—include the majority of his publications from 1930 to 1949. His half-dozen titles prior to 1930, in addition to *Hommes au soleil* and the novels *Trois hommes et un minaret* and *Héliotrope* cited above, include the poetry collections *Poème de la joie,* and *Ici-bas,* as well as two early academic works. For titles subsequent to 1949 the reader can consult the brief entry on Audisio in Pierre de Boisdeffre, *Histoire de la littérature de langue française des années 1930 aux années 1980,* II:799. Lacunae remain, however; among them, curiously, the present collection, *Fables.* (Note also that our poet should not be confused with his namesake, contemporary historian and author Gabriel Audisio, currently professor at the Université de Provence.)

Les Baobabs, les Bambous et le Coolie

Le chœur des baobabs chantait:
"Nous sommes grands, nous sommes beaux,
nous sommes exemplaires."
Et ils regardaient le ciel.
Le chœur des bambous récrimina:
"Si tous les arbres étaient baobabs, qui jugerait
de leur hauteur?"
Et ils regardaient le sol.
Vint à passer un pauvre coolie. Il regarda de bas
en haut, de haut en bas, et le silence se fit
dans la forêt.

The Baobabs, the Bamboo Trees, and the Coolie

The choir of baobab trees was singing:
"We're tall. We're beautiful. We're models of
our kind."
And they gazed at the sky.
The choir of bamboo trees took them to task:
"If all the trees were baobabs, then who would
judge their height?"
And they gazed at the ground.
Just then, a poor coolie happened to come by.
He looked down and up. He looked up and down. And
the forest fell silent.

A Quelque Chose Malheur Est Bon

Un mort sortit de son tombeau en s'écriant:
"Me voici!"
Alors, la veuve éplorée, joignant les mains:
"Cher Ludovic! Je t'attendais, je t'appelais.

An Ill Wind That Blows No Good

A dead man rose up from his grave and cried:
"I've come back!"
The weeping widow clapped her hands and shouted:
"Ludovic, darling! How I've waited for you... called

Enfin Dieu récompense mon attente.”
  “Mon nom est Antonio,” répliqua le mort.
  Et la femme, après un soupir:
  “La volonté de Dieu soit faite!”

to you!... At last, God rewards my waiting!...”
  “My name is Antonio,” the dead man replied.
  And the woman, with a sigh:
  “God's will be done!”

Le Hoche-queue

  Ce hoche-queue équilibriste, posé sur une feuille
de nénuphar, que pensait-il de la pesanteur?
  Il pensait que l'impondérable araignée d'eau est
bien heureuse de marcher sur la rivière.
  A ce moment un pêcheur chavire avec sa barque
et se noie.
  L'oiseau changea de nénuphar et se remit à hocher
la queue.
  Qui me dira ce qu'il pensait.

The Wagtail

  That acrobat wagtail, perching on a lily pad...
What was he thinking about weight, I wonder?
  He was thinking how lucky was the weightless
water spider, that she could walk on the river.
  Just then a fisherman keels over his boat and
drowns.
  The bird changed lily pads and wagged his tail
some more.
  Who can say what he was thinking.

Emile Martin   Les Fables de La Fontaine en Patois Lorrain (1976)

EMILE Martin has succeeded—unintentionally, I am
sure—in eluding my several attempts to unearth more than
the barest minimum of details about him and his work: to
wit, that he is (or was) a native of the village of Morey,
near Nancy, and that he contributed occasional anecdotes
in his local dialect to such journals as the *Revue lorraine
populaire*. These facts, the only ones I can offer, are provided in a brief preface by Jean-Marie Cuny to a curiously self-effacing volume of twelve of La Fontaine's
fables picturesquely adapted, in the same "folksy" manner as other Creole and patois imitations that we have
seen, into the language of Martin's province of Lorraine.
*Les Fables de La Fontaine en patois lorrain: une fantaisie
pastiche en patois de Morey*—privately printed, it would
seem, probably in Nancy and also probably in 1976—is
noteworthy, academically, for its relatively rare examples

of that dialect in written form;[1] and, graphically, for its
inclusion of a number of illustrations by the celebrated
French illustrator J.-J. Grandville (pseudonym of Jean-
Ignace-Isidore Gérard), reproduced from a two-volume
nineteenth-century edition of La Fontaine's *Fables* (Paris:
H. Fournier aîné, 1838). The above-mentioned Jean-Marie
Cuny, himself author of folkloric works centering about
Lorraine, remains, like the shadowy Emile Martin himself, quite silent regarding the present volume, except to
say in his preface that it is "un divertissement bien au
goût des Lorrains qui conviendra à leur esprit malicieux
et plein de bon sens," and that the author contrived his
versions with the "complicité" of his wife.[2]
  "Le Potat de Terre et le Potat de Fé," the eleventh
fable of the collection, is freely adapted from La Fontaine's "Le Pot de Terre et le Pot de Fer" (V, 2).

---

1. For an authoritative study of this somewhat recondite patois, see
Paul Lévy, *Histoire linguistique d'Alsace et de Lorraine*.
2. The latter detail would tend to prove, should there be any
question, that our author is not to be confused with an eminent

churchman of the same name, member of the Oratoire de France,
choirmaster of Saint-Eustache, and author of several musical trea-
tises and literary works.

Le Potat de Terre et le Potat de Fé

Le potat de fé, qu'atô pendu au crèmé de lè Bibi
E dit é potat de terre qu'atô eh'hute su î trôpis:
“Venant èvo me vo promouêner dans le mé.”
“Ve n'y pensè-me qu'è dit l'otèt î faè si bon tocé

The Earthen Pot and the Iron Pot

The iron pot, hanging by Mam'selle Bibi's hearth,
Said to the earthen pot, squatting on a trivet:
“What say we take a stroll in the garden, you and I?”
“Don't be silly,” the other answered. “It's very nice here,

Entenre fiûter les rèmeures dans l'aètre.
Je sus si fragile, j'aè lè teusse; î n'men faurôme lo pien
                                        po meuri!
Ç'a bon por vo qu'èvez lè pé pu dûh'h que les pîrattes."
"Là bon, ne dotèr'me je ve wèdrai, je v'soutainrai."
Que dit le potat de fé, en se r'drassant
Le porat de terre è rèpondu.
"Enlè je n'dime, èprovant."
Le potat de fé se mat banjoindant
Et les val envouyes su zoutes trôh pettes.
Le mé de lè Bibi atô pien d'embèches.
Et les potats se beugnîn' sovent înque contre l'autre
Le potat de terre pedô eune câye de temps en temps
Le val que trèbuche dans eune pîre
Et en rezombant contre l'aut' potat
Le val en cent câyes dans le mé de lè Bibi, l'y a qua!

"Ne frayon-me qu'èvo des gens de même migaine que no."

Listening to the branches whistling in the fire.
Besides, I'm too fragile. One cough and I'd be done for!
It's all right for you. Your hide is hard as stone."
"And all right for you too," the iron pot told him,
                                        puffing out his chest.
"I'll take care of you. Don't worry."
The earthen pot answered:
"Well, in that case, why not? Let's give it a try..."
So the iron pot comes over and stands very close,
And off they go loping, on their three little legs.
Now, Mam'selle Bibi's garden has lots to bump into,
And the two pots kept hitting up against one another.
Every so often the earthen pot lost a chip.
Then, all of a sudden, he stumbled on a rock,
Smashed into the iron pot, and dashed himself to bits.
He fell in a heap in Mam'selle Bibi's garden. In fact,
                                        he's still there.

"Better for us all if we kept to our kind."

Jean-Luc Déjean   La Feuille à l'Envers (1970)   L'Ordinateur Sentimental (1977)
La Surlune et l'Oizéro (unpublished)

Among the many strings in the bow of historian and novelist—and, indeed, historical novelist—Jean-Luc Déjean, there figure both the fable and the *roman jeunesse*.[1] Let the reader beware, however. That duo is strictly fortuitous: in no sense should it be inferred that his fables, sophisticated in the extreme—in expression as well as subject—are intended for the young. Or, for that matter, even for the literarily immature, aging or aged. On the contrary, these virtuosic exercises in verbal panache and gymnastics, *feux d'artifice* reminiscent of Raymond Queneau, are wry products of their age, facilely and capriciously juggled, sometimes within the genre's supple and sacrosanct form, other times in constructs that owe little or nothing to the formal structure of fables past.

Déjean, who lives in the town of Saint-Martin de Londres, near Montpellier, was born in 1921, a native of Languedoc, and spent his early professional years teaching French, Latin, and Greek literatures. Widely traveled, he eventually abandoned academe at age thirty to indulge his intellectual and aesthetic gifts in a double career as author and television writer. In the latter capacity he has a long list of programs to his credit, devoted to the arts—*beaux* and *décoratifs*—to history, especially, and, as he tells me (in a letter dated December 17, 1988), "à mes maîtres de toujours, les enfants." In addition to the two above-mentioned *romans jeunesse*, he has published some ten novels, two of which have received literary awards (*Les Voleurs de pauvres*, Prix Fénéon, and *Le*

Cousin de Pothos, Prix Alexandre Dumas); two histories of the French theater (*Le Théâtre français d'aujourd'hui* and *Le Théâtre en France depuis 1945*); and a pair of highly regarded historical studies (*Quand chevauchaient les comtes de Toulouse, 1050–1250,*[2] and *Marguerite de Navarre*), the latter a tribute to his avowed admiration for the sixteenth century, his "siècle préféré," as is his recent important study, *Clément Marot.*

His affinity for earlier times—even earlier than the sixteenth century, that is—is reflected in Déjean's affection for the fable as a primarily oral genre. "Les vers, fables, fariboles, charmes et incongruités qui suivent," he observes in a brief foreword to his first volume of verse, *La Feuille à l'envers,* "ressortissent à un genre malfortuné- ment délaissé: *La poésie orale.* Conçus pour être dits, au moins ronronnés à mi-voix, ils supportent mal l'œil muet, encore moins l'œil littéraire. En des temps plus heureux, je les aurais récités de rues en places, accompagné d'une caisse à cordes." There is, however, nothing of the antique flavor of the medieval troubadour or jongleur about the fables in that early volume. If a few are disarmingly sim- ple—like "Oceano nox," included here—most of the ten that are scattered among the "vers," "fariboles," "charmes," and other "incongruités" in *La Feuille à l'envers* are densely, often almost cryptically, modern in theme; and in form, they are really fables in name only. The forty- two that compose his second volume, *L'Ordinateur senti- mental,* taking its name from the longest of them, while no less up-to-date in spirit, are generally closer to the traditional fable in form and style. Hardly so, however, in their cast of characters, sporting such whimsical, un– La Fontainian titles as "Le Chat Cycliste," "Le Lièvre Célibataire," "Le Hippie et les Deux Agents," and "Un Scotch pour l'Ecureuil," among the more colorful.[3]

The five that I have translated illustrate the happy ex- tent to which tradition and originality come together in the work of this most engaging contemporary fabulist. They are respectively the thirtieth of the unnumbered poems in *La Feuille à l'envers,* the tenth and thirty-fourth of the likewise-unnumbered fables in *L'Ordinateur senti- mental,* and two fables from his recently completed col- lection, the second of which bears the date 1990.

1. Two of his children's novels have been published to date: *Le Pre- mier Chien* and *Les Chevaux du roi.*

2. A revised and augmented edition, entitled simply *Les Comtes de Toulouse,* has recently been published.

3. The author informs me (in a letter dated June 29, 1990) that a third volume of fables, numbering forty-nine, has just been completed, as well as another "roman pour enfants," but that publication—of the former, at least—is not imminent. It bears the punnishingly untrans- latable title "La Surlune et l'oizéro."

Oceano Nox

C'est dans l'armoire du second
qu'est enterré le capitaine...
D'ailleurs il n'en restait à peine
qu'une molaire et qu'un bouton:
les requins tortorent le reste
au large des côtes de Brest.

Et les clairons sonnent Aux Champs
le capitaine est dans l'armoire
les requins n'ont pas de mémoire:
mon Dieu que le monde est méchant!

1. This self-styled "fable" is Déjean's concise and antiromantic response to Victor Hugo's celebrated poem of the same name; a lengthy tableau of the fate of shipwrecked sailors, briefly mourned and eventually forgotten. Hugo's title is borrowed from Vergil's *Aeneid,* II, 250: "Vertitur interea caelum et ruit Oceano nox"

Oceano Nox[1]

The Captain's buried—second floor—[2]
laid in a chest. What's left, that is:
a button and a tooth of his.
Molar and button, nothing more.
The sharks, awash somewhere off Brest,
are grubbing up on all the rest.

The bugle sounds Salute, but not
for Captain. No, he's in his chest.
Sharks have short memories at best.
My God, this life's a nasty lot!

("Meanwhile the heavens turn round, and night surges up from the Ocean").

2. Although the French *second* corresponds, in fact, to the English third floor, I retain the original here, with no serious damage, I think, to the scenario.

Le Kangourou, le Casoar et Moi

Un jour un kangourou avec un casoar
        dans le *bush* à l'herbe grillée
(or, je passais par là: jugez de ce hasard!)
        se flanquait une dérouillée.

The Kangaroo, the Cassowary, and Me

A cassowary and a kangaroo,
    off in the toasty outback (just as I—
coincidence, perhaps?—came passing by),
    were raising quite a hullabaloo.[1]

Moi l'homme d'âge mûr, de combats contempteur
approchai pour offrir un mot médiateur.

"Bêtes, cessons! Votre querelle
du sens commun vous dériva:
crochet droit contre stylets d'aile
tout ça finirait chez malva.
Ce manchot, rêves-tu l'abattre?
Tu psychoses, fort kangourou:
va quimper chez ton psychiatre
chez ton curé, chez ton gourou!
Toi, casoar, t'armer en guerre
gager ton honneur pour des riens
quand la plume de ton grand-père
fleurit le front des Saint-Cyriens!"

Tel je prônois debout la foi stoïcienne
l'humble Non-Violence où mon cœur est certain
sous le soleil de feu, sur l'herbe australienne
    la main gauche au médiastin.

O puissance de mots! Le combat se délie
kangourou, casoar soudain vivent en paix
mais retournant vers moi leur pugnace folie:
"Que nous veut," braillent-ils, "ce faiseur d'ysopets?"
"Vit-il dans le quartier?" "Connaît-il nos familles?"
"En sait-il plus que moi?" "Nous prend-il pour des billes?"
    "Pour bien montrer ce qu'il en cuit
    de mettre un doigt dans nos querelles
casoar, prends mes poings!" "Kangourou, prends mes ailes
    et jetons-nous à deux sur lui."

Je m'enfuis (le repos du sage est dans la fuite)
non pour sauver ma peau, mais pour te dire ensuite:
pacifique qui vois des fous s'exterminer
porte plainte à l'ONU, mais n'y mets pas le nez.

Now, being mature and of a pacifistic bent,
thought I: "I ought to mediate their argument."

"Fighting is folly! Enough, you two!
If each one does his (or her) thing
(your right hook... your stiletto-wing...),
it's up the creek with both of you.
You, my marsupial friend, you're nuts
to think this armless bird will be
a walkaway, a cup of tea:
It's shrink (priest? guru?)-time! No 'buts!'...
And you, my struthioid. Shame, you hear?
A vulgar brawl! How commonplace
for one whose grandpa's plumes still grace
the valiant brows of old Saint-Cyr!"[2]

Thus, on the burning grass, beneath the Austral sun,
    sincere, I preached the Stoic faith canonic—
humble Non-Violent faith (when all is said and done)—
    with left hand poised in pose Napoleonic.

O power of the Word! Verb efficacious!
A trice, and my combatants quit the list...
only to turn on me their wrath pugnacious:
"What's with this mate? This blithering fabulist?"[3]
"Some neighbor?" "Family friend?" "Some
                            smart-ass writer?"
    "Must think we're loony, the blooming blighter!"
    "I say we jump him, you and me...
    teach him a lesson...." "I agree.
My wings, your fists." "My fists, your wings. We'll show
this good-for-nothing meddling so-and-so."

And so... I ran, as wise man should, resolved
to warn you (not just save my skin): "Do-gooder brother,
when you see fools about to slaughter one another,
    tell the U.N., but don't go get involved."

---

1. The author assures me that, his extensive travels notwithstanding, Australia is one of the few countries he has never visited, and that, in fact, the animals of the present fable were suggested by a picture book.
2. The elegant *shako*, headdress of the French military academy of Saint-Cyr, founded by Louis XIV in 1685, has sported its decorative cassowary plume since the middle of the nineteenth century.
3. The reader will not have forgotten that the several medieval French fable collections were grouped under the general name *isopet* (or *ysopet*), in honor of their supposed Aesopic progenitor. (See p. 7.)

Le Cercle et la Roue

Un mulet à hue à dia
rondtournait une noria
quand les dindons (cul qui pavane)
lui balancèrent plus d'un vanne:

"Esclave, tes chemins sont faits!"
"Du Devoir voici le profès!"
"Tourne!" "Il est rond!" "Cerne!" "Circule!"
"Voyez le plaisant curricule!"

"Ma foi, sans peine ni galop"
répond l'autre, "je monte l'eau.
Le maïs y boit: qu'il vous fasse
pour Noël la panse bien grasse."

Au bout de cette fable-ci
la morale ne m'a souci:
mulet, dindons? Vos saburrales
opinions électorales
plaindront l'un ou les autres, ou chacun d'eux. Merci.

Annoncez la Couleur

Le merle blanc disait à la corneille rose
              quelque chose
        qu'il faut par curiosité
              rapporter.

"Qui sont ces gens qui nous regardent,
ces béants, ces outrepassés?
Voyez: de nous ces insensés
        bavardent!"

"Merle, je sens pareillement
leur insistence insidieuse:
de vous à moi, corneillement,
suis-je une bête curieuse?"

"Corneille, nous prêtons le flanc
aux horreurs de la différence:
même beaux, même nés en France
vous êtes rose, je suis blanc."

"N'est-il point doux, n'est-il point rare
        d'être bizarre?
Méprisons-les. Puis, déféquant,
        levons le camp."

Ils s'envolent, ces dissemblables
à grandes ailes tout à coup:
d'autres, les jambes à leur cou
parmi des mots épouvantables
        savent le coût

The Circle and the Wheel

A loping waterwheeling mule
trudged round to shouts of ridicule
as turkeys (ass a-strut) jeered, jibed,
along the path he circumscribed:

"Such blind devotion!" "Duty-bound!"
"A veritable merry-go-round!"
"Gee up!" "Round, round, you rounder!" "Whoa!"
"It's ring-around-a-rosy, O!"

Replied the mule: "Friends, not to worry,
the wheel I turn—no fuss, no hurry—
waters your corn. Let's hope it's able
to fatten you up for the Christmas table!"

Now, what's the moral of my fable?
Turkeys or mule: former or latter,
who's to be pitied? That's up to you,
depending on your morbid taste and *mauvais goût*:
Him? Them? The lot? You choose. No matter.

The Color That Suits You[1]

A blackbird, white, said to a raven, pink,
              something I think
        we might do well to lend an ear to,
              hereto:

"Who are those foolish folks who gawk
        and ogle us?
Why all their highfalutin fuss
        and nasty talk?"[2]

"Friend blackbird, I resent, like you,
their sneer and would-be third degree:
really, in matters ravenly
am I so different, *entre nous?*"

"Friend raven, it's our fate to be
butts of their panic and rebuff:
though French and fair, what good are we?
You're pink, I'm white, and that's enough."

"It's nice to be an odder bird—
to be an *avis* 'rarer,' eh?
Damn 'em! Let's leave 'em with a turd,
        and fly away."

And off they flew, our matchless pair,
without delay... Now, others too
there are—the two-leg kind—and who
take to their heels (and not the air)
        'midst curse and swear;

d'avoir reçu pour tout partage
la couleur qui n'est pas d'usage
    chez nous.

who pay a price for having been
given a different color skin
    than ours to wear.

1. My title attempts to suggest, at least, the pun of the original, based on the double meaning of *couleur:* 'color' and 'suit' (of playing cards). In the latter context *annoncer la couleur* means 'to declare', and has the figurative meaning of "to lay one's card on the table."

2. Déjean's blackbird would seem to be a modern descendant of another literary figure: the hero of Alfred de Musset's semisatirical *Histoire d'un merle blanc* (1842), whose whiteness makes him a Romantic metaphor for the misunderstood artist cum social misfit.

Le Poète et la Tradition

La maîtresse m'était farouche.
La servante en ses dix-sept ans
le cœur m'en venait à la bouche
quand s'éparpillait le printemps.

Prenant pour exemple et repères
les aveux d'illustres confrères
riant j'effleurai ses rondeurs
de mes trente doigts baladeurs.

Hélas! cette enfant difficile
me réparplique tout de go:
"Laissez donc mes fesses tranquilles,
vous n'êtes pas Victor Hugo!"

Je m'émeus, m'inquiète, m'étonne...
L'Amour est un dieu capricant:
mais si l'on baise plus la bonne
les traditions foutent le camp!

Tradition and the Poet

Madame was cold, aloof, remote.
Ah, but her maid, plump seventeen...
As spring went spreading, young and green,
my heart came thumping to my throat.

Like many a poet predecessor
quick to confess his fleshly passion,
laughing, I tried to stroke, caress her—
Rump, bust—in lustful-fingered fashion.

Alack, no luck! Much though I tried,
a lusty "no!" was all I got:
"Hands off my butt!" she promptly cried.
"Victor Hugo, monsieur, you're not!"

And so, dismayed, I muse: "How odd!"
Cupid's a fickle little god!
Damn! If the maid won't let you screw her,
tradition's down the bloody sewer!

1. Toward the end of his life octogenarian Victor Hugo was, in fact, notorious for his backstairs amours, and is unfortunately often remembered by the French masses more for his wandering hands than for his prodigious pen.

Yves-Emmanuel Dogbé   Fables Africaines (1978)

Sᴏᴍᴇ ꜰɪꜰᴛʏ years ago a now-celebrated triumvirate of Black francophone student poets—Aimé Césaire, Léon-Gontran Damas, and Léopold Sédar Senghor—initiated a movement of cultural self-awareness and self-affirmation that early came to be known as Négritude, marked even from its beginnings by a rich diversity within a commonness of purpose.[1] Today their spiritual descendants carry the movement on in a variety of directions, proving, by a growing theoretical factionalism—even unto a questioning of the very validity of its philosophical underpinnings—that it has, indeed, come of age.

Yves-Emmanuel Dogbé, of Togo, is one of the more prominent and productive of those descendants, and a leading figure in his young country's budding literature in French.[2] Like most African intellectuals and men of letters, older and younger—vigorous hybrids of two contrasting cultures, of whom Senghor is the prototype—he does not take refuge in an ivory tower of art for art's sake or in a self-indulgent obscurantism. Poet, novelist, essayist, educator, his dozen-odd published works reflect both a committed "engagement," in the Sartrean sense, and a humanistic concern for the future of humankind in general and Africa in particular, in the best Senghorian tradition.

Born in Lomé, capital city of Togo, on May 10, 1939, Dogbé was educated in that country and in Ghana, where he studied English. After teaching school in Togo and in Dahomey for several years, he went to Paris where he studied philosophy and sociology at both the

Sorbonne and the Ecole des Hautes Etudes, completing his formal education with a doctorate in African Studies. He currently divides his time between Paris, where he is actively engaged in the encouragement of francophone African letters, and his native Togo.

Dogbé's works have been published by Editions Akpagnon, of Lomé and Le Mée-sur-Seine. In addition to his doctoral thesis, *Négritude, culture et civilisation: essai sur la finalité des faits sociaux,* his prose comprises three sociological monographs: *La Crise de l'éducation;* eight thoughtful and provocative essays grouped under the title *Lettre ouverte aux pauvres d'Afrique;* and *Réflexions sur la promotion du livre africain;* two novels: *La Victime,* a portrayal of the problem of Black-White relations; and *L'Incarcéré,* inspired by his own brief political imprisonment; as well as a collection of traditional *Contes et légendes du Togo.* Typically, Dogbé's earliest literary efforts were poetic. His first, privately printed collection of thirteen poems, entitled *Affres,* was followed by *Flamme blême,* which, while basically personal in inspiration, shows evidence of his admiration for both the stately *versets* of his elder, Senghor, and the militant rhythms of his contemporary, the late David Diop.[3] The collection *Le Divin amour* was recipient of the prestigious Prix Charles Vildrac for poetry, awarded by the Société des Gens de Lettres, in 1979. Besides a third volume of poems, *Morne soliloque,* he has also published an *Anthologie de la poésie togolaise,* a tangible example of his interest in and commitment to the advancement of his country's literature.

Given the genre, Dogbé's *Fables africaines,* though often sardonic, are, for the most part, written in a lighter vein than his other works, both verse and prose. He composed them to provide his own young pupils with moral exempla in African dress, and in a free-verse form reminiscent of the traditional folktales of the likes of Leuk the Hare, Bouki the Hyena, Ananzi the Spider, et al. (see p. 179, n. 1), only more concise and frankly didactic in intent. In so doing he recognized nonetheless the universality and continuity of the fable tradition, acknowledging his debt to "La Fontaine, Florian, Anouilh," and, appropriately, "notre père à tous, Esope," who—if he really existed at all—may well have been an African.[4] Unlike the Baron Roger's versions of Wolof fables (see pp. 136–37), Dogbé's crisp little apologues are of his own composition rather than direct translations of the folkloric corpus that inspired them. With their disarmingly deceptive simplicity and brief dramatic scenarios, they often recall the early La Fontaine, in spirit if not in form. The collection contains forty-six fables divided into three books.

The pair translated in these pages—the second and third of Books I and III respectively—are typical examples of the art of this modern African fabulist.

---

1. Among the many studies chronicling the movement's genesis, one of the most readable and informative remains the pioneering thesis of Lilyan Kesteloot, *Les Ecrivains noirs de langue française: naissance d'une littérature,* translated into English by Ellen Conroy Kennedy as *Black Writers in French: A Literary History of Négritude.* For a selection of the early poets translated into English, see, among others, my bilingual volume *Négritude: Black Poets from Africa and the Caribbean.*

2. For a brief discussion of Togolese literature in the African language Ewe, see Alain Ricard's entry in Leonard S. Klein, ed., *Encyclopedia of World Literature in the Twentieth Century,* IV:447–48.

3. David Diop (1927–60) was the author of the slim but much admired and very influential collection *Coups de pilon.*

4. At least according to the admittedly questionable authority of the fourteenth-century monk Planudes Maximus, who, in the first paragraph of his *Vita Aesopi,* tells us that the fabulist, black of skin, derived his name from the Greek word for Ethiopian. (For further discussion and additional references, see J[oel] A. Rogers, *World's Great Men of Color,* I:25–30.)

Le Hérisson et le Serpent

"La parole du plus puissant
Est toujours vérité."
(C'est un proverbe bambara qui le dit.)

Un Hérisson errait dans la brousse,
Prenant l'air tout à son aise

The Hedgehog and the Snake

"What the strongest one says
Is always the truth."
(That's what a Bambara proverb tells us.)[1]

A hedgehog was wandering along through the brush,
Out for a stroll, just taking the air.

Après avoir fait une bonne chasse
Et rempli son ventre de gros morceaux.
Au bord d'un étang, sous un arbre,
Il rencontra soudain un Serpent
Qui allait quitter la source
Sans rien trouver à croquer.
"Hé!" s'écria le Hérisson, "que viens-tu faire
Sur mon chemin? Vous avez toujours tendance,
Toi et les tiens, à me déplaire
Par vos hardies ingérences."
"Non, Seigneur," répondit le Reptile épeuré,
"Je n'ai aucune intention de vous déranger,
Et ne serais pas venu sur ces lieux
Chercher ma pitance
Si je les savais dans votre royaume…"
"C'est faux! pendard, malin, gueux!"
Cela dit, Maître Hérisson le saisit par le cou
Et le coupa en deux.

He'd had a good hunt,
And he'd filled his belly full of nice big pieces.
But all of a sudden, over by a pond,
Under a tree, he came across a snake;
He was leaving the water
Since he couldn't find a thing to sink his teeth into.
"Hey you!" cried hedgehog. "What do you think
                                    you're doing,
Using my path! You're all the same,
You and your kind. Always meddling in my affairs
And getting on my nerves!"
"Oh no, sir!" snake answered, quaking with fright.
"Really, I didn't mean to bother you at all.
I never would have come here
For my meager victuals
If I'd known this land was yours."
"Lies, lies! You wretch, you faker, you lowlife!"
So saying, Master Hedgehog grabbed him by the neck
And sliced him in two.

---

1. The Bambaras are one of the Mandingo peoples of West Africa, living primarily in present-day Mali, as well as in parts of Senegal, Sudan, and Ivory Coast. Their language is used extensively in trade throughout the upper Niger basin. Like most African languages, it is rich in proverb, riddle, and other oral forms. (See Martin-Samuel Eno-Beliga, *Littérature et musique populaire en Afrique* *noire*, pp. 227–30; and, on the African proverb in general, Richard F. Burton, *Wit and Wisdom from West Africa*. I cannot vouch for the authenticity of the proverb quoted here, though there is certainly no reason to doubt it. It and the fable it introduces present a striking parallel—differences of animal personnel notwithstanding—to La Fontaine's celebrated "Le Loup et l'Agneau" (I, 10) (see pp. 32–33).

La Fourmi et la Cigale

Une Cigale somnolait dans le creux d'une rivière.
Elle avait faim et n'avait rien à manger.
Toutes ses réserves étaient épuisées,
Et ses nombreuses chasses n'avaient rien donné.
Certaines fois, en temps de famine,
La Cigale avait prêté à la Fourmi,
Et la Fourmi tenait à lui rendre ses bienfaits;
Mais la Cigale était orgueilleuse.
"Tiens! ma bonne Cigale," s'écria la Fourmi,
En apercevant son amie,
"Justement, j'ai pensé à vous.
Vous ne devez plus rien avoir,
Avec la chaleur qu'il fait…"
"Non, vous vous trompez, ma pauvre Amie," dit la Cigale,
"J'en ai beaucoup, au contraire.
D'ailleurs, je n'ai pas faim;
C'est pourquoi je me repose ici."
La Fourmi n'était pas dupe.
Elle connaissait la Cigale
Et savait qu'elle ne disait pas vrai.
"Tant mieux, si vous avez encore des provisions,"
Dit la Fourmi,
"Je vous apporte quand même
Quelques grains de riz tout frais."
"Non, je n'en veux pas. Je n'en ai pas besoin.
Gardez-les! Je vous les demanderai
Le moment venu," dit la Cigale.
Puis elle quitta la Fourmi

The Ant and the Cricket[1]

A cricket lay dozing in the dry riverbed,
Hungry, and with not a bite to eat.
Whatever provisions she had put aside were gone,
And for all her foraging she had nothing to show.
At times, in the past, when famine had struck,
Cricket had loaned this or that to friend ant,
And ant was anxious to pay her back in kind.
But cricket was a proud one.
"Well now, friend cricket," ant cried out
When she saw her lying there.
"You know, just now you crossed my mind.
With all this heat,
You can't have very much left, I'll bet."
"You're wrong, poor friend, I do!" cricket answered.
"Plenty, in fact.
And anyway, I'm not hungry.
That's why I'm here, resting…"
Well, ant was no fool.
She knew cricket too well
To swallow her story.
"That's fine," she said.
"It's good you've got a lot.
Still, I'm going to bring you
A few grains of rice… Nice and fresh… Just a few…"
"No, no!" replied cricket.
"I don't want them… I don't need them…
Keep them. And later, when I do,
I'll let you know."

Et rentra dans son logis.
Mais elle y mourut d'avoir tant dédaigné
Les offres de la Fourmi
Pour sauver trop d'amour-propre.

Then, taking leave of ant,
She went back home
And promptly died, having spurned ant's offer
And saved too much face.

1. To any Francophone, this title cannot but raise expectations of yet another version of, variation of, or sequel to La Fontaine's very first fable, "La Cigale et la Fourmi" (see pp. 31, 60, 89–90, and 157); expectations quickly confounded by the ensuing scenario.

Gomar (pseud. Jean-Charles Talmant)
Fables Nouvelles (unpublished)

Fables et Chantefables (1982)

In 1982 a civil servant by the name of Jean-Charles Talmant published, under the pseudonym "Gomar," an unpretentious but impressive little volume entitled *Fables et chantefables*. The author, who assures me (in a letter dated January 1, 1989) that his biographical details "n'encombreront pas votre anthologie," was born in 1938 and currently lives in the north of France, in the town of Aulnoy-les-Valenciennes. His fables, brimming with verve and wit, and typically Gallic in their often sardonic view of the world, are all the more remarkable in that he is, apparently, largely self-taught.

Talmant's admiration—adulation—of La Fontaine would be obvious even if he didn't take pains, in a brief introduction, to affirm it. But, like his legion of predecessors, he is not daunted or discouraged from paying his present-day tribute to the master of the genre. ("Il m'a semblé que le domaine des Fables, quoique essarté pour sa meilleure partie par l'un des plus grands et beaux génies que la France ait produits—c'est à Mr Jean de La Fontaine que je pense—avait encore, ici et là, quelques arpents en friche qui méritaient qu'on les cultivât" [p. 7].) In so doing, he respects the capricious line-lengths, rhythms, and rhymes of the traditional La Fontainesque *vers libres* (though, it will be noted, not their usual typographical disposition): "Mais parlons tradition. C'est là toute mon ambition, outre la facilité de la lecture, de retrouver dans le rythme, dans la tessiture, dans l'enchaînement des vers, j'espère dans l'assonance des mots, cette harmonie, j'allais dire cette musicalité, et cet apprêt sans artifice qui faisaient chatoyer les contes d'autrefois" (p. 10). An ambitious aim, and one—"toutes proportions gardées"—nicely realized. As with Anouilh

and Déjean, and, for that matter, the inimitable Franc-Nohain (see pp. 198, 205–6, and 188–90), who subscribe to the same basic principles without specifically proclaiming them, the result is no mere "old wine in new bottles" but rather a thoroughly modern wine in bottles made intentionally—and a little nostalgically—conventional.

It would seem that the often mordant but not overpowering cynicism that typifies Talmant's engaging fables is carried over into his personal life. Though he has written other works, he takes a dim view of the professional literary establishment, which he sees, perhaps a little monolithically, as a closed society: "C'est qu'il faut s'introduire dans les cénacles, mendigoter des recommendations, s'aplatir devant telle ou telle célébrité, l'encenser, la louanger, devenir son thuriféraire. Je ne sais pas le faire. Alors, tout seul, au fin fond de sa province, il ne vous reste qu'à maudire le système." It would be easy to dismiss such recriminations as mere artistic pique were it not for the evident qualities that grace his pages. In any event, he has published only the single volume, *Fables et chantefables*. The continuation of the collection exists in manuscript, however, under the title *Fables nouvelles,* in which he is no less quick to "maudire le système" in his very personal style and with his undeniable talent. One hopes that it might also find its way into print.

Of "Gomar's" seventy fables, divided into four books, "La Rate et le Chat Maigre" and "La Poule et Ses Humeurs" are, respectively, numbers III, 2 and IV, 1. "Le Sultan et le Rossignol," "La Destinée du Coq," and the uncharacteristic, gently delicate "Le Papillon" are from among the seventy unpublished *Fables nouvelles,* where they appear as numbers V, 1, V, 3, and VI, 13.

La Rate et le Chat Maigre

Une rate replète
Daubait sur un chat maigre.
"Minet, minet, minet. Mon dieu, la pauvre bête.

The She-Rat and the Scrawny Cat

A chubby she-rat sat
Taunting a sick and scrawny cat:
"Misery me! Poor kitty, kitty, kitty!

Malingre, je vous dis. Pas de santé du tout.
Ça s'en va tout à rien. Ça part. Ça tourne à l'aigre.
Un si bel animal qu'on admirait partout.
Nous sommes peu de chose."
Le chat ne quitte pas son allure morose.
Un malade, une loque, une chiffe, on vous dit.
Du coup. "Hé," s'ébaudit
La rate, "après tout pourquoi pas.
Serait-il interdit,
Par un juste retour des normes d'ici bas,
De goûter,—pourquoi non?—, quel fumet ont les chats."
Elle avance aussitôt, tourne un peu, se balance,
Improvise un détour, enfin elle s'élance,
Puis se jette
Et trépasse.
"Ventre Saint-Gris, la noble bête,"
Ronronna le matou. "Une rate et si grasse.
Bénis soient les Dieux et le sort
Qui s'ingénièrent à nourrir
Un pauvre chat perclus qui ne sait plus courir."

Méjuger le danger vous expose à la mort.
C'est un très vieux proverbe
Que devrait méditer tout matamore en herbe.

My, how emaciated! What a pity!
Beauty and health awry, undone...
Done in, that handsome beast that everyone
Once contemplated with admiring eye.
Alas, what fragile creatures we!"
The cat, limp as a rag, mumpish and mopishly
Continues to sit sickly by.
Suddenly: "What if I..." chortles the rat,
"I mean, why not?... It's only tit for tat...
I don't expect it's breaking any law
To try a taste of cat." Whereat,
A trifle circumspect at first, with timid paw,
And many a hem and haw,
She takes two steps... Skirts round sidewise...
Stops... Turns... And finally plunges boldly on.
Whereupon
She straightway dies.
"Gadzooks, the selfless beast!" our tabby sighs.
"A rat... And fat! Praised be the gods, and Fate, who feed
This poor arthritic cat in time of need."

As in the ancient proverb, aptly stated,
"Deadly the danger underestimated."[1]
All budding braggart warriors please take heed.

---

1. The original certainly sounds like a proverb, as the author asserts, though I cannot confirm that it actually is one, "vieux" or otherwise. Proverb or not, like most such folk wisdom it calls to mind its diametric opposite; in this case, the moral of La Fontaine's "Le Renard et les Poulets d'Inde": "Le trop d'attention qu'on a pour le danger / Fait le plus souvent qu'on y tombe" (XII, 18).

La Poule et Ses Humeurs

Une poule couvait avec mélancolie,
Maudissant la folie
Des anciennes amours. "Le coq," gémissait-elle,
"Le coq, lui, continue. Ainsi, la vie est belle.
A lui, les complaisances;
A nous, les conséquences.
La femelle
Est maudite."
Et de se renfrogner, douloureuse et contrite.
Hors çà, le temps passa.
Eclose, la couvée
Fut bien vite élevée,
Et notre poule, enfin, peu à peu délaissa
Sa piaulante progéniture.
Il lui sembla que la nature
Retrouvait, alors, des couleurs,
Des saveurs
Qui, jadis, l'avaient fait tressaillir.
Comme elle sentit, au fond d'elle,
Ressurgir un désir
Fort et d'une impulsion telle
Qu'il fallait l'assouvir
Au plus vite, au plus vite.
"Et la suite, et la suite,"
Lui criait la raison.

The Hen and Her Moods

A hen, in melancholic mood,
Hatching her brood,
Was cursing yesterday's madcap amours. Groaned she:
"Ah, life! What vain futility!
The cock... That pampered, self-important he-male...
While he exults,
We, the vile female,
Bear the results."
Then on and on she droned her sullen, dour lament.
But time, as usual, came and went;
And soon her chirping chicks become adults.
No longer quite so malcontent, our hen
Is free to leave her offspring to their own devices.
Ah, then,
How quickly nature, once again, entices
And charms her with those colors, smells, sensations
That earlier made her thrill to love's temptations!
Again that feeling deep inside,
That all-compelling
Urge, surging and swelling:
Desire! Desire! Too strong to be denied,
Welling up, yearning to be satisfied!
And now! Today, today!...
Scandalized, reason cries: "Nay, nay!
Come to your senses!

"Reprends-toi, reprends-toi." Y pensez-vous? Que non.
La raison s'évanouit quand l'instinct se dessine.
Notre caquetante héroïne,
Conquise, près du coq vint refaire
La coquette.
La couvaison?... La belle affaire!
Dès l'instant qu'elle est poule, une poule y est prête.
"Et j'ai besoin du coq. J'en ai besoin vous dis-je."

Cette rétractation ne tient pas du prodige.
Telle fureur d'aimer prédomine sur tout.
Raisonnez, raisonnez.
Le vertige des sens vous mène par le bout
Du nez.

I pray, think of the consequences!"
But no... When instinct rears its head and joins the fray,
Reason grows weak and dies without defenses.
And so, same old duet:
Our cackling hen, again the cock's coquette.[1]
Another brood? Well, what's one more?
A hen's a hen, and that's what hens are for.
"I need that cock," she clucks. "I need him, hear?"

Her turnabout's no awesome feat. I fear
Love's folly rules. Whatever be your breed, you
Reason in vain. So? So it goes:
Passion is always sure to lead you
By the nose.

I. As the reader will appreciate at a casual glance, the play on words exists in the original as well as in my translation.

Le Sultan et le Rossignol

Le grand Vizir eut beau s'incliner jusqu'à terre,
Le cimeterre
Siffla
Et sa tête roula,
Pelote sanglante,
Sur le sol...
Tout cela pour un rossignol,
Dont le sultan voulait qu'il chante.
Perclus, froid, desséché, ce souverain
Devait, au dire d'un devin,
Trouver une vigueur nouvelle
S'il entendait perler le chant de Philomèle.
Capturer l'oiselet,
Un filet
Fit l'affaire;
Mais, dans sa cage aux barreaux d'or,
L'oiseau persistait à se taire.
Le sultan, suffoquant, s'affaiblissait encor.
Tout juste il ordonnait que l'on pendît le mage,
Quand, soudain, il mourut.
Stupeur parmi la foule, hourvari, grenouillage.
Les courtisans partis, une esclave crut
Bon d'ouvrir la porte de la cage.
Le rossignol
Reprit son vol.
L'azur, le bel azur, l'espace, l'allégresse,
L'alacrité de la vitesse.
Puis lorsqu'il se percha, quand vint l'obscurité,
On l'entendit chanter, chanter la liberté.

The Sultan and the Nightingale

In vain the Grand Vizier stood bowing,
Scraping, kowtowing...
The scimitar-blade
Made
A *whish!* one blow,
And lo!
His head dropped off—
Lopped off—
Rolling about, a bloody ball.
And all
Because a nightingale refused to sing!
A seer had told
The dying sultan—lying wizened, wan, and cold—
That Philomela's warbling song would bring
Him back to health.[1] And so
A net was set:
The bird was caught and caged... And yet,
Behind her gilded bars, ah no!
No song she sang!
The sultan, failing fast,
Managed to order that the seer should hang,
Then gasped his last.
Ah woe! The wailing courtiers stand aghast...
But once they leave, after the whole shebang,
A slave girl, wondering what to do,
Opens the cage. As for the bird,
Up, up she flew,
Swift-winged, into the joy of endless blue...
Come dusk, she perched. And now, at last, was heard
The nightingale—unfettered, free—
Singing her song: the song of liberty.

I. The mythological reference is to Philomela, who, with her sister Procne, was transformed by the gods into a bird in order to save her from the rage of her lover Tereus, king of Thrace, in an espe- cially lurid episode of familial skulduggery. We are told that Procne, married to the king, took revenge for his amours with Philomela by murdering his son and serving him up one night for supper.

One of the sisters became a swallow and the other a nightingale. Though sources disagree as to which became which, French tradition generally identifies the latter with Philomela. (The reader will notice that, in deference to this allusion, I have seen fit to make the present nightingale a female despite the masculine gender of the French *rossignol*.)

La Destinée du Coq

"Moi, je vais vivre, moi," coqueriquait le coq.
"On crie, on pleure, on se lamente.
Tiens là. Le maître est mort? d'accord, un choc.
Quel choc, d'accord, pour les commis, pour la servante,
La famille, bien sûr, oui mais pour moi?
Songez à ces repas... C'était toujours la fête.
Pour ceci, pour cela, pour un je ne sais quoi,
L'on vous coupait la tête
D'un poulet, d'un chapon, d'un coq, d'une poulette.
Nous vivions dans la peur. Un effroi journalier
Hantait le poulailler.
Cette mort nous délivre,
Nous qui savions pourquoi l'on nous tenait reclus.
Et vous voudriez, vous, la tristesse au surplus.
Cot, cot, cocorico, vivre, moi, je vais vivre."
Il en eût chanté plus,
Mais déjà dans la ferme
Une foule d'amis s'agglutine. On boit ferme.
L'éloge du défunt aiguisant l'appétit,
Il convient de pourvoir très vite à la mangeaille.
Et la servante aux yeux rougis se rabattit
Sur la volaille.
Une razzia. Sacrifié le chanteur
Aux mânes de son maître...

      Heur ou malheur,
Deuil ou bamboche,
Le coq doit finir à la broche.

The Cock's Fate

"Now I can live my life!" So crows
The cock, a-doodle-dooing. "See?
All of them weep and sigh their 'ahs' and 'ohs.'
And why? Because the master's dead. Well, I suppose
It's quite a shock. For them, that is... The family,
His friends, associates... And the maid... But me?
With all those meals? Each day, some bloody celebration!
For what? Who knows? Still, capon, cock,
Chicken, or hen, off to the block!
Why, all of the barnyard population
Trembled in constant trepidation!
At last, his death has set us free.
Now I can live!... Me? Mourn him too?
Ha! Doodle-a-cock, and cock-a-doodle-doo!"
Undoubtedly
He would have cackled on some more.
But at the farm, already, by the score,
The friends assembled... Drank their fill...
Soon all their eulogizing of the dear deceased
Whetted their appetites, until:
"Food! Food! And quick! Something, at least..."
And so, eyes red, the maid swooped down...
    Fast... Faster...
Raided the coop... Dispatched our crowing beast
To join his master.

Foul times or fair, nothing is truer:
Come funeral or fête,
You can bet,
The cock'll wind up on the skewer.

Le Papillon

Dans cet effort immense,
C'était, tout à la fois,
Souffrance
Et délivrance.
Après ces longs mois
D'espérance,
La chenille, en travail, devenait papillon.
Cocon-prison,
Adieu. Le vol, le ciel, l'ivresse,
La sensation enchanteresse
D'une totale liberté.
Cette existence, en plein été,
Parut au papillon d'une extase achevée.
Et la fin du jour arrivée,

The Butterfly

That longed-for transformation:
Immense
The effort, and intense
The pain. Then, liberation,
As caterpillar turns to butterfly.
The months of waiting,
Incubating...
Now prison-cocoon good-bye!
Sky, soaring flight,
Giddying height,
And heady joy of boundless liberty...
Life, shimmering in midsummer sun,
Seemed to our butterfly pure ecstasy,
Second to none.

Lorsqu'il sentit mourir cette félicité
Chatoyante et si brève,
Il remercia les Dieux d'avoir vécu ce rêve.

And when, too brief, the day at length was done,
Dimming his joy, barely a-gleam,
He thanked the gods that he had lived that dream.

Eugène Guillevic   Fabliettes (1981)

ONE OF the most highly regarded of the elder generation of contemporary French poets, Breton-born Eugène
Guillevic has produced a substantial body of characteristically spare, often fragmentary verse, no less enigmatic
and hermetic in its way than that of the Surrealists,
whose direct influence he disavows, and no less lapidary
than that of such younger moderns as Edmond Jabès,
whom he seems at times to anticipate. Lapidary indeed,
not only in its form but in much of its inspiration. His is
truly a universe of "blocks" and "stones"—to evoke
Shakespeare in different metaphorical context: "senseless
things," perhaps, from the human perspective, but imbued all the same with mysteries to be plumbed, and an
almost mystical relationship—or nonrelationship—with
Man to be defined. His is a poetry obsessed with the
existence of physical objects. In the words of Jean-Pierre
Richard, writing at Guillevic's mid-career: "De l'objet la
seule chose sans doute que nous puissions tirer, c'est le
savoir qu'il n'y a rien à en tirer: d'emblée il nous signifie
qu'il se situe ailleurs, en un autre espace que le nôtre,
qu'il relève d'un ordre auquel nous n'avons pas accès."
(See *Onze études sur la poésie moderne,* p. 189).[1]

From his first important work, *Terraque,* infused especially with the spirits of earth and water, as the two
syllables of its title suggest, critics recognized Guillevic
as just such a poetic conjurer of objects rather than as a
subtle sound-and-image magician. For Léon-Gabriel
Gros, perhaps his earliest critic, his poetry "n'est point
faite pour ces amateurs de poèmes qui attendent d'un
texte qu'il les éblouisse d'images, les envoûte d'une subtile et puissante musique. Ils n'y trouveront guère leur
compte, encore moins cette euphorie qu'ils recherchent."
And the same critic goes on to identify what was to become the poet's hallmark: "Tout se passe comme si
Guillevic s'incarnait dans l'objet de son poème, se faisait
tour à tour végétal ou minéral. Poésie dont la démarche
dernière, véritable rite de sorcellerie, serait une anima-
tion de l'inanimé." (See "Un exorciste: Guillevic," pp.
460, 462.) With the exception of a brief incursion into
traditional rhymed and metered versecraft, especially in
his *Trente et un sonnets,* ostensibly meant to express his
Communist social conscience in a form accessible to the
average reader, Guillevic has continued, throughout his
long career, to be a poet of the essences of concrete

things.[2] As for his style, it remains, in general, elliptical
and condensed, prompting more than one observer to
compare it—in spirit, at least, if not in precise tech-
nique—to the art of the Japanese haiku.[3] Albeit, to be
sure, haiku properly cross-fertilized with Breton inspiration. For Guillevic's ancestry cannot be overlooked, with
that substratum of otherworldliness—and othertimeli-
ness—virtually synonymous with his Celtic heritage. To
quote Richard once again, commenting on the current of
angst that runs through much of the poet's work: "Nul
doute que le terroir breton, traditionnellement fécond en
personnages fantastiques... n'ait ici fourni à l'angoisse
intime un admirable matériel imaginaire" (*Onze études,*
p. 192).

It is not of that Breton brand of mystery, however,
that another of Guillevic's American translators speaks
when commenting on the "mysterious" appeal that his
unique work has for his readers. "He is enjoyable and
shocking, obtuse and aggravating, humane and unhu-
man. But it takes no time at all for us to begin to inhabit
his world. And, as he begins to be translated into more
and more languages, admiration for his skill as an artist,
his poetic ability, becomes international." (See Teo Savory, "An Introduction to Guillevic," p. 45.)

Savory's prediction having come to pass, Guillevic's
vital statistics and artistic accomplishments are today too
well documented to require extensive elaboration here.[4]
Suffice it to say that he was born in Carnac on August 5,
1907, spent much of his childhood and youth in Alsace,
and most of his adult life in government service, filling a
number of posts and eventually being named Inspecteur
de l'Economie Nationale in 1946. Guillevic retired from
public life in 1967 to spend his time writing, traveling
extensively, and lending his support to a variety of
worldwide writers' causes. An *officier* of the Légion
d'honneur, he has received many awards for his *œuvre;*
among them the Grand Aigle d'Or de la Poésie at the
Nice Festival of 1973, the extremely prestigious Grand
Prix de Poésie of the Académie Française in 1976, and,
most recently, in 1984, the Grand Prix National for poetry awarded by the Ministère de la Culture. He has also
been honored with a number of foreign distinctions.

At first glance it might seem inconsistent that this
serious poet of the concrete object should have published

a rather more sprightly collection, late in life, of what he calls his "fabliettes," expressly (though not exclusively, one can easily suspect) intended for children.[5] Certainly the good-natured spirit of La Fontaine does not inform the body of his poetry, nor does his unmistakable style. Still, as Léon-Gabriel Gros astutely points out, Guillevic, in his beginnings, was a fabulist of sorts. "Il a aussi retrouvé la Fable . . . en tant que genre littéraire. Il n'est point d'objet proposé par Guillevic, d'épisode conté par lui, qui ne comporte en transparence une moralité." But a "moralité," he adds, proffered with "une sorte de sourire crispé qui dissimule mal un désespoir foncier" ("Un exorciste," p. 462). Indeed, his very first volume of verse—a half-dozen brief poems ("Bruyère," "Pin," "Vache," "Hanneton," "Ecureuil," and "Fourmi") grouped under the dour title *Requiem,* dedicated to poet Jules Supervielle, gave a somber foretaste, and strikingly so, of what was to become the present collection, published four decades later.

Fabliettes, brilliantly illustrated in its original edition (in the "Folio Benjamin" series for children) by Californian artist Laurie Jordan, contains thirty-eight unnumbered, unpaginated verses, more lighthearted for the most part than their animal and vegetal antecedents in *Requiem*—including, not atypically, a number of inanimates as well—but still concise and no less cynical in their implications. Those translated here are the first, tenth, eleventh, sixteenth, twenty-first, twenty-third, twenty-seventh, twenty-eighth, thirty-first, thirty-second, thirty-fourth, thirty-fifth, and thirty-eighth, in that order.

1. The almost mystical nature of Guillevic's objective world is also discussed in poet Alain Bosquet's article "Guillevic ou la conscience de l'objet."

2. Though defended by Aragon, who wrote a laudatory preface to the collection, Guillevic's sonnets were not an unqualified success in the world of letters. As one of his American translators, Denise Levertov, observes: "he seems—in the adoption of the sonnet form itself, as if to give to the common reader an absolutely familiar point of entry—to have been making a deliberate effort to write a kind of poem he felt . . . he *ought* to be writing: which he owed to the social struggle. . . . But Guillevic himself seems to have felt that it was not *his* way." (See Guillevic, *Selected Poems,* p. xi.)

3. See, for example, Etiemble's essay, "Guillevic est-il un haïjin?" in *Lire Guillevic,* ed. Serge Gaubert.

4. For the most nearly complete and (almost) up-to-date biographical and bibliographical data—including Guillevic's numerous translations from a variety of languages, such as Finnish, Rumanian, Ukrainian and Hungarian, to name only the more recondite—the reader should consult the above-mentioned volume edited by Serge Gaubert. In it he will find a chronology of the poet's life, a bibliography of his works and translations, and a critical bibliography, including three works devoted entirely to his poetry from different stages of his career, by Pierre Daix, Jean Tortel, and Jean Dubacq, respectively. (The critical bibliography, however, omits a number of the non-French studies of Guillevic, notably Teo Savory's article cited above.)

5. "Et pourquoi avoir écrit ces petites choses?" asks Guillevic rhetorically in the postface to his little volume, *Fabliettes.* "Facile de répondre: en marge des autres choses, dans des moments de détente. . . . En général les fables portent aux enfants la morale des adultes, des grandes personnes. Pourquoi ne pas, pour une fois, renverser les rôles? L'auteur croit être resté assez enfant pour jouer ce jeu."

Fabliette du Petit Chien

Que lorgnait le petit chien?
Un os qui était le sien,

Cet os que lui avait pris
Un chien tout gros de mépris.

The Little Pup

Little pup sat eyeing bone,
One he used to call his own.

Burly hound came swaggering up,
Snatching bone from little pup.

Le ciel ne rougissait pas
D'assister à ce repas.

L'un des chiens resta petit.
L'autre garda l'appétit.

Sky watched hound dine on said victual:
Didn't care one whit or tittle.

Pup's still little, as before;
Hound's still hungry, wants some more.

Fabliette du Petit Ver

Petit ver, ce n'était que toi
Qui faisais des trous dans le bois.

Je croyais que c'était le temps
Qui démolissait en partant.

The Little Worm

Who chews the wood to tatters? Who?
Why, little worm, it's only you!

And all the while I thought we ought
Blame fleeting time for what you wrought!

Fabliette du Ver

Le ver était dans le fruit,
Le soleil à la porte.

Lorsque arriva la nuit,
La pomme était morte.

The Worm

Worm was in apple, sun
Was overhead.¹

As soon as day was done,
Apple was dead.

1. I have taken the liberty of placing the poet's sun "overhead"—with little change in meaning, if any—for the same demands of rhyme that apparently made him place it "à la porte."

Fabliette de la Chaise

La chaise un soir se demandait
Si jamais elle ne pourrait

A son tour prendre pour perchoir
Un qui sur elle vient s'asseoir.

The Chair

A chair who'd had enough, one night,
Of being sat on, hoped she might

In time, perhaps, indulge her whim:
Turn man to chair and sit on him.

Fabliette de l'Ara

Perroquet, perroqui,
Perroquo, perroquoi—

Pourquoi l'ara
Il criait ça?

The Macaw

Caw-caws, haw-haws:
Macaws' guffaws...

And why?
Be-caws.

Fabliette de l'Œuf

Il y avait là deux œufs
Tremblant de paraître vieux.

Ils ne savaient pas qu'un œuf
A toujours l'air d'être neuf.

The Eggs

Two eggs stood atremble, fearing
They might grow too old-appearing.

Little did they know, however,
Eggs keep looking young forever.

Fabliette de la Souris

Une souris de bonne race
Qui n'avait pas été en classe
Et n'avait jamais rien appris
Ni d'un maître, ni de sa mère,

Savait pourtant ce qu'il faut faire
Pour se comporter en souris,

Et devint ainsi douce chair
Pour un matou de bonne race
Qui n'avait pas été en classe
Et lui aussi savait y faire.

The Mouse

A mouse of proper pedigree,
Unschooled, untutored by her mother—
Or, to be sure, by any other—
Versed all the same in mouseliness,

Knew what a mouse was meant to be;
And so, indeed, as one might guess,

Became a tasty fricassee
For tomcat quite untutored too,
But who, well-pedigreed no less,
Knew what a cat was meant to do.

Fabliette du Lapereau

Tout lapereau qu'il était,
Savait ce qu'on racontait.

Savait, mais n'acceptait pas
Et se vouait au combat.

Tant montait en lui la fièvre
Que presque il se croyait lièvre.

The Baby Rabbit

A baby rabbit's all he was,
But that was hardly proper cause

To shrink in fear from mortal fray,
Despite what anyone might say.

Full of the fire to do and dare,
He rather thought himself a hare.

Fabliette de l'Alouette

L'alouette monta
Au plus haut de sa joie

Et tomba tout à coup
A se rompre le cou

Pour avoir approché
L'infini recherché.

The Lark

Happy the lark went soaring
High as her joy's outpouring

But tumbled from the blue
And broke her neck in two

Because she wouldn't quit
Seeking the infinite.

Fabliette de la Laitue

Une laitue
Se plaignait: "Ça me tue,

Ce soleil
A mon réveil.

Je veux sur la table
Etre présentable."

Elle mourut de vieillesse
Et de sécheresse.

The Lettuce

"I'm dying," said
A fretful lettuce-head.

"More morning sun
And I'll be done.

I'd like to be able
To look nice on the table."

Instead, she aged, and dried...
And died.

Fabliette de la Fourmi

La fourmi se fit serment
De vivre plus largement

Et se mit à entasser
Ses raisons de dépenser.

The Ant

The ant resolved that she
Would live less frugally,

And so made lists, piled high,
Of things she ought to buy.

Fabliette du Chevreuil

Le chevreuil se savait joli,
Ravissant, mais savait aussi

Que ce n'était pas pour cela
Qu'on lui faisait cet hallali.[1]

1. Rather than second-guess the poet, I reproduce the unrhyming "cela" of his text even though I suspect he may have intended a "ceci."

The Roebuck

The roebuck knew how utterly
Delightful to behold was he.

He also knew that wasn't why
They hounded him with hue and cry.

Fabliette de la Fabliette

Une fabliette
Ne comprenait miette
Aux moralités.

Vit avec scandale
Qu'est loin la morale
Des moralités.

1. It seems so appropriate to conclude this collection with Guillevic's last *fabliette*, a pithy commentary on the nature of the fable—its moral (or nonmoral) notwithstanding—that I have seen fit to

The Little Fable

A little fable couldn't
Quite understand (or wouldn't)
The morals of fables.

He found, to his chagrin,
There's little moral in
The morals of fables.[1]

displace the preceding fabulist, Gomar, slightly from his logical (i.e., chrono-logical) position. My apologies.

Bibliography

GENERAL TEXTS

REFERENCE WORKS: BIBLIOGRAPHIES, ENCYCLOPEDIAS, DICTIONARIES, YEARBOOKS, ALMANACS, ETC.

Annales dramatiques, ou Dictionnaire général des théâtres. 9 vols. Paris: Hénée et al., 1808–12.

Annuaire administratif et statistique du département de la Loire. Monbrison: Bernard, 1851.

Annuaire de l'Ordre Impérial de la Légion d'honneur, année 1852. Paris: Imprimerie Impériale, 1853.

Beaumarchais, Jean-Pierre de, Daniel Couty, and Alain Rey. *Dictionnaire des littératures de langue française.* 3 vols. Paris: Bordas, 1984; 4 vols. Paris: Bordas, 1987.

Biographie nouvelle des contemporains. Edited by Antoine-Vincent Arnault, Antoine Jay, Etienne de Jouy, and Jacques Maufret de Norvins. 20 vols. Paris: Ledentu, 1827.

Biographie toulousaine. 2 vols. Paris: L.-G. Michaud, 1823.

Biographie universelle, ancienne et moderne, commonly the "*Biographie Michaud.*" 85 vols. Paris: Michaud frères et al., 1811–62. Revised ed. 45 vols. Paris: Delagrave, 1870–73.

Biographie universelle et portative des contemporains. Edited by Alphonse Rabbe et al. 5 vols. Paris: F.-G. Levrault, 1834.

Boisard, François. *Notices biographiques, littéraires et critiques sur les hommes du Calvados.* Caen: Imprimerie Pagny, 1848.

Boissier de Sauvages, Pierre-Augustin. *Dictionnaire languedocien-françois.* 2 vols. Nîmes: M. Gaude, 1756, 1785. 2d ed. (edited by L.-A. d'Hombres-Firmas). Alais: J. Martin, 1820.

Brenner, Clarence. *A Bibliographical List of Plays in the French Language (1700–1789).* Berkeley, 1947.

Caribbean Writers: A Bio-Bibliographical-Critical Encyclopedia. Edited by Donald Herdeck. Washington: Three Continents Press, 1979.

Celani, Enrico. "Additions et corrections au *Dictionnaire des anonymes* de Barbier." In *Revue des bibliothèques,* year 11 (1901): 323–61.

Cioranescu, Alexandre. *Bibliographie de la littérature française du dix-huitième siècle.* 3 vols. Paris: C. N. R. S., 1969.

———. *Bibliographie de la littérature française du dix-septième siècle.* 3 vols. Paris: C. N. R. S., 1965–66.

———. *Bibliographie de la littérature française du seizième siècle.* Paris: Klincksieck, 1959.

Dictionnaire de biographie française. 17 vols. and 2 unbound fasc. to date. Paris: Letouzey et Ané. 1933–[90].

Dictionnaire des lettres françaises: le dix-neuvième siècle. Edited by Georges Grente et al. 2 vols. Paris: Fayard, 1971–72.

———: *le dix-huitième siècle.* Edited by Georges Grente et al. 2 vols. Paris: Fayard, 1960.

———: *le dix-septième siècle.* Edited by Georges Grente et al. Paris: Fayard, 1954.

———: *le seizième siècle.* Paris: Fayard, 1951.

Dreher, S., and M. Rolli. *Bibliographie de la littérature française, 1930–1939.* Geneva: Droz, 1948.

Drevet, Marguerite L. *Bibliographie de la littérature française, 1940–1949.* Geneva: Droz, 1954.

Dufay, Pierre. "Esquisse d'une bibliographie du Loir-et-Cher (1900–1908)." In *Mémoires de la Société des Sciences et Lettres de Loir-et-Cher* 19 (1909): 227–334.

Encyclopedia of World Literature in the Twentieth Century. Edited by Leonard S. Klein. 4 vols. Revised ed. New York: Ungar, 1982–84.

Encyclopédie des gens du monde, répertoire universel des sciences, des lettres et des arts, etc. Paris: Treuttel et Würtz, 1833–44.

Huguet, Edmond. *Dictionnaire de la langue française du seizième siècle.* 7 vols. Paris: Champion (vol. 1), Didier (vols. 2–7), 1925–67.

Jacob, père Louis. *De claris scriptoribus Cabilonensibus.* Paris, 1652.

Jal, Auguste. *Dictionnaire critique de biographie et d'histoire.* 2d ed. Paris: Plon, 1872.

Lachèvre, Frédéric. *Bibliographie des recueils collectifs de poésies publiés de 1597 à 1700.* 4 vols. Paris: Henri Leclerc, 1901–5. Reprint. Geneva: Slatkine, 1967.

La Tour-Keyrié, A.-M. de. *Recueil de proverbes, maximes, sentences et dictons provençaux.* Aix: Makaire, 1882.

Lebreton, Théodore. *Biographie rouennaise.* 3 vols. Rouen: A. Le Brument, 1857–61.

Le Roux de Lincy, Antoine-Jean-Victor. *Le Livre des proverbes français.* 2 vols. Paris: Paulin, 1842.

New Grove Dictionary of Music and Musicians. Edited by Stanley Sadie. 20 vols. London: Macmillan, 1980.

Nouvelle Biographie générale. Edited by [Jean-Chrétien] Ferdinand Hoefer. 46 vols. Paris: Firmin Didot, 1852–70.

The Oxford Companion to Canadian Literature. Edited by William Toye. Toronto: Oxford University Press, 1983.

The Oxford Dictionary of English Proverbs. 3d ed. Oxford: Oxford University Press, 1970.

Le Petit Almanach de nos grands hommes, pour l'année 1788. Paris: Léopold Collin, 1808.

Picoche, Jacqueline. *Nouveau Dictionnaire étymologique du français.* Paris: Hachette-Tchou, 1971.

Quérard, J.-M., ed. *Les Supercheries littéraires dévoilées* [augmented edition of Barbier's *Dictionnaire des ouvrages anonymes*]. 3 vols. Paris: Paul Daffis, 1869–70. Supplement Paris: F.-J. Féchoz, 1889.

Qui êtes-vous? Annuaire des contemporains, 1908. Paris: Delagrave, 1908.

Richelet, Pierre. *Dictionnaire de la langue françoise.* Geneva: Wiederhold, 1680.

Rigoley de Juvigny, Antoine, ed. *Les Bibliothèques françoises de La Croix du Maine et de Du Verdier.* Revised and augmented ed. 3 vols. Paris: Michel Lambert, 1772–73.

Roman, Pau. *Lei Mount-Joio: voucabulàri dei prouverbi e loucucien proverbialo de la Lengo Prouvençalo.* 1 vol.; others projected and never published. Avignon: Aubanel, 1908.

Saint-Lanne, Emile. *Dictionnaire illustré des contemporains.* Paris: E. Dentu, 1891.

Sgard, Jean. *Dictionnaire des journalistes (1600–1789).* Grenoble: Presses Universitaires de Grenoble, 1976.

Les Siècles littéraires de la France, ou Nouveau Dictionnaire historique, critique, et bibliographique. Edited by N.-L.-M. Désessarts et al. 7 vols. Paris: "Chez l'Auteur," An VIII [1800]–An XI [1803].

Talvart, Hector, and Joseph Place; continued by Georges Place. *Bibliographie des auteurs modernes de langue française.* 22 vols. Paris: Editions de *la Chronique des Lettres Françaises,* 1928–76.

Tchemerzine, Avenir. *Bibliographie d'éditions originales et rares d'auteurs français des XVe, XVIe, XVIIe, et XVIIIe siècles.* 10 vols. Paris: Marcel Plée, 1927–34.

Thieme, Hugo P. *Bibliographie de la littérature française de 1800 à 1930.* 2 vols. Paris: Droz, 1933.

Thieme, Ulrich, Felix Becker, et al. *Allgemeines Lexikon der bildenden Künstler.* 37 vols. Leipzig: Wilhelm Engelmann (vols. 1–4), E. A. Seeman (vols. 5–37), 1907–50.

Thompson, Stith. *Motif-Index of Folk-Literature.* 6 vols. Bloomington: Indiana University Press, 1957.

Tudesq, André-Jean. *Les Grands notables en France, 1840–1849.* 2 vols. Paris: Presses Universitaires de France, 1964.

Viollet Le Duc, Emmanuel-Louis-Nicolas. *Catalogue des livres composant la bibliothèque poétique de M. Viollet Le Duc.* Paris: Hachette, 1843.

GENERAL ANTHOLOGIES, LITERARY HISTORIES, LITERARY MEMOIR AND ANECDOTE, ETC.

ab der Halden, Charles. *Nouvelles Etudes de littérature canadienne-française.* Paris: F.-R. de Rudeval, 1907.

Almanach des Muses. Paris: Delalain et al., 1765–1833.

Armand, Alain, and Gérard Chopinet. *La Littérature réunionnaise d'expression créole (1828–1982).* Paris: L'Harmattan, 1983.

Boisdeffre, Pierre de. *Histoire de la littérature de langue française des années 1930 aux années 1980.* 2 vols. Paris: Librairie Académique Perrin, 1985.

Brée, Germaine. *Twentieth-Century French Literature.* Chicago: University of Chicago Press, 1983.

Brunet, Berthelot. *Histoire de la littérature canadienne-française.* Montréal: Editions de l'Arbre, 1946.

Clouard, Henri. *Histoire de la littérature française du symbolisme à nos jours.* 2 vols. Paris: Albin Michel, 1947–50.

Crépet, Eugène. *Les Poètes français.* 4 vols. Paris: Gide, 1861–62.

Donnadieu, Frédéric. *Les Précurseurs des Félibres: 1800–1855.* Revised ed. Paris: Quantin, 1888.

Dussault, Jean-Joseph. *Annales littéraires.* 5 vols. Paris: Maradan et al., 1818–24.

Esprit de Rivarol. Paris, 1808.

Faguet, Emile. *Histoire de la poésie française de la Renaissance au Romantisme.* 11 vols. Paris: Boivin, 1923–36. [Note: a variety of Faguet's chapters, relating to specific poets, also appear in the *Revue des cours et conférences* 1896–1905, where they are, substantially, reprints of his Sorbonne lectures on the authors. Among those cited are: 5 (1896–97), nos. 6:241–48 and 7:304–27; 7 (1898–99), nos. 31:625–33, 32:678–86, 33:727–35, and 34:776–84; 8 (1899–1900), nos. 1:2–8, 2:57–61, 3:117–21, and 4:145–50; 12 (1903–4), nos. 22:193–202 and 23:241–54; and 13 (1904–5), no. 4:145–58].

Fournel, Victor. *Le Théâtre au XVIIe siècle: la comédie.* Paris: Lecène, Oudin et Cie, 1892.

Fréron, Elie-Catherine. *L'Année littéraire.* Amsterdam and Paris, 1754–75.

Geoffroy, Julien-Louis. *Cours de littérature dramatique.* 5 vols. Paris: Pierre Blanchard, 1819.

Godet, Philippe. *Histoire littéraire de la Suisse française.* Paris: Fischbacher, 1895.

Goujet, abbé Claude-Pierre. *Bibliothèque françoise, ou Histoire de la littérature françoise.* 18 vols. Paris: P.-J. Mariette et al., 1741–56.

Grimm, Friedrich Melchior von. *Correspondance littéraire, philosophique et critique.* Edited by Maurice Tourneux. 16 vols. Paris: Garnier frères, 1877–82.

Grudé de La Croix du Maine, François. *Premier volume de la bibliothèque du Sieur de La Croix du Maine.* Paris: Abel l'Angelier, 1584.

Guiot, Joseph-André. *Les Trois siècles palinodiques, ou Histoire générale des Palinods de Rouen, Dieppe, etc.* Edited by l'abbé A. Tougard. 2 vols. Rouen: A. Lestringant, 1898.

Holmes, Urban T., Jr. *A History of Old French Literature from the Origins to 1300.* Revised ed. New York: Russell and Russell, 1962.

Irailh, Augustin-Simon. *Querelles littéraires, ou Mémoires pour servir à l'histoire des révolutions de la République des Lettres, depuis Homère jusqu'à nos jours.* 4 vols. Paris: Durand, 1761.

Journal Literaire [sic]. 24 vols. The Hague: T. Johnson, 1713–37; Reprint. Geneva: Slatkine, 1968.

Jullien, Bernard. *Histoire de la poésie française à l'époque impériale.* 2 vols. Paris: Paulin, 1844.

Lafont, Robert, and Christian Anatole. *Nouvelle histoire de la littérature occitane.* 2 vols. Paris: Presses Universitaires de France, 1970.

La Harpe, Jean-François de. *Lycée, ou Cours de littérature ancienne et moderne.* 16 vols. in 19. Paris: Agasse, 1799–1805.

Laincel, Louis de. *Des troubadours aux Félibres: études sur la poésie provençale.* Aix: Makaire, 1862.

Lalou, René. *Histoire de la littérature française contemporaine, de 1870 à nos jours.* 2 vols. Paris: Presses Universitaires de France, 1947.

Lancaster, Henry Carrington. *A History of French Dramatic Literature in the Seventeenth Century.* 5 parts in 9 vols. Baltimore: The Johns Hopkins University Press, 1925–42.

Lareau, Edouard. *Histoire de la littérature canadienne.* Montréal: Lovell, 1874.

Mary-Lafon [Jean-Bernard Lafon]. *Histoire littéraire du Midi de la France.* Paris: Reinwald, 1882.

Mirecourt, Eugène de. *Les Contemporains.* 100 vols. Vol. 68: *Viennet.* Paris: Havard, 1856.

Moripeau, Louis, ed. *Anthologie d'un siècle de poésie haïtienne, 1817–1925.* Paris: Bossard, 1925.

Niceron, Jean-Pierre. *Mémoires pour servir à l'histoire des hommes illustres dans la république des lettres, avec un catalogue raisonné de leurs ouvrages.* 43 vols. Paris: Briasson, 1729–45.

Portal, E. *La Letteratura provensala moderna.* Palermo: Lauriel, 1893.

Ripert, Emile. *La Renaissance provençale, 1800–1860.* Paris: Champion; Aix-en-Provence: Dragon, 1917.

Rossel, Virgile. *Histoire littéraire de la Suisse romande, des origines à nos jours.* 2 vols. Geneva: H. Georg, 1889.

Roustan, F. *Pichoto Istòri de la Literaturo d'O: o prouvençalo despièi sis óurigino enjusquo à noste tèms.* Marseille: P. Ruat, 1914.

Roy, Camille. *Nos origines littéraires.* Québec: Action Sociale, 1909.

St. Martin, Gérard Labarre, and Jacqueline Voorhies. *Ecrits louisianais du dix-neuvième siècle.* Baton Rouge: Louisiana State University Press, 1979.

Titon du Tillet, Evrard. *Le Parnasse françois.* Paris: J.-B. Coignard fils, 1732–43.

Trouillot, Henock. *Les Origines sociales de la littérature haïtienne.* Port-au-Prince: N.-A. Théodore, 1962.

Van Bever, Adolphe, ed. *Poètes du terroir.* 4 vols. Paris: Delagrave, 1909–13?

Vandérem, Fernand. *Le Miroir des lettres.* 8 vols. Paris: Flammarion, 1919–29.

Voisenon, Claude-Henri de Fusée de. *Anecdotes littéraires.* Published by "Le Bibliophile Jacob" [Paul Lacroix]. Paris: Librairie des Bibliophiles, 1880.

THE FABLES AND THE FABULISTS

ANTHOLOGIES, HISTORIES, BIBLIOGRAPHIES, AND STUDIES OF THE FABLE

Carnes, Pack. *Fable Scholarship: An Annotated Bibliography.* New York and London: Garland, 1985.

——, ed. *Proverbia in Fabula: Essays on the Relationship of the Proverb and the Fable.* (*Sprichwörterforschung,* Band 10.) Bern: Lang, 1988.

Collins, William Lucas. *La Fontaine and Other French Fabulists.* Edinburgh and London: William Blackwood, 1882.

Doderer, Klaus. *Fabeln: Formen, Figuren, Lehren.* Zurich: Atlantis, 1970.

Ewald, Dieter. *Die moderne französische Fabel: Struktur und Geschichte.* [Rheinfelden]: Schäuble Verlag, 1977.

Le Fablier des dames, ou Choix de fables en vers pour les filles, les épouses et les mères. Lyon: J. Tasge; Paris: Louis Jannet, 1821.

Le Fablier du jeune âge. 2 vols. Paris: D. Belin, 1832.

Hasubek, Peter, ed. *Fabelforschung.* Darmstadt: Wissenschaftliche Buchgesellschaft, 1983.

———, ed. *Die Fabel: Theorie, Geschichte und Rezeption einer Gattung.* Berlin: Erich Schmidt Verlag, 1982.

Hérissant, Louis-Théodore. *Le Fablier françois, ou Elite des meilleures fables depuis La Fontatine.* Paris: Lottin le Jeune, 1771.

Hervieux, Léopold. *Les Fabulistes latins depuis le siècle d'Auguste jusqu'à la fin du moyen âge.* 5 vols. Paris: Firmin-Didot, 1884–99.

Illberg, G. *Les plus belles fables des 50 meilleurs fabulistes.* Paris: Editions André Bonne, 1964.

Janssens, Jacques. *La Fable et les fabulistes.* Brussels: Office de la Publicité, 1955.

Keidel, George Charles. *A Manual of Aesopic Fable Literature: A First Book of Reference for the Period Ending A.D. 1500.* Baltimore: Friedenwald, 1896.

———. "Problems in Mediaeval Fable Literature." In *Studies in Honor of A. Marshall Elliot.* 2 vols. Baltimore: The Johns Hopkins Press; Paris: Champion; Leipzig: Harrassowitz, [1911].

Leibfried, Erwin. *Fabel.* Bamberg: C. C. Buchners Verlag, 1984.

Levrault, Léon. *La Fable: évolution du genre.* Paris: Delaplane, 1905. Reprint. Paris: Mellottée, 1919.

Lindner, Hermann. "Bibliographie zur Gattungspoetik (5): Theorie und Geschichte der Fabel (1900–1974)." *Zeitschrift für französische Sprache und Literatur* 85 (1975), no. 3: 247–59.

———. *Fabel der Neuzeit. England, Frankreich, Deutschland. Ein Lese- und Arbeitsbuch.* Munich: Wilhelm Fink Verlag, 1978.

Mombello, Gianni. *Le Raccolte francesi di favole esopiane dal 1480 alla fine del secolo XVI.* Geneva and Paris: Slatkine, 1981.

Noel, Thomas. *Theories of the Fable in the Eighteenth Century.* New York: Columbia University Press, 1975.

Nouveau Fablier français. Paris: Capelle et Renaud, 1905.

Nouvelles Fables choisies, et mises en vers par les plus célèbres auteurs françois de ce temps. Amsterdam: Daniel De La Feuille; The Hague: Meindert Uitwerf, 1694–95.

Perry, Ben Edwin. *Aesopica.* Urbana: University of Illinois Press, 1952.

Reboul, Robert[-Marie]. *Fabulistes provençaux.* Paris: Techener, 1892.

Robert, A.-C.-M. *Fables inédites des XIIe, XIIIe et XIVe siècles, et Fables de La Fontaine, rapprochées de celles de tous les auteurs qui avoient, avant lui, traité les mêmes sujets, précédées d'une notice sur les fabulistes.* 2 vols. Paris: Cabin, 1825.

Ruben, Emile. *De quelques imitations patoises des Fables de La Fontaine.* Limoges: Chapoulaud frères, 1861.

Runte, Roseann. "The Paradox of the Fable in Eighteenth-Century France." *Neophilologus* 61 (1977), no. 4: 510–17.

Saillard, Gustave. *Essai sur la fable en France au XVIIIe siècle.* Toulouse: E. Privat, 1912.

Schlumberger, Camille. *Promenade au jardin des fables.* Dornach and Paris: Braun; Paris: Berger-Levrault, 1923.

Shapiro, Norman R. *Fables from Old French: Aesop's Beasts and Bumpkins.* Introduction by Howard Needler. Middletown, Conn.: Wesleyan University Press, 1982.

Soullié, Prosper. *La Fontaine et ses devanciers.* Paris: Durand, 1861.

FABLES—COLLECTIONS, TRANSLATIONS, SPECIAL EDITIONS—AND OTHER ŒUVRES OF THE AUTHORS REPRESENTED

Anouilh, Jean. *Fables.* Paris: La Table Ronde, 1962.

Arnault, Antoine-Vincent. *Fables.* Paris: Chaumerol, 1812. Reprint. Paris: Eymery, 1813.

———. *Fables et poèmes.* Paris: Bossange, 1826.

———. *Fables nouvelles.* Paris: Didot, 1834.

———. *Les Loisirs d'un banni.* Edited by August Imbert. Paris: "Chez l'Editeur," 1823.

———. *Œuvres.* 8 vols. Paris: Bossange, 1824–28.

———. *Souvenirs d'un sexagénaire.* 4 vols. Paris: Dufey, 1833. 2d ed. Paris: Garnier frères, 1908?

———. *Vie politique et militaire de Napoléon.* 2 vols. Paris: Babeuf, 1822–26.

Aubert, Jean-Louis. *Fables nouvelles.* Amsterdam and Paris: Duchesne, 1756.

———. *Fables nouvelles.* Paris: Desaint et Saillant, 1761. Revised ed. Paris: Duchesne, 1764. 4th, enlarged ed. Paris: Moutard, 1773.

———. *Fables et œuvres diverses.* 2 vols. Revised ed. Paris: Moutard, 1774.

———. *Psiché, poème en huit chants.* Paris: Moutard, 1769.

———. *Réfutation suivie, détaillée des principes de M. Rousseau, de Genève, touchant la musique françoise.* Paris: Chaubert, 1754.

———. *Le Vœu de Jephté.* Paris: Duchesne, 1765.

Audisio, Gabriel. *Fables.* Paris: Pierre Belfond, 1966.

———. *Feuilles de Fresnes.* Paris: Les Editions de Minuit, 1945.

———. *Héliotrope.* Paris: Editions de la *Nouvelle Revue Française*, 1928.

———. *Hommes au soleil.* Maupré: Charolles; Mâcon: Protat, 1923.

———. *Ici-bas.* Algiers: Basset, 1927.

———. *Jeunesse de la Méditerranée.* Paris: Gallimard, 1935.

———. *L'Opéra fabuleux.* Paris: Julliard, 1970.

———. *Poème de la joie.* Paris: Editions du "Solitaire," 1924.

———. *Trois hommes et un minaret.* Paris: F. Rieder, 1926.

———. *Ulysse ou l'intelligence.* Paris: Gallimard, 1945.

———. *La Vie de Haroun-al-Raschid.* Paris: Gallimard, 1930.

———, ed. *Cagayous, ses meilleures histoires.* Paris: Gallimard, 1931. 2d ed. Paris: Balland, 1972.

Baïf, Jean-Antoine de. *Œuvres en rime.* 4 vols. Paris: Lucas Breyer, 1573.

———. *Œuvres en rime.* Edited with a biographical introduction and notes by Charles Marty-Laveaux. 5 vols. Paris: Lemerre, 1881–90.

———. *Les Mimes, enseignements et proverbes.* Edited and with an introduction by Prosper Blanchemain. 2 vols. Paris: Léon Willem, 1880.

———. *Poésies choisies de J.-A. de Baïf.* Edited by Louis Becq de Fouquières. Paris: Charpentier, 1874.

Bastin, Julia. *Recueil général des Isopets.* Paris: Champion, 1929–30.

Beer, Jeannette. *Medieval Fables: Marie de France.* Limpsfield, Surrey: Dragon's World Ltd., 1981. Reprint. New York: Dodd, Mead, 1983.

Benserade, Isaac de. *Fables d'Esope en quatrains.* Paris: Sébastien Mabre-Cramoisy, 1678.

———. *Poésies de Benserade.* Edited by Octave Uzanne. Paris: Librairie des Bibliophiles, 1875.

Benserade, Isaac de, and Charles Perrault. *Le Labyrinte de Versailles.* With engravings by Sébastien Le Clerc. Paris: L'Imprimerie Royale, 1679.

Boisard, Jean-Jacques-François-Marin. *Fables*. Paris: Lacombe, 1773.
———. *Fables*. 2 vols. Paris: Lacombe, 1777. Second printing Paris: Pissot, 1779.
———. *Fables*. Caen: P. Chalopin, 1803.
———. *Fables*. Caen: P. Chalopin, 1804.
———. *Fables*. Caen: P. Chalopin, 1805.
———. *Mille et une fables*. Caen: P. Chalopin, 1806.
Boufflers, Stanislas-Jean de. *Œuvres*. 2 vols. Paris: Briand, 1813.
———. *Poésies diverses du chevalier de Boufflers*. With a preface by Octave Uzanne. Paris: A. Quantin, 1886.
Boufflers, Stanislas-Jean de, and la comtesse de Sabran. *Correspondance inédite de la comtesse de Sabran et du chevalier de Boufflers, 1778–1788*. Edited by E. de Magnieu and Henri Prat. Paris: Plon, 1875.
Boursault, Edme. *Artémise et Poliante*. Paris: René Guignard, 1670.
———. *Lettres nouvelles de Monsieur Boursault, Accompagnées de Fables, de Contes, d'Epigrammes, de Remarques, de bons Mots, & d'autres particularités aussi agréables qu'utiles*. Paris: Veuve de Théodore Girard, 1697.
———. *Théâtre*. 3 vols. Revised ed. in one vol. Geneva: Slatkine, 1970.
———. *Théâtre choisi*. Edited by Victor Fournel. Paris: Laplace, Sanchez et Cie, 1892.
Burgaud des Marets, Henri. *Fables en patois charentais*. Paris: Firmin-Didot, 1849.
———. *Noveau fabeulier jarnacoès* ("New Jarnac Fable-Book"). Paris: Firmin-Didot, 1852.
———. *Parabole de l'enfant prodigue, en dialecte saintongeais*. Paris: Firmin-Didot, 1858.
———. *Recueil des fables et contes en patois saintongeais*. Paris: Firmin-Didot, 1859.
———, trans. *Konrad Wallenrud*, by Adam Mickiewicz. Paris: Gagniard, 1830.
Burgaud des Marets, Henri, and Edme-Jacques-Benoît Rathery, eds. *Œuvres de Rabelais, collationnées pour la première fois sur les éditions originales*. Paris: Firmin-Didot, 1858–59. 2d ed. Paris: Firmin-Didot, 1870–73.
Corrozet, Gilles. *Le Compte du Rossignol*. Edited by Ferdinand Gohin. Paris: Garnier frères, 1924.
———. *Les Fables du très-ancien Esope mises en rithme françoise*. Edited by Auguste de Queux de Saint-Hilaire. Paris: Librairie des Bibliophiles, 1883.
———. *Fleur des antiquitez de Paris*. Edited by François Boucher. Paris: Editions de l'Ibis, 1945.
———. *Hécatomgraphie*. Edited with a preface by Charles Oulmont. Paris: Champion, 1905.
Couteau, Emile [the younger]. *Du Bénéfice de l'assurance sur la vie*. Paris: Auger, 1877.
———. *Le Centenaire de 1789 et l'impôt foncier*. Blois: E. Moreau, 1889.
———. *De la distribution des biens*. Paris: Durand, 1858
———. *Fables*. Nice: Imprimerie Niçoise, 1906.
———. *Fables*. Nice: Imprimerie Niçoise, 1907.
———. *Fables et apologues*. Paris: Collection de "La Poétique," 1910.
———. *Fables du vingtième siècle*. Paris: Delagrave, 1929.
———. *Lettres sur l'Algérie: De l'administration de la justice*. Paris: Goupy, 1866.
———. *Des Rapports à succession*. Paris: Durand, 1861.
———. *Traité des assurances sur la vie*. Paris: Marchal, Billard et Cie, 1881.
Déjean, Jean-Luc. *Les Chevaux du roi*. Paris: Hachette, 1986.
———. *Clément Marot*. Paris: Fayard, 1990.
———. *Le Cousin de Pothos*. Paris: Lattès, 1981.
———. *La Feuille à l'envers*. Paris: Gallimard, 1970.

———. *Marguerite de Navarre*. Paris: Fayard, 1987.
———. *L'Ordinateur sentimental*. Paris: Editions Saint-Germain-des-Prés, 1977.
———. *Le Premier Chien*. Paris: Hachette, 1984.
———. *Quand chevauchaient les comtes de Toulouse, 1050–1250*. Paris: Fayard, 1979. Revised ed.: *Les Comtes de Toulouse*. Paris: Fayard, 1988.
———. "La Surlune et l'oizéro." Unpublished collection, 1990.
———. *Le Théâtre en France depuis 1945*. Paris: Nathan, 1987.
———. *Le Théâtre français d'aujourd'hui*. Paris: Nathan, 1971.
———. *Les Voleurs de pauvres*. Paris: Gallimard, 1953.
Delaunay. *Le Complaisant*. Comedy: 5 acts. Utrecht: Etienne Neaulme, 1733.
———. *Œuvres de théâtre de De Launay*. Paris: Veuve Duchesne, 1766.
———. *Le Paresseux*. Comedy: 3 acts, verse. Paris: Le Breton fils, 1733. Reprint. Utrecht: Etienne Neaulme, 1734.
———. *La Vérité fabuliste*. Comedy: 1 act. Paris: J.-F. Josse; Utrecht: Etienne Neaulme, 1734.
Deschamps, Eustache. *Œuvres complètes d'Eustache Deschamps*. Société des Anciens Textes Français. Edited by Auguste de Queux de Saint-Hilaire and Gaston Raynaud. 11 vols. Paris: Firmin Didot, 1878–1903.
———. *Œuvres inédites d'Eustache Deschamps*. Edited by Prosper Tarbé. 2 vols. Paris: Techener, 1849.
———. *Poésies morales et historiques d'Eustache Deschamps*. Edited by Georges-Adrien Crapelet. Paris: Crapelet, 1832.
Desprez, Philippe. *Le Théâtre des animavx, avquel, sovs plvsievrs diverses fables et histoires, est representé la plus-part des actions de la vie humaine: Enrichy de belles sentences tirees de l'Escriture-Sainte et orné de figures pour ceux qui ayment la peinture*. Paris: Simon Douget, 1595.
Diouloufet, Jean-Joseph-Marius. *Le Don Quichotte philosophe, ou Histoire de l'avocat Hablard*. Lyon: Pélagaud et Lesne, 1840.
———. *Epître en vers provençaux*. Aix: Mouret, 1825.
———. *Fablos, contes, epitros et autros pouesios prouvençalos*. Aix-en-Provence: H. Gaudibert, 1829.
———. *Leis Magnans* ("The Silkworms"). Aix-en-Provence: Pontier, 1819.
Dogbé, Yves-Emmanuel. *Affres*. Porto-Novo, Dahomey: Rapidex, 1966.
———. *Contes et légendes du Togo*. Lomé, Togo; and Le Mée-sur-Seine: Editions Akpagnon, 1981.
———. *La Crise de l'éducation*. Lomé, Togo; and Le Mée-sur-Seine: Editions Akpagnon, 1975. Revised ed. 1979.
———. *Le Divin amour*. Paris: P.-J. Oswald, 1976. Reprint. Lomé, Togo; and Le Mée-sur-Seine: Editions Akpagnon, 1979.
———. *Fables africaines*. Paris: L'Harmattan, 1978. Revised edition. Editions Akpagnon, 1982.
———. *Flamme blême*. Paris: Editions de la Revue Moderne, 1969. Revised ed. Lomé. Togo; and Le Mée-sur-Seine: Editions Akpagnon, 1982.
———. *L'Incarcéré*. Lomé, Togo; and Le Mée-sur-Seine: Editions Akpagnon, 1980.
———. *Lettre ouverte aux pauvres d'Afrique*. Lomé, Togo; and Le Mée-sur-Seine: Editions Akpagnon, 1981. Revised ed. 1983.
———. *Morne soliloque*. Lomé, Togo; and Le Mée-sur-Seine: Editions Akpagnon, 1982.
———. *Négritude, culture et civilisation: essai sur la finalité des faits sociaux*. Lomé, Togo; and Le Mée-sur-Seine: Editions Akpagnon, 1980.
———. *Réflexions sur la promotion du livre africain*. Lomé, Togo; and Le Mée-sur-Seine: Editions Akpagnon, 1984.
———. *La Victime*. Lomé, Togo; and Le Mée-sur-Seine: Editions Akpagnon, 1979.

————, ed. *Anthologie de la poésie togolaise*. Lomé, Togo; and Le Mée-sur-Seine: Editions Akpagnon, 1980.

Dorat, Claude-Joseph. *Le Célibataire*. Comedy: 5 acts, verse. Paris: Delalain, 1776.

————. *La Déclamation théâtrale* [expanded version of *Essai sur la déclamation tragique* (1758)]. Paris: Delalain, 1771.

————. *Fables nouvelles*. The Hague and Paris: Delalain, 1773–75.

————. *Fables ou allégories philosophiques*. The Hague and Paris: Delalain, 1772.

————. *La Feinte par amour*. Comedy: 3 acts, verse. Paris: Delalain, 1773.

————. *The Kisses*. A translation of *Les Baisers*, by H. G. Keene. London: Vizetelly, 1889.

Dutramblay, Antoine-Pierre. *Apologues*. 4th revised ed. Paris: A. Eymery, 1818.

————. *Apologues*. 5th ed. Paris: C.-J. Trouvé, 1822.

[Dutramblay, Antoine-Pierre]. *Apologues*. 2d ed. Paris: H. Perronneau, 1806.

Florian, Jean-Pierre Claris de. *Fables*. Paris: P. Didot l'aîné, 1792.

————. *Fables*. Paris: Mame, 1811.

————. *Fables de Florian*. Preface by Charles Nodier. Paris: Delloye, 1838.

————. *Fables de Florian, suivies des poèmes de Ruth et de Tobie, et autres poésies, de Galatée et d'Estelle; des idées sur nos auteurs comiques, des lettres et du théâtre; de Myrtil et Chloé, et d'un choix de fables de Lamotte*. Paris: Firmin Didot, 1846.

————. *La Jeunesse de Florian, ou Mémoires d'un jeune Espagnol*. Paris: H. Nicole, 1807.

————. *Lettres au marquis A. de Florian, 1779–1793*. Edited by Alfred Dupont. Paris: Gallimard, 1957.

————. *Mémoires d'un jeune Espagnol*. Preface by André Bouis. Paris: Bossard, 1923.

————. *Œuvres posthumes de Florian*. Edited by Louis-François Jauffret. 12 vols. Paris: Le Clerc, 1803.

————, trans. *Don Quichotte de la Manche*, by Miguel de Cervantes. 6 vols. In *Œuvres de Florian*. 13 vols. Paris: Guillaume (-Déterville), An VII [1799].

Franc-Nohain [Maurice-Etienne Legrand]. *Les Chansons des trains et des gares*. Paris: Editions de *la Revue Blanche*, 1899.

————. *Fables*. Illustrated by Madeleine Franc-Nohain. Paris: Renaissance du Livre, 1923.

————. *Fables* [books I–III]. Paris: Renaissance du Livre, 1921.

————. *Fables* [books I–IX]. Paris: Grasset, 1931.

————. *Fables nouvelles* [books IV–VI]. Paris: Renaissance du Livre, 1927.

————. *Fables nouvelles* [books X–XII]. Paris: Editions Spes, 1933.

————. "Les Fables de La Fontaine." *Revue hebdomadaire* 7, (July 23, 1921): 405–19.

————. *Flûtes*. Paris: Editions de *la Revue Blanche*, 1898.

————. *L'Heure espagnole*. Comedy: verse. Paris: Fasquelle, 1905.

————. *Les Inattentions et Sollicitudes*. Paris: Vanier, 1894.

————. *La Vie amoureuse de Jean de La Fontaine*. Paris: Flammarion, 1928.

Franc-Nohain and Fernand Vandérem. *La Victime*. Play: 3 acts. Paris: *L'Illustration*, 1914.

Furetière, Antoine. *Dictionnaire universel*. The Hague: A. & R. Leers, 1690.

————. *Fables morales et nouvelles*. Paris: Louis Billaine, 1671.

————. *Nouvelle allégorique, ou Histoire des derniers troubles arrivez au royaume d'éloquence*. Paris: F. Lamy, 1658.

————. *Poésies diverses*. Paris: De Luynes, 1655.

————. *Recueil des factums d'Antoine Furetière*. Edited with an introduction and notes by Charles Asselineau. Paris: Poulet-Malassis, 1858–59.

————. *Roman bourgeois*. Paris: Louis Billaine, 1666.

————. *Roman bourgeois*. Edited by Edouard Fournier and Charles Asselineau. Paris: P. Jannet, 1854.

————. *Le Voyage de Mercure*. Paris: Chamboudry, 1653.

Fuzelier, Louis. *Momus fabuliste, ou les Nôces de Vulcain*. Comedy: 1 act, verse. Paris: Veuve Ribou, Pierre Simon, 1719.

Gacon, François [Poète Sans Fard, pseud.]. *Les Fables de mr Houdart de La Motte traduittes en vers françois par le P. S. F.* Paris, 1723?

Gacon, François. *Homère vengé, ou Réponse à M. de La Motte sur l'Iliade*. Paris: Etienne Ganeau, 1715.

————. *Le Secrétaire du Parnasse, au sujet de la tragédie d'Inés de Castro*. Paris: François Fournier, 1723.

————, trans. *Les Odes d'Anacréon et de Sapho en vers françois*. Rotterdam: Fritsch et Böhm, 1712.

Genlis, comtesse (née Caroline-Stéphanie-Félicité Du Crest). *Herbier moral, ou Recueil de fables nouvelles, et autres poésies fugitives*. Paris: Maradan, An VIII [1801].

Ginguené, Pierre-Louis. *Coup d'œil rapide sur "Le Génie du christianisme."* Paris: Imprimerie de la Décade philosophique, littéraire et politique, An X [1802].

————. *Fables inédites*. Paris: L.-G. Michaud, 1814.

————. *Fables nouvelles*. Paris: Michaud frères, 1810.

————. *Histoire littéraire d'Italie*. 9 vols. Paris: Michaud, 1824.

————. *Lettres sur "Les Confessions" de Jean-Jacques Rousseau*. Paris: Barois l'aîné, 1791.

Gomar [Jean-Charles Talmant]. *Fables et chantefables*. Paris: La Pensée Universelle, 1982.

————. "Fables nouvelles." Unpublished collection.

Grécourt, Jean-Baptiste-Joseph Willart de. *L'Œuvre badine de l'Abbé de Grécourt*. Edited by Guillaume Apollinaire. Paris: Bibliothèque des Curieux, 1912.

————. *Œuvres complettes de Grécourt*. 4 vols. Luxembourg [i.e., Paris (false imprint)], 1764.

Guéroult, Guillaume. *Le Premier livre des Emblèmes*. Lyon: Balthazar Andoullet, 1550. Reprint edited by DeVaux de Lancey (Société Rouennaise de Bibliophiles). Rouen: Lainé, 1937.

Guichard, Jean-François. *Contes et autres poésies, suivis de quelques mots de Piron*. Paris: Suret, An X [1802].

————. *Contes et fables, suivis de quelques mots de Piron*. 2 vols. Paris: Collin, 1808.

————. *Epigrammes faites dans un bon dessein*. N.p. 1809.

————. *Fables et autres poésies, suivies de quelques morceaux de prose*. Paris: Suret, An X [1802].

Guichard, Jean-Francois, and Monsieur Castet. *Le Bûcheron, ou Les Trois souhaits*. Paris: Chez l'auteur, 1763?.

Guillevic, Eugène. *Fabliettes*. Illustrated by Laurie Jordan. Paris: Gallimard, 1982.

————. *Requiem*. Paris: Librairie Tschann, 1938.

————. *Selected Poems*. Translated by Denise Levertov. New York: New Directions, 1964.

————. *Terraque*. Paris: Gallimard, 1942.

————. *Trente et un sonnets*. Paris: Gallimard, 1954.

Haudent, Guillaume. *Trois cent soixante et six apologues d'Esope traduicts en rithme françoise*. Rouen: Robert et Jehan Dugord, 1547. Reprint (edited and with an introduction by Charles Lormier). Rouen: Henry Boissel, 1877.

Hégémon, Philibert [Philibert Guide]. *La Colombiere et Maison Rustique de Philibert Hegemon, de Chalon sur Saone: contenant une description des douze Mois, & quatre Saisons de l'annee: avec enseignement de ce que le Laboureur doibt faire par chacun mois. L'Abeille Françoise du mesme Autheur. Ses Fables Morales, & autres Poësies. Et ses Louanges de la vie Rustique, extraites des Œuvres de G. de Saluste, Sieur du Bartas*. Paris: Robert Le Fizelier, 1583.

————. *Fables morales*. Edited with an introduction and notes by Laura Rovero. Paris and Geneva: Champion-Slatkine, 1987.

———. *Fables morales.* In Arthur F. Whittem, "Two Fable Collections." *Harvard Studies and Notes in Philology and Literature* 14 (1932): 151–79.

Héré, J. *Fables.* Saint-Quentin: Tilloy, 1830.

———. *Fables et poésies.* Saint-Quentin: Moureau, 1860.

———. *Leçons de rhétorique et de littérature française.* Saint-Quentin, 1852.

Houdar de La Motte, Antoine. *See* La Motte.

[Un ingénieur en chef honoraire des mines]. *Fables d'Amérique.* Paris: Imprimerie Lahure, 1895.

Jauffret, Louis-François. *Dictionnaire étymologique de la langue française, à l'usage de la jeunesse.* 2 vols. Paris: Dugour et Durand, An VII [1799].

———. "Dissertations sur Phèdre le fabuliste et sur le poète Saadi, auteur de 'Gulistan, ou le Jardin des Roses.'" In manuscript.

———. "Dissertations sur quelques fabulistes modernes." In manuscript.

———. *Fables nouvelles.* 2 vols. Paris: Maradan, 1814. 2d, enlarged ed. 2 vols. Paris: Béchet, 1826.

———. *La Gymnastique de la jeunesse.* 3 vols. Paris: Eymery, 1816.

———. *Lettres sur les fabulistes anciens et modernes.* Paris: Pichon-Béchet, 1827.

———. "Notices biographiques et bibliographiques sur les fabulistes Fumars, de Marseille, Vitalis, d'Aix, et Guichard." In manuscript.

———. *La petite école des arts et métiers.* 4 vols. Paris: Eymery, 1816.

———. *Petit théâtre des familles: drames à l'usage de la jeunesse.* 3 vols. Paris: Gide, An VII [1799].

———. *Quelques fables inédites, lues aux séances publiques de l'Académie Royale des Sciences, Belles-Lettres et Arts de Marseille.* Marseille: Achard, 1838.

———. *Trois fables sur la girafe.* Paris: Pichon-Béchet, 1827.

———. *Les Veillées de pensionnat, contenant des dialogues destinés à être représentés dans les maisons d'éducation et des comédies propres à instruire et à amuser la jeunesse.* Paris: Veuve Nyon, 1808.

———. *Voyage au Jardin des Plantes, contenant la description des galeries d'histoire naturelle, etc.* Paris: Houel, 1798.

Joliveau [de Segrais]. Madame (née Marie-Madeleine-Nicole-Alexandrine Gehier). *Fables nouvelles en vers, suivies de quelques poèmes.* Paris: Cordier et Legras, 1801. 2d ed. Paris: L. Collin, 1807. 3d, revised ed. Paris: Janet et Cotelle, 1814.

———. *Repentir.* Paris: Michaud, 1811.

Kaddour-Mermet. *Fables et contes en sabir.* 2d ed. Algiers: A. Jourdan, 1916. 3d ed. Algiers: Jules Carbonel, n.d.

La Fontaine, Jean de. *Fables.* Claude Barbin, 1668–93.

———. *Fifty Fables of La Fontaine.* Edited and translated by Norman R. Shapiro. Urbana: University of Illinois Press, 1988.

———. *Œuvres de J. de la Fontaine.* Edited by Henri Regnier. 11 vols. Revised ed. Paris: Hachette, 1883–92.

La Motte, Antoine Houdar de. "Discours sur la fable." Summarized by an anonymous author in *Journal literaire* (24 vols.) 11 (1720): 41–61. The Hague: T. Johnson, 1713–37.

———. *Fables nouvelles.* Paris: Grégoire Dupuis, 1719.

———. *L'Iliade, poème, avec un discours sur Homère.* Paris: Grégoire Dupuis, 1714.

———. *Œuvres de Monsieur Houdar de La Motte.* 9 vols. in 10. Paris: Prault, 1754.

LeMay, Pamphile. *Contes vrais.* Québec: Imprimerie "Le Soleil," 1899.

———. *Essais poétiques.* Québec: Desbarats, 1865.

———. *Fables canadiennes.* Québec: Darveau, 1881; 2d printing, 1882. 2d ed. Québec: Darveau, 1891. Granger, 1903. 3d ed.

Montréal: Librairie Granger, 1903. 4th ed. Montréal: Granger frères, 1925.

———. *Les Gouttelettes.* Montréal: Beauchemin, 1904.

———, trans. *Evangeline,* by Henry Wadsworth Longfellow. Québec: Delisle, 1870. Reprinted in *Evangéline et autres poèmes de Longfellow.* Montréal: J.-Alfred Guay, 1912.

Le Noble, Eustache. *Contes et Fables.* Lyon: Léonard Plaignard, 1697.

———. *Contes et fables tirez des entretiens politiques de M' Le Noble.* Paris: J. Moreau, 1710.

———. *L'Ecole des sages.* Paris: Martin Jouvenel et al., 1692.

———. *L'Ecole du monde, ou Instruction d'un père à un fils touchant la manière dont il faut vivre dans le monde.* Paris: Jouvenel, 1702. Reprint. Amsterdam, 1709.

———. *Esope.* Comedy: 5 acts. Paris: Guillaume de Luynes et al., 1691.

———. *L'Esprit d'Esope.* Paris: Claude Mazuel, 1694.

———. *La Grotte des fables.* 2 vols. Paris: Jouvenel, 1696.

———. *Œuvres de M. Le Noble.* 19 vols. [Primarily] Paris: P. Ribou, 1718 (several of the volumes following volume 1 bear earlier dates and diverse places of publication and names of publishers).

———. *La Pierre de touche politique.* Various publishers, 1690–91.

———. *Talestris, Reine des Amazones.* Tragedy: 5 acts. Paris: Veuve Châtelain, 1717?.

Maltrait, A. "Louis XIV et son siècle." *Comptes-rendus de l'Athénée Louisianais,* May 1, 1898: 278–90.

———. "Le Melon." *Comptes-rendus de l'Athénée Louisianais,* Jan. 1, 1899: 403.

Marie de France. *Das Buch vom Espurgatoire S. Patriz des Marie de France und seine Quelle.* Biblioteca Normannica, no. 9. Edited by Karl Warnke. Halle: Niemeyer, 1938.

———. *L'Espurgatoire Seint Patriz.* Edited by Thomas Atkinson Jenkins. Philadelphia: A. J. Ferris, 1894. Reprint. Chicago: University of Chicago Press, 1903.

———. *Die Fabeln der Marie de France.* Biblioteca Normannica, no. 6. Edited by Karl Warnke. Halle: Niemeyer, 1898.

———. *The Fables of Marie de France.* Edited and translated by Mary Lou Martin. Birmingham, Ala.: Summa Publications, 1984.

———. *Les Lais de Marie de France.* Edited by Jeanne Lods. Paris: Champion, 1959.

———. *Les Lais de Marie de France.* Edited by Jean Rychner. Paris: Champion, 1966.

———. *Die Lais der Marie de France.* Biblioteca Normannica, no. 3. Edited by Karl Warnke. 3d ed. Halle: Niemeyer, 1924.

———. *Marie de France: Fables.* Edited by Alfred Ewert and Ronald C. Johnson. Oxford: Blackwell, 1942.

———. *Marie de France: Fables.* Edited and translated by Harriet Spiegel. Toronto: University of Toronto Press, 1987.

———. *Marie de France: Lais.* Edited by Alfred Ewert. Oxford: Blackwell, 1944.

Martin, Emile. *Les Fables de La Fontaine en patois lorrain: une fantaisie pastiche en patois de Morey.* [Nancy?: privately printed? 1976?].

Mercier, Philippe. *Fables modernes et poésies diverses.* Paris: A. Jeande, 1912. Also Paris and London: Nilsson, n.d.

Mirault, Louis. *Au pas de nos bœufs: patoiseries nivernaises, poésies, et contes.* Preface by Claude Aveline. La Charité-sur-Loire: A. Delayance, 1935.

———. *Brindilles: recueil de fables et contes en vers.* Tours: A. Mame, 1923.

———. *Le Calvaire.* Play: 1 act, verse. Tours: Péricat, 1896.

———. *Fleurs de Touraine.* Preface by Edmond Porcher. Tours: Deslys frères, 1897.

———. *Jeanne d'Arc*. Paris: L. Vanier, 1900.

———. *Molène aux champs*. [La Charité-sur-Loire?]: A. Delayance, 1924.

———. *Roses d'automne: recueil de fables, chansons et élégies*. Loches: Daigremont, 1928.

———. *La Terre qui chante*. Paris: A Messein, 1910.

Mirault, Louis [Fanchy, pseud.], and Pierre Chambon. *Théâtre nivernais*. Preface by Simonne Ratel. La Charité-sur-Loire: A. Delayance, 1939.

"M. de L***" [Delaunay?]. *Poésies diverses de société*. London: La Compagnie, 1767.

Nau, François. *Les Fables de La Fontaine mises en chansons, vaudevilles et pots-pourris*. Paris: Veuve Duchesne, n.d.

Palvadeau, Paul. "Le Chêne et sa mousse" and "Les Deux tableaux." *Comptes-rendus de l'Athénée Louisianais*, May 1, 1885: 164–65.

Panard, Charles-François. *Œuvres choisies de Panard*. Edited with a introduction by Armand Gouffé. 3 vols. Paris: Capelle, An XI [1803].

———. *Théâtre et œuvres diverses de M. Pannard* [*sic*]. Edited by Jean-François Marmontel. 4 vols. Paris: Duchesne, 1763.

Péras, Jacques. *Fables nouvelles*. Paris: Delaguette, 1751.

Péras, Jacques, and François Nau. *Les Dieux protecteurs de la France*. Paris: F.-G. Mérigot, 1744.

Perrault, Charles. *Histoires et contes du temps passé*. Paris: Claude Barbin, 1697.

———. *Histories, or Fables of Past Times*. An anonymous translation of *Histoires et contes du temps passé*. London: J. Potevin, 1729.

———. *Les Hommes illustres qui ont paru en France pendant ce siècle*. Paris: Antoine Dezellier, 1696–1700.

———. *Le Labyrinte de Versailles*. See Benserade.

———. *Parallèle des anciens et des modernes*. Paris: Jean-Baptiste Coignard, 1688–97.

———. *Recueil de divers ouvrages en prose et en vers, dédié à Son Altesse Monseigneur le Prince de Conti*. Paris: Jean-Baptiste Coignard, 1675.

———. *Traduction des fables de Faërne*. Paris: Jean-Baptiste Coignard, 1699.

Pesselier, Charles-Etienne. *L'Ecole du tems*. Comedy: 1 act, verse. Paris: 1738. 2d ed. The Hague: Benjamin Gibert, 1739.

———. *Esope au Parnasse*. Comedy: 1 act, verse. Paris: Prault père, 1739.

———. *Fables nouvelles*. Paris: Prault père, 1748.

———. *La Mascarade du Parnasse*. Comedy: 1 act, verse. Paris: Prault père, 1737.

———, ed. *Le Glaneur françois*. 4 vols. N.p., 1734–37.

Piron, Alexis. *Œuvres*. 3 vols. Paris: Duchesne, 1758. Reprint. Amsterdam: Merkus et Arckstée, 1763.

———. *Œuvres complettes*. Edited by Rigoley de Juvigny. Paris: M. Lambert; Théophile Barrois, 1776. Reprint, 9 vols. Paris: Le Normant, An VIII [1800].

———. *Poésies choisies et pièces inédites de Alexis Piron*. Edited with an introduction by Honoré Bonhomme. Paris: Quantin, 1879.

Poète Sans Fard. *See* Gacon, François.

Porchat, Jean-Jacques. *Le Berger et le proscrit*. Paris: Meyrueis, 1857.

———. *Les Colons du rivage*. Paris: Dezobry et Magdeleine, 1849.

———. *Contes merveilleux*. Paris: Hachette, 1858.

———. *Fables et paraboles*. Paris: Meyrueis, 1854.

———. *Glanures d'Esope*. Paris: Belin-Mandar; Lausanne: Rouiller, 1840.

———. *La Mission de Jeanne d'Arc*. Play: 5 acts, verse. Paris: Dubochet, 1844.

———. [J.-J. Valamont, pseud.]. *Recueil de fables*. Paris: Fortic, 1826.

———. *La Sagesse du hameau*. Paris: Dezobry et Magdeleine, 1849.

———. *Trois mois sous la neige, journal d'un jeune habitant du Jura*. Paris: Dezobry et Magdeleine, 1848.

———, ed. *Le Fablier des écoles, ou Choix de fables des fabulistes français*. 2 vols. Paris, 1848–49. Reprint. Paris: Delagrave, 1881.

Prévert, Jacques. *Contes pour enfants pas sages*. Paris: Editions du Pré aux Clercs, 1947.

———. *Histoires: 30 poèmes de Jacques Prévert, 30 poèmes d'André Verdet, 31 dessins de Mayo*. Paris: Editions du Pré aux Clercs, 1946.

———. *Histoires et d'autres histoires*. Paris: Le Point du Jour, 1963.

———. *Paroles*. Paris: Le Point du Jour, 1946.

———. *La Pluie et le beau temps*. Paris: Le Point du Jour, 1955.

———. *Soleil de nuit*. Paris: Gallimard, 1980.

Roger, Jacques-François. *Fables sénégalaises, recueillies de l'ouolof et mises en vers français*. Paris: Nepveu, 1828.

———. *Kelédor, histoire africaine*. Paris: Nepveu, 1828.

———. *Recherches philosophiques sur la langue ouolofe*. Paris: Dondey-Dupré, 1829.

Roger, Jacques-François, and François-Xavier-Paul Garnier, eds. *Annales universelles de la législation et de la jurisprudence commerciales*. 7 vols. Paris: Renard, 1824–30.

Saint Gilles, le Chevalier de. *Je vous prends sans verd*. Comedy. Paris: Pierre Ribon, 1699.

———. *La Muse mousquetaire*. Paris: probably privately printed, 1709.

Saint-Glas, Pierre de. *Les Bouts-rimez*. Paris: Pierre Trabouillet, 1682.

———. *Contes nouveaux en vers*. Paris: Claude Barbin, 1670.

———. *Œuvres de Monsieur ***, contenant plusieurs fables d'Esope mises en vers*. Paris: Augustine Besoigne, 1672. Reprint. Paris: Pierre Trabouillet, 1677.

———. *Particularités remarquables des sauterelles qui sont venues de Russie*. Paris, 1690

Ségur, Anatole-Henri de. *Les Congrégations religieuses et le peuple*. Paris: Tolra et Haton, 1862.

———. *Fables*. Paris: Michel Lévy frères, 1847.

———. *Fables*. Paris: Hetzel, 1864.

———. *Fables complètes*. Paris: Bray et Retaux, 1878.

———. *Fables et poésies diverses*. Paris: Société de Sainte-Victoire, 1853.

———. *Grandes questions du jour, de la veille et du lendemain*. Paris: Tolra, 1877.

———. *Histoire de Saint-François de Sales*. Paris: Tolra, 1872.

———. *Un Hiver à Rome*. Paris: Bray et Retaux, 1876. Revised ed.: *La Rome de Pie IX*. Paris: J. Lefort, 1895.

———. *Monseigneur de Ségur: souvenirs et récits d'un frère*. 2 vols. Paris: Bray et Retaux, 1882.

———. *Nouvelles fables et contes*. Paris: J. Lecoffre, 1863.

———. *Premières fables*. Paris: Tolra, 1870.

———. *Témoignages et souvenirs*. Paris: Lecou, 1857. Reprint. Paris: Bray, 1862.

———. *Vie du comte Rostopchine*. Paris: Bray et Retaux, 1871. Reprint. Paris: Retaux, 1893.

Stevens, Paul. *Contes populaires*. Ottawa: Desbarats, 1867. Reprints. Montréal: Beauchemin, 1912, 1924.

———. *Fables*. Montréal: Lovell, 1857.

Sylvain, Georges. *Confidences et mélancolies*. Paris: Ateliers Haïtiens, 1901.

———. *Cric? Crac!: Fables de La Fontaine racontées par un montagnard haïtien et transcrites en vers créoles*. Paris: Ateliers Haïtiens, 1901. 2d ed. Paris: Imprimerie Dussand; Port-au-Prince: private printing, 1929.

———. *Dix années de lutte pour la liberté, 1915–1925.* 2 vols. Port-au-Prince: Editions H. Deschamps, 1959.

Sylvain, Georges, et al., eds. *Auteurs haïtiens: morceaux choisis.* Port-au-Prince: Imprimerie de Mme F. Smith, 1904.

Tandon, Auguste. *Fables et contes en vers patois.* Montpellier: Renaud, An VIII [1800]. Enlarged ed. Montpellier: Renaud, 1813.

Tardy, Marc-Louis de. *Fables et tragédies.* Paris: Sagnier et Bray, 1847.

———. [M. L.-M. de T+++, pseud.]. *Tragédies, fables et pièces de vers.* Roanne: E. Périsse, 1839.

Thierry-Faletans, Hippolyte de. *Fables et contes.* Genoa: Typographie de l'Institut Royal des Sourds-Muets, 1871.

———. *Le Nord et le Sud de l'Italie.* Paris: C. Douniol, 1864.

———. *Théâtre de société.* Paris: Librairie Internationale, 1866.

Vaudin. *Fables diverses, en quatre vers.* Paris: Laurent d'Houry, 1707.

Viennet, Jean-Pons-Guillaume. *Clovis.* Tragedy: 5 acts, verse. Paris: Ladvocat, 1820.

———. *Epître aux Muses sur le Romantisme.* Paris: Ladvocat, 1824.

———. *Fables.* Paris: Poulain, 1843.

———. *Fables et fables nouvelles.* Combined and augmented edition. Paris: Hachette, 1855.

———. *Fables nouvelles.* Paris: Amyot, 1851.

———. *La Franciade.* Paris: Plon, 1863.

———. *Journal de Viennet, pair de France, témoin de trois règnes, 1817–1848.* Amiot-Dumont, 1955.

Villedieu, Madame de (née Marie-Catherine Desjardins). *Fables, ou Histoires allégoriques.* Paris: Claude Barbin, 1670.

Young, Rodolphine. *Fables de La Fontaine traduites en créole seychellois.* Edited by Annegret Bollée and Guy Lionnet. Kreolische Bibliothek, 4. Hamburg: Helmut Buske, 1983.

STUDIES—BIOGRAPHICAL, BIBLIOGRAPHICAL, HISTORICAL, CRITICAL, ETC.—OF THE FABULISTS, AND RELATED TITLES

Archer, Marguerite. *Jean Anouilh.* New York: Columbia University Press, 1971.

Ashby-Beach, Genette. "Les *Fables* de Marie de France: essai de grammaire narrative." In *Epopée animale, fable, fabliau* (Actes du IVe Colloque de la Société Internationale Renardienne, Publications de l'Université de Rouen), edited by Gabriel Bianciotto and Michel Salvat, no. 83: 13–27. Paris: Presses Universitaires de France, 1984.

Augé-Chiquet, Mathieu. *La Vie, les idées et l'œuvre de Jean-Antoine de Baïf.* Paris: Hachette, 1909.

Baker, William. *Jacques Prévert.* New York: Twayne, 1967.

Barbier, J.-C. "Un Exilé de l'Académie." *Revue de la Société des Etudes Historiques,* 1888: 199–216.

Barchilon, Jacques, and Peter Flinders. *Charles Perrault.* Boston: Twayne, 1981.

Bataille, Georges. "De l'âge de pierre à Jacques Prévert." *Critique* 3–4 (Aug.-Sept. 1946): 195–214.

Batany, Jean. "Détermination et typologie: l'article et les animaux de la fable (de Marie de France à La Fontaine)." In *Au bonheur des mots: Mélanges en l'honneur de Gérard Antoine,* 41–49. Nancy: Presses Universitaires de Nancy, 1984.

Baum, Paul Franklin. "The Fable of Belling the Cat." In Pack Carnes, ed. *Proverbia in Fabula: Essays on the Relationship of the Proverb and the Fable,* 37–46. (*Sprichwörterforschung,* Band 10.) Bern: Lang, 1988.

Baum, Richard. *Recherches sur les œuvres attribuées à Marie de France.* Heidelberg: C. Winter, 1968.

Beaulieu, Camille. *Vie et travaux de Burgaud des Marets.* La Rochelle: Rupella, 1928.

Bellamy, Daniel. *Ethic Amusements.* London: W. Faden, 1768.

Bergens, Andrée. *Jacques Prévert.* Paris: Editions Universitaires, 1969.

Biard, Jean-Dominique. *The Style of La Fontaine's "Fables."* Oxford: Blackwell, 1966.

Bibliothèque patoise de M. Burgaud des Marets: livres rares et précieux. Paris: Maisonneuve, 1873.

Bosquet, Alain. "Guillevic ou la conscience de l'objet." *Nouvelle revue française* 11 (Nov. 1963): 876–82.

Bouchereaux, S.-M. "Recherches bibliographiques sur Gilles Corrozet." *Bulletin du bibliophile et du bibliothécaire* (1948): 134–51, 204–20, 291–301, 324–36, 393–411, 470–78, 532–38, 584–96, (1949): 35–47, 93–107, 147–54, 196–202.

Burgess, Glyn S. *Marie de France: An Analytical Bibliography.* London: Grant and Cutler, 1977.

Chapponière, Paul. *Piron, sa vie et son œuvre.* Geneva: A. Jullien, 1910.

Chatenet, Henri-E. *Le Roman et les romans d'une femme de lettres au XVIIe siècle: Mme de Villedieu (1632–1683).* Paris: Champion, 1911.

Chaudenson, Robert, and Guy Hazaël-Massieux. "Marbot, Sylvain, Young et les autres." *Etudes créoles* 10 (1987), no. 1: 35–54.

Claretie, Léo. *Florian.* Collection des Classiques Populaires. Paris: Lecène et Oudin, 1888.

Comandon, Odette. "Burgaud des Marets," in "Jarnac et ses poètes." *La Tour de feu,* cahier 117 (Mar. 1983):65–76.

Corne, Chris. "Remarques sur la langue des *Fables* de Rodolphine Young." *Etudes créoles* 10 (1987), no. 1:55–61.

Couton, Georges. *La Poétique de La Fontaine.* Paris: Presses Universitaires de France, 1957.

Cuénin, Micheline. *Madame de Villedieu (Marie-Catherine Desjardins, 1640–1683).* 2 vols. Paris: Champion, 1979.

Danner, Richard. *Patterns of Irony in the "Fables" of La Fontaine.* Athens: Ohio University Press, 1985.

Daudville, Charles. Obituary of J. Héré. In *Mémoires de la Société Académique des Sciences, Arts, Belles-lettres, Agriculture et Industrie de Saint-Quentin* 6 (1864–65): 514–23.

Daunou, Pierre-Claude. "Notice sur la vie et les ouvrages de M. Ginguené." In *Histoire littéraire d'Italie,* by Pierre-Louis Ginguené. I:i–xxvii.

Delafarge, Daniel. "Remarques sur les fables de Desmay et celles de La Fontaine." In *Mélanges de philologie et d'histoire littéraire offerts à Edmond Huguet,* 241–51. Paris: Boivin, 1940.

Della Fazia, Alba. *Jean Anouilh.* New York: Twayne, 1969.

Des Granges, René. *La Querelle de Molière et de Boursault.* Paris: A. Charles, 1899.

Desnoiresterres, Gustave. *Le Chevalier Dorat et les poètes légers au XVIIIe siècle.* Paris: Perrin, 1887.

Didier, Jean. *A la rencontre de Jean Anouilh.* Liège: La Sixaine, 1946.

Estrée, Paul d'. "Molière et les Jocondes." *Le Moliériste,* no. 62 (May 1884): 40–50.

Etiemble. "Guillevic est-il un haïjin?" In *Lire Guillevic,* edited by Serge Gaubert, 143–61. Lyon: Presses Universitaires de Lyon, 1983.

Ferrante, Joan M. "The French Courtly Poet Marie de France." In *Medieval Women Writers,* edited by Katharina M. Wilson, 64–89. Manchester: Manchester University Press, 1984.

Fontainas, André. "Revue de la quinzaine." *Mercure de France,* no. 565 (Jan. 1, 1922): 177.

Foreman, Jeanne. "Eustache Le Noble (1643–1711), témoin de son temps." Ph.D. diss., University of Colorado, 1970.

Fournel, Victor. "Un moraliste au théâtre." *Le Correspondant* 129 (1882): 966–81.

Fuzelier, Louis. *Discours à l'occasion d'un discours de M. D. L. M. sur les parodies.* Paris: Briasson, 1731.

————. Plot of his comedy *Momus fabuliste, ou les Nôces de Vulcain* summarized in *Journal literaire* (24 vols.) 11 (1720): 62–70. The Hague: T. Johnson, 1713–37.

Gaillon, Marquis de. "Un Fabuliste du XVIe siecle." *Bulletin du bibliophile et du bibliothécaire,* Apr. 1859: 238–45.

Gegou, Fabienne. *Antoine Furetière, abbé de Chalivoy ou La Chute d'un immortel.* Paris: Nizet, 1962.

Gignoux, Hubert. *Jean Anouilh.* Paris: Editions du Temps Présent, 1946.

Ginestier, Paul. *Jean Anouilh.* Paris: Seghers, 1969.

Gohin, Ferdinand. *Les Comédies attribuées à La Fontaine.* Paris: Garnier frères, 1935.

Gros, Léon-Gabriel. "Un exorciste: Guillevic." *Cahiers du Sud,* June 1943: 460–71.

Guillemin, Jules. *Philibert Guide, poète chalonnais (1535–1595).* Dijon, 1870.

Guillot, Gérard. *Les Prévert.* Paris: Seghers, 1967.

Guiton, Margaret. *La Fontaine, Poet and Counterpoet.* New Brunswick, N.J.: Rutgers University Press, 1961.

Hamel, Frank. *Jean de La Fontaine.* London: Stanley Paul, 1911. Reprint. Port Washington, N.Y.: Kennikat Press, 1970.

Hare, John Ellis. "A Bibliography of the Works of Léon Pamphile Lemay (1837–1918)." *Papers of the Bibliographical Society of America* 57 (1963): 50–60.

Harmand, Jean. *Madame de Genlis, sa vie intime et politique, 1746–1830.* Paris: Perrin, 1912.

Harvey, John. *Anouilh: A Study in Theatrics.* New Haven: Yale University Press, 1964.

Heger, Henrik. *Die Melancholie bei den französischen Lyrikern des Spätmittelalters.* Bonn: Romanisches Seminar der Universität, 1967

Herlet, Bruno. "Studien über die sogenannte Lyoner Ysopet, Ysopet I und Ysopet II." *Romanische Forschungen* 4 (1891): 219–309.

Hoepffner, Ernest. *Eustache Deschamps, Leben und Werke.* Strasbourg: Trübner, 1904.

Hudde, Hinrich. "Florians Fabeln: Regression angesichts der Revolution." *Zeitschrift für französische Sprache und Literatur,* Band 87, Heft 1 (1977): 99–141.

————. "Jacques Préverts Fabelparodie 'Le Chat et l'Oiseau': Über den besondern Nutzen der Fabel in den Schulen." *Literatur in Wissenschaft und Unterricht* 9 (1976) no. 4: 244–56.

Jacob, P.-L. [Paul Lacroix]. "L'Abbé de Saint-Ussans et ses ouvrages." In *Enigmes et découvertes bibliographiques,* 38–45. Paris: Ad. Laine et al., 1866.

Jambeck, Karen K. "The *Fables* of Marie de France: Base Text and Critical Text." *Text: Transactions of the Society for Textual Scholarship* 2 (1985): 83–91.

Jardel, Jean-Pierre. "Des quelques emprunts et analogies dans les fables créoles inspirées de La Fontaine: contribution à l'étude des parlers créoles du XIXe siecle." *Etudes créoles* 8 (1985), nos. 1 and 2: 213–25.

Jehasse, Jean. "De la fable aux *Fables:* Benserade et La Fontaine." In *Mélanges offerts à Georges Couton,* 323–44. Lyon: Presses Universitaires de Lyon, 1981.

Jolivet, Philippe. *Le Théâtre de Jean Anouilh.* Paris: Brient, 1963.

Junge, Ernst. *Charles François Panard.* Leipzig: Seele, 1911.

Kelly, Kathleen White. *Jean Anouilh: An Annotated Bibliography.* Metuchen, N.J.: Scarecrow Press, 1973.

Kohn, Renée. *Le Goût de La Fontaine.* Grenoble: Allier, 1962.

Laborde, Alice M. *L'Œuvre de Madame de Genlis.* Paris, Nizet, 1966.

Lachèvre, Frédéric. "Bibliographie des ouvrages de Gacon." *Bulletin du bibliophile et du bibliothécaire,* Mar. 1927: 131–40; Apr. 1927: 182–89.

Lacroix de Vimeur, René, comte de Rochambeau. *Bibliographie des œuvres de J. de La Fontaine.* Paris: Alexis Rouquette, 1911.

Lafouge, Jean-Pierre. "Madame de Villedieu dans ses fables." In Milorad Margitic and Byron R. Wells, eds., *L'Image du souverain dans le théâtre de 1600 à 1650, ... Papers in French Seventeenth Century Literature* (1987): 501–10.

La Harpe, Jean-François de. [Presentation of a sampling of Boisard's first collection of fables]. *Mercure de France,* Apr. 1773, no. 2: 117–31.

————. [Commentary on Boisard's second collection of fables]. *Mercure de France,* July 1777, no. 1: 79.

Lanski, Alan. *Jean Anouilh: Stages in Rebellion.* Atlantic Highlands, N.J.: Humanities Press, 1975.

Lassalle, Jean-Pierre. *Jean Anouilh, ou La vaine révolte.* Rodez: Editions Subervie, 1958.

Luppé, Robert de. *Jean Anouilh.* Paris: Editions Universitaires, 1959.

Lyoner Yzopet. Altfranzösische Übersetzung des XIII. Jahrhunderts. Edited by Wendelin Foerster. Altfranzösische Bibliothek, 5. Heilbronn: Henninger, 1882.

Marmier, J. "La Fontaine et son ami Furetière." *Revue d'histoire littéraire de la France,* Oct.-Dec. 1958, no. 4: 449–66.

Maugras, Gaston. *Dernières années de la cour de Lunéville: Mme de Boufflers, ses enfants et ses amis.* Originally published as *Dernières années du roi Stanislas.* Paris: Plon-Nourrit, 1906.

————. *La Marquise de Boufflers et son fils le chevalier de Boufflers.* Paris: Plon-Nourrit, 1907.

Ménard, Auguste-Louis. *La Fontaine et Mme de Villedieu, les Fables galantes présentées à Louis XIV le jour de sa fête, essai de restitution à La Fontaine.* Paris: Chavaray frères, 1882.

Mercure de France, no. 83 (Feb. 1762): 62–71; no. 105 (Aug. 1773): 73–87. [Anonymous reviews of Aubert's *Fables et œuvres diverses*].

Mickel, Emanuel J., Jr. *Marie de France.* New York: Twayne, 1974.

Millet-Saint-Pierre, J.-B. "Guillaume Haudent, poète normand du XVIe siècle." *Recueil des publications de la Société Havraise d'Etudes Diverses* (1864–65): 193–214.

Morrissette, Bruce. *The Life and Works of Marie-Catherine Desjardins (Mme de Villedieu), 1632–1683.* Saint Louis: Washington University, 1947.

Mourgues, Odette de. *"Ô Muse, fuyante proie..." Essai sur la poésie de La Fontaine.* Paris: José Corti, 1962. 2d ed., 1987.

Nivelle de la Chaussée, Pierre-Claude [attrib.]. *Lettres de Mme la marquise de *** sur les Fables nouvelles.* Paris: Pepie et Moreau, 1719.

O'Neill, E. Wesley, "A Trend in Fable Literature after La Fontaine: The Fable Play." *French Review* 24, (Apr. 1954), no. 5: 354–59.

Orieux, Jean. *La Fontaine ou La Vie est un conte.* Paris: Flammarion, 1976.

Parmee, Douglas. "'Cric? Crac!': Fables of La Fontaine in Haitian Creole: A Literary Ethno-Socio-Linguistic Curiosity." *Nottingham French Studies* 15 (1976), no. 1: 12–26.

Pauly, Alphonse. "Boileau et Boursault." *Le Livre* 5 (1884) no. 58: 305–11.

Poirion, Daniel. *Le Poète et le prince: évolution du lyrisme courtois de Guillaume de Machaut à Charles d'Orléans.* Paris: Presses Universitaires de France, 1965. Reprint. Geneva, Slatkine, 1978.

Porché, François. "Franc-Nohain poète, ou l'Esprit des choses." *Revue de Paris,* Mar.-Apr. 1932, no. 2: 34–49.

Porquet, Charles. "Le Fabuliste Boisard." In *Le Pays basnormand,* 11–17. Flers, 1913.

Pronko, Leonard C. *The World of Jean Anouilh.* Berkeley: University of California Press, 1961.

Queval, Jean. *Jacques Prévert*. Paris: Mercure de France, 1955.

Rachline, Michel. *Jacques Prévert, drôle de vie*. Paris: Ramsay, 1981.

Raitière, Anna. *L'Art de l'acteur selon Dorat et Samson*. Geneva: Droz, 1969.

Rat, Maurice. "Perrault." *Vie et langage,* no. 60 (Mar. 1957): 115–19.

Ravennes, Jean. "Les petits écrits du chevalier de Boufflers." *Revue hebdomadaire* 7, no. 30 (July 23, 1921): 467–76.

Reboul, Robert[-Marie]. *Louis-François Jauffret: sa vie et ses œuvres*. Paris: Baur et Détaille; Marseille: Lebon; Aix: Makaire, 1869.

Rochambeau, comte de. *See* Lacroix de Vimeur.

Rovero, Laura. "Plutarco, fonte delle *Fables morales* di Philibert Guide, favolista del Cinquecento." *Studi Francesi* 70 (1980): 73–81.

Roy-Chevrier, J. "Philibert Guide, poète châlonnais." *Mémoires de la Société Châlon-sur-Marne* 12 (1924): 105–66.

Saillard, Gustave. *Florian, sa vie, son œuvre*. Toulouse: Privat, 1912.

Sarradin, Amédée. *Etudes sur Eustache Deschamps*. Versailles: Cerf, 1878.

Savory, Teo. "An Introduction to Guillevic." *Books Abroad,* Winter 1971: 43–45.

Scharpe, L. "Van De Dene tot Vondel." *Leuvensche Bijdragen* 4 (1900): 5–63.

Scollen-Jimack, Christine M. "Marot and Deschamps: The Rhetoric of Misfortune." *French Studies* 42 (1988), no. 1: 21–32.

Séché, Alphonse, and Jules Bertaut. "Une Aventurière de lettres au XVIIe siècle: Madame de Villedieu." *Mercure de France* 65 (1907): 615–32.

Silin, Charles I. *Benserade and His 'Ballets de Cour'*. Baltimore: The Johns Hopkins Press, 1940.

Soriano, Marc. *Les Contes de Perrault, culture savante et traditions populaires*. Paris: Gallimard, 1968

Soudée, Madeleine. "Le Dédicataire des *Ysopets* de Marie de France." *Les Lettres Romanes* 35, (1981), no. 3: 183–98.

Stramignoni, Adriana. "Les Fables de Gilles Corrozet." In *Epopée animale, fable, fabliau* (Actes du IVe Colloque de la Société Internationale Renardienne, Publications de l'Université de Rouen), edited by Gabriel Bianciotto and Michel Salvat, no. 83: 585–95. Paris: Presses Universitaires de France, 1984.

Suarez, Georges. "Franc-Nohain." *Revue de France,* no. 23 (Dec. 1, 1932): 420–31.

Sweetser, Marie-Odile. *La Fontaine*. Boston: Twayne, 1987.

Taschereau, Jules. "Poètes du clergé au siècle de Louis XV." *Revue de Paris* 9 (1829): 209–17.

Thiébaut, Marcel. "Parmi les livres." *Revue de Paris,* Apr. 1957: 137–48.

Thody, Philip. *Anouilh*. Edinburgh: Oliver and Boyd, 1968.

Tiemann, Barbara. *Fabel und Emblem. Gilles Corrozet und die französische Renaissance-Fabel*. Munich: Fink Verlag, 1974.

Vaget-Grangeat, Nicole. *Le Chevalier de Boufflers et son temps: étude d'un échec*. Paris: Nizet, 1976.

Vandromme, Pol. *Jean Anouilh: un auteur et ses personnages*. Paris: La Table Ronde, 1965.

Weber, Verana. *Form und Funktion von Sprachspielen, dargestellt anhand des poetischen Werkes von Jacques Prévert*. Frankfurt am Mein: R. G. Fischer, 1980.

Wey, Francis. "Antoine Furetière: sa vie, ses œuvres, ses démêlés avec l'Académie française." *Revue contemporaine,* 1852, no. 2: 594–618 and no. 3: 49–78.

Williams, Perry A. "La Fontaine in Haitian Creole: A Study of *Cric? Crac!* by Georges Sylvain." Ph.D. diss., Fordham University, 1971.

WORKS OF OTHER FABULISTS CITED

Bertola, Aurelio. *Cento favole*. Bassano, 1785. Expanded ed.: *Favole dell' abate Bertola*. Capolago, 1834.

Boisard, Jean-François. *Fables*. 2 vols. Paris: G. Mathiot, 1817.

———. *Fables*. Paris: Vigor Renaudière, 1821.

Capaccio, Giulio Cesare. *Gli apologi di Giulio Cesare Capaccio*. Naples: Giovanni Iacomo Carlino, 1602.

Chrestien, François. *Les Essais d'un bobre africain*. Mauritius, 1820. 2d ed. 1831.

Coupé de Saint-Donat, Alexandre-Auguste-Donat-Magloire, chevalier de. *Favole*. Translated by Camillo Ugoni. Brescia: N. Bettoni, 1808.

Couteau, Emile [the elder]. Selected verse. In *Bulletin de la Société des Sciences et Lettres de Loir-et-Cher,* July 1873: 27–35; and *Mémoires de la Société des Sciences et Lettres de Loir-et-Cher* 7 (1867): 223–35; 9 (1875), no. 1: 129–36.

Desmay, L.-S. *L'Esope du Temps, fables nouvelles*. Paris: Veuve François Clousier & Pierre Bienfait, 1677.

Faerno, Gabriello. *Fabulae centum ex antiquis auctoribus delectae*. Rome: Vincentius Luchinus, 1563.

Gros, François-Toussaint. *Recuil de pouesiés prouvençalos*. Marseille: François Berte, 1734.

Guichellet, abbé Pierre-Philibert. *Fables nouvelles, suivies de pièces fugitives en vers*. Paris: Arthus Bertrand, 1816.

Hagedorn, Friedrich von. *Sämmtliche Poetische Werke*. Hamburg: Johann Carl Bohn, 1760.

Héry, L. *Fables créoles*. Réunion, 1828.

Heyns, Pierre. *Esbatiment moral des animaux*. Antwerp: P. Galle, 1578. Reprint. Antwerp: Le Livre Belge, 1925.

Lachambeaudie, Pierre. *Œuvres de P. Lachambeaudie. Fables et poésies*. Paris: Victor Lecou et al., 1854.

La Férandière, marquise de (née Marie-Amable Petitau). *Œuvres de madame de la Fér✳✳✳*. 3 vols. in 2. Paris: Colnet, 1806. Reprint. Paris: Janet et Cotelle, 1816.

Layet, abbé. *Le Fablier chrétien, ou Allégories nouvelles sur l'existence de Dieu, la Trinité . . .* Paris: Périsse frères, 1851.

Lebrun, Antoine-Louis. *Fables de Monsieur Lebrun*. Paris: Jean-Baptiste Mazuel, 1722.

Lessing, Gotthold Ephraim. *Fabeln*. Berlin: C. F. Voss, 1759.

Marbot, François-Achille. *Les Bambous: Fables de La Fontaine travesties en patois créole par un vieux commandeur*. Fort-Royal, Martinique: E. Ruelle et Ch. Arnaud, 1846. 2d ed. Aix: Makaire, 1886. 3d ed. Paris: J. Peyronnot, 1931.

Maréchal, Pierre-Sylvain. *Almanach des honnêtes gens*. Paris: n.p., 1788.

———. *Apologues modernes à l'usage du Dauphin: premières leçons du fils aîné d'un roi*. Brussels, 1788. Reprint. Paris: Editions d'Histoire Sociale, 1976.

———. *Dictionnaire des athées anciens et modernes*. Paris: Grabit, An VIII [1800].

Mérard de Saint-Just, Simon-Pierre. *Fables et contes mis en vers*. Paris: "Chez l'auteur," 1787.

Perret, Etienne. *Vingt-cinq fables des animaux*. Antwerp: Plantin, 1578.

Pignotti, Lorenzo. *Favole e novelle*. Pisa: F. Pieraccini, 1782.

Rabier, Benjamin. *Fables comiques*. Paris: Garnier frères, 1928.

Ségur, Louis-Philippe de. *Contes, fables, chansons et vers*. Paris: F. Buisson, 1801.

OTHER TEXTS—LITERARY, DRAMATIC, HISTORICAL, SOCIOLOGICAL, FOLKLORIC, ETC.—AND MISCELLANEOUS WORKS

Autreau, Jacques. *Œuvres*. Edited by Charles-Etienne Pesselier. 4 vols. Paris: Briasson, 1749.

Barbey d'Aurévilly, Jules. *Voyageurs et romanciers*. Paris: Lemerre, 1908.

Bausset, Louis-François-Joseph de. *Mémoires anecdotiques sur l'intérieur du palais et sur quelques événemens de l'Empire depuis 1805 jusqu'au premier mai 1814 pour servir à l'histoire de Napoléon*. 4 vols. Paris: Baudouin frères. 1827–29.

Berquin, Arnaud. *Œuvres complètes de Berquin*. Edited by Louis-François Jauffret. 22 vols. Paris: Le Clerc, 1802.

Beslier, G.-G. *Le Sénégal*. Paris: Payot, 1935.

Buffon, George-Louis Leclerc, comte de. *Œuvres complètes*. 2d ed. 40 vols. Paris: Verdière et Ladrange, 1824–30.

Bulfinch, Thomas. *Legends of Charlemagne*. Boston: S. W. Tilton, 1862.

Bulwa, Lillian. "Creative Ingenuity and the Engine: Esthetic Applications of the Invention of the Locomotive." (Unpublished.) Abstract in *Journal for the Humanities and Technology* 4 (1982), no. 1: 45.

Burton, Richard F. *Wit and Wisdom from West Africa*. London: Tinsley Brothers, 1865. Reprint. New York: Negro Universities Press, 1969.

Chamfort, Sebastien-Roch-Nicolas de. *Œuvres*. Edited by Pierre-Louis Ginguené. Paris: Imprimerie des sciences et des arts, An III [1795].

Champlain, Samuel de. *The Works of Samuel de Champlain*. Edited by H. P. Biggar. 6 vols. Toronto: Champlain Society, 1929–36. Reprint. Toronto: University of Toronto Press, 1971.

Chandler, John Greene. *The Remarkable History of Chicken Little*. Reprinted from the original edition by Herbert H. Hosmer, Jr. South Lancaster, Mass.: College Press, 1941.

Chateaubriand, René de. *Œuvres romanesques et voyages*. Edited by Maurice Regard. 2 vols. Bibliothèque de la Pléiade. Paris: Gallimard, 1969.

Cicero. *Academica*. Edited by James S. Reid. 1885. Reprint. Hildesheim: Georg Olms Verlagsbuchhandlung, 1966.

Claretie, Léo. *Feuilles de route aux Etats-Unis*. Paris: Dentu-Fayard, 1894.

———. *Les Héros de la Yellowstone*. Paris: Editions du "Monde Illustré," 1908.

———. *L'Oie du Capitole*. Ilustrated by Nicolas-Stanislas-Auguste Vimar. Paris: Société française d'éditions d'art, 1899.

———. *La Vallée fumante*. Tours: A. Mame, 1899.

Claretie, Léo, and Henri Potez. *Le Prêcheur converti*. Comedy: 1 act. Paris: Dentu, 1896.

Crane, Thomas Frederick. *The Exempla of Jacques de Vitry*. London: Folk-Lore Society, 1890.

Dacier, Madame (née Anne Lefèvre). *Des causes de la corruption du goust*. Paris: Rigaud, 1714.

———. *L'Iliade d'Homère, traduite en françois, avec des remarques*. Paris: Rigaud, 1711.

Delamain, Robert. *Jarnac à travers les âges*. Angoulême: Coquemard, 1954.

Deonna, W. "Quelques portraitistes genevois du XVIIIe siècle." *Genava* 21 (1943): 146–53.

Des Périers, Bonaventure. *Œuvres françoises de Bonaventure Des Périers*. Edited by M. Louis Lacour. 2 vols. Paris: P. Jannet 1856.

Diogenes Laertius. *Lives of Eminent Philosophers*. Translated by R. D. Hicks. London: Heinemann, 1925.

Diop, David. *Coups de pilon*. Paris: Présence Africaine, 1956. 3d ed. 1980.

Dupeux, Georges. *Aspects de l'histoire sociale et politique du Loir-et-Cher, 1848–1914*. The Hague: Mouton, 1962.

Duplessis, Georges. *Les 'Emblèmes' d'Alciat*. Paris: J. Rouam, 1884.

Durel, Petrus. *Léo Claretie, biographie critique*. Paris: E. Sansot, 1906.

Ecouchard, Ponce-Denis. *See* Le Brun.

Emeneau, Murray B. *Kota Texts*. University of California Publications in Linguistics. Berkeley: University of California Press, 1944–46.

Eno-Beliga, Martin Samuel. *Littérature et musique populaire en Afrique noire*. Paris: Cujas, 1965.

Fagan, Christophe-Barthélémy. *Théâtre*. Edited by Charles-Etienne Pesselier. 4 vols. Includes "Eloge historique de M. Fagan" (I:i–xvi) and "Analyse des Œuvres de M. Fagan" (I:xvii–lvii), by Pesselier. Paris: Duchesne, 1760.

Fin du Répertoire du Théâtre Français. Edited by M. Lepeintre. 45 vols. Paris: Veuve Dabo, 1824.

Fréchette, Louis-Honoré. *Les Lutins*. Montréal: Beauchemin, 1919.

Fuzelier, Louis, René Lesage, and d'Orneval. *Théâtre de la foire*. 10 vols. in 9. Paris: Pierre Gandouin et al., 1724–37.

Gautier, Emile-Félix. *Un siècle de colonisation*. Paris: Félix Alcan, 1930.

Gesta Romanorum. Edited by Hermann Oesterley. Berlin, 1872.

Gobillot, René. *La Comtesse de Ségur: sa vie, son œuvre*. Alençon: Imprimerie Alençonnaise, 1924.

Green, Henry, ed. *Andreae Alciati Emblematum fontes quatuor; namely, an account of the original collection made at Milan, 1522, and photo-lith fac-similes of the editions, Augsburg 1531, Paris 1534 and Venice 1546*. Manchester: A. Brothers, 1870.

Grenaud, Pierre. *Notre Algérie littéraire*. 2 vols. Oran: L. Fouque, 1958–59.

Guérande, Paul. *Le petit monde de la comtesse de Ségur*. Paris: Les Seize, 1964.

Guigou, Paul. *L'Arche de Noë*. Illustrated by Nicolas-Stanislas-Auguste Vimar. Paris: Plon et Nourrit, 1894.

———. *L'Illustre dompteur*. Illustrated by Nicolas-Stanislas-Auguste Vimar. Paris: Plon et Nourrit, 1895.

———. *Interrupta*. Preface by François Coppée. Paris: Plon et Nourrit, 1898.

Haag, Eugène, and Emile Haag. *La France protestante*. 10 vols. Paris: J. Cherbuliez, 1846–59.

Hardy, Georges. *La Mise en valeur du Sénégal de 1817 à 1854*. Paris: Emile Larose, 1921.

Hedouville, Marthe de. *La Comtesse de Ségur et les siens*. Paris: Editions du Conquistador, 1953.

Kesteloot, Lilyan. *Ecrivains noirs de langue française: naissance d'une littérature*. Brussels: Université Libre de Bruxelles, 1965. Translated by Ellen Conroy Kennedy as *Black Writers in French: A Literary History of Negritude*. Philadelphia: Temple University Press, 1974.

Le Brun, Ponce-Denis Ecouchard. *Œuvres*. Edited by Pierre-Louis Ginguené. 4 vols. Paris: Warée, 1811.

Leclerc, George-Louis, comte de Buffon. *See* Buffon.

Lévy, Paul. *Histoire linguistique d'Alsace et de Lorraine*. 2 vols. Paris: Société d'Edition: Les Belles Lettres, 1929.

El libro del Cavallero Zifar. Edited by Charles Philip Wagner. Ann Arbor: University of Michigan Press, 1929.

Libro de los exenplos por a. b. c. Edited by John Esten Keller, Clásicos Hispánicos, 2d series, ediciones criticas, vol 5. Madrid: Consejo Superior de Investigaciones Científicas, 1961.

El libro de los gatos: A Text with Introduction and Notes. Edited by G. T. Northrup. Chicago: University of Chicago Press, 1908. Reprint from *Modern Philology* 5 (1907–8), no. 4: 477–554.

Libro de los gatos. Edited with introduction and notes by Bernard Darbord. Annexes des cahiers de linguistique hispanique médiévale, 3. Paris: Librairie Klincksieck, 1984.

Lom d'Arce de Lahontan, Louis-Armand de. *Nouveaux voyages de Mr. le baron de Lahontan dans l'Amérique Septentrionale*. The Hague, 1703.

Lucas, Colin. *The Structure of the Terror: The Example of Javogues and the Loire*. Oxford: Oxford University Press, 1973.

Marx, Leo. *The Machine in the Garden: Technology and the Pastoral Ideal in America*. New York: Oxford University Press, 1967.

Maugras, Gaston. *La Cour de Lunéville au dix-huitième siècle*. Paris: Plon-Nourrit, 1904.

Metternich, prince de. *Mémoires, documents et écrits divers laissés par le prince de Metternich*. Edited by M. A. de Klinkowstroem. 8 vols. Paris: Plon, 1880–84.

Moussat, Georges. *A bon chat bon rat!* Comedy: 1 act. Algiers: C. Zamith, 1896.

———. *Sonnets*. Paris: A. Derenne, 1876.

———. *Les Trois intérieurs*. Rouen: L. Deshays, 1874.

Mouton, Eugène. *Les Vertus et les grâces des bêtes*. Illustrated by Nicolas-Stanislas-Auguste Vimar. Tours: A. Mame, 1895.

———. *Voyages et aventures du capitaine Marius Cougourdan*. Paris: Hachette, 1911.

———. *Zoölogie morale*. 2 vols. Paris: Charpentier, 1881–82.

Nau, François. *Esope au village*. Comic opera: 1 act. The Hague: Pierre Witte, n.d.

Nolhac, Pierre de. *La Création de Versailles*. Versailles: L. Bernard, 1901. Reprint. Paris: Conard, 1925.

Ossian, fils de Fingal. Translated by Pierre Le Tourneur, with preface by Pierre-Louis Ginguené. Paris: Dentu, 1810.

Pascal, Blaise. *Pensées*. Edited by Louis Lafuma. Paris: Le Club du meilleur livre, 1958.

Pataud, Emile. *Comment nous ferons la révolution*. Paris: Tallandier, 1909.

Pauli, Johannes. *Schimpf und Ernst*. Edited by Johannes Bolte. 2 vols. Berlin: Stubenrauch, 1924.

Prajoux, J. *Roanne autrefois et aujourd'hui*. Roanne: Souchier, 1900.

Régnier, Mathurin. *Œuvres complètes*. Edited by Gabriel Raibaud. Paris: Didier, 1958.

Richard, Jean-Pierre. *Onze études sur la poésie moderne*. Paris: Editions du Seuil, 1964

Rogers, J[oel] A. *World's Great Men of Color*. 2 vols. New York: J. A. Rogers, 1947. Reprint. New York: Macmillan, 1972.

Rousseau, Jean-Jacques. *Les Confessions*. Edited by Jacques Voisine. Paris: Garnier frères, 1964.

Sainte-Beuve, Charles-Augustin de. *Causeries du lundi*. 15 vols. 2d ed. Paris: Garnier frères, 1852–62.

Shapiro, Norman R., ed. and trans. *Négritude: Black Poets from Africa and the Caribbean*. New York: October House, 1970.

Signoret, Henri. *La Légende des bêtes*. Illustrated by Nicolas-Stanislas-Auguste Vimar. Paris: Plon et Nourrit, 1902.

———. *Le Mardi Gras des animaux*. Illustrated by Nicolas-Stanislas-Auguste Vimar. Paris: F. Juven, 1899.

———. *Les Noces fantastiques*. Paris: Marpon et Flammarion, 1879.

Silbert, J. *Auguste Vimar, artiste, peintre*. Marseille, 1917.

Tatar, Maria. *The Hard Facts of the Grimms' Fairy Tales*. Princeton, N.J.: Princeton University Press, 1987.

Vimar, Nicolas-Stanislas-Auguste. *A, B, C, D. La Ménagerie de Bébé*. Paris: Delagrave, 1902.

———. *L'Automobile Vimar*. Asnières: Manzi et Joyant, 1897.

———. *Le Boy de Marius Bouillabès*. Paris: H. Laurens, 1906.

———. *Clown*. Paris: H. Laurens, 1911.

———. *Les Maris de Mlle Nounouche: histoire de chats*. Paris: Floury, 1906.

———. *La Poule à poils*. Paris: H. Laurens, 1904.

Violot, Raoul. *Histoire des maisons de Chalon-sur-Saône*. 2 vols. Paris: Editions F. E. R. N., 1969.

Voisenon, Claude-Henri de Fusée de. *Œuvres complettes de Voisenon*. 5 vols. Paris: Moutard, 1781.

Index of Names

Index of Characters

236

A Note on the Translator

NORMAN R. SHAPIRO is professor of Romance Languages and Literatures at Wesleyan University and a leading translator of French prose, poetry, and theater. Among his works are *Négritude: Black Poetry from Africa and the Caribbean; The Comedy of Eros: Medieval French Guides to the Art of Love; Fables from Old French: Aesop's Beasts and Bumpkins;* and *Fifty Fables of La Fontaine.* His translations of George Feydeau and other French comic dramatists, published in several volumes, are frequently performed in this country and abroad.

A Note on the Illustrator

DAVID SCHORR divides his time between New York City and Rome, where he makes prints and drawings that have had solo exhibitions in New York, Chicago, Toronto, Montreal, Milan, Paris, Copenhagen, and Rome. He has illustrated many books, among them Phyllis Rose's *Parallel Lives,* and his portraits of authors have appeared for years in the *New Republic.* He is professor of art at Wesleyan University.